Maintenance,

Safety,

and Operating

Instructions

for Teens

THE GUY BOOK

AN
OWNER'S
MANUAL
FOR
TEENS

CROWN PUBLISHERS
NEW YORK

Mavis Jukes

Photo credits: page i copyright © Corbis Stock Market. Pages iv, 4, 7, 19, 37, 43, 50, 61, 62, 67, 72, 75, 105, 117, 118, 121, 122, 127, 128, 131, 137: copyright © H. Armstrong Roberts. Pages iii, viii, 20, 28–29, 35, 39, 54, 57, 71, 76, 89, 92, 132, 138: copyright © SuperStock. Pages 10, 22, 30, 44, 58, 81, 85, 95, 107, 114, 144, 147, 148: copyright © Getty Images. Diagrams on pages 12, 32, 36, 146 illustrated by Lisa Paterno-Guinta.

Published by Crown Publishers, a division of Random House, Inc., 1540 Broadway, New York, N.Y. 10036

CROWN and colophon are trademarks of Random House, Inc.

www.randomhouse.com/teens

Book design by Elizabeth Van Itallie

Library of Congress Cataloging-in-Publication Data

Jukes, Mavis.

The guy book : an owner's manual : maintenance, safety, and operating instructions for teens / by Mavis Jukes.—1st ed.
p.   cm.
Includes bibliographical references and index.

Summary: Provides information for boys on changes that occur in their bodies during puberty and offers advice on sexual topics, nutrition, drugs, girls, and more.

1. Teenage boys—Juvenile literature. 2. Adolescence—Juvenile literature. 3. Puberty—Juvenile literature. 4. Sex instruction for boys—Juvenile literature. 5. Sex instruction for teenagers—Juvenile literature. 6. Interpersonal relations in adolescence—Juvenile literature. [1. Sex instruction for boys. 2. Puberty. 3. Teenage boys.] I. Title.

HQ797 .J84 2002
305.235—dc21   2001047073

ISBN 0-679-89028-9 (trade pbk.)
ISBN 0-679-99028-3 (lib. bdg.)

Printed in the United States of America

January 2002

10 9 8 7 6

For Bob

Table of CONTENTS

DISCLAIMER

A Note to the Reader

The Guy Book: An Owner's Manual includes information that has been gathered through careful research by the author. Stories have been contributed by guys from a wide range of ages and cultural backgrounds. This book has been reviewed for accuracy by doctors in the areas of pediatrics and adolescent psychology. It has also been reviewed by an attorney. Laws that relate to sex, drugs, alcohol, violence, harassment, paternal responsibilities, and reproductive rights of juveniles vary from state to state. This book isn't a legal reference and shouldn't be used as one. If you have legal questions, talk to an attorney specializing in juvenile law.

Information in the field of sexual health for children and adolescents is continually changing. Every attempt has been made to ensure that this book is scientifically correct, but its purpose is to give general information; it shouldn't be relied on as a source of medical advice. If you have symptoms or specific questions or concerns related to your health, call your doctor. If you have any questions about the material in this book, please consult your parent, guardian, doctor, teacher, school counselor, or other informed, responsible adult.

Thanks

—for the editing: Nancy Hinkel
—for the art direction: Isabel Warren-Lynch
—for the book design: Elizabeth Van Itallie
—for review, in the area of adolescent medicine: Dr. Sarah Jane Schwarzenberg
in the area of adolescent psychology: Dr. Alice Siegel
in the area of law: Anke Steinecke
—for the backup: my family, especially my mom, Marguerite Jukes
—for ideas, insight, inspiration, and/or inside information: my friends—
with special thanks to Al, Alan, Bale, Bill, Bill, Bucca, Danny, David,
Dino, Dixon, Eldon, Fred, George, Jaimi, Jim, JoHarvey, Kearn, Lenore, Manuel, Marilyn,
Mary, Mary, Mary Ann, Mike, Milly, Pat, Richard, Richard, Sharon, Simon,
Sonia, Suzanne, Terry, and Wai-Yin

THE GUY BOOK

When your body begins to change from a kid's body into the body of a young adult, it means you're going through puberty. For most boys, puberty begins at about age 12½ or 13.

But it's also normal for it to begin earlier or later.

Going through puberty includes having your penis and testicles grow bigger. It also includes growing pubic hair and other body hair, sweating more, having oilier skin, growing taller, getting physically stronger, having your voice get lower, producing sperm, ejaculating, and maybe having stronger sexual feelings. All of these things are supposed to happen.

And they're all explained in *The Guy Book*. *The Guy Book* also contains other information that you may need down the road. It covers a wide range of information, too. Some material may be new to you, some familiar.

It's about sex and sexuality; it explains how sexual intercourse can cause pregnancy and how unplanned pregnancy can be avoided by using birth control.

It also discusses sexually transmitted diseases, including AIDS. It talks about condoms and the correct use of condoms. It deals with other health issues, including alcohol, tobacco, and drug use.

There's some advice included, too—like about how to choose a deodorant and how to shave, tie a tie, dance slow, and put together a wardrobe.

The Guy Book isn't meant to take the place of communicating with an actual person—it can't. Talk to your dad, mom, or another trusted adult about concerns or questions you may have that relate to the content of this book.

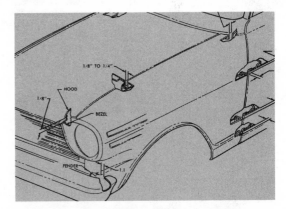

FEEL READY FOR THE INFORMATION?

If you're not sure, ask your parent or guardian if he or she thinks this book is right for you.

CHAPTER 1

Under the Hood:
PARTS

STANDARD EQUIPMENT

Human reproductive systems include primary reproductive organs, called **gonads**.

A male's gonads are his **testes.** Testes are commonly called "balls." They have dual functions: They produce reproductive cells (**sperm**), and they secrete the sex hormone **testosterone.**

Your reproductive system also includes accessory reproductive organs: a system of ducts that store and carry sperm, and glands that line and empty into these ducts.

The penis has more than one purpose and more than one function. The role of the penis in the reproductive system is to distribute sperm. It's also an organ of excretion: You pee out of it. The penis has another important function: producing intense physical pleasure.

PARTS

The end of the penis is called the **glans**. It's otherwise known as the "head." It's the most sensitive part to touch.

The glans is covered by a retractable layer of skin called the **foreskin**.

Some boys are **circumcised** at birth—which is when the foreskin is surgically removed. Circumcision is sometimes performed for religious reasons. In terms of appearance, it's considered fine to be circumcised or fine to be left intact.

The glans of an intact penis is reported to be more sensitive than the glans of a circumcised penis.

FYI Circumcision

Most doctors now agree that there is no medical reason to circumcise every newborn baby boy, and more and more parents in the U.S. are choosing not to do the procedure.

For one thing, routine circumcision of infants is no longer advised for prevention of penis cancer. (*Penis cancer?* Don't worry, young guys very rarely get this.)

Neither is circumcision considered necessary for prevention of infection. Keeping an intact penis clean is easily accomplished by gently pulling back the foreskin and washing under and around it with soap and water. This prevents smegma, the white substance secreted by the glans, from getting trapped behind the foreskin and causing infection.

There are medical reasons for circumcision

in some cases, though. It may be recommended if a guy's foreskin is uncomfortably tight or too big to be moved down over the glans.

Circumcision surgery is relatively simple and straightforward, and it need not be a cause of concern if it becomes necessary. However, it does require surgery for an older child or a man.

The rest of the penis is called the **shaft**. The structure of the penis and the blood flow to and from the tissue inside it (**erectile tissue**) allow the penis to become temporarily rigid at times. This is called having an **erection**. Boys get erections throughout their lives, starting when they are babies. However, erections take on new meaning during puberty (see page 11).

The testes hang down in a pouch of skin called the **scrotum**. One ball is called a **testis**. The scrotum is internally divided into two sacs: one for each testis. The testes-and-scrotum combo is often referred to as **testicles**.

A couple of months before the birth of a male baby, his testes descend into his scrotum. They drop down from his abdomen, where they are formed.

Sometimes a testis doesn't descend. It just stays up in the abdomen or only comes partway down. If you have an undescended testis or partly descended testis, make an appointment to talk to your doctor about it. He or she may recommend correcting this with hormone treatment or surgery.

OUTSTANDING DESIGN FEATURES
Cooling System

Sperm (more about them on page 11) are manufactured at a lower temperature than the internal temperature of the body. Air circulating around the scrotum keeps the testes cooler. Also, there's a heat-exchange setup in the blood vessels that supply the testes: a cooling system.

Compliments of Testosterone
1. Your penis, balls, and scrotum will grow and change.
2. You'll begin to grow pubic hair.
3. Additional hair will grow on your body, including in your armpits.
4. There will be changes in your sweat glands.
5. There'll be changes in your oil glands.
6. Your voice will change.
7. You'll grow taller.
8. You'll grow more muscular.
9. You may grow facial hair.
10. You'll have more erections.
11. You'll begin to manufacture sperm; you'll ejaculate.
12. You may have stronger sexual feelings.

Heat Regulation

The scrotum is capable of relaxing and tightening up. When it's chilly out, it pulls the testes as close as possible to the body—where they can warm up. When it's hot out, the scrotum gets all soft and droopy so that the testes can kind of swing in the breeze—to cool off.

This design isn't just to keep the testes at the absolute optimum temperature for sperm formation. The testes are unprotected by muscle or bone. This is risky, considering how important they are. To make the best of the situation, the scrotum tightens when a guy feels fear, drawing his testes closer to his body, where they will be safer if there is a confrontation.

It can also tighten when a guy feels nervous, and it tightens during sex.

One testis is usually a little bit bigger than the other. Both are carefully located in the scrotum so that one hangs lower than the other, usually the left one. This way, they aren't in a position to crush each other as a guy goes about an active daily life—that involves running, for instance.

CONTROL PANELS
Hormones

Hormones are part of a communication system called the **endocrine system**. They are chemicals secreted by various organs of the body, including the brain, heart, kidneys, liver, thyroid gland, and testes. Hormones act like tiny messengers, circulating through the bloodstream and giving signals to cells to make changes that affect everything from brain development to kidney function.

Even though hormones are carried by the blood throughout the entire body and reach all the body's tissues, hormones are very specific as to which cells they influence. Sex hormones are present in both males and females, and reproductive functions are largely controlled by them. Males and females share some of the same sex hormones.

The main male sex hormone is testosterone. It's secreted in the testes by **Leydig cells**, which are located in connective-tissue spaces between the tubules where sperm are formed.

Testosterone is famous for contributing to a boy's attraction to action. It enables guys to have the energy and concentration to perform well in a variety of situations.

Testosterone triggers many of the changes associated with puberty. It tells a guy's reproductive (sex) organs how and when to develop.

Secondary sexual characteristics aren't directly involved in reproduction, but they make up the many differences between male and female bodies. Testosterone influences the development of these characteristics. Among other things, it deepens the voice, increases lean muscle mass, cuts down on body fat, increases bone density and growth, and triggers the growth of facial hair.

It also increases sex drive (**libido**).

CHAPTER 2

IGNITION
System: HOW IT ALL WORKS

YOUR PENIS AND TESTICLES WILL GROW AND CHANGE

What to Expect

When puberty begins, the following changes take place over the course of a few years:

A very small amount of straight, almost colorless hair grows at the base of the penis; the penis becomes slightly enlarged; the scrotum becomes larger and less smooth than it used to be. On lighter-skinned boys, the scrotum will look pink. The coloring on darker-skinned guys will deepen.

The scrotum will get longer and looser and will hang lower. The testes will begin to grow. Oil and sweat glands will begin to develop on the skin of the penis and scrotum.

The hair at the base of the penis (pubic hair) gradually becomes darker (these hairs may be preceded by little bumps); the hair will begin to curl; the penis becomes longer and wider; the scrotum and testes will continue to grow. One testis will hang lower than the other.

The amount of pubic hair increases, and it becomes coarse.

The penis becomes larger (thicker), and the scrotum continues to grow; the skin on the penis and scrotum becomes visibly darker.

Pubic hair fills in. It can be red, brown, black, or blond. It can be very, *very* curly, or it can be almost straight. It makes a triangular shape (upside down) that spreads to the inner thighs (this is the adult pattern) and around the anus; the penis and scrotum reach adult size.

HEADS UP! Hood Ornaments

If you're thinking of piercing your penis, here are a few things to consider:

Piercing equipment needs to be sterile in order to prevent the transfer of germs—including those that cause AIDS and hepatitis. Piercing should only be done by a professional.

Body piercings don't always heal completely, and any unhealed wound, no matter how small, can provide an entry point for germs.

You'll grow armpit hair and you'll get furrier.

During puberty, boys grow hair in the armpits. Boys may also grow hair on the chest, back, and shoulders. Hair on the legs will thicken.

A line of fuzzy hair, sometimes referred to as a

PENIS SPECIFICATIONS

The average adult penis size is approximately 3½ to 4½ inches long. Shorter or longer is also normal. The average length of an erect penis is about 6 inches. Erect penises are pretty much the same size.

✔ Penis Size

Since penises are so noticeable, it's natural for boys to compare.

During puberty, there is quite a range of sizes. That's because boys go through puberty at different rates; some begin the process earlier than others.

✔ A Few Things to Keep in Mind

1. The notion that a large penis is an indication of great masculinity (or great sexual ability) is a myth.
2. All size penises work.
3. A relatively small penis will get significantly bigger when it becomes erect.
4. Science has never shown any correlation between ethnic background and penis size.
5. Penises look different from different angles; looking down at one from above makes it seem shorter than it actually is.
6. The size of a penis is not a measure of how often a boy will get an erection, how often he will ejaculate, or how his orgasms will feel.
7. Penis size doesn't relate to the ability a boy will have to please his sexual partner when he grows up. Pleasing a sexual partner has much more to do with communicating with, caring about, understanding the sexual responses of, and respecting the other person.
8. People don't generally choose partners based on what size penis a guy has.

"happy trail," may grow between a guy's belly button and his pubic area.

New sweat glands will begin to work. You'll sweat more. You'll smell stronger.

Puberty causes sweat glands to work overtime; you'll sweat more. Your armpits and genital area will have an odor that's different from when you were a little kid.

Wearing deodorant is helpful when it comes to armpit odor and perspiration control—but not all people feel a need to use it. Citations aren't issued for sweating. If you wash regularly and wear clean clothes, you'll smell fine—even if you happen to work up a sweat. But wash your clothes often. T-shirts, socks, and underwear, since they're worn very close to the body, get ripe fast once you've reached puberty.

OIL CHANGES
Your skin will become oilier. You may develop pimples on your face, shoulders, and back.

At puberty, oil glands start to produce an oily substance called **sebum**. Sebum is emptied onto the surface of the skin out of tiny openings called **pores**.

Bumps Ahead

During puberty, oil glands can get revved up by hormones and produce too much sebum.

Sebum can end up filling the duct, clogging the pore, and forming a blackhead. (Blackheads are not dirty pores. The black part of a blackhead is just sebum, which darkens when it comes in contact with the air.)

Sebum can build up and rupture the wall of the oil gland and escape into the surrounding skin tissue, causing inflammation and **pus** (a pimple).

GUY REPORT: THE LONELY ARMPIT

"Moving from grade school to junior high school, from the sixth grade to the seventh grade, from twelve to thirteen, was one of the most traumatic periods of my life. For the first time, I had to go to gym class and be in the shower naked with other boys! And all of them, it seemed, were fully developed 'hairy men.' They had it all over them . . . on their chests, their faces, under their arms. And most dadlike and manly of all—they had pubic hair!

"To my horrid chagrin, I only had hair growing in my left armpit . . . no hair anywhere else! It was terrifying and humiliating, and I spent the entire year trying to hide my freakish body—front to the bricks, right arm down, and left arm up. (I had to show something!) Finally, by the eighth grade, to my great relief, some fuzz started showing up."

Acne

Acne is the result of having many plugged-up oil glands. Some forms of acne require continuous, consistent treatment by a physician over a period of months or years. The good news is that acne can be successfully managed and almost everybody outgrows it, eventually.

A **dermatologist** (skin specialist) can develop a treatment plan for acne. The plan may involve applying medicated cream or gel directly onto the skin, washing the skin with medicated washes, and/or taking prescription medications orally (by mouth).

Make and keep appointments as advised.

Under some circumstances, blood tests may be required at intervals to make sure that your body is tolerating the medications safely.

Your voice will change.

At about age 14 or 15, your voice will change to a lower, adult tone. This is because the voice box gets larger during puberty and your vocal cords, inside the voice box, get longer.

Lowering of the voice usually doesn't present a problem, except for an occasional embarrassing squeak. Some boys try to control this by speaking in a calm and controlled manner.

Try not to worry about this temporary situation; the people around you, girls included, kind of expect this to happen—given that a voice change at puberty is a normal experience for every guy who walks the earth!

Eventually your voice will settle into its adult range, and the sudden shifts won't happen anymore.

You'll grow taller.

Once a guy's sex organs have begun to develop, he will experience a growth spurt of about 3½ inches a year (remember: this is average growth; more or less can still be normal). Fast growth usually continues for about 3 years, then slows down, stopping at about age 20.

Even though girls and boys begin to go through puberty at approximately the same time, the growth spurt for girls begins at an earlier stage of puberty than it does for boys (see page 65).

FYI Your Bones

If your feet seem big in comparison to the rest of your body, it's because . . . well, they are!

Not all bones of the body grow at the same rate during the growth spurt. Bones in the arms, legs, and (especially) the feet get a jump on some of the rest of the bones of the body.

For a while, it might seem as if your shoe size is going to get (or has already gotten) completely out of hand. If you're worried about this, there's good news. Your feet will stop growing bigger before you will stop growing taller.

So it all works out in the end.

You'll become physically stronger.

Your shoulders will become broader and more muscular, and muscles will grow bigger in your thighs, calves, and upper arms.

So you'll become physically stronger than you were when you were a little kid. How much bigger and stronger?

It's impossible to know what your body shape and size will ultimately be.

ACCEPT YOUR BODY TYPE

Sure, we admire and appreciate the bodies of professional athletes and Olympians. But we all aren't genetically programmed to develop the physique of an outstanding athlete or to attain the idealized male body images portrayed in the media. Try to maintain realistic expectations for yourself and the others around you.

A reasonable goal? Be fit. It's not a requirement to be athletic, but be active.

Live an active lifestyle and eat well. Build some form of exercise into your routine daily life. When you're growing, it's extra important for your body to get all the nutrients it needs. Eat for energy, eat to satisfy hunger, eat for enjoyment—and eat for nutrition. And eat on time! Being hungry can make it hard to concentrate or cause you to feel grumpy or down in the dumps and unmotivated (see page 31).

You may grow whiskers.

Most boys begin to grow facial hair between the ages of 14 and 18. Some guys just do not grow whiskers—not a mustache, beard, goatee, or sideburns. How much facial hair you have is genetically determined.

If you want to know how hairy your face will be, you may get some clues from checking out the other (adult) males in your family.

How little or much facial hair a guy can grow isn't a measure of masculinity.

FYI Breast Changes

Breast changes happen to boys as well as girls during puberty. Boys' nipples grow slightly bigger and get darker. The area around the nipple (areola) gets wider and darker.

Your breasts may ache as you go through puberty, and you may have some temporary breast growth. Don't worry! Temporary breast growth is so normal it even has a name: gynecomastia.

Gynecomastia disappears, usually before most people even learn the name of it, within about a year.

Questions? Ask your doctor.

You may have more erections.

Erections happen either spontaneously or when a guy becomes sexually excited.

Spontaneous erections happen on their own, without any physical encouragement. Guys often wake up with an erection.

An erect penis sticks out and stands up, away from the body. It becomes longer, thicker, and harder. It may bend to one side or the other.

Touching the penis, especially the head of the penis, can stimulate this reaction.

But so can certain thoughts, fantasies, emotions, sights, and smells.

Spontaneous Erections

Spontaneous erections are the result of a guy's fluc-tuating or high levels of testosterone. They slowly go away on their own if the penis is ignored.

Down, boy!

It's totally normal for a boy's penis to spring up several times a day and sometimes for no apparent reason—or for a very apparent reason. Like seeing somebody sexy!

It's also totally normal for this not to happen! There's no rule that says a teenage boy has to have continual erections at the drop of a hat.

A penis may simply react to the presence of naked bodies, regardless of gender. So if you get (or somebody else gets) an erection in the locker room, just ignore it. A penis is a very complex, excitable organ, and guys can't always get it to cooperate or be cool. Sometimes it just has its own deal going. If it goofs around in the locker room, don't let it stress you.

➤ Face it.

You wouldn't trade it in.

Your penis may get bigger (or smaller) at what seems to be exactly the wrong moment.

It will forever be capable of producing a certain amount of stress or embarrassment, and it might not be 100 percent dependable (including during sex). But it will be pretty much reliable. And definitely worth having!

The good news is that it will at least become more predictable as you get older.

You'll begin to manufacture sperm.

Sperm begins to be manufactured about a year or so after the penis, testes, and scrotum begin to grow—at about the time that your pubic hair is filling in.

Sperm contain half of the genetic information needed to create a baby. Once a boy starts producing sperm, it means that he has become physically capable of fathering a child (see page 73). A mature male produces about 30 million sperm every day, and the production of sperm happens round the clock—24-7.

SPERM

The head of a sperm contains DNA—which is the substance bearing the sperm's genetic information. The info is contained in 23 **chromosomes**.

The midpiece of the sperm provides energy for the sperm's movement, which is accomplished by a tail.

The tail is made up of filaments that produce whiplike movements. These movements propel the sperm forward—in search of a female reproductive cell (**ovum**).

Should the 23 chromosomes in a sperm be united with the twenty-three chromosomes contained in a female reproductive cell (ovum), the combined 46 chromosomes will provide the complete set of plans needed to make a new human being.

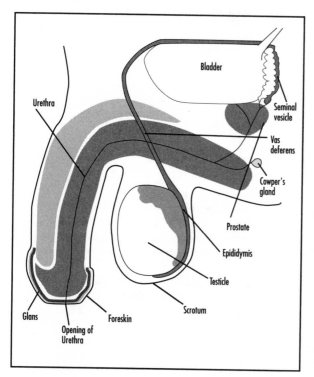

The duct of the **epididymis** drains each testis into a large, thick-walled tube called a **vas deferens**. The two vas deferens tubes and the part of the duct of the epididymis closest to the vas deferens tubes serve as storage reservoirs for sperm.

The vas deferens tubes are bound together in the **spermatic cord**, which passes through a small passage into the abdomen. Once inside the abdomen, they become the **ejaculatory ducts**.

Two large glands called the **seminal vesicles** feed into the vas deferens just before this transitional point. The ejaculatory ducts pass through the **prostate gland**, a single doughnut-shaped gland.

Seminal vesicles and the prostate gland secrete a milky-whitish fluid, which bathes, energizes, and nourishes sperm. The milky fluid, with millions of frisky sperm suspended in it, is called **semen**.

The ejaculatory ducts join up with the **urethra**, a tube that comes from the bladder and runs through the penis, all the way out to the tip.

The urethra has two jobs: one is to carry pee out of the body, and the other is to carry semen out of the body. Before semen is carried out, a valve automatically closes off the bladder so that peeing becomes impossible during this process.

Coils and Distributor

Spermatogenesis (sperm production) begins in tiny, tightly coiled **tubules** (tiny tubes) located inside your testes. This is how it starts:

Triggered by testosterone, original sperm cells (**spermatogonia**) begin to divide—initiating a cycle of cell division, which will continue throughout a male's life. The process of cell division results in the cloning (re-creating) of original cells so that the supply never runs out. But different cell forms are also created in the process. These different cells morph through a series of complex changes and are ultimately remodeled into sperm: cells that have heads, midpieces, and tails.

As sperm form, they are moved through the tubules into a system of ducts, ending up in a single duct inside of a structure called the **epididymis**. The epididymis is loosely attached to the outside of the

testis. Sperm continue to mature while traveling through the epididymis, a trip that takes about 12 days. The complete cycle of a sperm developing and maturing takes about 64 days.

You'll ejaculate.

As soon as you ejaculate for the first time, you will know that sperm production has begun. Ejaculation (commonly called "coming") is when semen is discharged from your penis. Ejaculation can happen while you're awake or asleep.

Having an ejaculation is a landmark event, similar to when a girl starts her period (see page 66). But even though ejaculating means you've become physically mature, it doesn't mean you've become a man—any more than it means that a girl has become a woman just because she's started menstruating.

Everybody remains a kid for quite a while after reaching puberty, and so will you. You'll still be a kid, entitled to the love, care, and protection of the adults around you. You won't (and shouldn't) be expected to take on adult roles and responsibilities.

Ejaculating while sleeping is called having a nocturnal emission, or a wet dream. Having a wet dream is a way of releasing sperm that builds up inside of your body.

Most guys have wet dreams, but some guys don't. Guys who release a lot of sperm by mas-

turbating (see page 15) don't usually have as many wet dreams.

Wet dreams can be accompanied by a feeling of intense pleasure (an orgasm), but often they're not. Ejaculation while sleeping can be a completely non-sensual event; it can just involve waking up with a wet spot on your sheets, pajamas, and/or underwear.

No Problem

Wet dreams are normal and should be expected. If you have a wet dream—good. Go back to sleep.

Sheets dry on their own just fine. It's not necessary to rip your whole bed apart and wash your sheets every time some semen gets on them, so don't.

If you do your own wash, note that washing semen spots out of light-colored fabric in very hot water can cause stains. Warm water is better.

Ejaculating While Awake

Some boys ejaculate for the first time while awake—kind of accidentally. And it surprises them.

How It All Happens

Before and during ejaculation, a nerve center at the base of the spine starts calling the signals, and nerve impulses occur, setting off a chain of reactions:

Blood vessels in the penis **dilate** (widen). Blood rushes in and fills the erectile tissue at high pressure. The penis becomes longer, thicker, and harder. Engorged with blood, the tissue expands, compressing the vessels that drain it. This helps keep the tissue rigid and the penis erect. Skin color darkens and the scrotum tightens.

The smooth muscles of the ducts and glands contract, emptying sperm and glandular secretions into the urethra. Semen is expelled from the urethra by a series of contractions of the smooth muscle that surrounds it—and also by contractions of the muscle at the base of the penis.

These contractions are associated with intense sensations of pleasure—called **having an orgasm**. Leading up to and during an orgasm, the heart rate increases noticeably, and breathing becomes faster than normal.

During an ejaculation . . .

About a teaspoonful of semen comes out. It comes out during a series of about four or five spurts that happen one right after another.

The semen can shoot out for quite a distance (a couple of feet), spurt out (a couple of inches), or even just dribble or leak out; the texture of the

semen can also vary. Sometimes it's thick; other times it's thin. It smells kind of sweet.

The experience of ejaculating and having an orgasm is completely variable. It can be more or less intense, depending on the occasion. Sometimes having an orgasm is nothing short of an earth-shattering event; other times it's just a quick, mildly pleasant feeling.

The amount of semen involved can also vary; the quantity can depend on how much time has passed since the last ejaculation. The more time between ejaculations, the more semen.

While it's possible to ejaculate without having an orgasm and possible to have an orgasm without ejaculating, these two events usually happen at the same time.

However, life is full of surprises. Boys are capable of having an orgasm without ejaculating—when experiencing something very sensual and exciting.

HEADS UP!

Before ejaculation occurs, a drop of clear fluid will appear at the tip of your penis. This is called "pre-ejaculate." Pre-ejaculate clears the way for semen: It neutralizes the pathway of the urethra in case there are traces of urine, which can impair sperm.

It is important to know that there is usually some live sperm in this fluid. It's not likely, but it is possible, for pre-ejaculate to cause pregnancy (see page 94).

The pre-ejaculate of an infected person can also contain germs, including HIV—the virus that causes AIDS (see page 87).

"Blue Balls"

If you remain sexually excited for a very long period of time without ejaculating, you may experience discomfort in your testicles (achy balls).

The discomfort has a nickname: "blue balls." Happily, your balls will not turn blue. The aching can be relieved by masturbating or by just wait-

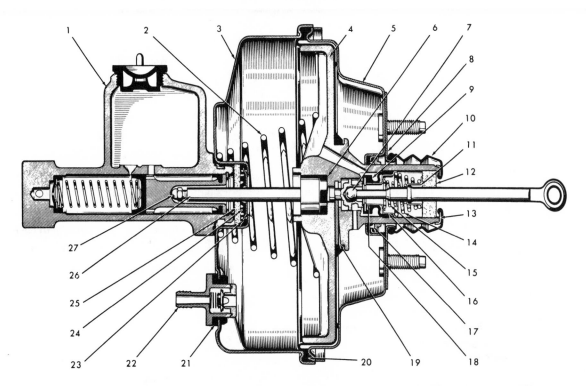

ing. The pain goes away by itself after a while.

Blue balls should not be used as an excuse for a guy to try to pressure his partner to have sex with him.

Masturbating (or "Solo Sex")

Some boys ejaculate for the first time by **masturbating.**

The purpose of masturbation is to give comfort. Masturbating can also relieve tension.

A guy masturbates by touching, rubbing, pressing, and/or stroking his penis (and maybe his balls). If he keeps on doing this, he will usually become sexually aroused, ejaculate, and have an orgasm.

Almost all boys who have reached puberty masturbate; many masturbate daily, some several times a day.

How often is too often? There's no easy answer to this question.

But becoming obsessed by masturbation or feeling compelled to masturbate over and over again as a means of escape are reasons for discussing masturbation with your doctor or other health care professional (see pages 27, 45).

Masturbation is rumored to cause problems with eyesight and athletic ability, but no way is this true. It doesn't cause hairy palms. Neither does it use up all of a guy's sperm. Sperm is made continuously, so the supply is endless. (However, it's usually necessary for some amount of time to pass between ejaculations.)

For boys who feel okay about it, masturbating is a perfectly safe form of sexual exploration—not at all harmful. It's a healthy, normal, natural expression of sexuality.

While it is perfectly natural and healthy to masturbate, it's also perfectly healthy and normal *not* to. Not all boys want to; not all guys feel good about it. Some religions prohibit it.

If it stresses you out, don't do it. There's certainly no obligation to masturbate.

Thar she blows!

Whatever you do, don't cap the opening of the tip of your penis with your finger when ejaculating!

This can drive the semen backward, and it can even end up in the wrong tanks—bladder and prostate gland—where it can cause problems.

Masturbating with Friends

Some guys masturbate in groups; others wouldn't even consider it.

If you don't feel good about group masturbation, don't do it. If you feel it's wrong, it *is* wrong—for you.

HEADS UP!

If someone outside of your own, similar age group (either older or younger) is present, definitely don't participate in group masturbation. A significantly older person shouldn't in any way be involved sexually with a significantly younger person. Child abuse is the issue (see page 120).

Inflation Issues

Sometimes, for no apparent reason (even when a guy is sexually aroused and ready to roll), there will be an unwelcome surprise: Your penis will just go limp.

As previously noted, the penis is not always cooperative, not completely predictable, and not consistently reliable. Loss of erection, or not even getting an erection in the first place, is an event that most males experience on occasion.

If it happens to you, don't panic. Understand that this is normal. Don't get down on yourself about it, and don't make doomsday predictions about your sexual ability. You're fine.

Try again later.

FYI Penis Check

When a guy's penis becomes consistently unreliable, it's advisable to see a doctor. There can be a number of causes for this treatable condition; stress can be a factor. Not knowing what's up and worrying about it adds to stress. He needs to get checked so he can get back on track!

Fantasies

You might spend considerable time imagining having sexual experiences. Lots of people do! It's called **fantasizing**. Fantasizing is a safe way for a kid to imagine being in a sexual situation without actually being in one.

Fantasizing while masturbating is a very common activity. And fantasizing can get pretty creative.

Same-sex fantasies are especially common during adolescence, when feelings about friendship can become a little confused, so it's not unusual to have fantasies that involve a best guy friend. These fantasies don't define sexual orientation (see page 80).

It's normal for some boys to fantasize about having a sexual encounter with a sister or other relative; many kids have fantasies about family members during their teen years. These fantasies are very different from actual incest within the family, which is a serious problem (see page 134).

If any of your fantasies disturb you, dream up something else to fantasize about or just stop fantasizing for a while. It's not like you *have to* fantasize!

Hazard Light

If you're seriously thinking about actually *acting on* an unlawful or inappropriate fantasy, don't. Talk to a counselor. Your doctor can refer you. A counselor can help you identify what might be causing you to contemplate doing something regrettable or harmful to someone else or yourself.

HEADS UP!

Flashing (exhibitionism) is never okay.

It is wrong and against the law for a guy to intentionally expose his genitals (or butt) for the purpose of shocking or getting a reaction from an unsuspecting person or persons.

A guy can get arrested for doing this, and if convicted, in addition to whatever other penalties a judge may impose, he may be required to identify himself as a sex offender wherever he goes.

Likewise, masturbating in public or in a

situation where you're "accidentally on purpose" likely to get caught by an unsuspecting person is a form of exhibitionism.

It's taken very seriously; it can have the same consequences as flashing, if not worse ones.

Looking at Sexy Pictures

Looking at regular old garden-variety sexy pictures, like mail-order lingerie catalogs or posters of supermodels, isn't exactly unpredictable behavior for teen boys and it's not exactly a crime! Don't guilt yourself out about it. But stay away from pornography (porn).

Pornography

Pornography includes X-rated videos, films, photos, or other images depicting explicit sexual material. It's commonly called "porn." If an adult offers to show you porn, consider it a sexual advance. Decline the offer, and report it to another adult. Showing kids porn is a tactic commonly used by molesters (see page 126).

Don't let curiosity get the best of you. You may be curious, but Internet porn sites are not good places for kids to learn about sex. Think about it: Why have a bunch of potentially weird sexual images floating around in your head before you've even figured out what's going on with your own sexuality?

You may have stronger sexual feelings.

During puberty, people commonly discover that they have increased sexual feelings. It doesn't mean there's something wrong with you if you don't. Not all guys do.

Romantic Attractions

Puberty is famous for being a time when people can have pretty strong physical reactions (attrac-

tions) to each other (see page 78). But not everybody experiences these.

Attractions to Adults

You may find yourself sexually attracted to adult movie stars, models, and other adult celebs.

You may also develop crushes on adults you know, such as your teachers, coaches, your friends' parents, etc.

These temporary attractions are a normal part of growing up. As long as they're not acted on, they're fine.

Hazard Light

Adults know that preadolescents and teens are prone to crushes on adults.

They also know it's totally wrong and against the law for an adult to respond sexually to a kid under the age of consent. If an adult you have a crush on wants to return your affection physically, the adult is out of line. Don't enter into the relationship. Tell another adult what's going on (see page 129)!

Attractions to Relatives

You might be surprised by sexual feelings toward your relatives of either sex. Getting a crush on a relative is very common. While it's perfectly natural for a kid to feel attracted to a family member, it's not okay to act on those feelings in a sexual way.

Hazard Light

Occasionally, an adult (or significantly older or more powerful kid) relative may try to get sexual with a kid (or kids) in the family. If this happens to you, refuse. Do *not* blame yourself. Tell another adult what happened and/or call the Child Help USA National Child Abuse Hot Line (see page 46). The hot line is for teens (and adults), too.

CHAPTER 3

EXTERIOR
Maintenance:
BASIC CARE

UNDERBODY MAINTENANCE

Caring for Your Genitals
Wash them every day or two with soap and water.

Detailing
If you're not circumcised, pay special attention to cleaning under your foreskin.

Self-Exam
About once a month, it's a good idea to examine your testicles. Why? Even though cancer is very, *very* rare among teens, testicular cancer does occur in young men. It begins in the cells that manufacture sperm. It grows into a lump that can be felt.

Testicular cancer can be cured if detected and treated early.

After taking a shower or bath, feel each testicle separately. Using the fingers and thumbs of both hands, gently roll each testicle around (fingers under the testicle, thumbs on top).

Note the epididymis, a structure that is loosely attached to the outside of each testis (on the back). It belongs there (see page 12).

If you discover a small lump, don't panic. Most lumps are cysts (lumps filled with fluid), not cancer. But do have all lumps checked by a doctor just to make sure!

Protect Your Genitals from Injury
A jockstrap (athletic supporter) hugs the genitals close to the body, supporting them and making them less vulnerable to injury during sports. A cup, which fits into the front of a jockstrap, affords extra protection.

Jockstraps are sold in stores that sell athletic equipment—uniforms and that kind of stuff.

They are also sold in department stores, usually the men's and boys' underwear department.

PREVENTING SURFACE DETERIORATION

"Jock Rot"
What an insulting name for a common condition: having a damp feeling and sore, red, itchy skin around your testicles and on your inner thighs.

Happily, when a guy has jock rot, nothing is rotting.

FIX-IT TICKETS

In terms of genital care, the following situations absolutely require a pit stop. Go to the doctor and get checked out if you . . .

- ☐ Have pain in your genitals or lower abdomen
- ☐ Have an injury to your testicles
- ☐ Develop a sore or tender spot on your testicles, groin, or genital area
- ☐ Notice a lump on a testicle, in the groin, or in the genital area
- ☐ Have a discharge (pus) come out of the tip of your penis
- ☐ Develop a yellowy-white discharge that's odorless
- ☐ Have a milky discharge (not semen)
- ☐ Have milky urine
- ☐ Have a burning sensation while peeing or have pain in your urethra
- ☐ Have an urgent and/or frequent need to pee
- ☐ Have a foul odor under your foreskin
- ☐ Have warts growing on or around your genitals
- ☐ Have itching, burning, redness, rash, or raised bumps in your genital area
- ☐ Have a painless, clearly visible ulcer on your penis
- ☐ Have painful sores or blisters on your genitals, butt, or thighs
- ☐ Have any other bothersome or painful symptom or condition that worries you

The way to avoid jock rot (or "jock itch") is to wear clean and dry clothing (cotton underwear); also, don't wear pants that are irritating to your crotch.

A little cornstarch is rumored to take care of jock itch in some cases, but it might require a **fungicide**—which kills fungus, the underlying cause of the problem. Fungicides are sold in the drugstore; just ask the pharmacist for a recommendation.

If the condition doesn't improve, be sure to contact your doctor. The rash may have a cause that requires medical attention.

GUY REPORT: JOCKSTRAPS

Guy #1: "When I was in the sixth grade, my family stayed with relatives in San Antonio, Texas. We temporarily stayed with my aunt and uncle—who sold graves to people before they were dead.

"I went to a huge school, and I had to change classes all day like in a high school. This was new to me. I had to take the city buses to get to the school; also, I had to look after my little brother. In gym class one day, the coach said, 'Okay. I want everybody next week to have your gym clothes—tennis shoes, shorts, T-shirt, and jockstrap.'

"Whoa!

"I was glad the stay in San Antonio was only temporary. I hoped we could hurry up and move so I wouldn't have to bring up jockstraps to my parents. I dreaded telling them I needed a jockstrap. Especially because I had no idea why I did need one! I didn't want to appear ignorant.

"Despite repeated warnings from my coach, I was able to hold out until we moved; I never had the conversation with my parents.

"My next school was also in Texas. The kids didn't even wear shoes much in that school and rejected shoes while playing sports; they felt shoes 'slowed 'em down.'

"There were lots of jocks there—just no straps."

Guy #2: "All I remember about my first jockstrap is the sense of relief I felt when I realized that the 'size: small' referred to the waistband."

WASHING THE SURFACE
Many guys shower every day.

Be considerate of the environment; be aware of the amount of water you use and the energy it takes to heat it.

In other words: Shower and get outta there!

Reuse your towel. If you arrange it nicely someplace to dry (like on the towel rack?), it will be more appealing to use again.

And of course, it always helps not to drop, step on, and stand on your towel between uses.

Not every guy has the opportunity to shower daily.

If your living situation doesn't allow for you to, no problem. All anybody needs is soap, water, and a sink or washbasin.

Wash and rinse your face, neck, behind your ears, armpits, genitals, and rear with water, soap, and a washcloth. In that order: face first and rear last.

Also: Brush your teeth, morning and night.

Keep Your Face Clean
To help avoid pimples, blackheads, and whiteheads, wash your face twice a day with warm water and mild soap. What's a mild soap? Ask your pharmacist. Pharmacists can be some

of the most helpful people on the planet.

If you are prone to pimples, avoid using perfumed or deodorant soaps, which can make matters worse.

There are over-the-counter cleansers and medicated soaps specifically designed for attacking zits, but don't overdo them. Overusing these products actually can make pimples worse instead of better.

Remember, a mild soap and warm water twice a day is probably all you need to keep your skin clean.

Spot Removal

It's tempting to try to pop and squeeze pimples and blackheads, but don't. Squeezing, rubbing, pressure, and friction all aggravate acne. Popping and picking can cause scarring.

If you have a habit of rubbing your face or sitting with your chin cupped in your hand, don't. Try to keep your hands off your face. Don't fiddle with bumps or scabs.

Avoid using oily hair and skin products. Check the labels of the products you buy. Many hair and skin care products are oil-free and those are preferable if you have acne.

Ingrown hairs causing zits? See page 9.

Unless you have identified or strongly suspect a

specific food allergy, don't stress too much about snacks. Snack foods—including chocolate and chips—do not cause acne. In moderation, snack foods are fine. But do eat well. There are plenty of options for healthy snacks. Eating well contributes to good health in general—including the health of the skin (see page 31).

HEADS UP!
Acne out of control?
Bummed about it?
Talk to your doctor. You may need to be on a supervised, long-term skin care program to get the results you want.

Lotion and Sunblock
Whatever the shade of your skin, it's the right shade. Nobody's skin is too dark or too light.

A little lotion (oil-free is available) will make dry skin feel soft and smooth. And lotion will bring out the deep, rich tones of darker skin.

The lighter the skin and the lighter your eyes, the higher your risk for developing skin cancer from exposure to ultraviolet rays of the sun. But anybody can get skin cancer. Wear sunblock (oil-free is available) and a hat (if practical) when you plan to be outside for extended periods—playing or watching outdoor sports, hiking, climbing, skateboarding, snowboarding, skiing, swimming, surfing, sailing, etc.

Unprotected exposure to the sun can cause damaging sunburns, which may contribute to developing melanoma (cancer of the melanocyte) and premature aging of the skin later on in life.

Stay out of tanning salons.

Tans fade, but unhealthy effects of exposure to ultraviolet rays linger on.

TRIM
Guy Advice: Instructions for Using an Electric Shaver
1. Plug the shaver in (keep it away from water, so you don't get shocked to death) and turn it on. If it's a rechargeable battery-operated razor, you won't have to plug it in—just take it off the charger and turn it on.

2. Rub it around your face. Use light pressure.

3. You may have to make some faces at yourself in the mirror to get to the hard-to-reach places, like under your nose.

4. When you're done, flip it open and brush the whiskers out. Or blow 'em out. Over the trash can or sink, of course.

5. If it's battery-operated, return the razor to the charger—which plugs into the wall socket.

6. If you want to, you can sprinkle a little aftershave (astringent) lotion into one palm, rub your palms together, and rub it on your face. It feels good.

7. If you use aftershave, don't get carried away with it.

FUZZ-FACE:
GUY REPORT ON SHAVING
"When I was old enough to stand at the bathroom sink and watch my father shave, it was still an art form. Shaving mug, brush, straight razor, and hot towels. Pulling the nose up to get under there. Pursing the lips and wonking them left or right. Lifting the chin to get at the neck. Finishing off the job with some smelly stuff.

"Later, shaving became a craft—still a ritual, but faster, and the tools less beautiful.

"Then came the electric shaver.

"What a disappointment.

"I had watched my father shave for many years so that I'd know what to do—with mug, brush, razor, and towels.

"What started out seeming like a grand adventure ended up being just like mowing the lawn."

GUY REPORT: INSTRUCTIONS FOR SHAVING WITH A SAFETY RAZOR

"Here's how I shave with a safety razor:

"I use a double-bladed cartridge and shaving cream for sensitive skin. (But you'll have to figure out which products work best for you.)

"I rinse my face with warm water.

"I dispense some shaving cream from the aerosol can onto the fingertips of one hand and apply the cream to the areas to be shaved: above upper lip, below lower lip, chin, sideburns, cheeks, neck.

"I usually start above my upper lip. I stick my tongue up between my top front teeth and my upper lip to make the area firm for shaving.

"I press lightly on my skin and drag the razor downward in short strokes.

"I do the same thing for the area under my lower lip, above my chin. (I put my tongue in there, too, to make the skin firm.)

"When the razor gets full of shaving cream, I rinse it under the faucet.

"When shaving my neck, I point my chin upward to stretch the skin nice and tight. I usually shave in downward strokes because it's awkward for me to turn the razor around to shave upward, although I think other people do this (in order to shave against the direction in which beard hairs grow).

"I try not to press too hard because when I do, I accidentally cut myself.

"I'm extra careful near my earlobes and nostrils because the sensitive skin in these areas is easily nicked or cut if I'm not paying attention."

FYI Cologne

If you want to, you can use cologne, but don't skunk up the place.

A little bit is good. Some people feel that none is even better!

Disposable (Throwaway) Razors

Disposable razors are popular and relatively safe to use, although it is easy with any razor to nick or cut yourself while shaving. Disposable razors should not be used more than a few times—they get dull.

Through trial and error, you can pick the brand of disposable razor that works best for you; many guys recommend double-bladed or triple-bladed. The more blades, the better.

Razors should not be shared. Although it would be very unlikely to become exposed to blood-borne disease through a shared razor blade, it is technically possible (see page 89).

HEADS UP! Ingrown Hairs

Sometimes whiskers bend at the tips, arch downward, and puncture the skin. These irritations cause pimples to form.

There are shaving techniques that can help avoid this recurring problem. One trick is not to get too close a shave. You may need to use a single-bladed razor (rather than a double- or triple-bladed one) or an electric shaver.

Talk to your doctor or dermatologist.

KEEPING THE UPHOLSTERY CLEAN

Your clothes need to be relatively clean for you to stay smelling good.

Ask for a lesson on how to use your washing machine. Here are the basics for beginners:

1. Don't stuff it full of clothes, you'll break it. It's better to do an extra load or two than it is to overload the washer and burn out the motor. Also, your clothes will get cleaner.

2. Check the washing machine settings. Don't run a full load on a low water cycle. There has to be enough water! Use the normal setting, unless you're washing clothes marked delicate on the labels.

3. Let some water run in first and dissolve a measured amount of detergent in the water before adding the clothes. Read instructions on the detergent box or bottle.

4. Balance the load—arrange evenly around the agitator. Otherwise, the washing machine will shake, rattle, and hop around the floor and possibly break.

5. Wash dark clothes with other dark clothes and lights with lights.

6. Check every label for washing instructions and follow them.

7. Check every label for drying instructions and follow them. This is critical!

Tip: If you take your clothes out of the dryer, flap or smooth 'em out and fold or hang them when still warm, they'll be less wrinkled.

If you stuff warm clothes into a laundry basket all balled up, they'll end up totally wrinkled!

8. Don't do other family members' laundry without their permission. It's so easy to ruin clothes during the washing/drying process.

Bleach

Don't mix bleach with other household chemicals! Lethal gases can form as a result.

Okay to use it in the washer along with standard laundry detergent, unless the directions say otherwise.

Begin the cycle that fills the washing machine with water. Once the washer is partly filled, carefully measure and add bleach to the water (don't just guess and glug it in) before putting in your clothes.

Do this before the agitator starts so you won't get clobbered by the agitator.

If not properly and evenly diluted with water, bleach will make splotchy marks and even weaken the fabric and make holes in it!

Basically, bleach is for white stuff. It makes clothes whiter and gets out certain stains.

Don't use bleach unless you've checked every label of everything you are going to wash. Lots of white clothes can't be bleached successfully.

HEADS UP!

Make sure you don't get bleach in your eyes, and if you do, immediately start rinsing them under a gentle stream of water (cup your hands and blink into the water as it flows) and keep on rinsing them for 15 minutes. Then call your doctor.

Meanwhile, if someone is home, have that person call your doctor, poison control, or the local emergency room for you and ask what else to do.

Got no washer/dryer?

If you don't have access to a washing machine, routinely wash out your underwear and socks in the bathroom sink or tub—with warm water and a bar of soap. Rinse well.

The Foolproof Drying Procedure: Lay the article of clothing (T-shirt, for example) on a towel, tightly roll the towel up, and then wring it as hard as you can. Then unroll the towel, flap out the shirt, and hang the shirt (and towel) up to dry.

Hamper Violations

Prowling through the dirty clothes hamper and sniff-testing your T-shirts as a kind of rotation method of selecting your outfit for the day is an absolute infraction.

Skid Marks

Skid marks keep showing up in your underwear?

These can be mighty unpleasant for whoever does the wash—including you. Plus, they stain.

Bathroom tip: Wipe and look at the toilet paper. If it's clean, wash your hands and you're outta there.

Otherwise, keep at it.

Another Bathroom Tip:

There's a handy little device in every bathroom called a toilet paper holder. When the roll gets down to the cardboard cylinder, be a good guy: Replace it!

Keeping Fluid Levels in Check

Deodorants (cover odor)/antiperspirants (block perspiration) are available in various forms: spray, cream, stick (solid), and roll-on. They all work pretty much the same. Some are scented, some aren't. If you're not sure which kind you want, it's safe to buy an unscented stick or roll-on deodorant. That way, you won't end up with one that smells too strong or has a scent you don't like.

Deodorants are sold all over the place; you're certain to find them sold in drugstores, grocery stores, and convenience stores. They cost about $3 or $4 each—maybe a little more. But a deodorant lasts quite a long time.

There's usually a men's section and a women's section of deodorants. They all work the same, but the women's types often have scents associated with girls—like "spring bouquets," for example. The guy ones have more "masculine" scents—whatever that means. Regardless, they're clearly labeled. Some are unisex. And again—many, both for men and women, are unscented.

To use deodorant, take off the cap and roll it around under each armpit for a few seconds.

If you're going to put on a dress shirt, you may want to wait a minute before putting the shirt on after using deodorant. That way, the deodorant will have a chance to dry and won't show up on the fabric. (A deodorant marked "clear" is the least likely to transfer onto your clothing when you're getting dressed.)

A good time to put on deodorant is after a shower—after you dry off and cool off a little. If you do it that way, it usually lasts all day, unless you become involved in a raucous game or sporting event.

If you shower at night before bed, it isn't necessary to put on deodorant. Just put it on in the morning.

Phantom Deodorant

With stick-type deodorants you have to occasionally dispense a little more deodorant for yourself by turning the bottom of the container. If you don't move it up, you'll just be rubbing the applicator onto your armpit without any deodorant going on.

ROUTINE SERVICING
Getting a Physical Exam

If you haven't had a routine physical (checkup) lately, now might be a good time to make an appointment to schedule one.

A checkup is different from a visit to the doctor for an earache or a sore throat. It's a special appointment (usually done once a year) during which a doctor or other qualified health care provider spends time looking at "the whole picture," such as your height, your weight, your vision, and whether all your immunizations are up to date. A physical checkup for a growing boy also includes checking his blood pressure and the general condition of his heart, lungs, and abdomen. It includes having a doctor check the boy's penis and testicles to make sure they're up to snuff.

A checkup provides a good opportunity to talk with a doctor about changes that may be going on in your body. If you have questions, you can ask them and get answers. It's appropriate for you to ask to talk privately with your doctor if you feel you want or need to. This means: no mom or dad in the room, if that's the way you want it.

It's a good idea to write your questions down before the appointment so you won't forget to ask them.

It is also a good time to talk with your doctor about problems you may be having at home, in school, or with friends.

Be honest with your doctor if he (or she) asks you questions, even embarrassing ones. Your health care provider may need to know information that you may consider private, in order to take good care of you. This includes information about sexual contacts you may have had.

Also, don't withhold information from your doctor about drug and alcohol use and/or abuse. A doctor needs to be aware of all drugs a patient is using, including illegal drugs and over-the-counter drugs.

You don't need to wait for a checkup to talk to a doctor if something is troubling you.

CHASSIS CHECKS YOUR FRAME
Scoliosis

Sometimes, as a kid begins to enter puberty, his (or her) spine starts to grow faster than it should,

and it begins to curve. This is called scoliosis, and in most cases, the problems associated with it can be avoided if a doctor becomes aware of it early. Scoliosis is one of many important reasons to have routine physical checkups.

Many school districts have programs in which the school nurse checks kids for scoliosis. Having your back checked for scoliosis doesn't hurt at all.

BLURRY WINDSHIELD?
Eye Exams

A brief eye test (reading an eye chart) is part of a routine checkup. Be sure to tell your doctor and/or parents if you have trouble seeing the chalkboard at school, if movies seem blurry, or if it's difficult to read books and magazines.

Your school may also offer eye testing. A teacher, a teacher's aide, the principal, or the school nurse may be able to help schedule an eye exam for you at school.

Some kids (and adults) are self-conscious at first about wearing glasses, but being able to see clearly more than makes up for it. Like anything new, it takes a while to adjust to wearing glasses— but after a short time, it's no big deal.

If you are interested in contact lenses, listen carefully to what your eye doctor has to say about them. Leave contacts in only for the recommended length of time. Also, follow all instructions on cleaning your contacts. This is really important to help prevent eye infections and injuries.

Dental Exams

Dentists recommend that kids have dental checkups twice a year. Teeth need to be cleaned in a dentist's office routinely in order to avoid cavities and maintain good health of the gums.

Brushing and flossing do make a difference; brush as soon as you can after every meal. Use fluoride toothpaste, especially if your water is not fluoridated. Chewing sugarless gum helps flush the teeth with saliva and may help prevent cavities, but brushing is better.

Smelly Emissions

Bad breath can be an indication of having a dental problem.

Don't avoid contacting a dentist if you get a toothache; a toothache may be an indication that you have a cavity (hole) in one of your teeth, which will just become bigger and bigger until it is filled. Untreated cavities can make dental treatment complicated and expensive. Decaying teeth may also pose additional health risks.

Do you have questions about getting hooked up with affordable dental care? You or your parent can begin by talking to the county health department, listed in the phone book.

Perhaps your school nurse has some additional information.

THE GRILL
Orthodontic Exams

A dentist may recommend that you make an appointment with an orthodontist. An orthodontist is a dentist who corrects irregularities of the bite. The orthodontist will evaluate whether or not you actually need braces.

Not every family can afford braces just for the purpose of designing the perfect smile. They're very expensive! However, it's usually possible to straighten your teeth or improve your bite when you're an adult, if you still want to by the time you grow up.

You don't have to have straight teeth to have a great-looking smile, though—and not every adult wants perfectly straight teeth. Neither does every kid.

Keep on smiling: crooked teeth, braces, and all.

What's behind the smile is what matters most: you!

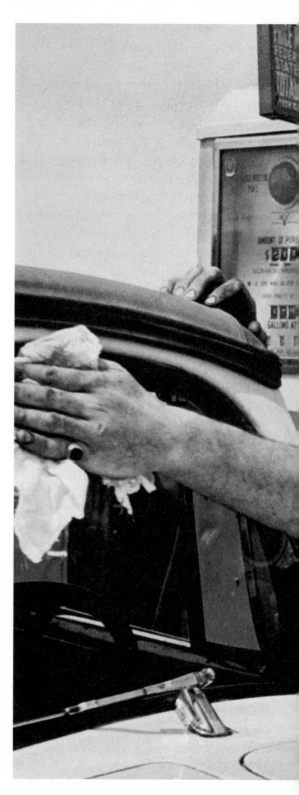

CHAPTER 4

OPERATING INSTRUCTIONS: KEEPING THE SYSTEMS RUNNING *Smoothly*

FILLING THE TANK: FOOD AND YOUR HEALTH

Everyone's body needs food to perform properly. A healthy diet includes appropriate combinations of proteins, fats, carbohydrates, and all of the vitamins and minerals required by the body. A well-balanced diet can be achieved by eating a variety of fruits and vegetables, low-fat dairy products, whole-grain cereals and breads, and lean red meat, chicken, fish, beans, nuts, and legumes.

Those who choose to eat a vegetarian diet must be extra careful to meet nutritional needs—especially during puberty, when the body is growing and changing very rapidly. Before deciding to eliminate meat and/or dairy from your diet, consult a health care professional. You'll need to be completely clear on how to fulfill your daily requirements, especially in the protein, iron, B vitamins, and calcium departments.

Fill 'er up!

Try not to skip meals—especially breakfast!

Kids who don't eat breakfast don't perform as well as they could in school. If you skip breakfast, it means that your body has had to go all night and then all the next morning until lunch to get the nourishment it needs. This can make you feel weak, irritable, sick, unable to concentrate, down in the dumps, and disinterested in your schoolwork.

At least eat a bowl of cereal (with low-fat or skim milk) in the morning. And grab a banana or an apple on your way out the door!

Do you like drinking milk?

If not, eat yogurt, frozen yogurt, cottage cheese, or other dairy products (nonfat and low-fat varieties are available). Your bones are still growing, gaining as much as 4 inches a year, and you need lots of calcium, which is found in milk products, to achieve your genetic potential for height and build strong bones.

If you don't "do dairy," you can get calcium from calcium-fortified juices, cereals, and other foods.

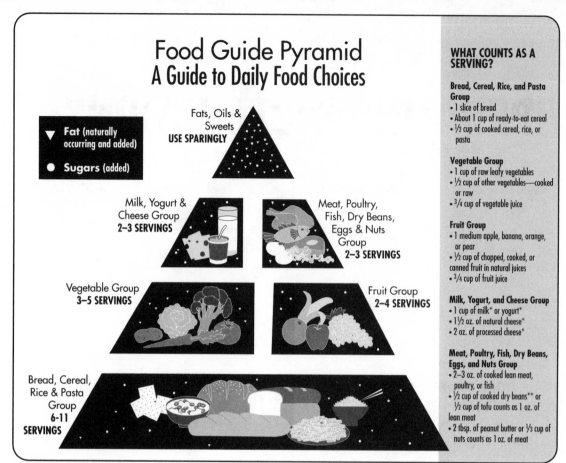

Food Guide Pyramid
A Guide to Daily Food Choices

▼ **Fat** (naturally occurring and added)

● **Sugars** (added)

Fats, Oils & Sweets
USE SPARINGLY

Milk, Yogurt & Cheese Group
2–3 SERVINGS

Meat, Poultry, Fish, Dry Beans, Eggs & Nuts Group
2–3 SERVINGS

Vegetable Group
3–5 SERVINGS

Fruit Group
2–4 SERVINGS

Bread, Cereal, Rice & Pasta Group
6-11 SERVINGS

WHAT COUNTS AS A SERVING?

Bread, Cereal, Rice, and Pasta Group
- 1 slice of bread
- About 1 cup of ready-to-eat cereal
- ½ cup of cooked cereal, rice, or pasta

Vegetable Group
- 1 cup of raw leafy vegetables
- ½ cup of other vegetables—cooked or raw
- ¾ cup of vegetable juice

Fruit Group
- 1 medium apple, banana, orange, or pear
- ½ cup of chopped, cooked, or canned fruit in natural juices
- ¾ cup of fruit juice

Milk, Yogurt, and Cheese Group
- 1 cup of milk* or yogurt*
- 1½ oz. of natural cheese*
- 2 oz. of processed cheese*

Meat, Poultry, Fish, Dry Beans, Eggs, and Nuts Group
- 2–3 oz. of cooked lean meat, poultry, or fish
- ½ cup of cooked dry beans** or ½ cup of tofu counts as 1 oz. of lean meat
- 2 tbsp. of peanut butter or ⅓ cup of nuts counts as 1 oz. of meat

*Choose fat-free or reduced-fat dairy products most often. **Dry beans, peas, and lentils can be counted as servings in either meat and beans group or the vegetable group.

But be vigilant! If you cannot get enough from food, talk to your health care provider about taking calcium supplements.

Lactose Intolerance

If you are lactose-intolerant (have difficulty digesting the sugar present in milk properly), your pediatrician can help you to make appropriate substitutions for milk in your diet and/or suggest a medication to help with digestion. Calcium supplements may be advised.

Other good sources of calcium include...

. . . canned fish with soft bones such as sardines, anchovies, and salmon; dark green leafy vegetables such as kale, mustard greens, turnip greens, and bok choy; tofu, if processed with calcium sulfate (read labels); tortillas made from lime-processed corn (read labels).

A daily multivitamin pill with minerals...

. . . is a good idea for a growing kid. You don't have to buy expensive ones; just standard daily multiple vitamins from the drugstore or grocery store work.

Do you shop for yourself?
If so, here's a handy list of what to buy.

HOPPING LIST OF
UTRITIOUS, LOW-FAT FOODS

uits and Vegetables and Legumes

Apples
Apricots
Bananas
Bok choy
Broccoli
Brussels sprouts
Cabbage
Cantaloupe
Carrots
Cauliflower
Chickpeas
Dried beans
  (navy beans, pinto beans,
  black beans, etc.)
Kale
Melons
Oranges
Peaches
Pears
Potatoes
Prunes
Raisins
Raspberries
Red and green peppers
Spinach
Strawberries
Sweet potatoes
Tomatoes
Winter squash

imal Products

Cheese (made from skim milk)
Chicken/turkey (remove skin)
Fish
Lean meats (trim fat)
Milk (nonfat/low-fat)
Yogurt (nonfat/low-fat)

reals and Grains

Brown rice
Corn tortillas
Pasta
Whole-grain bread
Whole-grain cereals

Source: American Cancer Society.

High-Octane Fuel

How much fast food do you eat?

Fast food, like cheeseburgers and fries, has a higher fat and calorie content than you may need on a regular basis. Be moderate in your consumption of fast food.

Fresh food—like fresh fruits and vegetables—and food that's prepared by baking, broiling, boiling, steaming, poaching, and grilling is generally more healthy than food that's prepared by frying, especially deep-fat frying.

Read the Map

Most fast-food restaurants offer heathful options: green salad, frozen yogurt with fruit topping, roasted chicken, tostadas piled with lettuce, tomatoes, onions, and beans. . . . Check out the menu!

Extra-large fries, huge soft drinks—and all for just a few cents more? Maybe it's best just to pass on these offers.

Snacks

Choose healthy snacks, like popcorn and fruit. Sweet between meal snacks promote tooth decay—especially chewy, sticky sweet snacks. If you can't resist them, brush after you eat them. If you can't brush, rinse your mouth with water. It at least helps!

Drinks

Sweetened drinks (like sodas, for example) have amazing amounts of added sugar—say, 12 teaspoons or more per drink. Experts in nutrition are beginning to advise us to pretty much give sweetened drinks the boot. They're considered one of the primary causes of **obesity** (being very fat).

HEADS UP!

"Nutraceutical" drinks promise health benefits, but a lot of claims are false. Some of the herbal additives can be straight-up bad for you!

Worried about being too light or too heavy?

Pediatricians are trained to evaluate growth, and a visit to discuss your weight can be very reassuring. Being slim usually isn't a medical problem at all, but it can be, especially if you are severely underweight.

Obesity is a growing problem in the United States. What makes it complicated is the fact that eating and body-image disorders are also problems! We don't want to focus too much on weight.

But you do need to pay attention to it so that you remain in the healthy weight range.

Our convenience-oriented culture, coupled with easy access to high-fat, high-calorie foods and the availability of fun things to do that just involve sitting, has contributed to a rise in obesity of teens.

If you think you're overweight, talk to your pediatrician. He or she can decide what is a healthy weight range for you. If he or she agrees that slowing your weight gain, maintaining your weight, or losing weight is a healthy choice for you, you can map out a program together.

Weight management for kids in puberty should be supervised by a health care professional who can recommend a specific nutritional/active-lifestyle program. In puberty, when you are growing and changing so fast, your body requires lots of specific nutrients.

Or you can ask for a referral to a registered dietitian, who can help you evaluate your eating habits and daily intake of food and advise you as to changes you may make regarding food choices. And follow your progress!

Your registered dietitian (or doctor) may also help you devise an exercise plan that fits your lifestyle and is workable for you.

Eat better. Be less inactive. Be more active. But . . .

Don't diet.

It's true that we can all live without that huge piece of cake or pie or that double-scoop ice cream cone or extra blob of butter and generous dollop of sour cream on a baked potato.

And yes, we can choose to eat a few cookies or chips rather than a whole stack. Or better yet, substitute fruit for cookies and chips.

But don't diet.

Diets, including fad diets, just plain don't work in the long run. They may even disrupt your normal metabolic rate and be counterproductive for weight loss. And dieting can be detrimental to the health of growing teens.

It's fine to cut back on or eliminate stuff—like sweetened drinks, candy, and desserts, for example—that has little or no redeeming nutritional value.

A switch from whole-milk products (milk, ice cream, cheese) to nonfat or low-fat milk products is also a fine idea. Nobody needs the quantities of saturated fats (bad fats, which clog the arteries) that are present in whole milk and other dairy and animal products.

It's also fine to cut back on portion sizes at meals.

HEADS UP!
A registered dietitian or otherwise qualified professional should be involved in any athletic program for teens that stresses weight loss or gain as part of training or competing. Look into it. Wrestlers: This means you!

PARKING VIOLATIONS

Failure to move around enough is one cause of weight gain. Odd as it sounds, prolonged TV watching is fattening. It's often coupled with turbo-snacking and intense exposure to ads for high-calorie, high-fat food. To get fit or stay fit, you may need to reduce the amount of time you

CHEF TIPS

Cooking for yourself or your family? Here are some tips for safe handling and preparation of food:

Separate raw, cooked, and ready-to-eat foods while shopping, preparing, and storing. This prevents cross-contamination. (Example: Bacteria present in raw chicken gets onto salad stuff when juice drips out of the package.)

Don't put cooked or ready-to-eat food on any surface, plate, pan, or bowl (or utensil) that has come in contact with raw meat, raw poultry, raw seafood, or raw egg—unless the surface (or plate, etc.) has been washed with hot, soapy water. Barbecuers beware!

Don't leave perishable food out of the refrigerator for more than 2 hours—1 hour if the air temperature is above 90° F.

Defrost frozen food in the refrigerator, microwave, under cold running water, or in cold water changed every 30 minutes.

Marinate food in the refrigerator.

Cook food to proper temperature. Thermometers designed to test the temperatures of food can be bought at the grocery store. Just make sure you follow instructions on the package.

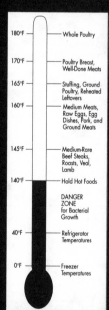

Temperature	Food
180°F	Whole Poultry
170°F	Poultry Breast, Well-Done Meats
165°F	Stuffing, Ground Poultry, Reheated Leftovers
160°F	Medium Meats, Raw Eggs, Egg Dishes, Pork, and Ground Meats
145°F	Medium-Rare Beef Steaks, Roasts, Veal, Lamb
140°F	Hold Hot Foods
	DANGER ZONE for Bacterial Growth
40°F	Refrigerator Temperatures
0°F	Freezer Temperatures

Make sure the microwave heats food evenly. Cover, turn, and stir, if necessary. Follow the instructions on the packaging.

Divide large amounts of leftovers into small, shallow containers for quick cooling in the refrigerator.

Don't stuff that refrigerator! Air needs to circulate for the system to work right.

Wash your hands for 20 seconds (count to 30) with warm, soapy water before handling food (or utensils) and after handling raw meat, poultry, fish, shellfish, and eggs.

Wash fruits and vegetables before eating.

Want to know more? Call 1-888-SAFE FOOD or visit www.foodsafety.gov.

spend sitting in neutral in front of the computer or TV. Adolescent health experts recommend 2 hours daily, max.

Check the meter.

Once you figure out how many hours a day you spend just sitting, you can make an adjustment. Set some limits for yourself.

Just do stuff.

You may think I'm working for your parents when I say this, but listen up: Lounging around burns way fewer calories than doing just about anything else (except sleeping, maybe).

Unloading the groceries, putting them away, vacuuming, sweeping, gardening, raking leaves, shoveling snow, organizing the garage, cleaning up your room—all these annoying chores assigned to you by your parents help keep you fit without your even leaving your home.

➤ **Identify the physical activities that you like doing and do them all year-round.**
It's best to build activity into your everyday routine.

HEADS UP!
If you are extremely overweight, check with your doctor before stepping up your activity level. Team up and make a plan. You can do this!

Have fun.

Participate in sports if you want to. If you don't, get some exercise in other ways.

Keep alternative sports in mind. If you don't like football, so what! Lots of guys reject football and other team sports. Play Ping-Pong!

Maybe it's nerdy—but it's a blast!

Play croquet!

Not good at it?

Be bad at it!

Just have fun.

Don't like games?

Noncompetitive activities that stress participation rather than winning may be the way for you to go.

HEADS UP!

Moderate exercise that focuses on strength, flexibility, and cardiovascular health is the key to creating and maintaining a balance for total fitness. To avoid injury, even a moderate workout should include stretching, warming up, exercising, cooling down, and stretching again. Find out how before you start!

Community Fitness Programs for Teens

Just about every community has supervised programs to keep teens fit and active—and occupied. The cost is usually low or free. Ask your parent or teacher to help you find what's available. Depending on where you live, you may be able to sign up for anything from basketball to ballroom dancing, from karate to yoga.

Water Ahead

Health clubs, country clubs, and backyard pools are the greatest, but we don't all have access to these terrific places.

If you don't, remember: Many communities do have a YMCA or other public facility where you can take lessons and swim for a reasonable fee or for free.

Why not call and check it out?

Go first with your parent or other trusted adult to scope out the situation. And never swim alone. Buddy up!

Just dance f-a-s-t.

Dancing fast is great exercise and fun all at the same time. You don't need a partner. Dance with the doorknob; dance with yourself in the mirror if you want.

Just go for a walk!

If you're in good health, walking briskly is great for physical fitness.

Unfortunately, we don't all have access to a beautiful walking path through a safe neighborhood. If you don't, choose another fitness activity. If you do—cool! Still, don't walk alone. And walk where someone could be called upon for help if needed (see page 136).

When you're out in the world, remain aware of your surroundings. Leave your disc player at home. Wear something bright so you're visible from a distance. Don't walk at dusk or in the dark.

Off-Roading

Does your parent or other adult relative like to hike?

Hiking in the out-of-doors may be the single most satisfying form of exercise if you love nature, but don't hike alone. Kids should hike with a responsible adult. A *short* hike on a well-marked trail is the way to begin.

Check it out.

Any marked hiking trails in the parks in your area? First, let your fingers do the walking: Use the phone book to find out. (Try looking under government listings under county, state, or national parks.) Ask when the park opens and closes and what trails are for beginners. Are maps provided? Where do you get one? It's best to hike with a trail map. Ask if there are any particular hazards you need to be aware of, like poisonous snakes or poison oak, ivy, or sumac.

Plan to stay on the trail. Scrambling around on rocks or on steep terrain or going cross-country should be avoided, unless you are hiking with an experienced adult guide.

High-tech equipment is the greatest, but if you don't own hiking boots, a sturdy pair of high-topped sneakers that support your ankles and feet and have good treads—and a small day pack—will be great for starters (on a beginners' trail). Bring a hat with a brim and sunglasses. Don't forget sunscreen.

Throw into your backpack a couple of plastic bottles of water. You'll need to drink plenty while you're on the trail, but don't expect to be able to drink from streams or lakes along the way. Unfortunately, most are contaminated.

Bring a healthy, high-calorie snack that doesn't spoil easily in your pack, such as trail mix, a couple of energy bars, and/or a peanut-butter-and-jelly sandwich or two. Oranges are also great to carry along, since they don't squash easily. And they're so refreshing! Empty a little water out of one of the bottles (so the bottle won't break) and freeze it; it will keep your food cool. Remember perishable food needs to be eaten within 2 hours, or 1 hour if the air temperature is above 90°F. Toss in a flashlight and a couple of extra batteries (it's a very good idea to hike with a flashlight no matter what time you expect to be home), a pack of matches or plastic lighter sealed in a plastic bag,

GO EASY ON YOURSELF

Achieving the "look" of a model is not a practical or meaningful goal for boys or girls. Accepting ourselves and each other, including our different body types, is.

People are genetically programmed to be a variety of sizes and shapes. Clothing ads, especially those featured in teen or fashion magazines, are famous for portraying unrealistic images of both men and women.

Photos of models in ads are often "enhanced" (faked); the photo's touched up. We see the same male body type over and over again in ads: tall, broad-shouldered, slender, very buff.

Certain models, entertainers, and actors have had plastic (cosmetic) surgery to achieve the "perfect" body; some guys even have biceps implants.

Many women in film, TV, and print ads may have had breast-implant surgery, "tummy tucks," butt lifts, rib removal, or liposuction (surgical fat-cell removal). Many struggle with eating disorders to try to maintain an unnaturally thin body.

Only a small percentage of girls will grow up to have the size and shape of breasts, hips, and thighs commonly seen on models wearing swimsuits, lingerie, or low-cut dresses; only a small percentage of guys will grow up to be proportioned like models.

It's reassuring to take a look around at the people you know—or even see walking around.

Most people, regardless of age, just look like people—not actors or supermodels.

and something warm in case the weather cools off. A pocketknife can come in handy, too.

A few Band-Aids are helpful in case you develop blisters on the trail. Are ticks or mosquitoes a problem? If so, use and bring repellent.

A wad of toilet paper or tissues is essential.

Now get your adult onto his or her feet—and you're on your way. Stretch before you start hiking and warm up by walking slowly for the first few minutes.

Hiking opens up amazing possibilities. Photography and bird watching are two of them, to say nothing of beginning a lifelong love affair with nature.

HEADS UP!
If your school pack is doubling as your day pack for hiking, make sure you take out your matches/lighter and pocketknife before going back to school with it.

FOCUSING ON THE EXTERIOR
Set and maintain reasonable standards for yourself.

There are good reasons to eat a nutritious, moderate-fat diet (with good fats) and to exercise regularly. It's appropriate to have the goals of being healthy, strong, and in good shape. But remember: You don't have to be buff to be physically fit. Only a handful of people are genetically programmed to be able to achieve the body of a professional athlete or Olympian. If you think you've got what it takes to become one of the few—go for it!

Consumer Alert

The media have invented an idealized male image that can cause some guys to feel as though they just don't "measure up." Preteen and teen boys are particularly vulnerable to these feelings. If you learn how to "read the media," you will recognize that many commercials are designed to make us feel like we're just, somehow, not good enough the way we are—that we need to buy something (which they're promoting) to be popular, successful, and powerful.

Bodybuilding

Dream of having big biceps and a six-pack?

For the moment, your body is busy building itself.

Talk to your doctor before embarking on a program to increase your muscle mass.

He or she will want to identify what stage of puberty you are in before advising you as to when and if it's okay for you to start bodybuilding (if you start too early, you can conceivably work against your own natural, healthy muscular development).

Likewise, before taking nutritional supplements (including herbal supplements) to gain or lose weight, run the products past your doctor, regardless of the safety claims on the container or what the salesperson promises you.

Unregulated nutritional supplements can be dangerous. There have been problems regarding quality control and contamination of supplement ingredients.

It's also hard to know what quantities (or combinations) might actually be bad for your health. And please keep this in mind: Just because something is labeled "natural" or "herbal" doesn't mean it's good for you.

Don't take steroids!

Unless they are prescribed by your physician to address a medical problem, don't take steroids.

HEADS UP!
Among other things, steroids can permanently damage the heart, cause dangerous mood

swings, and interfere with sexual drive and response.

Sharing needles used to inject steroids is one way people become infected with blood-borne germs such as HIV—the virus that causes AIDS (see page 88).

Be aware of eating disorders.

Focusing too much on body image may foreshadow the development of an actual eating disorder.

An eating disorder is an illness that causes someone to abuse himself or herself. Purposely starving, exercising way too much and too often, taking drugs for the purpose of speeding up the natural process of pooping and peeing, and binge-eating and/or throwing up on purpose to lose weight or to avoid gaining weight are all potential symptoms of eating disorders.

It's fine—in fact, good—to be aware of the nutritional content of the food you eat. Paying attention to nutrition facts labels is a good thing to do. But becoming obsessed with calorie counting and consumed by counting grams of fat are also signs that a preteen or teen may be developing a negative relationship with food and may be at risk for developing an eating disorder.

HEADS UP!

Anorexia nervosa is a condition in which a person restricts food intake too much and falls dangerously below his or her ideal body-weight range.

Bulimia is a condition in which a person regularly binges on food, then starves or uses laxatives or vomiting to avoid putting on weight.

Excessive exercising is a form of an eating disorder in which the person exercises for hours and hours every day to burn calories to lose weight.

Blind Spots

Often a person with an eating disorder does not recognize or admit that he or she has this problem. In fact, he or she hides the problem—or tries to. Denial of the problem may be a symptom of the disorder.

Eating disorders can inhibit normal growth and development and damage to the body, including the heart, skeleton, and brain. Many people succumb to the illness completely and die.

With help from health care professionals, it's possible to overcome the illness before irreversible damage occurs. A number of *very* effective medications are now available to help with the process of recovering.

Do you have questions about yourself, a sibling, or a friend?

Talk to a parent, doctor, teacher, or counselor.

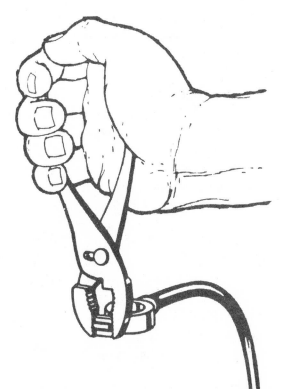

CHAPTER 5

INTERIOR
Care:
WHEN THE ROAD GETS ROUGH

A MAN AIN'T MADE OF STEEL

Face it: Boys are often discouraged from expressing (and feeling) certain emotions, such as sadness, fear, and anxiety.

But we need to get real with each other.

Everybody experiences feelings of sadness, vulnerability, loneliness, fear, anxiety, shame, and confusion at one time or another.

The Gender Conflict

The redefining of the roles of men and women can be a source of confusion for all of us.

Especially adolescent boys!

Here's the prob:

Historically, boys have been encouraged to be tough, strong, protective, aggressive, competitive, and independent. Right or wrong, these characteristics have been linked with being "masculine."

But hmmm. In recent years, boys have been encouraged to be more open, to share their feelings, and to be sensitive to the feelings of others. Males are now called upon to take on more active roles in parenting and homemaking—roles that have historically been reserved for women.

Girls can experience similar confusion. Our culture signals to girls that they're supposed to be dependent and in many ways weak, to be "feminine." At the same time, we encourage girls to be strong, assertive, competitive, and independent. And why not?

Why should these powerful traits be associated exclusively with males?

The roles of men and women have been continuously changing over the past few decades; it's okay to feel confused. But at least be sure of this much:

Both boys and girls (and men and women) feel all ways: strong and weak, powerful and vulnerable, confident and insecure, courageous and afraid.

These are human feelings. They're not attached to a particular gender.

Circuit Breakers

Talking about troublesome feelings with someone you trust and love makes having the feelings less painful. It also builds strong, healthy friendships and family relationships.

It's good to rely on your parents for emotional support and comfort. Letting your parents back you

up will make you stronger and more powerful as an adult, not weaker.

Mama's Boy?

You better believe it! It's outdated and old-fashioned (and sexist!) to believe that having strong communication with your mom will make you less of a male.

For starters, women can be just as tough, strong, assertive, and competitive as men. Some of the strongest men on earth have had women watching their backs.

More important, moms (like dads) understand the pressure boys are up against out in the world. They're also good at teaching boys the skills they need to grow into confident adults.

So many boys don't have a dad in their lives! Whether you do or don't, keep on hanging out with your mom; it's good for you. Chances are she's been there for some other guys, too. Like your dad, step-dad, uncle, or grandpa.

Why shouldn't she be there for you?

On Overload

Not all troublesome feelings or conflicts can be resolved by talking about them with your family and friends. If you are troubled by sad, worried, or anxious feelings that don't go away or keep coming back again, ask for help. If your emotions seem out of control, ask for help.

You can get help by asking your parents, doctor, teacher, or school counselor—or another adult you trust—to help you find a psychologist, psychiatrist, or counselor. Or you can call the county health department for a referral. (Ask the information operator [411] or look under county

government listings in the phone book.)

Or you can call a youth crisis hot line (see page 46). Call 911 or another police emergency number in any health emergency, including a mental health emergency.

Mental Health Care

Doctors and other adults are aware of the stress that can accompany adolescence, and just about every community has mental health care available for children and teens. Mental health care may include medication used in combination with therapy. Outstanding new medications have been developed for depression, anxiety, eating disorders, panic disorders, and other conditions.

Therapy is a process that involves talking and listening. With guidance from a trained health care provider, we can explore and identify what is making us feel bad and work through the problem. As the problem is resolved, positive thoughts and good feelings may replace the negative, sad ones.

It isn't necessary to feel sad, scared, anxious, or "out of control" to get counseling or help. Lots of people talk to mental health care professionals to gain insight and improve coping skills. Getting therapy doesn't mean you're crazy or can't help yourself. It enables you to understand your life better and feel more in control of it.

Drugs, Alcohol, and Stress

Some people may use illegal drugs or alcohol to try to manage stress or other uncomfortable or painful feelings. Although some of these substances may seem to offer temporary relief, they're actually harmful to emotional well-being and physical health.

Suicide Threats

If anyone talks to you about wanting to end his or her own life, tell a parent, a teacher, the school principal, a counselor, a health care professional, a police officer, or another adult you trust. Tell right away, even if you promised your friend you wouldn't tell. Don't try to decide whether or not the person might actually attempt suicide—all threats of suicide must be taken seriously. A person thinking about suicide should not be left alone.

HEADS UP!
Remember: In any emergency, call 911 or another police emergency number.

If you yourself have suicidal thoughts or feelings, tell your parent or another trusted adult such as a doctor, or teacher. And if you think you might act on these feelings, tell right away. Suicide is completely preventable. Depression is treatable. The trouble with depression is that it can feel like it will never end. But that's not true. There are many treatments that can help depression.

There are different causes of depression, including having a chemical imbalance in the brain. Depression can also be caused by real issues that teenagers have to deal with. There are so many medications available that can help you achieve a more positive, upbeat outlook on life! And counseling or therapy can help you identify and explore the source(s) of your desperate feelings—and do something to change them.

HEADS UP! Help is out there.
Suicide prevention hot lines are available 24-7. National Hope Line 1-800-SUICIDE (1-800-784-2433) or 1-888-SUICIDE (1-888-784-2433).

The Girls and Boys Town National Hot Line is also a suicide prevention hot line: 1-800-448-3000 (see page 46).

Other suicide prevention numbers can be found by dialing 411 or 0 and asking the operator.

Youth Crisis Hot Lines

Youth crisis hot lines are staffed by trained volunteers or professional counselors who help callers identify their problems, explore options, and develop a plan of action. They also offer referrals to community-based services, support groups, and even shelters, if necessary. You will find hot line numbers in the box below.

Sometimes hot line numbers change.

The front pages of the phone book often list hot line numbers along with other emergency numbers. Or you can call the information operator (411) or the regular operator (0) and ask for help in finding a hot line number that you need.

RUNNING AWAY

Some kids experience situations such as abuse, a serious breakdown in communication with parents, conflicts within the family, or other stressful circumstances that make them feel as if they just can't cope if they remain at home.

TWENTY-FOUR-HOUR EMERGENCY ROADSIDE ASSISTANCE

Dial **911** in most areas, or dial **0** for the operator and ask for help getting connected to the police emergency number. If you're on a cell phone, tell the emergency operator where you're calling from.

Also: The following hot lines are currently available for anyone to call, free, 24 hours a day. The call doesn't appear on your phone bill. Hang in there! It may be necessary to wait for a few moments for a counselor to come on the line.

Covenant House Nine Line (youth crisis line; call to talk about any problem): **1-800-999-9999** (U.S. only)

National Runaway Switchboard (youth crisis line for kids who are thinking about running away, for kids who have already run away, or for kids who want to talk about other problems):
1-800-621-4000 (U.S. only)
For the hearing-impaired: **1-800-621-0394** (TTY)

Child Help USA National Child Abuse Hot Line (if there are concerns about physical, sexual, or emotional abuse or neglect):
1-800-4-A-CHILD (**1-800-422-4453**) (U.S. and Canada)
For the hearing-impaired: **1-800-2-A-CHILD** (**1-800-222-4453**) (TTY)

Girls and Boys Town National Hot Line (youth crisis line—to talk about any problem):
1-800-448-3000 (U.S. and Canada)
For the hearing-impaired: **1-800-448-1833** (TTY)

The National Center for Missing and Exploited Children (and Teens) Hot Line:
1-800-843-5678 (U.S. and Canada)
For the hearing-impaired: **1-800-826-7653** (TTY)

National Hope Line 1-800-SUICIDE (**1-800-784-2433**) **or 1-888-SUICIDE** (**1-888-784-2433**).

There are times when it is in a kid's best interest for alternate living arrangements to be made, on either a temporary or a permanent basis. These arrangements need to be made by responsible adults who are in a position to safeguard a child's health and welfare.

Social service agencies run by the government are equipped to handle these arrangements. These agencies and groups can be found by asking a school counselor, teacher, principal, or health care professional. They can also be found by looking in the phone book under government listings (turn to "county government" and look under "health services" and "social services") or by asking the information operator (411) for government social services listings.

They can also be found by getting a referral from a youth crisis hot line (see page 46).

In any emergency, including a mental health emergency, call 911 or the police emergency number for your area, or dial 0 and ask the operator for help.

Most problems can be solved by remaining at home, with support from trained professionals.

There are thousands of agencies and support groups set up to help kids and their families find safe solutions to problems by taking advantage of services within their own communities.

The above hot line calls are free. Anyone can call, and the call doesn't appear on the phone bill.

Bullying

Bullying describes a form of aggression in which there is an intent to harm or intimidate somebody under circumstances where there is an imbalance of power. Over a period of time, a victim is made fearful by actions of one or several people.

Sexual harassment, rumor spreading, the taking of personal property, name calling, and teasing can occur in the context of bullying.

Some kids who are relentlessly bullied become depressed, anxious, and even suicidal. Who would want to make a kid that miserable?

Get over it.

Accept people's differences. Let it go at that. The world isn't entirely made up of kids who look, think, and act the same.

What's cool about bullying? Nothing. Be part of the solution, not part of the problem. Don't reinforce the behavior of bullies by laughing with them or otherwise backing them up. Rewarding bullying perpetuates the problem.

Socially powerful kids can be known to charm adults (and teachers) on the one hand and bully kids on the other. If you become aware that bullying is going on unchecked at your school, find a teacher or counselor (privately, if you want) and discuss the situation—as you see it. Schools need to maintain a bully-free, safe atmosphere for everybody. Adults in charge may be unaware of bullying unless students come forward to tip them off.

Feeling inclined to bully other kids?

Someone who experiences satisfaction in making other people miserable should identify why. Do you feel this way? If you do, ask your doctor to refer you to a counselor. Discover what's motivating or underlying your behavior so you can change it. You can find positive ways to use your power.

Being bullied?

Begin by telling your parent(s). They can help you develop a plan for dealing with the situation. Want to talk to a counselor? Ask your doctor for a referral.

If you're being bullied at school, you (and your parents) can schedule a meeting with your school counselor or other school official to discuss your options.

Meanwhile:

The fact that someone has a problem with aggression doesn't mean there's something wrong with *you*; never forget that. Believe in your right to be yourself and in your right to ask for help from the adults around you. Remember, even if the bully is threatening to harm you if you tell (or harm someone else, like your little brother), you still need to tell a trusted adult if you are being bullied, no matter how scared you may be. It's okay to be afraid, but don't let the fear keep you from getting help.

VIOLENCE
Violence in the Media

When it comes to viewing violence as entertainment, our culture seems to have crossed the line.

Be aware of the issues:

Experts believe that viewing violent images over and over again tends to make people desensitized to violence. This means that we can become detached from the emotions that would normally accompany the witnessing of a violent act.

It's also suspected that children who view excessive amounts of violence on TV, in video games, and in the movies may themselves be at risk for becoming more aggressive.

➤ An eye for an eye, a tooth for a tooth? Forget it. This approach to conflict leaves no room for peaceful resolution.

Imitating Fighting

Smashing people up against walls, kicking people in the face, head, neck, chest, or abdomen, strangling each other, breaking bottles over each other's heads, and so on is the kind of fighting most often modeled on TV and in the movies—where it's shown for entertainment.

In real life, these blows can kill people! People may also become paralyzed, sustain permanent brain damage, or suffer lifetime disabilities as a result of this kind of fighting.

The Myth—
You've Got to Fight to Be a Man

Sometimes people have to fight in self-defense. Under certain, specific circumstances, we can defend ourselves from physical attack, provided that we use no more force than is necessary to do so. If it's possible to retreat to safety from an attacker, we are expected to—and should.

But fighting just "to prove you're a man" is uncalled-for and can result in criminal charges being brought against you. So can using *excessive* force in self-defense (or defense of another).

Being a man involves realizing that it's okay to disagree, that conflict is a part of life, that disputes need not escalate to violence. It involves understanding anger and being aware of positive ways to express it. Being a man is about being able to keep anger in check. This means that unless you're lawfully defending yourself (or another), you've got to walk away from fights to be a man.

Cooling System

Overheating in an argument or dispute—sound familiar?

Anger is often a reaction to the action(s) of others.

If you get mad at somebody, step back. Getting in somebody's face, or allowing them to get in yours, makes matters worse. Develop a cool-down system. Take a deep breath. Think for yourself. What kind of person do you want to be? Ask yourself: Do you want to be the kind of person who reacts violently? Get a grip on yourself. If necessary, walk completely away. There are many appropriate (even creative) ways to express anger. It may be helpful to talk to an adult. Communicating your feelings can help you think constructively about how you can deal positively with the situation.

Releasing Steam
Physical activity is often effective in reducing levels of anger.

Blowing a Gasket/Boiling Over
Rages are NOT uncontrollable. Help is available for anger management.

Your pediatrician or counselor can point you in the right direction for finding help with controlling your anger—before it starts to control you (and your future). Violence is a choice. You CAN make choices that do NOT involve violence.

With guidance from a qualified health care professional, you can learn to reduce levels of anger. You can learn effective coping behaviors to stop the escalation of angry feelings and to resolve conflicts without fighting. You can also gain a better understanding of the wide range of feelings that can come under the category of "mad" (including feeling sad, hurt, rejected, or stressed).

You can learn to control your thinking by identifying what "triggers" anger for you. You can learn how to avoid jumping to conclusions or demonizing the person you're mad at.

You can learn to set realistic standards for yourself and the people around you, so that you are less likely to get mad to begin with.

Chill out.
Mmmmmmm. You can also acquire and use relaxation skills. Meditation, prayer, and yoga reduce stress for some people.

Be a hero.
Tell your parent or another responsible adult if you become aware of a threat of violence. It isn't your job to try to figure out whether or not the person is serious.

School Zone—Zero Tolerance
If you're aware (or even hear) that another kid is in possession of a gun or other lethal weapon at school, or has a plan to bring a gun or other lethal weapon to school, immediately tell a counselor, teacher, principal, or other responsible adult. Or call 911 or the police emergency number (anonymously, if you want).

You don't have to know whether or not the threat is serious—in fact, you can't know if the threat is real or if someone is playing a joke. So don't try to find out.

Just tell a responsible adult. This is the courageous (actually heroic) thing to do.

If it turns out the person was serious, you probably will have saved a life—or lives. In addition, you will have helped prevent the person making the threat from doing something completely regrettable—something that could negatively affect his or her life forever.

If it turns out the person making the threat was only kidding or making an idle threat, good. Nobody will have been hurt, and the person will learn not to make those kinds of jokes and threats.

Just like you can't make jokes at an airport about bombs and guns, you can't make jokes about guns and bombs at school.

Everybody understands that, or should.

CHAPTER 6

DANGER
Zones:
DRINKING, SMOKING, AND DOING DRUGS

TOBACCO, ALCOHOL, AND OTHER DRUGS

Now that you're getting older, you may hear about or know kids who are experimenting with tobacco, alcohol, or drugs. Knowing the facts about these substances can help you avoid the problems associated with their use.

The Effects of Alcohol

When a person drinks an alcoholic beverage, such as beer, wine, or hard liquor, the alcohol is absorbed into the bloodstream through the stomach and intestines. Since alcohol doesn't need to be broken down to be absorbed, like food, it enters the bloodstream quickly—within a few minutes.

Alcohol circulates throughout the body. It circulates through the brain, where it initially causes a sense of well-being. It can also cause feelings of great self-confidence, insight, and ability. In reality, though, alcohol diminishes ability: It dulls awareness, slows reflexes, impairs judgment, and interferes with physical coordination.

The more alcohol a person drinks, the more profound the effects are on the brain and other systems of the body. Drinking alcohol can cause a person to become confused, to stumble, to have slurred speech, to vomit, and to lose consciousness (pass out). Drinking too much alcohol can result in alcohol poisoning, which causes hundreds of deaths each year.

Alcohol Poisoning

Drinking too much alcohol can become a medical emergency. Too much alcohol can cause the brain to stop giving out the signals that tell the lungs to breathe. Without oxygen, the heart cannot beat— and a person can die simply because he or she has drunk too much. Too much alcohol can cause someone to pass out or fail to wake up or be woken up. A person who has passed out may throw up while asleep and choke on the vomit. If you suspect alcohol poisoning or believe that a drunk person's safety is otherwise in jeopardy, call 911 (or another police emergency number) and ask for paramedics (an ambulance) to come. Don't worry about whether or not somebody will get into trouble because of underage drinking. Just get help!

Why do people drink, anyway?

Adults who drink alcohol usually drink it to relax, often in a social setting. After having a few drinks, a person may become talkative or may "loosen up."

Although people may feel "high" while drinking, alcohol is a **depressant** (it slows the body's systems down). And many people experience feelings of "being down" after the initial effects of alcohol have worn off.

Responsible drinkers are aware of the effects that alcohol can have on their systems. They know their limits and stay within them. But drinking responsibly not only involves knowing how much to drink. It also involves knowing when, where, and with whom it is safe to drink. Managing the effects of alcohol can be tricky, and that's why the legal drinking age is 21.

Impaired Judgment and Alcohol

A person who is under the influence of alcohol has impaired judgment. He or she may make bad decisions or take dangerous risks, like driving a car or riding with a drunk driver, or going off someplace with someone he or she doesn't know well enough to trust.

Because alcohol impairs judgment and reflexes, people should not swim, dive, water-ski, wakeboard, surf, wind-surf, body-surf, snow-ski, snowboard, skateboard, rock climb, or participate in any other sports or activities that are inherently dangerous while under the influence of alcohol.

Bad judgment can also come into play regarding sex. Alcohol affects people's moods. Under the influence of alcohol, people may have romantic feelings or sexual urges that they act on but normally wouldn't or shouldn't—and later regret. Also, they may decide to have sex without regard for the risk of pregnancy or the spread of sexually transmitted diseases. For example, HIV—which causes AIDS—is often spread when people who have been drinking take a chance and have sex without using a latex condom (see page 94).

A person under the influence of alcohol is an easy target for being harmed, because he or she is physically and emotionally vulnerable.

Just refuse to go.

No exceptions: **Don't ride with a driver who's been drinking!** A person who has been drinking may reassure you that he or she can drive "just fine," but one of the effects of drinking alcohol is a false sense of confidence. The person cannot drive "just fine."

People under the influence of alcohol have impaired judgment and reflexes, which affect, among other things, how they react to sounds, to what they see, and to the speed of other vehicles. It causes drivers to operate vehicles recklessly, without regard to the safety of their passengers, other drivers, or themselves. People impaired by alcohol cause serious, often fatal, accidents with vehicles—cars, trucks, motorcycles, bicycles, and recreational vehicles, including boats, Jet Skis, and snowmobiles.

If a person who has been drinking offers to drive you somewhere, just don't go—and try to convince him or her not to drive. If you can get help from an adult, do. Hiding keys, calling a cab—even calling the police—are things people can do to prevent a drunk driver from going out onto the road.

What if he or she has drunk just a little bit?

Alcohol interferes with reflexes and judgment long before a person is visibly drunk. A kid is not equipped to judge whether or not another person is okay to drive; call your parent or another responsible driver you trust if you find yourself in a situation in which an adult or teen who is in charge of your transportation has been drinking alcohol.

Sobering Up

Taking a cold shower, drinking black coffee, or being walked around by a friend does NOT sober somebody up. The amount of time elapsed since the last drink, body weight, how many drinks have been consumed, and how much someone has eaten are the relevant factors affecting drunkenness and sobriety (the state of being sober).

Experimenting with Alcohol

Underage drinkers don't always understand that experimenting with alcohol can involve more than just "seeing how it feels" to get drunk. Here are some of the risks that can be associated with youthful experimentation with alcohol:

1. Being killed or injured in a drunk-driving accident.

2. Getting alcohol poisoning.

3. Spontaneously trying drugs/overdosing on drugs.

4. Getting a sexually transmitted disease.

5. Being sexually molested/assaulted.

6. Getting into a fight and getting hurt/hurting somebody else (which may involve criminal charges).

7. Getting a girl pregnant.

8. Getting arrested for being a minor in possession of alcohol.

9. Getting arrested for being drunk in public.

10. Getting suspended or expelled from school.

11. Being denied a driver's license or having a driver's license suspended—whether or not a vehicle is involved.

12. Being charged with a crime related to drunk driving (example: vehicular homicide).

HEADS UP!
When mentally and physically impaired by alcohol, a drunk person is considered unable to make responsible decisions about sex. Even if the drunk person says yes, appears agreeable to the prospect of having sex, or initiates the sexual encounter, it doesn't count as consent (see page 125).

Having sex (or sexual contact) with a drunk person is wrong and may constitute "date rape" (or sexual assault). These are serious criminal offenses (see page 125).

TOBACCO

Tobacco can be used legally by anyone over age 18. It is available in the form of cigarettes and cigars; loose tobacco comes in packages for pipes or for rolling into cigarettes. Smokeless (chewing) tobacco comes in small cans.

It's relatively easy to get hooked on tobacco, but it's hard to quit. There's a substance present in tobacco called **nicotine**.

Nicotine is powerfully addictive. Once people have used tobacco for a while, they feel compelled to keep using it. During the course of the day, at intervals, a person gets a strong yearning for a cigarette. Reaching for a cigarette may also become an automatic response to certain situations that include feeling worried, upset, nervous, anxious, or excited.

Some people first try smoking cigarettes or chewing tobacco because they're curious and/or because their friends are trying it. They're also responding to tobacco ads, which are designed by the tobacco industry to interest nonsmokers in smoking.

Tobacco ads try to make people associate smoking with popularity, confidence, success, beauty, and—sex. For that reason, adolescents can be especially susceptible to the ads.

After smoking a cigarette, a smoker's mouth tastes and smells like cigarettes. Smoke lingers in clothing and hair. Tobacco stains teeth. Its long-term use can cause gum disease, which contributes to tooth loss and bad breath. How gross is that?

It seems that the tobacco industry would like us to forget that tobacco is linked with profound

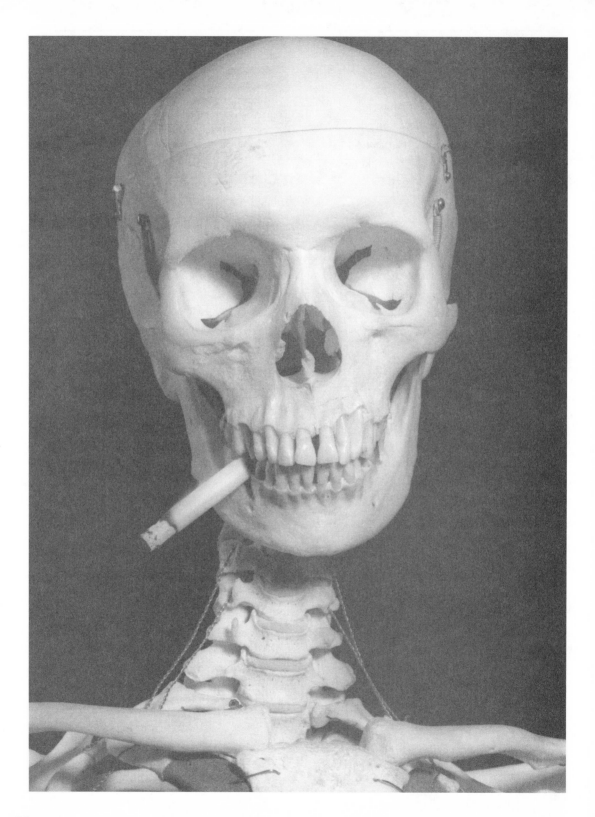

health problems, including cancer, heart disease, and respiratory illness, but 400,000 Americans die of tobacco-related illnesses every year.

This means that 400,000 fewer people will be buying cigarettes. The tobacco industry needs to recruit beginning smokers to replace them—like you, for example.

Many tobacco ads associate tobacco with fresh air and outdoor activity. They feature beautiful people having a great time while romping on the beach, hiking in the wilderness, wrangling cattle on the open range, skiing down snowy peaks.

What's *that* about? Smoking makes performing all of these activities more difficult, since it makes regular breathing more difficult.

Drugs

A drug is a chemical substance. Used correctly, drugs can prevent, treat, control, or cure disease. Others help people manage pain. Drugs can treat mental conditions, such as depression, or physical conditions, such as hay fever.

1. Legal drugs (medicines) include **over-the-counter** drugs, such as ibuprofen, which anybody can buy, and **prescription** drugs, such as antibiotics, which a pharmacist fills according to a doctor's request.

2. Illegal drugs include substances such as heroin, cocaine, "speed," LSD, "ecstasy," and many others.

Sometimes legal drugs are used illegally—such as when a person uses a prescription drug for a different purpose from what was intended when it was prescribed.

Taking Over-the-Counter Drugs

Over-the-counter drugs don't require a doctor's prescription, but they do require responsible, careful use. Ask your parents' permission before taking an over-the-counter drug, like a cough medicine, for example. Read the entire label, including the warnings, and check the recommended dose.

Don't take more than the recommended dose. Don't combine drugs without checking with the pharmacist or your doctor first. Combining drugs, including over-the-counter drugs, can be dangerous. So can drinking alcohol while taking drugs, including over-the-counter drugs.

> ➤ Don't take, or give anyone, medicine in the dark or when you're sleepy. It's important to be alert when taking medicine.
> If you need medicine in the middle of the night, wake up a parent and ask for help getting out the correct medicine and taking it.

Taking Prescription Drugs

Containers that hold prescription drugs sometimes look alike. Before you take any prescription medicine, make sure that it has your name on it, that it's the right medicine, that you know the correct amount to take, and that you're taking it for the reason for which it was prescribed. And don't skip doses.

Your doctor should be aware of all medications you are taking before prescribing additional drugs.

Remember

You can call the pharmacy and ask to talk to a pharmacist to make sure it's okay for drugs to be taken in combination with each other.

The call is free, and the pharmacist will be happy to give you this information.

ILLEGAL DRUG USE

Heroin, crack cocaine, cocaine, "crank" (speed), LSD (acid), and "designer drugs" (such as "ecstasy") are examples of illegal drugs that are used by people who want to alter the way they feel.

HEADS UP!
The "date-rape drug" is an illegal drug often used for criminal purposes. A person under the influence of the drug remains conscious but has

no memory of events that transpire while drugged.

People have been raped, sexually assaulted, and robbed by others who have sneaked the date-rape drug into their drinks. Death from overdose has also occurred. In the future, if you go to parties, don't let someone you don't know get you or give you a drink. Get it yourself and don't leave it unattended. If you forget and do leave it unattended (for example, to dance or use the bathroom), dump it and get a new one.

Drugs may seem to provide a temporary escape from reality and responsibility, tension, anxiety (nervousness), or boredom. But the feelings that drugs produce are unpredictable and don't necessarily provide this escape. If they do provide it, it's just an illusion. The drug wears off, and the person experiences a letdown. Plus, the person's problems remain unresolved.

If a drug is addictive ...

The person will feel a compelling need to take the drug again. The impulse can be so strong that the person will take it even though he or she knows it's damaging.

Some people turn to crime, including prostitution (being paid to have sex), to get money to buy the drug to which they are addicted. So, many people end up in jail as a result of drug addiction!

Drugs can cause permanent damage to the vital organs of the body, including the brain. Certain drugs cause people to become violent, homicidal (murderous), or suicidal.

Experimenting with Drugs

Teenagers may become curious about drugs and tempted to experiment. Just don't. Experimentation can lead to abuse, addiction, and emotional and physical harm. It can also lead to getting in trouble with the police.

The legal consequences of being caught in possession of illegal drugs are serious. Laws vary from state to state. Although some kids are ordered to attend drug education and rehab programs, not everybody is given this opportunity. It depends on the charges, the circumstances, and the type of drug use involved.

All people, including teens, are expected to know and follow laws—including laws involving alcohol and drugs. Kids who are caught possessing, using, and/or selling illegal drugs may end up spending a considerable amount of time in the juvenile hall, a youth-detention camp, or even jail if tried as an adult.

Impaired Judgment and Drugs

Like alcohol, drugs can impair judgment and make people less likely to think about consequences and therefore less likely to protect themselves (and others) against dangerous situations, including exposure to HIV, the virus that causes AIDS (see page 87). HIV is often spread in situations where people decide to have sex while under the influence of drugs or alcohol.

Different Kinds of Illegal Drugs

Some illegal drugs are swallowed, some are smoked, some are snorted up the nose. Others are injected into the body with needles (this is called "shooting up"). Shooting up drugs into a vein can lead to drug overdose and death. Sharing the needles and syringes used to shoot up drugs, including steroids, can spread HIV (see page 88) and other diseases.

Stimulants (uppers) make people feel "wired" or "fired up."

Depressants (downers) make people feel "slowed down."

Hallucinogens alter the perception of space and time and cause people to see and hear things that aren't real.

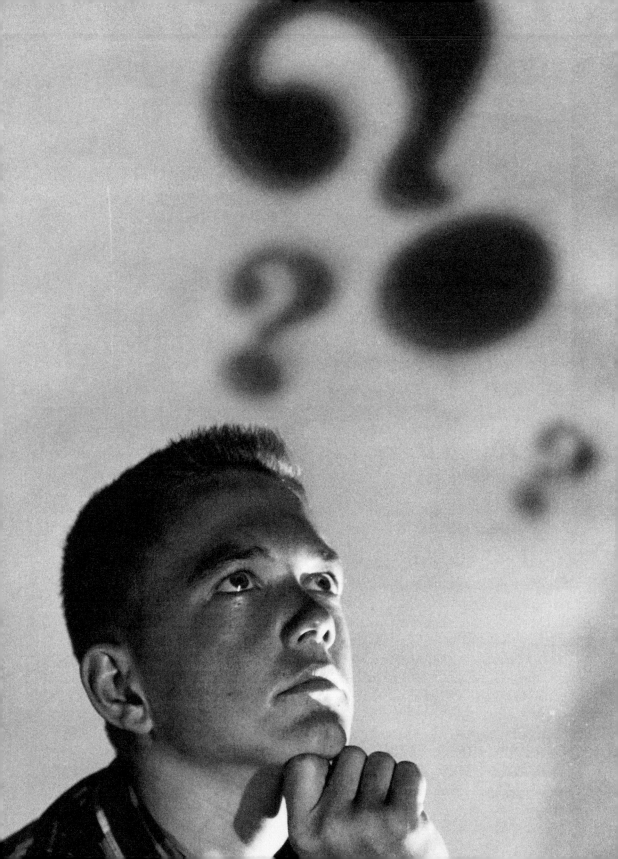

Steroids are used illegally by some people for the purpose of becoming more "buff" and/or improving their athletic performance. Abuse of steroids can cause dangerous mood swings, heart damage, sexual dysfunction, and other physical problems.

Sniffing Chemical Inhalants (Huffing)

Many products that can be purchased legally, including household products, can be dangerous or deadly when misused. It's extremely risky and unhealthy to attempt to "get high" by inhaling the fumes of household products; in fact, it's reckless. Huffing can cause permanent brain damage, heart damage, liver damage, and death.

Marijuana

Marijuana is a plant. Its dried leaves can be rolled up into a thin cigarette (sometimes called a "joint") and smoked. A few moments after the smoke is drawn into the lungs, it begins to take effect. Marijuana (also known as "weed" or "pot") is also sometimes eaten (after being baked into brownies, for example).

People who use marijuana do so because they like the way it makes them feel: Some feel relaxed; others believe it makes them think better; some just feel that it heightens their enjoyment of life. These feelings aren't consistent, though. Marijuana is also known to make people feel frightened, alienated, lonely, scared, or upset.

People have been arguing for years about whether marijuana is safe enough to be made legal. Regardless of these arguments, it is still absolutely against the law to use or be in possession of marijuana unless it has been legally prescribed by a physician for a valid medical reason under guidelines set by state and federal law—and even this is surrounded by controversy.

In any event, marijuana is still not considered a harmless substance. Marijuana smoke, like tobacco smoke, leaves a residue in the lungs. Also, it contains a mind-altering ingredient (THC). THC can cause psychological problems for some people who use it.

Like alcohol, marijuana can impair judgment. So, many of the problems associated with alcohol use apply to marijuana use—including the risks of driving while under the influence and of having sex while under the influence (and as a result: spreading or getting a sexually transmitted disease or causing an unplanned pregnancy).

The Munchies

Marijuana can also make you want to eat, a response sometimes known as "having the munchies." The munchies can cause you to overeat and, in the long term, become overweight.

FYI
Sometimes marijuana is "laced" with a more dangerous drug (heroin, for example), which has an unexpected, devastating effect on the person smoking it.

Frequent use of marijuana by teens...

Among other things, marijuana interferes with the natural development of coping skills. Teens who use marijuana may rely on it to escape the challenging feelings of everyday life, rather than experiencing the feelings and learning to deal with them.

Frequent use can cause bad grades, leading kids to drop out of school. That's because marijuana is known to interfere with motivation and concentration—two essential ingredients for being a successful student.

Legal Considerations

At the time of the publication of this book, the use of marijuana for medical purposes, such as controlling nausea during chemotherapy (cancer treatment), is allowed in some areas, but this may change. Where permitted, a prescription written by a medical doctor under a certain (narrow) set of circumstances is required if the marijuana use is to be considered legal.

But every state has consequences for people caught possessing and/or using marijuana illegally. Since the use of marijuana is widespread, people sometimes "forget" about the legal consequences of getting caught, or they feel like it's no big deal to get caught. But it is a big deal!

There are places where possession of even the tiniest amount of marijuana, like one seed, for example, is a **felony** (very serious crime).

Even in states that are more lenient toward possession of a tiny amount (considering it a lesser crime: a misdemeanor), growing a marijuana plant may still be considered a felony. And it's always considered serious to *sell* marijuana.

HEADS UP!
We *learn* to deal with stress, frustration, anxiety, and other uncomfortable feelings.

Those who use drugs to make the stressful feelings go away don't confront the feelings and don't develop good strategies for dealing with life's challenges.

As a result, teens who routinely use alcohol, marijuana, and other drugs can impair their development into strong and confident adults.

Anyone who has a problem with drugs can get help.

It's completely possible to get help with a drug or alcohol problem without getting in trouble with the police. The National Council on Alcoholism and Drug Dependence Hope Line number (for the U.S. and Canada) is 1-800-NCA-CALL (1-800-622-2255).

The call is free and confidential and won't appear on the phone bill.

CHAPTER 7

SHARING THE ROAD:
Girls

STANDARD EQUIPMENT

Just like with guys, the onset of puberty causes changes in a girl's body that relate to her reproductive system: Her external and internal reproductive organs grow and change.

The physical changes in a girl's external reproductive organs (**vulva**) are pretty subtle, and except for growing pubic hair on the outside, she might not notice them. It's hard for a girl to see what's going on down there. In fact, it requires a mirror to get a good look.

Parts

Like guys, girls have two gonads—called **ovaries.** And just like a guy's gonads, a girl's gonads have dual roles: They produce sex hormones (**estrogen** and **progesterone**) and they produce reproductive cells. Female reproductive cells are called **ova** (eggs). Each ovary produces just one tiny **ovum** (egg) every other month.

Eggs are produced in the ovaries at the same tem-

perature as the rest of the body, so it isn't necessary for a girl's gonads to hang down like a boy's do.

They are located inside her body, along with her **uterus** (womb), **fallopian tubes** (tubes that connect the ovaries to the womb), and **cervix** (bottom of the uterus). These make up her internal reproductive organs. The vulva includes the **mons**, the **outer lips**, the **inner lips**, and the **clitoris**, which is a small bump located at the top of the inner lips, where they come together. The **vagina** is the passage leading from the uterus to the vulva.

The Clitoris

Like the penis, the clitoris has a glans and a shaft. It also has erectile tissue, which swells and gets harder when a girl is sexually aroused.

An erect clitoris is only about as big as a pea— but like a penis, it's capable of producing intense physical pleasure: an orgasm.

When a girl has an orgasm, she doesn't release reproductive cells, like a guy does.

A girl is born with all of the eggs she'll ever have; her body isn't capable of making new ones.

Her eggs mature just a few at a time, over a period of many days, and are released just one at a time, every other month. Each mature egg is released according to an inner clock, which is regulated by her hormones.

Unlike the penis, the clitoris doesn't play a role in the reproductive system. Females can produce children without any help from the clitoris. The sole purpose of the clitoris is to provide pleasure. It doesn't produce or distribute anything. But since it does produce intense sexual pleasure when stimulated, the clitoris provides an incentive for a female to have sexual contact with a male.

The size of the clitoris, like the size of a penis, varies a little, but not much. Every clitoris is small, and every one works. Girls don't worry one bit about the size.

Just below the clitoris is the opening that a girl pees out of, her **urethra**, which is *not* part of her reproductive system. Below that is the vaginal opening, which leads into the vagina.

The Vagina

The vagina is like a soft, warm, moist passageway. Its opening is sometimes, but not always, covered by a fold of membrane called the **hymen**. The vagina plays a key role in the reproductive process. For one thing, it's the passageway through which a baby is born.

How can a baby come out of such a small opening? The walls of the vagina are stretchy. Nevertheless, it's a very tight squeeze.

The vagina has another role: to receive the sperm that the penis distributes.

The act of placing an erect penis into the vagina of a female and ejaculating is called having **sexual intercourse**. Sexual intercourse is described in detail on page 72. But briefly, what happens is this:

During sexual intercourse, about 6 million sperm are dispatched by the penis inside of a female's vagina. One lucky sperm may find the egg and get inside it, triggering a response that shuts all the other sperm out—kind of like slamming the door in their faces. A sperm uniting with an egg marks the beginning of a sequence of events that leads to a baby being born.

CONTROL PANELS: HORMONES

Hormones are secreted by various organs in a girl's body—just like they are in a boy's. Two key organs that produce hormones in a girl's body are her ovaries, which produce sex hormones.

Sex hormones are responsible for the regulation of the reproductive system and the changes a girl's body goes through during puberty. The two main girl hormones are **estrogen** and **progesterone**, and these basically run the show.

Girls are growing breasts.

One of the first, most obvious, changes that happen to a girl at the onset of puberty is that she begins to grow breasts.

Breasts are considered accessory reproductive organs.

A girl's body grows breasts to prepare her for the possibility of breast-feeding, in case she decides to have a baby once she becomes physically mature. But breasts have another function: They're capable of producing pleasant sexual feelings when touched.

The first signs that breasts are developing are that nipples become larger and the area around the nipple (**areola**) gets wider. Then the nipple and areola darken. A small bump, called a **breast bud**, appears behind each nipple. Breast buds can appear as early as age 8, but they are more likely to appear at around age 10 or 11.

Inside of her breasts, a girl's milk-producing organs (**alveoli** and **milk ducts**) are growing. Around these, a layer of fat tissue develops—to protect them.

Breasts come in a variety of shapes and shades. They can be big or small, round or flat, dark or light. Nipple color relates to skin tone. Nipples can be brown, plum-colored, dark pink, or pale pink. Breasts aren't always symmetrical (perfectly matched). It's very common for one breast to be a little bigger than the other one.

Big or small, breasts are famous for capturing the attention of males; most guys really like looking at them (and touching them, when permitted).

➤ Breast Etiquette for Guys
Commenting—complimenting a girl on her breasts—is offensive. Example: "Nice rack."
Criticizing breasts is also unacceptable. Example: "How flat is *she*!"
Even if a guy is being complimentary or just kidding around, remarks made that relate to sexual characteristics (including breasts and breast development) are embarrassing, unwelcome, and just plain inappropriate.
They're also considered a kind of sexual *harassment* (see page 123).

OGLING

Some boys feel like they can barely take their eyes off of a girl's breasts. During a conversation, it's sometimes hard not to look down. It's helpful to look into a girl's eyes or at her mouth when she's talking. Stay focused on the conversation.

Opportunities present themselves for a guy to subtly catch a glimpse without being obvious about it, and a quick glance shouldn't cause a problem. But don't stare! Girls are really tuned into guys checking them out. And girls can be just as self-conscious about their changing bodies as boys are about theirs, or more!

Objectification

Separating someone's body from who she or he is as a person has a name: objectification. Who wants to be scrutinized as an object? Nobody. Girls hate this!

"High Beams"

When a girl gets chilly, her nipples contract and become harder and poke out. Erect nipples can become pretty apparent under a girl's shirt. They may draw your eyes to her chest. Boys can't help but note this temporary, intriguing condition—but remember: A quick glance is all you get. Don't stare.

Hugs

When you casually hug a girl, you'll feel her breasts pressing against your chest for a minute. This contact is part of every friendly hug—and you won't be cited for it.

The same goes for when you're slow dancing: It's part of the dance.

CLASSIFIED INFORMATION

✔ About Bras

Girls usually feel more comfortable when their breasts are held snugly against their chests, especially when they jog, dance, or play sports. It's uncomfortable when breasts move around too much.

A bra provides support. A bra also provides a degree of privacy. It helps keep a girl's nipples from showing when she's wearing a thin shirt.

Some girls go braless (there's no law that says you've got to wear one). Others wear a tank top or a T-shirt under their clothes instead of a bra.

There are all kinds of bras—practical and fancy. Some hook in the back, some hook in the front. Some are strapless. Some are long—down to the waist (called "merry-widow bras" or "bustiers," à la Madonna).

Some are made from delicate material—very skimpy and flimsy. Not for soccer wear! Sports bras are made of thick, stretchy material. These really get the job done.

Bras aren't worn while sleeping.

✔ A cup, B cup—what's that about?

Most bras have a letter and a number for a size—like 36A, for example. The number relates to the measurement around the chest, below the breasts. The letter corresponds to the size of the breast itself. Cup sizes, from smallest to biggest, are AAA, AA, A, B, C, D, DD, and DD/E.

✔ Additional Random Bra Info

Nursing bras have flaps over the nipples that unhook and drop down so a baby can drink.

Padded bras? The name explains them. They're bras with padding inside—to make breasts look bigger. **Miracle Bras** and **Wonderbras** are two examples. These are craftily constructed with padding so that breasts are uplifted and pushed closer together, creating an illusion of cleavage (the "valley" where two breasts meet).

Some fashions don't allow for a bra (like backless formal dresses, for example). Girls can wear "stick-on bras" with backless dresses. These are basically two separate bra "cups" with adhesive around the edges. They work fairly well, except they're kind of uncomfortable to peel off.

But if a boy actually tries to feel a girl's breasts by rubbing his chest against her, it's different. The hug will have gone from friendly to sexual, and this will be totally obvious to the girl.

Will she like it?

Under most circumstances, no.

The girls are getting furrier.

Like guys, girls grow more hair on their bodies during puberty: pubic hair, underarm hair, hair on their legs.

This new hair grows to a certain length (short) and then stops, on both boys and girls. It doesn't keep on getting longer, like the hair on our heads. When shaved off, it grows right back in—like whiskers do on a guy.

Pubic hair, when fully grown in, looks like an upside-down triangle on a girl's body. It can be curly or straight, brown, black, red, or blond.

Occasionally, some girls style it—by trimming it a little bit.

Sometimes girls shave off some of their pubic hair so it won't peek out of a bathing suit. That's called the "bikini line."

The bikini line can also be adjusted by "waxing"—which essentially pulls the hairs out.

Ouch? You're right.

Not all girls care about trimming, shaving, or waxing the bikini line. Or de-fuzzing legs or armpits, for that matter.

Neither does every guy. A lot of guys couldn't care less if girls have hair on their legs and under their arms—in fact, they like it.

➤ De-fuzzing, Girl-Style . . .

Girls who shave their legs and armpits usually use a safety razor. They usually just shave between the ankle and the knee (not the kneecap) and under both arms. Stray hairs higher up on the fronts and backs of the legs (thighs) may also be policed.

A few girls shave with an electric shaver— not many, though. Some may wax their legs.

Some girls use hair-removing products. These are smeared on and rinsed off a few minutes later—after the hair has been dissolved by chemicals.

New sweat glands are beginning to work.

During puberty, the girls are sweating more. And like many boys, many girls are beginning to use deodorant/antiperspirant.

They're growing taller and gaining weight.

Girls also have a growth spurt during puberty, and it generally occurs earlier in the female's sequence of changes than it does in the male's.

That's why so many of the girls in middle school and junior high are taller and bigger than the boys are. Eventually the boys catch up and surpass the girls in size and strength. This is because the growth spurt of males lasts longer than the growth spurt of females.

A girl's growth spurt isn't only about height. Gaining fat is a normal, necessary part of female development.

Soft to the Touch

Girls get round during puberty. Fat tissue increases as part of breast development. A girl's hips increase in size and change in shape, and so do her thighs.

This increase in fat tissue is partly in anticipation of bearing children, when women need to have reserves of energy, which can be stored in fat.

Their skin is getting oilier.

They may be developing acne on the face, shoulders, and back.

The Main Event

They're starting their periods (or **menstruating**).

When a girl's period starts, it's major—comparable to when a boy ejaculates for the first time. Beginning to have periods means that her eggs have begun to mature. **Ovulation** may begin anytime during the next 2 years and occur unpredictably during that time.

Once a girl begins to ovulate regularly, her periods may become more regular as well. The cycle is controlled by hormonal activity and will repeat itself until she's about 50.

A girl's period usually begins when she's about 13—but it can happen at any time between the ages of 9 and 16.

When she's having a period, which lasts a few days, a small amount of bloody fluid trickles out of a girl's body via her vagina. But the girl isn't actually bleeding from an injury. Just a certain predetermined amount of blood is being released.

Then it stops.

And then the cycle starts all over again.

Once it starts, most girls have a period once a month. It takes a while for a girl's reproductive system to get into the rhythm of having a period regularly. Regularly means according to a routine schedule—for example, every 28 days. Not all girls have regular periods, but most do.

Q. AND A.

Q. Where does the blood come out?

A. It comes out of the vaginal opening.

Q. Where does the blood come from?

A. It originates in the uterus (womb)—a small, expandable, pear-shaped organ. It's located inside of a girl's body, about halfway between her belly button and her crotch.

When a woman becomes pregnant, the baby grows in the uterus—not in the stomach, which is an organ that both males and females have for digesting food.

Q. Why does blood come out?

A. Once a girl goes through puberty, her uterus makes a special lining of bloody tissue every month to prepare for a possible pregnancy. If a pregnancy were to occur, the lining would nourish the **embryo** as it grew and developed inside the uterus. (An embryo is a group of cells that develops into a **fetus**, which is the beginnings of a baby.)

If a pregnancy doesn't occur, the lining of the uterus isn't needed to nourish an embryo, and so the lining is released (as menstrual fluid). Releasing this fluid once a month is what having a period is all about.

Girls and women don't have periods during the months that they are pregnant.

That's why missing a period is usually the very first sign of pregnancy (see page 73).

Once pregnancy has occurred, the lining of the uterus isn't shed; instead, it becomes an organ called the **placenta**.

The placenta provides nourishment to the developing fetus. It acts as a filter between the mother and the fetus, keeping their blood separated. It allows nutrients and dissolved oxygen to enter the fetus's bloodstream. It eliminates waste. But the placenta is *not* a perfect filter. If the mom does drugs, drinks alcohol, or smokes, the fetus can be harmed.

The placenta is expelled from the uterus just after the baby is born.

Q. How does the blood get from the uterus into the vagina?

A. The cervix is the bottom of the uterus. The blood comes out of a small hole in the cervix. The hole, called the **os**, opens into the vagina.

Q. What does having a period *feel* like?

A. It feels like leaking a little bit of liquid. The leaking can't be controlled, like when people urinate (pee). It just comes out—whenever.

Q. Does having a period *hurt*?
A. Sometimes it involves having a big, fat, dull ache (**cramps**) in the abdomen or lower back, especially during the first day or two.

Girls can take over-the-counter or prescription medicine, lie in a comfortable position with a warm hot-water bottle on the abdomen—or even exercise to relieve cramps.

Q. Pads—what's with those?
A. Girls can wear throwaway pads (soft, absorbent ones) in their underwear during the days they are menstruating. The pads have sticky stuff on the back so that they stay in place (stuck to the underwear, not to the girl).

They are changed every few hours, or sooner if necessary.

Q. How does a girl know when she's going to start her period for the first time?
A. It's always a surprise. But at least she gets some clues: A girl won't start her period until she begins to grow breasts and also has quite a bit of pubic hair.

One day or night, she'll notice a smudge, stain, or dribble of blood in her underwear and . . . ta-da! Her period will have arrived. For some girls, this is cause for a great celebration. For others, it's a giant pain in the neck.

Sooner or later, though, everybody gets used to it.

Q. If a girl doesn't have a pad—then what?
A. For emergency purposes, she can use a wad of toilet paper, a stack of tissues, a folded-up paper towel, a clean washcloth—or even a clean sock.

A lot of girls and women carry pads in their purse or backpack and are happy to give one away if someone is in a pinch.

The school nurse and/or office manager almost always has a stash of pads for girls who start during the school day.

You may see blood on the back of a girl's clothes, and if you do, be cool. Don't put it on the ten o'clock news.

Pad Wrangling

Should you ever be asked to hook up your mom, your sister, or another female with pads, hey—you can do it! And it will really be appreciated.

Pads can be easily found in grocery stores, drugstores, and convenience stores. There's a sea of choices. Unless you have been given other instructions, any brand of pad that says "maxi" on it is a safe choice.

Don't choose "panty liners."

Tampons are not pads; if you've been dispatched for pads, don't bring back tampons, which are sold in the same area as pads.

James's Old Trick

Once upon a time, a long time ago, my friend started her period for the very first time when she was visiting her grandma and grandpa out in the country.

Her grandma wasn't home, so her grandpa volunteered to walk to the local store. An old trick when buying pads is to buy something else at the same time. That way the focus isn't so much on the pads. So her grandpa craftily selected a small box of Ex-Lax (poop medicine) for himself. Then he picked up a large box of pads and casually put both items on the counter.

The owner of the store, an old friend of his, stared at the Ex-Lax and at the box of pads. Then he leaned real close and said, "James? Are you all right?"

James was fine.

And so will all the other brave guys be fine who get dispatched to snag pads for sisters, friends, girlfriends, moms, grandmas. Or apparently, granddaughters.

Q. Not pads? Then what are they?

A. A lot of girls use tampons instead of pads. A tampon is carefully poked up into the vagina, where it absorbs menstrual blood before the blood leaves the body. Most tampons have a cardboard or plastic applicator, which helps the girl direct the tampon into place.

Like pads, tampons fill up with blood and must be changed regularly.

There is a string incorporated into a tampon for pulling it out. Tampons are either flushed or wrapped and tossed into the trash.

Tampons must be used responsibly because if used incorrectly, they can pose a health risk. That's why there are instructions on every box of tampons, and girls are encouraged to read and follow them carefully.

Q. PMS—what's up with that?

A. Hormone fluctuations during the course of each menstrual cycle can cause mood changes.

"PMS" stands for **premenstrual syndrome**, and, among other things, it's about feeling grouchy before a period. It can also be about puffiness in the hands, face, and abdomen and having tender breasts.

PMS can include general irritability, door slamming, toothbrush throwing, arguments with friends and family, and fits of sobbing over things like greeting-card commercials.

It may account for the times your mom, stepmom, or foster mom loses it—just because every article of clothing you own has been thrown on your bedroom floor, along with your bicycle helmet, snowboarding goggles, fish food, and clarinet.

➤ **Gr-r-r-r-r-r!**
Mentioning PMS, especially when somebody has symptoms of PMS, is extraordinarily risky.
If you suspect PMS, it's safest to say nothing.

It is so infuriating when somebody else brings up the topic, especially if it's a guy.

It's obnoxious to make PMS comments. Girls won't think it's funny because it's not!

PMS can go beyond grouchiness and/or weepiness.

It can be a source of serious physical and emotional upsets, and a number of girls and women have to alter their diets, take medication, and otherwise seek the help of health care professionals to establish a treatment plan for relieving the symptoms of premenstrual stress.

It lasts how long?!

Women have periods until about age 50. Then they stop. This is called menopause. After menopause, women are no longer able to conceive children. Their ovaries don't produce any more eggs.

Menopause has wide-ranging effects—the most famous of which are hot flashes, when a woman feels boiling hot for no reason. Do you have a 50-something woman in your family who randomly gripes about being hot?

So now ya know.

Handsome Knight in Hooded Sweatshirt

I'll admit it. As far as a boy-meets-girl story goes, this is an unusual one:

When my friend was in college, she unexpectedly started her period while in class—and didn't realize it until she stood up to leave.

A cute guy, a student, walked up to her and said, "I've got five sisters. Want to tie this around your waist?"

He took off his sweatshirt and handed it to her.

She tied his sweatshirt around her waist, and he walked her to her dorm.

After that, they figured out that they liked each other and started dating.

The moral of the story is: Be a cool guy—you never know what may happen as a result.

Girls are getting stronger sexual feelings.

Girls, like boys, experience a wide range of feelings during puberty because puberty has profound physical and emotional effects.

Girls get crushes, just like boys.

Many fantasize about sexual situations.

And many girls, like most boys, masturbate.

A girl masturbates by (gently) stimulating her clitoris. As she becomes more and more sexually aroused, her sex organs go through subtle physical changes (swell, change color). Her heart rate increases; her rate of breathing gets faster. If she has an orgasm, it will be of the same intensity as a male's. Unlike most males, a female can have several orgasms in a row without waiting for time to pass in between.

Fewer girls than boys masturbate because masturbating is a little harder to figure out for girls than it is for boys.

A boy's penis is pretty obvious; he can't miss it. And he routinely has occasion to touch it.

But a girl's clitoris is small and well hidden—in a place she doesn't pay much attention to, unless she's hunting for it.

Some girls don't even know they have one!

A girl can have an orgasm in her sleep, but since she doesn't ejaculate, wetting her sheets or pajamas isn't an issue.

She usually just wakes up momentarily and then falls back asleep—with the hopes of having the same dream again!

Z-Z-Z-Z-Z-Z-z-z-z-z-z-z-z-z-z-z-z-z-z . . .

CHAPTER 8

THE (RE)PRODUCTION LINE:
SEXUAL
Reproduction

To reproduce means to make anew; it means to make again. No species could continue to inhabit the earth without having the ability to reproduce.

All living creatures reproduce, from the tiniest moth to the hugest rhinoceros. But only some of them reproduce sexually.

When creatures reproduce sexually, it means that the male and the female parent each contributes genes to the offspring. Genes carry the information needed to form new life. They are contained in a female's egg and in the reproductive cells of a male and are united during the mating process.

Woof!

How does sexual intercourse between people relate to cocker spaniels?

Thankfully, it doesn't.

Neither does it really relate to birds, bees, and other creatures in the animal kingdom.

In the animal kingdom, two male hoofed animals paw the ground, charge each other, bash heads, and lock antlers until one gives up. The winner then briefly mounts a female, who's somewhere nearby flicking her tail. Afterward, he thunders off in a cloud of dust and disappears into the bushes, never to be seen or heard of again.

"THE TALK": GUY REPORT ON MAKING BABIES

"I first began learning about how people make babies from a children's book my parents gave me. I don't remember the title, but on the light green cover there was a picture of a boy and a cocker spaniel puppy. Inside the book were many stories about animals and animal babies and then a little section on people and human babies. The mechanics of reproduction were not described, but I got the idea that babies came from a mother and a father acting together in some way so the baby would start to grow and then be hatched.

"I never asked my parents about human reproduction. I got the feeling that this book with the boy and his puppy was about as far as they were willing to go."

WE DON'T JUST MATE
Sexual Intercourse

The following is an actual explanation of the act of people having (vaginal) sexual intercourse ("making love," "having sex"). Also explained is how sexual intercourse between human beings is related to making babies.

Under most circumstances, a woman, like a man, becomes sexually aroused during the activities that precede the act of intercourse (called foreplay). Foreplay can include making out, or going further and undressing together (see page 82).

When a woman is sexually aroused, slippery secretions are produced by the walls of her vagina and also by the membranes close to the entrance to her vagina. This makes it easier for the man's penis to enter.

During intercourse, the man's erect penis is placed in the woman's vagina. It becomes stimulated by the walls of her vagina as he moves it in and out and eventually ejaculates (and has an orgasm).

In the meantime, the woman's clitoris swells and gets erect. It withdraws under a hood of skin. During the act of sexual intercourse, the guy's penis tugs and rubs against the hood of skin, which indirectly stimulates the clitoris by friction.

This may or may not cause her to have an orgasm.

Having sexual intercourse is usually accompanied by strong, pleasurable emotional and physical sensations for both partners.

Adjusting the Timing

When people become sexual partners, they can teach each other what feels good so that the experience of having sex together is satisfying for both. Usually, it takes practice for both to have an orgasm.

Since the clitoris is stimulated only indirectly

during intercourse, an orgasm for some women may be more likely to happen during foreplay or afterplay (after intercourse).

How Pregnancy Happens

During intercourse, several million sperm zoom (well, wriggle, actually) through a tiny doorway called the **os** in the very bottom part of the uterus (cervix).

The sperm are basically on an egg hunt, and the odds of finding it first are 6 million to one!

Each sperm charges forward by lashing its tail tadpole-style. Millions frantically scout around in the uterus, where they will have absolutely no luck.

Some of the best navigators find their way up into the two fallopian tubes, which are attached to the uterus. In one of these two tubes, one tiny egg may be waiting. One (and only one) sperm will enter it. At this point, conception has taken place—the egg has been fertilized. The rest of the sperm will hang around, dying within a few days.

Genes . . .

Contain genetic information and are present in both the sperm and the egg. Once united, the genes combine to provide the plan for a totally new and unique human being.

Fertilized Egg

As soon as an egg is fertilized, it begins to grow by the process of cell division.

The fertilized egg (at first, one cell) divides. Then it divides again. And again. This process continues as the egg moves down the fallopian tube and into the uterus, where it will plant itself in the lining of the uterine wall.

After it is in place, its outer cells organize to form the **placenta**. The placenta surrounds the fertilized egg (now called an **embryo**) and grows along with it.

The placenta produces a hormone that causes changes in the mother's body that are needed to support a pregnancy. These changes include further development of the placenta and uterus, changes in the milk-producing glands in preparation for breast-feeding after the infant is born, and other changes that maintain a healthy environment as the embryo continues to grow.

First Stage

In the first few weeks of the development of an embryo, the basic systems of the body are formed. When the embryo's body structures are in recognizable human shape (at 8 weeks), it is called a

fetus. The placenta provides nourishment for the developing fetus and eliminates its waste products. It also acts as a filter between the mother and the fetus, keeping their blood separated. It allows nutrients and dissolved oxygen to enter the fetus's bloodstream. The fetus is attached to the placenta by the **umbilical cord**. Its life is entirely supported by the mother's body.

The placenta is not a perfect filter. It is unable to filter out drugs or alcohol if they are present in the mother's bloodstream. So, to protect her developing fetus from harm, a pregnant woman should not smoke, drink alcohol, or take any drugs, unless prescribed by her doctor.

After 9 months have passed, the baby is ready to be born.

Nobody knows what triggers the onset of a baby's passage from a mother's uterus into the outside world (called "labor and delivery"). But when the time comes, the muscles of the uterus begin to contract, and these contractions cause the os in the cervix to open wider and wider. Once it is all the way open, it becomes time for the mother to push (bear down) as hard as she can with her belly muscles along with each contraction.

The baby's head stretches the walls of the vagina and makes way for the rest of the baby's body to fit out of the vaginal opening. The process of labor usually takes between 8 and 26 hours for a first baby, but the "pushing out" and delivery happens relatively quickly at the end of the labor.

The baby is born. It cries out and breathes. Its umbilical cord is cut.

The placenta is expelled shortly afterward.

A baby will have a belly button where the umbilical cord was once attached.

> ➤ Often, the father of the child is present to provide support, encouragement, and physical assistance to the mom as she is giving birth. Dads can provide a lot of help to moms during childbirth.
>
> The thought of a woman pushing a baby out of her vagina may be a frightening image for some dads. But most discover that, since giving birth is usually a very long process, there is time to adjust to the situation.
>
> Participating in the birth of a child can be an extremely profound experience for a dad; not only can he help the mom, he can be present to hold, reassure, and help care for his newborn baby.

Alternative Insemination

Not all kids are conceived through sexual intercourse. Many are conceived through **alternative insemination** (or "donor insemination").

What happens is this:

A woman, usually in the office of a health care professional, receives sperm that has previously been collected from a male (through masturbating). The sperm is introduced into her vagina. If all goes well, the woman becomes pregnant.

In a more complicated medical procedure, a woman's egg(s) are **harvested** (removed) and mixed with sperm outside of her body. Later, the developing egg or eggs are introduced into her uterus, where they continue to grow.

All methods of human reproduction require both female and male reproductive cells—so it takes a guy's participation, no matter what.

Every birth is the result of the miraculous process of human reproduction, and every child is a natural wonder, regardless of whether conception of the baby takes place through intercourse or through an alternative method.

CHAPTER 9

Parking: SEX

Biologically speaking, sex is the compelling force behind human reproduction (see page 70). But sex isn't only about reproduction. If it were, couples would have only very specific sexual contact, and they'd only have it when they wanted to make a baby—and that's generally not how it works.

Unless actually planning a pregnancy, most couples intentionally avoid the link between sex and reproduction by stopping short of having sexual intercourse or by using birth control during sexual intercourse.

What is sexual intercourse? It's a kind of sexual activity that can lead to a woman's becoming pregnant. It's described on page 72.

Even though having sexual intercourse is sometimes called "having sex," and sex can be described as the compelling force behind human reproduction, sexual activity isn't necessarily a push toward sexual intercourse.

Far from it!

Sex is about exploring a whole range of sensations that feel good physically and emotionally, either with a partner or alone. And there are a variety of activities that go along with that.

Our sexuality develops as we grow from infancy into adulthood. And our awareness of sexual feelings often begins in infancy or early childhood, when we discover that touching our own bodies in certain ways feels good (see page 15).

SEX AND LOVE

Being in love is about having a profoundly tender, passionate affection for another person. Sharing sexual feelings can be a way of expressing that affection. Having sexual contact with a partner is a way of communicating feelings through touching.

Not all couples include sex in their relationship. Some choose not to. Couples can find many ways to express love without having sex.

Many people consider sex to be an expression so special and intimate that it should be reserved for partners who are married or otherwise committed to a long-term, mutually faithful relationship based on love and trust.

Some adults have sexual relationships with consenting adult friends or adult acquaintances—without being in love. But for most people, sex and love are linked.

When linked with love, sex can be one of the

most powerful, intense, and satisfying experiences two people can share.

However . . .

Sex, even when linked with love, isn't always powerful.

It would be unrealistic to think that every time two people have sex, the earth moves beneath them. More often, sex could be described as a comforting, reassuring experience that allows two people to snuggle up and touch bases with each other.

And sometimes (especially between inexperienced partners), sex can be downright disappointing!

Crushes

A strong physical attraction can easily translate into a crush, and the feelings associated with having a crush can be really intense.

Is having a crush the same as falling in love? Not really.

Having a strong physical attraction to another person is one of the components of being in love, but being in love involves other feelings, too.

A crush can be on somebody you hardly know; a crush can even be on somebody you've never even talked to.

Being in love is about being connected to another person in the deepest, most profound way imaginable. Actually knowing the person is an essential ingredient of being in love.

Unbelievably (and *totally* unbelievably if you're in the middle of having a crush), crushes can fade relatively quickly and often do.

Even so, having a crush can cause some emotional havoc, especially when you're young, because even though a crush isn't love, it can feel like the real thing!

Kids and Love (and Sex)

Sometimes kids do fall in love with each other. It may start with one or the other having a crush, with both people having a crush on each other, or with a friendship that moves in a romantic direction.

However it starts, it progresses into a situation where both people are extremely attracted to each other and acknowledge it. The feelings they share develop and deepen into a relationship that could be characterized as love.

Even so . . .

Most teens lack the experience needed to fully accept the responsibilities and assume the risks that go along with having sex with a partner.

The responsibilities that go along with having a sexual relationship include making and keeping appointments for routine medical exams for the screening of sexually transmitted diseases, as well as knowing how to reduce the risks of being exposed to, or exposing someone else to, sexually transmitted diseases. This is true of both heterosexual and homosexual couples (see page 80). With heterosexual couples, responsibilities also include knowing how to take precautions to avoid unplanned pregnancy and how to act responsibly should an unplanned pregnancy occur.

But the risks of having sex aren't limited to physical risks; there are also emotional risks. Preadolescents and young teens are not yet equipped to cope with the complex set of emotions that accompany a sexual relationship.

➤ Apart from the moral and ethical issues that accompany having put a baby on the planet, do you know that a male may be held financially responsible for the baby he produces until the baby grows up and reaches the age of eighteen?

This can apply even if the father had no intent to become a dad or to have a long-term relationship with the mother of the child and even if the guy himself used birth control (a condom) and/or believed the mother of the child was using birth control effectively while having sex (see page 93).

It can apply even if the guy wanted the girl to have an abortion (see page 102) rather than go through with the pregnancy and even if he offered to pay for the abortion and she declined his offer.

Peer Pressure About Sex

If you don't want to have sexual contact with a partner, don't. You don't have to give a reason—you don't even need to have a reason. You certainly don't have to have sex to prove your masculinity or to prove your affection for your partner.

There are lots of ways to show love that don't involve having sex.

Don't pressure yourself.

Peer pressure, when it comes right down to it, is really mostly about how we pressure ourselves. Most kids don't hound each other to have sex, smoke cigarettes, drink alcohol, or take drugs. Honor and respect your own ideas and instincts about what seems right for you.

Having a sexual relationship with somebody is a huge responsibility. If you don't feel ready to take it on, you're not ready—so don't.

You don't have to prove to yourself that you are capable of having sex.

"Being like the other guys" isn't a good reason to have sex—especially when you consider how many of the other boys are either exaggerating or just flat-out, full-on lying about it!

You'll Know When

Once grown and fully mature, you'll be aware of and ready and able to accept the risks and responsibilities involved in having sex with a partner.

You'll be able to recognize when the situation is right. You'll be able to make the commitment required.

You'll be able to responsibly have sex with someone you love and trust, who loves and trusts you, too.

Sex and the Media/Sex and the Myths

In our culture, sex is used to sell everything from toothpaste to chain saws. It's used to sell movie tickets, CDs, TV programs, magazines, and newspapers.

Since sexual images are used for the rather unimportant purpose of selling stuff to people, there's an unspoken message that sex is, well, not really all that special—but it is!

The media seem unrelenting in pressuring youth to have sex—and to be sexy. Young teens are bombarded by sexual images without being given enough actual information about sex and the risks and responsibilities associated with it. Kids are given the idea that "everybody" is doing it, or should be. They are also given the impression that adolescents are supposed to be sexy to be powerful and popular.

This may be part of the reason that so many boys feel pressured to have sex, even before they're ready to. But there's another reason: There is a societal myth that a guy has to have sex with a lot of girls (or even just one!) to prove that he's a man. Many boys exaggerate or just plain make up stories about sexual escapades to impress the other guys, and this just adds to the confusion.

Having sex doesn't make a boy a man—it just makes him a boy who's had sex. And if he just does it to get a feather in his cap—to impress his friends or to prove something to himself—where does the girl fit into the picture?

There's no good reason to rush into having sex, but there are a whole lot of good reasons not to.

Sexually transmitted diseases and unplanned pregnancy are only two of the reasons not to.

Sex can also put kids at risk of emotional harm if they're not actually ready for the experience.

> ➤ ~~Horse~~Studpower
> **At a time when people are particularly attuned to the health risks involved with having multiple sexual partners, boasting about sexual conquests isn't likely to get a guy high marks.**
>
> **Being a stud is important if you're a retired racehorse, a prize bull, or a blue-ribbon hog. Apart from that, it has no particular credibility.**

SEXUAL ORIENTATION

The words **sexual orientation** describe whether a person is attracted to people of the opposite sex, people of the same sex, or people of both sexes. The concept of how people get their sexual orientation is not fully understood.

Some people believe that our sexual orientation is something that we are born with. Others feel that it develops as a result of our experiences. Many feel that our sexual orientation is a result of a combination of both these factors.

Sexual orientation is sometimes thought of in terms of categories: **heterosexual** (when all or most of a person's attractions are directed toward someone of the opposite sex); **homosexual** (when all or most of a person's attractions are directed toward someone of the same sex); or **bisexual** (when someone has attractions toward people of both sexes).

Here are words you may hear describing sexual orientation: **straight** (men who romantically love women and women who romantically love men); **gay** (men who romantically love men); **lesbian** (women who romantically love women); and **bi** (men or women who romantically love both men and women).

All are natural ways of being.

Many people reject the notion of putting people into categories and labeling them. Not everybody believes that people fit into one category or another. In any event, the groupings don't apply to kids, who are in the process of developing in all ways—including sexually.

Liking to hold hands, hug, and snuggle with friends of the same sex or of the opposite sex, or both, is common among young children. Sometimes sexual feelings accompany these affectionate gestures. These feelings don't necessarily predict what a person's sexual orientation will ultimately be.

Having a few "gay" or "lesbian" romantic attractions as a young teen also doesn't necessarily mean that the teen will grow up to be gay or lesbian.

But it might.

Don't fix what ain't broke.

Homosexuality is a natural expression of human sexuality that has existed since the beginning of time. It's described by psychologists as a normal variation of human sexuality.

It's not regarded as a condition that needs to be treated, modified, medicated, changed, or fixed.

Understanding sexual orientation is the first step toward establishing healthy attitudes toward ourselves and others.

People can be strong, productive, respected, confident, healthy—and happy—regardless of sexual orientation.

Homophobia

A **phobia** is an irrational fear. **Homophobia** is an irrational fear of homosexuality.

The potential of being gay, or the idea of others being gay, is scary and threatening to some people. Sometimes the fear becomes translated into anger—and even hate. When this happens, homophobia can, and sometimes does, lead to

criminal violence directed against gays and lesbians.

It can also lead to unhealthy attitudes toward one's own sexual orientation.

HEADS UP!
If you have homophobic feelings that you think might lead to harming yourself or someone else, it's very important to talk to a counselor (see page 47).

Gay Parents, Friends, and Family Members

Lots of kids have gay parents, gay older siblings, other gay family members, and gay friends.

PFLAG (Parents, Families and Friends of Lesbians and Gays) is a national organization that provides support for lesbian, gay, and bisexual people and their families and friends. PFLAG's phone numbers are 1-202-638-4200 and 1-202-467-8180. You can call them 9:00 A.M. to 5:30 P.M. (Eastern time), Monday through Friday. (There is a long-distance charge, which will appear on the phone bill.) Or visit their Web site: www.pflag.org.

HEADS UP!
Sexual harassment (see page 123) includes inappropriate behavior and remarks regarding someone's sexual orientation. It's possible to express philosophical, cultural, religious or personal viewpoints without harassing (or, for that matter, judging) other people.

CRUISE CONTROL

It's very appropriate to set limits as to what, if any, physical contact you may have with a partner—now and in the future.

You are responsible for operating within reasonable limits for your age and experience.

Please keep this in mind as you read the material in this section.

Making Choices

Since people are unique beings, we like different things—different foods, different clothes, different music and movies. People also have different preferences regarding physical touching.

Family values and religious and cultural traditions, as well as health considerations and sexual orientation, play significant roles in the decisions people make about what kind of touching they believe should be included in a sexual relationship with a partner—and when.

All sexual touching requires consent from the people involved (see page 120). Basically, consent is permission freely given by someone who is considered old enough and sober enough to give it (and who is not otherwise impaired). Remember: Each state has its own laws that relate to sexual contact, including sexual contact between consenting juvenile partners. Specific questions? Talk to an attorney who specializes in juvenile law.

Definitions

Here are expressions you may have heard or may hear other kids talking about.

➤ Making out (sometimes called "getting together with") is when two people hug and kiss in a prolonged, romantic way. Sometimes they "French-kiss." French-kissing is open-mouthed kissing, including using your tongue.

➤ Going further refers to other ways that people can touch each other sexually while making out. Going further can include caressing any part of the body, with or without clothing. It can include touching the breasts, clitoris, vagina, or behind of a partner; it can include touching the penis and testicles of a partner. It can involve mutual masturbation (masturbating each other).

Making out and/or going further can

arouse strong sexual responses. Often one or both people have orgasms while making out.

➤ **Oral sex** refers to sexual activity that includes stimulating one's partner's genitals by using the lips, mouth, and tongue.

➤ **Anal sex** refers to partners having sexual intercourse by way of the anus. (This is also referred to as **sodomy**.)

The anus is a very delicate, fragile organ of the body. It's easy to bruise or tear the tissue in and around it. Tears in the tissue can take a long time to heal. They can also provide an entryway for germs and infections. Anal sex presents an **extremely high risk** for getting sexually transmitted diseases.

➤ *Sexual Intercourse*

Vaginal sexual intercourse is a major landmark in a romantic relationship between heterosexual partners (see page 72).

CHAPTER 10

Hazardous Conditions: STDs

Sexually transmitted diseases include genital warts, chlamydia, genital herpes, gonorrhea, syphilis, hepatitis B, AIDS, and others. They're caused by germs—either bacteria or viruses.

Before you read on, keep in mind that most germs that cause STDs die shortly after they leave the comfort of a human being's body. So it would be highly unlikely to catch an STD from, say, a toilet seat.

And you **can't** get an STD from "solo sex" (masturbating by yourself).

HEADS UP!

Remember: Every attempt has been made to ensure that the info in this book is scientifically correct, but its purpose is to give general information; it shouldn't be relied on as a source of medical advice. If you have symptoms or specific questions, call your doctor or the national STD hot line (see page 90).

➤ If you haven't yet had sex with a partner, your chances of now having a sexually transmitted disease are approximately zilch.

Be informed.

Vaginal fluid, cervical secretions, menstrual blood, semen, and pre-ejaculate often contain the germs that cause sexually transmitted diseases. Remember: For the germs to be present, the person must be infected.

In some cases, STD germs may be present in sores, warts, bumps, or blisters, or (uncommonly) just plain on the skin. Germs also thrive in mucous membranes, which are the slippery, moist places of the body.

Occasionally, STD germs are present in the mouth, on the lips, or in the back of the throat of an infected person.

Bug Deflectors

When used correctly, latex condoms can provide protection against the spread of many STDs (see page 86). But not all. There are lots of people who have used condoms responsibly but have still ended up getting exposed to an STD—like herpes or genital warts, for example.

Treating Sexually Transmitted Diseases

Some sexually transmitted diseases, such as syphilis, gonorrhea, and chlamydia, are completely curable provided they are treated in time. Remember: People can be *tested* for STDs, even if there are no outward signs of infection (symptoms).

This is one reason why sexually active people need to **schedule routine checkups**.

STD OVERVIEW

Syphilis is a relatively rare disease. If treated in time, it can be cured. Left untreated, it may eventually lead to death. Symptoms may include a painless, clearly visible ulcer that appears between the legs or on the penis, vagina, anal area (butt), or mouth two to four weeks after sex. This may be followed by feeling sick, getting bumps and spots on the hands and feet, having a rash, and developing a sore throat, sores in the mouth, and lesions between the legs.

Gonorrhea and **chlamydia** often have no symptoms or may have very mild symptoms, which can go unnoticed.

Gonorrhea may present itself as a yellowy-white, odorless discharge from the penis, pain or burning while peeing, the need to pee often, and/or flulike symptoms. If treated in time, it can be cured. Untreated, gonorrhea can cause a male to become sterile (unable to have children).

Chlamydia is especially troublesome, since it is very common and so often has no symptoms. Most young men who contract it don't realize they are infected. They pass it to future partners. Unnoticed (and untreated), chlamydia can spread and cause permanent damage to a woman's reproductive organs (resulting in her becoming unable to conceive a baby). Symptoms for males who do actually have symptoms include having a drip from the penis and pain when pee-

ing. If treated in time, chlamydia can be cured.

Other sexually transmitted diseases, such as **genital herpes** and **genital warts**, cannot be cured, but they are manageable. Early detection helps.

Symptoms of **genital warts**: raised or flat, single or multiple, growths or bumps in the area of the penis, scrotum, or groin (or vulva or vagina in women).

Symptoms of **genital herpes** may include pain and itching—then small, very tender red bumps that become blisters that may appear on the penis, scrotum, buttocks, anus, thighs, or urethra. In women? They may appear on the vaginal area,

vulva, buttocks, anus, thighs, or cervix. These blisters fill with a clear liquid, break, and cause ulcers, then scabs. Ouch!

These breakouts clear up—but may return periodically.

Chancroid is a sexually transmitted disease caused by bacteria. It can have symptoms similar to those of genital herpes. The good news is that, unlike herpes, chancroid is totally curable by antibiotics.

More? Are you kidding?

There's a list of other sexually transmitted diseases that don't usually lead to serious medical problems for boys, but they can if left untreated.

Nonspecific urethritis (NSU) is one of these. It causes urinary symptoms, including discharge from the penis, burning when urinating, burning/itching around the opening of the penis, and inflammation of the urethra. Untreated, it can lead to bladder, kidney, and/or urinary tract infections and permanent damage to the reproductive organs.

HEADS UP!
All painful or troublesome symptoms should be reported to your doctor (see page 20). Remember, *The Guy Book* isn't a medical reference book.

HITCHHIKERS

As you read the info that follows, don't be surprised if you feel the need to scratch a little; it's a well-known phenomenon that reading about crabs and scabies makes people itch.

Crabs

Crabs (pubic lice) are tiny beasts that jump or crawl from one person's pubic hair into another's. They take up residence in this warm, moist nest and multiply faster than rabbits. Symptoms: itch-

ing! Also, they're visible. They can be seen prowling around in pubic hair. After hanging out in pubic hair for a while, they get the urge to travel. They'll break camp and migrate to other favored spots: underarm hair, eyebrows, and eyelashes.

These can be zapped with a prescription lotion from the doctor or over-the-counter medication. Talk to a pharmacist.

Scabies

Scabies are frightful little mites that burrow into the skin. They're not necessarily related to sexual activity, but a person could pick them up from sleeping with someone in a scabies-infested bed.

If scabies set up shop in the genital area, they, too, will cause major itching. Scabies can be terminated by a lotion prescribed by the doctor.

THE TURBO-THREAT—HIV AND AIDS

AIDS (acquired immunodeficiency syndrome) is caused by a virus called HIV (human immunodeficiency virus). AIDS has absolutely swept the earth and millions of people have died from it worldwide. We are just beginning to get a handle on it. As yet, there is no cure for AIDS—only medications to help manage it.

HIV lives in the blood (including menstrual blood), vaginal fluid, and cervical secretions of an infected female. It's also present in the pre-ejaculate, semen, and blood of an infected male. It can be present in the milk of a nursing mother who is infected with HIV.

The HIV virus can be passed from one person to another if any of the above-mentioned body fluids from an infected person enter someone else's body.

The virus can enter a male's body through a break in his skin or through the mucous membranes of his mouth, penis tip, or anus (or nose or eyes). It can enter a female's body through a break in the skin or through her mucous membranes—in her mouth, vagina, or anus (or nose or eyes).

The virus can be passed from an infected pregnant woman to her unborn child, and it can be passed through breast-feeding.

Most HIV infections occur when people have sex without effectively using a **latex** (*not* lambskin) condom, or when people share the needles and syringes used to inject illegal drugs, including steroids.

Anyone—young or old, rich or poor, gay, straight, or bisexual—exposed to the HIV virus can become infected. People who are infected are said to be "HIV-positive." You can't tell by looking at someone if he or she has been infected by HIV. There are no outward clues until a person gets sick, which may be years after the virus has entered that person's body. A person infected with HIV may not know it and can infect others without meaning to.

HEADS UP!
Only a test can determine whether someone is infected with HIV. The sooner HIV infection is diagnosed, the better.

HIV attacks the immune system—which is the body's system for fighting off infections. Over time, as the body loses the ability to recover from sicknesses, the infected person reaches a point at which he or she is said to have AIDS.

Don't let your guard down!

Medications that prolong life for people with AIDS are now available. So are medications that help keep the HIV virus from causing full-blown AIDS.

Still, we are not in control of this disease! Results are not as promising as we had initially hoped.

AIDS still must be regarded as potentially fatal. And HIV is spreading at a *very* alarming rate. Our main defense against AIDS still remains not becoming infected with HIV to begin with! Knowing how HIV is spread can help us protect ourselves and one another from contracting this devastating illness.

> ➤ If you don't have sex with a partner and don't share needles or syringes, and if you avoid contact with other people's blood, you won't be at risk for becoming infected with HIV.

Symptoms

HIV often causes no symptoms at all. However, it can cause flulike symptoms after someone is initially infected. Later, more symptoms may appear. They include swollen lymph glands in the neck, underarm, or groin area; recurrent fever, which may cause "night sweats"; rapid, unexplained weight loss; diarrhea and decreased appetite; and white spots or unusual blemishes in the mouth. Women may also experience yeast or other vaginal infections that are recurrent or hard to treat.

HIV and Blood

Skin acts like a protective barrier, but skin can't protect us from HIV if the skin is broken. If skin is scraped, cut, or scratched, or if there is a rash, the virus can easily pass through. Remember that HIV can pass into mucous membranes (even if there is no break in the membrane). Mucous membranes are the slippery-type places on our bodies, like the insides of our mouths, for example.

Coming into direct contact with other people's blood, including menstrual fluid, should be avoided.

Sharing needles or equipment used to shoot up (inject) drugs—including steroids—is a way the virus is commonly passed (see page 56).

Avoid other people's bloody noses, cuts, sores, scratches, bloody tampons, pads, and bandages.

Ear-piercing "guns" and body-piercing equipment must be sterile to prevent transmitting the HIV virus. If you have your ears or body pierced in a store or salon, have your parents make sure that the equipment is properly sterilized. It's safest to have piercing done by a health care professional.

Unsterile tattoo equipment can spread HIV, hepatitis, and other blood-borne diseases.

Should you ever decide to get a professional manicure, be aware that there are guidelines for manicurists. Tools should be sterilized or disposable so that only clean instruments come in contact with nails and skin. Concerned? Bring your own tools.

To stay on the safe side, don't share toothbrushes, razors, or jewelry for pierced ears or body piercing. However unlikely, these things could conceivably have some fresh blood on them; if HIV were present in the blood, it might find an entry point on your body.

Do you know someone with HIV or AIDS?

Many babies have been born in the United States (and continue to be born in the United States) infected with HIV. This is because some (not all) infected pregnant women end up passing the virus on to their unborn children.

Lots of these children are now in their teens.

If you are infected or know someone with HIV or AIDS, remember that you can't pass it or get it through casual contact, like sitting near, talking to, or hugging an infected person. If you want to show affection in this way, do. People with HIV or AIDS are entitled to support, compassion, understanding, and acceptance—just like everybody else.

Making Out and STDs

Under certain conditions, making out can pose a risk of exposure to sexually transmitted diseases.

Although hepatitis B is usually spread through sexual intercourse, the virus that causes it may be present in saliva. It's considered technically possible for hepatitis B to be spread by kissing, although it's very unlikely. Talk to your doctor about becoming immunized against hepatitis B—if you haven't already been immunized.

The germs that cause gonorrhea may be present in the back of the throat of an infected person.

A syphilis sore may be present on the mouth of an infected person.

Herpes: What's Up?

Herpes is in a special category. The basic rule is: The place a herpes sore touches your skin or mucous membrane may become the site where you become infected. Uncommonly, infection can happen without a sore present.

A cold sore on the mouth (oral herpes) isn't considered an STD. But oral herpes can be spread through kissing. **The herpes virus present in a cold sore can be passed to the genitals of a partner during oral sex.** Once spread to the genitals, the partner will have genital herpes.

A herpes sore on the genitals (genital herpes) can be spread to a partner's mouth during oral sex, whereupon the partner will have oral herpes.

Genital herpes can be spread during genital-to-genital contact or skin-to-skin contact in the genital area.

HIV and Kissing

Small amounts of the HIV virus have been found in saliva, but at the time of publication of this book, there have been no documented instances of HIV having been spread by kissing alone. However, it should be pointed out that HIV could be spread through kissing if blood is present in the mouth of an infected person and saliva is exchanged. (HIV present in the blood could be absorbed by the mucous membranes of the mouth.)

HEADS UP!

If you have cuts, scratches, or other breaks in your skin—including the skin on the hands—avoid physical contact that would allow another's blood, vaginal secretions, semen, or pre-ejaculate to get on to these breaks. Be aware that "sex toys" (vibrators, dildos, and whatever . . .) can have fluids on them that contain STD germs.

SEXUAL INTERCOURSE AND STDS

Sexual intercourse is high-risk activity for spreading sexually transmitted diseases, since STD germs may be present in pre-ejaculate and semen, vaginal fluids, menstrual blood, and cervical secretions and in sores, warts, and blisters or on the skin on and around the genitals.

Oral Sex and STDs

Oral sex is risky activity for spreading STDs. Germs that cause STDs may be present in the mouth as well as in the genitals.

Information about sexual contact and sexually transmitted diseases can be confusing—and can change. If you have specific questions about exposure to sexually transmitted diseases through kissing, making out, "going further," or other contact, you can call the **Centers for Disease Control (CDC) National STD Hot Line**, and they will answer your questions or refer you to someone in your area who can. The call is free, confidential, and won't appear on the house phone bill.

1-800-227-8922 (U.S. only) 24-7
For the hearing-impaired: **1-800-243-7889** (TTY), 10:00 A.M. to 10:00 P.M. (Eastern time), Monday to Friday
In Spanish: **1-800-344-7432** 8:00 A.M. to 2:00 A.M. (Eastern time), 7 days a week

Or check out their Web sites: www.ashastd.org and, for teens, www.iwannaknow.org
Questions? Send an e-mail to hivnet@ashastd.org
Information about tests for sexually transmitted diseases is available through the local health department, at family planning clinics such as Planned Parenthood (1-800-230-7526), or at a doctor's office (or by calling the CDC National STD Hot Line—U.S. only).

Oral Sex and HIV

Since HIV may be present in pre-ejaculate and semen, vaginal secretions, and menstrual blood, and since HIV can be absorbed through mucous membranes, which line the mouth, oral sex is in the category of risky sexual contact for exposure to HIV.

HEADS UP!

Household plastic wrap, a latex condom (see page 94) cut in half lengthwise, or a dental dam can provide a protective barrier to separate the mouth from the vaginal area during oral sex performed on a female, although the effectiveness of this method has not yet been proved.

An infected male can pass HIV and other STD germs to his partner if he doesn't wear a latex condom while oral sex is being performed on him. A condom prevents pre-ejaculate and semen from coming into contact with the mucous membranes of his partner's mouth. It also prevents STD germs that may be present in his partner's mouth from contacting his penis.

Anal Sex and STDs

To recap, anal sex is very, VERY high-risk sexual activity for becoming infected with HIV and other STDs (see page 86).

A condom can easily break during anal sex. A water-based lubricant (see page 94) spread on the outside of a latex condom (after the condom is on the penis) makes breaking less likely. Again: Do not use petroleum jelly or butter, which can weaken the latex and create a higher likelihood of the condom breaking.

The CDC National HIV/AIDS Hot Line may have other information relevant to protecting oneself and others during sexual contact, including anal sex.

➤ If you have questions about HIV, HIV testing, or HIV/AIDS counseling, call the CDC National HIV/AIDS Hot Line and ask.

It's free; the call won't appear on the phone bill. The numbers are:

1-800-342-AIDS (1-800-342-2437)
For the hearing-impaired: 1-800-243-7889 (TTY)
In Spanish: 1-800-344-7432

In Canada, you may consult your local health department, listed in the municipality section of the white pages in the phone book, or call the information operator (411) for an HIV/AIDS hot line.

HIV and Shooting Up Drugs (Including Steroids)

Since blood from one person can be left in a hypodermic needle and syringe, sharing equipment used to shoot up drugs is a common way for HIV (and other diseases) to be passed from one person to another. And once infected, people can go on to infect their sexual partners as well as those people with whom they may be sharing needles and syringes (see page 56).

Remember:

People who are sexually active may **reduce** the risk of becoming exposed to HIV by way of sexual contact if:

1. The male wears a latex condom that's been lubricated with a water-based lubricant during every single act of sexual intercourse or anal sex.

2. There is a barrier between partners' mouths and genitals during every single act of oral sex (see above).

3. Partners stay informed regarding new developments and information about HIV and new kinds of protective products and strategies.

Don't forget: Other methods of birth control—such as birth control pills—**do not protect either partner** from being exposed to HIV.

CHAPTER 11

MAPPING
the Journey:

BIRTH CONTROL

RISKS AND RESPONSIBILITIES FOR DISEASE PREVENTION AND BIRTH CONTROL

As you read the material that follows, keep in mind that the most effective way of avoiding unplanned pregnancy is to abstain from having sexual intercourse.

The most effective way to avoid becoming infected with a sexually transmitted disease is to abstain from having sexual contact with a partner.

The topics of disease prevention and birth control should be discussed with parents, a trusted older relative or friend, the school nurse, or a doctor or other health care professional in a family-planning clinic before making a decision about having sex.

Before having sexual intercourse, a visit to a family-planning clinic, the health department, a doctor's office, and/or a drugstore is in order.

Or call Planned Parenthood; they're set up to talk to teens.

PLANNED PARENTHOOD
1-800-230-7526 (toll-free)
Or call 411 for the office nearest you.

Condoms

Most kids have at least heard the word **condom**, but not every kid knows what one actually is.

A condom is a covering for the penis, and a guy wears it while having sex. It's made of very thin, delicate material—usually latex, a kind of rubber. That's why another name for a condom is a "rubber."

Unrolled, a condom looks a little bit like a long, thin, clear, unblown balloon with a very wide opening for blowing it up.

Condoms are used for two purposes: (1) to help prevent the spread of sexually transmitted diseases (STDs) and (2) to help prevent unplanned pregnancy.

1. Helping Prevent the Spread of Sexually Transmitted Diseases (STDs)

Remember: Germs for certain sexually transmitted diseases (STDs) can be found in the vaginal fluid, cervical secretions, menstrual blood (all blood, actually), semen, and pre-ejaculate of an infected partner. Some germs can be present in sores, warts, bumps, blisters, or mucous membranes, or on the skin.

A condom provides a thin barrier between a male's penis and the body of his partner. When used correctly, latex condoms help protect both partners from the spread of germs that might enter the body through the mucous membrane at the very tip of the penis, the inside of the vagina, or the inside of the mouth—or through cuts, breaks, scratches, or sores, or by other contact with the skin.

> ➤ But it prevents skin-to-skin contact only between the *shaft* of the penis and the other person's body (see page 4).

If a condom is put on as soon as the penis is erect, a male's **pre-ejaculate** (preseminal fluid), which appears at the tip of a guy's penis when sexually aroused, will be prevented from coming in contact with his partner's body. If ejaculation occurs, the semen will be trapped in the condom.

Not all condoms are made of latex. Those made of natural membrane (lambskin) **are not reliable** for disease protection. Germs can pass through condoms made of natural membrane, including the HIV virus (see page 87).

A condom worn to prevent the spread of sexually transmitted diseases **must be made of latex**. If you (or your partner) is allergic to latex, talk to your health care professional about **polyurethane** condoms.

➤ Using a Lubricant

A latex condom needs to be lubricated on the outside (made slippery) in order to make sure it won't tear during intercourse (from friction).

The lubricant *must be water-based.*
Remember: Oil-based lubricants (such as Vaseline or butter) can damage (weaken) condoms and make them more likely to break.

Note: The medications for vaginal yeast infections (which girls get) can also cause a condom (or diaphragm) to weaken.

Water-based lubricants usually come in tubes or little plastic containers. They're sold in drugstores (and sometimes in grocery stores and convenience stores) and usually found near the condoms.

The lubricant is put on the outside of the condom after the condom has been rolled onto an erect penis (see page 99). A water-based lubricant should be used in addition to the lubricant that may already be on a packaged latex condom.

Some water-based lubricants also contain spermicide.

2. Helping Prevent Unplanned Pregnancy

Since a condom prevents pre-ejaculate and semen, both of which contain sperm, from landing near or inside a girl's vagina, a condom, if used correctly (with a water-based lubricant), will prevent pregnancy.

It's especially effective for birth control if the female uses **spermicide**, which kills sperm in case the condom leaks or breaks (see page 100).

Condoms and spermicides have another name: **contraceptives**.

Spermicides

Spermicides are products that kill sperm on contact. They also can help knock out some (not all) STD germs. Spermicides come in many different forms: foams, gels, and suppositories. They must be used in combination with a condom in order to be effective for birth control.

The combination of a latex condom worn by the male and lubricated on the outside with a water-based lubricant to help prevent it from breaking PLUS an additional spermicidal foam, gel, or suppository used by the female (put into her vagina before intercourse) both helps prevent pregnancy and reduces the risk of becoming infected with a sexually transmitted disease. This combination is not 100 percent effective, but it is very, very effective if the products are used according to directions. These products don't require a prescription.

And, when used correctly, they're probably the most effective combination of birth control products available that are under the guy's supervision and control; that's why guys need to know about them.

A guy knows if his condom's on right and if it's properly lubricated. Also, he can be present when his partner puts in spermicide.

Since these products are commonly available, relatively affordable, and usually sold with no questions asked, they're a good choice for teen couples who have decided to have sex.

But remember: Condoms can break; spermicide isn't a 100 percent effective backup. Sperm are determined to cause pregnancy, and when you

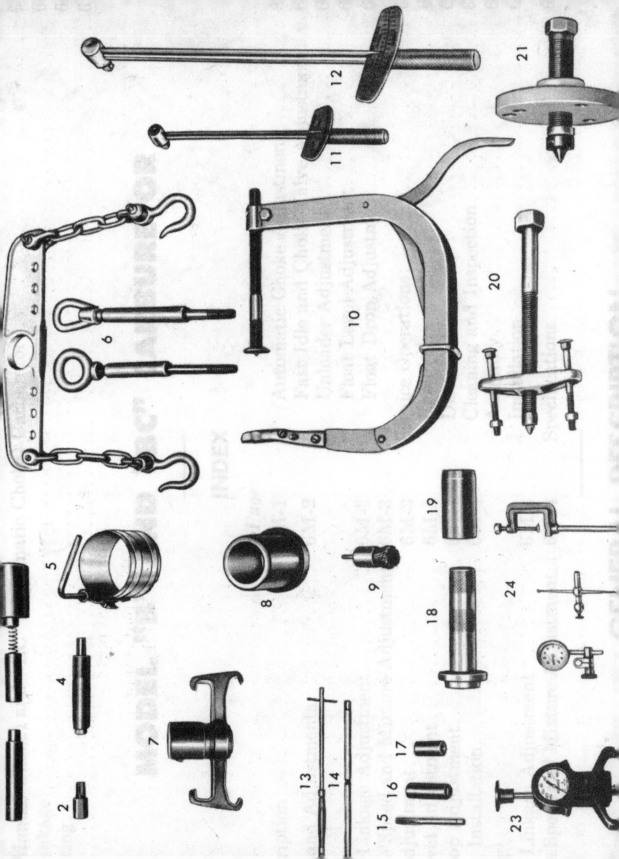

consider that 6 million of them hit the trail at the same time—look out!

Every guy who's having sex with a girl should also know about **emergency hormonal contraception** (see page 99).

There are many other forms of birth control. They are reviewed on pages 101-102. It's your responsibility to discuss birth control with your partner before having sex. It's not "up to her."

And remember even if she's using birth control, condoms are necessary for disease protection! So plan on using them! Age restrictions on buying contraceptives in your state? Probably not. But you can call the drugstore or Planned Parenthood (see page 93) in advance if you want to make sure.

Condoms: What to Know

A box of condoms often has a romantic picture on the front, such as a man and a woman looking deep into each other's eyes with the moon rising behind them.

The brand name is usually in large print on the box. Inside, condoms come rolled up and individually wrapped in foil or plastic packets. There are also detailed instructions inside the box or printed on an inside wall of the box.

There are many different styles of condoms: lubricated, unlubricated, reservoir-tipped, textured, with spermicide, without spermicide. . . .

As long as the three guidelines below are followed, any style of condoms works (as well as condoms work—which is not 100 percent).

HEADS UP! Guidelines
1. The condom should be made of LATEX (not lambskin or natural membrane).
2. A "disease prevention claim" should be present on the box. The claim will say something like "These latex condoms, when properly used, may help reduce the risk of catching or spreading many sexually transmitted diseases."

3. There should be an expiration date on the box, and it should not have expired.

➤ At the time of publication of this book, latex condoms are considered the safest condom choice. However, other materials are being investigated and tested. Stay informed! Talk to your pharmacist or health care professional about any new developments. Or call the STD hot lines on page 90.

Shopping for Condoms, Etc.

One fact of life is that if you want to have sex responsibly, sooner or later you're probably going to have to either persuade a friend or family member to score condoms for you—or face up to buying them yourself!

By the time you're old enough to have sex, it probably won't seem like a big deal to walk into a drugstore and buy what you need.

If it does, here's a strategy to keep in mind:

At the time of publication of this book, a box of three condoms costs under $5. Before entering the store, make sure that you have enough money in your pocket or wallet to cover the cost—so you can just bust it out without having to dig for dimes, nickels, and pennies to make the transaction.

➤ Background Info
The cost of condoms depends on how many are in the box. A first-time buyer may want to choose a box of three. (A box of 12 is larger and more expensive, and may draw undue attention to itself or you.)

If you should buy condoms from a machine, be aware that condoms shouldn't be stored in hot places or direct sunlight. Where is the machine located?

On your mark . . .

The condom section is usually fairly obvious—but of course you'll have to hunt for it.

And naturally, it will hide from you.

In a convenience store, condoms will probably be located near the spot where drugs (like Tylenol) are sold. They may also be found inconveniently near where the cashier is ringing stuff up—a nightmare if the cashier is a cute girl. Or the leader of the church choir.

. . . Get set . . .

In larger stores—drugstores or grocery stores—condoms will probably be somewhere in the aisles that display drugs, vitamins, Band-Aids, and that kind of thing—not housewares or other stuff.

. . . Go!

Once you find the condom section, go about your business of picking up the boxes on the display and looking for a box with the magic words "latex" and "disease prevention" on it. Then, find and check the expiration date. It will probably be printed or etched into the side of the box. It will look something like this: JAN 2000-something.

Bingo

You've snagged some. Maybe they won't ultimately be your favorites, but they'll work. (Save the colored, flavored ones or the ones wrapped in golden, coin-shaped packages for next time.)

You probably won't need to buy condoms marked "large" or "extra large." Unless your penis is HUGE, the regular-size ones should fit. If you get home and discover that regulars can't be rolled all the way down to the base of the penis, you'll have to shop again.

Remember: Condoms are supposed to be tight so they don't slip off!

One Down, One to Go

On to the area that displays lubricant! Yes—we know that the condom box may say the condoms are already lubricated, but to be safe you still need more, to minimize the chance of the condom breaking from friction during sex.

Water-based lubricant is almost always VERY close to the condoms. Find a product that says "personal lubricant" and "water-soluble" on the box. It will probably say something like "Ideal for use with condoms." (K-Y Jelly, by the way, comes in convenient small tubes, three per package.) The prices will vary, but you should be able to land some for under $5.

Don't get water-based lubricant confused with spermicide; they're two different products.

Nab the lubricant, and you're done.

Unless you need to buy spermicide for your female partner—which will cost about another $5 or so.

In that case, somewhere close to the condoms and lubricants, you will find another section or shelf of products. Look for the word "spermicide" (sperm killer) on a box that also says "vaginal contraceptive foam" (or "jelly" or "suppositories"). It should also say "applicator included" if one is necessary. Check the expiration date. Is it current?

Reel it in.

Mission accomplished.

Now you'll have to bite the bullet and proceed to the cashier. Whatever you do, don't be tempted to stick any of these products in your pocket out of embarrassment and just make a break for the door. Number 1, it's shoplifting, and number 2, contraceptive products usually have little hidden security strips that can set off every alarm in the store.

If you are very, very embarrassed by the prospect of approaching the cashier with these items, try James's old trick, minus the poop medicine (page 68). You can casually shop for this and that—a pack of gum, a magazine, whatever. That

If a condom breaks or leaks, or if another method of birth control (or self-restraint) fails, be aware of emergency hormonal contraception, also known as the emergency contraceptive pill (ECP).

The emergency hormonal contraception pill is not the same as the "abortion pill" (see page 103).

Doctors, hospital emergency departments, and family-planning clinics may be able to provide emergency hormonal contraception for a girl or woman when a couple experiences a condom failure or otherwise has unprotected sex.

If you are aware that your condom has failed, it's your job to tell your partner.

The medication works by either keeping the ovary from releasing an egg or by changing the lining of the uterus so that a fertilized egg cannot attach and develop.

Emergency hormonal contraception is effective only if taken within a certain time frame, and it must be given under appropriate medical supervision. At the time of publication of this book, the time frame is within 72 hours, but check. It may have changed. Regardless, the rule is: the sooner the better! A health care professional must be notified as soon as possible after the unprotected intercourse—even if it happens on the weekend.

Emergency hormonal contraception is not 100 percent effective and is not a routine method of birth control.

Although it can be administered many hours after unprotected sex, its effectiveness diminishes with the passing of time. Questions? Call Planned Parenthood (see page 90 for the number), the emergency room of your local hospital (always open), your doctor's office or family clinic, or the county health department.

way, when you go to buy your contraceptive stuff from the cashier, the condoms won't be lying on the counter all by themselves calling, "Look at me! Look at me!"

They'll be in the company of other objects—innocent ones.

Pay, and you're outta there.

Test Driving

The first, most useful condom tip is this: A few practice sessions when you are all by yourself are extremely helpful. It's easy to goof up when putting on a condom for the first few times, and it's way better to mess up when there's nothing big at stake.

You will need to have an erection to accomplish this feat.

Don't be surprised if you lose your erection while wrestling with a condom. Until you get the

process down pat, it can throw you off track.

Note that condoms should be stored in a cool place.

Getting It On

There are instructions enclosed or printed on the inside of almost every box of condoms.

1. Carefully take the condom out of the packet—they're delicate.

A condom should be inspected in good light before putting it on. A condom that's been previously unrolled, is brittle or torn, or is sticky or stuck to itself should be thrown out.

2. Position the rolled-up condom on the top of your penis so that the rolled-up ring is facing out. The rolled-up ring can't be in or you won't be able to roll the condom down. (If your penis is intact, move your foreskin back *first*.)

3. Leave a half inch of space at the tip, hold the

condom by the tip to squeeze out the air, and gently pinch this space closed before and during the unrolling of the condom. This is true even if there is a "reservoir tip." (You also have to pinch closed the reservoir tip.) Why? During ejaculation, there must be some space available inside the condom to hold the semen. Otherwise it will be forced along the sides of the condom and leak out or cause the condom to break.

4. Unroll the condom all the way to the pubic hair, covering your entire penis.

5. If the condom doesn't roll on correctly the first time, begin again—with a new condom. A potentially dinged-up condom is a high-risk item. It belongs in one of two places: in the trash or flushed down the toilet.

The Real Thing

For a condom to be the most effective for birth control, a guy's female partner should put spermicide in right before sex (see page 95). The spermicide acts as a backup, in case the condom breaks or leaks. Used alone, spermicide is NOT a reliable approach to birth control.

How a Girl Uses Spermicide

A girl puts in spermicide while lying on her back—just before having sex. She fills the applicator as per instructions that come with the spermicide. She pushes the applicator into her vagina. She pushes the plunger, and the foam or jelly comes out of the applicator. It blankets the walls of the vagina with a protective shield that kills sperm on contact.

An additional "applicatorful" is required each time intercourse is repeated.

➤ A girl may be interested in helping you put the condom on, but supervise! Most girls don't realize that you have to pinch the tip of a condom to get the air out.

A water-based lubricant must be spread on the outside of the condom, once the condom is completely rolled down over the erect penis. Use it even if the condom is labeled "lubricated" (see page 97). Put the condom on before the penis touches the vagina, mouth, or anus. Don't "poke around" beforehand!

After sex, while the penis is still erect, the male should pull his penis out of his partner's body slowly, holding the condom at the rim with his fingers to avoid spilling semen. He should turn and move completely away from his partner before letting go of the condom.

If there's going to be a victory lap, remember that a new condom, more lubricant, and more spermicide must be used each time a couple has sex.

Don't just pull out.

A fast way to cause an unplanned pregnancy is to reject using a condom and plan to "just pull out" before ejaculating.

Since pre-ejaculate contains sperm, it's possible to make a girl pregnant simply by having the penis enter the vagina. Also, it's very easy to lose control and—just *not* pull out in time!

If ejaculation happens partway into or even near the entrance to the vagina, look out. Whenever and however semen gets into or near the entrance to the vagina (even on somebody's fingers), there's a potential for pregnancy to happen.

Sperm live for only a few minutes out in the air, but they can live for days (days!) inside of a female's body. **Every time sex happens without using a condom or other form of birth control, there's a significant chance for pregnancy to occur.** Sperm just hang out in there and wait for an egg to show up. Trying to guess when a girl is ovulating and avoiding sex at that time is NOT in itself an effective means of birth control.

Timing intercourse is sometimes called "the rhythm method."

The rhythm method doesn't work reliably, so forget it until you're in a position to raise a child.

Yup, she can.

Yes, a girl can get pregnant if she is on her period, or if she thinks she is just about to start her period. Yes—a girl can get pregnant if the couple has sex standing up. Yes, a girl can get pregnant the first time she has sex. Yes, a girl can get pregnant if she is using birth control.

> ➤ **No form of birth control is 100 percent effective.**

Pregnancy Test Kits

Pregnancy test kits are available in drugstores. They cost about $10. Read the box to find out *when* the test should be taken. To find out results, a girl pees on a little testing device and checks it a few minutes later. Some kits ("early result" kits) can detect pregnancy as early as three days before an expected period. Pregnancy testing can also be done at the doctor's office or at Planned Parenthood (see page 90).

Positive Result?

If your girl is pregnant, she should not smoke, drink alcohol, or "do" drugs. She needs to make an appointment to see a doctor right away. Meanwhile, she should also call the doctor and ask if it's okay to continue whatever prescription medication or over-the-counter drugs she may be taking *and* find out what she should do to protect the developing fetus from **listeriosis** and **toxoplasmosis**. Among other things, she will be advised not to change the cat litter box, not to play with kittens, not to dig in the dirt without gloves, not to eat raw or undercooked meat or other foods that might contain the bacteria.

BIRTH CONTROL

A condom is the ONLY form of birth control used for disease prevention. Every other method of birth control requires a condom **in addition** to the birth control to prevent the spread of disease.

Barrier Methods

Barrier methods physically prevent sperm from coming in contact with an egg. Condoms are worn by the male. There is also a female condom available. The diaphragm and cervical cap are barriers worn by women. Prescribed by a doctor, these small latex cups are inserted into the vagina before intercourse. They fit snugly over the cervix. They are used with spermicide (see page 95).

Diaphragms and cervical caps fail if they don't fit properly, if they are taken out too soon after intercourse, or if the girl doesn't use enough spermicide. The medicine used for yeast infections can weaken a diaphragm (as well as a condom).

Hormonal Contraceptives

Hormonal contraceptives change the way a female's reproductive system is regulated by hormones, and so prevent pregnancy.

"The Pill" is very, VERY effective—provided the girl takes the Pill every single day at about the same time. Bouts of vomiting and/or diarrhea as well as certain medications (including certain antibiotics) may compromise the effectiveness of the Pill.

Birth control pills are a good deal for a guy. If the girl is using them correctly, that is.

If she's not, he can be having sex with a false sense of security. Even really responsible girls can space out on taking their pills on time and exactly according to directions (if one or more pill is missed). A boy's future may depend on whether or not a girl is using contraception effectively.

Hmmm. Since a guy is morally and financially responsible if he fathers a child, maybe he should stay in charge (see page 103).

Besides, a condom is necessary for disease prevention. So why not just plan to use one?

> **See Emergency Hormonal Contraception, page 99. This is different from taking a daily birth control pill.**

Injectable Contraceptives

Injectable contraceptives are available (they are injected by a health care professional), but they are effective for a shorter time—about three months per injection. Many teen girls choose this method because they don't have to remember to take a pill every day.

Contraceptive implants are injected into the arms of women by health care professionals and last for years.

Intrauterine Device (IUD)

An intrauterine device is a small device a doctor puts into the uterus of a woman to prevent pregnancy on a long-term basis (until it's removed by a doctor). This is NOT recommended for young women because of the high risk of infection that is associated with its use.

Surgical Sterilization

Sterilization surgery is permanent. It can be performed on males (**vasectomy**) or females (**tubal ligation**).

A vasectomy is when the vas deferens tubes are cut so sperm can't travel from the testicles to the penis. A tubal ligation is when a woman's fallopian tubes are tied so that a sperm can't reach an egg.

Permanent sterilization surgery is considered inappropriate for young people, who aren't experienced enough to know for sure whether or not they will eventually want to have children. (In some cases, these surgeries are reversible—but successful reversal is not a sure thing.)

ABORTION

Abortion is not a method of preventing pregnancy. It is a way of actually ending a pregnancy. For some people, there are strong moral, ethical, cultural and/or religious concerns associated with ending a pregnancy once it's begun. Others don't share these concerns.

Most people would agree on this much: If you don't want to have a child, it's far better to avoid becoming pregnant (or causing a girl to become pregnant) in the first place by using birth control or just not having sexual intercourse than it is to have an abortion.

How do you feel about abortion?

Think about it in advance of having sex with a partner. And find out how your partner feels.

If you're totally against abortion, don't have sexual intercourse unless you're sure your partner shares your viewpoint. Abortion is the girl's (or woman's) choice—not the guy's. A guy can't stop a girl from having an abortion. Neither can he make her have an abortion.

Plus, a girl can change her mind about how she feels about abortion once she finds out she's pregnant.

Currently, girls have two options for abortion:

1. Taking "the abortion pill"—a drug (or, when necessary, a combination of two drugs) that blocks progesterone (a natural hormone needed to sustain a pregnancy) and causes a developing embryo to be expelled from the uterus in the very early stages of pregnancy (within the first seven weeks). This is called having a pharmacological abortion.

2. Having a procedure performed by a doctor. Whether or not the procedure may be performed depends on how far the pregnancy has progressed and the health of the pregnant person.

What basically happens is that the doctor vacuums out, or otherwise removes, the lining of the uterus (which has become the placenta), and the developing embryo attached to it.

Both of the above methods of abortion are relatively safe—but are not risk-free.

> ➤ **A Review**
> 1. **Birth control pills:** These pills prevent conception from happening in the first place (used daily).
> 2. **Emergency hormonal contraception:** These pills either keep an ovary from releasing an egg or keep a fertilized egg from implanting in the uterine wall (should be used within about 72 hours—the sooner the better).
> 3. **Pharmacological abortion:** This method uses pills to cause a pregnancy to fail and the uterus to expel the embryo that has already been implanted (must be used within 49 days of the first day of a girl's last period).

If She Keeps the Baby

If a girl decides to have the baby, the guy has rights and responsibilities—once the baby is born. Rules vary from state to state.

Rights Vary from State to State

The dad may be given permission to visit the child throughout the child's childhood and teens.

If the girl (or woman) decides not to raise the child once it's born, the father may be given the chance to demonstrate that he can raise the child himself or with the help of his family.

He also may ask to have a say in whether or not the baby will be placed in a foster home or placed with an adoptive parent or parents.

Responsibilities Vary from State to State

The father may be held legally responsible for the financial support of his child until his child becomes an adult (reaches age 18).

If the mom and baby are financially helped by a government agency (welfare system), the government may ask for reimbursement from the father.

The mom may sue the father of the child for continuing child support. Adjustment of the payments may be made as the dad's salary increases.

The Most Awesome Responsibility of All

The dad will have put a kid on the planet. The kid will reasonably have expectations that his dad will be his daddy.

CHAPTER 12

DRIVER
Etiquette:
RULES OF THE ROAD

Someone to Roll With

Sure, it feels great to be popular, but it isn't necessary to be in the center of a social scene (or even to be included in a popular group) to be happy and fulfilled by friendship.

One or two really good friends to roll with is all you'll ever need.

> ➤ **Remember: To have a good friend, you need to be a good friend.**

Being There

If you're not sure how to respond to a friend who's feeling down, that's okay—being there is a good start. Hanging out with your friend—just being physically present—may be all that's called for in the situation.

Doing something together (like playing catch or going for a walk) is another way to show you care.

Listening helps; you're not required to have the answer to the problem. If you do want to advise or make a comment, try to imagine yourself receiving that bit of advice in just the same way you intend to give it and see how it feels—before you say it to your friend.

HEADS UP!
Worried? Trust your instincts. Your friend's telling you about the situation may be his or her way of asking for help. If your friend's problem is serious, encourage him or her to talk to a trusted adult and/or refer him or her to the hot lines in this book (see page 46). And talk to a trusted adult yourself, even if you promised you wouldn't.

GUY REPORTS: THREE STRATEGIES FOR GETTING NOTICED

#1: "My first scheme wasn't very romantic. It was a scheme to get the birthday girl at a party to notice me. It was totally unpremeditated. I went around and stomped on some of her birthday balloons.

"I got the girl's attention as well as everyone else's.

"I realized afterward that it was a dumb thing to do."

#2: "Two young beauties about my age (14) were sitting down by the boat dock, at Jump-Off Joe, where my family was vacationing.

"I had my own fly rod and a new green-and-black woodsman shirt. I put on my shirt, got my rod, and strolled down to the dock, where nobody had caught a fish in a hundred years.

"I started shooting out some long casts and doing some tricky retrieves. I worked out to the end of the dock and after a few more casts, was knee-deep in water.

"As it turned out, I was standing on a boat-launching machine and was being launched.

"I decided that rather than lose my cool and scramble back up on the dock, I would continue my performance. I refused to look back. At sunset, with my head and shoulders above water, I made my last cast."

This may be your best bet:

#3: "I just sidled up to 'em and hoped they'd notice me."

Teasing

Teasing is a timeworn (or is it just worn out?) way of guys getting girls to notice them.

Teasing is hurtful. Don't tease.

If you can't help yourself, you should know that teasing shouldn't ever include remarks about a person's physical appearance. Sexual harassment is pretty big territory, and it does include making jokes and wisecracks that focus on sexual characteristics, even if the comments are meant to be complimentary (see page 123).

No Visual Inspection

You're probably attracted to a certain body type; most guys are. But appreciating a girl's body is not the same as evaluating, sizing up, or rating her figure. Who likes to be inspected? Nobody.

Honking Your Horn/ Backfiring

Loudly farting and belching may be a competitive sport, and it may be somewhat impressive, but, well, duh. Don't rely on it to get the attention of somebody you have a crush on.

Pileups

Boisterous roughhousing with other guys is universally and historically a way that boys try to get girls to notice them. Wrestling, hat snatching, chasing each other, and rolling in the dirt are among the favored maneuvers.

How effective is this behavior in gaining a girl's attention?

Not very. But it's fun!

A swarm of boys gathered by an outside trash can in the school yard karate-kicking yellow jackets isn't a bad thing.

But it's not like a cute girl is going to come up to you when you've just successfully nailed one and say, "E-e-e-yeah!"

If you want to capture the attention of a girl,

you've got to buckle down and actually make the commitment to communicate.

At least say hi.

Bonjour!

A friend told me that when he was in junior high, he went to the beach. While sitting in the sand, he noticed two cute girls, about his age, sunning themselves on a blanket nearby. They were wearing bikinis and lying on their bellies. He couldn't help but note that they had unclipped the straps of their bathing suit tops to avoid getting tan lines.

My friend sat pensively looking out at the waves. How could he get to talk to them?

He could barely hear what they were saying, but he was able to identify that they were speaking French.

Fantastique!

He'd already had a few French lessons!

After a while, my friend got up his nerve and casually wandered over.

"Bonjour," he said in his best French accent.

Both girls popped up and cheerily said, *"Bonjour!"*

They sat there, smiling at him.

Inspired by the experience, he took French every year in school from then on.

CRUISING

Into girls? The following section covers a few things you might want to keep in mind.

Actually Getting to Know Her

Most parents set age limits on dating, and most preteens and young teens aren't allowed to date. But preteen kids who like each other romantically often talk on the phone and spend time together in groups. For example, at school activities; at a church, temple, or community center; at sports events; or at restaurants, the movies, or the mall.

It might seem hard to talk to a girl at first, but when you're in a group, it's easier because there are other kids to interact with at the same time.

But what do you say?

Just talk. Don't use standard "pickup lines." Girls don't fall for these much. (Nobody does.)

You can start by asking her questions about herself, but not overly personal ones. Find out what she's into—sports, music, whatever. The conversation will build from there.

You might ask for her phone number—if she gives it to you, you can call her up. Don't call before about 9:00 in the morning or after about 9:00 P.M. It may wake up younger siblings or otherwise annoy her parents.

If you call when she's not home, leave your number so she can call you back. If she doesn't, it's probably fine to call back once more and leave your number.

After that, if she doesn't return your call, it probably means that she doesn't want to talk to you on the phone, after all. She may have given you her number, but she changed her mind. So stop calling.

If it turns out that she actually was out of town or away from the house for an extended period of time, she'll end up calling you eventually.

If she doesn't give you her number but asks for yours, that's not a bad sign. Lots of girls don't give out their numbers. Maybe she'll call you, and maybe she won't. If she does end up calling you, you'll know it's because she *wants* to talk to you—rather than just having happened to pick up the

GUY REPORTS: FIRST DANCE

I interviewed a 21-year-old about his first school dance.

"My first school dance? Yeah, I remember it. It was in the sixth grade."

I said, "I want you to think about it and try to remember details. I need information for my book for boys."

My friend then told me he didn't have to think to remember. He remembered the whole thing perfectly, from beginning to end: "Me and three of my friends stayed by the wall for the whole dance."

"That was it?"

"Yup. We just stood there the whole time, at the wall. It was fun."

"It was?"

"Yeah."

"Did you interact at all with the girls?"

"Yeah. We tossed pieces of broken cookies at them. They liked it."

"They did?"

"I think so."

"Well, when did you actually get up your nerve and ask one of them to dance?"

"About five years later."

phone and discovered that you're on the other end of the line.

During a conversation, on the phone or in person, it's fine to talk about yourself, but also steer the conversation in her direction.

Be *very* careful not to talk negatively about her family, her friends, your friends, or kids you both know—this will come back to bite you.

If the opportunity arises, you can always ask:

Is she going to the dance?

Slow dancing may be the first romantic physical contact a boy makes with a girl. When you are slow dancing with someone, your heads may be close together. Your cheeks may be touching. Your heart may flutter. Or pound is more like it.

Holding someone in your arms and dancing can be a way of expressing sexual feelings; it may be the first romantic encounter you have with a partner.

Wait a minute!

If you're 13 and haven't completed (or even started) your growth spurt—and you're slow dancing with a girl—it just may not be cheek to cheek. It might be cheek to chest. (Uh—that would be your cheek on her chest.)

This minor detail shouldn't keep either one of you from having a good time dancing with each other.

Who says a guy has to be taller than a girl, anyway?

Slow-Dancing Instructions

If you're at a dance or party and don't want to wait 5 years to dance with a girl but don't actually know how to dance, here are some tips for first-timers:

1. Walk up to a girl and say, "Want to dance?" When starting out, it's not a bad idea to ask a girl who's a friend—rather than someone you have a crush on. That way, you can practice with somebody you feel somewhat comfortable with.

2. If she says yes, then take her by the hand. You may want to lead her deep into the group of people who are dancing. That way, you'll feel less conspicuous.

3. If you turn to her and hug her—gently, with your arms around her waist—she'll undoubtedly hug you gently back, with her arms around your neck. Your face will be close to her face, or touching it.

Or you can hold her right hand with your left hand and dance with your right hand on her back, and she'll dance with her left hand on your back.

4. Keep on gently hugging her as you slowly move to the music. If you haven't danced slow with a girl before, it works just fine to just sort of rock back and forth. Most of us have some natural instincts about dancing if we just relax and listen to the music. Don't look at your feet.

Don't dance to the saxophone! Dance to the drums or whatever instruments seem to actually have some kind of a predictable rhythm going on.

If you feel brave, walk around a little bit while hugging. The girl will follow along. (Or try to.)

The tradition is, the boy "leads" and the girl follows his lead. But there isn't a law against the girl leading and the boy following.

But what if she says no?

If the girl says no, politely accept her rejection. Return to where you were standing. Your friends can have opportunity to cheer you up by making fun of you and punching you on the shoulder.

ASKING FOR A DATE

When you ask for a date, you should look for some kind of a green-light response. If somebody says, "Sorry. I'm busy," and leaves it at that, that's a no.

CHEAT SHEET: DATING TIPS
Essential pointers:

• Checking out other people when you're on a date won't exactly boost your date's confidence.

• Have an opinion on how fast or how much your date is eating? Save it.

• If you're into someone, go for the gold. Don't try to get in through the grapevine by dating a friend or relative first. It will put you "off limits" for the future.

• Kissed your date? Even though it's tempting to talk it up with your buddies, don't. Talking about it sends a message: Your date isn't worth keeping your mouth shut for.

• Have a cell phone? Switch it to OFF and pay attention to your date.

• Find out you're wrong in an argument? Credit goes to the winner.

• Be considerate—but not selfless! You count, too. Don't be a doormat or servant for your date.

• Wondering what your date would like to do? Ask. But have some of your own ideas on where to go and what to do.

• No need to be the strong, silent type all the time. Communicating your feelings will encourage your date to communicate with you.

• Being overly possessive and jealous will work against you.

• There's a time and place to verbalize your obsession with celebrity beauties. It's not good to do this on a date.

• Watch your slang. Certain expressions for body parts are offensive.

• Shallow? Making negative comments about people's bodies tends to project the image that you have a superficial view of people.

• Narrow? Racist/religious/cultural/gay "jokes" and slurs reflect ignorance and hurt everybody. Your date won't be impressed.

• Nervous? Don't forget to smile.

• When you really care, it shows. Ask how your date is doing and then listen to the answer.

• Be yourself. How else will your date know the real you?

• An occasional gift is a good thing; don't overdo it.

However, if someone responds with: "Sorry. I'm already busy. What about next weekend?" that's a green light. Try again.

If someone says, "Ohmygosh! I'd so love to but, uh . . . I have to, like, wash my dog," take it as a no. If the person even owns a dog, this urgent dog bath could easily be postponed. Besides, you wouldn't want to be placed in line behind a stinky dog—if it were actually true.

If someone has an actual reasonable reason to say no, it's fine to ask for a date on a different night.

Oh, yeah!

Okay. So you get a yes.

Now what? Be sure to discuss the plan, especially the transportation part, in advance—so your date will be able to clear it with a parent. And know when to be ready.

If you're arriving at the house or apartment, rather than meeting someplace, go up to the door. Don't honk, whistle, or call on a cell phone from the driveway.

If the parent is home, say hi and tell the parent where you're going and what time you expect to return.

If you're the inviter, plan to pay.

It's an unfair and annoying convention (to both genders) that the guy should somehow be the one to pay—or even the one to do the inviting. But this convention persists. Remember that being traditional is a choice, not a requirement.

If your date *offers* to pay or pay half, that's okay, too. Also, if your date has invited you out, your date should be planning to pay! (Or at least planning to pay half.) Some couples take turns paying when they go out.

Unless you're eating at a fast-food restaurant, leave a tip. It's unclassy to stiff a server. Leaving 20 percent of the total bill is a good tip in most places.

Most dates like to get something to eat, talk, walk around, and hold hands in a setting where there are other people around. A movie or a school, community, or sports event is a good place to go on a first date.

Bowling alleys, skating rinks, miniature golf courses, and family fun centers are places young teens seem to like. But be on the lookout for sleazeball adults who frequent these places *because* young teens seem to like them so much!

Get your date back on time so parents won't worry and/or get mad.

Kiss good-bye?

The actual truth is this: Just about every girl who walks the earth knows how to signal to a boy that she'd like to be kissed. Then again, she just might go for it and kiss the boy herself.

Almost every girl also knows how to signal that she doesn't want to be kissed.

You've got radar; we all do. Just read the signals.

And you know what? You can always just straight-up ask her. Lots of guys do.

Decoding

If you and your date have had a good time and you're unclear as to whether or not you might kiss each other good-bye, and don't want to ask, here are a few things to consider:

When it's time to say good-bye, if she searches your eyes for a minute or watches your mouth while you're saying you had a good time, it's probably okay to try for a kiss.

If you bump noses, that's fine because it happens all the time.

If she looks down, turns her head away from you, hurries to find her key, or makes a grab for the doorknob, better luck next time. Say good night.

Wait till she gets into the house and shuts the door before you leave.

THE INNER CIRCLE

Maybe you've found a girl that you like spending time with, and she invites you to her house. Here're a few pointers to help prepare for the test.

Meeting Her Family

When you are relatively young and want to spend time with a girl you like, without being in a group setting, it's probably going to involve seeing her at her house. An event that is sometimes dreaded by guys is meeting the family of a girl they like—especially her parents.

House rules and customs vary in our multicultural society. But here are ten good rules to guide you. If you follow them, you're bound to make an excellent impression:

1. Unless you wear it for cultural or religious reasons, take off your cap/hat/beanie when you enter the house. If you are invited to leave it on, then put it back on if you want to.

2. If you are sitting down when introduced to a family member, stand up. After saying hey, hi, or hello and/or shaking hands, it's fine to sit back down again.

3. You don't have to talk your head off, but try to answer questions asked, as long as they're not too personal. "Please" and "thanks" are essential for showing that you have good manners, and you get lots of points for using these words.

4. Ask permission if you want to use the phone. (Unless, of course, it's an emergency of some sort.) Avoid making long-distance calls, if possible.

5. Don't assume it's okay to visit with your girl in her bedroom, because it's probably not going to be. In some cultures this is absolutely, positively not okay. If it is allowed, make sure that the door remains open.

Generally speaking, parents don't like guys in a room with their daughter when the door is closed—especially not the bedroom. They may not say this, but they expect you to know this and will undoubtedly hold it against you if you do it.

6. If you are in your girl's room visiting, you can chill on the floor, chair, couch, beanbag, box, or bench—but don't stretch out on the bed like you belong there. Parents usually don't like this.

7. Clean up. Throw out empty wrappers; bring empty cans, bottles, or glasses you've used into the kitchen.

8. Don't criticize your girl's family members or make fun of the family pets. If she does, just listen. Don't agree.

9. Avoid outward displays of affection, especially if you are in the girl's home for the first time. Kissing your girl hello or good-bye in front of her parent isn't a good idea, especially in the beginning.

10. When you leave, locate the parents (unless they've gone to bed) and say good-bye and thanks.

Sit-Down Dinner Regs

If you are invited to eat with the family at the table in a formal family setting, etiquette will vary according to culture. Keep your eyes open and watch what others are doing.

Generally speaking, here are ways to make a good impression:

• Unless your hat is on for a cultural or religious reason, make sure you're not wearing it at the table.

• If there's a napkin at your place, put it on your lap after you sit down.

• It is extremely polite and helpful to help seat an elder; if a very old (or disabled) person is going to be sitting next to you and needs assistance, help with the chair. Pull it back from the table, wait for the person to sit down, and help scoot it in (gently).

• If food is served by *passing serving plates* and bowls around the table:

When you are passed a serving plate or bowl, offer to hold it for whoever is sitting next to you, especially if it's an elder. Wait for him or her to serve him- or herself before you put food on your own plate. And, if there's a really little kid next to you, help him or her with the serving. If food is served by someone at the head of the table onto plates that are then passed, keep passing the plates past you until you end up with one.

• If a prayer is said before eating, listen. It's not necessary to do anything whatsoever during grace except remain quiet (don't eat).

• Generally speaking, it's best to wait until an adult at the table starts eating before you start eating. But do look around to see if others have started. In some cultures, it's considered an insult to let the food get cold.

• There is a lot of variance in cultural standards of politeness regarding the mechanics of eating. Regardless, take medium-size

bites. Don't stab huge chunks of food with your fork and bite from them. Cut into bite-size pieces first. Try not to herd food onto your utensils with your finger. And hey! You! Look up occasionally when you eat; it's not polite to stare continuously at your plate.

Picking up certain food with your fingers to eat it is okay in most situations. Ribs, moo shu pork rolled in a pancake, fried chicken, flautas, tacos, and other mmm-mmm delicious foods are traditionally eaten with the fingers. Don't do it if you're invited to eat with the queen of England,

though. With Her Majesty present, every last thing has to be eaten with a knife and fork—except maybe your roll!

Avoid talking with your mouth full—although we do know that people inevitably ask questions of other people who have just loaded the food in.

• Okay (in fact, good—the chef will like it) to have seconds if offered, but stay tuned in to how much food is available for how many people. If there's not much, just take a little bit more. Tip: Don't talk about calories, fat grams, or dieting while people are eating. It spoils the fun.

• If someone starts clearing plates into the kitchen, at least make a gesture toward helping. The point is: You're not really there to be "served" by your girl's parents. Unless somebody tells you not to, carefully clear the plates (without stacking them).

• Under no circumstances should you leave your plate, utensils, and dirty napkin sitting on the table if you are completely done eating and getting up from the table; remember, you're not at a restaurant.

• Thank the provider for the meal.

• When you leave the table, push your chair in.

• Offer to help with the dishes.

Very Formal

Dah-ling! If there are two forks, use the one with the shorter prongs for salad and dessert. The long prongs are for the main dish.

If there are two spoons, the big one is for soup or broth or dessert (ice cream, say) and the small one is for putting sugar into coffee or tea at the end of the meal—or helping yourself to small blobs of mustard, jelly, etc.

If there are small bread plates at the table, yours is the one to your left—nearest your fork.

Break pieces of your roll or French bread before eating and butter/jelly up each piece separately; don't sink your teeth into the whole roll at once. And don't slather the whole piece of bread with butter or jam.

Pass the salt and pepper together if someone asks for one or the other, and don't nab salt, pepper, soy sauce, or other spices. If someone at the table has asked for something to be passed, you're not supposed to hijack it!

When you're done eating your main course, neatly place your long-pronged fork and knife right next to each other, touching, pointing to the middle of the plate.

Keep your short-pronged fork for dessert.

> ➤ If there are chopsticks instead of forks, knives, and spoons, use those for everything except for broth (you will be given a spoon for this). Remember not to serve yourself with the ends of the chopsticks that you eat from. Serve yourself with the large serving utensil provided, or, if there isn't one, flip your chopsticks around and serve yourself with the squared-off ends that haven't touched your mouth.

IT'S A FORMAL AFFAIR

It's unlikely that you'll be attending an actual formal before, say, midway through high school or later (or it could be never—some people are able to escape these things altogether!), but for future reference:

It can take *days* to prepare. You'll probably want to enlist your parent to help you.

You'll need to know who your date is going to be well in advance of the occasion. So . . . ask!

Penguin Suit

If "black tie" (tux) is called for, you'll probably have to go to a rental shop a total of three times: once to order and get a fitting, once to pick up the tux, and once to return it.

Start by calling a rental shop and asking how much lead time they'll need to fit you, and ask about how much you can expect to pay for a (standard) rental. Call around to do some comparison shopping. There should be at least *something* available in the $50-to-$70 range, which should include a white dress shirt, "studs" and cuff links, bow tie (already tied), jacket, pants, and a choice of either a plain vest or a cummerbund (fabric

belt). Patent-leather shoes may cost an additional fee. You can save some money by wearing plain black leather dress shoes if you own them or can borrow them. Just make sure they're polished and in good shape.

When you choose a tux, unless you have a particular "look" in mind, it's safest to tell the salesperson you want to stick with traditional black-tie attire. Your look will be understated—and you'll for sure be classy, stylin', and cool. (The general idea is for the guy to not upstage his date.)

It may be worth buying the insurance (about $7 to $10 additional in most places), if you even *think* you and your friends might get into a spontaneous wrestling match just before or during the event. If you rent a white tux, by all means get the insurance.

If you are more the artist type and want to make a more alternative clothing statement, you may want to rent a tux from a vintage-clothing store. Call around and see what's available.

Corsage/Boutonniere

A corsage (a little pin-on bouquet of flowers and ribbon) or wristlet, described below, will be expected by your date if your date is a girl.

Guys wear boutonnieres. A boutonniere is usually a single flower specially prepped for (one hopes) easy pinning to your left lapel. Your date will be responsible for getting you one.

The corsage/boutonniere exchange happens upon your arrival at wherever you're meeting or picking up your date. The flowers should be kept in a cool place, but not necessarily the refrigerator. Ask the flower salesperson about this.

It's your date's job to pin on your boutonniere. This is an act of faith. With luck, you won't get stabbed. The pin goes through the little wrapped boutonniere stem, through the fabric of the lapel, and then out through the wrapped stem again.

A "wristlet" is a corsage attached to an elastic bracelet, and it's worn on the girl's (left) wrist. A wristlet is a mighty good idea, since it isn't pinned on and you won't have to worry about wrinkling, snagging, or rumpling your date's dress. If a corsage is the flower arrangement of choice, it's pinned above the girl's left breast. Good luck—because you, too, may become the designated pinner (if her mom or big sis isn't available to do the job).

A wristlet, like a corsage, generally costs between $10 and $15.

Ordering the Flowers

Ask your date what color dress she's planning to wear, because the flowers should generally match it. Make sure you order a corsage or wristlet that won't clash with her dress. (Example: If her dress is red, don't order a corsage of pink and orange flowers. You can discuss all this with the salesperson.)

Visit a flower shop (or grocery store that makes flower arrangements) about a week in advance. With help from the salesperson, you can decide on the flowers and establish the pickup time, which will usually be on the morning of the event.

Photo Ops

There is often a photographer at a formal dance, ready to take your picture under some kind of a gazebo or another—and collect about $25 from you and/or your date. Photos are optional.

Also, either or both sets of parents will probably be waiting in the wings at home to snap a few pics before you roll. Say *cheese*! Formals are very time-consuming and expensive, and all the parents have to show for their effort and dough are a few lousy snapshots!

So cooperate!

Hmmmm

Let's see:

Tux: $65

Tickets: $50

Flowers: $15

Photos at the event: $25

Something to eat before or after the event: $40

Do you *really* want to rent a limo?

The Ride

Limos are justifiably discouraged (even banned) by many schools because of the expense and one-upping involved.

However, if you're planning to share a limo with another couple or couples, also call around and ask the per-hour rate. Discuss payment arrangements with the company—in advance.

Make sure that one responsible person collects the money from everybody before the event. Otherwise, someone is bound to get stiffed for the money—and it's probably whoever made the arrangements originally. Don't forget the tip (about 15 percent) for the driver.

The driver will open the door for everybody, including the guys. Keep in mind that being classy involves being polite and considerate to people who are "serving" you—in this case, the driver.

Arrival and Departure

When you arrive, compliment your date. Your date will probably be a little nervous about getting all dressed up—just like you are. Hearing a compliment is very reassuring. Especially after all the shopping and getting ready!

Of course, walk your date to the door when it's time to go home.

Whether or not you kiss good-bye is up to both of you. It will either happen or not.

Prom Versus Morp

Do you know that some schools have an alternate event called a morp on prom night? This event is for kids, boys and girls, who like to socialize but hate proms, hate getting dressed up, can't afford formal events, can afford a formal event but have more important things to spend the money on, or don't have a date for the prom.

Kids arrive casually dressed (in pajamas at some schools) and sit around till the wee hours of the morning in the gym or cafeteria and eat pizza and other food provided by parent sponsors, listen to music, watch videos, talk, hang out, and complain about proms.

Sound like fun?

Talk to your student council rep about organizing one.

MOVING ON

Initiating a breakup with someone is never easy, but it's possible to be classy about it. Keep in mind the ol' golden rule: Treat others with the same degree of respect and consideration you'd like to be given yourself—under similar circumstances.

Breakups can be hard for both parties. Remember to communicate with your parents and/or other trusted adults during stressful times. Most adults have been on both sides of a breakup at some point or another, and can be really helpful and understanding.

Taking Another Route

If you are in a relationship, particularly a sexual relationship, and your romantic interests have shifted to someone else, it's advisable to break up before actually pursuing another love interest. Rejection is an emotion we all need to cope with in some way or another as life goes on. But feeling both rejected and cheated on can make rejection harder to accept and may also make it harder to trust someone else in the future.

What do you say?

Someone else in the picture?

"I don't want to be in a relationship" is fine—if it's true. But if you're planning to immediately start dating someone else, it's probably better to come clean. "I'm interested in seeing someone else," or "I'm attracted to someone else" may be hard to hear, but if it's true—you've been truthful. And you've given your ex a heads up for the future.

Just want to "uncouple"?

Most people would agree that it's best to be honest about your feelings. You shouldn't be given a citation for not telling the whole and complete truth, and a lengthy explanation shouldn't be required. But it's hurtful to be straight-up lied to. Examples: "I've suddenly decided to become a priest." (Really? But you're not even Catholic!) "I can't go out with you anymore because you're just too good for me." (Yawn. Nobody—and I mean *nobody*—falls for this one.)

Before speaking, take a minute to think how you would feel receiving the information yourself.

Would you rather hear "My feelings have changed" or "You're not attractive anymore"? Probably neither one—but given the choice?

Talking about your own feelings can be the best way to go (I feel this way or that way. . .). Talking about or criticizing the other person (you do this, you do that . . .) may not be as effective.

Example: "I feel trapped in this relationship" is an alternate way of saying "You're too possessive! You act like you own me!"

Just Friends?

"I just want to be friends" is fine—if it's true. Many couples remain in good standing with each other and go on to being just friends.

But not every former couple can manage this type of change, at least not at first. Don't be surprised if your ex says no to being "just friends." And if you don't think you want to continue a relationship as friends, avoid proposing it. "I think it would be best if we don't see each other for a while" is fine.

When and where?

Many people consider it classier to break up in person than on the phone or in a letter or e-mail (unless you've moved or live far away).

Having a friend break up for you can be pretty tacky. So is breaking up right in front of other people. Avoid it if possible.

How's your timing?

Can some recovery time possibly be built into the plan? For example, a Saturday afternoon at your soon-to-be ex's house (where support is available) may be better than springing a breakup on a Monday morning at school. Breaking up just before a really important event, performance, or exam may be regarded as sabotage.

CHAPTER 13

THE
Right of Way:
CONSENT

An Age Issue

Sexual contact between two kids who aren't in a similar age group may be regarded as a form of child abuse, even when both kids agree to it.

Why?

When one kid is significantly older than another, the older one is felt to have an advantage over the younger one, especially at certain critical stages of physical and emotional development. So even if the younger person agrees to sexual contact, we don't consider him or her to have had a fair choice.

In other words, the two aren't equals—they don't have equal experience in the world. If the younger one says yes, we presume that the older one has influenced the decision. So we don't count it as consent.

What does "similar age group" mean?

Rules vary from state to state.

Romantically involved with someone older or younger?

Questions or concerns?

Call the Child Help USA Hot Line to discuss your situation (see page 134 for information about this 24-hour hot line, which is staffed by professional counselors).

More About Consent

Our laws protect all people of all ages from being forced (by either physical force or verbal threat) into sexual contact. This is true even if they have agreed to have sexual contact with each other in the past.

A person who is very drunk or stoned is not in any condition to give consent. Consent given by a drunk or stoned person doesn't count (see page 125).

Consent is valid provided the person is in a similar age group and is not impaired by alcohol, drugs, or disability—or has not been in any way coerced (tricked, blackmailed, threatened, or unfairly manipulated in some other way) into giving consent.

"No" Never Means "Yes"

Once given, consent may be withheld or withdrawn by either partner at any time. As soon as one person says no, the other person *has* to stop. That's the rule, and that's the law.

➤ In the Movie

We've all seen this one:

In the movie, the beautiful, sexy woman fiercely resists being kissed and then gives in—passionately!—once a handsome, buff male forces the issue (by maybe grabbing her shoulders and pulling her close to him and kissing her anyway). She's "swept away" by the heat of the moment and melts in his arms. She really, truly does want him—in the movie.

In real life, she really, truly doesn't want him.

In movies, actors may be considered sexy when they force themselves on women. In real life, this has a different name: sexual assault.

Overpowering anyone—male or female—who doesn't want to be kissed or otherwise touched in a sexual way is against the law.

Back off.

When one person says or otherwise indicates no, it means one thing: No. This is true for all couples: pre-teens, teens, and adults. It's even true for married couples. Becoming physically aggressive with a person who doesn't want to have sexual contact or who wants to end sexual contact is totally against the law.

And there are lots of ways people indicate no without saying the word "no."

Examples? "I don't want to do this"; "I'm not ready for this"; "My mom wouldn't want me to do this"; "I don't feel right about this"; "Stop"; "I think we should stop"; "I'm scared"; "Don't"; "That hurts." These all mean: No.

Signaling No

There is also body language that indicates no.

Examples? Pulling away, pushing away, turning the head away (to avoid being kissed), struggling to get free of someone's grip.

Mixed Messages

A mixed message should also be interpreted as no.

What is a mixed message? It's when someone signals both yes and no, or if the other person interprets the signals to be both yes and no.

HEADS UP!
Yes + no = no.
An example:

A girl sits down very close to a boy on a couch. He puts his arm around her shoulder. She tips her head onto his chest and then looks up at him, directly into his eyes. He leans closer to kiss her—but she turns her head away from him.

She smiles a little, snuggles up closer, and looks up at him again.

Has she changed her mind?

Who knows!

Is it okay for him to try one more time to kiss her?

No, it's not.

Unfair?

Some people would think so.

Regardless, it's a no.

By turning her head away, the girl has indicated that she doesn't want to be kissed. Apparently, she just wants to sit by him and look into his eyes.

Is she just being playful?

How do you know?

You don't, and you can't. So take it as a no.

Any form of a no means no, and stays no regardless of when and how it's given. A mixed message also means no—and stays no.

After a no or a mixed message, it's up to the person who says no to make the next move, if there's going to be one.

Have a girlfriend who's giving you mixed messages? Confused?

Talk to her about it. Words are more reliable than signals. Straight-up ask her: What's going on? Is this okay—or isn't it?

WRONG WAY: SEXUAL HARASSMENT

The material that follows deals with sexual harassment, which consists of comments and behaviors that are harmful to the development of a positive, healthy attitude toward one's own body, sexuality, or sexual orientation.

Caution: School Zone

Sexual harassment is almost universally considered grounds for disciplinary action at school, at school-sponsored events, on the way to school, and on the way home from school.

Sexual harassment includes but is not limited to the following:

1. Touching somebody's body on purpose in a sexual way (example: patting someone's rear); making unwelcome comments about somebody's physical sexual characteristics (either compliments or criticisms).

2. Making uncalled-for sexual remarks or propositions.

3. Accusing people of being gay or lesbian and/or hounding people who are gay or lesbian.

4. Flirting with someone who has indicated that they're not interested.

The rules apply to everyone: Both boys and girls are protected.

In other words . . .
Some of the Don'ts!
Hands off.

Don't touch, don't grope. Don't make fun of girls' (or boys') bodies. Don't make a big scene about what a babe somebody is. Don't whistle or catcall at people who pass by. Don't make random sexual remarks. Don't make wisecracks about how much you'd like to have sex with a certain other person. Don't tell sexual jokes to a person or audience you don't know well.

Permanently lose gay slurs. Omit the words *fag, faggot, dyke,* etc., from your vocabulary.

Avoid making verbal predictions about someone else's sexual orientation.

HEADS UP!
An inherent human characteristic is that we long for connection, not separation. Not only is it against the rules to harass other people, it is also socially unacceptable, uncool, and will end up isolating you. Feel a need to harass and/or bully? See page 47. You may need help with an underlying problem.

Don't tailgate!
If you have a romantic interest in another person who isn't interested, back off!

Following someone home, hanging out in front of somebody's house, calling over and over, sending unwanted gifts or flowers, making hang-up calls, repeatedly e-mailing and writing letters, waiting to catch glimpses of the person as they go about their daily life, or otherwise hounding another person may fall into the category of stalking, which is against the law.

Is it okay to hold open a door for a girl?
Sure. If it seems like a polite thing to do, go for it—especially if she's carrying packages, walking with an older person, holding a baby, or leading kids through a doorway.

But use your head: If she's on your soccer team and you're heading through the door to the gym, she'd probably rather be treated like one of the guys.

Is it okay to offer to carry something heavy for a girl?

Sure, why not? But the operative word is *offer*.

"Want some help?" would be a good thing to say—rather than "Here, let me do that. You'll hurt yourself."

SEXUAL ASSAULT
Since sexual contact requires both partners' consent, all forms of unconsented-to purposeful sexual touching are illegal.

Oops!
What if you accidentally touch someone, like if you accidentally brush up against a girl's butt?

As long as it's not "accidentally on purpose," which we all know means intentionally, it's okay. It would be appropriate to say, "Sorry—it was an accident." And everything should be fine.

Girls (and boys), like women (and men), almost always know the difference between an accidental touch and an on-purpose one.

Rape
Rape is forced sexual intercourse.

It is highly uncommon for a boy to be forcibly raped by a girl or woman, but guys can be forcibly raped (sodomized) by other males.

Rape Crisis
Anyone who is raped should get medical attention immediately.

If a doctor can treat a victim right away, he or she may be able to help protect a victim from getting infected with certain sexually transmitted diseases (or from getting pregnant) from the assault. The medical facility can hook the victim up with psychological help and support.

Also, evidence can be collected to help convict the rapist.

If you are raped, tell your parent. Call the police, your doctor, the emergency room of the hospital, or the Child Help USA National Child Abuse Hot

Line (see page 134) or call a rape crisis hot line number in your area. (Call 411 or 0 and ask the operator or look in the front of the phone book or in the white pages under "rape crisis.")

Statutory Rape

At age 18, anyone who is not developmentally delayed or disabled, boy or girl, is felt to be lawfully old enough to give valid consent to sex. (But other elements of consent still apply. See page 120.)

Statutory rape is when two people agree to have sexual intercourse, but one of the two people is legally considered *too old* (the laws may vary from state to state) to have sex with a person who is legally *too young* to consent to sex (the laws may vary from state to state). Complicated? It can be. Questions? Call Child Help USA (see page 134). Remember: The hot line's for teens, too.

Date Rape

Otherwise known as "acquaintance rape," date rape is an assault that happens in the context of people getting to know each other romantically. Basically, what happens is that one person fails to honor the word "no" or other indications of "no" and forces the other into having sexual intercourse—often after they have been kissing, making out, or touching each other sexually.

Date rape is just as wrong and illegal as rape and statutory rape. All are serious criminal offenses—felonies, punishable by incarceration in jail or a juvenile facility.

Although acquaintance rape usually involves a guy assaulting a girl, it can also involve a guy assaulting another guy. It rarely, if ever, involves a girl raping a guy.

Rape and Alcohol and/or Drugs

What if someone has sex with somebody who seems willing to have sex, yet is profoundly impaired by alcohol (or drugs)?

If intercourse occurs under the circumstances of one person being too drunk (or drugged) to give valid consent, the intercourse is considered "unconsented to" and, therefore, *rape*.

Having sexual intercourse with someone who is passed out (unconscious) or totally out of it as a result of having taken or been given drugs is rape.

CHAPTER 14

ROAD
Hazards: KNOWING
WHO AND WHAT TO AVOID

At some point during your journey, you're bound to run into roadblocks here and there. The best way to handle 'em is to get informed, trust your instincts, and do your best to avoid those types of situations. This chapter is intended to help you become aware of potential dangers and scenarios and to help you learn how to deal with them.

Perv Alert

When my husband, Bob, was about 7 years old, he lived in a trailer park with his parents and big brother, Richard. Richard was much older than Bob. He was in his late teens and about to join the army.

One afternoon, a neighbor—a high school student that Bob had seen around the trailer park—invited Bob into his family's trailer to "show him something."

Nobody else was home when they went in.

The guy turned to Bob and said, "Let's take off our clothes." This seemed like a bad idea to Bob. But before he could even say no, the guy had unzipped his pants and stepped out of them, along with his underwear.

Bob didn't know anything about sex or kid

molesters. He did know this much: It was pretty weird for some guy he hardly knew to suddenly be standing buck naked in front of him for no good reason.

So Bob charged back out of the guy's trailer and raced home.

"Did you tell your dad?" I asked him.

"No."

"Why?"

"I don't know."

"Did you tell your mom?"

"No!"

"Why not?"

"I told my big brother."

"What did he do?" I asked.

"I'm not sure. There was some kind of confrontation. After that, the kid and his family left the trailer park."

Some people think of a kid molester as a dirty old man—or a guy who looks like a sleazeball. But a child molester can be young or old, single or married, clean or dirty, male or female, rich or poor, gay, straight, or bisexual.

Some people think of a molester as a guy that

looks like he just crawled out from under a rock. But molesters can be distinguished-looking—some wear expensive suits and ties. They can be uniformed. They can be handsome and buff, and stylin'. They can be jocks.

Most people think of child molesters as adults or older teens, but even a kid can be a child molester if he or she forces sexual contact with another kid or has "agreed to" sexual contact with a significantly younger person.

HEADS UP! Questions about "significant" age differences? Call the Child Help USA National Child Abuse Hot Line (see page 134) to speak to a trained professional.

We're not just talking about stranger danger.

Young children, preteens and teens, boys, girls, or both may become targeted by a molester.

Preadolescents and adolescents are often

targeted by older teens and adults, so stay on your toes!

Most molesters are known and trusted, and sometimes they're in a position of authority.

The molester is often a relative (see page 134).

A molester may be a teacher, coach, or religious leader. Often, molesters get jobs or work as volunteers in situations where they will have easy access to children.

Or they just choose careers that will put them in positions where they have an opportunity to get close to children.

Child molesters take advantage of younger people because they're smaller, less experienced, easier to confuse, and more vulnerable to attack—both physically and psychologically. But even a very small kid can have power against an older person who attempts abuse. The power lies in:

1. Trusting the feeling that something is wrong.
2. Saying no, getting away.
3. Reporting what happened, without delay.

HEADS UP!

The laws against child abuse are made to protect children and teens, including those who don't recognize that sex with a significantly older person is harmful.

The rules protect the victim even if he or she initiates and welcomes the contact. This is true even if the sexual contact felt good to the victim physically.

It's not the victim's fault!

Anyone who says something different is lying.

➤ In addition to experiencing physical and emotional trauma, children who have sexual contact with adults are at risk for getting sexually transmitted diseases (see page 86). Girls can also become pregnant.

BUILT-IN RADAR SYSTEM
Trust your instincts.

Kids have an instinctive feeling that something is wrong when an adult or significantly older person tries to start up sexual contact. It's very important to pay attention to these gut feelings. It seems wrong—because it is wrong.

If a situation is making you feel weird, pay attention to that feeling. Your inner voice tells the truth.

Listen when it tells you, "Something's happening that doesn't seem right. . . ."

Don't dismiss your instincts.

Instead, rely on them.

Say no, get away, tell a responsible adult what happened (see the Child Help USA National Child Abuse Hot Line info on page 134).

Know fear.

If you feel "creeped out" by something somebody says or does, don't try to talk yourself out of it. Accept that you feel afraid. Respect the feeling of fear. Your senses are giving you information so that you can act to make yourself safe.

Hmmmm . . .

Feel confused about something that's already happened—and not sure why?

Good communication with parents can help keep you safe. Most adults are protective of children—and are quick to identify inappropriate behavior patterns in others. If a person or situation makes you feel uncomfortable, uneasy, embarrassed, worried, sad, confused, or afraid, these feelings may be danger signals. **Talk to your parent about these feelings**, even if you don't know why you have them.

Protect yourself—stay in charge.

You may have been taught that kids are supposed to be respectful of adults, but kids aren't supposed to be respectful to all adults. Be rude to an adult who tries to have sexual contact with you—even if the person is in a position of authority, like a religious figure, camp counselor, teacher, coach, or someone else that's trusted by the community.

"Get the hell away from me!"

You don't have to be nice to anyone who's trying to take advantage of you sexually.

So don't be.

Get away from the person. Say no in whatever way you think will be most effective in getting him (or her) to leave you alone. Then immediately tell another adult what happened. Tell even if you are scared or embarrassed, even if you are afraid no one will believe you because you have no witnesses to back you up. And keep telling until someone really listens to what you are saying and takes it seriously.

Leave it up to a responsible adult to decide what to do about the situation. Your only job is to tell—then let the adults take over. Tell right away, without waiting or worrying about the consequences. If the abuse involves a parent, tell the other parent, a stepparent, or another adult relative (see page 134).

Or tell your doctor, your teacher, your principal, a nurse, or any other adult you choose—like your best friend's mom or dad, for example.

You can call the police or the county's child protective services number (see box on page 46).

You can also call the Child Help USA National Child Abuse Hot Line (see page 134).

READING THE ROAD SIGNS

Perv behavior includes a wide range of activities.

Unless the person is in your similar age group, is unrelated to you, and has your consent, a person should NOT touch any part of your body or act in any way calculated to cause sexual arousal.

Kisses between kids and older friends and family members should be regular old garden-variety affectionate kisses, fast ones. Not sexy kisses! Not open-mouth kisses, not long kisses or French kisses—and not gentle, tender kisses on the neck, ears, shoulders, or private places of the body.

"No way!"

Hugging someone or sitting on somebody's lap should never involve having an adult or significantly older person purposefully rub their genitals against your body.

What's up with that?!

Regular old snuggling in bed with your family and friends is fine. But an adult (or older teen) should not secretly creep into bed with you in the middle of the night and get weird under the covers.

Give 'em the boot! Then get right up and tell somebody what happened.

There's a wide range of perv behavior, and it doesn't always involve touching.

Exposing oneself (one's genitals); showing pornographic pictures (pictures of people having sex); and asking kids to pose for photographs naked, partly dressed, or in sexual positions are other examples of perv behaviors—and there are lots more.

How do you know if perv behavior is going on?

Almost always, you just know.

Trust

Among other things, trust is when somebody who's vulnerable isn't afraid to believe in the goodness and honesty of another person.

Kids can become vulnerable because of their age, size, and ability to cope emotionally, and the limits of their experience in relation to those around them.

Believing in, and not being afraid of, an older person in charge is about trust.

Being molested by a trusted older person is one of the saddest, scariest, and most troublesome

things that can happen to a kid. It's just such a letdown! The betrayal of trust can be so huge, and the event can be so staggering, that you just can't make sense of it.

A kid who's molested . . .

By a trusted older person or adult will typically feel embarrassed, ashamed, betrayed, humiliated, and afraid. And confused.

The molester gambles that because of these feelings, the kid won't want to tell anybody that he or she has been molested (or is being molested on a regular basis).

The molester also gambles on something else: that the victim will somehow feel responsible and blame himself. And the victim will be afraid that other people will blame him, too. But . . . the victim is never to blame!

The victim is never responsible and never to blame.

Most sexual abuse of boys is perpetrated by adult (or teen) males.

Most kid/teen abusers are heterosexual (straight) males. Many are homosexual (gay) or bisexual males.

When boys are molested, it often involves their father, stepfather, grandfather, uncle, or older (or more powerful) brother, or another male family member or extended-family member, like a mother's live-in boyfriend (see page 134).

It's unusual for an adult woman to want to molest a preadolescent or adolescent boy—but it definitely does happen.

Some people call this situation "being seduced by an older woman." But it's really "being abused by an older woman."

That there's a female perpetrating abuse doesn't make it any less harmful to the kid.

Don't be flattered if an older woman seems interested in you sexually.

Stay away from her!

She's a perv!

And to top it off—she may have a sexually transmitted disease!

Get away from her and report her to your parent—or another trusted adult.

HEADS UP!

Why would an adult or significantly older person propose that you do something together and keep it secret from your dad and/or mom? What might be proposed? Smoking cigarettes, smoking weed, drinking alcohol, looking at porn—or going to some forbidden place.

➤ **Ask yourself:**

What normal older person would rather secretly party, secretly look at X-rated pictures, or do other secret stuff with a young kid—than hang out with someone his (or her) own age?

An adult or significantly older person asking a kid to keep an activity secret is a signal that the person may want to separate a kid from the people most likely to protect him: his parents.

If this happens to you, what should you do? Say no. Then tell your parents about the conversation right away.

Sometimes the molester makes threats.

Whether or not he or she will really carry out these threats depends on the situation; regardless, it's nothing anyone (especially not a kid) should try to guess at. The police need to be notified immediately. Kids and their family members become much safer once the police are notified that threats have been made.

The police, the people who work for kid protective services, and the counselors who answer the calls on the child abuse hot line can make immediate moves to rescue and protect children in dangerous situations (see the Child Help USA National Child Abuse Hot Line on page 134).

Once a kid has been molested . . .

A complex set of psychological responses comes into play. If provided with a chance to recover from the trauma, he or she will probably end up being just fine. With the support of family, friends, and health care providers, kids bounce back.

But if the kid keeps the secret, there can be negative, lifelong consequences instead. He or she can become depressed (even suicidal). Shadowed by the secret, he or she may be unable to gain the confidence needed to live a happy, productive life.

And there are other troublesome possibilities. One is that a kid who's been molested and isn't given the opportunity to recover might go on to become a child molester in the future.

This is one of the reasons why patterns of child sexual abuse can repeat themselves for generations (see the Child Help USA National Child Abuse 24-Hour Hot Line on page 134).

Help is just a phone call away.

If you or any kid or teen you know has a problem with being abused by anyone—including a relative—you can call the Child Help USA hot line number, the police, or your county's child protective services. (Dial 0 or 411 and ask the operator for the number. Or look in the phone book under "county government" listings under "social services," or in the white pages under "child protective services." Or call a youth crisis hot line [see page 46].)

If you need emergency help, call 911 or the police emergency number.

➤ Child Help USA National Child Abuse 24-Hour Hot Line (for Children, Teens, and Adults)
This is the number:
1-800-4-A-CHILD (1-800-422-4453)
For the hearing-impaired:
1-800-2-A-CHILD (1-800-222-4453 [TTY])

This hot line is set up to help with any kind of abuse, including sexual abuse, physical or emotional abuse, and neglect.

Anyone with questions or concerns about abuse can call it at any time of the day or night. It's free, and the call will not appear on the home phone bill.

If you call the hot line, you will get to talk to a trained professional. After you call, stay on the line. Keep waiting, and soon someone will answer and help you.

The purpose of the hot line is to help stop abuse. So, even someone who is afraid of abusing somebody else (or has) can call the hot line and get help.

Incest—The Definition

The definition of incest may vary from place to place, but the following is a pretty universal guideline:

Incest refers to sexual relationships that take place between close family (or extended family) members:
parents and their offspring;
siblings;
close cousins;
aunts and nieces or nephews;
uncles and nieces or nephews;
grandparents and their grandchildren.

These sexual relationships are always against the law, even when the family members who are sexually involved with each other are consenting adults.

The unlawful relationships include people in a "step" or "half" relationship. They include people related through blood or marriage.

Innocent sexual experimentation between very young siblings of similar ages isn't considered particularly harmful—as long as it ends when kids are still very young.

Incest often involves children or teens being sexually abused within the family. Just like in the outside world, child molesting within a family is totally against the law. All of the rules are the same. Consent is never valid, even if the kid agrees to it. The molester gets in trouble when it's reported, not the molested person—and it's never, EVER considered the molested person's fault, no matter what.

This kind of sexual abuse within families involves an older or otherwise more powerful family member persuading, coercing, threatening, or somehow manipulating a younger or weaker or disabled kid in the family (or extended family) into tolerating or performing sexual acts, such as kissing, fondling, oral sex, anal sex, or intercourse.

When boys are molested within the family, it usually involves their father or stepfather. It also commonly involves a grandfather, uncle, or other stronger or older male member of the family or extended family—like a mother's live-in boyfriend.

But it is also possible for a boy to be molested by a *female* relative.

Telling Versus Not Telling . . .
No Contest: Tell.

Kids who are victims of incest usually don't want to tell because they think the family will be damaged if they do tell, and they're afraid that the relative who is abusing them will go to jail. Incest victims usually blame themselves. They feel guilty—even though it's not their fault. They don't want to talk about it.

Incest is one of the most frightening and upsetting situations imaginable for a kid. Some kids endure it silently—sometimes for years. But telling someone is the way to end the pain and confusion and start the healing process.

A family is already very damaged when a kid has suffered abuse by a relative. When abuse is reported, the family can be repaired. The kid can heal. The abuser is forced to confront his or her problems, often by participating in therapy or other programs.

Sometimes the abuser does go to jail, but not always.

In some cases, after the abuser gets treatment and counseling, it is possible for the family to be reunited under the supervision of the court— as long as the responsible adults in charge are convinced that the abuse won't happen again.

When incest happens to a kid . . .

He or she may feel completely alone in the world, as if the situation has never occurred before. But the situation has occurred before, in many thousands of families.

Unfortunately, incest is common.

Since it's common, specially trained adults are able to help a kid and his or her family take steps to overcome the pain, fear, and confusion associated with it.

Counselors know how hard it is for a kid to ask for help in a situation involving incest.

Friends don't let friends be abused.

Don't keep the secret if a friend (or family member) tells you about abuse. Kids who are being abused often tell other kids about abuse because they don't know where else to turn.

Even if you promise to keep the secret, don't. Get up your courage and tell a responsible adult.

You may feel like you'll be betraying the person who confided in you, but you won't be. You'll be asking a trusted adult for help on your friend's behalf. Ultimately, your friend (or family member) will understand that you did the right thing, the thing you were supposed to do under the circumstances. He or she will also understand that it was hard for you to break the confidence and that you did it because you cared.

CHAPTER 15

SAFETY
Zones: STAYING SAFE AND IN CONTROL

Being alert, aware, and prepared to act helps keep you safe when you're out in the world alone (or with your friends).

Remember: Acquaintances, not just strangers, can pose a threat to a kid's safety. Think on your feet; stay in control of your situation. Don't give someone the opportunity to mess with you.

• Whenever possible, go places with a friend or family member rather than alone.

• Don't accept rides or enter vehicles without your parent's permission. Don't hitchhike.

• Don't take shortcuts alone through alleys, wooded areas, creek beds, railroad tracks, or other out-of-the-way places where you couldn't be seen or heard if you cried out for help. When you're alone, avoid parking lots and parking garages.

• If you become separated from your family, class, or group when traveling in an unfamiliar city, go to a pay phone and call 911 or dial 0 for the operator and ask to be connected to the police emergency number. Or ask someone who works in a store (wearing a name tag or working at a cash register) to call the police for you. Wait in as safe a place as possible. The police will come and help reunite you with your group.

• If you go to a sporting event, concert, fair, or mall with your friends, decide in advance on a safe meeting place if you should get separated. Go there right away if you do get separated.

• If you're out with your friends and there's a change of plans, call your parent or one of the other kids' parent to discuss it. A responsible adult should know where you are and whom you are with.

• Unless there's a clear public safety emergency involving uniformed officers, or unless you need help from a uniformed officer, treat guys in uniforms as you would any other stranger. Uniforms are easy to rent or buy. If someone in a uniform approaches you with a concern or accusation, request that your parent be contacted. **Don't go anywhere** with him or her.

• Don't get an attitude or make personal remarks, comment on appearance, or say or do anything that might provoke a violent response from a kid not known to you. And don't respond violently if remarks are directed at you. Walk away. Kids out looking for a fight are usually dangerous—often armed. A kid with a problem

with violence can present a real danger to you, even if you're bigger. Back off; if you need help from an adult, get help.

• Don't allow adults you don't know well to engage you in conversations when you're out alone. You have no obligation to be polite or interact with adults who are strangers to you—so don't. When out alone, don't display your name visibly on your clothing, backpack, gym bag, or other belongings. It's easier for someone to trick you into talking to them if they know your name.

• Say no if someone you don't know well asks you to pose for a picture, video, or film; asks for your name, address, or school name; offers you a job or gift; offers you alcohol or drugs; or offers to show you pornography. Then tell your parent what happened.

HEADS UP!
Obviously, we need to be wary of strangers. But sometimes it's possible to find ourselves in a position where we have to reach out for help! If you urgently need help and there's no phone available, no law enforcement available, and no apparent safe place for you to go, you may need to ask someone you don't know to assist you. If you have a choice, ask for help from a woman, a family, or an adult who has kids with him or her.

Don't be lured away.
Beware of an adult or older teen you don't know well who offers to show you something cool (like a motorcycle) and wants you to follow along alone to see it (like into a garage or house, for example). Responsible adults do *not* invite kids they don't know well and who are alone into houses, garages, or other isolated places.

If you discover that something of yours (like your bike or pack) has been moved close to a vehicle or place where someone could ambush you, leave it there. Don't walk up to it. Go get help from an adult.

If someone in a car pulls up to talk to you . . .
Stand back and be ready to run. Cross the street or otherwise retreat to safety. Be suspicious of any adult or older teen who asks you for assistance or directions. Let the person get directions or assistance from someone his or her own age.

If you see a car circling the block or cruising your street, call the police and report it. Be ready to describe the car. It's fine to call anonymously (tell the police you don't want to give your name) if you want.

It would be very, *very* unlikely for someone to try to abduct you. But if grabbed by someone, fight your way free and make a lot of noise doing it. Cause the biggest scene you can so other people around can hear that you're in trouble and come to your aid.

Most adults will instinctively protect kids and teens in danger—but you need to get their attention first.

FYI
Some experts in law enforcement have the opinion that we should not agree to get into a vehicle with someone who's threatening us—even if they have a weapon. Those who have this opinion advise us to do the following:
1. Refuse to get into the vehicle, fight to get away, and make a lot of noise.
2. If pulled into a vehicle by an abductor and you can't get free, grab the wheel and cause an accident as soon as possible, while the vehicle is still moving relatively slowly. Act quickly! Turn the steering wheel into a parked car, sign, pole, or ditch (*not* into oncoming traffic or pedestrians).
   Why?
   There's no guarantee, but we're considered more likely to survive this type of low-speed accident than we are to survive being abducted and transported away in a vehicle.

The National Center for Missing and Exploited Children (and Teens)

There is a national center set up to help all missing, lost, abandoned, abducted, or runaway children. Every family and community wants missing children returned—no matter how far away they may be from home, no matter how long they've been gone, and no matter what has happened to them while they were gone. The National Center for Missing and Exploited Children (and Teens) hot line numbers are:

1-800-843-5678 (U.S. and Canada)
For the hearing-impaired: 1-800-826-7653 (TTY)

Home alone?

When you answer the phone, don't give out information—get information. If someone asks, "Who's this?" answer with the question "Who's calling? Who do you want to speak to?"

Don't reveal that you are home alone. Say, "My dad (or mom) is unavailable to come to the phone right now. What's your number? I'll have him (or her) return the call."

Or use your answering machine to screen calls—picking up the receiver only when there is a familiar voice on the line.

Keep the doors locked. Don't open the door to anyone you don't know well. If someone hangs around after it's clear you're not going to open the door, call the police.

Sometimes people pretend there's an emergency to gain entry into a house.

If a stranger comes to your door and says they need the phone to call the police, ambulance, or fire department, pick up your phone and call **911** (or the other police emergency number for your area). Tell the dispatcher there's someone outside the door needing to report an emergency. Ask that an

officer (and ambulance and/or fire truck, if that's what the person claims is needed) be sent over.

Then call through the door, "I've already called 911. The police are on the way here."

If there's an emergency, good, you've called 911. Now keep your door closed and locked until the police show up.

If there's not an emergency, even better that you called. You'll need the assistance of the police if somebody's trying to lie their way into your house. And good that you called through the door to say the police were coming. A person with bad intent would undoubtedly leave you alone once the police were on the way.

TOURING ALONE ON THE INTERNET
Chat Rooms

If you wouldn't interact with a stranger in a mall, why would you interact with a stranger on the Net?

The Internet is full of amazing, valuable information! It opens the door to so many interesting, exciting, and educational places.

But it can also open the door to weasels, sneaks, snakes, psychos, and pervs.

Make sure you don't "let them in." Have no expectation of privacy when on the Internet. Don't give out your name, address, phone number, school address, or parent's credit card information.

> ► **Chat Rooms**
> Adults posing as kids are continuously trying to get kids to interact with them on the Internet.
> The cute girl you imagine yourself to be chatting with could actually be some 45-year-old guy with a sex problem. Or a teen guy with a sex problem! Who cares how old he is! He's not who he's pretending to be!
> Talk on the phone? Exchange mail? Meet in person? Don't do it!

140

Chat rooms are perv paradise.

There have been lots of cases where pedophiles have used the Internet to trick or lure a kid into meeting—then raped, assaulted, and abducted the kid.

Or they've somehow weaseled information out of the kid and showed up at the kid's home or school.

If you do chat in a chat room, stay aware that you are communicating with an identity—a character—someone has created on a screen. There's a person behind this character.

Who is he or she, anyway?

➤ FILE A COMPLAINT

If someone proposes sex to you on the Internet, tell your parent. Your parent can report it to the Cyber-Tipline (www.cybertipline.com). This tipline is operated by the National Center for Missing and Exploited Children (see page 140).

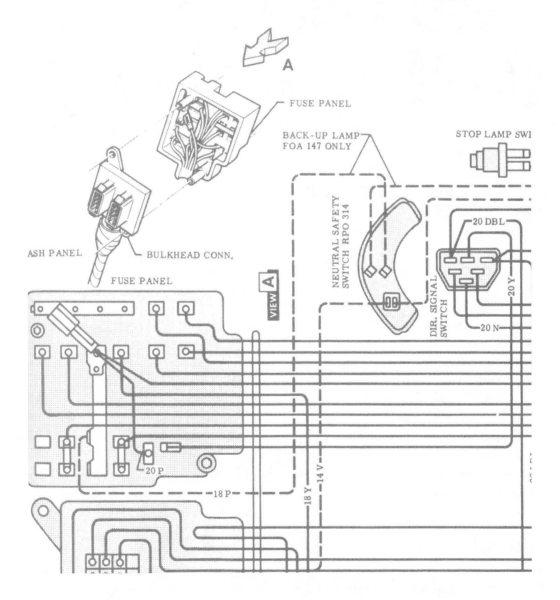

CHAPTER 16

Customizing:
DEVELOPING YOUR
OWN STYLE

DEVELOPING PRESENCE AND STYLE

Developing a unique presence and sense of style doesn't happen overnight. It begins with the realization that appearance is more than just how a person looks and that style is more than appearance. Style involves attitude—beginning with your attitude toward yourself.

Your Presence (Vibe)

Everybody has a vibe, a way of being in the world; be aware that things you say and do are making a statement about who you are.

Your Style

You're born with certain looks, but you'll create your own style. You're about you. So don't measure yourself against other guys.

UPHOLSTERY

No matter who you are, there will always be somebody with more expensive, more stylin', and just plain *more* clothes than you. It's possible to have a lot of style even if you don't have much money to spend on clothes.

Shopping with a Parent

When you shop with your parent, you might run into some conflicts about what clothes you should wear. This is a normal part of growing up and establishing your identity.

The following suggestions may help you find some middle ground.

Shopping Tips

1. After buying clothes, keep the tags on. Keep the bag and receipt until you have tried on the items at home. Try them on in front of the mirror. Like them? Still, wait until you're ready to roll: Wait till you've actually made the decision to wear each item before taking off the tags.

Keep the tags, receipt, and bag in your closet for a while—in case there's a flaw that doesn't show up until, say, after you wash or wear it a few

times. It's much easier to return clothing when you have the tags, bag, and receipt.

If you've bought something that has a defect, it's a very good idea to call the store and ask to talk to the manager. Explain the problem. Write down his or her name and find out when he or she works.

Return the merchandise when the manager is there—or ask the manager to make a note that you're coming in for a refund or exchange.

Since you've already discussed the problem, there shouldn't be a hassle when you show up.

2. Buy clothing loose enough to fit comfortably after being washed and dried a few times. Washing shrinks stuff, especially cotton. So does the dryer, even on "cool." Regarding pants and shorts: Is the waistband tight when you button or snap it? Do they ride up in the rear? If so, buy a bigger size—or you'll be miserable after they're washed and dried.

Jeans shrink in length over time, and you'll be getting taller. Pay close attention to the length of your pants—or they'll be floods after you wash them and put them in the dryer. Before you buy them, ask a salesperson how much you can expect them to shrink. If they shrink more than you were warned, bring 'em back!

Black pants, shorts, shirts, and jackets made of cotton (and denim) fade. You can hold off the fading process for a while by washing them inside out in cold water. Still, they won't remain as black as the day you bought them. And they'll keep on lightening over time. So ask yourself: Will I still like this if it's a couple of shades lighter? If not, don't buy it.

3. Read labels for washing instructions before buying. If it's dry-clean only—a shirt, for example—expect to spend about $5 or $6. Uh, each time you clean it? Yup. Avoid dry-clean-only clothes, unless they're for a really special event.

4. Unless you like to iron, think twice about buying clothes that require a lot of ironing to look good.

Basic Threads

If you don't have someone to boss you around and pick out your clothes for you, here are some suggestions for a basic wardrobe.

Dress Clothes

1. One pair of plain leather shoes, brown or black (these can easily be polished).

2. Two pairs of plain, dark, thinnish (not athletic) socks. Both pairs the same, in case the washing machine eats one sock.

3. A plain leather belt, with a plain buckle, that matches your shoes (brown or black).

4. One long-sleeved, collared cotton shirt (that can be bleached to rejuvenate it in case you get into a food fight wearing it).

5. One T-shirt to go under it.

6. One pair of cotton khakis, long enough to at least touch the tops of your shoes—but no so long that they eclipse the heels of your shoes in the back.

7. One tie—whatever one you like. Look in magazines for clues as to what's fashionable if you care.

8. One mid-weight dress jacket, sports jacket, or blazer—the most versatile would be a solid color. Navy, brown, or gray will work. Be positive the sleeves are long enough, since jackets are relatively expensive and your arms are growing—and will soon be dangling out of the cuffs. Better yet: Can you borrow a jacket? When you're growing fast, this may be the best option.

Casual Clothes

1. Jeans. As mentioned previously, don't buy jeans that are threatening to be floods in the immediate future! Jeans shrink—a little or a lot, but always at least a little.

Is dark or light denim in style? Are flares, bells, or boot-cut, baggy, or slim-fit jeans in style? If you care, check this out in a magazine before shopping. (In the library, if you don't want to buy one.) Otherwise, just buy jeans you like that fit comfortably—not tightly.

2. A few colored T-shirts and/or other everyday shirts you like.

3. One solid-colored (goes with more things) warm sweater or sweatshirt—nice and big.

4. A jacket—if the climate calls for one. A hood is helpful.

5. One pair of flip-flops.

6. Pajamas—or at least one pair of pajama bottoms.

7. One pair of athletic shoes.

8. Some white athletic socks—all the same. That way, you won't have to match them; there will be endless possibilities for sock partnerships.

9. A few pairs of underwear.

Seat Covers
Boxers or Briefs?
Who cares!
Wear what's comfortable.

Great Condition—Previously Owned

Wearing hand-me-downs from family or friends is one more way of recycling, being environmentally conscious, and being considerate of your parent's budget.

Any great "vintage" clothes available in the attic or way, way back in the family's closets? It's a fashion phenomenon: Styles that went out 20 years ago come back to haunt us.

Ask.

It's possible to put together a great look with hand-me-down clothes and clothes bought at garage sales, flea markets, and thrift stores. Artists, actors, models, musicians, and dancers (even movie stars) have been doing it for years.

Also, you can mix new stuff with used stuff; that's an old trick.

A tip if you shop in secondhand stores or flea markets: Plan to wash before you wear. Always give armpits a "sniff test." If the underarm doesn't smell good, don't buy it unless you're sure it's washable in **hot water and detergent**. (Buying a stinky used leather jacket is an example of what would be a bad choice; leather isn't washable, and dry-cleaning it would be really expensive.)

HOW TO TIE A TIE

1. Situate the tie so that the end **A** is longer than end **B** and cross **A** over **B**.

2. Turn **A** back underneath **B**.

3. Continue by bringing **A** back over in front of **B** again.

4. Pull **A** up and through the loop around your neck.

5. Hold the front of the knot loosely with your index finger and bring **A** down through front loop.

6. Remove finger and tighten knot snugly to collar by holding **B** and sliding knot.

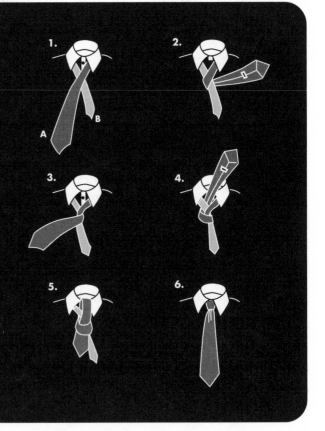

If you have clothes that you've grown out of or are sick of and they're still in good shape, get into the habit of stuffing them into a bag (an old pillowcase works) in your closet. Eventually the bag will fill up.

Then donate the clothes to a charitable organization—like your younger brother.

ROOFTOPS
Hairstyles

Hair grows naturally in a variety of colors and textures. All hair can look good in its natural state. Just keep your hair clean and trim it occasionally. It will look and smell great.

There are lots of hair products available for guys. They can make your hair shine, stick straight up, or lie down flat. They're commonly sold in drugstores. If you're curious, check them out.

Note conditioners (displayed near shampoos). They can be rinsed out or left in after washing, and they increase manageability.

You can stand up against frizz, too—with a little help from the products developed to tangle with it.

And speaking of tangling, detanglers can help you untangle long hair.

Interested in alternative hairstyles? Lots of kids are, especially kids who are artists or musicians and appreciate a more unconventional look.

As long as you have your parent's okay, and as long as your school's dress code allows for it, there's no reason not to experiment.

Use products responsibly.

There are countless products that alter the natural state of hair. *Always ask* permission of your parent before using these.

Read the warning label on the package carefully before you buy any of these products. Most products such as relaxers, perms, bleaches, and dyes require adult supervision. Why? They can damage your eyes. Study the warnings on the packaging and follow all directions, paying close attention to the protection of your eyes.

Don't *ever* bleach or dye your eyebrows or eyelashes.

HEADS UP!

If you accidentally get a potentially damaging hair product in your eyes, *immediately* begin flushing your eyes with water.

Catch a gentle stream from the faucet in your hand and blink into it, or use an eye cup, or ask a helper to pour water gently into your eye from a clean cup or pitcher while you tip your head back. Forget about getting wet. You can change your clothes later.

Continue flushing your eyes for 15 minutes—then call a doctor or poison control center number for additional advice. The poison control number for your region will probably be listed on the emergency page in the front of the phone book. Or call the information operator for the number.

Moon Roof

In some parts of the United States, a shaved head is considered an emblem of extremist viewpoints linked with ignorance, racism, hatred, and violence.

In other areas, having a shaved head is just another hairstyle.

Make sure you know what's up if you're contemplating shaving your dome. And do ask your parent's permission.

A helper is usually required to do a good job and/or to avoid totally nicking up your scalp.

Remember not to share safety razors. It is possible (although improbable) for somebody else's blood to be on the blade; blood carries germs, including HIV (see page 89).

Door Dings

During adolescence there's a tendency to focus on very small physical imperfections and stress over them, as though physical perfection actually exists.

Which it doesn't. Guess what—you're not perfect. You're not supposed to be! And the really good news is that neither is anybody else.

Bumps, moles, warts, flaky skin, cowlicks, hairy nostrils, and pointy heads aren't factory defects. They're just small variations in human design.

GUY REPORT: ERASERHEAD

"When I was in grade school and the weather was bad, we played games in the classroom instead of going outside to recess. One of the games was an 'eraser relay.' Two groups of kids could get at each end of the room and race down the aisles between our stupid little desks trying to balance black chalkboard erasers on our heads while moving as fast as we could to transfer it to the next kid's head.

"This was the time of the early flat-tops, so most of the boys could accomplish the feat with ease. My own case, however, was different. Because my mother had a terrible time during my birth, I was extricated into this world by large forceps . . . pliers. The result was my having a very pointed head.

"Instead of a flat top, I had a roof top. I had to lay my head cheek-to-shoulder to get the proper flat angle to carry the eraser.

"I always dreaded this foul-weather game because I could not do it well and it pointed out my awful physical oddity."

Be real.

People come in all shapes and shades and sizes. Appreciate your unique characteristics.

You don't have to look like a model or a movie star to be handsome.

You don't have to be handsome to be beautiful. You don't have to be buff to be powerful.

You don't have to be big to be strong.

And besides, you don't have to be strong—not all of the time, anyway.

Who you are is defined by what you do, say, and think. It's defined by how you act and who you are, not how you look. What's in your head and what's in your heart are the most important things. In the long run, success is less about appearance—and more about performance using life skills that you've developed like integrity, courage, and compassion.

Low Mileage

You're a kid. Pubic hair and ejaculations don't change that. Looking physically like an adult male doesn't mean you're supposed to take on the roles and responsibilities of a man. You're a kid—entitled to the care and protection of the adults around you.

Life isn't a race. So take it slow and easy. You're not supposed to know exactly where you're going or where you'll end up.

The journey is the destination.

An Insurance Policy

Communicate with your family and friends—especially about things that trouble you. Talk! It'll help keep you covered, bumper to bumper.

Keep your lifetime warranty in effect.

Wear your seat belt. Wear your helmet!

Don't do drugs. Don't let anybody who's drunk or stoned drive you anywhere.

Postpone having sex with a partner until you are fully mature and able to accept the risks and responsibilities.

Look for non-violent solutions to conflict.

Maintain realistic expectations of yourself and the people around you.

Think for yourself; don't give into the feeling that you have to do what other kids are doing to belong. You belong!

Accept yourself. Hear your own ideas and pay attention to your own instincts about what is right, or wrong, for you.

Work hard.

Play hard.

Make plans.

Dream.

INDEX

P9-DWK-095

NORTH
VIETNAM

DMZ

Khe Sanh

Hue

LAOS

Da Nang

THAILAND

Dak To

SOUTH
VIETNAM

CAMBODIA

Ban Me Thuot

Nha Trang

Tan Son
Nhut

Long Binh

Bien Hoa

Hong Nhu

SAIGON

CAM RANH
BAY

My Tho

GULF
OF
THAILAND

Can Tho

MEKONG DELTA

SOUTH CHINA SEA

N

km. 100

mi. 100

A TIME OF WAR

Michael Peterson

POCKET STAR BOOKS

New York   London   Toronto   Sydney   Tokyo   Singapore

ACKNOWLEDGMENT

To Al Zuckerman,
without whose faith and guidance
this book would not be.

A Pocket Star Book published by
POCKET BOOKS, a division of Simon & Schuster
1230 Avenue of the Americas, New York, NY 10020

ISBN: 0-671-70126-6

First Pocket Books paperback printing April 1991

10 9 8 7 6 5 4 3 2 1

POCKET STAR BOOKS and colophon are trademarks of
Simon & Schuster.

Printed in the U.S.A.

To Patty, who suffered all my wounds.
To Clayton and Todd, whose suffering, I pray,
   is only in my nightmares.
To the dead.
And to those whose suffering cannot be relieved.

AUTHOR'S NOTE

This novel is set in a matrix of fact: certain aspects and events of the conflict between the United States and North Vietnam in 1967 and 1968. Actual military and political leaders are also part of the background against which this fictional drama is played. *A Time of War* is, however, entirely a novel—a fictional account of the fictional Bradley Lawrence Marshall and what happpened to him during those years in those places. Marshall's mission to Saigon is wholly imaginary, as are his conversations with real persons, such as Lyndon B. Johnson, and his involvement in real events, such as the Tet Offensive. These fictional dialogues, ideas and actions were created out of my imagination in order to enhance the novel's plot and authenticity. I also changed the topography of Khe Sanh; anyone who was there knows the terrain was neither sand nor desert.

To every thing there is a season, and a
    time to every purpose under the heaven;
A time to love, and a time to hate; a time
    of war, and a time of peace.

—Ecclesiastes

Alas, said the king, that ever this unhappy
    war was begun.

—Le Morte d'Arthur

CHAPTER

• 1 •

Looking out through the French doors of the Oval Office, Marshall watched the President pad through the Rose Garden, appearing as out of place as a polar bear. The huge man, his powerful gait oddly cumbersome, his dark blue suit already rumpled—it was only noon—stalked through the garden, looming over the profusion of flowers. If only he had a parasol, Marshall thought, it could be a scene painted by a crazed Monet.

The President bounded up the patio stairs and disappeared into the White House.

Alone in the Oval Office, Bradley Lawrence Marshall stood gazing out on the garden, then turned away. As always, the room surprised him; it was huge, yet smaller than expected, perhaps because a room that housed such power should be without dimensions, too vast to be contained by walls, let alone bordered by a bank of television sets, and tables on which newspapers and telephones were strewn.

The electronics were unfortunate, Marshall thought, too mundane for the lofty setting, but elegance was not what one associated with Lyndon Johnson. Little bronze oil derricks and cattle figurines, a straw "Howdy" mat thrown on the floor over the thick carpet with the Great Seal of the United States: that was more the Johnson style.

Marshall felt no disdain. It was just that since his being

1

left alone here had been so carefully orchestrated, he felt sorry that the desired effect had not been achieved; he was meant to be awed and humbled by the setting, not critical of the decor.

But Marshall knew the President too well, had worked with him too closely to be taken in by such heavy-handedness, and the past hour's performance had been as ham-handed as they come—a great show by any standard, terrific theater, but in the end it was the actor one applauded, not the play.

Marshall almost laughed aloud remembering the President sitting across from him, leaning forward, his face pressing closer, the great jowls waggling, his eyes as mournful as a basset hound's, the voice a stricken plea—"Bradley, you've got to help me. You can't leave me stranded among these wolves."

But the image fled and Marshall grimaced. His arm hurt. He rubbed it gently; at least it was bruised, possibly even dislocated.

A large man himself, six feet two and in excellent shape for his forty-two years, he nevertheless had flinched under the President's crushing grip. Johnson was a toucher; the large hand would reach out in a handshake, then the other hand would start to work—stroking and coaxing, tugging and pulling, molding and manipulating. A hand would squeeze the arm, test the flesh, then an arm would reach around the shoulder, drawing the person closer. In some acts of persuasion, Marshall had seen Johnson put a head-lock on a man, literally drag him around the room, all the while pleading and cajoling with florid calls for reasonableness.

Marshall had witnessed many such performances, and though himself now immune to them, he enjoyed the show: political opera buffa at its best, a bogus extravaganza. Johnson was great theater, ham masquerading as ham—the voice rising in rage, dropping in sorrow, the heavy lids, the agonies, injustices, and betrayals he suffered, the stirring calls to duty and glory.

Who could resist: the President of the United States

leaning close, pressing forehead to forehead, the eyes entreating, the entire Free World in the balance—"Help me"?

They had started by sitting across from one another in the leather library chairs before the fireplace, and Johnson had come directly to the point.

"What do you know about Vietnam, Bradley?"

"I could locate it on a map, Mr. President."

Then the arms began to wave and the show was on. "That's only because it's still there, because I won't let Curtis LeMay pound it into a cow flop. Bomb, bomb, bomb—that's all I hear!" he shouted, his hands flailing the air, warding off the rain of shells exploding on the carpet.

The aggrieved tone suddenly changed; the eyes narrowed. Where did the eyes go, Marshall wondered—lost in the wrinkles and folds, or withdrawn altogether?

"You didn't know anything about Central America when I sent you there, but you saw right to the heart." He leaned forward, wringing four vowels from the word: "Poverty."

"There aren't any isms in hunger, that's what you told me. The Marines can't cure hunger. I remember it perfectly, Bradley—'the peasants don't give a fuck about communism, only food.'"

Hardly my words, Marshall thought.

"And what about the Jews and A-rabs? Remember what you told me when I sent you to the Mideast?"

Marshall sat straighter, wondering what form his advice had taken.

"Stay out!" Johnson shouted.

More or less, remembered Marshall.

"Let the silly bastards blow each other away."

Marshall did not even blink at that incredible distortion.

"I remember it clearly, the only sensible advice I got." Johnson wrung Marshall's arm in gratitude. "'Stay out—ten centuries of warfare between Christians, Moslems, and Jews: a few Marines aren't going to solve the problems. Caesar Augustus and Richard the Lionhearted couldn't do anything, and neither can you'—that's what you told me."

Remarkably accurate, Marshall remembered. There was always a danger in Johnson's recollections for usually he

3

heard only what he wanted to hear, and remembered only what he wanted to remember. Therefore, his recollections were highly selective reconstructions put together to serve the need at hand, and subject to immediate and innumerable revisions.

Suddenly the voice saddened. The President sat back in his chair, slumped in somberness and regret.

"Remember in the beginning, that awful period after Jack was killed?"

Who could forget that, thought Marshall. Though nearly four years ago, Kennedy's assassination was still as vivid to him as if it had happened yesterday afternoon.

Even the glare of sunlight through the windows could not brighten the moment. Johnson took off his glasses and held them in his lap, his sad gaze on the dance of light on the parquet floor. Marshall glanced involuntarily toward the rocking chair, not similar to Kennedy's bentwood, but nonetheless reminding him of the slain president.

Marshall entered government service under John Kennedy; a Harvard classmate of the president's younger brother, Marshall was persuaded by Robert to join the administration. As a lawyer, and known to Bobby, he expected to be in the Justice Department, righting wrongs, equalizing justice; instead, the president asked him to be assistant chief of protocol.

At first flattered and enjoying the position, he soon chafed—one could greet just so many pretentious dignitaries, set up so many appointments, attend so many dinners. Moreover, he came to feel used and resentful of the reasons why he had been chosen—his family wealth, equal to and much older than the Kennedys'; his looks and poise and bearing; his youth—eight years John Kennedy's junior, he made the president look not so disturbingly young to the foreign ministers and heads of state.

He had been on the verge of returning to private practice when Kennedy was murdered.

Indeed he remembered that awful time and a very unsure Lyndon Johnson trying to maneuver through the shoals of those first days, seeking the proper stance during the national mourning, overcoming the resentment and apprehen-

4

sions, even suspicions, of the Kennedy loyalists, then trying to assert himself to the foreign leaders who had come to Washington for the funeral.

Later Johnson thanked him for his service during those early days.

"You were one of the few, and I mean *damn* few Kennedy people who really tried to help me."

Now the voice was bitter, the jowls shook, the hand stabbed in anger at the memory of those who had turned on him, at the resentment and hatred he had suffered for succeeding Kennedy. "You were never patronizing or condescending; you never laughed or sniped at me. And you never kissed my ass either. And when that fandango of foreigners came, de Gaulle and Mikoyan, and people whose names I couldn't even pronounce, you were right beside me, telling me what to say and how to say it, who to shake hands with, and who not, who to bow to, who to salaam—and you did it without being a fucking know-it-all."

He reached out and grabbed Marshall in appreciation. "I'll never forget what you did for me, and someday when you need something, I'll be there for you."

Except Marshall thought, it never worked that way. It was always Johnson calling on him for help, as in Central America.

The Bay of Pigs had been Kennedy's biggest embarrassment. Johnson, determined to avoid a similar misfortune, asked Marshall to go to the Central American countries as special envoy. But Marshall had demurred, because of his new law practice, and because he knew little about the area.

Johnson had dismissed the excuses out of hand. "I don't want anyone who knows about Central America. I want someone without prejudices. I want a fresh approach. Don't you understand, Bradley, I *need* you. Your country *needs* you. Bradley, you don't need any more money—that's just greed working for that law firm, and those corporations that hire you for five hundred dollars an hour."

So he had gone, knowing next to nothing about Honduras, Guatemala, El Salvador; and months later he returned with a clutch bag of observations that a blind person could have gathered: poverty and social injustice were the root problems, land reform was essential, political corruption and economic exploitation had to be overcome.

Castro and communism aren't the problems, he told Johnson—poverty and corruption are. Unless we do something to help those people, the communists will succeed. It won't do any good to send guns when what they need is food. The Marines can't cure poverty and ignorance.

Perhaps Marshall had said, "There aren't any isms in hunger." He hoped he had; it was a good line, and true.

Johnson had listened as raptly as if Marshall had lugged in new tablets of stone, had thanked him profusely and told him that he had solved all the problems. Three months later the President sent the Marines to the Dominican Republic while Luci Baines was being crowned queen of the Azalea Festival.

Marshall was neither surprised nor upset. He liked and understood Johnson. Though vastly dissimilar, they struck a chord in one another. Despite all the man's bombast and duplicity, Marshall believed there was in Lyndon Johnson great good and genuine commitment to justice. His Great Society was not a sham; the President ached for the poor and oppressed. Marshall knew Vietnam meant nothing to Johnson—his Great Society mattered, not some foreign war in some faraway place where he wasn't even on the ballot.

Yet Marshall understood Johnson's dilemma; here was a man who could not admit error and walk away. What Texan could quit a fight, risk being called cowardly and unmanly? How could he turn tail and run? Did they do that at the Alamo? Would Sam Houston have fled? Would John F. Kennedy? Johnson had been drawn in gradually, pulled and pushed by Kennedy advisors and his own generals until he was embroiled in a full-fledged war. Though his heart was not in it, he was beyond the point where he could, as he put it, "Say whoops and go home."

But he'd like to, Marshall knew; Vietnam did not interest him, his Great Society did. Yes, Johnson was outrageously bogus, a notorious liar, and probably dishonest besides—how did a man get to be a multimillionaire on a government salary?—nevertheless, this man raised in poverty on the Pedernales, whose first job was as a teacher in a small

Mexican-American school in Cotulla, Texas, this terribly flawed man, vengeful and mean and petty, distrustful and driven, yearned to help people.

And Johnson, though he distrusted and feared the Eastern patricians, saw in Marshall—a man born in luxury, from the most privileged class, a man with good looks who attended the best schools and was surrounded by women, proud and rich—a man who sought to do good and help people.

In 1966, Johnson implored Marshall to go as special envoy to the Mideast. "You've got to help me, Bradley. The whole area is a crapper ready to explode. Of course you don't know anything about Lebanon—who does? But go and find out. Tell me what to do there, Bradley. Your country is counting on you."

Six grueling weeks he shuttled between Cairo, Jerusalem, Beirut, Damascus, Amman, Riyadh—talking with Nasser, Hussein, Eshkol, even tribal chieftains in the desert—and brought back a report that there was no imminent solution.

Stay out was his advice; a battalion of Marines wasn't going to resolve centuries of conflict between Christians, Moslems, and Jews. He told Johnson that he could not succeed where Caesar Augustus and Richard the Lion-hearted had failed; but he had not said, "Let the silly bastards blow each other away."

He did not speak or think that way. Other peoples' beliefs were serious matters not to be trod on or interfered with; to do so invited war, and that he never wanted to see again.

Once Johnson had shown Marshall his security clearance file, tossing it casually across the table to him.

"I hope there's more in your life than this," Johnson had said. "That's the most boring goddamn thing I've ever read."

Marshall flipped through the report with minor anxiety—his life had not been *that* boring; certainly there were things he did not want to read about, let alone have others read.

But Johnson was right, the report was boring. When he learned that an aide's report had been "compromising," Marshall was somewhat envious, and more than a little curious as to what qualified as "compromising." He realized later, of course, that the differences were merely the results of agency bunglings, oversights, and errors.

The succinctness in his own report was exemplary: "1942–1945, military service, honorable discharge." And again, "1951–1953, military service, honorable discharge."

Because he seldom thought about it, and never spoke of it, the four words "military service, honorable discharge" seemed appropriate, though two more words that could have been included, "Guadalcanal" and "Chosin," would have markedly changed the context of the entry and hinted at the depth and complexity of the later man.

Yet even momentary recollection on the entry gave that hint. Born in 1925, why would a seventeen-year-old from one of the oldest families in America run off to war? Why, at twenty-six, would he go again?

Then, before the dead on the beaches and the dead sprawled in the snow pulled him down to them, Marshall closed the file and placed it on the desk.

"Anything you want to add?" Johnson asked.

"No sir, everything's in there," he said quietly. "It's been a pretty unexciting life so far."

"Well goddamn," said Johnson. "Get busy."

Now again he was at the White House, across from the President. The moment of commemorative silence was over.

Johnson's eyes narrowed conspiratorially and he glanced around suspiciously; his voice dropped to a whisper and Marshall had to restrain himself forcibly from looking over his shoulder to make sure that they were alone, as if spies freely roamed the corridors.

Johnson moved his chair nearer so that their knees touched. To get any closer, Marshall thought, he's going to have to sit on my lap. Invading personal space, literally encroaching onto another person, was a frequent Johnson ploy, but Marshall did not mind because he did not feel threat or intimidation.

"I need you again," the President said. "Vietnam." He nodded his head slowly and let the word hang for effect. "I gotta get out of that shithole."

Johnson jerked forward, brought back to life by the threat

8

that he took personally, as he did everything—legislation, budgets, space programs, wars—and Vietnam was a personal affront, as well as a mortal danger to his place in history, and his reelection hopes.

He shook his head mournfully. "Oh, Bradley, I've done what I could; I walked more than half of the mile, but I can't get anywhere with those bastards."

Marshall wasn't sure if he meant Hanoi or his own advisors.

"That pissant country is going to sink my presidency." He held his aggrieved heart. "Nothing has worked. I've bombed, I've stopped bombing, I've pleaded, I've promised, I've threatened." He leaned forward. "I've prayed."

Looking forsaken and betrayed even by God, he said in stricken tones, "I don't know what else to do. That's why I've called you."

He jumped up. "What do *I* care about that goddamn place?"

He started to pace. "I don't want to be there." He said it as if a rifle were slung over his shoulder and it was he trudging the paddy dikes.

"What does that have to do with poverty and hunger and ignorance? Nothing!" he shouted at a lamp.

He grabbed a chair for support, as if stabbed in the back by traitorous advisors. "All I've heard since I've been here is bomb, mine the harbors, bomb, napalm, send more men, more guns, bomb."

He ducked a shell. "Just a little more and they'll cave in. The light's at the end of the tunnel." He groped blindly toward the light.

"And I'm getting nowhere."

Marshall knew the planes were bringing home the silver caskets in mounting numbers and Johnson feared that unless victory came soon, sentiment would turn bitterly against the war, and himself. There would not be another term unless there was a quick resolution to the war.

"I've fallen into a deep shitter, Bradley." His hands clawed the air, then he clutched the back of the chair and shook it. "You've got to get me out of that war. For three years I've sat here listening to people tell me about Vietnam, and you know what? Nobody knows a goddamn thing. All they know is bombs, an.' more men. And it's not working. I'm sinking deeper and deeper into the shitter."

He clutched his throat as if strangling in manure.

"Go there for me. Tell me what to do. Tell me the truth." Tragedy etched his face; the wrinkles deepened, the jowls and mouth fell mournfully. "Boys are dying over there, Bradley. You're a father, help those boys. Your country needs you. This is the most important thing you can do. When you were a soldier, you risked your life for your country. Now, as Commander in Chief, I'm asking you to serve your country again. I want you to save lives."

Marshall felt like applauding. But he sat perfectly still, waiting.

Johnson's face leaned into his. "Go to Vietnam for me. Talk to everyone. Find out what's going on there—I can't believe anyone here. The Joint Chiefs tell me one thing, the Defense Department another, the CIA something else. I need someone I can trust, someone who sees things clearly, someone who can't be fooled, someone who won't lie to me—I need you. Listen to everybody, and come back here and tell me what I have to do to end that war."

He fell silent a moment, then brought his hands together and held them up in offering.

Now the dangle, Marshall thought.

"It's no secret that some cabinet members are ready to move on."

He paused for effect. "Do this for me, and you can name what you want."

As if this offer was not enough, he sat back, seemingly lost in thought. "You know, the person who ends this war, he's going to get himself a Nobel Peace Prize."

His face fell in sorrow, his best basset look, overcome by the injustice of it all. "Not me, of course. I could crawl on my knees to Hanoi and kiss Ho Chi Minh's ass at high noon on Ding Dong Street and they'd just revile me. But someone else, the one who finds the solution to this war . . ." He gazed out the window, absorbed in the spectacle of the Peace Prize winner being paraded triumphantly through the streets.

Dear God, thought Marshall, I'm going to have to put on hip boots soon. No wonder the Rose Garden is thriving; they must just open the doors in here and shovel it out.

The show was over, but Marshall sat calm and unresponsive.

"Well?" demanded Johnson suspiciously.

Still Marshall did not answer, knowing that Johnson, having committed himself, would have to plunge on; he could not accept a rejection, especially after revealing his desperation.

Johnson wriggled himself deeper in his chair, hunkering down, knowing that he was not going to bully or cajole Marshall into submission. Now it was going to be bare-fisted horse-trading, except that Johnson had erred by showing how much he wanted the horse, while Marshall hadn't even indicated that the horse was for sale.

"Bradley, it *can't* be money. I know you make more in an hour in that highfalutin law firm than I can pay you in a day, but you're a rich man, Bradley. And don't talk to me about your practice and all those cases you have pending—I'm discussing *lives,* not corporations."

Johnson looked at him expectantly, then exploded, "Well, goddamn it, what is it?"

"Mr. President," Marshall said easily, "it isn't money or my practice. It's simply that I don't want to go. I don't trust you."

"What?" Johnson's shock was genuine. "What do you mean you don't want to go? And what do you mean, you don't trust me? Goddamn!"

"I think you're just playing games, Mr. President; I don't think you're ready to face issues squarely, or make difficult decisions."

Johnson started to erupt from his chair—no one had ever talked to him in such a manner; but Marshall waved him back, dismissing further theatrics.

"I know how the game is played, Mr. President. You have a problem too hard to deal with, so you buy yourself some time by appointing committees to make studies, and you send envoys to bring back more information. You know as well as I what to do about Vietnam—get the hell out. Why

11

should I waste my time gathering information you already know? You're just using me to buy you more time, to avoid making the decision you know is right."

Johnson brought his hand to his heart as if stricken, but again Marshall waved away the show.

"I've got better things to do than play that game. You're going to have to make me a much better offer, and I'm not talking about a cabinet post or an ambassadorship—I don't need self-aggrandizement any more than I need more money, Mr. President."

Johnson looked momentarily confused—if Marshall wasn't interested in money or position, what else was there?

"I'll go, Mr. President, and I'll conduct a fair and objective study, but if I bring back a recommendation, I expect you to do something about it."

"Well, of course I will, Bradley, you know—"

"If my finding is that the troops should be withdrawn, then I expect you to withdraw them. Or withdraw yourself from reelection." Marshall gestured to the bank of televisions. "Go before the people and tell them you won't be a candidate, that in the interest of peace, you're withdrawing from the race."

Johnson started to say something, opened his mouth, then closed it.

"And I want it in writing also. This is September—let's give it six months, March. If you don't have the courage to withdraw troops by March first, then you'll make your announcement. This is conditioned, of course, on my recommendation's being in fact for withdrawal, and that there's been no tangible progress in the war."

Johnson's eyes lit, sensing an escape route. "What do you mean, 'tangible'?"

"I mean a clear, easily identifiable, commonly agreed upon improvement in the military situation—I don't mean more 'light at the end of tunnel' bullshit: I mean the end of the tunnel."

Johnson shook his head sorrowfully. "I'm shocked at you, Bradley; that's blackmail."

"No, sir. In law it's called a contract—'If I perform such

12

and such, then you will, in consideration for my efforts, do this and that.' It's very straightforward and aboveboard. That's why I insist it be in writing, as evidence of our good faith, our straightforwardness, our desire to be aboveboard."

"And so you can blackmail me with that goddamn piece of paper, don't try to kid me."

"Why would I need to do that? As an honorable man, you would comply with the conditions of the contract anyway."

"Well, I'll have to think about it," Johnson said petulantly.

"Fine," Marshall said, standing. "Let me know."

"All right, goddamn it, I'll do it." Johnson stood up angrily, glared into Marshall's eyes, then smiled. "You're probably worth all that money they pay you."

Marshall nodded gravely in the best Johnson manner. "You can't put a price on truth and justice, Mr. President."

Johnson whooped and slapped him on the back. "And Catherine, how's that wife of yours? I'm surprised she doesn't have writer's cramp." He gestured toward his desk. "I've got a hundred petitions with her signature on them, telling me to get out of Vietnam, calling me a war criminal. A war criminal! I hear from her as often as I do that Fondue woman in Hollywood, and that goddamn singing woman, Joan Buzz. I'll bet she'll be happy to have you go over there on this blackmail mission."

For the first time Marshall smiled. "She won't see any need for me to go—she thinks all you need to do is bring the troops home now."

Johnson did not say anything. He went to the window and stared out on the back lawn. "Women have the damnedest vision, don't they? Lady Bird . . ." He stopped, shook his head slowly, then said, "You have sons, don't you?"

"Yes sir, two."

Johnson said softly to the window with a conviction so earnest that the words passed like light through the glass to the world beyond, "May God have mercy on them all."

Marshall stood beside him at the window. "Yes, sir," he said. They were looking beyond the lawn, past oceans, to lands far away. Marshall could feel the burden on the man beside him. "I always found the Second Horseman the most terrible," he said.

Johnson nodded. "He is."

"We can't do much about the others—famine, pestilence, death—they'll carry us off no matter what. But war, surely we can do something about that."

Johnson turned to him and put a hand on his shoulder. "God, I hope so," he said sincerely. Then he smiled. "Now go convince that Ho bastard. And Westmoreland. And Robert McNamara."

He went to his desk and stabbed the intercom. "Get those appointment papers for Ambassador Marshall. I'm going to lunch."

He shook hands with Marshall. "I took the liberty of signing them before you came—in anticipation of your devotion and patriotism," he said snidely.

Then he crossed the room. At the door leading to the Rose Garden, he turned.

"You've got to unfuck that mess," he said, and walked out.

A presidential aide, sensing Marshall's impatience to leave, hurried in, carrying a leather folder embossed with the presidential seal.

Marshall declined it and pointed to Johnson's desk. "Leave it there for him—he's going to add a memorandum. When he does, have it all sent to me."

"Yes, sir. Your offices will be next door, Mr. Ambassador, in the Executive Office Building; we've arranged for secretaries and aides, and we'll arrange briefings with State, Defense, the Joint Chiefs, the CIA, and anyone else you'd care to contact, at your convenience. If there's anything you need or any questions you might have, we'll get on it immediately. The President wants to assure you that you'll have anything you want, whenever you want it."

When Marshall stepped outside, he raised his hand to block the sun's glare, and he exhaled quickly at the smothering humidity. At least he would be escaping the Washington summer, he thought. Wasn't it winter in Saigon? Weren't they below the equator? A Mercator projection of the world flashed into his mind; of course not, he realized, angry at himself for the lapse.

A Secret Service agent held the door to his limousine. "Good day, sir."

Now it begins, he thought, all the power of the President behind him—the attendants, security, and deference, the limousines, helicopters, and airplanes: speed crystallized, power distilled.

He would use it for good purpose.

The car pulled away from the White House.

He would accomplish great things; he would bring an end to that awful war. He would save lives.

Thank God his own sons weren't there, he thought. Chris was only fifteen, and Ryan was safely deferred in college. That was one thing he could not bear, he knew, for suddenly in his mind he saw the dead, floating facedown in the water, swollen on the beaches, frozen in the snow. Guadalcanal. Chosin.

He forced the images away and drew a deep breath. He turned to the window.

It was a beautiful summer day. His children were safe. He would find a solution. The world would be better.

The limousine passed through the gate and turned onto Pennsylvania Avenue, accelerating. Marshall saw the crowd before the White House. The People. They were not a blurred streak to him; The People was not an abstraction, and he believed them basically good, and he trusted in their better instincts.

The limousine sped down Pennsylvania. It was a beautiful city, he thought, representing the noblest spirit in men— freedom, justice, equality.

He sat back. Saigon, he thought; then he mouthed the word. It sounded exotic and mysterious, and Vietnam—so far away.

But he was strong, his vision clear, his heart good, his purpose right and just. How could he fail?

CHAPTER

· 2 ·

Sung always thought of the land as a green ocean of jungle and rain forests, but now it was shell-pocked and defoliated. The rice fields and rubber plantations that seemed limned from a jade canvas were now mutilated and scarred, the composition vandalized by an angry god, gouged and ripped in random fury.

The graves of her ancestors were cratered by bombs, the dead reannihilated in free-fire missions.

The temples she used to pray at were in ruin and disrepair, pathetic little pantheons where she imagined the minor deities, covetous of the scraps of rice and small bony fish placed before them, hid in dark corners and bickered among themselves.

Now Sung sat with her father on the veranda in the evenings, staring across to the heavy, damp jungle gradually being swallowed by the night and mist.

Who are these people who want my land and my ancestors? he asked the dark. It had been the land of his family for generations. He could not leave it. The graves of his ancestors were here. Who would honor them if he left? What would become of him with no land on which to be buried and no one to tend him?

Sung Le Vinh was seventeen, almost five feet seven, tall

for a Vietnamese, with long black hair and features of porcelain beauty.

She had been born in this house in Ban Me Thuot in the Central Highland province of Darlac, not far from the hunting preserves of the former emperors. She was the last of five children and the only daughter. Her father was of a family of landowners and mandarins, and her mother was distantly related to the Emperor Bao Dai and had once lived at court in Hue.

Her mother had once brought Sung as a small child to see the dowager empress, a woman so old and tiny that when the empress told her that Sung reminded her of herself as a child, Sung could not believe the dowager had ever been young.

She could not take her eyes from the empress's fingernails; they were long as knives, and when the old woman reached out to touch her, she'd been frightened, but the touch was as soft as feathers.

"It is not the style anymore," the old woman had said in her whispery voice, holding out her hands, displaying the nails. "But before they were even longer. It was to show that we never did anything for ourselves."

She smiled faintly: "It is not so practical now."

After the empress had taken her nap, she called again for the child.

Sung was given slippers to walk the wood floors of the palace, so polished she could see her reflection. The floors creaked so loudly that she was embarrassed by the noise she made, but her mother told her they were made to creak to give warning to the royal family.

The empress had her sit beside her on the sofa in her private chamber, and they had fruit and tea while the old woman told her of her ancestors.

"Weak men, that is the story of our dynasty," the dowager said in a light singsong voice. "If we," and she meant the women, "had ruled, there would have been no French or Japanese, and we would still be on the throne."

Her grandson, the Emperor Bao Dai, had abdicated ten years ago and fled to Paris; the dowager stayed in Hue.

"I was born in the reign of Tu Duc, the fourth Nguyen emperor, and the last before the French enslaved us."

She shook her head in disgust. "Weak men. A thousand years of Chinese rule, then one strong man in 1802—Gia Long. Minh Mang was his son, and he too was strong, but then the blood got weak; so when the French came, our emperors tried to accommodate them, as if one accommodates a thief by letting him in the house."

She closed her eyes and folded her hands in her lap, sitting very straight. "The French came for spices and silk and jewels. They thought we were like India and China, but even when they found we had nothing to offer except ourselves as slaves, they stayed, and brought their missionaries, wicked men dressed in black who swept through the country like roaches."

Her eyes opened; she did not move otherwise, but the anger in her eyes and voice made it seem as if she were standing in defiance.

"Tu Duc ceded independence in his last years, weak and afraid. I was your age in 1883 when I became a slave."

"Really a slave?" Sung asked in wonder. Her family had many servants; surely the dowager had never bowed or bent a knee as they did.

"Vietnam became a colony. Ants live in colonies; men who live like ants are called slaves. The emperor became a puppet dangling from French strings, except when the strings were Japanese during the war. After that the puppet became a rag doll, cast to a corner and forgotten."

She stood. "Weak men," she said in dismissal, then she went to an old teak chest and brought out her dolls to show Sung, and she placed them on the cushions and chairs around them; they smelled of camphor.

Another time Sung went with the dowager to the River of Perfumes. It was only a short outing but the preparations were elaborate. They drove in an old black limousine with a chauffeur dressed in yellow, the imperial color, and three ladies in attendance.

At the riverbank, the empress got out to pray. Though very old and frail, she would allow no one to help her. She prayed to the spirits of the river. She told Sung that the warriors of the old emperors used to do this to drive away evil. Now the soldiers don't believe in spirits and there are no more emperors, she said. But the dowager told her there still was evil.

Sung learned later that the dowager was driven from Hue and abandoned by her attendants, a frightened old woman clutching clean undergarments to her breasts as she fled on foot, pushed and shoved off the road by deserting soldiers who had long ago deserted the dead dynasty.

Though it was through Sung's mother that the irresolute dynastic blood flowed, it was she who proved more resolute than her father.

"We must leave Ban Me Thuot," she said. "We cannot stay any longer."

"Leave? Leave the land? Abandon the ancestors? And go where?"

The huge estate of rice paddies and rubber trees supported a luxurious lifestyle. Her four brothers had been sent to the university in Hue, and she had been privately tutored and taught excellent French and English.

Because her father had kept his distance from the French, he was able to expand his holdings when Dien Bien Phu fell, but afterward he could not strike a balance among the factions: Saigon, the Viet Minh, Catholics, Buddhists, the Cao Dai, the Americans, became too much for him.

"There can be no peace," her mother said. "And it will do no good to choose a side because then the other would come for you. We must go; our time is past."

"But all we have is the land," her father said.

"That is what they want," she said. "That is what they will kill us for. That is why we must leave."

Sung watched her mother; she sat like the dowager had, with her back straight and her hands folded in her lap. She spoke to her husband with quiet finality.

Yet her father could not accept her words. He had been a fair man who treated his workers well; he did not understand when they deserted him.

"They are afraid," his wife told him. "The Viet Minh will kill them if they work for us."

Then the household servants ran off.

Other landowners fled, and all their relatives.

The fields went fallow. Sung's brothers returned from Hue to help, but the land had become a battlefield for the warring sides whose soldiers roamed at will.

At night, as enemies moved and probed the darkness outside, the family huddled in frightened vigil inside like doomed guardians in a forsaken temple, awaiting the barbarian rampage.

One day a Viet Cong cadre came to the house. They were polite, but frightening. They demanded ten million piasters, payment on a debt long overdue the people, they said.

"What debt? What people?" her father asked.

"You and your family have been parasites, living off the labor of others. You must return the land to the people, its rightful owners, and your entire family must undergo resettlement and education. It will do you good to work for others, and for your sons to erase the family stain by joining us."

When they left, her father went to the province chief in Ban Me Thuot. The man, an appointee from Saigon, listened with lugubrious sympathy. Alas, he said, his forces were already overextended. Of course, if her father was willing to underwrite the expense of the soldiers, then he, the province chief, might be able to do something; but the cost would be high.

"You are as bad as they!" her father shouted. "You are all extortionists. You are all corrupt."

"Now do you see that we have to leave?" said his wife.

But now more than ever he refused. He would not give in to terror and corruption. He would never abandon his land to such people.

Sung was in the kitchen with her mother the morning the soldiers came.

"Run," her mother said, but without urgency, in such a normal tone that Sung did not grasp her meaning.

Then she said it again, this time with force and anger.

Finally she screamed it, and Sung ran in panic, but she did not know where to flee or why. She ran to the back of the house, thinking to escape across the fields to the jungle, but then she saw them, seven soldiers with rifles, and they had her brothers and father.

They saw her at the same time. Three soldiers broke away to chase after her but she could not run; she was transfixed by the scene before her.

Her father's and brothers' hands were tied behind them. They stumbled and fell as the soldiers pushed and prodded. Even from the distance she saw blood. From their bent and subdued carriage she could tell they had been beaten.

Her mother reached Sung's side just as the soldiers did. Her mother struck at them, then dug her nails into the neck of the soldier who grabbed Sung. Another soldier struck her mother in the side so hard that she fell, but she struggled up again and threw herself on the soldier, her screams rending the morning. Finally the third soldier smashed the butt of his rifle against her head.

There was nothing Sung could do for her mother, lying at her feet. No one could help now. The horror of what she knew was going to happen numbed her. In self-defense her mind separated from her body; she viewed the scene as a faraway observer.

When the soldiers brought her father and brothers before her, they kept their gaze riveted to the ground.

Her mother stirred when she saw her sons and husband above her and she crawled to them. She put her arms around the legs of her nearest son and tried to stand, but a soldier stomped on her arms. Sung heard the bones break.

The soldiers never spoke. One grabbed her mother by her hair and dragged her to the courtyard in front of the house while the others herded Sung and her father and brothers there.

The soldiers forced her father and brothers to sit and propped her mother beside them, slapping her until she responded. Three soldiers stood behind them with rifles.

The other four grabbed Sung.

They ripped off her clothes. One soldier, the youngest, a boy no older than she, quickly stripped off his trousers, but the others pushed him away.

Before they attacked Sung, they dragged her before her

21

family and made them all look at her, jabbing them with rifles in the neck, raising their chins with the barrels. Her father and brothers clamped their bloodied eyes shut, but her mother met her gaze.

Sung saw her jaw set and watched the rage fade from her eyes, seep away until it was replaced with the most sorrowful love. She never took her eyes from her daughter and her expression never changed.

The soldiers raped and sodomized her, and when they finished, they placed the bores of their rifles against the heads of her family and fired a single bullet into each.

Sung lay on the ground, her head turned to her mother, their gazes locked together until her mother's head erupted in blood.

Above her, the boy soldier grinned. He jammed the barrel of his rifle into Sung's vagina, pushed it farther, impaling her like a pig, then his eyes glinted wildly, and he pulled the trigger.

The click echoed in the morning stillness, then the boy laughed and withdrew the barrel.

The incessant buzzing of flies roused her. They were all over her, a swarm alighting on the semen and blood coagulating in her vagina. They were in her mouth and nose and eyes, and when she swiped at them, they buzzed back greedily.

Her mother was sprawled in the dirt, the flies feeding on her open eyes, but when Sung tried to crawl to her, she could not move.

Then she saw her father.

But it was not her father.

At first it made no sense to her. Where was his head?

Then the full horror struck her, and she tried to push herself away, whimpering as her fingers dug into the dirt.

Her father's body lay only fifteen feet away. The head had been cleanly severed in midneck; the stump had emptied into a pond of blood.

Suddenly her father's hand moved. The fingers straightened as if reaching out toward her. She screamed. Then all the bodies were moving. They writhed on the ground beside her. The severed neck twitched and blood spurted from the stump.

She screamed until she lost consciousness.

When she woke, she was cold. The sun was setting and the flies were gone.

She turned her head to where her father lay. The fingers on his hand were stiff, his entire body awkwardly rigid in rigor mortis. So were her brothers and mother.

She tried to move but seemed unable to exert any power over her body; it was as if she too lay dead, except that she hurt too much, and then she lost consciousness again.

When she woke, the moon was so bright that she could see the gaping exit wounds of the bullets in her brothers' foreheads; but under the starry sky, her brothers seemed peacefully asleep and she didn't want to move for fear of waking them. She cradled her head in her arms and fell asleep.

Birds woke her at sunrise. Her arms were so stiff they ached when she moved them, but as soon as she did, she heard furtive scurrying beside her. She turned, then screamed. Rats were on the corpses. They had eaten into the body cavities. A rat crawled out of her brother's chest and bared its teeth at her.

She flailed her arms and kicked herself away, but she could not stop screaming. Then she stumbled up and ran across the field, waving her hands before her face to wipe away the sight of the rats feeding on the corpses.

She ran blindly until she collapsed, sobbing, choking for air. The fields were damp from the morning dew and wet dirt clung to her. She lay shivering until she caught her breath.

When she reached a neighbor's house, a friend of her father's for all her life, she knocked on the door. She heard people inside, but no one answered.

"Help me," she cried. "Please help me."

Finally the door cracked open and she saw her father's friend hiding behind it.

"Go away," he hissed.

He knew, she realized. Everyone knew what had happened and they were afraid.

23

"Go," he said, throwing a few bills at her.

She picked them up and said simply, "There is nothing more they can do to me."

"There is always something else they can do," he said, and closed the door on her.

No, she thought, they have done the worst.

Her mother had said they should flee to Saigon; that was the only safe place. She would go to Saigon; there would be help there.

She stuffed the bills in her ripped blouse and walked toward the road. Even at this early hour there was traffic, a few vehicles, but mostly families pulling carts, all traveling south to Saigon.

She followed after them and had walked for only a few minutes when she came to the edge of Ban Me Thuot. On the side of the road facing those who would enter the city was a little forest of staff pikes, a severed head on each. Her father's choked eyes and tongue bulged out a warning to those who would not help the communists.

She wanted to cry, but she had no tears left. She turned away. I will not think, she said to herself. I will not feel.

As the day wore on, more people filled the road. She walked with a woman whose husband had been killed in the army and she was going to Saigon to plead with . . . she did not know whom, because she had no money and the district government would not give her any for her two children.

Sung helped carry the baby, too weak to cry or nurse.

On the third day the woman handed the baby to Sung to carry. The day was hot, the road dusty. They had not spoken for hours, just trudged along with the multitude.

As soon as her fingers touched the baby, Sung knew it was dead. Sung jumped away and the woman stood in the road, her arms outstretched to Sung, holding the dead baby.

She stared at her dead child for a long time, then placed it in the middle of the dirt road and wandered away with her other child, crossing the fields, simply disappearing.

People walked past the child without even looking; its stomach was distended, and open sores covered its body.

A pack of dogs ran up to the corpse, but Sung chased at

them. The dogs ran into the field, then circled back and crouched, waiting.

Sung looked from the child in the road to the people walking past to the dogs lying in wait, then she turned away and continued on. She did not look back, and did not listen for the dogs, and did not think or feel.

Each day more people were on the road, thousands, their belongings on their backs—the old and feeble, children, cripples, the wounded, the widowed, the orphaned, fleeing from the edges of disaster to its center.

Sung kept moving with the thousands, six days on the road, prey to the box people who lived in discarded wooden ammunition crates lining the road and who would dart out to wrest away whatever anyone carried, or to strip the clothes from the backs of the refugees.

At night she huddled with the others on the side of the road, but the box people sorted through them as through heaps of trash. Sung lay motionless as bugs and rats and men scavenged.

The road was like a choked vein coursing septic blood to a diseased heart, but finally she knew that she was nearing the city.

Saigon began miles out, with clumps of cardboard dwellings before which wasted women sat listlessly and skeletal children stared dull-eyed. Two million refugees had fled to the city, were sucked in, then washed out because there was nothing for them, spilling over into human eddies that trickled back out into the devastated marshland, camping beside the dirt road.

The road widened as it approached the city. Huge military vehicles laden with troops and munitions hurtled along, horns blaring, scattering smaller vehicles, carts, and the refugees. The fumes were noxious and the noise painful. Soldiers jeered and shouted obscenities at the refugees; sometimes they tossed rations, but this only caused more chaos as the refugees fought for them.

Cardboard boxes and ammunition crates gave way to shanties as the dirt road turned into a potholed, cratered highway. The shanties seemed nailed one onto another, but suddenly there appeared a stab at commerce—a noodle vendor or a bike repair shop. Then pedicabs and motorcycles. The shanties gave way to ruins, former dwellings of stucco and stone, single homes now shared by five and ten families.

The highway gradually turned into a boulevard lined with shops and apartment buildings. Trash and garbage rotted everywhere. A rush of beggars, cripples, thieves, and children shoved and pushed her. The city swirled with frenzy, the people drawn like rats to the center of an overcrowded cage.

Suddenly she was by herself, lost down a side street, surrounded by people with looks of cunning and purpose. She tried to find her way back to the boulevard but found herself on yet another side street.

All along she had said to herself, "Everything will be all right when I reach Saigon," as if she expected refuge there, someone to meet her, but now she saw there was nothing and no one.

She wandered all day, and late at night, hopelessly lost in the back streets of the Cholon district, she begged two girls to let her stay the night in their room. They worked in the bars and stayed in the room only those nights soldiers didn't take them to a hotel.

The three sat on the floor of the barren room and drank cold tea. A bare bulb cast harsh light as the cord dangled in the light breeze coming from the paneless window.

"Find a man," one said, an eye bruised and swollen closed, her hair knotted in filth. "In war a woman has only her cunt. Learn to use yours, and hope someone wants it."

"Things will get better when the communists come," the other said.

The other spat. "It's all the same bone and flesh and cock."

"Go to the Chinaman," they said. "There are worse things to be than a whore."

Three days later, after finding there was nothing for her to do, without money or food or a place to stay, she went to the Chinaman.

The brothel was a two-story, shambling dwelling set amidst a maze of back alleys. Behind a crumbling stucco wall was a small courtyard littered with trash where nothing grew and cats sunned themselves on the warm concrete.

But the Chinaman chased her away. "I have whores enough," he said.

She went timidly up the stairs again. "I have no money and nowhere to go. I can speak the Americans' language."

He laughed. He was a small man and very old. His half-hooded eyes were filmy and red and what teeth he had were yellow and broken. There was white stubble on his face and he was dirty, constantly wiping saliva from his mouth with his sleeve. He spoke rapidly in a strange dialect, his hands and feet never still.

"What good are words? We need noises, animal noises. I need you to sound like a dog." He laughed. "Can you sound like an American dog?"

There were four other women in the small dirty room, bare except for the bench on which they were sitting. They looked up when she came up the stairs but turned away when they saw she was not a customer.

"Let me see you," the Chinaman said shrilly.

He ripped her gown away. When he jerked two fingers inside her, he laughed. "The Americans are going to hurt you. You'll make noises enough." He ran his hands over her back, caressing her buttocks.

"Suck me," he said.

She backed away. The other women looked up with faint interest.

"Then leave. What do you think a whore does?"

She bowed her head and made no movement, then she dropped to her knees before him.

"Think of what is done in these times," he said in a bored voice. "What does it matter what you do, daughter?"

She opened her eyes on him inches in front of her. The other women watched with mild curiosity, but when she took him in her mouth, they lost interest and looked away.

"You are no good," he said, and withdrew. "But they pay to have you do it, not for how you do it. For the Americans, how is never important."

27

He brought her to the next room where there were fifteen cubicles partitioned by hanging sheets, each with a cot. He pointed. "That is yours. Make noises, grunt, moan, and move quickly so they will come quickly. Your work is easy."

He pointed to a wash basin in the corner. "Wash the men before and yourself afterwards. If you get a disease or pregnant, you must leave. I pay for each man, three hundred piaster, and I give you food."

Then he took her to the waiting room and she sat on the bench. No one spoke to her. She pulled her torn clothes about her and huddled back against the wall, so ashamed and afraid that she could not raise her eyes. What would the men do to her? What would become of her? Then she thought of her mother and she began to weep.

A hand pressed on her arm and she looked up into the eyes of a woman no older than herself. Her face was as heavily made up and as lifeless as a Kabuki player's. The hand patting her seemed to have a separate, feeble existence, the last expression of an expiring soul.

Sung bowed her head; the hand continued softly stroking, and she fell asleep, but dreams plagued her—her butchered father, the rats, the soldiers, the baby—and she jerked awake.

Finally she rested her head back and closed her mind to it all. Each time a thought or memory entered her mind, she burned it away. That is how to survive: she would become like the woman beside her, a body with only flickering movements and no thoughts.

She woke to charged tension in the room; it was dark and the Chinaman came in, went to the window, then shuffled to the head of the stairs and looked down.

Then she heard shouting and laughter in the courtyard and the women moved closer together, their faces tightening.

In a moment four men burst in, followed by the China-man. They were larger and noisier men than Sung had ever seen, laughing and joking among themselves. One put his arm around the Chinaman. "How much fucky-fucky, papa-san?"

"One thousand piaster." He pointed to Sung. "Virgin two thousand."

They howled with laughter. "There ain't no virgins in Vietnam. The whole country's been fucked."

"You gotta be shittin' us, papa-san. Two thousand P for a cunt?"

The women drew closer, understanding nothing.

"Five hundred P, papa-san. Five hundred."

The Chinaman shook his head violently. "One thousand, GI, one thousand. Number-one girls. Suck good. Number-one suck."

"All right. All right." They chose women and were led off through the beaded curtain.

Sung heard the tap from the basin, unintelligible talk and laughter, then the noises of coupling and cries from the women. "Too big, GI. You fuck good. You number one, GI."

The girls on the bench settled back, oblivious to the next room, and when the other girls came back out, the Chinaman gave each a bead.

Later another group of soldiers came in and one chose Sung. She did not look up at him, never saw him above the chest. She washed him, then took him to her cot. She dropped her gown and closed her eyes tightly when he moved over her. She tried to blank her mind, but the pain was intense, a terrible stabbing, and in her mind she saw the soldiers. She turned and twisted under him, which he mistook for passion, and he did not notice when she began to cry.

When spent, he lay on her, crushing her until finally she squirmed away and ran off to douche herself. When she came out, the Chinaman gave her a bead. She had no place to put it, so she clenched it in her fist, so tightly she could not feel it.

Later, Vietnamese soldiers came and one chose her. He did not speak to her, merely forced her mouth over him as he lay on the bed and worked her head up and down. His movements made her gag, and when he came in her mouth, she choked and heaved up on the bed. He laughed and dressed, then swaggered into the other room.

That night, as she slumped against the bench, a hand took hers. She whimpered and drew away, but the hand forced hers open and placed a small rag doll in it. The doll had no clothes, and stuffing popped out from where the button eyes had been.

She never knew who gave her the doll, maybe the woman who had stroked her arm, but she never asked and soon that woman disappeared. Another took her place, then she left, and others came and went, but she kept the doll, stroking it while she sat on the bench, and carefully placed it under her cot when she was with a soldier—one of a hundred thousand whores in the city, any man's woman for fifteen minutes and five dollars.

The Chinaman gave her heroin the second week, after three soldiers paid five thousand piasters to have her at once. They hurt her as much as the soldiers in the courtyard, and when they left she could not move. The Chinaman gave her heroin; she liked it, feeling freed and eased, and soon she was giving all her money back to him. She would lie all day in a dream state, wandering out to the other room only in the afternoon, no longer caring what happened to her, never thinking long enough to care, never wanting to think, just stroking the doll that brought the faintest memory of camphor.

CHAPTER

• 3 •

Luke Bishop had never known what fear was before this. It hurt so much that he thought he might throw up. He felt as though a great hand had reached into the pit of his belly and squeezed, making him want to double over, but he could not move and knew his bowels would give if he did.

The chopper banked sharply, and through the open doors he saw the jungle below.

A heavy artillery barrage had prepped the area because the landing zone was expected to be hot; an enemy battalion had been sighted. The choppers were going to set them down on higher ground, a ridge now smoldering from the fires set by the shelling.

To him, the jungle below seemed a green dragon from whose mouth fire and smoke belched.

This was his first insert, only his sixth day in combat, and he could not catch his breath. Only through a great force of will was he able to stretch out his legs and lean back against the vibrating hull in an effort to calm himself. He could not show his fear to his men.

Not even a week, he thought, exactly as long as Keith Sterne had lasted, the first officer in his class killed, a bullet in the brain in his first insert too.

"They might as well have shot the dumb bastard at OCS and saved the government the airfare," someone had joked when the word came that Sterne's body was on its way back before most of the class even got to Vietnam.

And they'd joke about him too, Luke Bishop knew, thinking of the disgrace, worse than the prospect of death. Perhaps dishonor was worse than death, but being a joke surely was: Hear about Luke, the dipshit never even fired his rifle.

Surely his men could see him shaking; they must know how afraid he was.

Only one other man in the platoon had not seen combat, Scott Sutherland, but he was just a rifleman, and no one expected anything of him; he was not going to have to make decisions, or call in air strikes and artillery, or medevacs.

Bishop glanced at Sutherland to see if he was afraid too. Sutherland was nineteen, blond and lean, with green eyes as piercing as a cat's. He had shadowed Ron Mead since put in his squad; now he was sitting beside Mead, unsuccessfully attempting to copy his composure, but Sutherland's darting eyes and clenched fist gave him away. Yes, Sutherland was afraid.

But Mead appeared to be sleeping, and from what Bishop had heard of him, he might well be. Mead was a hero, personally decorated by President Johnson at Cam Ranh Bay. Even the platoon's gunnery sergeant, Anthony Brock, seemed intimidated by him, and Brock, with three ex-wives, Korea, and a previous tour in Vietnam behind him, was not a man easily intimidated.

Bishop studied Mead to see if his nonchalance was genuine. He was a poster Marine, tall and muscular, with sharp, strong features, but lacking, as far as Bishop could tell, any friendliness, or sense of camaraderie. Bishop since sophomore year had been a starting halfback at Oklahoma and felt he had spent his life on football fields and in locker rooms, yet he had never encountered anyone like Mead. In the week he had had the platoon, Bishop had not seen Mead talk to anyone. He stayed completely to himself; and to Bishop he had said only "yes sir" and "no sir."

"Does he ever speak?" Bishop asked Brock.

"Not much. He does what he's told, doesn't ask questions,

and has the brains and balls of a buffalo; that's all there is to know about him."

"And you don't like him."

Brock considered the question. "I don't trust him. I think he likes the killing; people like that bother me."

Though only twenty, Mead seemed older than the other men, who treated him with wary deference. Bishop knew that to win over his platoon, the only person he had to impress was Mead, but he wondered if he would be able to do that.

Suddenly Mead opened his eyes directly on Bishop, as if he had known all along that he was being watched. When Bishop did not avert his glance, Mead yawned and closed his eyes again.

Bishop turned to stare out the open doors. For him, the jungle below was an inevitable extension of the football field in Oklahoma, the Marines foreordained, the war inescapable because from where he came, patriotism was not acquired, but genetic. Not good enough for the pros, he joined the Marines because he believed in his country, and what it said was right. His beliefs were so simplistic that even he joked about being such a dumb jock, and he understood when a girl he thought of marrying broke off the relationship because of politics.

After one fight she yelled at him, "I can't fuck a Nazi." Then they both laughed, because he was not that at all, and both knew it. And they remained good friends, because no one could dislike Luke Bishop. He was just gung ho: "What do you want to do, shoot me because I'm a patriot?" he asked her.

"I don't, but someone probably will, you stupid animal," she had said.

And there they were in that jungle, just waiting to shoot him.

Suddenly he felt everyone staring at him.

They were, he realized, and Landis, his radio operator, next to him, was saying something, but he couldn't hear over the roar of the chopper. Then Brock signaled him, tapping his head and pointing to his crotch.

Bishop looked down to check his fly, then realized that was crazy—who would care about such a thing? Finally Landis tapped Bishop's helmet, reached over and grabbed his crotch tightly, and made the gesture of a bullet coming up from below.

Bishop looked about and saw everyone sitting on his helmet, except for himself and Sutherland, and they were all laughing.

Sheepishly he took off his helmet and sat on it.

The chopper plunged suddenly and his stomach bottomed out. They were going in.

Mead sat straighter but did not open his eyes. The others all stared out the doors, fully armed, grim-faced warriors ready to meet the battle, but their harsh appearance was belied by the fear and innocence in their eyes.

He had not expected his men to be so young. They were boys, high school boys. Though only twenty-two he felt a generation older. They shouldn't be so young, he thought. They don't even know why they're here. Christ, he thought, and laughed, thinking of Kathy who stopped fucking him, they're even dumber than I am.

Then Mead's eyes were on him, a quizzical look, wondering why a man making his first combat insertion was smiling.

Machine gun fire erupted from the chopper. The hull shook so violently that Bishop thought it would come apart.

The jungle mouth yawned wider. Men frantically unhitched their seat belts and stood, clutching the overhead straps as the chopper rocked and tossed.

All Bishop could hear was machine gun fire and the roaring engine.

The chopper hovered just off the ground. Men raced toward the open hatch, and Bishop jumped, the fourth man out.

He followed those charging toward the treeline, their rifles firing on automatic. He held his own hip-level and fired, dodging and weaving toward the trees, no thought in his head.

It was over before he understood what had happened. The

choppers were gone, everything was quiet, and Landis crouched beside him, holding out the radio handset.

When Bishop did not seem to know what to do with it, Landis said, as though to an obtuse child, "You should call the CO and tell him the LZ is secure."

Jesus, thought Bishop, anybody could run this platoon better.

He radioed the company commander, then signaled his squad leaders to move out, and he watched in minor amazement as his men fanned out through the jungle as ordered.

His relief at finding no resistance bordered on elation, but at the same time he wished the LZ had been hot, for now he still had to undergo his first firefight; he was still untested.

The first hour, the platoon crept its way through the brush, each man probing with his rifle, no sound at all except for the buzz of insects and the crush of foliage. There was no sign of the enemy.

The second hour, Bishop spread the squads farther apart and quickened the pace. The third hour he placed them in a classic V formation, two squads forward, one back, and the platoon traversed the ridge at a heightened pace, reaching the day's objective, a rise overlooking the upper tip of the A Shau Valley near the Laotian border, about twenty miles from the Demilitarized Zone, by noon. Below, the valley shimmered like green foil, the jungle canopy reflecting the blinding sun.

"That's where they are," said Brock, standing beside him. "Sending a platoon down there would be like tossing us naked pussy."

"It's not our mission to go down there," Bishop said.

"Not today, but they'll send us soon enough." Brock gestured to the men who had set themselves in a defensive position without being told. "We ought to stop for chow, Lieutenant. Four hours of humping is a long time." He said it with slight disapproval, but also with a hint of respect, and surprise that Bishop could have managed his first long insert with such ease, seemingly less affected by the heat and strain than anyone else.

Bishop took off his helmet and ran his hand through his closely cropped hair. "Gunny, this is only my sixth day—I don't know what the hell I'm doing. You gotta tell me things. Jesus, I'll listen." He grinned, an ingenuous smile that won even Brock. "I was scared shitless coming in on that LZ. You see me making a mistake, let me know."

"Don't worry—fuck up, Lieutenant, and I'll let you know in a big hurry."

Brock yelled at the men to take a break; they immediately dropped down, shedding helmets, flak jackets, rifles, and drank greedily from their canteens.

Brock turned back to Bishop. He tossed his own gear down and wiped sweat from his face. He was thirty-five, a hard man who had fought in two wars, and right now, though he was trying to hide it, he felt what he was—twice as old as some of his men. He was of medium height but powerfully built, with finely chiseled features marred only by the glow of harshness that emanated from him.

He could tell that the new officer was wary of him, and now he said in appeasement, "Lieutenant, *everyone* was scared shitless."

"Mead wasn't. I think he was asleep."

"That's because Mead doesn't care if he gets killed. He's been here too long—he's just looking for a bullet. You better get rid of him soon. I seen guys like Mead before. They get to be a hero, then they gotta live up to it every time. We had a guy like that in the unit a while back—Bobby Yates—big hero, had a Silver Star and was shooting for a Navy Cross or the Congressional Medal. Stupid motherfucker."

"What happened to him?" Bishop asked, not really wanting to hear casualty stories on his first mission.

Brock just shook his head and flicked an ash from his cigarette. He pointed to it on the ground. "See that ash—that's more than went back in the coffin."

He took a deep drag on the cigarette. "It only ends one way. And with Mead it's worse because he doesn't want to go home; he doesn't have anything to go home to."

Brock stroked the barrel of his rifle and pointed it to the jungle below. Bishop followed his aim. The jungle was mysterious and wonderful, alive and beckoning.

"How do you go back to the farm after that?" Brock asked.

He turned to Bishop and smiled. "War is like my first wife, Lieutenant—a real bitch, but God could she stiffen your dick."

He laid the rifle down and walked off.

Bishop was about to lie back when his radio operator suddenly appeared. He carried the radio and the batteries because he was the strongest man in the unit, having dropped out of school after the ninth grade to—from what Bishop could see of him—spend all his time working out in a gym. He had incredible muscular development, and in addition to the burden of the radio, he had to suffer the gibes of the other men who told him that everybody knew all bodybuilders were homosexual.

Matt Landis thrust the radio handset out to Bishop and said in minor admonishment, "Sit rep time, Lieutenant. You gotta keep the CO informed of where we are and what we're doing."

After radioing in, Bishop checked his men, clustered in four-man fireteams in a defensive perimeter. Bishop spent a moment with each group asking how they were and answering questions.

"You could tell we were cherries, Sutherland," Bishop said when he joined his group. "Didn't even know enough to protect our balls."

Bishop saw that even Mead smiled faintly at the self-deprecation.

"The gooks couldn't have hit a target that small on Sutherland," one joked.

"I don't think they could have hit mine either," Bishop said. "They were up in my throat."

He left them laughing and returned to where he had dropped his pack. He was opening a can of C rations when Brock crossed to him and took them out of his hands.

"Never eat apricots in the field, Lieutenant."

Though Bishop had heard the superstition, he did not believe Brock would give it credence.

"Every one of the last eight guys who ate apricots got zapped. I told Lieutenant Taggert the week before you came

37

not to eat them. He laughed at me. Next day when we got hit, we couldn't find enough of him to put in an envelope, let alone a body bag."

Then he started one of his favorite refrains: "I know you could give me ten good college reasons why it ain't so. I'm just a dumb grunt who never even finished high school; I seen my records—I got a GCT intelligence score of sixty-two, which probably means I'm a certified moron, but I seen what I seen, and that's a lot.

"I'm thirty-five, old enough to be these guys' father. I was in Korea, and this is my second time here. I spent more time in combat than you did in college. I was chasing nooky in Pusan while you were playing with rubber duckies. And this is what I learned"—he flung the can into the valley—"don't eat apricots."

He crouched next to Bishop. "The guys are watching you carefully, Lieutenant. Our lives are in your hands—you fuck up and we die; you get the coordinates wrong, or don't know exactly where we are when you call in air or artillery, we get blown away. You send us up the wrong ridge, or miscalculate that map, we're dead. So far the guys think you may be all right—you made your first insert and nothing happened. You might be lucky, and that's better than being God. And they seen you hump four hours without even sweating, and they watched you check everybody before you ate your chow, and you talked with them and made them laugh. So far you done real good. All you gotta do is keep it up so that we all get home safely."

He stood up. "I'm holding you personally responsible for my ass, Lieutenant. So don't eat no fucking apricots."

He walked away, then turned. "Sir."

For another two hours the platoon worked through the jungle brush without a sign of the enemy. A battalion of six hundred could not have vanished without a trace, so Bishop knew the intelligence must have been wrong.

Gradually Bishop relaxed. His men moved expertly, and he was having no problems controlling them, or following the map. He knew that war was ninety percent boredom, days and weeks of patrols like this, sloughing through jungle without enemy contact. He knew too the dangers of fatigue and carelessness, and he realized that his men should not go much farther.

The platoon was moving in V formation, two squads forward on the left and right slopes of the ridge.

Suddenly the radio crackled and Landis gave him the handset.

"Bravo One, got something here you should check."

"That's Mead," Landis said unnecessarily.

Bishop radioed the other squads to set in and he moved up to the left flank.

Though he moved as stealthily as he could, Bishop felt as though he were riding an elephant through the brush. He cringed at his own noise and would have walked past Mead had the corporal not grabbed his trouser leg and pulled him down.

Mead pointed into the foliage before them. Bishop stared but saw nothing. Mead pointed again, and still Bishop did not see anything. Mead shaped a mound with his hands, then drew his finger across it. Bishop knew he was telling him of an enemy ambush with a slit aperture, but though he strained his eyes, he could not see it.

Crouching together, their faces inches apart, Mead placed his hand on Bishop's shoulder, forcing him down. Though a powerful man over six feet, Bishop felt no match for him. Mead was in charge; he wanted Bishop to stay out of this.

Mead signaled Sutherland to cover them, then motioned the others in the fireteam to circle around the camouflaged bunker.

Mead crawled from cover beside Bishop and snaked toward the mound.

Two men, Coney and Frizzell, worked to the right of the ambush; a third, Dutton, was on the left. Only Mead was exposed, crawling directly toward the bunker.

Bishop barely breathed as Mead edged closer. Suddenly he saw Mead stop; he didn't move for a full minute, then he began to grope delicately in the heavy brush with his eyes closed, concentrating all sensation in his fingers. He pulled away his hands twice to wipe off sweat, then Bishop saw Mead find a wire, and another above it at knee height, and he severed them.

He crouched and moved behind the mound, signaling that he'd found an underground entrance.

As he unclipped a grenade from his flak jacket, an enemy soldier suddenly came out. He was smiling, as if he had just heard a joke, but when he saw Mead he froze. Then he reached for his rifle.

With no time to aim his own, Mead threw the grenade as hard as he could into the man's face and kicked him in the groin, knocking him backward into the bunker.

Mead dove for cover as the explosion rocked the jungle.

Two men jumped from a camouflaged hole in front of Sutherland. A third popped from a spider trap behind Dutton.

Sutherland brought his rifle to his shoulder and squeezed off a round at the nearest man. The second threw down his rifle and fell to the ground before him.

Bishop did not have a clear shot at the enemy soldier behind Dutton. He jumped up and yelled for him to duck. Dutton looked stunned, staring at Bishop, his weapon aimed at the man on the ground. Dutton looked at Bishop as if puzzled, seeing him wave frantically and bringing his rifle to his shoulder so that it was pointing at him. Dutton's head tilted quizzically, knowing that the lieutenant was not going to shoot him, but still not understanding. Then Dutton heard the click behind him. He whirled, his eyes releasing the grieved, almost apologetic look on Bishop's face. He spun into the barrel of the rifle with no chance to aim his own as a burst threw him to the ground.

When Dutton collapsed, Bishop fired. The bullets caught the man in the back, and his rifle flew from his hands as he was slammed against a tree.

Mead raced to Dutton.

He dropped down beside him and knew immediately it was too late; blood seeped through his clothes. He looked at Dutton's face, saw the teeth bite through the lips and blood spurt from his mouth.

Mead stood.

Bishop could not move as he watched Mead walk to the enemy soldier on the ground. The man was on his knees, his

40

hands clasped behind his head, his eyes pleading quietly. Mead's face was expressionless.

Mead brought his rifle to his shoulder and leaned into it, the muzzle only inches from the man's head. The man stared into the barrel, then raised his eyes to Mead. Mead looked deeply into them and pulled the trigger.

The man's head exploded, splattering fragments of flesh, bone, and blood onto Mead's clothing and rifle.

Coney and Frizzell burst from the brush and froze, watching Mead shoot the man kneeling before him.

Bishop was the first to move. He ran to Dutton and tore at the clothing.

The bullets had entered one side, caught the kidneys, and exited in a massive wound. Dutton gasped for air and tried to form words, but only blood bubbled from his mouth.

Mead knelt with him and grabbed his hands. Dutton clutched them desperately, as if they alone could save him. His nails dug into Mead's hand, puncturing the skin, drawing blood, but Mead did not flinch.

Bishop tore open his first-aid kit. Dutton watched frantically. He half-raised himself, his eyes filling with fear, then he convulsed and fell back motionless.

The rest of the platoon broke from the brush.

Bishop stood slowly, clutching soaked bandages.

Sutherland dropped his rifle and walked to a tree and buried his head in his arms.

Still stunned, Bishop looked about to see the men staring at the bloody scene. Then he was filled with rage, for losing a man, at his own inability to save Dutton, and at Mead.

"Spread out," he yelled. "Set up a perimeter."

Then he snarled at Landis, "Give me the radio."

He watched Mead as he gave a situation report.

Mead rolled the enemy corpses over, squatting to examine the one he had shot, then he looked back toward the underground bunker.

Brock stood beside Bishop, motioning Landis away.

"You okay, Lieutenant?"

Bishop nodded.

"There was nothing you could have done. Coney and

Frizzell said Dutton was in the way and they couldn't fire either without hitting him. That's how it usually is: it just happens—a guy steps on a mine, he takes a bullet. You can't blame yourself."

"I know. It was just so . . ."

"Fast."

Mead came up to them, his expression unchanged. "There's at least one more down that bunker, Lieutenant. None of these gooks is the one I threw the grenade at."

Bishop could not hold his anger. "How can you tell? The one you shot doesn't have a face anymore."

"The one in the bunker was older," Mead said evenly. "His teeth were betel stained."

Brock was incredulous. "You do dental checks before you kill people, Mead?"

Mead ignored him. "The guy I saw is still down there, Lieutenant. Maybe he's dead, maybe not, but he was much older, like an officer. Maybe there's a whole bunker complex under here."

Bishop looked to Brock.

"Drop a satchel charge," the sergeant advised. "You can't risk sending someone down there."

"But maybe this is what we've been looking for. They sent us out to find a battalion CP. We gotta check it."

"Then call for some tunnel rats, people who know what they're doing. Battalion has a team; they're the only ones qualified to go down there."

"It'll be dark before they get here."

Brock drew a deep breath. "Lieutenant, you give an order, and we gotta obey it, but I wouldn't order anyone down that hole." His eyes were a dark warning.

"You're telling me—"

"Nothing," Brock said.

Mead lit a cigarette and studied Bishop's face. "What he's not telling you, sir, is that if something happened to the guy you sent down there, his buddies would get you. And even if nothing happened, you would have scared everybody. They wouldn't trust you."

Mead let smoke seep from his mouth and he stared directly into Bishop's eyes. "They'd frag you, sir."

"Shut up, Mead," hissed Brock. "You're talking court-martial."

Mead didn't break his gaze. "I think he's a good officer; I'm trying to save his ass."

Bishop studied the incredibly hard eyes, then he looked about to his men, all watching quietly.

He drew a deep breath then took off his helmet and unfastened his web belt; he knew what he had to do. This was what he was here for.

"You got no business going down there, Lieutenant," Brock said.

Bishop checked his pistol and chambered a round. "It's this simple, Gunny—I'm an officer, it means something to me. I couldn't live with myself if I backed away from the first mission I got. I was told to locate an enemy CP. That's what I'm going to do."

"This isn't a fucking John Wayne movie, Lieutenant," Brock exploded, gesturing to the surrounding jungle. "All this is bullshit. This war is bullshit. Not one of these guys knows what it's about, and neither do I. Best I can figure, it's a game. We're *playing,* Lieutenant. It's cowboys and Indians for big kids. Dutton's dead. What did he die for? Not a fucking thing. It's not your fault he got killed. You haven't got to prove anything."

"It's not a game to me, Gunny, and I'm not trying to prove anything." Bishop started toward the bunker.

Mead blocked his way. He dropped his helmet and flak jacket and held out his hand. "Give me the pistol, I'll go."

Bishop tried to shove past him but Mead didn't move.

"Lieutenant, I can do it a lot better than you. You're the only one who can get us out of here—we don't even know where we are, and the gunny can't read a map any better than he could *War and Peace.* The gooks would nail us sure."

When Bishop did not move, Mead said, "I know you believe everything you said. Once I did too. So did the gunny. But it's best you stay up here."

He took the .45 pistol from Bishop and dropped into the bunker.

The cramped underground was damp and smelled of cordite. It was built like a little pillbox, the aperture giving a perfect line of fire on the only trail leading through the jungle. Though meant for several men, Mead had to bend uncomfortably because of the low ceiling, and when he found the tunnel, he wasn't sure his shoulders would fit through the passage.

The bunker was not a command post for there was neither radio nor communication wire leading to any other bunker. This was a listening post, an isolated bunker serving to warn the main unit of an approaching enemy. By now the larger force would have fled, or have had time to prepare for an assault. The men here had died protecting the main unit.

And Dutton?

Mead no longer gave him any thought. Born in Arkansas, the oldest son of sharecroppers, Mead joined the Marines after high school, not to fight for anything, but to get away—he didn't want to be a tenant farmer, and there were no other opportunities.

He came believing in the rhetoric, but belief died with his closest friend—his only friend, and after that he never opened himself up again. He understood the lieutenant and respected him for his belief, but the gunny was right, he knew—the war was bullshit. But so was Arkansas.

He became a hero his third week, when the platoon was ambushed. The others ran for cover but he charged the enemy, killing four, sending the rest fleeing.

He was put in for the Navy Cross and decorated at Cam Ranh Bay by President Johnson.

When he returned to the unit, he was sullen and never spoke of the honor. He seemed to resent the medal, isolated himself, and grew more bitter. He had no friends, and though everyone in the platoon wanted to like him, held him in awe, they were frightened of him. No one else would have entered this bunker.

Dropping to the ground, holding the pistol out in front of him, he started to crawl, his shoulders scraping against the tunnel walls. The tunnel floor was wet and dank. He dipped his hand in a pool of liquid and brought it to his nose; it was blood.

Then he heard breathing, labored and pained.

44

He crawled another twenty feet before he came to the man.

The tunnel branched, one passage running to the spider trap, the other to the concealed entrance where the two men had jumped out before Sutherland.

At the branch, propped against the wall facing him, was the enemy soldier. Mead could make out only the dark outline of the slumped figure, and his eyes, half-closed and tortured.

Mead knew he did not have a weapon; the rifle had been dropped at the bunker entrance.

Suddenly there was the slash of a match, then a burst of flame.

Mead closed his eyes against the blinding light. When the phosphorus burned down, he looked up.

The man held out the match, then he brought it close to his own features so Mead could see him.

It was a scene from a horror movie.

Shrapnel from the grenade had ripped his face and torn off his jaw. Blood spilled from the mouth and wounds.

Then the match went out.

Mead buried his face in the dirt.

Then the man struck another match.

Mead looked up. The man lowered the match to his chest, exposing metal-gouged flesh, and two gaping wounds from which blood bubbled, then was sucked back.

The match went out. The only noise was the man's labored breathing.

Then he spoke, a plea, and Mead understood.

"No," Mead moaned. "No."

The soldier spoke again, an agonized plea, more insistent. Then he struck another match and brought it to his face again. He was crying, and his eyes begged release.

"Oh, God," Mead cried. He could not shoot him in the tunnel; the noise would burst his own eardrums. But neither could he leave him to die like this.

The man, perhaps understanding, began to speak. The words were choked painfully, almost drowned in blood, but the tone was reassuring. Mead realized the man was praying.

Mead drew a deep breath and crawled to him. The soldier closed his eyes but continued to pray as Mead drew up to him.

"I'm sorry," Mead cried, closing his own eyes on his tears as his hands reached around the man's neck and squeezed.

The soldier did not resist.

Mead strangled him, his hands slipping for tighter grip in the slick blood.

As soon as the body went slack, Mead grabbed the pistol and clawed back through the tunnel.

His fingers dug into the dirt and his shoulders slammed against the tunnel walls.

When he reached the bunker, he scrambled up and burst into the jungle, crying out from the blinding light, throwing up his hands to shield his eyes.

He stood among them like a ghoul, his hands and face dripping blood.

The other men backed from him in horror.

He staggered toward Bishop.

"Jesus Christ," said Bishop, unable to move.

Mead stood before him, eyes unfocused, his breath gasping, holding out the pistol.

Bishop looked at the bloody hands, then to the face streaked with blood.

"It wasn't a CP, sir. There wasn't anything there except a dying gook."

No one spoke; they merely stared at him, standing limp in their midst, covered with blood.

Finally Bishop took the pistol, and without wiping it off, he put it in his holster.

"Okay, move out, V formation," he said. Then he radioed a report to the company commander and requested extraction because their location had been compromised and they could not risk the night surrounded by an enemy battalion.

After returning to base camp and briefing the company commander, Bishop requested that Mead be transferred.

"I don't know what happened in the bunker, but he has to be sent to the rear. The gunny is right, he's looking for a bullet."

"You sure, Luke? He's a good trooper, your best squad leader."

"Positive, sir. He's done his share; we owe him."

"No problem," said the captain. "He's overdue for rotation. Battalion has a quota for embassy-duty slots in Saigon. He looks the role, and has the medals—and you can't get more to the rear than that; send him out tomorrow."

He pointed to his map. "The rest of us are going here."

Bishop saw a circle drawn in a remote mountainous area: Khe Sanh.

The captain spat chewing tobacco against a sandbag. "It's going to be a long goddamn war, Lieutenant. You've been here a week, right? Just think, only fifty-five more to go."

Bishop sent for Mead and the two men walked to a little rise overlooking the perimeter. The night was cool and lit so brightly by stars that they could see the mountains rising over the plain.

Bishop reached for a handful of dirt and let it sift through his fingers. "I'm having you sent back tomorrow. You've been in the field too long." He laughed and threw the remaining dirt at the wire. "So have I. Six days has been plenty. But you've been here ten months. That's enough."

"I'm okay, Lieutenant."

Bishop shook his head. "You saved my ass today. Now I'm going to save yours. Tomorrow you're going to the rear. You're going to be an embassy guard in Saigon—hot chow, showers, pussy. I tried to volunteer, but it's not an officer billet."

"I don't want to go to Saigon, Lieutenant."

"I don't want to go to Khe Sanh, Corporal."

"Is it an order, sir?"

"Yep. I'm ordering you to eat hot chow, take a hot bath, get drunk, and get laid. You gonna frag me?"

Mead smiled. "I guess I can handle that." He was silent for a long time, then he said simply, almost a question, "Saigon."

But Bishop didn't hear. He was staring beyond the wire to the mountains, thinking of fifty-five more weeks.

47

CHAPTER

• 4 •

Bernard Lacouture darted across the street in front of the National Assembly in Saigon and studiously avoided a glance to the left, preferring to be hit by a pedicab than to gaze upon what he considered was the gray blight of the Marines' Memorial.

Safely reaching the opposite curb, he raised his eyes and let out a little sigh of happiness at the sight of the green-canopied terrace of the Continental Palace Hotel. He almost clapped his hands, such was his pleasure.

It was midmorning, the very best time, he thought, before it became too hot, and before the Americans arrived to ruin the day. Ten A.M. was a civilized hour, consequently unappealing to the Americans; he would have the entire terrace to himself—the ghastly "breakfasters" were gone, and the journalists had not sufficiently sobered up to stagger in for the even ghastlier "lunch." Lacouture shuddered at the word; it sounded like masticating jaws, wholly appropriate, of course, for the way Americans ate. *"Déjeuner"*—that was dining: "lunch"—that was eating.

Suddenly he was seized with anxiety, then wild depression—what if he was not alone? He envisioned pagan hordes, all speaking English, at every table.

The prospect was too awful: a gorgeous, cloudless day ruined. He held the railing for support and bowed his head

48

under the potential tragedy; then he gasped, casting out the barbarians on the terrace. His white trouser cuffs were splattered with mud, and his gleaming shoes streaked with —oh, God, he thought, let it be just mud.

He reeled at the base of the stairs.

Then Trinh was there, beckoning from the top of the stairs, in white jacket and black bow tie, a napkin on his arm. Everything was all right after all, he sighed in relief.

Lacouture stood straight, adjusted his white linen suit jacket, brushed at his trousers, and went up the stairs.

"Bonjour. Bonjour, Monsieur Lacouture," Trinh said with the exactly correct tone, striking the perfect balance between friendliness and deference.

The terrace was deserted, Lacouture saw; the horde had broken camp, and the next sack was not until noon. No journalist slumped over a table, no GI to be seen, no whore buzzing about.

"Bonjour, garçon," he said in more than greeting, in satisfaction and congratulation to Trinh: the empty terrace was a triumph; the day was saved.

A short man, immaculately groomed, and properly stout for a sixty-two-year-old Frenchman, Lacouture followed the even shorter, more immaculately groomed, stouter, older Vietnamese waiter past empty tables to his own at the back of the terrace, slightly removed from the others, and providing a complete view of the other tables and the street beyond.

Trinh held his chair, then disappeared, returning almost immediately bearing a silver tray. He set the basket of breads—one croissant, one brioche, and two wedges of toast—on the table, arranged little porcelain dishes of butter and jam, and poured strong French morning coffee into a large cup.

Lacouture sipped while Trinh waited as a sommelier might; this was not coffee served to the Americans, only to the regular diners from the nearby French embassy, a dwindling group, a very few high-ranking Vietnamese who had served under the colonial power, and to Lacouture.

Lacouture closed his eyes and sighed; the chicory blend was perfect. *"Bien. Très bien,"* he murmured.

Trinh bowed and left the coffeepot on the table.

It was going to be a wonderful day, Lacouture thought: nothing could go wrong now; even if it did, it would not matter, not after coffee and Trinh's ministrations.

Then Trinh reappeared with the silver tray, on it a selection of newspapers, and placed the tray on the table, not close enough to distract from the setting, but within easy reach. One did not have *petit déjeuner* to read the newspaper—the newspaper was there if one wanted to read it with *petit déjeuner*.

Lacouture did not glance at the papers: he admired the bursting brioche, the curve of the croissant, the snippet of bougainvillea vine on the table, its purple brilliance heightening the crispness of the linen and the luster of the silverware. And he savored the coolness of the terrace, almost mosquelike with its pillars and arabesque tiles.

Soothed and fortified, he could now look beyond the terrace to the frenetic life from which he had found momentary refuge, for he believed that just as one requires the heat of hell to appreciate the coolness of sanctity, so he needed to step onto the terrace to savor the saturnalia that was Saigon.

He loved Saigon; sitting here, raised slightly above the street in pampered respite, he shivered with pleasure and excitement for his city.

For him, Saigon was an exquisite *fleur du mal* whose overripe ovary burst with seed, its odoriferous scent heavy and soporific. It was a grotesque carousel—carnal and cruel and brutal: urchins and beggars, whores and amputees, a reeking, cankerous carnival of freaks pitched on garbage-littered, excrement-rotting ground, a dizzying, pungent charnel, intoxicatingly rancid, his wormy, writhing, lice-ridden city—the grave, teeming and alive.

He broke a wedge of toast, lathered it with butter and plum jam. He popped it in his mouth, chewed delicately, and wriggled the crumbs from his fingers.

Then he chose a newspaper from the tray.

The papers, all French, were weeks old, the news stale, the great crises long decided. He read with interest, amusement, and detachment, knowing that the resolution, so important on the page, was of no consequence whatsoever.

He loved old newspapers. For him it was death in print, a yellowing, crinkling, disposable tombstone: names and dates, a few squiggles—pretentious, momentous, fateful—ephemeral and destined for the gutter, torn, tattered, shit- and piss-stained.

He finished the wedge of toast and dabbed his mouth with his napkin, then gazed with expectancy toward the street. Who was going to come by today? he wondered. He sat, a patient, appreciative audience for whatever spectacle the city offered.

And there, as on cue, came Father Dourmant. Oh, wonderful, thought Bernard Lacouture. He wanted to call out *"Allô, allô"* to his dear, dear friend Father Dourmant.

The gaunt, tall, white-haired priest, sensing perhaps the intensity, glanced toward the terrace, and seeing Lacouture, shuddered visibly and looked away, striding to the corner, turning right.

Going where? Lacouture wondered. Certainly not to the cathedral up the street, since the Jesuit resolutely refused to cross the threshold after Rome had appointed President Diem's older brother an archbishop.

Lacouture missed the Diems: while it lasted, it had been a wonderful little tent show in the carnival—Diem, Madame Nhu, the archbishop, roasting Buddhists on every street corner. The show had turned tawdry after the Diems. He found no one amusing anymore. All the Minhs—big, little, and otherwise—Thieu, the Kys, were only paltry substitutes, though at one time he had had some hopes for the Kys, with their rhinestone sunglasses and matching flight suits, zippers, and gleaming buttons. Alas, Ky was too stupid, and she, despite her surgically rounded eyes and garish makeup, was only a little neutered gecko compared to the wondrous dragon lady—"Buddhist barbecues" indeed, he remembered with delight. Dear Madame Nhu, come back! We need you!

"I can't imagine why you're so upset with his eminence, the archbishop," Lacouture had told Father Dourmant back when they were on speaking terms. "It's not as if what the Vatican did was new; they've been selling indulgences for centuries, along with red hats, masses, and novenas, bartering heaven and hell, creating a celestial bourse with purgatory—what's a little archdiocese in Indochina? You're just being obstreperous—go kiss his ring and stop being petulant."

He loved Father Dourmant: such a good man, a true saint. It was a source of endless enjoyment to Lacouture to watch the priest's vain struggles. There were few pleasures for him as consistent and gratifying as observing this selfless man being thwarted, defeated, and humiliated at every turn. There was nothing wrong with good triumphant, Lacouture reasoned, only that it was so tedious: the trouble with goodness was that it simply was not amusing.

He told Father Dourmant that "not only would it be better to reign in hell than serve in heaven, but even if one merely has a gallery seat in the audience, surely the spectacle in hell would be more entertaining."

"Doubtless you'll have a box seat in the inferno," Father Dourmant had answered.

Box seat indeed! Lacouture raised his coffee cup to toast the disappearing priest. Probably the poor Jesuit was returning from another unsuccessful attempt to get money from the French embassy for the orphanage and clinic, Lacouture reasoned.

The prospect of getting anything from the French embassy made him giggle; only Father Dourmant would think it possible and relentlessly fling himself on that broken, dull sword.

No! he almost cried aloud: the Americans think it possible too. After all, weren't they paying Sûreté Générale for information? France, having lost an empire, its army totally defeated, its informers wholly discredited and unreliable—of course, the CIA would pay for their expertise. He clapped his hands: the dumb teaching the dumber; oh, exquisite!

Lacouture knew everybody at the French embassy, all Sûreté's spies, all their informers, and he knew all the American spies, and all their informers, and the Vietnamese government's Special Branch, their spies and informers, all the Viet Cong, and all the Chinese too.

He knew everyone in Saigon; he was a matchmaker, connecting the right man to the right information, for a price corresponding to value and ability to pay. He was the black market for information—any bauble or bead, any gem or trinket, a stick of gum or refrigerator of information—he had anything anyone wanted.

Unencumbered by country, duty, or principles, motivated only by amusement, and guided by a pragmatic, unerring sense of self-preservation, he was the conduit for all spies and informers, the holder of all information, the one indispensable link in the tatty, linkless chain.

Lacouture was born in 1904 in Saigon during the reign of the bizarre puppet emperor Tahn Thai, soon declared insane by the French and replaced by his seven-year-old son.

Lacouture's father, the youngest son of a wealthy shipping family in Marseille, brought the family enterprise to Indochina in 1882. He also brought his wife, who, unlike other French wives, found everything in the exotic land agreeable. Their colonial life was unbridled license and luxurious indulgence, unrestrained by any convention— moral, practical, or financial.

Reared with pleasure as the only sensible pursuit, and in a place where abnormality was a convention, Lacouture found the restrictions and conformities of religion, country, and society impossible.

Moreover, when he was sent to Paris for schooling after World War I, Europeans bored him with their affectations and ennui, and he returned to Indochina as soon as his education was completed.

Europe was lifeless for him, but Indochina throbbed; Saigon blossomed and blossomed, never even taking time to renew, simply adding more colorful foliage. The Japanese had come and gone, his own countrymen were for the most part gone, but now the Americans were here, bringing new excitement and challenge—and unfortunately themselves with their boorish behavior to the Continental Palace, but he knew there had to be trade-offs. Besides, there were ways around such inconveniences—he merely rearranged his schedule to avoid Americans.

His inconvenience was minor compared to what he felt the Americans brought—priceless time. They would give him five more years, until 1972, he reasoned. By then he would be nearly seventy, and ready for retirement in Nice or Antibes. He doubted the Americans could last beyond 1972, but surely they could manage until then. However, he was hedging his bet by transferring money out of the country: the Americans were just not that reliable; they were too excitable and adolescent. They didn't know anything about seduction, only rutting, just as they didn't know about dining, only eating.

But, he thought fondly, the dear Americans gave him time. He knew he would not survive the communists. They were exact and dogmatic and principled. They were fanatics, ruthless and uncompromising—perfectly stupid, absolutely blind, and utterly deadly. And worst of all—boring.

He heaved a deep sigh. His lovely, lovely Saigon would wither and die; there would be no fun and no amusements. He brightened: he would go to the Côte d'Azur. The Americans would go home. But where would poor Father Dourmant go? What would happen to all those orphans?

Father Dourmant was as old as himself. Perhaps he would offer to take him with him to Nice. Yes, he decided; they could sit together under blankets and wraps and reminisce. Father Dourmant was not boring or self-righteous. And the stories he could tell after forty years in Vietnam! But Father Dourmant would have to promise never to mention that Teresa Hawthorne woman—there was a limit! Better the communists, Lacouture thought, than having to listen to stories of the sainted Teresa with her blessed GI orphans.

When he first heard of her, an American ex-nun in Saigon, Lacouture had great expectations; surely this would be an amusing person. Supposedly she was working for something called the Pearl Buck Foundation, an organization for helping the illegitimate children of oriental women and American servicemen.

He believed it a front, of course: that anyone could care about the bastard children of American GIs and Asian whores passed beyond belief into fantasy. Then he learned it was true, but still he held out hope that Teresa Hawthorne was really a CIA agent or a nymphomaniac or had some ulterior purpose, but alas it seemed that the whole disgusting affair—his mind always conjured little Asian babies emerging from slop buckets of sperm—was nauseatingly, boringly true.

"Ah," Lacouture cried aloud at the sight of Bui Cao Kim, by whom he could set his watch, and who had arrived to save him from further thoughts about Teresa Hawthorne.

Though no one was on the terrace except for Lacouture, and though Kim came every morning at this hour, the small, wrinkled Vietnamese looked about furtively before darting to Lacouture's table.

Lacouture called him The Fly, for Bui Cao Kim was everywhere—in every alley, on every wall, thriving on manure and garbage, dipping his feelers and legs in it, then flying off with the little bits and pieces of filth, bringing them to Lacouture, who sorted, cleaned, and polished them, then sold them as nuggets.

Their bond was need and years of familiarity that nearly bordered on trust.

Kim drew nervously to the table and placed a dirty piece of paper, painstakingly written in Japanese characters, before Lacouture. Not deigning to touch it, Lacouture bent forward and read the script.

Kim had learned Japanese while a prisoner from 1940 to 1945; he took great pride in this ability and was almost sorry the Japanese were gone. They were no worse than the French, and he was too old and tired to learn English. Now he had no one with whom to use his Japanese except Lacouture; it was their secret code.

Lacouture's Japanese was strictly a business practicality, as was his English. Forty years ago when he saw the Japanese emerging as the dominant Asian power, he learned their language. Then, when the United States began to underwrite the French war in Indochina, Lacouture knew it would only be a matter of time before the Americans replaced the French. If they were willing to send *money,* they certainly weren't going to quibble about sending soldiers. Anticipating the Americans' coming, he learned their language. The practicality was also self-serving—by learning English, he would not have to listen to them mutilate French.

Yet, to his horror, some Americans insisted on speaking French, so proud were they of what they had learned in universities, or "abroad," as they termed the civilized world.

Lacouture found that the higher-echelon CIA were the worst offenders: schooled at the best American universities, they flaunted their sophistication. The amusing but thoroughly obnoxious CIA chieftain, Wilson Abbot Lord, was the perfect example. Lacouture had almost stopped meeting with him because of Lord's French. The man knew the words, even the grammar was proper, but the noise! Doubtless one could hammer out the "Ode to Joy" on an anvil and get all the notes right, but think of the din.

Yet even he was better than his protégé, Jeffrey Gibbon, who looked to Lacouture as if he had tumbled out of a vapid Hollywood movie, what with his blocked, chiseled-out-of-granite features, and carefully tousled blond hair. He was absolutely beautiful, Lacouture thought, but in the glistening, cold way a cobra is—one could admire, but one wouldn't think of touching.

It was right here, Lacouture remembered, at this very table where Gibbon had delivered the line, perhaps the only one that had ever left Lacouture speechless.

Gibbon had been speaking, his mouth doing such strange things that Lacouture could not take his eyes off the lips and teeth and tongue, all twisting and contorting in an obscene mash.

"I love French," Gibbon had said. "It's so wet and soft and fleshy. It reminds me of a cunt."

Lacouture had rattled his cup so badly that he spilled coffee on himself. Despite Gibbon's beauty, Lacouture would never forgive him, he thought.

Lacouture bent closer over Kim's yellowed, grimy sheet of paper; it looked as if it had been pulped from cholera. The characters were remarkably fine, calligraphy Emperor Hirohito would have esteemed, but they were all wrong and misplaced, as if a dyslexic artist had done the work—the trees were in the sky, the man was upside down.

But Lacouture made out the meaning: more Viet Cong infiltration and the location of several weapons caches; the South Vietnamese were appointing General Tran as Saigon area commander; the North Vietnamese commander General Khanh was seriously ill with dysentery.

Wonderful nuggets, thought Lacouture; how did Kim do it? He reached for his wallet and dropped four five-hundred-piaster notes on the paper.

Kim put out his hand after the second note; but then, as the notes continued, withdrew it in surprise bordering on alarm.

Lacouture was moved to generosity today; it was a gorgeous day, everything was right, and he was happy.

Kim bowed slightly, thanking him in Japanese. Lacouture bowed too in dismissal.

Kim stuffed the notes in his trousers but carefully folded the paper he had labored over and put it in his shirt pocket; then he nodded another bow and left.

The information on the arms caches alone was worth ten times what he gave Kim, but the valuable news was about General Tran. Tran was an honest, competent, and courageous soldier—the last person one would expect President Thieu to appoint. What was happening? Of course, he thought, it wouldn't make any difference if Alexander the Great were appointed, the disaster could not be averted. Still, competency could at best lead to a coup.

And General Khanh ill? he mused. That was significant, and highly marketable—all he had to do now was match the information to the buyer.

Perhaps he would have a little cognac in celebration, he decided; he rarely indulged himself so early, but today was special. He looked up to signal Trinh.

No! he gasped. Trinh was leading a soldier to a nearby table.

It can't happen, thought Lacouture, and he nearly stood to shoo them away with his napkin.

Oh, wretched day, he thought, almost in tears. What was an American soldier doing here at this hour? He'd be loud and insulting and demanding.

And he'd speak English. Lacouture wanted to stamp his foot. The man had no right to ruin his day like this. How could Trinh allow this? Oh, wretched little gook!

The American chose a table only three from Lacouture, looking away from the street, so that the two faced one another, and he gave a curt but polite nod to Lacouture as he sat.

He had a face that seemed familiar, Lacouture thought. His features were handsome, but not movie star quality like the CIA Gibbon's, nor were they particularly masculine. He looks, Lacouture decided, like an extremely attractive big baby, and the closely cropped blond hair enhanced the effect.

How odd; a big baby in a crisp, sharp uniform with an utterly comfortable military manner, as though he were born in the uniform.

But what was he doing here at this hour? Military men never came this early; they would never dare leave their offices before noon. They manned their desks, turrets armed with paper and pens, until the senior officer departed, and they rarely had lunch at the Continental; officers went to the military hotel, the Brinks, for lunch, had hamburgers and two beers, and talked military talk and whores.

The war was getting dangerously out of control if officers were wandering into the Continental in midmorning, Lacouture thought. Such daring was out of place for a mere lieutenant colonel. What was wrong with this man?

Suddenly Lacouture realized that Trinh and the American officer were speaking French. He inclined his head to listen. Extraordinary! No American spoke French that well. There was an accent of course, but not disagreeable, merely indicating that the language was not the native one of the speaker.

Then it struck Lacouture. Of course the face was familiar! He had seen the image a thousand times, in newspapers, magazines, on posters, and in newsreels. This was the great war hero, the savior of France—Robert R. Romer.

Fool! he thought. Of course Romer's been dead twenty years. This was his son.

There could be no mistake; the face was too distinctive. After the Liberation, Romer was almost as celebrated as de Gaulle; every schoolchild knew about him. Not just a great general, he was intelligent and erudite, clever and outspoken, and he spoke excellent French.

It all rushed back to Lacouture, a true legend. Raging Romer, that is what he was called, Lacouture remembered —raging at his men, driving them beyond endurance to victory, raging against the Allied High Command, castigating his military and civilian superiors for timidity and incompetence, raging at the Germans, and raging at the Russians. He raged and stormed across Europe and at the war's end, wanted to press on to Moscow.

A towering figure who *had* to die after the last battle, his death had been so inconsequential that Lacouture could not even remember how he died—an accident of some kind.

Now here was his son, a soldier in another war; the mind boggled. How could anyone be Romer's son? Lacouture wondered. How could one survive such a reputation, or live up to the expectations that must accompany such a name? But to don the uniform, to enter the same arena from which the father had been carried in triumph—only a very strong, or a very weak man would do that; a most psychologically interesting one. An amusing man.

This was too exciting! He must leave; if he had a cognac, he would swoon.

He placed a five-hundred-piaster note on the table, dabbed his mouth with his napkin, brushed his clothes, then left, nodding slightly at Romer as he walked past.

What a curious, prissy little frog, thought Robert R. Romer III; not what you'd expect to see in the middle of the war, he mused. But then, nothing here was what he had expected; Saigon had turned out to be just another papermill.

Still, he knew it was better to have a desk here than in Washington. The real war would come soon enough—he would get his troop command one way or another, he knew. But he was going to have to fight for it; while he had patrons, senior officers who remembered and revered his father, he had enemies too, equally senior officers prejudiced against him because of his father.

He knew that he was not perceived as himself, but as the son of Romer. He had long accepted this; it was the primary fact in his life, and it did no good to rail against the incontrovertible.

Now his concern was to get out of the troop study he was on, and into a command billet.

General Arthur Shaw, once a battalion commander of Raging Romer's, a man who had patterned himself on the WWII hero, down to the pistols and cigars, had been sent to Vietnam to conduct a troop study to ascertain whether a few more divisions could win the war.

The conclusion—querying the military whether they wanted more men and munitions—was foregone. As General Shaw put it, "We're going to ask them if bears shit in the woods."

Shaw had brought Romer with him from his Pentagon staff job. They had been in Saigon a month, "documenting bear shit" according to Shaw, and now Romer was ready to move on.

For the moment, being Raging Romer's son prevented him from getting a battalion, but it also enabled him to walk out of MACV, Military Assistance Command, Vietnam, headquarters to sit here on the terrace of the Continental.

Something would turn up, he knew; or rather, he would turn up something. Until then, he would enjoy what he could of Saigon, and practice his French, which he had not spoken since his youth in France where he lived with his mother in her exalted widowhood.

Father Dourmant was so distracted by the sight of Lacouture that he stumbled over an amputee sprawled on the sidewalk.

"Damn," he said. He had been thinking for days of having coffee at the Continental, not as a reward even, just for sustenance. A woeful weakness, he knew, but what could it harm or matter? Quite a bit, apparently; it was too much for the Lord to grant even that small thing, so He had arranged for Lacouture to be there.

What was God doing? That was not a reminder of earthly

foolishness or even a reprimand—that was just being small, the priest thought.

God was very personal to Father Dourmant; he had long ago passed from theology and philosophy to intimacy, and the older he got, the more angry and exasperated he grew at the Lord's increasing pettiness and incompetence.

After forty years as a missionary, it was time to face facts—the failure of the world, all its misery, was either by design or ineptitude—either God meant it, or He couldn't help it. Knave or fool, one or the other. Forget free will, there was no such thing for most souls. Teresa Hawthorne's clinic wasn't filled with souls who had a choice; no one there had willed himself into despair.

He glanced back at the hotel furiously. Just a cup of coffee, that's all he wanted, but God knew full well that He could stage the Resurrection on the Continental terrace and that he, Father Dourmant, would not attend if Bernard Lacouture were there. It was just spite, that's all.

Turning the corner, the cathedral loomed before him.

He stopped and stared at it. Then he sighed. Maybe it was a reprimand after all: what did it matter who was archbishop? Did He really care about such matters? Or orphans or amputees either; those were all temporal vanities. And coffee? Father Dourmant hung his head.

He took a deep breath. He would go back to the clinic. For his lapse against his Lord, for penance, he would spend the evening at Teresa Hawthorne's clinic; working with unwed mothers and their syphilitic, retarded children would be his penance.

He sighed at his unworthiness: one night of penance, whereas she did it every day and night.

As exasperating as she was, as angry as he got with her, he knew she was probably a saint.

Then he was angry again; she didn't even believe in God; the damn woman was a heretic.

Another of God's spites on him, and in a fury about Teresa Hawthorne, the archbishop, and his cup of coffee, he stormed off, cassock flapping.

* * *

In his top-floor office in the Joint General Staff headquarters, General Huy Chi Tran, the newly appointed Saigon area commander, stared out the window at the U.S. military headquarters across the street.

He had only learned of his selection yesterday; it had to have come about at the insistence of the Americans, and over the wild objections of older, more senior generals, and probably President Thieu himself.

The door opened and his aide, whom he had told not to disturb him no matter who called, stepped in. "General Westmoreland would like to speak with you, sir."

Tran said patiently, knowing it was going to take a long time to change things, "Major, I said no one."

The aide was confused; he did not know what to say to Westmoreland's aide.

"Tell General Westmoreland that I shall return his call as soon as I can."

The aide hesitated, then saluted and left.

Tran was a tall, thick, muscular man with a hard, almost coarse face, yet with a manner inconsistent with his appearance; he was soft-spoken, almost gentle, with the courtly equanimity of a mandarin. His quiet air seemed incongruous to the rows and rows of battle ribbons on his uniform.

The general sat in his overstuffed chair, stretching out his legs, resting back his head, torn by both exhilaration and exhaustion.

Though he had wanted this command, he feared it. He was the only one who might possibly save his country, the best general, the only one who could rally the forces, he knew—but what if he should fail?

The struggle ahead was going to be overwhelming, not just against the communists, but against the corruption and cowardice of his own government. How could he rally an inexperienced army led by cowardly, unscrupulous officers to fight for a corrupt government?

Then there were the Americans to face; he knew their contempt—he was the general of the *gooks, slopes, dinks,* and *zipperheads.* They laughed at his army and his men; he hated their patronizing smugness, yet he was ashamed before them of his army's failures, and of the self-serving men who led his country.

But it was his country and he loved it. He wanted peace and freedom for his people. But how do you make others brave and honest?

The Americans talked so glibly about democracy and were so self-righteous, yet they were generous and sincere in their desire to help; their intentions were good, he knew, and they were a hundred times better than the communists.

But Americans did not understand the complexities. They did not understand history; they were as contemptuous of it as an untutored schoolboy. And their insistence on quantifying everything—totally ignoring subtleties and shadings —created a rigidity and naïveté inappropriate for dealing with the rest of the world.

They wanted to help, but they did not begin to understand—as if millions of people could forget a thousand years of Chinese domination, centuries of corrupt emperors and French exploiters, and then suddenly write a constitution, find an honest president, and immediately become free and democratic.

And now Westmoreland was on the phone. What's wrong with you gooks? Why can't you zipperheads get it together?

Westmoreland wanted to tell him what to do and where to deploy his men. Westmoreland didn't want to listen, and he certainly didn't want to hear about the enemy buildup or that Tran feared a major enemy offensive either at Christmas or during Tet. But still Tran would tell him.

He buzzed his aide. "Return the call to General Westmoreland, please."

Westmoreland would probably come to regret pushing his appointment, Tran felt, because he was going to tell him at every opportunity about the enemy buildup. He knew they were going to attack—but how does a zipperhead tell an American anything?

In a thatched hut in a remote village sixty miles from Saigon, the North Vietnamese general Xuan Tien Khanh lay on a straw pallet. He had to relieve himself again, but he did not think he could get up. Even the ignominy of lying in his own excrement finally failed to give him the strength to move.

Had it all come to this, he wondered, all the struggles, all the sacrifices of thirty years?

To come this close—to the outskirts of Saigon, this near victory—after the Japanese and the French brought him to such despair that he finally laughed at himself and his seriousness. He was taking this too personally, forgetting the historical overview.

Long ago, before joining with Ho Chi Minh to fight the French, he had been a history teacher; he was a scholarly man who even now could see matters from a historical perspective.

Lying on the pallet, he wondered how Moses felt when brought to the mountain to see the Promised Land, knowing that he would never himself enter it. Was he angry? Did he have any humor left with which to see the irony?

The years of his own deprivation had sapped him of humor and irony; these had been used up in the all-consuming struggle for independence.

Probably Moses lost his humor, he decided; he probably turned into an angry, cranky old man.

Confucius, the Buddha, Lao-tzu, they kept their humor, but they did not struggle for anything; they were not revolutionaries.

That would make for an interesting discussion with his oldest friend, General Vo Nguyen Giap, he thought: humor and irony in revolutionaries. He had known Giap since they were schoolboys in Hue forty years ago. They had studied together at the Lycée Albert Sarrault in Hanoi and had gotten their law degrees together from the University of Hanoi.

They both had humor then, he remembered. Giap lost his first, when his wife and infant child died in a French prison in 1941, and his sister-in-law was guillotined in Saigon for terrorism.

How could there be laughter after that? Indeed, had he himself ever laughed after burying his own sons?

Ho Chi Minh could still laugh, but then he had no family. He had suffered and struggled, but there had been no personal losses; he was still a mild and gentle man.

He and Giap were not; they had lost too much. The struggle had been too long and too hard. Dien Bien Phu had been only the midpoint, thirteen years fighting the Japanese and the French, and now thirteen since.

He turned his head toward the sunlight streaming through the doorway. The small movement exhausted him, but though ravaged by amoebic dysentery and malaria, he still had the will to live. He felt it now just as he had in all the other awful moments—as a prisoner of the Japanese, tortured by the Sûreté, and worst of all, when he buried his sons.

He remembered digging tunnels with his hands, clawing dirt until there was no flesh on his fingers, until others had to pull him away. He remembered digging a son's grave.

He raised his hands to his face. They were dirty and scarred, and they shook uncontrollably: hands that had held his dead sons, hands that had killed; hands that had not caressed or loved in longer than he could remember. Bloodied, scarred, burned hands that for thirty years had crawled and dug to freedom.

Hands that would not fail him now. He would win; he would lead his men to victory. His sons had not died in vain; the suffering would be avenged.

His eyes narrowed on the sunlight, and his hands reached for the ground, felt the cool earth, and the fingers dug in and pulled him to the door, and the sunlight outside.

Bernard Lacouture was so excited that he had to take a long walk to calm himself. The city would soothe him; seeing everything in its proper place would restore his tranquility.

It did; he was reassured to see everything as it should be, all the flotsam up on the city's surface, nothing sunk.

He walked happy and pleased: the black market thrived, Tu Do Street bustled with whores and dope peddlers and money changers; the beggars, cripples, and amputees were all where they belonged; the starving woman in front of the Catinat Hotel with her dying or dead baby in her arms was faithfully at her post; the buzz and roar of traffic, the litter and trash, the smell of rot—all was intact.

Lacouture beamed as he walked: the theater was open, the stage set for the Grand Guignol that was Saigon.

CHAPTER

• 5 •

Morning light streamed through the bay windows of the dining room, mingling and dancing with the crystal and silver of the breakfast setting.

The room was large, formal yet comfortable, with a blend of Chinese and European furniture, rosewood and mahogany; on the floor was an antique Persian rug, an Isfahan of intricate Shah Abbas design in an azure blue that reminded Marshall of the Gulf of Oman. On the walls, a world away, Gobelin tapestries of Flemish court and hunting scenes provided a muted backdrop for celadon porcelains and matching Ming vases.

The art was not decoration to him; each piece had meaning, and its own life. In the rug he saw Islam, caliphs with scimitars, and he heard the call to prayers from minarets, and he saw sun-baked villages where weavers sat before broad looms. In the Gobelins, beneath the wild eyes of the bloodied boar and the melancholy unicorn, lusty lords and seductive ladies, he saw Gothic towers and heard Gregorian chants, and he could see medieval, winter-grim cities where guild weavers shivered in ateliers before their looms.

The art was fixed and lasting, giving him a sense of the nobility and permanence in man's work. There was beauty in what men could achieve, not just individually—a paint-

67

ing, a poem, a symphony—but collectively, in the artistry required for tapestries, carpets, architecture; in the orchestration as well as the conception.

The art could not be undone. The Isfahan would survive murdering mullahs, shahs, and emirs, and the Gobelins would endure NATO and the Warsaw Pact as they had all the other alliances, tyrants, and wars.

The art could be destroyed—unraveled, marred, burned—but that would not diminish the achievement.

If only there could be art in our politics, he thought. There was a Declaration and a Constitution, a *Utopia* and a *Republic*—concepts, but no orchestration; there was so little artistry in human relations.

Still one tried, he thought, staring out to the great lawn and garden. He was no artist; there was no art in his work—no symphony, no "Pietà," no *King Lear*—he was merely one of the guild weavers in the dark atelier, threading the weft and warp: a little mission here, gathering information, work on a treaty. But in his mind he saw the grand design, a world of peace, and it was enough for him to be a minor craftsman in the workshop.

Perhaps in Vietnam he would achieve something. He was leaving the day after tomorrow; maybe, just maybe, he could weave something fine and lasting and meaningful.

Above him, in the bedroom, he heard Catherine moving about; she would be coming down in a few minutes.

The thought of her depressed him. The celadons turned to plastic, the Mings were only carnival glass; the Isfahan was straw, and the Gobelins—wallpaper.

Then he laughed and reached for his coffee: Catherine was kind and good, generous and caring. She was a wonderful person who gave to the poor, tended the sick, and wept true tears for the sorrow of the world. She was intelligent and attractive; she didn't smoke, hardly drank, and wasn't pathological in any way he knew. She was a faithful wife and a loving mother.

He just did not want to see her this morning. The marriage was a failure; it was his fault, and he did not want the reminder of her presence.

He had thought endlessly about his marriage, delved as

obsessively and indefatigably into himself and his marriage as certain Jewish novelists quarried their Jewishness. He had tunneled through motives, burrowed beyond weaknesses and faults; he had strip-mined the lode and at the bottom he found no ore, any more than the Jewish novelist found the essence of his Jewishness. What he sought to find, his specialness, was just the common dirt at the bottom of everybody's shaft.

The problem was sex; nothing lofty, no nugget of exclusiveness. The failure was common and banal, as tacky and trashy as a grocery checkout tabloid. The problem had always been not enough sex. When they were married at twenty-two, he wanted to spend the whole day in bed. He loved sex; it consumed him. It still did.

He was a man of learning and sensitivity, wit and polish, he knew, but he had a caveman's penis: he was a Renaissance man with a Hun's cock. He simply could not reason with his penis, though it seemed to respond to everything else.

Catherine was a warm, sensual woman, sexual and responsive. She was utterly feminine and generally uninhibited, but she was not obsessed with sex; she did not want to spend the whole day in bed.

The problem was not technique, not quality, just quantity. He wanted to revel in sex.

"You're basically just a gutter person," she had told him, not even unkindly.

It was true, he knew. He had loved the whorehouses of his youth in the Marines, loved raw, raunchy sex, and he did not want to outgrow it. So, slave to his Hun penis, he sought sex outside the marriage. There had been many women, and also guilt. He did not like being unfaithful; adultery filled him with remorse and guilt.

"You are an upper-class man, with low-class desires, and middle-class morality," she told him.

That was true too; he pursued infidelities, then felt great guilt for infidelity.

"I wouldn't mind your other women, if you were just kind to me," she told him once.

But that was not true. She could not countenance the

69

other women, and she could not forgive him: she had not failed, he had. He was the betrayer; he had wronged her—people shouldn't spend whole days in bed.

Now the marriage was only a polite facade.

Behind the facade he had Deborah. It was his midlife crisis, he assumed, labeling it that as a ready-made convenience, an acceptable alibi for the embarrassing disparity in their ages. She was twenty-two, a recently graduated art major working for the Smithsonian, on whose governing board he sat.

But maybe it wasn't his midlife crisis, he reasoned; he hadn't been struck blind, he wasn't in love—Catherine was far more intelligent and interesting—it was just sex: he hadn't grown up, just gotten older, and he wanted to sleep with the same kind of girl that he always had.

Deborah was impressed with his wealth and manner, that he was called "Mr. Ambassador" and met with the President. She was too young and not good for him, he knew, and this mission to Vietnam provided him with a graceful way to disengage. She would hardly be hurt, he reasoned; he did not believe a woman her age could fall in love with a man his age, nor should she—it was not right physiologically or psychologically, and certainly he was not the only wealthy, well-connected middle-aged man in Washington.

Behind Catherine's facade were her many interests—the children, activities, causes and commitments, boards, foundations, and charities she served on. Now she was dedicated to ending the war.

She worked too hard, he thought, was as obsessive and compulsive about that as he was about sex. She was a perfectionist in a very imperfect world, as fanatical as an Arab. Trying to impose order on everything, she invited disappointments; everything and everybody failed her. She made everything difficult. It would be far better for her and everyone else if she spent more time in bed, he thought.

"I would be a wonderful queen for the world," she once said. "There would be no poverty, no injustice, no wars."

That was true, he knew, but it would also be a world of headless people, his being the first lopped off. He had told her that.

She had laughed. "No, I would just have your penis cut off." She reconsidered. "Actually that would be the same thing, wouldn't it?"

So there they were, civil and irreconcilable in their marriage, in a holding pattern until the children were grown and gone.

Ryan, at eighteen, was in college, safe from the draft, and doing well at Brown. Sarah, sixteen, and Chris, fifteen, were doing less well.

"Sex, drugs, and hippies: all because of that damn war of yours, Brad," Catherine had said. Actually his wife was a great deal like Lyndon Johnson, Marshall thought, and it would do no good to point out to her that the war was not his.

"Good morning, Brad," Catherine said, entering the room with her purposeful, energetic stride, moving as though to meet a challenge head-on. She was a tall woman, nearly five feet ten inches; she carried more weight than when younger, but it gave her a smooth, soft appearance. Her face, large, full, and expressive, looked exactly its age and looked exactly what she was—intelligent, sure, wealthy.

She touched him on the shoulder as she passed to the buffet table.

"You're up early today," he said.

"Yes, I've got a great deal to do before I chain myself to the White House gate this afternoon."

Marshall gazed up from his newspaper; she was quite capable of the act, but she was joking.

He smiled. "It's unnecessary; he knows how you feel. He's read all your petitions. He said he hears more from you than he does the cheese lady."

Catherine brought her coffee and a plate of eggs and bacon to the table but waited for the explanation before sitting.

"Jane Fonda," he said.

She waited patiently.

"Fonda—Fondue."

She sat down. "And you, what morass today?"

"CIA."

She held up her hand. "I hope you get a Medal of Freedom

71

out of this. Last week the Joint Chiefs and the State Department, this week the CIA." She shook her head. "Forget the medal, Brad, ask him for an ambassadorship. Let's go to France."

"I thought you were chaining yourself to the gate. He may leave you there."

"Lady Bird would let me out; I'd mar her beautification program. Besides, now that you've gotten all the information from the Pentagon and the State Department, and after the CIA briefs you today, you should be able to end this war by Friday."

He smiled.

"Well, it's not very complicated, Brad. It's not a *mystery*, for God's sake. All it requires is an admission of error."

"What a curious thing for you to say, Catherine. Would the Queen of Hearts casually admit error?"

Her mouth tightened in annoyance. "*I* wouldn't have made such a mistake to begin with."

"Of course not. How foolish of me."

But to give her credit, she probably wouldn't have made such a mistake, he thought. Even if she had, she would have quickly extricated herself, not by admitting error, of course, she was no more capable of doing that than Lyndon Johnson was, but simply by changing her mind. It was not quite a matter of "This war doesn't go with my gown after all," but a woman's decisions were not tied to ego as a man's were. The prerogative to change her mind was not a woman's flaw but a strength; the flaw lay in man's inability to change his, to casually reverse direction without its becoming a major matter of face and pride. There was no penis to lay on the line, as she might say.

And that is what seemed to be on the line in Vietnam. Strip away everything he had heard from State and the Pentagon, behind all the data and charts, all the iron curtains and stacked dominoes, was a—not even raging erection, just an exposed, vulnerable bud of a penis.

In the Pentagon briefing, he was given the whole "dog and pony show" as it was termed, though that hardly captured the Lippizaner extravaganza staged for him, a dazzling sound and light show, lacking only a firefight in the corridors of E Ring, and the Joint Chiefs raising the flag in the War Room.

But Marshall knew that some things could not be charted or graphed; there was no computation for what he had felt in the landing boat off Guadalcanal, and in the charts and figures presented to him, he did not see the enemy soldier in Vietnam.

The true test of strength, Marshall believed, was not the numbers or proficiency of those willing to kill, but of those willing to die, but in the Pentagon analysis, it was not a factor for consideration.

At the State Department he saw a similar show—different costumes, stage, and sets, more somber lighting and muted sounds, but the plot was the same. Marshall was given a global picture of a world threatened by falling dominoes, and he was shown the microscopic slide—democratic nation-building in South Vietnam.

What he did not get was the historical perspective. He wondered if at the Southeast Asia desk there was a volume on the history of Vietnam, or if there was, whether anyone had read it.

"You're still leaving on Wednesday?" she asked.

"Yes. The CIA isn't going to tell me anything I don't know."

"I doubt they know more than you do, or than I do, for that matter, unless of course they tell you what they're *doing*, which they won't."

"Catherine, you've turned into a terrible cynic. You've become jaded."

She leaned forward and patted his cheek. "Dearest Brad. No, I've become olded. Since you've been less than candid in what you've been doing these past twenty years, I have little faith in the CIA's willingness to be frank about *their* little peccadillos."

"Catherine, why do all our conversations lead back to this?"

"Peccadillos?" she asked innocently. "I suppose because they all start with that."

"Jesus Christ, it's not even eight o'clock in the morning," he said in exasperation.

She smiled, then reached over and touched his hand. "That wasn't nice, I know. Is there anything I can do before you leave?"

"Thank you, but I think everything's taken care of. Is there anything I can do for you?"

She shook her head. "I'm glad you were able to stay at least until the children were back in school; that makes it much easier for me. Worrying about their schoolwork is a relief after a summer of—"

"Worrying where the hell they are."

"It was a hard summer," she allowed.

They both fell silent on their children, having been through this many times without getting anywhere. Were they lacking as parents or was it the times—or were there no problems, just exaggerated concern?

"Well," he said in resignation, "what's done is done."

"My God, Brad, you make it sound like we've raised psychopaths. Ryan is doing very well. Sarah . . . is . . ."

"Certainly not sweet sixteen. And that's hardly puppy love she's carrying on with what's-his-name—Bosco. Bosco, for God's sake!"

"Brad . . ."

"I know times are different. I know everybody has long hair and never washes, and little girls have diaphragms and spermicides for their Barbie dolls, and Ken has a cock ring . . ."

"I find your outrage somewhat hypocritical," she said calmly. "Name someone, including your own dear Jack Kennedy, who wasn't promiscuous. What kind of children do you expect from such parents? If *you* set a better standard, your children might come closer to it. And look at our society—slavery and segregation and prejudice for centuries: our children are rebelling against it. They're marching and having sit-ins. I say wonderful. The government tells lie after lie about Vietnam and sends young men off to die. Our children protest. Thank God."

She leaned toward him, her voice intense. "I'm glad our children don't accept the way things are. I'm not happy Sarah is sleeping with her boyfriend, but she is a good and caring person. There are things you do that I don't like or agree with, but you are still a good and caring man. I'm glad you are going to Vietnam: I hope desperately you will succeed. I could not bear it if Ryan or Chris had to go."

"Ryan is student deferred, and Chris . . . well, it is hardly likely he would be drafted."

Catherine sat back and suppressed a sigh. They were both confused and uncomfortable with what no longer seemed a concern but reality—their son's homosexuality. Chris never liked the games boys played. Since puberty, the homosexual tendency grew more pronounced; this summer it became overt.

There had been no tears, no condemnations, merely sorrow and resignation. It was accepted but not discussed, and Catherine acknowledged the primacy of her husband's pain and admired the equanimity with which he handled it. Even this brief reference was rare.

Marshall pushed himself from the table. "I'd better go: the car is waiting."

The CIA headquarters at Langley, Virginia, was like a corporate cloister, a calm sanctuary of confidence and efficiency. It was an imposing contrast to the bristling tension of the Pentagon, and the doughy blandness of the State Department.

The expansive lawns, the muted corridors and nearly somnolent atmosphere, were soothing and reassuring. Surely in such a sedate setting no decision would be hasty or ill-considered: deliberation, dispassion, sober judgment, were what this serenity inspired.

There was no aura of crisis, nothing furtive; a moment here would dispel any thoughts of cloaks and schemes, coups and assassinations.

But Marshall knew that the master poseurs would be able to strike the proper pose; that is what he liked about Langley, the production was always perfect. The FBI show was too mechanical and contrived, as though everyone were reading from a script, entering and exiting on cue; the production showed the heavy hand of the producer.

Langley's did not; it was seamless—theater as opposed to theatrical, the royal troupe in a sophisticated production, not dinner theater by traveling players. Of course, a turkey put on by the Royal Shakespeare was still a turkey, Marshall knew, but at least one could admire the performers.

Marshall had no delusions about the show; he was familiar with several CIA flops, but he thought they would present a more accurate and balanced picture than what he got from the Pentagon and State.

He was not disappointed.

The director and senior staffers sat around a seminar table and discussed the war with him. Instead of an Agency "presentation," there was deliberation, theorizing, ruminations—doubts and unanswered questions, reasoning, not concluding.

It was of course, he knew, a well-rehearsed, well-hedged presentation that concluded the military situation was not as optimistic as the Pentagon made out, and the political situation worse than the State Department admitted.

The picture painted was almost candidly negative. It was, Marshall knew, the CIA's Pontius Pilate routine—they were washing their hands of the debacle they were not quite warning you about: covering their asses while still stirring the pot.

Their consensus was that more of the same would not achieve victory—more men and weapons would not alter the outcome. Only direct military, political, and economic confrontation with the North on their own territory would make a difference.

To cap the show, Marshall was left alone with Andrew Maynard, a friend since they had served together as Marine lieutenants in Korea. Maynard was now in the upper level of the directorate.

"Do they expect me to believe you?" Marshall joked. "You're the biggest liar I've ever known."

"They don't know what to expect from you, Brad," he said seriously. "They're not sure of your game. Nor of your power and influence with the President. Nor of your weaknesses."

"Christ, that's simple—I have no game, no power, no influence, and no weaknesses."

"That's what I told them—Bradley Lawrence Marshall is the most dedicated, unselfish public servant in America, uninterested in power and self-aggrandizement. And I told the truth about your weaknesses too."

"Yes?" Marshall said, waiting.

"I told them you were cunt-crazed."

Marshall laughed.

"I told them about that cathouse in Seoul and the time you—"

"Jesus Christ, is this room bugged?"

"Probably. That's what we do for a living, you know. But this is on the level; I'm supposed to answer any questions you have but weren't comfortable asking the others."

"And of course you'll answer them truthfully."

Maynard considered. "I won't lie to you, you know that. If there's something I can't answer, I won't answer. So phrase your questions carefully. . . . How're Catherine and the kids?"

"Catherine's fine. The children . . . teenagers."

Maynard held up his hand. "Say no more. I wonder what I did to deserve mine."

"Probably by going to that whorehouse in Seoul with me."

"Shhh. You know this place is bugged." Maynard laughed. "You look good, Brad." He patted his own paunch. "I've dedicated myself to truth, justice, and the American way, and all I've gotten for it is fat."

"That's called feeding at the public trough, Andy—too many expense account meals."

"No, it's too much sitting around, too many meetings, and too much talk. I need to get back in the field."

"You're too old to be a spy, Andy. Besides, you couldn't pass for anything else. Face it, we're middle-aged bureaucrats."

Maynard sighed. He was as tall as Marshall but stockier—an aged athlete, still powerful and quick, however. The two had been close friends since they were junior officers; their careers had occasionally intersected, and though they saw each other infrequently, there was the bond of combat and shared youth.

Maynard said, "We've come a long way, haven't we? But I'd go back in a minute. Wouldn't you?"

Marshall shook his head. "No, Andy, I wouldn't."

Maynard nodded, his hand reaching out and grabbing Marshall's elbow. Maynard was the only man who knew what happened in Korea and how it affected Marshall.

"Tell me about Diem," Marshall said, smiling a challenge.

"We didn't *pull* the trigger that killed him and his brother," Maynard said evenly, his eyes steady on Marshall.

"Cambodia?"

"Same as in Laos. We're working out of both, but only minor activity—they're too fragile: resupplies, drops, incursions, Air America traffic. Thailand is the main base."

"Thieu and Ky?"

"The George Washington and Ben Franklin of Vietnam."

"What are you people doing there that violates the principles of decency and democracy?"

Maynard shrugged. "A little murder and torture here and there, some counter terror now and then—we don't want to get rusty."

"And the CIA's true assessment?"

"Ah. Now there it is."

"The question you can't answer?"

"The question that doesn't have an answer—or rather, has several. Some think Vietnam's a complete bag of shit that we ought to drop immediately; others see it as a vital interest and think we should dig in. You see, it's not *our* war, so unlike the military and State, we haven't got a policy, we're just providing some support."

"And you personally?"

"It's a bag of shit. Get us out of it."

Marshall smiled.

"Now a word of advice, Brad . . . no, make that 'warning.' I want you to be careful over there—I mean that literally and seriously. I just told you, the Agency is divided on Vietnam, but those who believe in it—if they think you're out to undermine the war effort—they'll nail you. I mean it, Brad, they believe in the war—and don't forget, they're professional killers. Remember this name: Wilson Abbot Lord."

"Wilson Abbot Lord."

"Wilson Abbot Lord. You watch out for him, Brad. He *believes.*"

When the limousine dropped him off at home in McLean in late afternoon, Marshall was surprised to see his son's car in the driveway. The drab, unpretentious, ten-year-old car, small and practical, built in an age of automotive ostentation—fins and grille—seemed as incongruous in the neighborhood of mansions as it did with the teenager behind the wheel.

Ryan had bought it with the money he had earned the previous summer, refusing any support from his parents. He had not made an issue of it, nor had he of anything—"understated" best described him—he merely wanted to make his own way. He was, Marshall knew, his mother's son, as stubborn and independent as she.

A calendar flashed into his mind. September. Labor Day was circled red. There were no other holidays, and it was too early for exams—the semester had begun only three weeks ago, Ryan's sophomore year at Brown. There was no reason for him to be home.

In his distraction, he only nodded to the maid who opened the door as he reached the top step. "Ryan?" he called anxiously.

His son was coming down the stairs in the jeans and plaid shirt that seemed to have been issued to him in 1964.

"Are you all right? My God, what happened to your head?"

Ryan stopped on the stairway; his hand went to his head, then he grinned and bounded down to his father.

Marshall hugged his son to him, gripping the back of his neck. "With all that hair you used to have, I'd forgotten you had a neck. And ears. Jesus Christ, Ryan, you have ears."

Ryan laughed, breaking away. "Come on, Dad, it wasn't that bad. Everybody has long hair." Then in mock affront at the unfairness, he said, "Sarah's is much longer. You never said anything about hers. How come you're always picking on me? It isn't fair. I can't stand it anymore. You always loved Sarah the most."

"Did you teach that to Chris? I swear he said those exact words yesterday. Or does it come in *The Teenagers' Manual to Drive Their Parents Crazy?* And what are you doing home? You couldn't have flunked out already." His voice could not hide his anxiety. "Are you in trouble?"

"No."

"You can tell me, Ryan, you know that. I'd stand by you no matter what. I wouldn't even get mad. What is it?"

Ryan bowed his head. His foot dug into the rug. "It's about this girl, and the 7-Eleven." He shrugged, head down. "She was pregnant, and . . . well, we didn't have any money, and nothing to eat . . . and . . . Christ, what were we supposed to do? So we knocked over this 7-Eleven store in Providence and took some Slurpees—"

"What!"

"You said you wouldn't get mad, Dad."

"God damn it, Ryan, don't do that to me. Now what are you doing here? And why'd you get a haircut? You haven't had a haircut since junior high school. You look perfectly normal—what's the matter with you?"

Ryan backed away a step from his father. Though the same height, and with similar builds, they did not otherwise resemble one another. Ryan was much fairer, his features softer and less angular. The son was more classically handsome, where the father had the more striking and powerful look.

"Maybe we ought to sit down and talk about it," Ryan said, then playing for time, added, "Maybe we ought to wait for Mom. Is she coming home soon?"

"Let's talk now," Marshall said, walking toward his study. "I don't know when your mother is coming back, maybe not for a couple more hours—she's chaining herself to the White House gate today."

He sat in a leather library chair and gestured for Ryan to sit across from him. "Am I going to need a drink for this?"

"You've never needed a drink for anything, Dad. But I could use one."

Marshall went to a built-in cabinet. "What would you like?"

Ryan shrugged. "I don't know. What's a guy supposed to drink with his old man?"

Marshall could feel his heart clamping. Something awful had happened, he knew. The world had changed forever. He could not bring himself to look at his son. Strangely, it did not matter what had happened, only that the moment had arrived: the mystical bar had somehow come without his knowing it, had appeared without warning, without giving him a chance to prepare or protect Ryan, and the defenseless boy had crossed it. Oh, God, he thought, I didn't know it would come so soon. He was only a baby yesterday. Give me more time.

His hand fumbled with the decanter, knocking it against the glasses. He tried to steady himself. "I don't know," he said. "Since my old man was a drunk, I never had a drink with him. How about bourbon?"

"Fine."

"Straight up all right?"

Ryan grinned sheepishly. "I'm not much of a drinker. What does that mean?"

"It means I don't have any ice."

Marshall brought the glass to him and sat, raising his own. "To you."

Ryan took a deep swallow and was unable to suppress a grimace. Their eyes met. Finally Ryan said, "I dropped out of school, Dad."

Marshall said nothing, merely waited.

"I joined the army."

Marshall inhaled sharply at the blow, much worse than any physical strike he could have suffered.

"I already signed the papers. I have to report to Fort Bragg, Monday." He pulled a copy of his orders from a pocket and held them out.

Marshall glanced at them, then took a drink and exhaled. "I think I liked the girl and the Slurpee story better," he said, trying to smile.

"You're not pissed at me?" Ryan asked anxiously.

"Pissed?"

"Angry."

"I know what 'pissed' means, you idiot." He jumped up furiously. "Of course I'm pissed. What the hell's the matter with you?"

Ryan laughed. "That's better. Now we can act this out like we're supposed to."

Marshall felt foolish, standing over his son, spilt bourbon dripping from his hand. He sat down, wiping his hand against his trouser leg. "You know, I have an international reputation for calmness. I am world famous for aplomb and never losing my temper. I have listened to the most notorious assholes in the world without batting an eye. Only you and your mother can reduce me to quivering jelly in seconds." He flicked droplets of bourbon onto the rug.

He looked at his son, then the full horror struck. "Don't do this," he pleaded.

"I have to, Dad."

"Why, Ryan? For God's sake, why?"

"Because if I didn't go, someone would have to go in my place; I couldn't live with that."

"I don't understand," Marshall said.

Ryan finished his drink and put the glass down. "When I got back to college, everybody was joking about Vietnam and the draft, about how they got out of it because of the student deferment, about how only the dummies have to go, dummies and blacks—the dregs. That's what they say— 'Let them be the fodder, they won't be missed.' Nobody in college has to go and everybody jokes about it, how they're going on for their master's degree, then a Ph.D.—anything to stay in school and out of the war."

He stared at his father. "That's wrong. You know that's wrong, Dad. I don't have to go. Nobody I know has to go—we all can get out of it. Anybody with money and connections can get out. Every guy I know could get his old man to make a phone call, or they could get a doctor to sign a paper. It's a joke. But somebody has to go; for every one of us who gets out, someone else takes our place. Somebody would go for me. Maybe he would get killed. I can't let that happen."

He smiled. "I like my shitty little car. It's *mine*. It's the sorriest-looking thing at Brown, maybe in all New England, but it's mine. A lot of guys I know have Porsches. I know you would have bought me one."

"The hell I would."

Ryan laughed. "Okay, an Oldsmobile. And you'd get me out of the draft, get me in some reserve unit if nothing else, but . . . Can't you see, I couldn't do that."

"Ryan—"

"Dad, I think I know how you feel. I know how you care about us. And maybe even how you feel about war; you never talked about it, ever. Other guys' dads have all their medals in cases in their dens, pictures of themselves in their uniforms, all decked out and ready to storm beaches, and they tell the same old war stories over and over."

Marshall bowed his head; he closed his eyes and massaged his temples.

"I understand, Dad."

"No," Marshall whispered. "You can't." He looked up, and through his tears all he saw was a bloody blur, and he was deafened by shelling and screams. The glass fell from his hands. "Oh, God, Ryan, don't do this. Please."

"Father, I have to."

The word was a blow. *Father.* Yes, that was what he was above all things, the strongest male tie, the most complex gene, protective and destructive at once, generous and jealous, loving and hating, sacrificial and murderous. A man might fight his children every inch of their growth and his own displacement, yet he would lay down his life for them, sacrifice name and fortune, endure any pain, lie, steal, betray, and kill for them.

"No," he said, standing angrily. "You can't go. I won't let you."

"Dad—"

"No!"

Ryan stood. "It's too late, Dad. It's my decision; it's my life."

Marshall grabbed him. "You don't understand. You don't know what it's like." He shook him. "You'll die. My God, Ryan, you'll get killed. I know you will."

"I can take care of myself."

"That's not how war is! You'll die. You're just the type. People like you don't make it. Ryan! Ryan!"

Ryan backed away. "You don't think I'm strong enough? You think you can go but I can't? You think it's all right for others to go? Other people's sons can go and get killed? The war is only wrong when it touches us?"

"If you think the war is wrong, protest. March, burn your draft card. Do anything!"

"Except go."

"Yes!"

Ryan shook his head. "The war will end only when people like us are touched. I have to go. You know I do." He went to his father and put his arms around him. "What would you do?"

Ryan let go, then turned and left the room.

Marshall went slack. He stared after his son, tried to raise his hand, but couldn't move. He wanted to run after him, grab him, hold him, never let him go, but his limbs would not respond. He was straining but not moving, like running in water.

And there he was in the water, and shells were bursting, and there were screams, and blood everywhere, and before him a body floating facedown, and he ran and ran, and then he finally reached it, and turned him over and held him in his arms, and it was Ryan, it was his son, and he raised his face to the sky, and he screamed, No. Over and over, No.

CHAPTER

· 6 ·

Wilson Abbot Lord finished reading the dispatches on Ambassador Marshall's mission for the second time and laid the file on his desk on the third floor of the embassy in Saigon.

The only other papers on his desk were Marshall's security file and biography. Those he reread, then stacked them neatly on the dispatches from Langley and sat back, a tall, lean, sharply angular man of forty.

He had known vaguely of Marshall's previous missions for the President, but now with the full file before him he was profoundly disturbed.

Despite Langley's dispassionate tone, he felt certain that Marshall was not coming to make an objective analysis— Marshall was coming to seek a way out of the war for Johnson.

Others had come for the same purpose, which perhaps explained Langley's nonchalance, but Lord felt that Marshall was different and more dangerous, and everything he'd read in the record confirmed his fears.

"Military service, 1942–1945" and "military service, 1951–1953" spoke volumes to Lord. A seventeen-year-old from one of the wealthiest and most distinguished families in America was not meant to have joined the Marines to storm beaches on the Pacific islands nor should that same man at twenty-six have gone off to Korea when he had no need to.

This was a formidable man, Lord realized, not some career diplomat or political dilettante. No one was going to fool him. Unlike the Washington bureaucrats and congressmen, he would not be "brainwashed" by the martial extravaganza MACV staged for visiting dignitaries: he would see the political fiasco for what it was, and the military stalemate as well.

He would conclude, Lord felt certain, that the war was not winnable, and that Johnson should pull out. He would take that recommendation back to the President and perhaps become the deciding factor in America's sellout of Vietnam.

Lord sat perfectly still, his face expressionless, giving no hint of the fury he felt.

He had been in Korea too; that fight had ended in a draw, and that was the best America had ever done against the communists—everywhere else had been defeat, even in Cuba.

Well, not here, he vowed; he had not invested four years of his life fighting communism in Vietnam to have Bradley Lawrence Marshall destroy his work and the only hope this country had to remain free.

His marriage had been wrecked by Vietnam; after ten years, the stresses and separations of his work were too much. When he was posted to Vietnam, his wife told him that he would have to choose—husband and father, or spy. He loved his wife and children, but he had come here; she divorced him that year. Though bitter, he understood her decision and bore her no ill will. The settlement called for a division of property and a third of his salary for child support—he gave her all his property and sent half his salary.

He did not blame his divorce on Vietnam, his work, or his wife; Lord was a practical man and rarely assessed blame to any shortcoming. He seldom pictured right and wrong but instead saw fittings and accommodations—neither ends nor means hindered him from finding the best solution to every problem. He had summed up his view to his protégé, Jeffrey Gibbon—"Nothing is either/or; it's all ands/buts."

He had sacrificed his family life for his conviction—one of the few blacks-and-whites he knew—that communism was an evil that had to be defeated. Now Bradley Marshall was coming to negate his sacrifice and undo his work.

He still did not move, but he replaced his fury with granite resolution: I won't let that happen, he promised himself.

Then he looked at his watch and frowned; it was after seven P.M., much later than he liked to stay, because no matter how often he had told Gibbon and his secretary to leave at five, or whenever their work was done, they wouldn't go until he had. Frequently he left early only so he could come back after they had gone home.

Wilson Abbot Lord inspired others; those who worked for him were devoted.

He picked up the files and stood, grimacing at the pain in his legs and back, a grimace that would never have crossed his features if someone else had been in the room. No one, even his wife, had any intimation of the agony he sometimes felt. Hiding that pain from his torturers in Korea had been the most brutally difficult thing ever; disguising it from everyone since had been easy. During moments such as this, he could indulge the pain, vent the agony. In Korea, because he was watched every minute, he had not been able to. He had even taught himself to sleep with a part of his brain always alert, holding his face expressionless, and his tongue silent.

Lord limped across the room, but by the time he reached the door, his stride was powerful and smooth.

He walked down the corridor, noting that everyone was gone, all lights off, every door open as was station policy—anything sensitive locked in safes—all quiet except for his secretary typing in her office.

"Carol," he said, entering, "if you don't go home, I'm going to throw your typewriter out the window."

"Oh, Mr. Lord, you startled me; I never hear you."

"Spies aren't supposed to crash down corridors," he said.

"I hear everybody else," she said.

"Even Jeffrey?"

"*Especially* Jeff."

"Has he left yet?"

"No, sir, he's still in his office."

"Now listen, I want you to go home. I'm going to talk to Jeff for a few minutes, then I'm leaving."

"Actually, I was just finishing up," she said.

"Good, go home," he said, leaving the room. "Good night, Carol."

Lord tapped lightly on the only closed door on the corridor and walked in.

Jeffrey Gibbon, barefooted and wearing only gym shorts, scrambled up from the floor where he had been doing sit-ups. He glistened with sweat and grinned sheepishly, standing at an approximation of attention.

"Evening, Mr. Lord."

"Jeff, it's after seven—what are you doing here? I can see you're working out, but why don't you go to the Cercle Sportif? I got you a membership there."

"Yes, sir, and I really appreciate it, sir, but I thought I'd just . . . get a little workout before I left." He stepped over his barbells and reached for a towel.

"You're not impressing me, you know—with the workout, yes, but not by staying late."

Gibbon toweled sweat from his torso and grinned. He was twenty-eight, tall, blond, and muscular, a former Green Beret officer and helicopter pilot now in his third year with the CIA, his first overseas posting.

He was not afraid of Wilson Abbot Lord; he wasn't afraid of anyone. He wasn't staying late to impress Lord; he was staying in the hope that he could be useful, and that he might learn something from Lord. Gibbon did not want Lord to know that he idolized him, and even felt uncomfortable in his feelings for Lord—an admiration and respect he had never felt for anyone else—but he supposed Lord knew that. Lord seemed to know everything, and no one else even knew for sure what Lord himself did.

Lord was the senior agent at the embassy; theoretically he reported to the CIA station chief, but Gibbon knew that was just for the flow chart. Lord operated autonomously, receiving orders from the directorate in Langley, and reporting only to it.

He had a secretary, and though he could have had numerous assistants, and whichever ones he chose, he had picked Gibbon as his sole aide. He had also told Gibbon to call him by his given name, but Gibbon couldn't bring himself to do it—he was Mr. Lord to everyone, except to the station chief and a few other very senior, and much older, agents.

In their shadowy world, the only agent who possessed the special aura that separated him from all the others was Lord.

Lord stepped carefully over the barbells and sat down on a metal folding chair, the only piece of furniture in the room besides Gibbon's desk and chair. It was, Lord knew, an emulation of Lord's own austere office, Spartan in the extreme, and devoid of any personal mementos.

He made the slightest motion with his head, and Gibbon immediately sat down, but carefully drawing his chair away from his desk to avoid any appearance that it was he who might be interviewing Lord.

"Anything for me today?" Lord asked.

For Lord to come down to his office was a rare event, and Gibbon was flattered and pleased.

"No, sir, except that your assistant took it in the ass today."

"How is that, Jeffrey?"

"That faggot, Lacouture, really stuck it to me today. Jesus, he gives me the creeps; he's like a slug, and he keeps staring at my crotch. As soon as I left him, I went back to my place and fucked Ca Li twice—she didn't understand what was going on, me coming home in the middle of the afternoon and throwing her down on the floor, but I just had to get Lacouture out of my system. But then I came back here and found out how the bastard stuck it to me. Actually that was why I was working out with the weights, just burning off anger."

"He's not a total loss, is he? He's doing wonders for your libido and your muscles. But tell me, Jeffrey, how did Monsieur Lacouture 'stick it' to you?"

"He contacted me earlier and told me he had some valuable information to sell. So I met him. I kept scratching my crotch until I got the price way down."

"And what did you buy for your bruised balls?"

"Not a fucking thing as it turns out—the big so-called scoop was that the NVA general Khanh is seriously ill with amoebic dysentery."

Lord sat expressionlessly, long legs crossed, arms folded, leaning back in the chair.

"Then I got back here and found out that Khanh's dead; he died two days ago of gangrene—it's in the MACV intel report."

Lord scratched his chin. He didn't say anything for a minute, his gaze noncommittal on Gibbon. "Now tell me, Jeffrey—why is it that General Khanh is dead from gangrene rather than just ill from dysentery?"

"Well, sir, because MACV is Category One intelligence, and Lacouture is . . . about a Category Ten faggot."

"Jeffrey, Jeffrey," Lord said in mild reproach. "You're not confusing the message with the messenger, are you?" He uncrossed his legs and stood smoothly, no sign whatsoever of pain in his long-ago broken and battered knees and limbs. He bent and deftly picked up the barbell.

"Tell me, Jeffrey, is this morally good or bad?"

"The weight, sir? It's . . . just a dead weight, sir."

"Dartmouth is such a good school—yes, you're right. But if I use it to build my muscles, and burn away anger, it is a good thing. Conversely, if I drop it on my foot, it is a bad thing."

"I guess maybe I didn't get my money's worth at Dartmouth, sir. I don't follow you."

"Dartmouth didn't cost you a penny—you were on a baseball scholarship. My point is, don't be moralistic. Morals and values and prejudices just get in the way, Jeff. One man's morals are another man's prejudices—they're all clutter. Free yourself of all that. You can't think straight if you're hampered with all kinds of preconditions; thought should be as clear and unfettered as gazing through a telescope—not like trying to see the stars through a kaleidoscope." He put down the barbell.

Gibbon lowered his eyes in chastisement.

Lord said gently, "Moral judgments have the very bad habit of—"

"Clouding vision," Gibbon said.

"*Becoming* vision, Jeffrey," he said more sharply. "Let's keep our vision clear, and concentrate on what matters. I'm glad you like to fuck girls—I think that's healthy and wholesome. But Joe Stalin liked to fuck women too. What does that have to do with anything? Communism is bad, not communists; democracy is good, not, however, all democrats."

"Yes, sir."

"You have a star pitcher who can strike out every man on the other team. Do you care that off the field he likes to diddle five-year-old girls, or likes getting buttfucked by the shortstop in the showers? Not if you want to win games it doesn't. All it teaches you is to—"

"Take separate showers."

"Exactly." Lord tossed the files on Gibbon's desk. "This is trouble, Jeff. I want you to read it carefully, but not tonight. Lock it in your safe and look at it first thing in the morning with a clean, unfettered, microscopic gaze."

He stepped over the barbells and went to the door. "And open the windows in here—it smells like a gymnasium."

"Yes, sir. Good night, Mr. Lord."

When Lord entered his house, a light blue, two-story stucco home of former French colonials on a quiet residential street less than a ten-minute drive from the embassy, a little boy jumped up from the rug on which he had been playing with his blocks, took three tottering steps, and fell down. He clambered up, took three more steps, and crashed down again, then scooted across the rug on his knees to Lord, who seized him and tossed him into the air until the child squealed with delight.

Lord set him down and they played the child's favorite game, in which he would scramble away as fast as he could, and Lord would grab him by the foot or diaper and drag him back on his belly, and it would start again until the boy made it safely into the kitchen, his father pounding the rug behind him, just missing his toes as the boy reached his mother.

"Hurry! Hurry, Lance," Lord called, pursuing the child,

who was shrieking with glee, scampering across the kitchen tiles, and throwing himself into his mother's outstretched arms.

Lord tousled the boy's black hair as he kissed the woman, a long, lingering kiss. The boy finally grew bored and poked Lord in the eye with his finger.

"Little oedipal monster," Lord said, breaking away. "Sorry I'm late, Ahne."

"You are always late," she said with a smile.

"I know; I'm sorry about that, too."

"You're not going out again tonight, are you?"

"No. Let's get rid of the kid and go to bed early."

"Do we have time for dinner?"

He smiled. "If we hurry—I'm really beat; at my age you'd better grab it when you can."

"Forty is not old, Wilson."

"Exactly what a mistress is supposed to say. Thank you. But a forty-year-old man knows exactly what forty means, and having a fifteen-month-old son only underscores it. Do you know, when he'll want to throw a football around, I won't be able to; I'll be too old—he'll laugh at me." Lord playfully stuck his finger in the child's cheek. "Better not, you little bastard."

Ahne made hushing, censoring sounds. She did not like profanity, his saying the word "mistress," and especially his reference to the child's illegitimacy.

Lord took the child from her arms. "I'll play with him in the living room until you get dinner ready."

Lord stretched out on the carpet and placed large colored blocks all over his body; the boy gathered them up and tried to stack them on Lord's chest.

He had not wanted the child, had tried to persuade Ahne to have an abortion, but she insisted that she wanted a child by him and none of his arguments—racially mixed parentage; illegitimacy; his, Lord's, age; the unpredictability of his job; the war—had dissuaded her. But at her desire to name the child after him he had drawn the line. "I never liked my name," he told her. "It would just sound stupid on a half-Vietnamese child."

92

"I like your name," she had told him. "It is distinguished, and I won't have a Vietnamese name for him."

So Lord had come up with Lancelot, and she had liked that, especially when she learned who Lancelot was. But he chose it because the child would be called Lance, and that was an acceptably oriental-sounding name.

"Why don't you choose a new name for me too," she had said.

"I love Ahne. If I were to choose an American name, it would be just the same—Anna."

That had pleased her very much; but everything about him pleased her—it had from the beginning when they first met.

Lord had arrived in 1963, four years ago, in the final days of Diem's rule. Ahne's father, a colonel in the South Vietnamese army, had been put to death by Diem in one of his brother's earlier purges of Buddhists. She, because of her family connections and her fluency in French, had gotten a clerical job at the French embassy when she was eighteen. She met Lord on one of his first liaison calls to Sûreté. All other Americans had spoken pidgin English to her, but she rebuffed them all, as she had all the French, because she was a very shy, chaste girl who had been strictly reared.

Lord was gracious to her, and despite what she thought was his inept French, he spoke to her without self-consciousness, and as an adult woman deserving respect.

Then one day when she returned from work, she found him at home talking with her mother and uncle with whom she was living. He had explained his marital situation to them and asked if they had any objection to him as a suitor.

They were impressed and posed no objections. Then he asked her if she would have dinner with him. Four months later they rented a house together and she quit work. He had been apprehensive for her about her family's reaction, but Ahne had told him that in Vietnam women were expected to be strong and independent.

"Vietnamese women never bound their feet, and you'd never see a Vietnamese woman giggle and hide her face when talking to a man, like Japanese women do."

"I've certainly noticed that," Lord had answered; her forthright manner often revealed an obstinate core.

"Vietnamese women have always been able to own and manage property, and I think that's only recent in many Western societies, isn't it?"

Her obstinacy culminated in the child, but now he was glad she had stood up to him. He had missed the childhoods of his other children; seeing Lance's growth was like witnessing the wonder of babies for the first time.

As Lance built with the blocks, Lord felt his diaper.

"Hey, stinky, when are you going to learn to use the potty?"

No one who had ever worked with Lord could imagine him changing a diaper, but now he did, happily and deftly.

"We'll eat in about fifteen minutes," Ahne said, coming into the room, finding them both back on the floor again.

She dropped down on the rug with them and stroked Lord's forehead. "You look tired tonight. And something's bothering you."

He smiled. "How can you tell?"

"You didn't whistle when you changed the diaper; you always do."

He laughed. "You can't smell anything when you whistle."

"I know. But tonight you didn't; that means you are troubled."

"How can there be any secrets from women?"

"Why should there be?" she countered. "Anything men do in secret is probably no good."

"Well, so much for the CIA," he said with a laugh.

"What is troubling you?" she persisted.

The child crawled onto him and straddled his chest. "Nothing really, just an annoyance at work."

She nodded, knowing that he would never discuss his work; the mere mention of "work" signaled the end of the conversation. Then he surprised her.

"You do the best you can; you work years for something —you really want to help people, and then some asshole comes and in a mindless minute ruins it all."

In four years, this was the only reference he had ever

made to his job; she didn't say anything, just sat quietly beside him.

Lord picked his son up, raised him over him as he lay on his back on the rug. He let go, then caught him; he did it again and again to the boy's delight.

"He deserves to be free, doesn't he?"

"Yes," she said.

"And you too?"

She smiled. "I only care about him; it's not important what happens to me."

He put the child down and took her hand. "It's important to me."

Then he truly surprised her, venting an anger and determination she had never seen. "I'll be goddamned if I'll let him sell out everyone in this country." He lifted his son high and promised, "I'll kill him first."

CHAPTER

· 7 ·

Teresa Hawthorne cradled the infant in her arms. The child's breathing was smooth only as long as Teresa held her, momentarily calmed, as though soaking up some life-sustaining force. The rest of the time the infant whimpered, flinched, and twisted, a pathetic creature, syphilitic and heroin-addicted, emaciated and covered with oozing sores.

Teresa rocked and hummed softly. She did not feel the crushing heat or stifling air, nor did she hear the screams from the ward, the wails and cries of the women and children.

The baby in her arms would die soon, she knew; it had already suffered numerous convulsions. It could not feed and would perish from dehydration. The hospitals, hopelessly overcrowded, unable even to care for the wounded soldiers, would not take such a child.

Usually these babies were left on garbage heaps. Teresa had found many newborns, sprawled like rag dolls in the rubbish. She had gathered the little corpses and brought them to the church for burial until the nuns told her they could no longer accept them. Now she simply left them.

Yesterday, a girl perhaps twenty, barefoot and dirty, her clothes tattered, had wandered in with drug-vacant eyes and simply held out the day-old baby. As soon as Teresa took it, the girl turned away and left, wandering back to her alley or brothel.

Probably it was not even hope that had brought the woman to the hospice, any more than it would have been malice to lay the child on the refuse; most likely it was as unconscious an act as the conception had been, or its death would be.

Teresa's clinic was a former French hospice run by nuns in a once quiet neighborhood; the white stucco, two-story building was now a crumbling ruin in a slum of tenements, on a filthy street choked with motorcycles and pedicabs. The front entrance was boarded shut to keep out looters; access was from a trash-littered alley where beggars and cripples camped. Inside, cots and cribs were so close together that there was barely space to stand between them, and no passageway through the long, narrow room to the doorless toilet. The staff—Teresa and six other women—shared small cubicles in what previously had been the supply room; the nuns' quarters had been converted into rooms for sicker children, and for the women who had not yet delivered. A part of the kitchen was set aside for deliveries.

Yet the hospice was immaculate; anyone idle was thrust a broom or mop or rag. Cleaning was the only activity, except for painting, whenever paint could be scrounged.

The interior was psychedelically colored, bright blues and reds, yellows and purples, whites and greens, whatever color paint had been found or contributed, and splotched onto the wall wherever the painter chose. The effect, however, was pleasing, as though it were a happy nursery; and interspersed on the walls were little drawings, here and there a woman's expression of hope or longing or memory—a flower, a bird, a sun.

The number of women and children remained constant with the number of cots and cribs: one hundred fifty. Women came to deliver, others returned to the brothels or just wandered away; infants died or were placed in orphanages, others took their places.

Teresa Hawthorne had run the hospice for a year; she had been in Saigon for three, before that in Taiwan and the

Philippines, altogether thirteen years in the Orient, a third of her life. Before that she had been a Catholic nun. Before that she could hardly remember, though inside she felt herself still to be the solitary figure of her childhood, an almost ethereal, otherworldly child, large and awkward, out of place with childish concerns and play.

Simple, that is how she was described. And simple is how she felt about herself now: plain and horsey and simple—though that is not how she appeared or how others would describe her.

She was like her clinic, strained and wan on the outside—a tall, thin woman with short brown hair and brown eyes—yet inside, there was color and humor and life, so rich and vibrant that they seeped through the skin to infuse her with a lustrous beauty. Though her face was worn through work, there was no tiredness or sadness in it, but instead, an open freshness and expectancy.

Born of elderly, wealthy, and very devout parents, she was reared in privileged isolation and was overly protected—no makeup, no frilly dresses, nothing light or frivolous: life was serious and meant to be dedicated to God.

But Teresa was a goose with no mind for studies. "No mind for anything," her father grumped. "She's detached," her mother said. "A holy detachment." "A holy fog, more like it—the girl's a clod," her father answered.

She did not play with other girls, was not interested in dolls, makeup, or clothes, did not read mysteries or romances, and showed no interest in boys. Even when her parents thought it was time, when they bought her dresses and sent her to beauty shops, she was indifferent; she liked bright clothes and liked her hair done up, but then her hair would fall, the clothes would rumple and tear, and she would not notice. She had no aptitude for music, went without complaint to years of violin lessons without ever, as far as her father discerned, learning a single tune. And she could not dance; a closet full of tutus and ballet slippers in ascending sizes only brought her father grim memories of sitting white-knuckled at a hundred recitals as his daughter galumphed out of step, pirouetted with alarming unpredictability, and sometimes fell, once off-stage into the audience.

But she had kindness and humor, and as she grew older, she had friends. People liked her; there was nothing in her to dislike, to envy, to covet. She was straightforward and sensible; girls confided their secrets to her, and she developed an ease with boys because none of them thought of her in a sexual sense—she was no more sexual than she was musical or graceful. But in this instance it was not a lacking, but a transcending.

Once, on a dare, the high school star athlete took her out. On a deserted lane, in a closed car, he had forced himself on her, crushing her on the seat, mashing his mouth against hers, thrusting under her clothes, and then, stripping off his pants, he had stopped. Ashamed and apologetic, he pulled away. She had been frightened, but later she laughed about it, and there were no recriminations. There was simply an aura about her; she was never asked out again, yet there yearned in her a desire to give and share of the love that overbrimmed her being. There was no reticence or squeamishness about sex or touch, and always there burned in her the embers for husband and children, but it was not to be—boys and men could sense the fathoms of love and giving, knew the depths were too vast for them, and they lingered on the shore, digging their toes into the sand, drawn but afraid.

What her mother called detachment, her father doltishness, was in fact spiritual purity; she was as precocious spiritually as Mozart had been musically, but because kindness and decency cannot be marked, she was merely thought simple.

Her beliefs were indeed simple, too simple to be categorized as theology; she gained no more from catechism than from music or ballet lessons. None of the liturgy and ritual, the pomp and ceremony, made any impression on her. The teachings of Christ, the lives of the saints, the lessons of denial, sacrifice, and martyrdom, had little or no effect on her. In the same way, she did not understand Christmas decorations—putting baubles, lights, and tinsel on a tree that was beautiful in itself.

What the church taught—sacrifice, helping, giving—she felt instinctively; what was demanded—worship and obedience—she ignored. That, of course, was her undoing in the church.

The idea of God never rooted in her mind—she never conceptualized a being behind goodness or kindness, nor were her acts motivated out of love or fear of Him.

As her spiritual purity was mistaken for simple-mindedness, so her goodness was mistaken for devoutness. Yet it was not dedication to God that brought her to the nunnery; rather, it was her belief that as a nun she could best help others.

Instinctively she knew that desire was painful, insatiable, and destructive, so she tried to free herself of wants and desires, but she failed daily because she so much wanted to help others. She understood the paradox—that wanting to end pain and suffering was itself a want—a paradox more acute in the Orient where there was so much suffering.

She left the Catholic church when she realized that it was irrelevant for her. The demands of worship and obedience were too great and detracted too much from the simple good she sought to perform.

Finally, God became irrelevant too. She did not need mystery or transubstantiation—spirit was enough, the oneness or nothingness of Eastern thought.

"You're nothing but a Mason," Father Dourmant told her. "A freethinker. Like Voltaire, and Rousseau, and Ben Franklin. And the Buddhists. It's the same damn nonsense —spirit, nature, nirvana: a theological lobotomy."

Perhaps he was right, she allowed; she had no time to think about such things. "I have no answers," she said. "I try not to have any questions either."

Leaving the church was no more difficult than shedding useless skin. Eventually she found her way to the Pearl S. Buck Foundation, working in the Orient to help the illegitimate children of Asian women and Western soldiers. Through her work with the churches and orphanages she met Father Dourmant. Last fall, with his help, she took over the hospice, but the care it provided was woefully insufficient—the women were too diseased, the children too sick, and for the addicted nothing could be done. There was virtually no money, only enough for food and basic supplies; medicine was stolen long before it reached the hospice.

Funds trickled in from a few charities, and Father Dourmant came almost daily with a few piasters. She had no idea where he got them, probably from his own collection box, because the bills were so torn and dirty. Her efforts to raise money from the American embassy had all failed. The government was not going to acknowledge illegitimate children; that was a problem for the local authorities—but the local authorities were not interested in the illegitimate babies of U.S. servicemen born to prostitutes and drug addicts.

So this baby in her arms would die. Probably it was a mercy; death would solve all its problems: the syphilis, the sores, the deformity, the black father.

In the doorway suddenly was a tall, gaunt man with white hair. He stooped to enter, his black cassock the only somber color in the ward.

He started toward her with determination, then slowed as he made his way through beds and cribs, slowing further as he stopped, touching and soothing, all the while his face, at first fixed, even angry, easing, until by the time he reached her, his look was mild and gentle.

"Good afternoon, Father. How are you today?"

He sat on the edge of a bed. "Well, thank you. And you?"

"Very well."

The priest bent forward to take the infant. The baby's eyes opened, the body tensed, but when the priest cradled her in his arms and brought her close to him, the infant eased.

"I haven't seen this one before," he said.

"She came yesterday; she can't nurse, and the convulsions are more often."

"Do you want me to bring some heroin?"

She laughed. "Are you dealing dope now, Father?"

He shrugged. "What's a little therapeutic heroin? You can withdraw her gradually, though I don't think she will live long in any case."

He handed the child back to Teresa. "I should baptize her."

"Would that make a difference, Father? Do you imagine that your God would care about such a thing?"

"I have no idea what my God cares about, or what He is up to. I can't even count on Him for a cup of coffee anymore, but it can't hurt if we send the child off to your Perfectly Harmonious Nothingness baptized, can it?"

Then, stung about the heroin, he said testily, "I send all the wretched women of the parish to you for birth control pills and contraceptives. What's wrong with easing a little pain with drugs?"

"Here," he said, handing her a large roll of bills.

She accepted them gratefully.

"I hate to imagine the sin this money is supposed to be absolving. The man didn't even make a confession, just came up after praying for a few minutes and handed me the money."

"He meant the money for the church," Teresa said.

"He meant the money to save his worthless soul. But God doesn't accept bribes."

Teresa smiled.

"Besides, if the church kept the money, the bishop would only steal it." He shrugged. "Better that I should."

"Thank you," she said. "You've been so good to us."

"I'm sure God will reward me."

"The preparations will be very great," she said solemnly.

"I have no doubt." He looked about the ward, saw the pain everywhere, heard it too. "I can hardly wait to see what He's managed in the next world. Well, enough theology; did you have any luck at the embassy?"

She shook her head.

"Bastards," he said.

"They're afraid. If they acknowledge that their soldiers are having illegitimate children, they may have to provide for them always."

"As well they should," the priest said indignantly.

"Did the French?"

"Of course not; when did we ever set a moral example? We're *supposed* to be hypocrites, the Americans aren't."

"They see all kinds of complications," she went on.

102

"Medical care, questions about citizenship, foster homes, orphanages."

"Money," he snorted. "And you know what else?" he asked, waggling a finger at her. "They can't bear the thought that their precious sons are over here screwing oriental women. They're over here bringing democracy to the savages, not pumping them up with dope and babies."

She laughed; she loved his anger and indignation, loved the way he worked himself up so that the most unpriestlike things spilled off his tongue.

"At least *we* were honest," he said. "We didn't want the little bastard babies in France, but we certainly knew what was going on."

He snatched the startled baby out of her hands. "Something has got to be done."

"I know," she said, eyeing the infant worriedly, expecting it to break into screams, but the movement had been so deft, the grip so sure, and his hold so firm and comforting, that the baby immediately relaxed.

"Well?" he asked.

She shook her head. "I don't know what else to do, Father. They see me coming now and have it all worked out—they pass me from one office to another. Everyone is polite and sympathetic, and isn't it wonderful what we're doing here? I go round and round and get nowhere. And it will just get worse—the more babies there are, the less willing they'll be to do anything."

Father Dourmant, his hands wrinkled and mottled with age, rocked the baby quietly. He closed his eyes, but Teresa could tell from the frown and pursed lips that he was not calm.

"Someone has come up with a way that she thinks will force the Americans to help," he said. He opened his eyes on Teresa. "I've never violated the confessional before, never betrayed what has been said to me. Priests suffer martyrdom to protect the sanctity of the confessional."

He paused on the magnitude of his sin, then said, "A woman came to me yesterday, one of the mothers from here, and told me that she was going to set fire to herself and her

103

baby in front of the American embassy. She asked me to forgive her and grant her absolution."

He had begun matter-of-factly, but then grew angrier. "I told her I would not. I told her that she would burn in hell forever, that the flames from the gasoline she poured on herself and her baby would be balm compared to the flames of hell. I almost dragged her out of the confessional and throttled her before the altar."

His anger subsided, replaced by deep worry. "But I don't think I convinced her. We talked for a long time, but she left intent on killing herself and the baby."

Teresa listened placidly, her hands folded in her lap.

"I think she might do it," Father Dourmant said. "Her family is dead, she has nowhere to go, and she says hell could not be worse than here. The child is like this one, with a black father, and probably diseased too. Death would be better for it, she says. She says she can't go back to the brothel. I told her I would find her work in the parish somewhere, but she said that would solve nothing—there would be more prostitutes and more babies. She said someone has to do something to stop it, like the Buddhist bonzes did to help their people. She said that when the bonzes immolated themselves, there were television cameras, and protests and demonstrations against the government, and all that brought the end of the Diems."

"She is right," Teresa said.

Father Dourmant's jaw set. "I am not remotely interested in what worked for the Buddhists, or the Tartars for that matter; I am not about to condone infanticide in the parish."

Teresa took back the child, who was beginning to stir at the priest's agitation. "What should she do?" Teresa asked.

"Well, hardly set fire to her child!" He dropped his head into his hands. "My God, birth control pills, dope, compromising the confessional, and now I'm talking to a woman about burning babies on Tu Do Street."

"What do you want me to do?" Teresa asked mildly.

The priest looked up incredulously. "Do you think I want you to hold the match? I want you to stop her!" he shouted. "I want you to talk to the wretched woman."

Teresa smiled. "The church used to burn heretics at the stake; there's considerable precedent for what she wants to do."

The priest was about to jump up in fury, but he drew a deep breath and sat back. "You're doing this just to vex me," he said. "I am an old man, Teresa, a frail old man who deserves respect and kindness. You should be ashamed of yourself."

"I am not trying to anger you," she said. "Nor am I suggesting Lin—it must be she, only Lin is that strong—do such a thing."

She stood, suddenly very tired and frail herself. She placed the infant in a crib, then stretched, arching her back. She brushed stray wisps of hair from her face and turned to Father Dourmant.

"This baby is going to die. What does it matter if it's from a drug-induced convulsion in her crib, on a garbage heap in the alley, or burned with her mother in front of the U.S. embassy?"

She looked down on the twitching child. "Maybe it would do some good. What good will there be to her life or death otherwise?"

The priest shook his head sadly. "This is what comes from falling away from God, child. I know you are tired and discouraged, and I cannot condemn you, but there is right and wrong, good and evil: moral choices must be made. As sure as I know anything, I know that ends do not justify means. Such an act screams with wickedness. Perhaps that poor woman in the throes of her agony cannot hear the evil, but you can—listen to your heart."

The priest stood. He patted her arm, then he smoothed her brow with his fingers and smiled. "Rest, Teresa, don't think. You will do what is right. Poor souls such as I have to wrestle with our consciences before we do the right thing— you do it naturally. I'll stop by tomorrow. Good-bye."

After he left, Teresa turned back to the child. She lay stiff in the crib, shaking violently, her eyes rolled back in her head, her tongue protruding, choking for air.

Teresa did not move; she stood before the crib, hands folded in front of her, watching.

The shaking increased, the limbs were rigid, the fingers as stiff as sticks, and the face turned blue.

She watched the color spread like dye, moving down the neck and torso. Then, as if the infant had been struck, it jerked, then went limp.

There was no expression on Teresa's face as she stared at the lifeless form.

When she looked up finally, a young woman was watching her.

Once beautiful, but now with hair partially fallen out, puffy skin, and needle marks up and down her arms, the woman held an infant in her arms, a pathetic thing, blind and brain damaged, its palate so badly cleft it would barely nurse.

For a long moment Teresa and Lin stared at one another, then Lin turned and walked away with her baby.

Teresa looked at the dead infant in the crib.

Would it do any good? she wondered. God doesn't care what happens to them, whether they live or how they die. The Americans don't care about them either; but if one were burned to death in front of the U.S. embassy, perhaps they would.

She herself would try the embassy one more time—just once more, and then if no one would listen or help, she would not stop Lin.

CHAPTER

• 8 •

"Hey, hero."

Ron Mead froze at the sneering voice; he stood motionless in the corridor of the embassy, his back to the man mocking him. The three Marines with Mead stopped too.

"Come here, shitbird."

The men beside Mead felt him tensing, a palpable stiffening; he was like an armed barricade in the hallway. One of the Marines put his hand on Mead's arm, a warning grip. "Easy," he whispered.

"I said come here, asshole."

Finally Mead turned. Others in the corridor quickly moved aside.

The Marine sergeant, a man equal in size to Mead, in his late twenties, coiled and tense as a boxer, immaculately groomed, brass gleaming, his uniform crisp and starched despite the heat, gestured to the men with Mead. "Move out."

"We'll catch you later, Ron," one said, backing away, then whispered again in warning, "Easy, easy."

The sergeant beckoned with a finger to Mead.

But Mead had regained control of himself. He yawned, then ambled back to Sergeant Robson Holman, standing so close that their chests brushed together, and their faces almost touched. Their eyes locked.

"Move back, fuckface," snarled Holman. "I only let someone I'm gonna screw or kill get this close to me."

"You're a dead nigger, either one you try," said Mead without moving.

"I'm still making up my mind which one it's gonna be, white boy," Holman said, pressing his face even closer.

Mead had been surprised at the speed and intensity of the hatred that developed between them. The distance he kept from others deterred friendship, but also deep animosities; yet the dislike he and Holman had formed for one another was instantaneous, and overwhelming.

"He's out to nail you," the other Marines at the embassy told him when he arrived. "You have more medals than he does—until you came, he was the hero. You have the Navy Cross, he can't handle that; he's gonna do everything to break you. It happened to another guy a couple months ago; they sent him out of the field too. He had a Silver Star like Holman did, and Holman was on his ass the minute he got here. Most everybody here never saw combat—we came right from Embassy School in Washington—so Holman can rub his medals and ribbons in our faces, but he can't do that to you. By the way, the other dude lasted two weeks."

"He's just a lifer," another said in contempt. "He looks good by making everybody else look bad; he's a career puke who'll stab you in the back—just be glad you ain't black like me. A black with a Navy Cross? Shit, he could just hang it up."

But even without Holman's enmity, Mead was having problems and had already been counseled by his officers and warned of possible court-martial.

He had never spent time in garrison; after basic training, he had been sent to Vietnam where he had been a year in combat. The adjustment from combat to the demands of embassy life—the inspections, spit and polish, drills and parade practice for visiting dignitaries—was more than he could handle.

He was too wired; every noise set him off—a slammed door or dropped book, a vehicle's backfire, sent him diving for cover; a rush of people, a crowd on the street, even clusters in the embassy corridors made him nervous.

His dreams were worse. They were blood red, and he would jerk awake covered with sweat, gasping for breath, his hands sometimes numb from being so tightly clenched, squeezing the air that in sleep was the blood-slick neck of the enemy soldier. The dead would not leave him alone. Every night he heard their screams and pleas and saw their mangled bodies.

He saw them everywhere. At a bar he saw Mitchell, dead four months ago, a bullet through the brain; Donnadio danced on his stumps with a whore, and Gonzalez toasted him with his own blood, his face a macabre leer. On the barstool beside him was Dutton, whose death grip now made him flinch, and before him, kneeling on the floor, was the enemy soldier without a face.

He dreaded sleep; his dreams were as alive as the jungle, dark and menacing, crawling with horror. Alcohol and drugs only aggravated the terror, twisting the images, turning sleep into demon-filled nightmares.

"Permission to touch you, Corporal," Holman said, and without waiting, stuck his finger in Mead's throat and pushed until Mead had to back up. "Don't ever come that close to me again. I don't like your smell. I don't like anything about you, Mead. You make me puke. You're weak. You got a medal and think you deserve special treatment—we're supposed to feel sorry for you because you suffered: you saw your buddies die, you can't sleep. So fucking what? You're just a worthless cunt."

He drew the skin down on Mead's cheekbones, exposing the raw eyes, then before Mead could react, Holman ripped Mead's sleeve, revealing his forearm dotted with needle tracks.

With a viselike grip he forced Mead against the wall and brought his knee into his groin. "Move, motherfucker, and I'll drive your balls into your throat."

Mead strained with fury, every muscle in his body bulging, his eyes flashing.

Holman stepped back contemptuously. "You wouldn't dare. You haven't got the guts, you doped-up cunt. C'mon, move on me."

But as he had a hundred times in combat, Mead went

cold, draining himself of emotion, in total control of himself, now so assured and relaxed that Holman, who himself had survived with that ability, knew that Mead was not going to make a mistake.

"I was trying to make it easy for you, Mead, but you can't even fuck up properly. Now I gotta get rid of you the hard way."

He stepped on Mead's boots and grabbed his brass belt buckle. "Since you can't bother spit-shining and polishing, I found something else for you to do. You're off guard duty—you just been assigned to be the personal bodyguard, flunky, waiter, kissass, to the President's special envoy. You're going to be responsible for his safety, needs, and happiness—providing his security, getting him his coffee, polishing his shoes, wiping his ass—and you're going to fuck up *so* bad."

Holman smiled wickedly, his eyes glinting. "You're gonna hate it, and feel sorry for yourself, and do dope, and get shitcanned so fast and so far that even that redneck hole you crawled out of will look good."

His manner changed to astonished innocence. "And I wouldn't have done a thing, just assigned a war hero, a Navy Cross winner, to protect the President's man. How was I to know he was a doper? A fuck-up, a crybaby, a cunt?"

Holman straightened Mead's sleeve and brushed up his uniform. "This is an important man coming, Mead, the personal representative of the President of the United States. When he says 'Jump,' General Westmoreland says 'How far?' and old Ellsworth Bunker starts hopping down the corridor. They're worried about this man, Mead. I heard he's tough too—ex-Marine, so you can imagine how impressed he's gonna be with a shitbird like you."

Holman grabbed Mead's uniform and pulled. "Come with me; I'll show you where you work from now on."

Mead raged within as he followed Holman through the corridors, up the stairway to the top floor of the chancery.

Painters, carpenters, and workmen were readying a special wing that was sealed off from the rest of the floor.

In a suite of offices at the end, four men—two civilians and two army officers—and two women worked at desks.

"Sergeant Holman reporting with Corporal Mead," Holman said to a tall, precise-looking colonel in his early forties.

Colonel John C. Waggoner, designated as senior aide to the arriving envoy, looked at Mead, saw potential trouble in his unkempt appearance, and said curtly, "Glad to have you with us, Corporal. We've all been chosen specifically for this task. We'll be working for Ambassador Bradley Marshall. You will answer to me, but Captain Latham will be your immediate superior—he'll brief you on your duties."

He pointed to two attractive women in their midtwenties, one blond, the other with long black hair. Mead, who as an embassy guard knew everyone who had access to the embassy, had never seen these women before.

"Miss Toland," he nodded to the blond woman, "is the ambassador's secretary."

"Dolores," she said without interest, then added so that there would never be a misunderstanding about their roles, "Corporal."

"Ann Fincher is an administrative assistant," Colonel Waggoner said, introducing the other woman, who smiled tightly.

"Mr. Beecher and Mr. Navasky are with the State Department and will be the ambassador's civilian assistants," he said of two men in their early thirties who merely glanced at him.

Nodding dismissal to Holman, Colonel Waggoner said to the younger officer, "Captain Latham, tell the corporal what to do."

Captain Benjamin Latham, a solidly built, very professional-looking soldier, slightly shorter than Mead, motioned him out to the hallway. "First, go polish your brass and boots. I never want to see you less than perfectly sharp. Understand?"

"Yes, sir."

"Get your hair cut, and shave again. I want you 'strac' at all times. That's a paratroop term for perfect, and that's what you're going to be. Forget the Marines, Corporal, you work for me now, and my standards are a lot higher. When

111

you're strac, which will be at two P.M., come back and see me. Dismissed."

Mead saw how perfectly Holman had set him up—these men would court-martial him for any infraction that might reflect on them.

At two he was back with a haircut and polished brass, and for the next weeks he suffered the indignities of a menial—getting coffee, emptying wastebaskets, sharpening pencils, sweeping and mopping.

No one spoke to him except to give him an order.

He came to hate them, and a murderous fury grew in him for the man he was to serve. The arriving envoy, Bradley Lawrence Marshall, came to personify all his humiliations and degradations, represented for Mead all the liars and cowards and sycophants and backstabbers he had encountered in Saigon.

The others talked of Marshall with awe and fear. One day, moving furniture at the direction of the two civilians, Mead listened to them.

"They flew in this desk from the Philippines—I think it was MacArthur's," said Navasky of the State Department, about the massive carved teak desk Mead was pushing into place.

"Everything was flown in from Manila, including the cunt," said Jerry Beecher. "That poor bastard won't even be able to muster for the dog and pony show after they finish with him—Dolores is supposed to be able to suck-start a B-52."

"They don't need to worry—he knows how to play the game. You don't get to the top by pissing in the boss's ear. He's not coming over here to bring back bad news, any more than we're here to give him any."

Beecher feigned horror. "What? You mean to tell me that we are supposed to be less than candid?"

"Figuratively speaking, we're supposed to be able to suck-start a couple B-52s ourselves."

They laughed, and left Mead to finish arranging the furniture. He was accustomed to that kind of talk. He knew that he was so inconsequential to them that they never considered his presence. "They don't think snuffies have brains or ears," he told the other Marines.

Daily his anger grew and his dreams worsened. Now he saw the dead, their bodies bleached bloodless, limbs mangled, being laughed at by the others in their civilian suits and starched uniforms, and the women pointing in disgust at the stumps.

Mitchell, Dutton, Donnadio, Gonzalez, and all the others had died for nothing. They had been killed, and not by the enemy, but murdered by those here and in Washington.

He had been a fool; they all had been.

The idea rooted in his mind.

And the dead would not leave him alone, not just those he had fought with, but those he had killed.

Over and over he saw into the eyes of the man who had knelt before him, pleading for life.

And the soldier in the tunnel, the last man he had killed. The first man he had killed had brought him elation and pride, and the esteem of others. He never thought about the enemy soldiers he had killed; they were simply numbers, and he lost count of how many.

But now they came back to him. He saw each one, frozen in the instant before death, before he squeezed off the round that severed their spines or ruptured their hearts or exploded their skulls. He saw their deaths in slow motion, and himself standing over them.

The dead came to him every night, but they no longer screamed; now they were silent and they just stared at him, like the man in the tunnel seeking release.

The weekend before the ambassador's arrival, Mead was granted two days off as the offices were given a final security sweep and secured.

He began drinking in late afternoon, planning to waste himself into oblivion, but Marines coming off duty, the weekend before them too, their pockets heavy with pay, persuaded him to go into the city. They started in the center, on Tu Do Street, in the bars and dope dens, then worked their way out to the darker, nether regions of Cholon, eight of them at first, a raucous group looking mostly for excitement and fights. Several dropped off along the way, content with the looks, price, and promise of a particular woman, but five of them, including Mead, ended up at three A.M., wild on dope, down a maze of back alleys, before a shambling two-story building where an old Chinaman enticed them inside.

Sung heard them outside in the courtyard. She had been in the brothel five months; though now almost mercifully comatose from drugs, she flinched at the sound of the men, at the shouting and guttural, primal noises coming from below. She closed her eyes tightly but could feel them outside in the dark, boots stomping, eyes wild, bodies sweating and heavy.

In her hands she clutched a rag doll. She brought it closer to her body, and beside her on the bench she felt the other women tense.

She wore a loose-fitting brown wrap that tied about her waist; she had no undergarments, and her hair was dirty, clumped in knots. There was no luster to her skin; her body and her eyes were vacant and red. She sat on the bench as limp as the doll, her legs spread wide, barefooted.

The drugs no longer brought her pleasure, only release, but neither did she feel pain, no matter what the men did to her; her mind and body were conditioned now to endure what happened, for it did not last long.

When men came into the brothel, she never looked up. Sometimes one would grab her, or the Chinaman would pull her off the bench and push her to a man, but sometimes the men would make a game of choosing the women, stripping their clothes, mocking and laughing until they settled on which ones to take.

A few of the women, those who could no longer work in the bars, who were too old, or now too ugly, with their teeth knocked out, their features misshapen from beatings, would giggle and seek to entice, but tonight not even these women sought to be picked by this group. The women huddled together, pressed close to avoid being chosen, for there was an aura of danger about these men.

One stood before Sung; she felt his dark presence and could see his boots, yet she could not look up.

Beside her a girl was pulled up roughly, and two other men grabbed women from the bench and dragged them off through the beaded curtains, but the man before her just stood waiting.

"Number-one fuck; suck good." The old Chinaman danced at Mead's side. "Doggy fuck number one."

The Chinaman pulled her up, then grabbed her hand and forced it to Mead's crotch, rubbing and groping.

Still without speaking, Mead pulled some bills from his pocket and gave them to the Chinaman, then he took her shoulder and led her into the other room.

At the basin, she worked at his trousers. She held him in her hands, as large a man as she had seen, and she looked up in fear, knowing how he could hurt her, and she saw his own eyes, burning into her.

She held him, mesmerized by the eyes, until he pulled away and said, "I'm clean."

She led him to the cot and stripped off her gown. She waited for him to undress, but when he didn't, she moved closer to help with his clothes, but he held her away.

"I don't want to fuck," he said.

She dropped from the bed to kneel before him, reaching into his trousers, but he lifted her up with one hand and sat her back on the bed.

"Just tell me when I have to go."

She had been with men who did nothing. Some lay on her without moving; others just sat until their time was up. Some beat her. She had asked the Chinaman about these men.

He waved his hand in exasperation, moving back and forth in his nervous dance. "They love other GIs and come here to pretend they are men. Or they love some god. Religion is no good for women. Or for whoremasters. Or they are ashamed of their organs. Those are the meanest, those with small organs—a small organ is a curse on the world."

But this man was different. He was on heroin, too, she

could tell, for his eyes focused with fierce penetration, then went blank, and it was as though she were looking into an empty room. His head nodded but would snap back, wary and alert.

She saw that he was young, but even at rest and while vulnerable, he conveyed power and danger.

From his pocket he pulled a handful of money and let it fall over her, onto the bed and floor.

She was afraid to move, so he bent over to pick up the money, and his hand felt the doll under the bed.

He pulled it out and she began to whimper.

She was afraid to reach for it, afraid he would strike her, but seeing the doll in his huge hands, she knew he was going to rip it apart.

She dropped her head, not wanting to see, and she cried.

He held the frayed doll curiously, then he put it in her hands. She grabbed it to her and clutched it tightly, and he saw that she was shaking.

He held the money in his hand, then gave it to her, not wanting to put it on her naked body, just offering it out to her until she took it shyly, still without looking up.

They sat side by side on the bed for several minutes, then he said, "I forgot. I need five hundred P for a cab to get back."

She held the money out to him.

He looked at her curiously. "You understand me? You speak English?"

She did not raise her head. "Yes," she said.

He nodded. They sat silently for several more minutes, then he left.

When he was gone, she counted the money. Nine thousand piasters. That was as much as if she had gone with thirty men. She put the money into the gown, and when she went back to the waiting room, she almost forgot about the bead-token the Chinaman gave for each man.

Sung thought about this man as she had no other man—because of the money, and because of the doll, but there was something else about him too: it was in his eyes, and the way

116

he held his body; he hurt too, she knew. She almost wished he would come again.

For days afterward, Mead could not get her out of his mind. When he saw the two women in the office primp and fret about their clothes and makeup, he thought of the woman in the brothel, naked and shaking on the bed. She bored through all his thoughts; no matter where he was or what he was doing, he saw her clutching the doll, crying and afraid.

She even entered his dreams and gave the dead rest.

Yet the dreams were not erotic; his dreams had not been sexual for a long time. And when he thought of the woman, it was not with desire or lust. Before the war, in high school, he had had girls in the backseats of cars and in abandoned shacks; sex was easy and pleasurable, without any edge of anger or violence.

But after combat that changed. He hurt the first woman he had had in Saigon; in the brothel, lying in her arms, her body under his, he turned brutally aggressive. Each time afterward, sex unleashed a violence that he had felt only in combat. He wanted to hurt another, to use his body to cause pain. At the time, cock hard, he could not control himself, but the desire to hurt repelled him and filled him with disgust and shame.

He had not had intercourse in a month, since one night in a brothel when he had lain on a woman, pounding her with his body, oblivious to her cries and screams until he felt small fists striking him, and looking up he saw two children hitting him, sobbing, as he fucked their mother.

He wanted a woman badly; he hurt from the need to be with one, but he did not trust himself anymore.

Yet he could not get this woman out of his thoughts.

Like most of the Marines, Mead had his own dingy tenement room away from the barracks where he escaped to get wasted, but unlike the others, he did not have his own woman.

But now it worked into his mind: this woman was not like the others, and she hurt, and it would be nice to have someone—just someone to see and talk to.

Finally, four days later, he went back to the brothel.

Men seldom came before dark, and hardly ever alone, so Sung looked up when she heard heavy boots on the stairs. She was sitting on the bench with the other women and recognized him immediately, though he seemed even taller and more threatening than she remembered.

She wondered if he wanted his money back, if he would hurt her for it, and she held the doll tightly against her.

Even the Chinaman seemed wary and stood a distance from him.

The man looked at all the women on the bench. All glanced away except Sung. For the first time she felt a positive emotion—she wanted him to choose her: not for the money he might give her, but simply to be recognized— one little thing, a soldier in a whorehouse pointing at her.

He did. He paid the Chinaman and motioned to her.

She stood and led him through the beaded curtain, holding his fingers gingerly as she brought him to the basin.

She worked at his trousers, but he said, "I'm still clean."

She went to the cot and unfastened the straps to her gown.

"Don't," he said. "You aren't a whore."

"No one here is," she said.

He sat on the cot beside her, staring at her curiously. "How come you can talk so good?"

She lowered her head, remembering what she had tried to forget. "I learned a long time ago."

He watched her hands shake, then he tilted her face up so he could see the addiction in her eyes.

"Come with me," he said.

She could not move her head; he held her face in his hand. She closed her eyes.

"I won't hurt you," he said. "I promise I'll never hurt you. Come with me."

She did not open her eyes. "I can't leave here."

"You can leave anywhere. That's the easy part."

She opened her eyes and saw his face, deadly hard, harsher than any man's she had ever seen, and yet she saw that he would not harm her, and she knew that she would go with him because she somehow knew that with him there might be a chance—though a chance for what she did not know.

He pulled her up from the cot and led her away, then stopped and went back. He dropped to a knee and felt under the bed, returning with the doll in his hand. He pushed through the beaded curtain with her, quickly past the Chinaman, then down the stairs, pulling her after him, out into the courtyard, into the street.

He took her to a two-story wooden building pressed into blocks of others exactly alike, leading her down a trash-littered corridor to a room where peeling wallpaper hung loosely and a torn curtain fluttered at an open window.

There was no furniture but two sleeping bags rolled in one corner; a toilet and basin were in another.

"You can stay here as long as you want and leave whenever you want. I'll bring you food."

"Why?" she asked him. "Why are you helping me?"

"Because you're not a whore," he said. "And because I'm not . . ." *An animal, a murderer,* he wanted to say, but instead he just looked away.

"The Chinaman said it would hurt worse than anything if I stopped the drug."

"There are worse things," he said.

That night she waited for him to say or ask something, but he didn't, and when they lay together on the sleeping bags, he did not touch her but fell asleep immediately.

She woke in pain, her throat dry and her muscles cramping. She slipped away from beside him, but he jerked forward and grabbed her by the neck, but in a second his hand relaxed and he released her, easing back, watching.

"Be careful when I'm asleep," he said.

"I was thirsty." She went to the sink and drank deeply.

He lit a cigarette and she could see only the red bud, but she knew he could see her.

At the window she looked out over the shanties. Clothes hung from every window, and although it was before dawn, people darted furtively in the streets. A truck rattled by with beer and ice for the bars.

"What is going to happen to me?" she asked.

She watched the red glow move slowly in the dark. His voice was tired. "What do you want to happen?"

She turned back to the window and stared for a long time. Her mind was blank.

She went to him and looked down. He was asleep, but he looked tense. There was nothing gentle or innocent in his slumber.

In the morning he was gone but there was a woman with her, much older, coarse looking and stocky, with a broad, fleshy face. She smiled and brought Sung water when she woke.

"Do you hurt?" she asked.

Sung nodded. Her skin was on fire and her bones throbbed, but she tried to concentrate and not cry out. "Who are you?" she asked.

The woman told her she was Han and had worked the bars on Tu Do Street for many years before going to live with a Marine embassy guard. Since then she had passed from one to another as they came and went.

"You are lucky Ron took you. Now you will always have a man to care for you."

"Is that his name? He never told me."

"Yes. Ron Mead. He is a friend of my man; he asked me to stay with you while he was gone. They say he is dangerous and has killed many men. I feel safer with my man. His name is Bill. They tell me it is a common name for Americans, and it must be so. He only eats and drinks and fucks, and he is very common about them all. Still, you are lucky, for when Ron goes, you will find another man. They are all jealous of one another and want each other's woman. There can be a thousand women in the streets, but they want the one in another man's bed."

She smiled, showing a mouth of missing teeth. "Then you will be a virgin again. A virgin for every man. They will fuck you, then give you things. In other times and places they give you things first then fuck you. And every year one goes and another comes."

"For how long?"

"There will always be men to fuck you and give you things. Until you are too old. But don't ask about then."

120

When Sung told her about herself, Han listened stoically, her face as masked and expressionless as the women's in the brothel, then she said, "You could stop anyone on the street and weep with them."

"And you?" Sung asked.

"You could weep for me too," she said simply, "but you were lucky—the drug was a blessing. All Chinamen are whoremasters. And the French all whores. Our own men are fools, and the Americans are children. What a place for a woman!"

"What do the men do?"

"They guard the American embassy. They are Marines. They are supposed to be special." Han laughed.

That night, after dark, he came back. She was in great pain and only intermittently conscious of his presence. She could not eat, and he had to help her drink because she shook so much.

She cried out and tried to claw her skin, and he had to hold her tightly to keep her from hurting herself.

She slept in snatches, and he would doze when she was quiet, but then would wake and sit with her when pain overcame her.

He was holding her, rocking her gently as she moaned, when there were loud raps at the door and two Marines came in. It was four A.M., and he had slept perhaps an hour all night.

"They sent us to get you, Ron. Your man's coming in."

"He's not due for a couple more days. I can't go in now. I can't leave her like this."

"Han will watch her. You better take off. The whole place is in a panic. They just got word that Marshall was coming in ahead of schedule, probably just to fuck'em up, but the brass is running around like roaches. You're supposed to be at Tan Son Nhut when he arrives."

"Fuck him," said Mead. "Fuck all of them."

The two men crouched beside him.

"You gotta go," said Bill Catton. "They'll throw you in the brig if you don't show—then how could you help her? I'll get Han. You get dressed. Everything will be all right."

"Aw shit," Mead said, almost in tears from exhaustion

121

and anger, but he laid Sung back on the sleeping bag and got up.

He put on a starched uniform, spit-shined boots, and polished brass that he had readied days ago, then he went to Sung, who lay shivering and moaning on the sleeping bag.

Han, squatting beside her, a blanket pulled about herself, looked up into his eyes. She had never seen such an expression, at once tender and pitying, yet cold as death.

He bent down, placed the doll in Sung's hands, and left.

CHAPTER

• 9 •

The stack of metal coffins reflected the sunlight so intensely that it seemed to be a source of energy itself, a dazzling, burning core able to melt through the tarmac of Tan Son Nhut.

A forklift raised the last silver coffin onto the pile as if it were a matchbox. There were twenty caskets, four neat rows of five on a pallet, slightly off the runway, ready to be loaded for return to the United States.

They had been in the way—a jarring sight for the President's special envoy—so they had been moved to a less conspicuous location; it would not do to have the President's representative blinded on arrival by the dead.

A ground crew moved about the pallet, trying to fit a canvas tarp over it, but the tarp was too heavy to toss, and the stack of caskets too high to reach over.

Ron Mead stared at the coffins from a short distance down the runway, where in a few minutes the envoy's plane was to arrive.

The ground crew scurried, thwarted in every attempt to cover the stack; finally they scaled the caskets and lifted the tarp over them, slightly disarranging them and marring the symmetry.

The men clambered down, shook themselves off, and

brushed their hands against their trousers, then they tied the flaps of the tarp and secured them to stakes in the ground.

Mead started toward the mound angrily, but then he caught himself; yet he could not shift his gaze. He stared as though trying to see into the caskets themselves.

In his mind he could see—not faces, only cadaverous flesh, the naked, anonymous corpses sealed in plastic, tagged and embalmed, any loose limbs or pieces of body likewise wrapped in baggies.

Twenty dead, he counted. Maybe Landis or Lieutenant Bishop, or Sutherland; or Snags, but he hoped not him, for Snags should be about ready to go home. He strained to see, but the faces in the caskets were absolutely blank, devoid of features or expression—just dead.

Mitchell had passed through here, and Gonzalez and Donnadio and Dutton; all of them.

Had they been hidden too, he wondered, an embarrassment to be moved out of sight so as not to offend the eyes of some dignitary?

He wanted to rip off the canvas and drag the coffins over to where the great man was to arrive; open them, and make him walk past and peer inside.

"Mead!"

He jumped.

"Wake up, for Christ's sake. Stand over here; this is where you'll be when he arrives."

Mead walked to where Colonel Waggoner directed.

"No," Waggoner amended, and pointed a few feet away. Mead moved.

Waggoner considered, then shook his head and motioned him back.

Like furniture, Mead thought, moving again.

"Good," Waggoner said. "Now stay there, and stay alert. You know what to do?"

"Yes, sir."

"Tell me."

"I'm to guard him, the ambassador, and make sure no one gets too close to him unless he wishes the contact."

"Not everyone, damn it."

"I know," said Mead in slight confusion, not about his duties, but how to express them. "Not General Westmoreland, or Ambassador Bunker, just . . . little people."

"Right. And be unobtrusive about it."

"Sir?"

"Jesus," Waggoner snapped. "Are you going to push them out of the way? Stab them with a bayonet?"

"No, sir, just sort of block them. Like in football."

"Right. But don't tackle them."

"I know what to do," Mead said, offended.

Waggoner patted his arm. "I know you do. We're all just a little nervous."

Waggoner wiped sweat from his forehead and moved away. Almost everyone was sweating, Mead saw; all the fresh uniforms were drenched, except for his, and a very few others.

It was eleven A.M., and though a cloudless sunny day, a beautiful bright morning, it did not seem so hot to him, but he had known jungle heat, and these men hadn't; they worked in air-conditioned offices and slept in air-conditioned quarters. Only a man of great importance could bring them out in such heat.

From his vantage, in front of the group, facing them, so that when Marshall arrived he would be able to fall in behind him, Mead looked out on the choreography of the reception committee.

Even when President Johnson had decorated him at Cam Ranh Bay there had not been this many generals and dignitaries. Mead had stood for hours in the sun that day, too, and had rehearsed over and over their little scene, heroes in formation, marching out to receive their medals, and marching back.

A major, a strange-looking man, Mead thought, all hands and expressive gestures, had arranged everyone not just by rank, but by size within ranks. The four three-star generals stood in descending heights, and so it was with the other generals and civilians—after Ambassador Bunker and General Abrams, Westmoreland's deputy, the supporting cast was arranged for esthetics.

125

For diversion, Mead tried to count the number of stars, but there were too many, and the sunlight blurred the gleaming silver on their uniforms so that little heaps of dazzling light blazed like miniature replicas of the mound of caskets.

Mead recognized only Ambassador Bunker, General Abrams, a few generals and senior State Department officials, and The Phantom, as he was called by the Marines in the embassy—Wilson Abbot Lord, officially listed as consular officer, but known as the senior CIA officer.

Lord was not sweating, Mead noticed without surprise, and his face expressed what no one else's did—boredom. Abrams looked annoyed, Bunker anxious, others showed discomfort or nervousness; Lord alone indicated no interest whatsoever in the proceedings. Several times Mead felt his scrutiny, an almost laser-intense look, but each time Mead glanced at him, Lord's expression was distant and detached.

Lord was the only person who interested Mead. The others seemed not so important and powerful as they were overweight, out of shape, sweaty, and old. But Lord was different. Mead sensed danger about him as in no other man. Lord would be the first man here Mead would choose to have on his side in a fight, and the last one he wanted as an enemy.

Though part of the reception committee, Lord somehow remained separate and aloof, with a relaxed stance that nevertheless seemed coiled to spring.

It was a game among embassy personnel to guess the CIA employees and hierarchy. Because Marine guards kept the arrival and departure logs, and knew who had access where, they spotted Lord as the senior agent, calling him The Phantom because he kept no scheduled hours, often arrived to work in the middle of the night, never was seen with anyone, and never spoke to anyone as far as the guards knew.

Several times at three or four in the morning, Mead had been confronted by Lord, holding out his pass. "Good morning, Mr. Lord" was met with a faint nod—not haughty or rude, just an acknowledgment.

It was Lord's presence, not Abrams's or Bunker's, that made Mead realize the importance of the man arriving.

Again Mead felt the scrutiny, but again Lord was not looking at him. The extraordinary fine profile with the straight nose and sharp chin was turned toward the approaching marching band and honor guard. Mead suddenly spotted a motorcade racing onto the runway from behind the terminal, escorted by police on motorcycles and soldiers in jeeps.

"The gooks," Mead heard, an audible chorus of surprise at the flashing lights and wailing sirens of the arriving representatives of the government of South Vietnam.

The dignitaries tensed at the sight of the armed motorcade, and Mead clicked off the safety on his rifle.

The Vietnamese dignitaries got out of their limousines; a wide area before them was cordoned off by Vietnamese paratroopers, two of whom positioned themselves directly in front of Mead.

The awkward moment was diffused by Ambassador Bunker, who stepped forward to greet the ranking Vietnamese. Then everyone shook hands and bowed. The paratroopers gave a curt but friendly nod to Mead, then the soldiers jumped back into their jeeps and the motorcade sped off.

The Americans moved to accommodate the Vietnamese with great deference, too much so, Mead thought, except for Lord, who acknowledged the man beside him with the same faint nod that he used to give Mead.

The major reappeared and reset the stage, but the symmetry was hopelessly destroyed: with the shorter Vietnamese standing mostly on the left, the runway seemed tilted. Looking out on the reception committee, Mead felt off balance.

Mead had no idea who all these people were; President Thieu and Vice President Ky were the only Vietnamese he would have recognized, except for Ho Chi Minh, but having attended a course on protocol, he knew that the ranking Vietnamese here would hold a position equal to that of the arriving American.

The laser gaze was on him again, but when he looked

quickly at Lord, the man was staring into the distance, at a tiny silver dot that had appeared on the horizon.

A young air force officer tapped his shoulder gently. "Sir, we'll be touching down in a few minutes."

Marshall opened his eyes; for an instant he had no idea where he was or whose face he was looking into.

"Saigon," the officer said helpfully.

Marshall smiled. "Thank you. I knew I was supposed to be somewhere today." He glanced at his watch; it read three, but he didn't know if it was day or night; the cabin was dark, the shades drawn.

"You might want to reset that, sir. It's eleven A.M.; you slept nearly four hours. Can I get you something? Coffee? Juice?"

"You have any amphetamines?"

The officer looked so surprised, then dubious—as though debating whether the question was serious, and how he was to answer—that Marshall laughed. "Coffee will be fine, thank you."

He stood and went into the bathroom to clean up, slapping cold water on his face.

In the mirror, he decided that considering the length of the flight, he did not look too bad. Direct from Washington, and with touchdowns for refueling in Anchorage and Tokyo, he had been airborne for eighteen hours—with about six hours' sleep altogether.

His arrival was three days early.

An hour beyond Washington, Marshall notified Tokyo that he would not be stopping over, merely refueling, then continuing on to Saigon. He did not want a cumbersome and time-consuming layover in Tokyo, and he wanted to avoid ceremonies there and in Saigon.

While many affected disdain for ceremony, Marshall genuinely hated the trappings of diplomatic protocol. His aversion dated back to Korea when his combat unit was ordered to prepare for a general's inspection. Wounded men picked up paper and pulled weeds on the battlefield; a slit trench latrine was filled in to spare the inspecting team, and when Marshall would not order men to trim the grass around a drainage ditch, he was threatened with court-martial, so he did it himself.

When the general inspected, it was in his jeep, and he did not even slow down as he passed by.

Now when he undertook a mission, Marshall made it clear there would be no reception committee, no honor guard, no welcoming speeches. He preferred not to feel the resentment of those forced to meet him, and he hated the spectacle of the public stroking. It made him feel dirty.

And there was Ryan, already at Fort Bragg; in three months he would be in Vietnam, and Marshall knew with horrible certainty what his son's fate would be.

He did not have three days to spare in Tokyo, nor even thirty minutes to waste in ceremonies in Saigon if he was going to save his son.

What he felt went beyond fear; fear was small and petty, what he had felt for himself in the launch off Guadalcanal and at Chosin. What he felt now for Ryan was dread, so heavy and hurtful that the mere contemplation of it was crushing him.

When he returned to the cabin, the shades were up, the bed folded away, and the compartment remade into a comfortable executive office. Coffee and a small breakfast buffet were waiting.

Sipping coffee, and looking out the window, he beheld the cloudless day, and the earth coming into focus as the plane dipped lower: the South China Sea, the jungle, the delta with the Saigon River snaking through it—blues and greens so bright as to be hallucinogenic. From this height, the land seemed serene and peaceful; a tranquil, verdant, and azure world beneath him.

But dropping lower, the beauty showed gapes and gouges. The jungle was defoliated, giant barren swathes in the earth, and the landscape was blighted with metal boils—armed camps of Quonset huts and water towers, trucks, tanks, and airplanes.

Then the city rose, a pollution cloud on the horizon, a smudge pot spewing noxious vapor.

The 727 presidential jet, embossed with the Great Seal of the United States, started its final approach. Sampans and water buffalo dotted the waterways; fields were surgically stitched with concertina wire; huts and squalid camps formed a brown scab around the city; and the city itself seemed to reach up for the plane, a giant insect with a million antennae.

Marshall fastened his seat belt and folded his hands in his lap. He watched out the window as the plane banked sharply, then—an arrow to the heart—streaked toward the runway.

He saw the band and color guard, and the red carpet before the plane touched down.

"God damn," he said, so loudly that the officer, strapped in at the front of the cabin, said, "Sorry, sir," for what he thought was criticism of the rough landing.

As the plane taxied, Marshall saw the size of the awaiting welcome, and anger flashed through him. He did not want this. He had told them that there was to be no reception. What did these people take him for?

Then the anger subsided to mere irritation—nothing could be done; there was no point in creating furor over a misunderstanding, or what was well-intended.

He unbuckled and stood, resigned to the ceremony.

But he was not prepared for the blast of heat that struck him, or the blinding sunlight or the cacophony of band instruments and plane engines. The heat, light, and din were dizzying, and he caught himself from stumbling backward. He started down the stairway tentatively and off balance, unable to see the steps.

Anger surged back, at his own awkwardness, the discomfort, and the unexpected reception. By the time he reached the bottom rung, his calm was gone, and only out of politeness toward the seventy-three-year-old Ambassador Bunker did he restrain his temper.

They performed the formal ritual and exchanged personal greetings. Then the elderly man escorted Marshall down the red carpet to meet the others.

The officers saluted, Marshall shook hands with them, and accepted from General Abrams the regrets of General Westmoreland that pressing military matters prevented his appearance.

Then the Vietnamese foreign minister stepped forward and introductions were made.

The band played both national anthems, the flags were presented, Bunker made a short welcoming speech and the foreign minister a longer one, expressing gratitude for past assistance and pledging cooperation in the struggle for freedom.

Marshall had no prepared speech, and when the microphone was turned over to him, he could not remember the name of the foreign minister. In the stifling heat, even the most innocuous platitude wilted in his mind.

"Mr. Foreign Minister, Ambassador Bunker, gentlemen: thank you for this gracious reception. I am here at the behest of the President of the United States, and bring you . . ."

At that moment, a blast from a jet engine blew off the canvas tarp covering the caskets. The midday sun reflected a dazzling, blinding burst of light from the metal, forcing Marshall to raise an arm to shield his eyes.

Then he lowered his arm and stared at the stacked coffins.

The sun, shimmering off the metal, mesmerized him; the light gleamed as it had on the beach at Guadalcanal and blinded him as it did on the snow at Chosin. He saw his son; clearly he saw Ryan in the coffins—in all of them: Ryan lay in every one of the caskets.

Everyone turned to follow Marshall's gaze when he stopped speaking. For a moment there was stunned silence.

To Mead, behind him, it looked as if Marshall had been struck. Marshall recoiled, then slowly straightened, his back arching in what Mead knew was anger—he could feel it emanating from the man.

Lord saw the anger too. He had watched the canvas straining the stakes, and at the moment the tarp tore off, he glanced back to observe Marshall's reaction.

Shock came first, the recognition of what was exposed, then a curious blend of anguish and defeat, a very personal wounding; then anger, growing to such fury that Lord, a man seldom surprised, was taken aback.

In that instant, he realized that Langley had completely miscalculated—*he* had been right about Marshall. Here was the enemy, Lord thought—the soft underbelly of America, whose dainty sensibilities would lose a world to communism; here was the rotten core.

Lord was filled with sudden loathing. Marshall represented what he despised: the naïve, hand-wringing, bleeding-heart liberal who would cede the war to the communists, betray the very men whose caskets so moved him.

Here, Lord realized, was the most dangerous man in Vietnam, a man who could achieve what the North Vietnamese and the Viet Cong never could—a victory for the enemy.

Marshall was not here to observe—he was here to appease and betray. And he could do it, Lord knew.

But he would not let him. He, Lord, saw through him, and he would stop Marshall.

Lord turned his gaze from Marshall to the Marine standing behind him. Lord considered him for a long moment, and when Mead felt the eyes and looked at him, Lord did not glance away. Their gaze locked, then Lord nodded slightly.

". . . greetings," Marshall said sharply, and stepped back from the microphone.

Ambassador Bunker shook his hand again and led him to a waiting limousine.

The door was held open and final salutes rendered. Marshall got in, and Mead, directly behind him, bent to get in also.

"Who's he?" Marshall demanded, more sharply than he intended.

Mead stepped back, stung. "Sir, I . . . I'm . . ."

General Abrams was at the door. "He's your bodyguard, sir."

A cluster of dignitaries formed a half-circle around the car. Mead stood awkwardly among them, humiliated by the spectacle he had become.

"A bodyguard?" Marshall said contemptuously. "I thought this was Saigon, not Hanoi. Isn't it secure here? Though those coffins are answer enough, I suppose."

Abrams leaned into the car, his face stern and unappeasing. "There is no secure area in a combat zone.

Your safety is my responsibility—I ordered the bodyguard, Mr. Ambassador."

"I don't want a bodyguard, General."

"I regret that it is necessary, Excellency."

The two men stared at one another, then Marshall relented. "If that is your considered judgment, of course."

"Thank you," said Abrams, who then half-shoved Mead into the backseat.

Mead edged as far away from Marshall as he could get.

Marshall ignored him; his gaze was on the caskets.

Not knowing what to do, Mead also looked out the window. Lord was standing by himself, staring directly at him.

CHAPTER
• 10 •

In the underground bunker on the forward slope of Hill 742, the northern Khe Sanh outpost, Luke Bishop stared through the night scope to the enemy ridge. A mile away, rising steeply from the plain, the craggy formation looked to Bishop like a dark, evil fortress.

Through the starlight scope, the plain between the hill and the ridge seemed a lunar wasteland, still and lonely, a cratered moonscape, endlessly dead.

Yet Bishop knew tonight the enemy was out there; he could feel them. He scanned slowly but saw no movement on the plain, and finally he laid the scope aside and rubbed his eyes; exhausted, he rested his head against the sandbags.

Bishop's platoon had been on the hill a month; two nights ago, a patrol from the ridge had struck the hill, killing two of his men. Now there were twenty-three left.

The hill is the final promontory before the Demilitarized Zone, a shell-pocked, defoliated waste that was once, before the war, a green ocean of rain forest and jungle. It is a blue circle on detail maps of Khe Sanh, a smaller circle on battalion and regimental maps, a tiny dot on division maps, and does not appear on corps and army group maps. On enemy maps it is a red circle, a red dot, and likewise nonexistent at higher headquarters.

Just inside the DMZ lies the ridge, the enemy's forward

outpost; the hill and the ridge face each other across the seared plain like two colonies of bacteria on an infected sore.

Days on the DMZ are scorching; light shimmers over the sand and the men shield themselves from the heat in their bunkers. But nights are cool; the wind blows off the desert, and in the moonlight, the dunes look like a menacing sea.

The enemy was out there now, Bishop knew, and dutifully he raised his head to scan again.

Three months of combat had etched his lean, angular face with strain. He looked more tired than sleep could restore, and older than twenty-two.

Since his first insert and Dutton's death, seven others had been killed, yet even so, Bishop believed in the war. Now, however, his belief had transmuted into a dogged determination to affirm that the carnage had not been in vain. The holy fire of his patriotism was doused, the altar of cause lay in ruins, he no longer knew what he believed, only that he believed, but the sacrifice was sacred: the dead consecrated the fire, their blood anointed the altar.

Behind him, the wood-plank stairs groaned under the weight of boots. Bishop turned to see Brock drop into the bunker. Brock more and more radiated cynicism and bored anger. An excellent platoon sergeant, Bishop thought, but an excruciating companion.

"They're out there tonight, Gunny," Bishop said.

Brock dropped onto an ammunition crate and unbloused his boots to massage his feet. "They're out there *every* night, Lieutenant. They live here. It's their fucking country."

Bishop did not want that tirade to start again so he picked up the scope to scan. Brock's conversation was women, old war stories, and the futility of this position, and Bishop felt that he had been married to him for twenty years. In fact, Bishop thought, if he ever was married to a woman for twenty years, he would not want to know her as well as he knew Brock.

Suddenly there was a snap and the bunker filled with the loud, high-pitched screams of a rat.

"God *damn* that Landis," Brock said angrily. "I told him a hundred times to stop setting traps."

Brock grabbed his rifle and went to the squealing, struggling creature pulling against its crushed leg. The animal thrashed at the sergeant's feet. Brock let the rifle fall casually, the butt crushing the rat's head, then he went back to his ammo crate.

Without turning from the scope, Bishop said, "One of these days, the rats are going to rise up and finish us off."

"They better hurry before the gooks get here first," Brock grunted. He rubbed his toes sensuously and contemplated the dead rat. "How come they don't make traps that kill rats right away?"

Brock mused a moment on his own question. "Probably it's better they're not killed right away," he decided. "If the bastard suffers, then the other rats will hear him and stay away."

Bishop scanned the desert. "Why is the place crawling with rats then, and why do they keep going into the traps?"

Brock puzzled the questions. "The same reason you and I are sitting in this goddamn bunker, Lieutenant," he said at last.

Then, to make sure Bishop got his point, Brock grabbed his rifle and held up the bloodstained butt. *"Marines* don't hide in bunkers, Lieutenant. Marines don't sit on hills. Ants do. And *army* people," he said with great disdain.

"Gunny, don't get started," Bishop said, putting down the scope. "My orders are to hold this hill. You know I think it's stupid." He pointed to his lieutenant's bars. "But what can I do?"

"Dien Bien Poo, that's what this fucking place is. I know I'm just a gunnery sergeant, and didn't study strategy and tactics at OCS, but—"

"You take first watch, okay?" said Bishop, ignoring him. "I need a couple hours sleep; nothing's going to happen for a while."

He crossed to his sleeping bag in a corner. The bunker was black and quiet; the floor was dirt, moist from seepage, and the low, reinforced ceiling compressed stale air that smelled of cramped living, sweat, and tobacco.

Bishop stripped off his torn, camouflaged jacket and lay

down, propping his field jacket under his head for a pillow and pulling his poncho around him. He had not bathed in two weeks; he felt crusted with grime and dirt, and his mouth was gritty.

Scrunching into himself, he felt the briefest flash of sexual longing, a pulsing in his crotch, but his exhaustion quickly extinguished it.

He may have dozed, but dreams, memory, and reality were so intermingled and sleep so troubled that sometimes he was not sure when he was awake or asleep, yet an insistent call on the field radio roused him.

"Bravo One, Bravo One, this is Bravo Six, Bravo Six."

Brock keyed the handset. "Bravo Six, this is One Alpha."

The company commander came back with insulting emphasis, "Bravo *One,* this is Bravo Six."

Brock tossed down the handset. "This must concern the total war effort—some grand strategy. He doesn't want to talk to sergeants, he wants you, *Lieutenant.*"

Bishop dragged himself up, grinning despite his ruined sleep. "Bravo Six, Bravo One."

"Bravo One, stand by to copy coordinates for Lima Papa insert."

Though he had heard perfectly, Bishop keyed the set incredulously. A two-man listening post could not be sent out this late; a night insertion in open terrain, with the enemy already on the move, would be suicidal. "Bravo Six, Bravo One. Say again?"

"One, Six; copy coordinates for Lima Papa insert."

"Bravo Six, that's a negative; not possible to comply," Bishop said with quick anger.

There was a pause, then the transmission with threatening deliberation, "Bravo One, you *will* send out a Lima Papa. Possible enemy rocket site at following coordinates. Ready to copy?"

Bishop started to dispute the order further, but instead he just stared at the handset, knowing that the decision had been made by superiors, and he had to comply. "Ready to copy," he said at last.

Captain Evans ended the transmission. "Give me the

departure time, and run the horses on this net so I can monitor. Out."

Bishop held the dead radio. "Jesus Christ," he whispered.

Brock was calmly oiling his disassembled rifle. "Call him back in fifteen minutes and tell him the men just left, then fake the whole thing on the radio. Don't even think of sending anyone out there tonight. He's such an asshole," Brock said, wiping the barrel. "College graduate." Then he looked up. "Begging the lieutenant's pardon."

"Why?" Bishop asked, more to himself than aloud.

"Because he's playing games, Lieutenant, clean and safe back at Khe Sanh with his maps and colored pencils. His butt's not out here on the line." Brock assembled the rifle without even looking at it. "Fuck him."

"It's an order, Gunny."

"Jesus, Lieutenant," Brock said disgustedly. "Spare me the bullshit. I'm not going to get involved in a fucking college argument about duty, ethics, and all that horseshit. Some orders are good, some bad—some you follow, some you don't. You been here long enough to figure that out. Now cut out this crap and go back to sleep. I'll run this thing for you."

"Gunny," Bishop said softly, "I can't disobey an order, you know that."

"Lieutenant, you *better* disobey that order. You're not some boot lieutenant who stumbled off the airplane this morning, you *know* better than to send anyone out there."

But then, realizing how young and inexperienced Bishop was, and sensing the danger of the situation, Brock went over to him, and though a smaller man, he pushed on Bishop's shoulders, forcing him down on an ammunition crate.

Brock crouched eye level to Bishop, so close that Bishop could see beaded sweat on his upper lip and stubble on his jaw.

"Listen, Lieutenant, I been in the Corps twenty years; I've spent more time in combat than you did in college. I seen . . ."

He stopped, and in his eyes Bishop could see—the frozen waste of Korea, men trudging, bent double in the snow, blood icy slush; then deeper in the eyes he saw the jungle and more blood and the desert and this hill.

Bishop blinked and saw his own reflection in the pupils.

"You're a good officer, Lieutenant, but let me tell you something—there's nothing sacred about orders. Sometimes orders are wrong, Lieutenant. You can't always do what you're told."

"Maybe there *is* a rocket site out there," Bishop said.

"There probably is. They've probably got a shopping mall going up too."

"A listening post could find it."

"For Christ's sake!" Brock exploded. "An LP wouldn't last an hour out there. They'd see them as soon as they left the wire. You send two men out there, Lieutenant—you're killing them."

"I don't have a choice, Gunny," Bishop pleaded.

"You haven't got a right," Brock countered. "No one's got the right to kill two men like that. Not for an order. Not for anything."

Brock reached out and shook him. "How many men have we lost? Eleven? Twelve? I can't even remember exactly. But you didn't kill them. You done your best here and haven't made any mistakes, except maybe a long time ago when you let Mead go down that tunnel, but even that worked out okay. None of the blood is yours, Lieutenant, but this will be. I don't see how you can still believe in this fucking war, but that's your business. What people believe . . . well, that's up to them, even crazy stuff like religion. But God damn it, not when it starts killing other people."

He looked straight into Bishop's eyes. "Don't do it, Lieutenant. Don't send two men out there."

"Gunny, I *can't* disobey an order; I can't choose what to obey and what not to. I'm just a lieutenant. He didn't give me an illegal order—this isn't goddamn Nuremberg. It's a valid order."

"It's a death warrant, and you know it." Brock let the words hang in the silence. "I thought you were different, Lieutenant," he said at last. "I thought you were better than the others."

Bishop dropped his head. "Don't," he said softly.

139

Brock stood before him coldly. "Then you write those names on paper, Lieutenant. Write down the men you want to die tonight. You're going to kill two men because you're afraid to do what you know is right. Write their names down and put them in your wallet, then carry them the rest of your life, because you will have killed them."

Bishop turned away; he was trapped. Brock was right, but right had nothing to do with this. For many minutes he stared out on the desert through the starlight scope; it remained as before, still and dead, eerie and forbidding. If death were a place, Bishop thought, it was out there.

Finally he wrote down the two names on a scrap of paper and handed it to Brock.

Brock did not take the paper, merely glanced at the names, then he left the bunker without saying a word.

Bishop stared at the paper for a long time. Am I killing them? he wondered. He looked about the cramped bunker, saw his rifle and gear in a corner, his sleeping bag rumpled on the ground, scattered C rations and loose ammunition—his home for the last month. I don't have a choice, he told himself; it's not my decision. He folded the paper with the names. It's a valid order—it's as if the President chose them, or Congress voted on them. Then he put the paper in his wallet and held the wallet tightly. He closed his eyes; please, God, let them be all right. No more dead; please, God.

On the berm facing the ridge, Scott Sutherland and Larry Miller huddled close together in the darkness, hunched over a machine gun, straining to see beyond the wire to the plain.

Miller was nineteen, with a wife and child, and he had been terrified every minute of the seven weeks he had been in combat. When the enemy had struck two nights ago, he had knelt impotently beside a man ripped by shrapnel, beating the sand with his fists as he listened to the screams, then kneading the sand as the screams softened into pleas for release, then sitting perfectly still when the man died.

Now he wanted to speak, rend the fearful silence, but no words came, only images, the dead, and he envisioned himself among them, their open eyes fixing him.

"Sutherland?"

"What?"

"I keep seeing Mitchell." Miller brought his arms around himself, hurting from fear. "No man ought to die like that."

Sutherland shrugged. "One way's no worse than another. Dead is dead."

Miller fell silent, giving himself to the night, seeing the dead. He clutched himself tightly. "Jesus, I'm so scared, Scott."

Sutherland was nineteen too, lean and darkly tanned, with hair bleached almost white by the sun, bleached as dry as his feelings after three months in combat. He had survived hard fighting since his first insert, sitting so afraid, trying so hard to hide it, beside Ron Mead on the chopper, the day Dutton was killed. There had been eleven others killed after Dutton, and it wasn't over yet, he knew.

There was no sense in those deaths; it could have been himself any number of times. He had been only a few feet away from Dutton on that first insert—the gook could have shot him instead, and it would be himself, not Dutton, rotting underground the last three months.

The thought filled him with anger. He felt that he had been tricked into this war, thrown out here for nothing. No one cared, and he was bitter. No one cared about those who were killed, and no one would care about him if he died, and that thought fueled his resentment, and his determination to live.

He was going to make it, he promised himself. He had survived his mother and father, who didn't give a shit about him, and he had survived Los Angeles gang wars, and he was going to survive this. Except this was different. . . .

"Everybody's scared," he said softly. "Even the gunny and the lieutenant."

"You too?" asked Miller, who had only seen Sutherland's scorn and swagger. Sutherland never seemed to let on to fear. He carried himself with such force and anger that Miller had never thought of him as being afraid.

Sutherland peered into the night and said quietly, "Sometimes I get so scared I want to throw up, but . . ." The futility swallowed the words. He laid his rifle aside and rolled away, punching his field jacket into a pillow.

"You take first watch, okay?" He drew his poncho around him and tried to sleep, but the dead came to him, the same cries from the same dead, every night now for three months. He forced his eyes tighter, squeezing out the dead, and in their stead came women. He moaned to himself, clutching his body.

Miller stared into the night for a long time after Sutherland fell asleep, then suddenly he jerked forward, grabbing the machine gun. "Scott."

Sutherland sprang awake instantly, blood pumping, his eyes straining in the darkness. Time passed, but Sutherland neither saw nor heard anything. Tiredness overcame him; his eyelids fell. He kept them closed, jerked them open, but finally gave in. "I don't see anything."

"There's something out there."

Sutherland spat. "The whole fucking gook army's out there somewhere." He lay back and in a few minutes was asleep, the women upon him again.

Then Miller saw it again. "Scott!"

His urgency brought Sutherland scrambling up, with his rifle positioned even before his eyes focused on the wire. "Where?"

"Just outside the wire."

Sutherland scanned the black terrain, then he said disgustedly, "That's a bush." He untensed, rubbed his eyes, and put down his rifle. "Larry, I gotta get some sleep. They're not gonna get into the wire. We spent two days booby-trapping that wire. Nobody's gonna sneak through now we done it right."

He spoke contemptuously, burrowing into his field jacket, drawing his poncho tighter. "Remember when the captain saw that goddamn John Wayne movie and we spent eight hours putting empty C ration cans on the wire so the gooks couldn't get in, then the wind came up that night and there was so fucking much noise from those cans clanging together that the gooks could have ridden Harley-Davidsons up here and we wouldn't have heard them? Well, nobody's getting in now, so let me sleep."

He was dreaming of soft naked flesh when he felt a sharp jab in his side and heard Miller hiss, "They're just outside the wire."

Sutherland jerked up again. Fear vised the back of his neck. He shivered, moving closer to the machine gun, yet when he refocused, there was nothing. "That's the same goddamn bush, Larry. Goddamn!" He grabbed his rifle and stood. "I'm going over to Coney and Frizzell's to sleep."

Miller hissed. "It just moved."

"Yeah, the wind just came up." He started away. "Jesus."

"Scott, I swear it's getting closer."

Sutherland sighed but crouched down. He peered into the night, then slowly raised his rifle.

Miller moved near and brought up his own rifle. "You see something?"

Sutherland nodded, prone in the sand, rifle on his shoulder. "Yeah."

Miller tensed and flipped off his safety. "What?"

"I see a bush."

"God damn it, Scott."

Sutherland sat up, laughing. "Relax. Think about other things."

"What? Mitchell and Donner? Blake with his guts all over the wire and pieces of him they couldn't find? For Christ's sake, I don't want to think about Mitchell, but I keep hearing him scream."

Miller put down his rifle and held his sides. "All I want to do is get out of here." His voice was a cry. "I want to see my wife. And my kid."

"Oh, Jesus," Sutherland moaned. "Not that again," and he stood up.

Miller watched him crouch, then ease away, vanish in the dark. Awful darkness settled over Miller too, and he pulled the machine gun closer. He heard noises at the wire. Instantly his wife and child disappeared, and he turned to call Sutherland, but Scott was gone. Oh, God, Miller thought, remembering two nights ago.

Sutherland crossed the hill noiselessly, his body flowing into the black pool of night, his rifle weightless in his hands, metal merged with flesh, all becoming one with the darkness.

Then he froze as a rifle safety unclipped.

"It's me, Sutherland," he said quickly.

"Where you going?"

"To get laid."

Another voice came from the dark. "Who's watching your post?"

"Fourteen gooks."

The voices snickered and he went to them, dropping into the bunker beside two men as motionless as warrior statues in darkened ruins. The blackness laid a pall on their features; only their eyes were alive and gleaming.

"You're just in time," said Matt Landis. "I'm gonna kill Snags if he tells me how short he is again."

"Forty-two days, motherfucker," said Snags.

Landis pulled out his bayonet and flung it; the blade embedded in a sandbag inches from the other man.

"Forty-two days, motherfucker," said Snags, unperturbed.

"That's not short," said Sutherland.

"That's tomorrow, compared to you, Sutherland. What do you got, three hundred left? And Landis isn't going home at all—they're not even going to find enough pieces of him to send back. Want to know what I'm gonna do first when I get home?"

"No," Sutherland and Landis said in unison.

"Eat pussy."

Landis laughed. Greg Pozinski, a blond, burly youth who had survived nearly a year of combat, was nicknamed Snags because his missing and oddly angled teeth marred what otherwise was a handsome face. "Any woman who'd let you down there might as well take a buzz saw to her cunt," Landis sneered.

"It's all in the tongue," said Pozinski.

"You got teeth on your tongue, you gooney-faced fuck," said Landis.

Snags considered him, then said with profound satisfaction, "Forty-two days, motherfucker."

To Sutherland it did sound like tomorrow; every man knew to the day how much longer he had in Vietnam. A combat tour was thirteen months, and Sutherland had three hundred and four days left; Landis, the radio operator, had one hundred seventy-nine.

Sutherland stuck close to Pozinski and others like him who had survived in the hope that he would discover the secrets they possessed.

From Ron Mead he had first learned that you needed to be brave, and to trust your instincts. He hated Gunny Brock, but Brock had taught him discipline and caution. Snags had taught him singlemindedness, absolute self-mastery—he never got mad, never lost his patience, could sit for hours in an ambush without moving a muscle or dropping his concentration. Others taught him too; the dead and wounded also had lessons to pass on.

"Do you get more cautious, the closer you get?" Sutherland asked, breaking the taboo by inquiring directly.

But Snags knew better than to risk the taboo. "You talking about eating cunt? No, when you get that close, you just take a deep breath."

"Shit," said Sutherland, standing up. "It's been so long since I seen one, I forgot what they look like."

"A taco," Landis said.

"In forty-two days and ten minutes I'll send you a picture of one," Snags said, and added, turning to Landis, "With tooth marks on it."

Sutherland jumped out of the bunker and headed for the next, making his nightly social rounds. He hated to be alone, loved the camaraderie, like at home only months ago, sitting on the hoods of cars at drive-ins, talking with his buddies.

He approached the bunker of his two best buddies, Dennis Coney and Leslie Frizzell. "The password tonight is 'Suckmydick.'"

"It must be a gook," said Coney. "That was last night's password. Shoot him, Frizzell."

Sutherland dropped beside them. He took the cigarette dangling from Coney's mouth. Smoke curled about Sutherland's face, emphasizing the sharpness of his features.

"You got nothing to worry about tonight. Miller's so scared a fart couldn't get through the wire. He woke me ten times about some bush creeping up on him."

Coney took back the cigarette. "They're out there all right, like flies buzzing a turd. Or my wife sniffing—"

"Jesus," said Frizzell, "don't get started on that." Frizzell was eighteen, six feet and taut, with chestnut hair that would not stay out of his eyes, and a smile he could never quite suppress, even now. He turned to Sutherland, his face unlined and untroubled, happy the night vigil was broken. "Hey, what's a semaphore? I asked Coney"—his voice filled with mock respect—"'cause Coney went to college for a year, but he didn't know."

"How do you spell it?" Sutherland asked.

Coney spat. He was two years older, a big man with handsome dark features who had fled his wife and the confines of marriage. "Shit. You wouldn't know even if he could spell it, which he can't."

The word *spell* caught Sutherland and he leaned back against the bunker. "You guys ever have spelling bees in school, where everybody had to stand up by the blackboard till they didn't know a word, and some ugly fucking girl with glasses would win, or some dipshit with zits?" He turned to Coney and smiled. "I always had to sit down after the first word. Sometimes I wouldn't even bother to stand up."

Frizzell broke in. "C'mon, what's a semaphore? I read it in a story on peace."

"A piece of ass?"

"No. The other kind. You know, no war. I'll get it for you." He dropped to his knees to rummage through his pack.

Sutherland rolled his eyes at Coney in their mutual agreement about Frizzell's simplemindedness, then he jumped out of the bunker. "Christ, I won't get any sleep anywhere tonight. What the fuck do I want to know what a semaphore is? It's probably some kind of plant; maybe it's what's creeping up on Miller."

Frizzell found the magazine, but Sutherland was already gone.

Coney shook his head. "Scott's right, you are one dumb fuck—three hordes of gooks are at the wire, and you're asking what a semaphore is."

Frizzell was unperturbed, used to everyone's gibes. "You're just pissed 'cause you didn't know what a semaphore was." He settled against the sandbags, resuming the vigil, staring up at the sky, then he remembered something he had always wanted to know. "Dennie, how come sometimes there are stars and sometimes there aren't?"

Coney followed his gaze to the black canopy, respecting the question and mindful of Frizzell's near worship of him. "Because they're behind the clouds."

Frizzell pondered the answer. "Oh." Then he turned to Coney. "I never should have quit high school." He shook his head wistfully. "But there was all that shit about gerunds and things. I mean, how does that help a guy? But now . . . I think I'll go back." He closed his eyes and promised, "I will. A guy can't be dumb all his life."

Brock sat on the floor in a corner of the bunker, arms around his knees, his gaze intent on Bishop.

Bishop felt the searing eyes but concentrated on his map, plotting artillery coordinates. Then he went to the starlight scope to scan the desert again, awaiting the two men.

In a few minutes their boots pounded down the stairs and Bishop turned.

"Yes, sir," said Pozinski. Despite his rifle and ammunition belts, grenades and blackened face, he stood timidly before the officer.

"You ready too, Miller?"

Miller could not meet his eyes, merely nodded his head.

"You're going to set up a listening post in the desert on the infiltration route. It's not an ambush, you're not to engage the enemy, just watch and listen, mostly see if they're setting up a rocket site out there."

Pozinski stared at him dubiously.

"I know," said Bishop soothingly, "we don't send out LPs at night, but this is special. It's very important." He told them the coordinates and showed them the position on the map, then gave them the compass azimuth readings to follow.

"You have any questions?" he asked when he finished.

They stood silently before him, fully armed and equipped, warriors with drawn faces shadowed under their helmets; but the fierce illusion was defeated by the fear and innocence in their eyes.

Miller strapped the field radio onto his back.

"Your call sign is Tiny Tim," Bishop said.

They lingered another few seconds, then backed awkwardly toward the stairs, then they were gone.

For a long time Bishop stared after where they had been.

"You know what war is, Lieutenant?" Brock said from his corner. He struck a match; the slash on flint and burst of flame rent the fetid, dark bunker. "It's not maps and plans, generals and presidents, tactics and grand strategy. War is personal tragedies, Lieutenant—individual deaths; it's people dying one by one."

He blew out the match.

Miller and Pozinski moved down the hill to the break in the wire.

They crouched, listening, searching for a sign; finally they slipped into the dark arena.

Miller shivered as he switched off his rifle safety. He said to himself, but Pozinski heard, "We're gonna get hit, I know it."

They moved due west, stopping every hundred meters to listen. In thirty minutes they reached the night position, a small indentation in the middle of the desert on the infiltration route, a mile from the hill, a barely visible speck on what looked like a vast lake.

Bishop watched through the starlight scope, holding his breath each time they disappeared in the dunes. Finally when they set into position, he relaxed slightly. "They're okay," he said to Brock, who had not moved from the corner.

Pozinski settled into the sand, feeling better now that they were safely in. Maybe it would be all right, he thought. There was enough moonlight so that he could see the dirt in his fingernails. He concentrated on cleaning them, ears cocked for any noise.

Beside him, Miller did not relax. All he thought was how far they were from the hill, alone.

The wind picked up; it grew colder.

Bishop's eyes hurt from staring so intently. After an hour he felt mesmerized by the stark scene through the scope, so still yet alive, a black-and-white photograph developing surrealistically as he watched.

Then he lurched forward and stabbed the handset. "Tiny Tim, movement spotted to your sierra, four of them."

Miller and Pozinski moved together, scanning to the south.

The radio crackled again with Bishop's voice, slow and assured, but with a trace of tension. "I see two more to the west. I don't know if they see you or not."

Fear slashed Miller's stomach; he felt sick.

Pozinski's fingers softly stroked his rifle barrel; two small groups weren't so bad, and the lieutenant hadn't seemed worried. The enemy would probably walk right into them. His pulse quickened at the prospect of killing them.

Miller began to tremble uncontrollably; he had to root himself in the sand to keep from jumping and running.

Pozinski felt Miller's nervousness and reached over to touch him. Miller flinched at the contact, but Pozinski held his hand on him.

Then the air came alive with sounds, a quickening in the wind, a feeling they knew was desperately wrong.

And Bishop suddenly knew. He saw fifteen men moving in on them from the north. He started to yell but caught himself and said into the handset with as much control as he could, "Get out, get out quickly."

He watched in horror as enemy soldiers moved swiftly over the dunes, streaking for the two men, a claw closing. "Hurry! Move back now. They're all around you."

Bishop's words struck Miller like a bullet. He jolted upright and grabbed Pozinski. The two clambered from their position, groping sand to get out.

Bishop yelled to the posts on the hill and called for artillery. Brock raced from the bunker to set up a defense at the wire.

Suddenly there was the hollow crump of mortars, and everyone on the hill hugged earth, trying to bury themselves as enemy rounds screamed in.

Bishop shouted into the radio, "Run, run, don't get down."

Miller was terrified. He had never heard fear in Bishop's voice. Then he saw the hill erupt in a barrage of bursting shells. The radio bore down on him and his feet sank into the sand; he felt as if he were running in water. He stumbled. Pozinski grabbed him and pulled.

Bullets hit at their feet; rounds seared past.

Miller fell behind under the radio; he cried out in terror. Pozinski ran back to him.

The first artillery rounds landed a hundred meters away. The explosion blinded them and knocked them to the ground. They began to crawl, grappling their way to the wire as bullets hit beside them.

Bishop's fist pounded the sandbags as he watched. "Hurry. Hurry."

Pozinski reached the outer strand of wire. He heard men on the hill yelling. He saw Brock crawling through the wire to get him; behind him Miller screamed.

Then the hill and the wire exploded.

Brock threw himself over the wire and pulled Pozinski through. He searched for Miller, but he wasn't there anymore; all he could see were enemy soldiers racing toward him. The wire ripped his flesh as he went back over. Hands grabbed him and Pozinski, pulling them up the slope.

Bishop was directing artillery when they brought Pozinski to the bunker; at first he could not tell who was wounded for all the blood. Bishop dropped to his knees to wipe it away, then ripped at Pozinski's clothing. Blood bubbled out of his chest, then was sucked back in.

Pozinski's voice came dully. "Lieutenant?"

Bishop could not take his eyes from the wound.

"I hurt, Lieutenant, I hurt. Please help me."

Bishop lifted him in his arms. "Greg. Greg," he pleaded softly.

Pozinski opened his eyes, seeking the voice calling his childhood name, but he couldn't see and was falling so far and so fast, out of the world, the second before sleep. "Mom? Mommy?"

Then there was the softest cry, and his head fell sideways. For a moment Bishop blanked, holding the man in his arms, smelling the wet, hot blood, hearing the shouts from the wire. Fear and confusion overwhelmed him.

He looked about in terror, then with a desperate force of will he laid the body back and ran down the slope as bullets embedded at his feet. "Fire," he yelled. "Spray the wire."

He saw enemy soldiers making the final assault on the outer strand. None of his men was firing. He alone stood before the wire, facing the enemy, his rifle bursting automatic.

Sutherland yelled at him. "Miller's out there."

"Fire. Clear the wire," Bishop commanded.

Sutherland screamed, running to the wire, "No! Larry. Larry!"

Men grappled him to the ground and a machine gun exploded point-blank into the enemy. Bishop saw them recoil, individuals thrown back as bullets hit them. For five minutes the barrage raged at the wire.

Then it was over. The enemy suddenly withdrew and firing ceased. The entire perimeter was lost in smoke.

Bishop ordered his men back to the crest of the hill.

Sutherland didn't move. "Larry's out there."

Bishop crouched beside him. "He's dead, Scott. We'll get him in the morning."

"You killed him, Lieutenant. You motherfucker!" he screamed. "You killed him." He dove at Bishop.

Men restrained Sutherland, and Bishop returned to the bunker; Brock checked the posts and set the men in position.

For hours Bishop sat on the forward slope of the hill staring at the wire. Finally light broke from the horizon, a lid slowly opening. Gray mist wound from it, rolling toward the hill, settling over the crumpled bodies, obscuring them.

Then the mist passed and the figures reappeared one by one, a ghastly resurrection of the dead, still dead, lying on the plain like elemental fixtures.

Bishop went to the bunker and returned with a green body bag.

"Do you want me to go with you?" Brock asked without accusation or recrimination.

Bishop shook his head and went down the slope; alone he slipped through the wire and searched through the dead until he found Miller.

A mortar had hit him, blowing off his head, scattering his torso. Bishop willed away all thought and for twenty minutes picked up flesh, placing meat and bone in the bag. At last he reached down for the head, closing his own eyes, gently placing it in the bag; then he shuddered and wiped his hands on his arms.

The stench made him dizzy and he wanted to vomit; his mind reeled and he turned his back to the rising sun to see his shadow stretching over the dead. He moved aside, but in each position his shadow fell on a corpse.

From the hill he saw his men watching him. He picked up the green body bag, and like a ghoul, struggled with it up the hill.

An hour later a helicopter clattered overhead, circled several times, then dropped ponderously to earth.

A stocky man of average height, in his middle forties, emerged from the vibrating hull. On his shoulders and helmet was a gleaming silver star.

Bishop ran from the bunker and saluted.

The general did not return his salute but appraised him with utterly cold, gray eyes. "The enemy hit every outpost on the DMZ last night, Lieutenant. Your position was the only one not overrun. You should be very proud. Your company commander has put you in for a Navy Cross. I've already approved it."

He spoke without emphasis, as though he knew the emptiness of the words.

The general gazed about the hill, his eyes emotionless on

the two body bags. Then he turned to Bishop. "Come with me," he said, walking to the forward crest that looked out on the desert.

They stood side by side without speaking for a long time, then the general said, "Tell me about it, Lieutenant."

Bishop stared out into the desert. It was cold and lonely and the wind howled over the sands.

He opened his mouth but there were no words. "I . . . I . . ." He closed his eyes and bent forward, holding his stomach.

The general put his hand on his shoulder. Bishop buried his face against the general's chest and sobbed.

"Go ahead and cry, Lieutenant," the general said, looking out expressionlessly on the desert. "A day will come when you'll want to, but there won't be any tears left."

Sutherland stood alone on the crest of the hill before the two body bags, drawn by an overpowering desire to understand.

How did it happen like that? They had been talking, and Snags was joking. He stared at the mounds and reconstructed the night before. There must have been a sign, something he had overlooked that would explain it.

Miller, yes; he could see Miller's death. But not Snags. Snags should not have died; there was no warning, no sign.

He dropped to his knees and unzipped the bag.

There was no mystery in the uncovered face, nothing revealed in the features, just absolutely cold, gray death.

And if it could happen to Snags, then it could happen to him too. Unless there was some design he could not see, unless God decided these things. Did God reach into the jungle and leave a man like this?

No. He knew He didn't. No god cared about Snags or Miller. There was no design.

But if not, what?

Was it just that their luck ran out? Was there nothing he could do to protect himself? Could he end like this too, without warning, so quickly, just another poor dumb bastard caught and used and squashed, bagged and sent home?

He zipped the bag and stood.

No. No matter what, he would not end like this. He would not die.

His eyes were hard and fixed, staring at the body bags, then he looked beyond them, to where Bishop and the general stood, and past them to where the enemy lay.

"I won't," he said aloud, a defiant promise: I'll make it, no matter what I have to do.

CHAPTER

• 11 •

Marshall woke to the slow, rhythmic clacking of an overhead fan. The sheets were still drawn tight; he had slept soundly, apparently without even turning over, and he felt refreshed.

The only sound was the fan; he watched it sleepily, lulled by the soft breeze and gentle whir, but then his eye focused on the ceiling, and he started at the sight above him, a frieze of lizards. Then one moved, and another, and the ceiling seemed suddenly alive.

Geckos. He relaxed. That's why he had slept so well, untroubled by flies and mosquitoes. He was in Saigon, it was seven forty-five in the morning, and he had slept thirteen hours.

Rising stiffly, aching from so long in bed, Marshall went to the blinds and peered through the wooden slats. The bedroom overlooked the gardens and inner courtyard of the villa. Already a man was pruning oleander bushes bursting with white blossoms. The garden was a bit overgrown, like the villa itself, overripe and slightly decayed.

A villa of the French legation, the estate was now infrequently used because dignitaries preferred the service and safety of hotels; it had hastily been commandeered from the French when Marshall stated that he would not stay in a hotel and he also refused to impose on Ambassador Bunker's hospitality.

His demand for total privacy had created a crisis for the embassy staff, and only minutes after the welcoming reception was the villa readied for him and staffed with service personnel who had worked all through the night preparing it to accommodate the President's special envoy. While he slept, a cleaning crew scoured the villa, provisions were stocked, and furniture brought in, literally carried out of the homes of lesser bureaucrats.

Gardeners had been working long before dawn, weeding and pruning, cutting away years of overgrowth; the fountain had been cleaned, the fish pond drained, refilled, and restocked.

After this frenzy of activity, the villa was now quiet. The gardener's shears clipped outside, and in the kitchen the staff prepared breakfast.

Marshall saw his white linen suit pressed and his clothes laid out. The setting was comfortably, agreeably colonial, and he did not regret in the slightest the pandemonium he knew he had caused.

His demand for privacy had been implacable, even when told such accommodations could not be arranged—"for security reasons."

"What the hell have I got a bodyguard for then?" he asked General Abrams. "If I'm going to stay in a hotel, I can call room service if I need help. If you people can't provide better lodging than a hotel room, and chant safety and security every time I want to do something, then I'm wasting my time here. I can call the President right now and give him my analysis."

Abrams swallowed his fury and ordered that the villa be readied.

Marshall then told Ambassador Bunker that he would not attend any more receptions or social functions.

The impression Marshall had made was negative, but wholly calculated. He wanted to be thought difficult and demanding. He wanted to be feared, and he intended to use fully the awesome power of the presidency.

The greatest challenge was going to be to cut through the

bureaucracy, to burrow through the propaganda and reports and briefings to find the buried truths—gems or sand, whatever lay at the bottom. He could not allow himself to be handled or railroaded; he had to assert himself from the beginning.

He knew the military and the bureaucracy—nothing could be coaxed from them. They were a bog that offered no resistance, sucking in any tentative step, drawing the unwary in farther, and swallowing whole well-intentioned reformers.

He had sloughed through the mire before, in the Mideast and in Central America, but here he wasn't going to wade through it. His time was too precious, his mission too crucial. He would blast through it; he had already begun.

At the reception he had been polite but distant, letting small talk curdle on men's lips, and inanities resound in silence. He told the State Department liaison that he would make no appointments, accept no invitations, and that he wanted no visitors. He would make his own arrangements and notify them when he wanted assistance.

He left the reception knowing full well the fear and discomfort he had created.

After shaving and dressing, and remembering the night before with satisfaction, Marshall opened the bedroom door, confident and ready for the challenge before him.

Ron Mead, scrambling up, startled and unprepared, knocked over the chair he had been sitting on and awkwardly came to attention with his rifle, shouting much too loudly, "Good morning, sir!"

Marshall jumped back. "Jesus Christ," he said.

Mead stood stiffly, rifle raised, blocking the doorway.

"Oh, for God's sake," Marshall said in disgust, now remembering the Marine assigned to protect him.

Seeing the ambassador's annoyance, Mead brought the rifle down and moved aside.

"Don't ever do that again," Marshall said. "My God, I thought you were going to shoot me. And put that damn thing away." He gestured at the rifle. "I'm going to breakfast, not on a search and destroy mission."

"Yes, sir," Mead said, casting about for a place to lay the

M-16, but finding none, he held it behind him and stood in a parade rest position.

Marshall studied him, saw the youth's confusion and trepidation, and remembered guiltily his curt behavior of the previous day.

"Relax," he said, and he reached out and shook Mead into a looser position. He smiled. "Let's start over again. What's your name?"

"Mead. Corporal Mead, sir."

"I mean your real name."

Mead looked even more confused and uncertain. "Sir, that is my real name."

Marshall grinned. "What does your mother call you? Surely she doesn't call you Corporal Mead."

"Oh. No, sir. Ron. Ron Mead, sir. Corporal Ronald F. Mead."

Marshall nodded and glanced at the overturned chair. "How long have you been here?"

Mead shifted uncomfortably. "Well . . . all night, sir."

"You mean you slept there, on the chair? Didn't anyone tell you to go home?"

"No, sir. I, I just supposed I was to stay near you. That's all I was told . . . to, well, to guard you."

Marshall nodded solemnly and kept a straight face. "Well, you did a good job." He tapped him on the arm. "C'mon, let's have breakfast."

Mead didn't move. "With you, sir?" he asked, perplexed.

"Would you rather I brought it up here for you?"

Mead stifled a grin at the image of the ambassador bringing him his breakfast. "No, sir. I mean, well, I didn't think you'd want me to . . ."

But Marshall was already walking down the stairs, and Mead hurried after him.

At the bottom of the stairs, presenting themselves in order of rank, was the household staff: the majordomo, valet, chauffeur, cook, housekeeper, and two maids. Each stepped forward with name and greeting, and Marshall bowed to each and thanked them, ruefully thinking of the privacy he had forgone by insisting on quarters rather than a hotel.

The dining room table was set for only one. Marshall

directed a setting for Mead and motioned him to a chair. The Marine stood until Marshall sat, then he dropped down quickly, sitting rigidly ill at ease.

A servant poured coffee, but Mead did not drink until after Marshall had.

Marshall contemplated him for a moment, then said gently, "We better have a little chat, Corporal; otherwise we're going to have a very trying time. I'm sorry I was rude to you yesterday. I shouldn't have been; I was just surprised and disturbed to have a bodyguard. It's not personal, just that I didn't count on having someone with me constantly. I imagine you're not terribly eager to baby-sit me either. Surely there's someone else you'd rather be spending time with. But apparently we're stuck with one another and we're going to have to make the best of it."

Scrambled eggs and bacon were served, and a variety of breads and rolls brought around.

Mead did not touch anything until Marshall finally directed, "Eat."

Watching Mead, stiff and formal, afraid to speak or spill, cutting his bacon and buttering toast almost daintily, Marshall suppressed a laugh at the contrast of breakfast with this Marine, and the memory of his last one with the President.

Johnson, a napkin stuck under his chin, had reached across the table to spear a biscuit with his fork, knocked over his orange juice, sucked butter off his fingers, threw newspapers and reports to the floor, shouted for hotter coffee, and sprawled over the table like a lord at a medieval banquet. There had been little conversation, but no silence, instead a harangue against the injustices of the press, punctuated with a stabbing of Walter Lippmann masquerading as eggs Benedict.

"Tell me about yourself," Marshall said.

Mead stopped chewing; he looked as if struck by a rock.

"Where are you from?" Marshall coaxed.

"Arkansas, sir."

"A big family?"

"No, sir."

"Are you married?"

"No, sir."

Marshall smiled. "I see. Well, I'll tell you about myself. I have children your age, a son who just joined the army as a matter of fact, and a long time ago I was in the Marines too. Then I became a lawyer, and now I work for the President. And that's what we have to talk about, Corporal."

At the mention of the President, Mead sat even straighter.

"We're going to be spending a great deal of time together, it seems. Rather than have a number of bodyguards, I think I'll just have you; that will make it much simpler. But you're going to have to understand something—that you work for me, only me, no one else. You won't report to any gunnery sergeant or captain or major, just to me. Understand? No one else gives you orders. If there's ever a conflict, tell them to see me. Is that clear?"

"Yes, sir."

"I work for the President, no one else. I don't report to anyone; no one can fire me, no one outranks me—not General Westmoreland, not Ambassador Bunker—only Lyndon B. Johnson. I work directly for him, and you work directly for me. I have to be able to trust you completely. Your commander in chief is the President of the United States; I am his direct and personal representative. Do you have any doubts or questions?"

Mead shook his head. "No, sir, I understand."

"Good. Now I want you to go home."

Mead started. "Sir?"

"Go home, or back to the barracks. Do you have a girlfriend?"

Mead flushed.

"Good. Go home to her, or go get some sleep. I don't care what you do, but I'm going to the embassy and will be there most of the day and I won't need you. Nobody is going to shoot me there. Well, that's probably where they will shoot me, but never mind. So take off and come back around . . . two in the afternoon."

"Sir, I . . . I can't . . ."

"Whom do you work for, Corporal?"

"You, sir."

"And what did I just tell you to do?"

Mead swallowed.

160

"You have any money?"

"Sir?"

"To get home; for a cab." Marshall smiled. "Corporal, I was a corporal once too. I'm old, but not senile. I remember how it was." He took out his wallet and handed Mead some piaster notes. "Pay me back later. You finished with breakfast?"

Mead looked at the bills in his hand, then at his empty plate.

"Then go. I'll see you at two."

Mead stood, pushed in his chair, looked uncertainly for a place to put his napkin, stuffed it in his pocket, and backed from the room in confusion. "Thank you, sir," he mumbled, and fled.

Jostled in the back of the cab as it fought its way through morning Saigon traffic, Mead tried to sort his thoughts. He had expected to hate Marshall; certainly he had not anticipated any kindness.

Since he had been at the embassy, no one in authority had even acknowledged his existence, except to give him an order or to harass him. The last person to take any personal interest in him had been Lieutenant Bishop, and now suddenly the most important man in Vietnam, a man who could order generals about, had asked him his name and sat down with him for breakfast, had in a few moments shown him more warmth than his own father had in all his years.

He seemed—the only word that came to him was *nice*, and Mead could not remember anyone's being nice to him; usually he was ignored, and he was accustomed to that.

Mead did not think Marshall's manner had been calculated or false; he knew himself too insignificant for the ambassador to waste time trying to impress, so that made Marshall's behavior even more remarkable to him.

He remembered an old farm dog they had had, one of many that lasted a couple years, then wandered off, or was run over or shot, or just disappeared. Like all dogs, it was mostly ignored, left to fend for itself, thrown scraps, never let in the house, never played with, and maybe now and then scratched behind the ear—a farm dog, not a pet. One day he and his father went into town, the dog in the back of the pickup, and when they came out of the store, two young black boys were with the dog, petting him, and they had set a dish of milk before him.

He, Mead, remembered it clearly because he thought it was so funny, petting that mangy old dog and giving it milk, funnier still because the dog didn't understand what was happening either, standing there perplexed, wondering why he was being touched, and staring—not suspiciously, just curiously—into the dish set before him. The dog followed after them back to the pickup; but as they drove away, Mead saw the dog staring back at the boys, and later he knew the dog always looked at him wonderingly, as if questioning why he had never petted him. Afterward, he always felt guilty, though he still never patted the dog.

Then he remembered what Sung had asked him—"Why are you helping me?"

Why was he? It was more than pity and feeling sorry for her. And pity wasn't why Marshall had been nice to him. He didn't have an answer for Sung, any more than he had one about Marshall.

The cab bounced down side streets, horn blaring, and finally stopped before his building. Children swarmed about him as he paid the driver, and an old beggar woman pulled on his arm and screeched at him.

He dropped coins and bills onto the street and ran up the stairs as they all fought, the old woman the fiercest, clawing the children with her nails.

Mead walked the trash-littered hall anxiously, listening for Sung's cries, but all was silent, and he stood fearfully outside the door before letting himself in.

The stench of vomit and urine overwhelmed him.

Sung lay on the floor, her hands bound by a belt, with Han crouched over her.

Sung's eyes were open, staring sightlessly up to the ceiling, and she moaned in a continuous monotone, rocking from side to side. Her skin was red and scraped from her own clawing, and her hair was clumped in sweat and filth.

Mead knelt beside her and stroked her brow; her skin was

162

dry and hot, the flesh gray, and her eyes sunk in deep dark hollows.

Han struggled up stiffly. "Water," she said. "Make her drink."

"Will she be all right?" Mead asked.

"What does that mean?" Han answered. She looked haggard and old, a broken-toothed middle-aged woman trying to survive in a war, sleeping with rifle-laden boys young enough to be her sons.

"I'll come back when you go," she said, and let herself out.

For several minutes Mead stood in the middle of the room, staring at Sung and the squalor about him.

Discarded empty C ration cans and crumpled cracker wrappings were tossed in a corner; that had been their breakfast.

Mead felt in his pocket for the napkin; it was white linen and still clean except for a small butter stain. Smoothing it out and folding it on its sharp ironed creases, he held the napkin in both hands. The contrast between this room and the one from which he had just come was immense—the powerful man ensconced in his villa, surrounded by servants, and the drug-addicted woman lying on a filthy floor, attended by a broken-toothed old whore. And in his mind he saw the gleaming coffins on the tarmac, then the mangled, shrapnel-riddled face of the soldier in the tunnel, and looking at his own hands that had squeezed out life, dripped blood and gore, he saw the crisp napkin with its faint glistening stain of butter.

He let the napkin slip from his hands to fall near where Sung lay, then he stripped off his uniform and set it carefully in a corner.

His body hurt from tiredness, but the exhaustion was different from combat; his mind was tormented, not with fear, but thoughts. Everything was twisted and confused and he wanted away from it all, but it swirled around, pressing on him.

He moved his sleeping bag near Sung and dropped down on it. Lying beside her, his eyes open, he watched her face contort in pain. Her mouth grimaced and her lips stretched grotesquely. Too weak to thrash, she rocked from side to side, her hands pulling against the belt, rubbing her wrists raw.

She choked on the water he gave her, but some managed to trickle down her throat. He tried to pat off what had spilled with the napkin, but when he touched her, she pulled away and cried out.

Finally he closed his eyes, and sleep swallowed him while she lay beside him, moaning and twisting.

CHAPTER

• 12 •

Jeeps with armed soldiers and police on motorcycles screamed Marshall's limousine through the crowded streets. As he saw carts upturned and bicyclists thrown to the ground, his fury mounted, but even more disturbing to him were the expressions on the faces of the soldiers and police, and of the people they scattered.

Arrogance shone on the faces of the soldiers and police, a cold luster of power and cruelty, though the power was only derivative—it was his power and authority they wielded vicariously, viciously, and wrongly—little Martin Bormanns with rifles and pistols in jeeps and on motorcycles. His driver too. All of them, maggots feeding on the flesh of power; here and in Washington. Everywhere.

And off the street, faces with curled lips looked at his procession with hatred, gleaming resentment and incipient revolution—Madame Defarge at the guillotine.

Yet on the faces was something else—envy.

That is what frightened him—he knew that they all could change places, those on the street be put in the jeeps, and the police disarmed and cast into the gutter, and the expressions on the faces would be exactly the same—Defarge would become Bormann. Tyrant and slave were after all just matters of birth. Pauper or prince was just a changeling in a crib: a troll's jest. Or God's.

Or, Marshall thought, drawing the curtains in the limousine, and thinking of the Marine and himself, nothing more complex than Arkansas and Newport. Troy and Agamemnon dead, Vietnam and Lyndon Johnson—all just shudderings in the loins.

The motorcade screeched into the embassy compound to a fanfare of salutes and slapped rifles.

The State Department liaison met him at the portico.

"I never want that again," Marshall said, nodding toward the jeeps and motorcycles, the helmeted soldiers and police gleaming in the bright sunlight. "Get rid of them."

"Excellency, for your security, General Westmore—"

"Get rid of them," Marshall said coldly, striding into the building, nodding acknowledgment to the guards standing at attention, presenting arms.

The liaison officer followed quickly.

Inside, the massive lobby was filled with people eager for a glimpse of the President's emissary; a cordon of soldiers held the crowd back.

Marshall walked into their midst. He looked about in surprise, finding himself the center of attention and not knowing where to go. The State Department aide rushed to his side.

"Am I expected to do something?" Marshall asked. "A trick perhaps?"

"No, sir," the aide stammered in embarrassment. "I'm sorry about this too, it won't happen again. This way please."

He led Marshall down a corridor to a private elevator that brought them to the top floor; a guard met the elevator and escorted them to a wing that was sealed off by bulletproof glass. On the inside another guard pushed a button that released a sliding glass door.

"Is all this really necessary?" Marshall asked.

"We hope not," said the aide, "but it would reflect rather poorly on us if something happened to the President's representative while he was here. We're not trying to embarrass or inconvenience you, sir, it's just that—"

"I understand," Marshall said. "But surely the precautions and security can be less obtrusive. I don't want the pomp and ceremony; do what must be done—I too would be upset if something happened to the President's representative while he was here—but hide it from me as much as possible."

"Yes, sir. Here we are," he said, leading Marshall into a large, luxuriously furnished reception room where his staff was assembled.

"I will leave you with Colonel Waggoner, your aide. My office is in the next corridor. I am at your disposal at all times, to assist, coordinate, intercede—whatever, as unobtrusively as possible, of course."

"Thank you very much," Marshall said, shaking his hand, and turning to his staff.

"Colonel John Waggoner, sir," said the senior aide, stepping forward and introducing the others. "Dolores Toland, your secretary; Ann Fincher, your administrative assistant. Jerry Beecher and Tim Navasky of the State Department. Captain Benjamin Latham."

Marshall shook hands with each, smiling pleasantly, concealing his annoyance; he did not want a large staff—they would bog him down, generate useless papers. He saw what was being done to him: a staff, a ready-made little bureaucracy, would then become part of the larger one and his report would fall into the pile of other reports, become part of the colorless collage that was titled "government."

The bureaucracy, amorphous and alive, would absorb him, swell even larger, a protoplasmic entity without brain or heart, bloating and expanding.

And Dolores Toland. Jesus Christ, he thought, where did they get her? With her platinum hair, high heels, and heavy makeup, she looked as if she had walked in off the set of a porn film. What the hell did they take him for?

Having absolutely nothing to say to them, and seeing no sense or dignity in giving a little pep talk, he walked away toward what he felt must be his private office, but it was his secretary's, and beyond hers was Colonel Waggoner's. His own was last.

"What do I need all these guards for?" he asked. "An enemy would be so exhausted by the time he finally got to me that he couldn't hurt me. Isn't there a shortcut I could take?"

"You have a private entrance onto the corridor—you don't have to pass through Dolores's office or mine, sir—but you're still at the end of the corridor, and the only exit or entrance is at the other end."

"What if there's a fire at my end? Do I jump out the window? What if the VC charge down the hall and Miss Toland isn't able to stop them, and you're in the toilet? Where is my escape route, Colonel?"

Waggoner stared at him, uncertain whether Marshall was joking or in earnest; he also didn't have any answers. "I never thought of that, sir; I don't think anyone else did either. Would you like a back exit, sir?"

"Is fire a possibility? Is an attack conceivable?"

"Fire? I suppose so. Yes, sir. An attack? No, sir, that's not conceivable. There probably should be another exit though. That's a very good point—someone should have thought of that. I'll get right on it."

"Colonel, please don't bother. I'll jump if necessary. And if, inconceivably, the VC do attack and Miss Toland can't stop them, maybe while they're ravishing her I'll be able to sneak away."

Waggoner didn't know what to think. The envoy's manner was now known to everyone at the embassy. His appearance today had been anticipated with apprehension and fear. Certainly Waggoner had not expected any humor, and he was still unsure if Marshall meant any. He was also loath to risk misinterpreting a serious remark from a man of Marshall's power and reputation.

Sensing his confusion and concern, and seeing that Waggoner was a well-meaning and probably highly competent career officer, Marshall motioned for him to sit on one of the high-backed leather chairs.

The room, for Marshall's taste, was uncomfortably large and overbearingly masculine, too dark and heavy, a room meant for a Tudor baron, lacking only a boar's head and a suit of armor. The drapes were beige, the carpet brown, the walls military khaki, and the furniture leather and mahogany, except for the elaborately carved teak desk.

Looking about, and noting his white linen suit, Marshall said, "I don't go with the room. Either I'm going to have to get a loincloth, or we're going to have to brighten this place up."

Waggoner smiled for the first time. "We'll get you a loincloth, sir. Perhaps Corporal Mead has a spare."

"I doubt I would fit in one of his."

Waggoner frowned. "Speaking of Corporal—"

"He's running errands for me." Marshall settled on the leather sofa and crossed his legs comfortably. "Which leads nicely into what I want to discuss with you." He nodded to the outer offices. "My staff. I don't need them either. Apparently General Abrams was willing to go to the mat with me over a bodyguard, and since he looks like a man who truly belongs in a room like this, I capitulated.

"But I have no need for two military aides, two State Department assistants, and two secretaries. If Ambassador Bunker wants to fight me over that, I know I can take him—he's seventy-three."

Marshall gestured to the room about him. "I don't need any of this. I'm here to look and listen, to consider and analyze, then I am going to fly back to Washington and tell the President what I have seen and heard, and what I think. I am not going to put my thoughts on paper; I am not going to make a written report. I don't need any of those file cabinets out there because I am not going to generate any paper. I am not going to do any dictation, or send memos. I won't have any work for a large staff, and I don't want any busywork done; I don't want any pretense of work when there isn't any work to do. So I'm going to leave this office and all these people for you to manage, or to dismiss, as you see fit—but I want you to understand that I will have very few needs and requirements: someone to make and answer phone calls, make appointments and travel arrangements, get me reports and information."

"I think the problem, Mr. Ambassador, was that no one knew what to expect—you were given a large staff to cover whatever contingencies might develop."

"I understand. I just want you to be aware that I will have no need for such a staff, any more than I do for a private wing, guard booths, and bulletproof glass. I plan to spend much of my time traveling and observing. I doubt I will gain anything meaningful for the President by sitting here in Saigon reading reports and going to briefings. Neither do I plan to go on any prescribed tour set up by others. Right now I am just testing the waters."

"Is there anything I can do?"

"Yes—run this office: collate materials sent to me, give me what you think might be helpful in coming to a broad understanding of the military and political situation in Vietnam—and I don't mean body counts and captured weapons."

"Something like rice harvests?"

"Yes. Medical care, orphanages, church attendance, schooling, drug abuse, taxation, land distribution—all the things that make up a society and country. A little thing like—how many prisons are there in the country? What's the most common crime, most severely punished? What are people imprisoned for?"

He leaned forward on the sofa. "You see, Colonel, I don't know much about Vietnam. I don't think many Americans do. But telling me how many VC were killed yesterday, how many weapons were captured, how many bombs were dropped, how much more of the countryside is under our control—that hardly adds to my understanding."

"I see, sir," Waggoner said, then added with genuine feeling, "I think you're doing exactly what is needed; I'd be very grateful if you'd let me continue working with you. It's sort of like the fire escape—nobody ever thought of that, myself included."

"Exactly," Marshall said. "I think that rather than sealing ourselves behind bulletproof glass, we'd better make sure there's a back exit. Fire escapes are unnecessary until there's a fire—but you don't wait until there's a fire to build one."

"I'll do the best I can, sir, but this is all new for me so you might have to give pretty direct and specific guidance sometimes."

"I think we're going to get along just fine, Colonel. Soon

I'll give you a list of people I'd like to meet with—President Thieu, political leaders, field commanders, and I'll have you set up the appointments."

"Is there anything specific I can do right now? I've left your schedule completely open, pending a talk with you. You've been invited to numerous meetings, briefings, receptions, social functions."

"Acknowledge them all, and inform me of them, but I will attend very few. My time is limited and I don't want to waste any of it listening to—"

"Propaganda."

"—what I know I am going to be told. Certain people will tell me very predictable things that I don't need to listen to."

"Then I can probably decline everything you've been invited to today."

"Is there anything you feel I should attend?"

Waggoner considered, then shook his head with a slight smile. "General Westmoreland's office asked if you'd like to attend a COVIA briefing, but you wouldn't need to sit through it to know what will be said."

"COVIA," Marshall repeated, remembering the acronym from a Washington briefing. He held up his hand to silence Waggoner, wanting to recall it from his memory, both as a test, and to put it in its proper setting—who had discussed it, in what context, with what facial expressions and tones of voice.

He sat, seemingly relaxed, appearing only faintly interested, but Waggoner studied his face and saw the incredible concentration in the eyes, laser intense, unseeing. Marshall held perfectly still for a full minute, then he said easily, "Combat Operations Vietnam, Infantry and Armor. The Defense Department study to determine whether more troops will help end the war."

Marshall stretched comfortably. "I sat in on a Pentagon briefing on COVIA some months ago with Secretary McNamara. It was mentioned only cursorily—a study to analyze combat effectiveness and to determine if a few more mechanized infantry and armor divisions might speed victory."

He smiled. "Probably I could guess its findings and conclusions. What time is the briefing?"

"This afternoon at two, at General Westmoreland's headquarters—MACV: Military Assistance Command, Vietnam, a few minutes from here."

"I'll go. How something is said, and who says it, is often more important than what is said. Call MACV and tell them I'll be there. And have some lunch sent up here, something light. I'll spend the rest of the time going over what you've piled on my desk."

He arched his brows. "And Miss Toland? Can she type?"

Waggoner laughed outright. "Yes, sir—hard to believe, but she actually can. As a matter of fact, she's extremely competent. I don't think the VC would get past her."

"I can't imagine why they would want to."

"Do you want to keep her, sir, or should I get someone more . . . subdued?"

Marshall grinned. "Oh, let's keep her. One rarely encounters someone like Dolores outside of wet dreams." He shook his head. "Who assigned her to me? Never mind, I can imagine. No, Colonel, we'll keep her. I think I can safely manage around that pitfall."

When Marshall left his office at one forty-five, smiling pleasantly at his secretary and the others with whom he had not spoken all day, Mead jumped up from the metal chair he had been sitting on in the corridor.

"Jesus!" Marshall said, flinching in surprise. "You've got to stop doing that, Corporal." He gazed about the corridor, empty except for the chair. "Is this where they have you? We'll find you someplace else; I'm not going to have you sitting out in the hall. You get any sleep?"

"Yes, sir, thank you," Mead said, and reaching into his pocket, pulled out money, clean bills he had spent an hour in line to get at the military bank, and handed them to Marshall.

Marshall put them carefully in his wallet. "All right, let's go."

The lobby was empty, obviously having been cleared, and his limousine waited outside, motor idling, two motorcycle police in front, a single jeep with four soldiers behind.

Two guards saluted, one held the door; Mead got in the front seat, and with a single siren, the procession left.

Just beyond the compound gate, Marshall told the driver to stop. The car immediately pulled to the curb. The motorcycles continued on a block, then raced back. The soldiers jumped from the jeep, and Marshall and Mead got out of the car, Mead racing around with his rifle raised.

"Gentlemen," Marshall said to the soldiers and police standing before him in alarm, "there has been some misunderstanding about my orders. I do not want an escort. You make me feel very uncomfortable, and besides, you draw unnecessary attention to my presence—you are making me a target. I want you to go back. Tell your superiors what I've said. Tell them also that the man who questions my command will be relieved immediately."

Marshall got back in the car, waited until Mead jumped in the front seat, and told the driver to go, leaving the others staring after them.

"What's that building?" Marshall asked the driver, pointing to a massive complex flying Vietnamese flags. Though obviously of importance, surrounded by soldiers and police, it looked in need of paint and maintenance.

"That's the Joint General Staff headquarters, sir," the driver said. "The gooks."

Marshall only nodded and the limousine pulled into an immaculate, fortresslike complex flying the U.S. flag. Guards stood aside and saluted as the car pulled up.

As Marshall started up the stairs, General William Westmoreland, in crisp battle fatigues, his four silver stars and paratroop wings gleaming in the sunlight, strode from the building. He gave a sharp salute and held out his hand.

"Welcome to Vietnam, Mr. Ambassador. I'm very happy to meet you, and pleased you could be with us today." He glanced over Marshall's shoulder to the limousine parked solitarily in front and smiled faintly, his eyes glinting beneath the brushy brows. "Sneaked up on us, as it were."

"Next time I may take a cab," Marshall replied good-naturedly.

"We have strict per diem rules," Westmoreland said. "Cabfare might not be reimbursable." He motioned inside, and Marshall followed, thinking that the general was even more impressive than his pictures, absolutely made for the role of command, someone central casting could not improve upon, with his square jaw and aquiline nose, strong features and piercing eyes.

Marshall found the entire setting cinematic, as though he had just walked onto a Hollywood sound stage. The direction was flawless; power and confidence throbbed—everything perfectly rehearsed, no cue missed, the supporting cast polished professionals; lighting, costumes, sound—all ideal.

Of course it was rehearsed, Marshall knew. How many times had some dignitary been met in this way, escorted down the pristine corridor as crack troops broke before him like waves parting at a ship's prow? Who could be immune to this? Marshall thought. The aura was of imperial splendor—armed warriors in starched uniforms, polished boots striking marble floors, the headquarters of a great army in the midst of war.

"I don't believe," Westmoreland said smoothly, leading Marshall down the hall past the legions, "that General Abrams got an opportunity yesterday to convey his and my willingness to assist you in any way we can."

"No. We never got much beyond discussion of a bodyguard."

Westmoreland grinned. "And now today, dismissal of all your security. We may have to get you to sign a personal liability disclaimer. But I'm sure you understand that we're at your disposal for whatever we can do to assist you. I appreciate your desire to remain autonomous, so I won't impose on your time in any way, nor put you in an awkward position of having to decline any invitations—just let me know if you desire anything, or if there is any problem that I might be able to help you with."

"Thank you. I'll try not to impose on your time either, though I'll be grateful for your views and expertise, and I'll want to get together with you before I return."

"Whenever you wish. Is there anything now that I might do for you?"

"I'm going to need an aircraft," Marshall said. "I'm not sure of my schedule or travel plans, and they might be very spur of the moment. I don't want to sap the war effort, but I also don't want to have to requisition a plane every time I decide to go somewhere."

Westmoreland nodded. "I'll have an aircraft ready for you at all times, on call just as they are for me, jet or chopper, depending on where you desire to go." Then he smiled. "Would you like a pilot for the aircraft, or will you make do on your own, as with your security?"

Marshall laughed. "A pilot, please."

They reached a doorway flanked by armed guards, who saluted, and as Marshall heard "Attention" shouted, Westmoreland stepped aside to allow Marshall to precede him into a small amphitheater.

Thirty officers, mostly generals, and half as many civilians stood until Westmoreland showed Marshall to one of the three front seats facing a stage, then walked to the podium and told them to be seated.

Marshall shook hands with General Abrams beside him, then turned to those behind and nodded, recognizing several from the airport and reception yesterday, including Wilson Abbot Lord, who had been identified as being with Central Intelligence, though acting under the aegis of State.

"Gentlemen," said Westmoreland in his confident tenor with its hint of Southern graciousness, a voice accustomed to command and public speaking—just months ago, triumphantly before a joint session of Congress, "I want to welcome Ambassador Bradley Marshall to MACV. Ambassador Marshall is in Vietnam as the personal representative of the Commander in Chief, President Johnson. The ambassador does not stand on, nor for, I might add, much ceremony."

General Abrams snorted.

"So I will merely express welcome to him and best wishes for a productive and successful visit to Vietnam. I am very pleased Ambassador Marshall has taken the time, only twenty-four hours after arrival, to join us for a briefing on what has been the most important and comprehensive study of combat operations in Vietnam. The study was commissioned by Secretary McNamara. General Arthur Shaw headed the group composed of military experts and civilian systems science analysts. General Shaw."

A pit bull of a man strode to the stage. Though older than Westmoreland, he had only two stars. With ill-concealed impatience, he waited until Westmoreland took his seat, then he stared at the audience with what could only be described as belligerence.

Well, thought Marshall with relish, no one is going to sleep through this—they could have sold me a ticket. Arthur Shaw was one of the few living legends in the military, a man known even beyond military circles.

A battalion commander under Patton during World War II, Shaw was a colonel when Westmoreland was a young lieutenant, but in the last twenty years he had advanced only two ranks, and now men who had served under him were his superiors, though that did not affect the way he treated them, nor they him.

A swaggering, blustering man of proven courage, daring, and military brilliance, he, like his mentor Patton, was not well-suited for times other than war. Finding a place for him in peacetime had been difficult, for unlike a battleship, he could not be mothballed, then reactivated. One had to take him as he was, and he was very difficult, especially when sober, for then the powers of his intellect and personality were concentrated.

Vietnam came too late for Arthur Shaw; though not sixty, he was too old to lead armies in the field. A younger corps of officers, untested in battle but now in command positions, led the battalions and regiments and divisions. With his two stars, he was too junior to direct the armies or determine strategy; he had made too many enemies, and Vietnam was a political war that was not going to be fought conventionally. Curtis LeMay in the air and Arthur Shaw on the ground would indeed have put Vietnam back in the Stone Age, but this war was going to be civilized, fought by technocrats, not Neanderthals.

An unrepentant Neanderthal—"The only thing better than fucking is fighting, and those with the biggest balls are the best at both"—Shaw knew that his time was past, but he was not going gracefully. He almost went out with a court-martial. Instead, he was banished from the Pentagon, exiled to Saigon with a study group to reach a foregone conclusion. Now that the study was completed, he was to return to Washington to retire.

The banishment was a compromise—the Chief of Staff of the Army wanted to court-martial him, and Shaw wanted to be court-martialed. To avoid such an uproar and to deny both officers, the Secretary of Defense appointed Shaw to head this staged study.

The problem had been long developing. Shaw was publicly contemptuous of the conduct of the war and reviled the air force general, Earle Wheeler, who was Chairman of the Joint Chiefs, and General Harold Johnson, Army Chief of Staff. But those feelings paled in the disgust he held for the civilians who micromanaged the war.

The exact cause of his final outburst was unknown; probably it was accumulated frustration, but it might also have been the martinis he had at lunch. However, there were no doubts about the nature of the outburst itself.

Returning from lunch, Shaw encountered the Chief of Staff in the corridor of the inner ring of the Pentagon, not far from the offices of the Secretary of Defense.

"He makes me puke," said Shaw to an aide as he passed Johnson.

The remark was clearly audible to the twenty or so people in the corridor, and there was no doubt at whom the words were directed.

General Johnson broke stride, then gathered himself and continued on.

Shaw clutched his own throat and pretended to gag, then he made the most awful retching noises and doubled over.

Johnson stopped and turned to face him. Shaw stood straight and bellowed, "You lipless cunt."

Johnson reeled, then he charged at the same time Shaw did.

What happened next was never agreed upon by all witnesses; whether Shaw actually attempted to strangle the Chief of Staff was disputed, but all confirmed that in the melee, Johnson ended on the marble floor with Shaw on top of him.

Two days later Shaw was en route to Vietnam.

Now he stood before the gathering, eyes glinting like a

boar's. He would return to Washington for retirement and oblivion in a few days. He knew he would not brief McNamara or the President; Marshall was the highest-ranking man he was ever going to address. This would be his last opportunity to express his views, an unexpected chance he was not going to let slip by.

He folded the pages of remarks he held in his hands and put them on the podium.

Beside him, Marshall felt Westmoreland stiffen.

Shaw took his spectacles from his pocket and put them on, slowly adjusting the wire harps over his ears. Then he gazed out on the assembly, his pugnaciousness suddenly transformed into a kindly, wise grandfatherliness, his voice vibrating with a deep, soothing resonance.

"I am an old soldier," he said. "Older than one should ever get. There will be no more bullets nor battles for me. I have dedicated my life to the call of arms, and I have loved it. It is a noble calling, manly and glorious, and it is true as Homer said that men tire sooner of sleep, love, song, and dance than of war. Achilles and Ulysses, Caesar and Hannibal, Wellington and Lee have been my brothers.

"I have seen men die bravely, and others live cowardly, and seen the wrong man honored, and the weak one prevail. As there is no dishonor in dying on the field, there is none in losing a just cause. But there is disgrace in a life cowardly lived, and shame in winning an unjust cause.

"I am a warrior. You are warriors. We are charged to fight bravely, and God deciding, die bravely. We are charged to take care of one another and be merciful to our foe. We are charged not to hurt women or children. We are charged to do our duty. As officers, our foremost duty is to our men and their welfare.

"I do not know if our cause in this war is just, but I am certain that the principles behind it are not unjust. I do not feel like Galahad questing for the Holy Grail; probably more like what Hector felt at Troy, some misgivings and alarm, but not enough to overcome devotion to country, and trust in king.

"But as I said, no more bullets and no more battles for me; no armies to lead, no enemies to meet."

He walked to a table on the stage and brought back a thick volume. "Only a report to make."

He held it up, then placed it back on the table.

"You will be briefed on the report, but not by me. It is my duty to disassociate myself completely from it. I disagree with everything in it. It is not a prescription for victory, but only for more of the same—two aspirin for a patient bleeding to death.

"More men will die in a cause, just or not, that will not be advanced. It is my duty to tell you that it is wrong and cowardly and immoral. I would be derelict not to tell you this. Warriors love combat, not carnage; the field of battle, not"—he gestured to the room about him—"this.

"Either meet the enemy or strike the tent. Leave this building and lead your army to the battlefield. Attack the enemy on his soil, at his heart; don't let him sneak by night to murder your men while you and they hide on hills and in bunkers, behind 'perimeters.' We are violating every rule of engagement, every law of combat and arms that every soldier knows. We are letting our own men die. Stop, I say. Either win this war as we know how and can, or take us from the battlefield. In the name of honor and decency, in God's name, stop killing our brothers. Our sons."

He took off his glasses, put them back in his pocket, and walked from the stage, then out of the room.

There was absolute silence, then a single man clapped.

Westmoreland turned and glared at the man, but he continued to clap.

Finally the man stood and walked to the stage.

Marshall leaned toward Westmoreland and said, "You should have charged admission."

Westmoreland's jaw was set in concrete, but Abrams laughed. "We will," Abrams said. "For his execution."

The man at the podium, a lieutenant colonel, tall and fair, was familiar to Marshall; he knew he had seen that face before.

The colonel appeared perfectly composed, confident and relaxed.

"General Shaw and my father served together; their respect for one another was mutual and profound. My

179

father probably would have given the same speech, and walked out, and gone to the bar and cursed us all. He then may or may not have come back in here to give the briefing.

"When my father died, Arthur Shaw treated me as a son. I honor and revere both men. That is love. Now it is my duty to give you the . . . majority report on the study."

What followed, without notes or pause, was the most brilliant presentation Marshall had ever heard, so assured and professional, so faultlessly executed, never boring, condescending, or contrived, so utterly masterful of material and audience that Marshall almost forgot that he was listening to the son of Robert R. Romer, Raging Romer, whose men kept going even after Patton's tanks ran out of gas.

Lieutenant Colonel Romer evoked a mighty army with inspired leadership prevailing in a struggle against evil and darkness. Only an artillery barrage and an air strike could have made the presentation more compelling.

After two hours, General Shaw was forgotten. More troops were not aspirin, they would be a transfusion, the lifeblood of victory; more men would save lives by bringing the war more quickly to its inevitable end—the triumph of freedom and democracy. Without new divisions, the war would be prolonged, victory delayed, and lives needlessly lost. Combat operations in Vietnam were an unequivocal success—witness the maps of vast terrain under American and South Vietnamese control versus the tiny patches of land under VC and NVA control; witness the body count of dead enemy troops, the weapons captured, the rice confiscated.

By every conceivable standard, operations in Vietnam were a resounding success. The only possible way the effectiveness of combat could be enhanced would be by increasing the infantry and armor. Two more divisions, with logistical support, would have a quantum effect on the successful execution of the war.

"Are there any questions?" Romer asked in conclusion.

General Westmoreland stood up. "Colonel, there could not possibly be any questions. No man here could be so obtuse not to have understood everything you so clearly and simply explained."

Then he turned to those behind him. *"Are* there any questions?"

There were none. He turned back to Romer. "Thank you, Colonel. I want to congratulate you and the study group on an exemplary piece of work. Absolutely first class. I will endorse the report today without changes or qualifications. I want your group to take this study back to the Pentagon immediately—I want the Joint Chiefs and the Secretary of Defense apprised of its contents without delay. Thank you again."

Westmoreland turned to Marshall expectantly, waiting for him to rise so that he could escort him from the amphitheater.

Marshall remained seated. "General, lacking the military expertise of everyone here, there are just one or two points that I am still a little obtuse about. I wouldn't dream of subjecting anyone to having to go over those again, so I would like to sit here alone, and have Colonel Romer touch on those one or two things again."

Westmoreland stared at him. His face set. Finally only his lips moved. "Of course." He turned and walked out so quickly that he was gone before an aide shouted "Attention" and everyone jumped up.

General Abrams smiled as he walked past. "You're two for two," he said.

Several rows back, Wilson Abbot Lord fumbled with papers and a briefcase so that he could be among the last to leave. As the aisles filled with men filing toward the exit, he kept his eyes on Marshall.

Throughout the meeting he had observed the envoy intently, watching his reactions, absorbing every nuance.

The ambassador had loved Arthur Shaw, had soaked up every word of the old rummy's, and when the sodden fraud had ended his maudlin plea to spare the "sons," Lord had seen Marshall visibly flinch.

The coffins; the sons; his own sons. It was all perfectly clear, his conclusions already drawn, his report to the

President determined within twenty-four hours, and nothing would change it.

There was no alternative, Lord saw—Marshall would either have to be discredited or his report somehow intercepted.

Marshall had appeared to concentrate on Romer's presentation, but Lord knew that he had not bought a word of it.

Romer's report would go to Washington, be heralded by the Joint Chiefs and Defense, and Marshall would torpedo it with a single word. The entire study would sink without trace.

Lord raged within. How could people like Marshall be so blind? How could the same errors of appeasement of communism be repeated over and over again? How often did America have to be duped before her leaders acted with force and resolution?

England was rot, an empty shell whose heart and muscle had been eaten away from within. She had not been deceived by a Trojan horse but betrayed by traitors within her own walls, not by enemy sappers or even her own disaffected class, but by men of privilege, of her upper class—intellectual effetes at Oxford and Cambridge.

Marshall was no traitor like Kim Philby, Maclean, and Burgess, no mole leaking secrets to the enemy, but the havoc he could wreak would be no less. What did intent matter if the result would be the same? Gullibility was as bad as betrayal. Whether freedom and principle were sold or ceded, they were gone nonetheless; semantics and sophistry would not stay the tyrant's fist, nor unbind the slave's chains.

Men such as Marshall, with principles and ideals and clean hands, who disclaimed the grubby toil of those working in the alleys and gutters and cesspools, could sanctimoniously intone from their penthouses "democracy," "justice," "freedom," and above the fray could piously inveigh against ends tainted by means.

Lord knew—anyone whose hands were dirty from sloughing through the shit of other men's freedom and justice knew—there were no ends, there were only means. Where was justice in the poor fighting and dying for the rich? Sons! The hypocrite, thought Lord in disgust: those poor boys in the coffins! What about the poor bastards in the gutters and slums, the diseased and addicted, the ignorant bastards who couldn't spell or define "democracy"?

Ends and means. What utter horseshit, thought Lord. There are only means. Or call them ends, it makes no difference—there is no final computation, only the sum or difference of the moment, an ever changing number in the infinite calculation.

The aisles were emptying, only a few people were left beside Marshall and Romer.

Lord took a tiny, highly sensitive tape recorder from his briefcase and placed it within a crumpled piece of paper, then he carefully placed the paper on the floor, closed his briefcase, and followed the last person out, closing the door behind him, nodding to the two guards who stood before it.

He, Lord, had a son too—did Marshall care about him? No, Lord thought bitterly, the bastard wouldn't give a damn about the Vietnamese sons he was selling out; he'd never give them a thought, and he'd never realize that other men such as Lord cared just as much about their own sons.

CHAPTER

· 13 ·

When the door closed, Marshall stood and walked to the stage.

"That was a very fine presentation, Colonel. I'm sorry to trouble you, but I'm just a civilian and need a little more clarification on a few things."

"I'm sorry I didn't make it clearer the first time, sir."

Marshall smiled. "The fault may not be yours, Colonel. Nor mine, for that matter."

Romer grinned. "You mean, it might be in the data?"

"I couldn't imagine it, but perhaps I could look back on a few items. Could I see the topographical slide on the Mekong Delta, and the one on the Central Highlands? Slides twenty-seven and thirty-one, I believe."

Romer nodded appreciatively and went to the projector to flash the slides onto the screen.

Marshall studied them. "Thank you. Now forty-two and forty-six, the specifics and logistical data on weaponry."

They were flashed onto the screen.

"Thank you. Finally numbers seven, fourteen, and eighty-five, on unit deployment, current and projected."

After they were screened, Marshall nodded, then brought a chair over to the table and motioned for Romer to sit across from him.

Romer's manner had not changed; confident and relaxed,

he seemed neither intimidated nor anxious in Marshall's presence.

"Now, Colonel," Marshall said, "I want you to tell me what wasn't in that report. I want you to tell me what you *think*."

"Think?" Romer deadpanned. "I'm only a lieutenant colonel, sir."

"At what rank does one begin to think?" Marshall asked.

"Some get four stars without ever having a thought," Romer said.

"Yes, I know some of those generals. They're the ones who dreamed up this study, and its conclusions." Marshall leaned back in his chair and folded his hands on the table. "But then there are other generals with only two stars who seem to think a great deal."

Romer nodded. "General Shaw said everything that wasn't in this report."

Marshall stared at him, then looked to the screen. Finally he said, "How is it that the tanks and armor won't sink in the Delta?"

Romer met his gaze, then he leaned over the table and pushed on the massive report, sliding it across until it fell heavily to the floor. "This *report* would sink in the Delta."

"And more infantry and armor?"

Romer made a loud sucking noise, closed his fingers, and lowered his hand, dragging the infantry and armor down into the swamp.

"Can we win?"

"Absolutely."

"How?"

"Put General Shaw in command. Invade the north. Drop H-bombs. Use nerve gas."

Marshall could just imagine making that recommendation to Lyndon Johnson. "I think," he said, "that the President might demur from such a suggestion."

Romer pointed to the report on the floor. "There's always that. Which, I suppose, will go to him after it's endorsed by the Pentagon. And in six months the divisions will be sent over."

185

"My son in one of them, I suspect," said Marshall with more sadness than he meant to convey.

"Surely you can get him deferred," Romer said.

"He doesn't want to be deferred."

"Surely he doesn't believe in the war," said Romer with more surprise and cynicism than he intended.

"Oh, no. It's some twisted sense of moral principle—that someone else will have to go, and perhaps die in his place, if he refused to go. I couldn't get through to him at all."

Romer smiled. "I see. One of those kinds of son."

Marshall laughed. "You probably know the type. Did your father want you to join the army?"

"He was killed when I was sixteen, before joining was a question, but he always told me never to become a career officer, and I think he meant it. He was always frustrated with the army except when he was in the middle of battle. Like General Shaw, he was a terrible peacetime soldier. He thought the military was filled with incompetents and pygmies, and though he loved war, truly did, according to Mother, and his diaries and letters, that was just for himself—I don't think he could have stood having his son on the battlefield. Certainly he could not have led me in battle. How could he forgive himself if his son was killed? Deep down, he was a soft and sensitive man—like General Shaw. There's a lot of bluster and swagger and bravado about Shaw, but he meant that speech he gave today. And I honestly believe my dad would have given the same one. Both are—were—very honorable men."

"Where are men like that today?" Marshall mused.

"We haven't become generals yet," Romer said with a smile. "And never will unless I get a battalion to command."

"Is that what's important to you?"

"Critical. Essential."

"I'm sure many men have been promoted to general without combat experience, plodders not even able to give stunning briefings."

Finally Romer's composure cracked. "Raging Romer's son? Untested on the battlefield? A lieutenant colonel who gives briefings? A staff officer?" His voice was bile and pain. "My father was a military hero, a legend on par with

Washington, Grant, Lee, Sherman, Pershing. Mention World War II, and it's MacArthur, Eisenhower, Patton, and my father. I don't resent him, envy him, hate him—I just want to be myself. For Christ's sake, I'm not going to win the Vietnam War, march triumphantly into Hanoi. Fifty years from now, a hundred years from now, there'll be only one Romer—my dad—and that's okay by me. It's just that *today,* I'd like to be the Romer. I want my own turn."

He stopped, chagrined. "I'm sorry, sir. I don't normally carry on like that; I don't know what brought that on. I beg your pardon. That's certainly not what we're here for, to have me rave before the President's envoy. I guess it started with the mention of your son. My father would have nightmares to see me on the battlefield, though he himself would have run naked and unarmed to get on one."

Marshall smiled and asked softly, "Why won't they give you a battalion to command?"

Romer shrugged. "I don't think there's any one reason—the fact that I am Raging Romer's son and they don't want to give an impression of favoritism; some residual resentment of my father and of General Shaw—though both were heroes, many people hated them; some fear that I might fuck up and disgrace the name—it would make great news copy if Raging Romer's son led his men into a massacre, or got captured and became a POW. On the other hand, what if I became a hero too, entered Hanoi and captured Ho Chi Minh? That would be even worse. How could the army deal with another Romer—a prima donna's prima donna? And finally, I give good briefing—that's what they're sending me back to Washington for day after tomorrow."

"You don't want to go?"

Romer leaned forward and said forcefully, "I want a battalion."

Marshall considered him for a long time. Finally he said, "May God and your father forgive me. How about a deal, Colonel?"

Romer looked directly into his eyes. "Name it."

"Be my aide for the next month or so, and I'll get you the battalion."

"What's the trick? The deal? My part?"

"Be my aide. I need someone here to work for me—I have someone to manage my office, but I need someone who has absorbed all the information you have. I want to travel to the places your study touched on. I suppose I could take General Shaw, but probably we would not be compatible traveling companions. After a month or so, I'll get you your battalion. I am not without influence."

Romer laughed outright. "Indeed."

"I have no idea what kind of battalion commander you'll make, but you would be an ideal aide for me—you're quick, savvy, not intimidated, and have, I think, a perfectly clear, uncluttered view. You could save me a great deal of time by pointing me in directions I would take longer finding on my own. Is it a deal?"

"I don't want to sound like I'm trying to flatter you but . . . I'd be honored to work for you. I'm very grateful for your confidence in me. And by the way, I'll make a terrific battalion commander."

Marshall stood. "Excellent. I'll tell General Westmoreland. He'll be disappointed that you won't be making the presentation in Washington, but I'm sure he'll accede to my request."

"Yes," Romer said, nodding, "I expect he will. I'll unpack and wait until I'm told to report to you."

They shook hands and Marshall left.

Moments later, Lord returned. Showing his credentials, and explaining that he had left classified notes crumpled on the floor, he retrieved the tape recorder.

After the briefing, Lord had spent twenty minutes with Westmoreland and his senior staff, getting the end-of-day wrap-up on combat activity.

The only matter of note, to Lord, was Westmoreland's obvious ire with Marshall, and his casual direction to an aide to have aircraft and a pilot detailed to the ambassador for whenever he desired them. Both the ire and the pilot were fortuitous developments; Lord thought he knew just how to exploit them.

*　*　*

When Marshall returned to the embassy, the lobby had again been cleared.

Mead, accompanying him, looked about apprehensively. "This is kind of spooky," he said.

Marshall snorted, "It's stupid. Why the hell can't people do something simply?" Surely there's a compromise between a midway and an empty tomb, he thought; he couldn't come and go with a huge crowd always gawking, nor could he have people locked in closets every time he arrived.

He had crossed the lobby, going toward the elevator, when a voice suddenly cried out, "You there! Stop!"

Marshall and Mead turned to see a woman walking toward him. Then there was a rush of movement behind her. She, glancing over her shoulder and seeing guards pursuing her, started to run toward Marshall.

Marshall hesitated, confused and slightly alarmed, but Mead acted immediately. He stepped in front of Marshall, shielding him, and brought his rifle up, not pointing it at her, but raised menacingly.

The guards gained on the woman. One grabbed her but she screamed and broke free.

"The children!" she cried. "You've got to save them."

Mead stepped forward to block her, thrusting his rifle against her breasts.

"How dare you!" she yelled. Then she stepped back and slapped him across the face. "Get out of my way!"

The slap was so loud and unexpected that everyone—the guards, Marshall, Mead, and the woman—stood still.

The woman recovered first. "Oh, my God," she said, "I'm terribly sorry." She reached out to touch Mead's cheek, already red from the blow.

Mead did not flinch, just held her back firmly with his rifle.

Then the guards moved. They seized her and pulled her away, forcing her arms painfully behind her back.

Finally Marshall moved. He stepped forward, in front of Mead. "Let go of her," he said.

The guards hesitated.

"Release her!"

The guards did, but very unsurely, and they stood ready to grab her again.

"I must talk with you," the woman said rapidly, stepping forward. "Please. Please. Children will die unless you help. Please!"

Marshall stared at her. Though her clothes were shabby and her hair in disarray, Marshall could see that she was no madwoman. Her face, pained in desperation, was strikingly intelligent and appealing.

"What can I do for you?" Marshall asked.

"Listen to me. Oh, please, just for five minutes." Her eyes brimmed in plea and hope.

"Of course," Marshall said, and motioned the guards away.

"Sir," one started. "She's . . ."

Marshall waved his hand. "It's all right. Thank you," he said to the guards.

They backed away reluctantly.

"Come"—he gestured to Teresa—"we'll go to my office."

He led her to the elevator, and the three got in. Again she put her hand out to touch Mead's cheek. "I'm so sorry," she said. "Forgive me. I never meant to hurt you."

Marshall smiled. "I think you embarrassed him more than you hurt him."

"You could have shot me," she said to Mead.

"We have strict rules about gunning down women in the embassy lobby," Marshall said.

Mead edged to the back of the elevator to avoid further solicitude from the woman.

"I am Teresa Hawthorne," she said, extending her hand to Marshall. "Thank you very much for seeing me. No one else would."

"Bradley Marshall," he said, shaking her hand.

"You must be very important."

"You didn't know who I was when you ordered me to stop?"

"No. I just knew you must be important. They moved everybody out of the way before your arrival, herded us like cows, saying, 'He's coming, he's coming,' so I knew you had to be somebody. You are somebody important, aren't you?"

"Just an envoy, I'm afraid. A diplomat."

"Indeed; I could have guessed. You look like one, quite distinguished, and you handled that business in the lobby most diplomatically. You were very impressive and forceful."

"Thank you, and now this way please."

"My goodness," she said, seeing the guard meet the elevator, then escort them to the glass booth. "I *am* surprised he didn't shoot me downstairs."

At the entrance to the suite of offices, Marshall said to Mead, "Corporal, would you wait until Mrs. Hawthorne—"

"Miss Hawthorne."

". . . Miss Hawthorne and I have finished talking, then you can escort her out." He smiled. "You might want a backup, but I think it will be all right." He turned to Teresa. "You're not going to hurt me, or attack my Marine again, are you?"

Inside his office, Marshall directed Teresa to a chair. "Would you care for coffee? Or tea, or something else?"

"Oh, no, thank you. You are being very kind. I really never expected to be treated like this. Father Dourmant will hardly believe this—he's a French priest; he doesn't think much of Americans, I'm afraid."

"I've never met a Frenchman, secular or cleric, who did."

Teresa looked about shyly, took in the opulent setting, and self-consciously smoothed the hem of her dress that had come unstitched.

She looked exhausted and overwhelmed, but Marshall saw in her face a kindness that was ethereal, almost as if a mist separated her from the world. She sat pleased and happy, utterly ingenuous, and he was charmed.

"I think I'll have coffee," he said, standing and going to the door. "Are you sure you won't have something? It won't be any trouble."

"Well . . . yes. Coffee would be wonderful. I hardly ever get coffee. It's so expensive on the black market."

Marshall opened the door. "Colonel Waggoner, would you have Miss Toland bring coffee for two? And some cookies, or whatever she can find. It's getting late; there's no need for you or anyone to stay on. I'll see you in the

191

morning; there are numerous matters I'd like to go over with you first thing. I'll be in around eight. Good night."

He returned to the chair across from Teresa. "Now what is it you'd like to tell me? Whose children can I save?"

Teresa spoke for nearly an hour, telling him of the clinic and orphanage, her work, all their problems. She told him of her many trips to the embassy to get help, and of being turned down every time, and that now she was desperate, the South Vietnamese government would not help.

"I have a woman in the clinic who wants to set fire to herself and her baby in a public protest, an immolation like the Buddhist bonzes did. Father Dourmant is outraged, but I honestly don't know what to tell her."

"Well, I certainly hope you tell her not to do it."

"Why?" asked Teresa tiredly. "So she and her child can be bombed? Or die of starvation? The baby's deformed and retarded. Many of them are that way, and drug-addicted and with sores all over their bodies. They have no hope: if they live, can you imagine what their lives will be? Outcast children, brain-damaged, wandering the streets, sorting through garbage. Truly, what difference does it make if the woman sets fire to herself and her baby? Their lives will never get better; there's only going to be more pain and suffering. It's cruel to hold out hope when nobody cares."

The room was getting dark. Through the window Marshall saw lights turning on, bright neon flashing, signaling the carnival of night. He sighed, too tired and overcome to turn on his own lights in the office.

He had not expected this; the horror overwhelmed him.

Who was this woman who had just entered his life, this remarkable woman who shone with an attraction so strong that he had to turn away his gaze?

"How many orphanages are there?" he asked at last. "How many children altogether?"

She shook her head. "I don't know. I don't even know how many clinics and orphanages there are in Saigon, but there must be hundreds throughout the country. And children? Thousands and thousands. More every day, not just orphans from the bombings and killings, but illegitimate babies by the score, and the Catholic hospitals won't do abortions, and the soldiers—they don't care enough to use contraceptives."

She sighed too, then smiled. "I never get this discouraged until I take time to think about it. Now that I've talked it all out, it seems impossible. Just absolutely overwhelming and awful."

"Indeed it does," said Marshall, mustering a faint smile too. "Lord. I don't know what to tell you. I certainly can't give you any answers or solutions. Frankly, I've never given thought to what you've told me; I wasn't even aware of what you've described. I can see why you've been rebuffed here. The problem seems monumental; and politically . . . well—I can't imagine who would champion the cause of the illegitimate children born of soldiers and prostitutes."

"But morally . . ."

Marshall held up his hand. "I said politically; the moral and political coincide only randomly, and only when it's expeditious. But I promise I will do what I can. I will look into the matter tomorrow."

He stood up and went to his desk. "Would you write down your name and the address of the clinic, and a phone number if there is one."

When she did, and handed him the paper, she said, "I am so . . ."

Marshall waved his hand. "No, please don't. You're the one who should be thanked. I . . . I'm not at all sure I can do anything to help."

"You've already helped; you've given me hope."

"That may be a cruelty."

"I'll thank you anyway," she said, extending her hand and shaking his. "Thank you also for the coffee and cookies, but mostly for listening. That's a wonderful help sometimes. I wish Father Dourmant could meet you; I know he'd like you."

"That would spoil everything for him, ruin a cherished prejudice."

"Thank you again," she said as he led her to the door.

"Good night, Miss Hawthorne," he said, then looked down at the hand she held out to him.

He took it. It was so warm, and he could feel its soothing, comforting power, and he did not want to release it.

"Corporal Mead will show you out," he said at last, then he watched her leave and stood motionless for many minutes after she was gone.

In his office on another floor, Lord for the second time finished listening to the tape. He had been right, there was no question of Marshall's position. Taking on Romer as his aide was a masterstroke—he would be able to document with authority his refutations of the COVIA study. He was a very clever, dangerous bastard, Lord thought, and he had to be stopped.

Lord spent a long time thinking. He could sit motionless for an extraordinary period, for so long that others in the Agency had compared his ability to that of a lizard.

Finally he moved; he reached for the phone to call Da Nang. He would get Bradley Lawrence Marshall a pilot all right.

When he finished making the arrangement, he went down the hall to Jeffrey Gibbon's office.

Gibbon stood when Lord entered, then he went to his safe and brought out the file on Marshall, handing it back to Lord.

"He's stirred up a lot of shit since he got here," Gibbon said. "How did you know he was going to be trouble? There's nothing in his file or background to indicate it."

"It's in the file," Lord said, sitting comfortably on the metal folding chair.

"I sure missed it," Gibbon said. "To me he came across like the ultimate Establishment character—makes Ellsworth Bunker look like a hippie."

"Jeffrey, the Founding Fathers came from the best families—revolutionaries usually do. The rabble rarely produces a successful revolutionary; they all come from Establishment families, and knowing the system and how it works makes them all the more dangerous. Marx, Engels, Lenin, Mao, Che, and Ho did not come from the oppressed proletariat."

"You don't think Marshall is a . . ."

"Communist? Of course not. There *aren't* any communists in America, Jeffrey—we're the most communist-free society in the world. Do you know any communists? Have you ever met one? At any communist cell meeting, two-thirds of the people are FBI agents. It's the damnedest canard in the world—the nuts on the right paranoid about communists in America and . . . there aren't any."

Lord liked Gibbon, his dedication and eagerness, but he was finding Gibbon to be exactly what he looked like—too good to be true; he wasn't proving to be as quick or perceptive as Lord had hoped. Probably, Lord thought, it has to do with his looks: handsome men and beautiful women can't avoid a glance in the mirror—it's a harmless conceit, but it breaks concentration, and in this business, a second's lapse can be fatal.

Still, Lord decided, he would be able to use Gibbon.

"'Trouble' is what I said, Jeff. Marshall is going to be serious trouble. He's much worse than a communist, far more dangerous."

"You mean he's a liberal?" Gibbon asked with a grin.

"The worst kind," Lord answered. "A true, honest-to-God concerned man with—"

"His head up his ass."

Lord nodded approvingly. He stood up. "You're still flight qualified, aren't you?"

"Yes, sir."

"You remember how a Huey works?"

Gibbon smiled. "Flying's like fucking, it's not something you forget how to do."

Lord stared at him coldly. "You remember how they *don't* work?"

Gibbon was confused. "Sir?"

"You might want to break out a manual on the Huey UH-1B, Jeffrey. I want you to know it backwards and forwards in the dark."

Gibbon smiled. "A Huey, a woman—I can handle them both in the dark; I don't need a manual."

Lord went to the door. "Jeffrey, either you're going to have to grow up, or I'm going to have to grow down if we're going to have meaningful discussions."

Gibbon nodded solemnly. "I think you should grow down, sir."

"Indulge me, Jeff. Get a manual on the Huey. Good night."

After placing a call to MACV, requesting Romer's transfer, Marshall left his office.

When the limousine pulled up before the villa, he told Mead and the driver to go home.

"I'm going to bed and may sleep for sixteen hours. I won't need you, Corporal. If someone wants to shoot me, they can."

"What time should I report in the morning, sir?" Mead asked.

"Don't," said Marshall. "Take the morning off. Take your girlfriend somewhere. Come in after lunch."

Marshall climbed the steps wearily; the door was opened for him, and his entire house staff stood at attention, smiling.

Oh, my God, Marshall said to himself.

Mead got back in the car. The limousine left the villa compound and started back toward the embassy.

"I'm not going back to the embassy," Mead said. "Drop me off at the corner so I can get a cab."

"You got a gook cunt?" the driver asked, pulling to the curb.

Mead got out. "No," he said, shutting the door and running to a cab stopped at a traffic light. He flung open the rear door.

A middle-aged Frenchman squealed in surprise and terror when Mead jumped into the seat beside him.

"But this cab is taken," he said petulantly.

"Shut up," Mead said, raising his rifle into his face and giving an address to the driver.

"Delighted to share the cab," said Bernard Lacouture, and he murmured in French to the driver, "Take our deliverer to where he wants to go."

Lacouture settled in the seat, squirming delicately, and admiring the soldier beside him, easily the most handsome trooper he had ever seen, a stunning specimen, savage and

196

dangerous. He reminded Lacouture of a French Legionnaire he had had years ago. Lacouture fairly swooned at the memory and the nearness, and he entirely forgot his mission, to reconnoiter the residence of the new American envoy.

Lacouture wriggled a little closer. "Could not I invite you—"

"Don't talk to me, faggot," Mead snarled.

Lacouture gasped in pleasure. Exquisite! he thought. I must have him.

When the cab pulled up, Mead reached for his wallet.

"No, no," said Lacouture. "My pleasure. *Enchanté.*"

Mead mumbled, "Thanks," and slammed the door, then ran up the stairs.

The cab started down the street. "Stop!" shouted Lacouture. "Go back."

The cab backed up. Lacouture leaned out the window until he saw a light go on in an upstairs room, *"Bien,"* he said, scribbling the address, then he shouted happily to the driver, "Go!" He had a plan, a wonderful plan that would bring him enough money to retire on the Riviera, and let him possess this centurion too. An exquisite plan!

CHAPTER

• 14 •

Luke Bishop had only thirty minutes' notice before being pulled from the hill and sent back with the bodies.

"It's an order, Lieutenant," said the company commander, who had himself received it from battalion, which got it from regiment, and they directly from General Haggan at division headquarters.

"Send the man out for a couple days," said Haggan after returning from the hill and seeing Bishop's exhaustion. "That's the only position that wasn't overrun last night. The gooks will be back, but not for a while—I want him ready. I can't win a war with officers dead on their feet."

"Anything I should do while you're gone?" Gunny Brock asked, waiting beside Bishop.

Bishop shrugged. "You know as much as I do. I don't think they'll hit again for three or four days. Probably you could cut the guard to the minimum and let everybody get as much sleep as possible. During the day, I'd have them work on the wire, setting more traps. There's nothing else *to* do, except wait. And try not to get killed."

"We'll do our best, Lieutenant." Brock had intended to make a joke about getting laid, and officers having all the privileges, but he just stared at the two green body bags lying before them, shook his head, and watched the chopper approach from the horizon.

Bishop took only his rifle and a shaving kit, not even a change of clothes. On the short flight he sat strapped in by webbed belts, the body bags at his feet. Below he saw the massive buildup at Khe Sanh, ring upon ring of bunkers and tunnels, an ugly sore on the land that had been cleared for miles around. Far in the distance he could see the little welts of forward outposts, but he could not make out Hill 742.

At division headquarters in Quang Tri, he was placed on a C-130 flight to Da Nang, listed on the cargo manifest as "Bishop, Lucas M., 2Lt. 0104422, and Human Remains."

When they landed, a truck was waiting with two Navy men who grabbed the body bags and tossed them into the flatbed. He started to jump in back when one of the men called out, "You can ride up front with us," but he ignored them and squatted beside the bags, oblivious to the dust and blinding sun.

The truck bounced across the airfield to a remote white building where they carried in the body bags. Bishop handed over the paperwork and personal effects, then stood awkwardly, not knowing what to do.

"You don't want to see this, Lieutenant," said a corpsman. "Why don't you go over to the BOQ and get cleaned up. You have to take back some copies to your unit headquarters, but we won't finish with the files until tomorrow."

They directed him across the massive base to the BOQ, where he was given a room. He fell onto the cot without taking off his clothes and passed into a mercifully dreamless sleep.

Pounding on the door slammed him awake. He threw himself on the floor, fumbling for his rifle, unable to focus, completely disoriented.

Finally it all came to him and he went to the door; checking his watch, he realized he had slept to late afternoon.

One of the sailors from the mortuary stared at him, his mouth smacking gum. "Somebody fucked up and didn't sign the right papers. You gotta come identify the bodies."

Bishop pushed on the door. "It's them. I've been with them the whole time."

"You gotta come anyway, Lieutenant. Things gotta be right—they can't go sending the wrong fucking guys home."

"I told you, it's them. Get out of here."

"Listen, Lieutenant, Commander Hartman said to come. That means you come. *Sir.*"

Bishop reached out for the sneering face but the man was gone.

It took him thirty minutes to walk back to the mortuary where a neatly painted white sign read "Graves Registration."

Inside he was led down a long corridor to a slate, antiseptic room of slab tilt tables. There were bodies on all the tables, and stacked like cordwood against the walls were others, still in their uniforms, some stiff in rigor mortis.

The bodies on the tables were naked, some without arms and legs, some twisted and horribly deformed. On one, drained and scrubbed the color of the colorless walls, his blood in pails, arms dangling off the table, his eyes fixed on the fluorescent light, was Pozinski.

Bishop turned away, but on the next table were just pieces of flesh, meat, and Miller's head.

Bishop grabbed his stomach and whirled around.

A naval officer in a blood-splattered surgical gown steadied him. "I'm sorry, Lieutenant, they shouldn't have brought you back here. I'll talk to them. It's macabre work here; it gets to them sometimes—they take it out in cruel ways. Are you all right?"

Bishop nodded, eyes riveted on the floor.

"Can you identify them?"

Bishop nodded again, then he drew himself straight and turned to the tables. "Corporal Pozinski. Gregory S.," he said evenly. "They called him Snags. And that is PFC Lawrence F. Miller. Will that be all, sir?"

"Yes, Lieutenant. Thank you. Just sign these forms, please."

His signature was steady and his hands did not shake when he handed back the papers. "May I ask a favor, Commander?"

"Of course."

"I don't want to go back to the BOQ, sir. I don't think I could."

"I understand, Lieutenant. Do you have any friends in Da Nang? I could have one of our drivers drop you at another unit."

"Thank you. I have a friend with the Marine Air Wing. We went to college together."

"That will be no problem." The pathologist looked over Bishop's shoulder to the table. "I . . ." Then he merely shook his head. "Take care of yourself, Lieutenant."

When Bishop knocked on the screen door of the Quonset hut and poked his head inside, a huge man in skivvies bent over a flight bag open on his cot looked up curiously.

The man cocked his head, momentarily puzzled, then he straightened.

"Jesus Christ! Luke!" He bounded across the room and grabbed Bishop in a bear hug. "My God, what happened to you?"

Bishop pushed him away. "Nothing happened to me." He grabbed a fist of flesh on the other man. "I been fighting a war. I haven't been getting fat like you."

"Yeah? Well, no wonder we're losing—you look worse than the gook I napalmed yesterday."

Then he grabbed Bishop again and held him so that he could see him. "No shit, you look awful. I don't see many grunts—is this what you guys look like? War must be a motherfucker."

Bishop laughed. "It is."

"Glad I ain't in it." Then he shook his head. "I didn't even recognize you. You look like you haven't slept in months. You must have lost twenty pounds."

"Do I really look that bad?"

Jim Magnuson pulled him over to a mirror. Standing beside his friend, Bishop could see. They had played football together at Oklahoma; once the same size, Bishop felt shrunken and wizened. Magnuson was robust, his face full and energetic; Bishop's own face was drawn, his eyes sunk; he looked wasted.

"Okay," he said, and shrugged. "I should have been a pilot."

"I told you that at OCS, asshole. But no, you were going to be a hero, go hand to hand with the gooks. What a dipshit!"

Magnuson swept everything off his cot and pushed Bishop down on it. Then he ran to a small refrigerator, smashed an ice tray on top of it, filled two glasses with cubes, and poured them full with Jack Daniel's. He brought them back to the cot, singing the Oklahoma fight song.

"Jim, if I drink this, I'll get sick."

"Well, goddamn, you couldn't look any worse. Or smell worse." He raised his glass. "Sooners."

Bishop clinked the glass and sipped, then he gagged.

"What a disgrace," shouted Magnuson, raising the glass again. "Sigma Nu."

Bishop raised his and drank again, this time without gagging.

"All right," said Magnuson. "Now tell me what you're doing here. No, first we have to drink to Barbara."

Bishop had been best man in Magnuson's wedding and he drank to his friend's wife.

"Now to the Corps," said Magnuson, filling the glasses. They had both joined the Marines after college and were together at Quantico until Magnuson went off to flight school. "Never mind," he said, tossing the whiskey to the floor. "Fuck the Corps. What are you doing here?"

Bishop told him, and Magnuson listened.

When Bishop finished, Magnuson said nothing for a long time, then he emptied the bottle in both their glasses. "Reminds me of the joke about the woman with two cunts."

He told it to Bishop, then another; soon they were laughing, retelling jokes and stories, pushing each other around and throwing ice cubes.

Finally, as it grew dark in the room, Bishop sat on the cot quietly. "You haven't told me about yourself, Jim, anything about what you're doing." He pointed to the flight bag and clothes strewn on the floor. "You going somewhere?"

Magnuson shrugged, looking a little sheepish. "I'm a pilot—what's there to say? I drop big bombs on little gooks, defoliate forests . . . that kind of thing."

"So where are you going?"

"Saigon. The unit got a call this morning; they need a pilot at Tan Son Nhut. I'm elected."

"Saigon? Why do they want a Marine pilot? That's all Air Force down there."

"Beats me. But just like a grunt, 'ours is not to reason why,' just do what we're fucking told." Then, eager to change the subject, he pulled Bishop up. "Go take a shower, then we'll get something to eat. I'm not leaving till tomorrow, so we got the whole night to party. I'll take you places, and show you sights that your little Okie brain won't believe."

"Forget that shit," said Bishop, heading for the shower. "Show me something my big Okie cock can fuck."

After they cleaned up, they pushed and shoved each other out of the Quonset hut, then, arms around each other's shoulders, they sang their way across the unit compound and commandeered a jeep to drive into Da Nang.

"Jesus!" Bishop said as Magnuson careened the jeep into III MAF Headquarters. "I don't want to go in here."

"I have to park the jeep here—I can't leave it on the street downtown, they'd booby-trap it. Besides, it's fun to take the launch into town—it's the only sea duty I ever hope to do."

"A launch?"

"The navy runs a shuttle from the Officers' Club across the river into town. It's great—you stagger out of the club, some sailor salutes you and helps you onto the boat, then ferries you across the river to the cathouses—it's exactly how war should be."

Magnuson parked the jeep near the Officers' Club and they went inside to drink, but Bishop felt uncomfortable and self-conscious. His uniform was torn and dirty, his boots unpolished, and everyone else wore starched fatigues and their boots and brass gleamed.

"Let's get out of here," Bishop said after one drink. They went out the back and crossed the manicured lawn to the dock where two sailors saluted them smartly.

"Shit," said Magnuson. "I wanted the admiral's boat."

"The admiral's using it, sir," said a sailor. "He's at the

Stone Elephant—the launch waits there until he's ready to leave."

Magnuson jumped aboard and explained to Bishop, "The admiral has his own launch; needless to say, it's a lot nicer than this—it's a cabin cruiser, top of the line—and when he's not using it, it's used for the shuttle too. Maybe we can ride it back."

"What's the Stone Elephant?" Bishop asked.

"The old French officers' club. It's like a restaurant on the Riviera. Hey, we'll go there."

Bishop shook his head. "Not the way I look; let's just go get laid."

"We have plenty of time for that. You gotta see the Stone Elephant, I mean, we have the war down right—booze, pussy, three-star restaurants. It would be a *tragedy* if we lost this fucking war."

But when they arrived at the Stone Elephant, an elegant restaurant set back from the tree-lined boulevard, surrounded by gardens lit by lanterns hanging from sculpted trees, Bishop was not allowed in because of his uniform.

The maître d', a tall Frenchman in a white tuxedo, firmly barred the entrance.

"This man is single-handedly holding Khe Sanh," Magnuson yelled, pushing the maître d' out of the way, but immediately three tuxedoed waiters grabbed him.

"Arrest those men," a voice shouted, and Bishop turned to see an admiral storming across the dining room toward them.

Bishop kneed a waiter in the crotch and dropped another with his right fist. Magnuson broke free and they ran, chased by the admiral and twenty others in the dining room.

"I'm gonna strafe this place tomorrow—your asses are gonna fry in napalm," Magnuson yelled over his shoulder.

They ran through the garden and jumped the hedge, then bolted down the street and ran into an alley.

As soon as Magnuson saw they were not being pursued, he stopped to catch his breath, but immediately beggar children appeared from nowhere. They closed on Bishop and Magnuson, coming from behind garbage cans and from doorways, so many that Bishop couldn't count them. He started to back away, but Magnuson grabbed his arm and at the same time he hurled a handful of coins and money. As the children scattered to grab the money, Bishop and Magnuson ran through them.

"This is worse than the goddamn DMZ," Bishop said when they reached the main street, but there, too, they couldn't stop because beggars and cripples hounded them incessantly.

"That looks like the gook I dinged last week," Magnuson said about a legless, one-eyed man sprawled on the sidewalk, holding out his hand, yet he stopped and gave the man a large bill from his wallet.

Magnuson stopped numerous times for amputees and cripples. "The reason I don't come down to get laid very often is because it costs so goddamn much—not the pussy, just the tolls."

Bishop sobered up quickly as figures darted toward them from alleys and shadows. He moved away from the buildings, walking almost in the street, but there motorcyclists and cars nearly hit him and horns blared constantly.

"You know," Magnuson said, oblivious to Bishop's mounting anxiety, "Da Nang used to be a small, almost sleepy colonial town up until four years ago. There were only about eighty thousand people here. Beautiful bay and beaches, quaint little shops—they say it was like the French Riviera. Now there are more than eighty thousand whores alone, and the only things for sale anymore are dope and cunt."

Magnuson stepped over a cripple. "But that's all I want to buy, so it's okay by me."

Bishop jumped from the curb; he kept looking about nervously. Instincts and senses he had sharpened and lived by for the past months shrieked warnings to him.

"How can you joke about this?" he asked.

"Da Nang? Or you mean the war?" Then Magnuson stopped on the sidewalk and grabbed Bishop's arm. "Hey, let's get something straight here," and he pointed to the buildings about them.

"French colonial architecture, nice homes in their days—note the pastels, pinks, and yellows and blues under all the pollution and grime; it's like a postcard from Nice. And that bay out there is where the admiral has his ship that his Chris-Craft yacht takes him out to whenever he wants to feel salty. And beautiful beaches up and down the coast. But let's keep it in perspective—the French landed here a hundred and twenty-five years ago, and they robbed and stole what they could and made slaves of the people, then they bailed out and we came, and now it's just one gigantic whorehouse."

Bishop looked at him curiously. "Jim, this isn't you. This isn't how you came over here."

"You're right, man, but this is what I've seen. You might still believe in this fucking war, but to me, it's bullshit, just one big lie on top of the French lie—the big Western lie of saving the gooks, or whatever they happen to be, and we're gonna turn them into white folks like us even if we have to kill every fucking one of them in the process."

He pointed to the children and beggars. "There aren't any minds and hearts to be won here—just cripples and amputees and whores and kids: everybody else we kill. That's what *we* do. You got that—I mean, really got that? We kill people. You and me, Luke Bishop and Jim Magnuson from Bumfuck, Oklahoma—we kill people. That's our job, our line of employment. We fucking kill people for a living. You want me to take that seriously?"

Magnuson shook his head. "I thought this war was going to be John Wayne and Sergeant Rock. I *believed* in the comic books. I came over here for democracy, truth, and the American way. I went to flight school to be the Red Baron—not to drop bombs from thirty thousand feet and napalm water buffalo. I didn't come over here to defoliate forests."

He said curtly, "Or other things."

"What other things?" Bishop asked. "What's happened to you? This isn't you."

"You bet it ain't. Now I just want to get out. I don't want to think about anything, Luke. I have a job—I'm doing it. Tomorrow my job is to go to Saigon—I'll go. They pay me to do my job. I don't get paid for teeth gnashing, soul-searching, remorse, conscience. I'm not paid to think, and thinking wouldn't change a fucking thing—they'd just put someone else in my place. Yours too."

He put his arm around Bishop. "You bet I joke about this. If I didn't, I might come to believe in what I'm doing."

He pointed to the bright lights and flashing neon several blocks away. "Now, you want to continue the geopolitical discussion, or you want to get laid?"

"I may have forgotten how," Bishop said.

"I'll get you one with an operator's manual."

Before long they were pushing their way along a sidewalk crowded with sailors and Marines, past bars and whore-houses.

The first bar they walked into, a girl ran up to Bishop, calling, "So handsome. Such a pretty boy. You fuck me?" She grabbed his crotch.

Bishop turned to Magnuson and grinned. "This is just like it was back in college."

"Right," he said, heading for the bar, pushing two women away from him.

In a minute Bishop joined him, but the woman was still with him, her hand inside his zipper.

Magnuson pushed a beer toward him and glanced down. "She still looking for it?"

Bishop drank his beer and watched her stroke him. "You know, I got a feeling I'm gonna score tonight."

"C'mon," Magnuson said, "let's check out a few other places."

"What's the matter with this one?" The woman bent over and blew warm air over his jutting cock. "I like the ambience."

Magnuson grabbed him off the stool, and Bishop shoved himself back into his pants. "I can't hold out much longer, Jim—it's been months."

"I know a much better place," Magnuson said. "Away from all this; a good quiet place where we can do it right." He led Bishop outside, down a maze of back streets to a quieter neighborhood. He pushed through an unmarked door on a row of buildings into a courtyard where nothing grew and startled cats darted over the wall. He knocked on the door of what was once a fashionable house and an old man looked them over carefully before letting them in.

He brought them to a small dark room and gestured for them to sit.

"We want to be happy, papa-san. We want to forget," said Magnuson, taking out his wallet.

The old man was small and very old. His half-hooded eyes were filming and red, and what teeth he had were yellow and broken. He snatched the bills with birdlike speed and disappeared behind a beaded curtain.

"Where'd you find a place like this?" Bishop asked. He looked at his friend questioningly. Maybe in the mirror it was only he, Bishop, who had changed, but beneath the skin and the eyes, it was Magnuson who was different. "What have you been doing?"

Magnuson raised a warning hand but didn't answer.

In a moment the old man returned with a tray on which was a water pipe and a smudge of what looked like paste. The old man heated the opium over a candle flame, then kneaded the ball of paste on the convex margin of the bowl at the end of a foot-long bamboo pipe. After inserting a needle into the cavity, releasing the opium, he turned the bowl over, holding it over the flame. When the bead of opium began to bubble, he handed the pipe to Magnuson, who drew on it deeply, then gave it to Bishop.

"What is it?" he asked.

"Magic."

Bishop drew it into his lungs and held it. An anesthetizing numbness spread mercifully through him. He drew again, but Magnuson took the pipe away. "Too much magic is dangerous," he said.

Though Bishop had not moved, sat perfectly straight, he felt his body settling, sinking into the cushions while his mind rose, escaping his body, floating about in luxurious freedom and safety. Magnuson looked far away.

When he spoke, each word had its own life. "What happened to us, Jim?"

"We're Oklahoma boys sort of out of our territory, Luke."

"But . . ."

Magnuson raised his hand again. To Bishop the hand was disconnected, hanging separately in the space between them. "Don't think, Luke. Forget. I came over here to be the Red Baron. Instead, I've done . . . things I'm not proud of. Things I'm never going to think about."

"What?" whispered Bishop.

Magnuson's face was a mask. "No," he said softly. "Don't make me think about it, Luke. I can't joke about that."

Suddenly Bishop was conscious of a girl beside him. From above, his mind watched her ease into his lap. Her hands unbuttoned his uniform to stroke his chest.

Then she led him up a stairway into a dark room and all he had was the exquisite sensation of hands and mouth on his body, and he was naked staring down on her lying on the bed, looking up at him, beckoning.

He knelt on the bed and moved over her. She spread herself open for him and eased him inside, drawing him deeper with slow undulations, but it had been so long since he had been with a woman that he could not hold back. He crushed against her, and as he came to an explosion of release, twisting, straining into her, he looked into her face and it was not the girl but Pozinski beneath him, and when he recoiled, Snags pulled him back. He struggled up and there lying on the table was Miller's mutilated corpse, and it was not the girl's head in his hands but Miller's. He threw it down and yelled.

Suddenly there was blood everywhere and screams. The room filled with people and hands pulled on him. The girl shrieked relentlessly and others hit him. Then Magnuson grabbed him and helped him into his clothes.

"Run!" Magnuson yelled, pushing him out of the room and down the stairs.

Bishop ran. They were outside, racing down alleys when Bishop became violently sick. He doubled over and threw up. He gagged and could not breathe.

Finally when he recovered, he looked up at Magnuson, who was staring at him curiously.

"Apparently you didn't read the instructions right," Magnuson said.

Then Bishop began to cry.

"Oh, God, Jim, I killed them." He dropped on his knees to the street. "I killed them. Oh, God," he sobbed.

Magnuson knelt beside him, his voice low and pained. "Luke, you can't think about this. Now or ever. We'll never be able to deal with this."

"But you didn't do anything!" he cried. "You didn't kill them. *I* did. I can't live with that."

They knelt together in the middle of the trash-littered dark street. Magnuson put his hand on Bishop's shoulder and made him look up.

"You know what I do, besides dropping bombs and napalming gooks? I work for the CIA. It's my plane that takes up those poor bastards to get information out of them—maybe NVA who know something, or maybe just farmers.

"You ever seen a guy held out of an airplane door at five thousand feet, screaming, begging, pissing and shitting all over himself? How would you like to be one of those, tormenting and laughing at him as he bit off his tongue, not to keep from talking but because he was so afraid?

"Ever seen a guy free-fall from five thousand feet, his scream ripped out of his throat as he went down? Then cleaning up the shit and piss afterwards? Not once, but again and again because they only want one pilot for that."

Then he was crying too. "Don't make me think about that, Luke. I don't ever want to think about what happened over here."

In the morning they went to the airfield together.

Magnuson's flight to Saigon left first. He held out his hand. "Well, let's do this again real soon—maybe in another fifty or sixty years."

Bishop laughed. "I can hardly wait. Hey, did I get laid last night or not?"

"Man, I don't know what you call what you were doing, but do some woman a favor—don't marry her."

"Maybe I'll get down to Saigon. You can show me a good time there—things my Okie eyes ain't seen."

"You get to Saigon, Bishop, you stay the fuck away from

210

me. Stay up north where you grunts belong and kill gooks like you're supposed to."

Bishop shook his hand. "Take it easy. If you get a chance, look up one of my men—Ron Mead; he's a corporal at the embassy. Real good man; give him my regards."

"Will do, Luke." He punched his arm and they stood together awkwardly, then they grabbed each other, then turned away quickly and left.

"Holy shit, Lieutenant, you look even worse than when you left," said Gunny Brock when Bishop returned to the unit late in the afternoon. "I went cunt-crawling in Okinawa for a week and came back looking better than you."

"I don't think I quite got the hang of it," Bishop said with a grin. "I may need to go again to practice." Then he shook his head. "But another practice like that may kill me."

"Well, goddamn, Lieutenant, tell me about it."

"I'm an officer and a gentleman, and I did nothing to bring discredit on the Corps. And I'd certainly never tell you if I did."

Brock laughed. "You're full of shit, Lieutenant."

"So what happened here?"

"Nothing. Maybe you oughta go away again. We redone the wire like you said, but mostly we just took it easy."

"That's what I need to do," Bishop said, dropping onto his sleeping bag. "I gotta get a couple hours sleep. Get me up when it gets dark."

"You think they'll hit tonight?"

Bishop rolled over and pulled his field jacket over his head. "I don't know. But you oughta see what's going on at Khe Sanh. They're getting ready for something big."

"And we're just the fucking bait," Brock said in disgust.

On the forward slope of the hill, Dennis Coney began to nod off to sleep. He shook himself awake, stared again into the blackness, but tiredness overcame him. He looked to the man sleeping beside him, his head cradled on his field jacket, smiled to himself, and tried again to stay awake. He didn't want to wake Frizzell, knowing that Frizzell would do anything for him, certainly take on another watch to let him sleep.

He liked Frizzell, but Jesus was he a burden, Coney thought; he had never known anyone as . . . *simple* was the nicest word he could think of, nor had anyone ever looked up to him as Frizzell did. Coney had been in combat five months, the only man in the platoon who had been to college except for Bishop, and he had watched men form special bonds, relationships almost like marriages, and at first he tried to discourage any closeness with Frizzell when they were teamed together, but Frizzell was not to be discouraged, and now Coney was comfortable in the big-brother role.

His head snapped forward, and he realized he had dozed off.

"Frizzell," he said sharply, knowing he could not stay awake any longer.

There was no answer. He nudged him. "Frizzell, wake up, I can't make it any longer; it's after two."

Frizzell groaned, tried to rise, but fell back. "Fuck."

Coney poked him with his rifle. "You gotta get up; I'm gonna crash."

Frizzell mumbled with his eyes closed, "Go ahead, I'm awake."

Coney stretched back, pushed his field jacket into a pillow, and pulled his poncho over himself.

Frizzell brought himself up reluctantly. He pulled his rifle into his lap and stared into the darkness, where far in the distance he saw dull flashes of artillery. "Fuck, I'm tired," he said. "I was so tired I didn't even get a hard-on when I was sleeping. Usually I—"

"Shut up, Frizzell."

Frizzell fumbled for his canteen and heat tablets. "You want some coffee?"

"No, asshole, I want to go to sleep," Coney said, pulling his poncho tighter.

"Jesus, I hate watch." Frizzell added a packet of coffee granules to the hot water. He sipped gingerly. "What do you think about, Dennie, when you're standing watch? I never can think of anything to think about. It's really hard to sit in the dark with nothing to think about. It's like being a fucking watchdog. I wonder what dogs think about to stay awake."

Frizzell pondered that a moment, but he couldn't imagine what dogs thought about, so he gave it up. He nursed his coffee. "I gotta come up with something to think about during watch so I can stay awake. Landis thinks about his car, that's all he ever thinks about, you know—what kind to buy and what color and all that shit. And the only thing Sutherland ever thinks about is cunt, but I can't do that— fuck, I'd spend all my time on watch jacking off. What do you think about?"

There was no answer.

"Dennie? You awake?"

"No."

"Sure is quiet, ain't it?"

"No."

"You trying to sleep?"

Coney threw off his poncho. "Jesus! All right, all right, I'll talk to you for a few minutes, okay? But then you gotta let me sleep."

Frizzell handed him the canteen of coffee. "What do you want to talk about, Dennie?"

"*I* don't want to talk about anything, you dumb shit— you're the one doing all the talking, so talk; I'll listen."

Frizzell frowned in concentration. "My problem is thinking, Dennie. It's not that I'm dumb—"

"Listen, if my kid's as dumb as you, I'm gonna drown him."

"Fuck you. It's just that I can't come up with anything to think about. You know, maybe I should take one of those correspondent courses. You seen the ads, on those match-books, how if you send away for the course, they'll give you a high school diploma. You think I oughta do that?"

"When would you do your homework?"

"After patrols, or in the mornings. Or like now—it would give me something to do."

"What happens when we move out? You gonna hump schoolbooks all over this fucking country?"

Frizzell sighed. "Yeah. I guess that's no good. Shit. So

what do you think I should think about? What do you think about?"

Coney took a deep breath. "Oh, just different things—my wife, my kid, what it's going to be like when I get home."

"Well, I haven't got a wife or a kid." Frizzell didn't say anything for a moment, then he said softly in a shy voice, "You know, I only ever had one girl, I mean like a steady girl. And I only fucked her a couple times. Well, three times. Then she found another guy. And then there was this other girl, Becky. Becky Blowjob—that's all she ever did, but she'd do it to anybody. And that's the only girls I ever did anything with."

He looked at Coney. "What's it like, being married, and . . . you know."

Coney closed his eyes at the thought of his wife. He didn't speak for a long time. His mind flooded with sex; carnality ripped through him like a tide, and he inhaled sharply. "Oh, man, don't talk about that."

"I know," Frizzell said suddenly, having thought of something to talk about, or a question he remembered, something he had always wanted to know—like about why you couldn't see stars sometimes—but there had never been anyone to ask.

He had never had a friend like Coney, no one this close, someone he really cared about. He loved Coney; he had told Coney that once, and Coney had gotten very angry.

Frizzell grinned suddenly as that memory popped into his mind. "You were so pissed off at me. Remember that time after Donnadio and Perez got zapped, and I kept thinking about what if it had been you, and I told you—"

"I remember," Coney said curtly.

"And you got so uptight."

"Well, guys shouldn't say things like that."

"It didn't have anything to do with sex—it was just love, like if I had a brother. I never had anybody to love."

Coney shifted uncomfortably. "Let's not talk about this, huh?"

"Oh, yeah," Frizzell said, remembering the question he wanted to ask. "What good does circumcising do? I always wanted to know that."

Coney stared at him incredulously. "Where do you get these things? Is someone sending you asshole questions to ask me?"

Frizzell grinned. "No, it's just something I wondered about. There are lots of things like that, things you want to know about—not bullshit things like gerunds and the capital of Peru, shit that they teach you—but important things that you want to know that they never tell you. So you gotta find somebody to ask those things, and I never had anybody before. That's why, well, it's one of the reasons I like being with you—you know things. Anyway, a lot more things than I do, and you're not too much of an asshole about it. So what good does circumcising do?"

"Well, for one thing, it's cleaner."

"Bullshit, you ain't any cleaner than me."

"And it's better for women."

"How is it better?"

"Because you don't come so quickly when you're fucking."

Frizzell stared at him to see if Coney was putting him on—he never knew for sure sometimes. Finally he asked, "So what good is that?"

"Oh, Jesus," Coney said, and lay back on the ground, punching his field jacket into a pillow again.

"What's wrong?"

"Nothing. I'm just tired. I can't stay awake anymore. Why don't you send off for one of those matchbook sex courses?" He wrapped himself in his poncho and scrunched against the sandbags.

"You never helped me come up with anything to think about," Frizzell said petulantly.

Coney buried his head under his field jacket. "Why don't you pray? Quietly. Or jack off. Quietly."

A little way down the perimeter, Scott Sutherland stared into the black. He tried to imagine the enemy moving out there, strained in the darkness, but he could not see beyond the wire.

Every item that had belonged to Miller had been sent back with the body; there was nothing in the bunker except

Sutherland's own rifle and pack. He moved the rifle into his lap and sat cross-legged, peering through the entrance into the night.

He was alone for the first time in the war, and though he tried to remember Miller, he could not raise his image. His hand massaged his face, then dropped to the rifle. He stroked it absently.

Before the war had been easy, he thought. He thought it was hard then, Los Angeles, and trying to make it on the streets—worrying about not getting cut, and staying out of his old man's way, getting laid, and scrounging quarters, but that was nothing compared to this.

He traced circles in the sand. All that was cheap shit, he thought; now he had to worry about staying alive. And unless he was careful, he was going to end up just like Miller. And who would give a shit? Not anyone in L.A., that's for sure. Or any of the assholes who sent him over here. He had been conned, and like a dumb bastard, he had fallen for it. Like Miller had, and look where it got him.

Staring into Miller's empty corner, he was suddenly overcome with sorrow, and he left the bunker and made his way across the perimeter.

He came to Frizzell on the berm, and he dropped beside him. "I couldn't take it there alone anymore," he said softly. "I kept thinking about Miller."

Sutherland closed his eyes and said dully, "You know, the first man I killed was that time with Mead. The guy was a hundred feet away, and I shot him in the chest. When I went to him, he was staring up at me. I turned him over and there was a big hole in his back. I used to count them. It was a game; all that was important was the numbers. It was like playing pinball—you get a bigger and bigger score and all you can win is another game. You could spend your whole fucking life watching the score get bigger and playing the same machine. For goddamn what? Then I stopped counting. They're not even numbers anymore."

He lowered his head. "Except Miller."

He turned his head so that Frizzell could not see him, and he brushed at his eyes. "You know, that night we talked, and before he showed me pictures of his wife and kid, and now . . ."

His body shuddered, then he bent forward and began to cry.

Embarrassed, Frizzell placed his arms around his shoulders.

"Oh, Jesus, I'm so sorry," Sutherland cried.

Beside them, Coney groaned. "Oh, for Christ's sake. How can I sleep listening to this shit? Look, I'm sorry about Miller, and Snags too, and all the other poor dumb bastards. And I'm sorry for you too. I'm sorry for all of us. Miller shouldn't have been sent on that patrol. The lieutenant fucked up. But that's just the way it goes. None of us should be here at all, but we are, so what are we gonna do about it, cry all night? I fucked up coming over here. Before that I fucked up getting married and having a kid. I'm twenty years old—I got a kid and wife I don't want, and a million fucking gooks are trying to kill me because I'm sitting on *their* fucking hill, which I don't even want to be on. And now, I can't even sleep because some asshole is crying because *he's* sorry."

Sutherland pushed at his helmet, then said softly, "Would you guys mind if I stayed here tonight?"

"If you're quiet, you can stay forever. Just let me sleep."

Frizzell leaned forward eagerly. "Hey, why don't you move in with us? There's room. It'll be just the three of us from now on. They can't beat the three of us."

Frizzell grew excited. "We'll make a pact, the three of us sticking together, looking out for each other. If we can do that, everything will be all right." His mind tossed. He wanted to use bigger words, say it better, make them understand what he felt inside. He searched their faces. "A pact. Buddies. All right?"

Coney pulled the poncho over his head.

"All right, Dennie? Buddies."

"Oh, God," Coney moaned. "All right, all right. I'll be your fucking *lover* if you'll just shut up and let me sleep."

"Okay, Scott?"

Sutherland looked at the two men, then he nodded. "Yes."

217

"But we gotta make it official," Frizzell said in agitation. "I know, we'll give each other something. C'mon, Dennie." He pulled the poncho off Coney. "Give Scott something. Here."

He fumbled for one of his dogtags, worked it off, and handed it to Coney. "Now you give something to Scott."

"Are you shitting me?"

"I mean it, this will protect us. Everything will be all right if we make a pact."

Coney held Frizzell's dogtag. "What am I supposed to do with this piece of shit? Never mind. Jesus!" He struggled with the school ring on his finger and handed it to Sutherland. "Don't lose it. I want it back when this horseshit is over. Or if I ever get any sleep. Whichever comes first."

Sutherland stared for a long time at the ring in his hand, then he put it on his finger.

"Now give me something," Frizzell said.

"I don't have anything."

"Sure you do."

Sutherland felt for the amulet around his neck, a piece of shrapnel extracted from his leg that had become his secret talisman sealing his private pact with his God. He stared at Frizzell, reached to pull off the amulet, then stopped, searched in his pocket, and found his pocketknife.

Frizzell took it solemnly and put it in his own pocket.

Coney looked at them both, grabbed the poncho back, and pulled it over his head. "Jesus Christ."

Sutherland and Frizzell smiled at each other, sitting side by side, almost touching.

Suddenly the ridge flashed with bright lightning strokes, and there was the dull crump of mortars.

Frizzell yelled, "NO!" and threw himself across Sutherland.

The hill rocked with a tremendous string of explosions. Sutherland struggled under Frizzell's weight, and the world seemed to end in an explosion of light and noise.

Shrapnel slammed into the sand about them. The ridge erupted again. Sutherland broke free of Frizzell and grabbed the machine gun, chambering a clip of shells.

Coney called the sighting over the radio, then dug in as

the hill was ripped by huge metal fragments. When he looked up, a trip flare burst into white phosphorus only meters in front of him, exposing three men in the wire.

Frizzell jumped up, flipped his rifle to automatic, and fired, even before Sutherland opened fire with the machine gun.

Coney shouted into the radio, "They're in the wire."

The mortars had thrown Bishop and Brock against the walls of their bunker, but Coney's shout sent them scrambling for their rifles, and Brock raced to the stairs, cursing furiously.

Bishop turned cold. He switched the radio frequency to the company unit and his voice was tightly controlled. "They're in the wire."

"How many?"

"I don't know. Give us defensive artillery fire against the ridge."

"On the way."

Bishop dropped the handset, chambered a shell in his rifle, and moved steadily up the stairs, crouching at the bunker entrance, trying to focus in the confusion of light and sound.

Flares illuminated the entire perimeter, and there was steady firing from his seven posts that circled the hill.

His eyes burned into the night and his body tensed, then he sprang, racing across the hill toward the post doing the heaviest firing.

He dropped into the bunker with Frizzell, Coney, and Sutherland as a mortar burst behind. Flattening himself on the ground, he called over the explosion, "How many?"

Coney shook his head frantically. "Trip flare . . ."

Bishop shouted to Frizzell, but he was unhearing, firing mechanically into the wire.

"Cease fire," Bishop yelled at him, but when he didn't, Bishop grabbed the rifle. Frizzell turned, and Bishop saw a fury he had not imagined possible. Bishop was transfixed by eyes that registered a rapturous, exalting hatred. Bishop had never seen such a look.

Frizzell grabbed for the weapon but Bishop pushed him back. Frizzell came at him again and Bishop struck him in the chest with the rifle butt, knocking him to the ground. Frizzell looked up dumbly, and Bishop shouted at Sutherland, "How many?"

"I only seen three, Lieutenant."

"You get any?"

"I don't know, sir."

Overhead artillery screamed past, bursting red and orange on the enemy ridge. When the shelling stopped and the echoes drifted across the desert, a single flare came from one of the posts. Slowly the sky above the wire lightened as the small glow drifted to earth.

There was eerie silence over the plain. Clusters of smoke hovered over the ground, clung to the wire, and finally began to disperse like vanishing ghosts.

The men watched with drawn faces, listening, scanning the silence.

Bishop turned to Sutherland, searching for a trace of the malice he had seen in Frizzell, but it wasn't there. The face, covered with sweat and dirt, was hard under the helmet, and the eyes were stark, but there was no hate.

Sutherland threw his helmet to the ground. "Motherfuckers!"

Bishop sought Frizzell's face in the diminishing light. The virulence was gone, and there was no trace of the fury that had possessed him. He no longer even seemed concerned; he stood as mildly as he might at a drive-in hangout on any Friday night.

Bishop cast a final glance to the ridge, then went back to his bunker to make a report.

Inside, he brushed off his body, picked sand and dirt from his chest and legs, and knelt to make coffee. When the heat tablets burst into blue flames, Bishop remained kneeling, hypnotized by the fire and his exhaustion. This had happened so many times he could not number them—a probe, mortars, firing, then nothing.

The boiling water brought his attention back. He sighed and massaged his temples, then stirred in coffee granules and stretched back against the wall. His hand fell to his groin, and he squeezed the hardening. In the beginning he had been surprised at the erotic response he had to combat, but now he took it for granted and rubbed his erection.

But sex was not what he had seen in Frizzell's eyes. That was hatred.

Suddenly the stairs groaned under Brock's fury and Bishop's hand disengaged.

Brock threw his helmet at the wall. "Those goddamn motherfuckers. They were right on top of us."

"You're all right, aren't you? They missed."

"God damn it, Lieutenant. We were lucky tonight; only you and I know how lucky. But we're gonna die unless we get out of here. And for what? This fucking hill?"

Bishop picked up his coffee and brushed his lips with the hot cup. "You're gonna die for Khe Sanh, Gunny. That'll make it all right."

Brock exploded. "Khe Sanh!" Too beside himself to even argue, he finally sank down on an ammunition crate. "Oh, for Christ's sake."

Bishop poured a cup of coffee and handed it to him. "My orders are to hold this hill. I don't want to hear any more about it, Gunny."

Brock grabbed the cup.

Bishop settled back against the wall, studying Brock's face. What he saw in it differed from the others. There was neither anger nor hatred, but outrage, and the dignity that comes from it—indignation at the affront to sense and principles, to the code of war and soldiery.

"What do you think of Frizzell?" Bishop asked.

Brock looked up in surprise. "Frizzell? *Think* about Frizzell? Who the fuck would ever think about Frizzell?"

"All right then, tell me about him."

Brock went to his rifle and emptied the magazine; his words dropped like the bullets. "Eighteen. Comes from Kansas. IQ about eighty. As complex and trustworthy as a Doberman. Pat him, stroke him, feed him, and he's yours."

He wiped down his rifle and spread a thin coat of oil over the metal. "He and Sutherland are the best men we got. They kill the best. Frizzell because he's dumb, Sutherland because he's smart. They're not cowards, and they don't ask questions. What more could you want?"

221

"You really think Sutherland is good?"

"Yep. He comes off the street like I do. He's hard and he's smart and you can't fool him. He's from L.A.; old man is a drunk, mother is a pig; he's one mean bastard who'd blow you away in a minute if he thought he had to."

"And you don't trust him."

Brock looked up from his rifle. "I don't trust you, Lieutenant. You'd blow me away in a minute too."

Bishop looked hurt and he shook his head. "No, I wouldn't. You know I wouldn't, Gunny."

"Not to save your own ass; no, you wouldn't do that. But you'd do it for something else. Like for this hill. Or if someone gave you an order."

Stung, Bishop looked away.

Brock went back to his rifle. "Lieutenant, everybody could be Judas. You can't be *for* something without being *against* something else. It's just choices. I think they call it ethics. I learned about it in school, in detention. Trouble is, I keep making the wrong choices."

"How about Coney?"

"Trouble. He's smarter than the other two, but not as hard. He's bitter. Like me, his dick got him in trouble too early. You can't unfuck a woman or shove the baby back in."

"How come you know all these things?"

"My life depends on them. I can tell you about every one of those assholes out there, everything you want to know. I can tell you exactly how far to push them, and how they'll respond. I don't make mistakes about my life, Lieutenant— except the big one, getting caught in this shithole."

Bishop finished his coffee and ran his hand through his hair tiredly. "I don't know. It just seems that the killing gets too easy."

"Lieutenant, killing *is* easy, and takes less time than jacking off." He finished with his rifle and propped it against the wall. "A hard cock doesn't have a conscience, and neither does a hungry gut. You don't have a conscience when you're scared to death. Conscience comes when you've got time. It's what comes afterwards, like babies, and guilt, and history."

Brock emptied his coffee onto the ground and tossed the cup toward the fire.

Bishop rested his head on his knees. "I'm scared, Gunny," he said quietly. "I don't want to lose anyone else. I don't think I could stand it." He looked up pleadingly. "I don't *like* the killing, Gunny."

Brock looked at him, a man thirteen years younger than himself—a boy really. "I'm glad you're scared, Lieutenant. I'd be worried if you weren't. And I'd be really worried if you liked the killing. Stay scared, and hate the killing—and get us out of here."

Bishop smiled. "If you handled women as well as you handle lieutenants, you'd only have had one wife, Gunny."

Brock laughed. "I never wanted just one wife, Lieutenant."

"You may want another lieutenant after I tell you to take a patrol out tomorrow to see if we got any of them. I want you to go to the ridge. I want to know what's there."

"I can tell you that without going—gooks: big ones, little ones, fat ones, thin ones."

"Good, then you'll recognize them when you see them." He picked up the radio handset to call the company commander to make his report.

Across the hill, the three men stood together in their bunker.

"Those sons of bitches," Coney said angrily. "They're gonna get us some night."

Sutherland kicked the sand. "They're not gonna get me." Defiantly he lit a cigarette. "Bastards." He waved the cigarette in signal. "Come on, motherfuckers, shoot." Then he threw the cigarette toward the wire and leaned against the bunker. "Screw it."

Coney dropped down onto his sleeping bag and wrapped himself in his poncho. "I'm going back to sleep. I was having the best dream. It was about the most fantastic piece of ass. She was all over me, had a hold of my cock . . ."

Sutherland pushed him. "That wasn't a dream. That was Frizzell."

They laughed, the tension gone. Watching the quiet, Frizzell and Sutherland shared a cigarette, caught in the intimate bond of fear and death.

"They're still out there," Frizzell said. "You think we got any of them?"

"Nope."

Frizzell was quiet a moment, then he sighed. "Jesus, I'm tired of this. You think they ever get tired of it too?"

"Who? The gooks?" The idea surprised Sutherland. He had never pictured the enemy as having feelings. He debated the possibility, then dropped it immediately. He distrusted thought. He liked the smooth surface of sensation and action; he knew that the murky depths beneath were best left unplumbed.

Besides, thinking made no difference. People were always talking about right and wrong, but nothing ever changed. There were so many things wrong, like killing and wars and lies, but what good did it do to think about them? It was all like Frizzell's semaphore: it might make perfectly good sense, but it didn't make one goddamn bit of difference. You killed or got killed; that's all there was to it.

Frizzell was staring at the black canopy of night. "I wonder how much longer this is going on."

"Till we're all dead," Sutherland said bitterly; but he caught himself immediately and said to Frizzell, though it was to himself, and to whoever decided, "We'll be all right."

Then he sighed, drained of feeling. "It doesn't do any good to get mad. I didn't want to go to school but they made me. And I didn't want to go to church, but they made me. And I didn't want to come to this fucking war, but they made me."

He turned to Frizzell. "I haven't done one goddamn thing yet that I've wanted to. I've just been putting in my time. But one of these days, I'm gonna do just what I want. Just me. Just Scott Sutherland in the world. Then *watch* out. First, though, I gotta get out of this mess. But I will. Count on it."

Beside them, Coney rolled over and looked out from his poncho.

"Now that we made that pact, you got nothing to worry

about. Good thing you were wearing my ring, Sutherland, or those mortars would have blown your ass to the moon. And if I hadn't had Frizzell's dogtag, those gooks would have got through that wire and cut my balls off. But all us buddies better get to sleep so we can be ready for that patrol tomorrow."

"What patrol?" Sutherland asked anxiously.

"The patrol tomorrow to find the gooks you didn't kill tonight. That's what it's all about, dummy—killing gooks: if you miss tonight, then you gotta go tomorrow and try again." He rolled over, pulling the poncho over his head.

Neither Frizzell nor Sutherland said anything. They moved closer together and stared out over the dark plain.

Unconsciously Sutherland's hand went to his neck, and he softly stroked the amulet.

CHAPTER

• 15 •

Blood. The smell of it, hot and slick, penetrated his consciousness; he was drowning, submerged in an ocean of blood. He struggled up and finally broke to the surface, lungs bursting, and he yelled, his hands clawing the air.

Confused by the light, he reached for his rifle, but beside him a person thrashed, then screamed. Mead threw himself on the person who struggled furiously. His nostrils filled with the stench of blood, and now it was on his hand.

The blood was real, and the person beneath him a woman, screaming in terror.

Mead pushed himself away and focused.

On the floor beside him was Sung; her eyes and mouth were open, and her face and arms were streaked with blood.

Mead struggled to understand—it was morning, he was in his room on his sleeping bag; Sung was beside him. But what had happened? Why was there blood, and why was she screaming?

His hand was bloody, but he hadn't hurt her; he knew he hadn't.

Though there were streaks of blood on her face and arms, there were no cuts.

Then he saw that the blood was menstrual and that her hands had come unbound.

He moved closer to her. "It's okay," he said. "I'm not going to hurt you. I'm sorry I scared you. I was dreaming."

She did not look at him, and he was not sure she heard his words, but the tone must have calmed her for gradually she stopped shaking.

He went to the sink and brought her back a cup of water. Lifting her head gently, he helped her drink; then he got a washcloth and wiped her face and arms, but he did not touch between her legs for fear of frightening her.

Her eyes were clearer, and the drug spasms seemed to have stopped.

"Can I get you anything?" he asked. "Do you want anything to eat?"

When she didn't answer or move, he turned her face softly toward him.

"Can you hear me? Do you remember what happened and where you are?"

She stared at him, then tried to speak, wetting her lips and moving them, but no words came.

"I'll get Han," he said.

It was after nine, the latest he could remember sleeping, but he didn't have to be at the embassy until noon. He had three hours on his own, and he wasn't exhausted. He felt what he had not felt in all the time he had been in Saigon, and long before that even—almost good, a glimmer of happiness.

"I'll be back tonight," he said. "I'll get you something."

He dressed, then went down the corridor and knocked on another door.

The door was cracked open before he could knock twice; Han's face was anxious, and behind her he saw Bill Catton, naked and asleep, sprawled on a mattress on the floor.

Han came out into the hall. "He sleep. Duty late last night, then beaucoup drinking. He wake . . . then trouble."

Mead understood; Bill Catton, when drunk, became mean and violent. Several times Mead had stepped in when Catton had been hitting Han. Yet no matter how drunk Catton got, he never fought Mead. No one did; sensing his violence, even the most aggressive Marines in the barracks were careful not to provoke him.

"I have to go," Mead said. "Could you look in on Sung? I think she's better. But she's bleeding. Can you . . . you know, help her? Or give her something?"

Han looked at him sharply. "What do you mean, bleeding? What did you do?"

"No, I mean bleeding . . . from . . . you know," he stammered, and pointed toward his groin.

Han grunted and shook her head. "You must get her things. Go to PX." There was the faintest hint of warmth and humor in her eyes. "Girlfriends big problem, Ron—not like Tu Do Street boom-boom."

"Okay," he said. "I'll go to the PX; but will you stay with her today?"

"You buy me something too?" Han asked. She gestured to the closed door and said disgustedly, "He never remember; he get me nothing."

"I'll get you something," Mead said. "But you'll stay with Sung?"

"I'll stay." Then her face changed; the skin crinkled and she looked excited, like an aged little girl. "What you buy me?"

"What do you want?"

She hooted, then covered her mouth as she remembered her sleeping man. "Just present me," she said happily, then added cautiously, knowing men that well, "But pretty present."

"Okay," he said. "I'll be back tonight."

She grabbed his arm. "And candy too. Hershey candy, but no nuts," she said, pointing to her gap-toothed mouth. "Kissy Hershey candy. You know kissy candy?" She made a little triangle with her fingers.

"I know," he said, leaving her in the corridor, staring over his head, fixed on a vision of chocolate.

The main post exchange was the favorite destination of all cabdrivers. In the suburb of Cholon, thirty minutes from downtown Saigon, the PX was the earthly realization of heaven's promise. GIs with money went in, emerging laden with wonders and abundance. There seemed no end to the marvels wrought from this building that sprawled an entire block.

Ships and planes brought the wonders that were carried in truck caravans from the airport and piers—not just orthodox treasures such as cigarettes and whiskey, perfumes and candy, food and clothing, but wizardry: electronics, televisions, tape recorders, stereos. Then there were the luxuries beyond luxury, beyond the aspirations even of cabdrivers—jewels and toys.

After fending off the driver's entreaties to buy him cigarettes and whiskey and a television set, Mead had to run a gauntlet of money changers, merchants, and black marketeers, plus women and children and cripples and amputees.

Brushing past booths that sold Fords and Chryslers and the *Encyclopedia Britannica,* insurance, and stocks and bonds, he entered the massive complex of goods—huge departments for clothing and cameras and cosmetics, household goods and hardware, a store much larger than any he had ever been in at home.

Bewildered by the myriad offerings, he did not know where to look. He started down different aisles, hoping to stumble upon what Sung needed, the proper name of which he could not remember.

Down one aisle he found toys, and there was an entire shelf of dolls. He stopped before them—dolls that wet their diapers and cried "Mama," Barbie dolls in ensembles for beach and balls, Heidi dolls, and others in gowns and costumes. Then he saw the one he would buy Sung—a princess doll, in a long white gown, wearing a little jeweled crown: Cinderella. He picked up the box carefully and cradled it under his arm. He found the Hershey's kisses next and grabbed six big bags. Then he returned to the front of the store for a shopping cart.

For Han he had a difficult time choosing. He did not want to pick something too personal, for fear Catton would mistake his intent and become jealous, but he did not want to disappoint her with anything practical either. At last he selected a bracelet that he was told was jade, and he supposed it was because it cost twenty-five dollars.

After he had it wrapped, it was past eleven and he knew he

would have to hurry to make it to the embassy by noon, and he still had not found the main thing he had come for.

Finally he summoned his courage and asked a clerk, though he had to search to find a male one.

"Where can I get some . . . something for a woman when she's . . . you know, bleeding."

"You mean a Band-Aid?"

"No." Then he blurted, "When she's on the rag."

"Sanitary napkins."

"Yeah, that's it."

"Aisle six, under Feminine Needs."

Asshole, thought Mead, knowing the rear-echelon GI clerk had said that just to make him look stupid.

Standing before the shelf, looking at a vast array of different brands, he was lost, and when people pushed past him in the aisle, he felt self-conscious and foolish. He reached out for a box, then quickly withdrew his hand as someone approached.

But the person, a naval officer, did not pass by: he stood beside Mead, then pulled a large blue box from the shelf. When he turned away, Mead grabbed a similar box, then another, and two for Han.

The naval officer stopped and looked at him. "That's an awful lot of Kotex," he said.

Mead, standing in the aisle with four boxes, froze in shock.

"If she's bleeding that much, maybe she should see a doctor." Then, seeing Mead's confusion and embarrassment, the man said, "You need some help?"

Mead shrugged. "I just didn't know what to buy."

The officer nodded, then pointed to the boxes. "You probably want to buy a belt too." He grabbed a package from the shelf and handed it to Mead. "Is she very small?"

Mead stared at him in a look approaching terror.

The officer saw the misunderstanding. "No, I mean her waist and hips. Vietnamese women are so small that tight, girl-size panties work better. But try the belt first," he said, and walked off, suppressing a laugh.

Mead grabbed another belt, tossed everything in his cart, and wheeled it to the checkout.

After paying in military scrip, he fled.

When a cab dropped him in front of the embassy just minutes before noon, Mead knew he did not have time to put the shopping bag in his locker at the barracks and would have to carry it inside.

The Marines on duty knew him and didn't bother to security check the bag, but when he reached the fifth floor, he realized he had no place to put it.

Dolores Toland was leaving her office for lunch as Mead entered the corridor.

"I wish I had your hours, Corporal," she said pleasantly. "Coming in at noon, going to the PX—I should have joined the Marines too. What did you buy?"

Mead pulled the bag away. "Just stuff," he said.

She moved past him. "Colonel Waggoner wants to see you as soon as you get in—he's very anxious. He's in the ambassador's office. He wants everything moved before the ambassador gets back, so you better hurry."

Just then Waggoner stepped into the corridor from Marshall's private office. "About time," he said. "Get in here, Mead, I need your help."

"Put that down, behind the door," he said to Mead, pointing to the bag. "Give me a hand with this desk; the ambassador doesn't like it. Then I want you to bring up another one from the basement. We have to hurry; he's having lunch with Ambassador Bunker, then he's going to a briefing at ARVN headquarters and you have to be with him."

For an hour and a half Mead moved furniture and hung new drapes, then Waggoner sent him to Bunker's office to wait for Marshall.

Lacouture's "Fly," Bui Cao Kim, had been on the street across from Mead's building since early morning, and though several Americans wearing the special embassy uniform had come from it, he knew none was the one the Frenchman had described—"Le Sauvage."

Kim had squatted on the sidewalk, holding out his hand for alms, and had gone unnoticed. By midmorning, he wondered if perhaps he had missed the man. He might have

gone to work at dawn or left after Lacouture saw him the
night before and never returned.

Lacouture had sent word last night through one of their
contacts that he must see Kim immediately. When Kim
found him, Lacouture was in a frenzy; the last time Kim
had seen him like this was seventeen years ago when Lacouture had found a young French Legionnaire. It was the only
lapse Kim had ever seen in Lacouture. The Frenchman had
fallen foolishly in love with the soldier, had showered
him with money and gifts; his judgment had been so
impaired that years passed before Kim trusted him again.
The affair with the soldier had ended just in time, Kim
thought; the young man had begun to abuse Lacouture
physically so that eventually he might have killed him.
As it was, the youth got into a knife fight with another
soldier and was wounded so badly that he had to be evacu-
ated to France. Lacouture was disconsolate, and though
over the years he had a steady stream of soldiers, there
had never been a relationship like the one with the Legionnaire.

Kim made no moral judgments: pederasty ranked no
higher or lower than any other human activity; a homosexual, a Buddhist, a fisherman, were all the same to him.
Collecting boys, girls, stamps, or coins—preferring flowers,
puppies, or feet—were merely choices, in themselves without merit or value.

What disturbed Kim about Lacouture's involvement with
the soldier was that it had cost him money, and in those
early days, Kim relied almost entirely on Lacouture for his
living. Lacouture had not been able to work, so infatuated
was he, and every centime he had, he spent on the Legionnaire.

So last night when Lacouture went into raptures about
this savage American, Kim was alarmed, knowing that the
most foolish of men was a foolish old man. Lacouture was
too old, Kim thought, and so was he himself. At this age
Kim could not allow such a distraction. There was too little
time left; the communists would win soon and he would
have to get out, and that meant he would need a lot of
money.

So, yes, he would indulge Lacouture, but not very far—
not if it was going to be costly or endanger his livelihood.

"You must find out *everything*," Lacouture had said.
"Who he is, where he works, his hours, where he goes after
work, what his weaknesses are—*everything!* I will pay you
very well, my dear, dear Kim."

So Kim had waited for the American since early morning,
across the street from the building Lacouture had described.

"The third floor, the fourth window on the left of the
stairway," Lacouture had said.

Since there had been no sign of movement in four hours,
Kim decided to investigate inside.

He had crossed the street and was approaching the
building when the man came out. It had to be he; there
could be no mistaking this man, and just as quickly Kim saw
how dangerous this man could be, and that he could never
allow Lacouture to become involved with him. But Kim
knew, too, that everyone had a price; any and everything
could be bought. Failing that, it could be stolen; or coerced.

Lacouture could get the man, of that he had no doubt, and
Lacouture would pay Kim handsomely. And Kim would
help, but the price would be great now that he had seen this
man—and after Kim got the money, he would make certain
that the involvement was short.

The man stopped as soon as he emerged from the
building, and his eyes took in everything warily. He looked
directly at Kim, then beyond him, then quickly back as
though sensing something amiss.

The unexpected encounter, and the intensity of the man's
gaze, unnerved Kim. Should he pass on, or would that be
more suspicious?

Deciding intuitively, Kim confronted the man; smiling
ingratiatingly, he held out his hand. "Cigarette, GI? American number one. VC number ten. You give me cigarette?"

Kim waited for the expected response; in the nearly
twenty years he had approached soldiers and foreigners for
cigarettes or money, the responses seldom varied: "Fuck off,
gook," a soldier would say, often accompanied with a shove,
or they would ignore him. Only rarely would someone stop
and give him a cigarette.

This man did none of those; he considered Kim with appraising eyes, then said, "I don't smoke either."

Kim did not know the word "either," but he understood from the way the man looked at him, and from his tone, that the man guessed that he did not smoke. It was his teeth; he prided himself on them: they were white and unstained even by betel nut chewing, and this man had noticed.

Knowing that the best course of action was now to stand there with a foolish look on his face, pretending to know nothing, Kim did not move, continuing to hold out his hand, his mouth a grimace of a smile.

For a few seconds the soldier studied him, then finally stepped out onto the street and waved for a pedicab; he did not look back at Kim. He did not need to, Kim knew. He had decided, probably because of Kim's age, that he was not a threat—he was too old to be a Viet Cong, an informant perhaps, but not an active agent. The soldier had dismissed him but would remember him if he encountered him again. Kim was going to have to be very careful.

Kim moved away at last, crossed the street, hovered for another thirty minutes, then recrossed the street and entered the building.

The stench of stopped-up toilets and rotting garbage brought back his confidence; this was familiar. He understood this world.

On the third floor he listened a moment before the fourth door, then he opened it and stepped inside.

Two women were there, an older one sitting on the floor beside a much younger one lying on a military sleeping bag. Despite the open window, the room was rank with the smell of vomit and blood.

The younger woman did not turn as he entered, but the older one jerked up.

"What do you want?" she demanded sharply. "Who are you?"

He knew this type of woman; not much younger than himself, she had survived on her body and wiles. She would be easy to deal with for she understood how the world worked.

He crossed the room and squatted down beside her,

noting the wasted, drug-addicted condition of the girl on the floor.

"Who do you want me to be, sister?" he asked Han. "Who could help you?"

She made a spitting noise as she studied his face. There was nothing there, she saw—no feelings of any kind, not even the embers were left; he was dead cold. His eyes were depthless, only mirrors reflecting surface images. She knew men like this. She had moved under such men, thrashed and grunted beneath them and sped them on their way, but now one had come for her as she had always feared. She had hoped to stay out of the way of such men, service them and have them never linger, but now one had opened the door and stepped on her life.

"You are too old to fuck the Americans," he said. "You are too loose in the cunt." He did not say it contemptuously, just matter-of-factly.

"But you are lucky, sister. Someone has taken an interest in you. You have what he wants."

She did not speak; there was no need for words. He would tell her what he wanted, and then she would give it to him for the best deal she could strike. Otherwise he would force it from her for nothing. It was all fated: an opening door. Then it would close, and the room and air would be still again, nothing disturbed, nothing changed.

Kim squatted silently for a full minute; he considered her, then the woman lying between them, a beautiful girl, he could see, but filthy and sick.

"Your daughter?" he finally asked.

Han shook her head. "A young whore. With a tighter cunt—better for fucking the Americans."

Kim laughed and slapped the floor. "Hah! Old whores are the best."

"How much you pay me?" she taunted, spreading her thighs.

"Maybe I pay you a lot. More than you believe. More than you ever saw. Who is the man who just left here, the big American with eyes that see?"

"Ah." This could be a great deal of money, she thought; but very dangerous. It must have to do with the important man all the Marines talked about. But then it could be very treacherous.

The less she knew, the better off she would be.

"How much will you pay me?" she asked.

He pulled a soiled and crumpled twenty-dollar bill from his pocket.

She shrugged. "My man gives me that much for swallowing him."

Kim merely stared at her. It was not necessary to threaten her; he did not need to take out a knife or slap her. She knew that he was capable of any vile act. The understanding was silent. Now she would have to tell him what he wanted, what he felt was worth the money he offered, and when she felt she had told him the value of what he offered, she would stop.

"His name is Ron Mead. He is a Marine at the American embassy. This is his woman."

Then she told him about Sung.

"Why did he take her from the brothel?" Kim asked. "She is pretty, yet . . ." It was inexplicable to him; every brothel had beautiful women. But the streets, too, were filled with hustlers and with soldiers, and he did not understand Lacouture's pursuit of this particular one—it certainly wasn't love.

Han touched her breast. "The foreigner is soft where we are not. Even the hardest one has it. Pity." She shrugged. "Hope too."

Kim grunted. Then he reached into his pocket and pulled out a large roll of bills. He took a one-hundred-dollar note and put it before Han.

"Tell me about him," he said.

She thought he meant the important American, of course. No information about Mead, or any Marine, could be worth that amount of money. That is why Kim had come, she assumed, for information about Marshall.

"Ron does not talk about him much, even to my man, and they are close friends. Ron says he is more important than anyone, and lives in a mansion with many servants, but that he treats everyone well. I can tell that Ron likes him. These days are the only times I have ever seen him not unhappy."

Kim had no idea of whom Han was speaking, but he had learned over the many years not to interrupt or question, that if one only listened carefully all the necessary information would unfold. Since she assumed that he knew about the man of whom she was talking, he let her talk on.

At first he thought she was talking about a rich, powerful American who was keeping Mead as Lacouture sought to do, but gradually he realized that the man was a high government official who had just arrived, and that Mead was his personal guard.

The man was so important that everyone in the embassy was cleared from his path, and he had private meetings with General Westmoreland.

When she finished speaking, she reached out for the money, and he was so distracted by what she had told him that he did not stop her.

He sat cross-legged on the floor, trying to absorb it all. But it was too much for him. Lacouture did not know of this important American, or if he did, he did not know of his tie to the soldier of his desires.

In his mind he saw a massive, black, unscalable obelisk. What was he to do with this information? How could he turn it to his advantage?

He knew he was not as clever as Lacouture, his mind not as labyrinthine.

Perhaps Lacouture was not the man to have this information. What would the Viet Cong pay for this? But could they be trusted to pay?

Like a bone dragged back to his burrow, he would have to gnaw on this for a long time in secret.

Kim was about to ask about Mead when a door slammed and a man bellowed. "Han! Where are you?"

Then the door was flung open, and a naked young man staggered in. "Han! I want to fuck. Come back to bed."

Then he saw Kim. "Who's the gook?" He stumbled closer. "What's going on in here?" He moved threateningly on Kim. "Stand up, asshole. Who are you?"

Han motioned Kim to stand. Bill Catton was a full foot taller, and at least eighty pounds heavier.

Han jumped up between them. "Billy, he doctor. Sung very sick."

"Doctor, my ass. He looks like shit."

Han put her hand on his thigh and spoke soothingly, all the while stroking him softly, moving her hand closer to his groin. "Not like American doctor, Billy. Medicine man. Does special things, has special teas to drink to help different problems. Like Chinese have acupuncture, sticking needles in body, he give Sung special things for heroin. Make her much better."

"Yeah? Well, he oughta take something for himself. He looks like dog shit."

By now he was half erect and had lost interest in Kim. He grabbed Han and pulled her toward him. "C'mon, let's go."

He started away with her, then stopped. "Hey, think he's got anything for my head? It hurts like a motherfucker."

Han grabbed his erection and tugged. "I got something." Then she pulled his head down to her and licked in his ear.

He laughed and nuzzled her neck as she steered him out of the room and closed the door behind them.

Kim exhaled slowly and sat back down on the floor. Suddenly he felt old, watching the soldier go off with the woman; he was tired of ridicule, and loneliness. The Japanese, French, Americans—humiliation all his life. Now there was youth to mock him—the strapping soldier with his taut body flaunting his power before him.

But his feeling passed quickly; he could not afford even a moment off guard. Life ended that quickly—in the flick of a gecko's tongue for a fly.

The girl stirred beside him. "Water," she said.

Kim contemplated her. What was it the old whore said the foreigner suffered? Pity. And hope.

He gazed on the girl's pain-wracked face and body. Yes, he felt sorry for her; for the old whore too, laboring under the crude youth, and sorry for himself. But there was no pity, just the wish that fate had been otherwise. And hope? No, that did not exist at all—that was to deny fate. Hope was only salt for thirst.

Kim grabbed the girl's jaw and yanked her face toward him. Her eyes focused; she would be rid of the drug in a few

238

days—the worst was over. He lifted her head by the hair and brought her face up to his. "You hear me, daughter?"

Her eyes widened in pain and fear.

He shook her head. "Are you listening, daughter?"

Her lips moved as she struggled to talk.

"You fuck the American good. You make him happy. You understand?" He shook her by the hair again. "Understand?"

"Yes," she choked.

Pity was good, he thought, but love was better. And sex was best of all.

His face pressed against hers. She could not recoil from his eyes that were more fearsome than death. "Oh, daughter, what I will do to you," he rasped. "Please him."

Then he lowered her head to the floor and stood. He must think this out carefully. The old whore and the girl were his; they would never say anything. But the young soldier would—if he remembered. He would mention it to Mead at some point, the funny-looking old gook who came to see Sung, and Mead would remember seeing him in front of the building. But the old whore would explain and the story would be just barely plausible.

But what was he going to tell Lacouture? He was to meet the Frenchman this afternoon at the Continental; he would be frantic with anticipation.

If only he could think of what to do. What did fate mean by all this? The signs were portentous: the dragon stirred; his eyes opened. Kim felt himself at the dark mouth of the lair.

CHAPTER

· 16 ·

At the residence of the American ambassador, a few blocks from the embassy, Marshall sat at the dining room table having lunch with Ellsworth Bunker.

Marshall had come to hear the older man's observations. Bunker, a seventy-three-year-old career diplomat, a fellow New Englander of succinctly acid speech, had arrived in Vietnam only a few months ago; Marshall knew his impressions would be relevant and fresh.

The two had first met several years ago when Bunker was ambassador to the Organization of American States, and Marshall was special envoy to Central America. Though Bunker was older than Marshall's father, their relationship was collegial, and because of Bunker's intellect, vigor, and friendliness, Marshall tended to forget how much older Bunker was.

The meal—appropriately light for the midday heat and served impeccably—was over, but Marshall purposely lingered over the wine. The past two hours had been so pleasant, and the conversation so engaging—the only civilized time he had spent in Vietnam—that he decided that he deserved the indulgence. Besides, his villa had been stocked with inferior wine.

Bunker had suggested that they move to the garden, but

Marshall declined. Beautiful though the oleander and bougainvillea were, and despite Bunker's urging him to see his rare orchids, Marshall did not feel like moving; it was too hot and humid outside, and the air reeked of gasoline fumes. He did not want to leave the crystal and silver and linen; the Meursault was soothing, and the clacking overhead fan lulling.

"I'm going to call on Thieu and Ky later," Marshall said, lifting the glass of pale yellow liquid to the light. "What can I expect?"

Bunker sipped his wine delicately. "Nguyen Van Thieu is an army general of no charisma, ideas, abilities, or accomplishments. Last month he got himself elected president. Previously he was merely a figurehead chief of state under the prime minister, Nguyen Cao Ky, an air force general particularly fond of purple jumpsuits that match his wife's—a most bizarre man. Now Ky is the vice president, outmaneuvered by Thieu in influence among the other generals."

Bunker put down his glass and blotted his lips with his napkin. "They rigged last month's election, yet still managed to get only thirty-five percent of the vote. That's the kind of incompetence we're dealing with. Finishing second was a disreputable lawyer who had once used his wife as collateral for a loan. Can you imagine?"

"I'm sorry I missed the campaign," Marshall said with a smile. "How are people like that going to unite this country?"

"They can't. Thieu replaced Ky; Ky led a military coup that overthrew Dr. Quat, a medical doctor who led a coup four months earlier overthrowing another government. Before that there were other coups. Since Diem's assassination four years ago, there have been seven major changes of government. It makes the banana republics look like bastions of stability. But what is the alternative—the communists?

"There can't be a political victory," Bunker said. "It has to be a military one."

"But how feasible is that?"

241

"I'm optimistic, Brad," Bunker said. "The South Vietnamese army is making great progress—the appointment of General Tran as area commander is a healthy sign."

"I'm meeting with him as soon as I leave here," Marshall said. "I've heard he's their ablest general; I want to hear his assessment. Do you think he'll speak frankly?"

"I do; he's very forthright." Bunker smiled. "It took a considerable amount of my time to persuade Thieu to appoint him. Thieu rose to power through intrigue and conspiracy, therefore he sees it everywhere. Most of his time and efforts are spent consolidating power and removing threats, leaving no time for leadership or nation building. A competent general like Tran terrifies Thieu—competence could mean a coup. I had to assure him that we would support him in the event of difficulties with Tran. Actually, he wanted my wife as collateral."

"Tran is that good?"

As Marshall prepared to leave, he broached the subject of the illegitimate children of American servicemen. "Is there anything that can be done for them?"

Bunker pursed his lips. "No," he said.

Marshall had expected at least a token offer from Bunker to have his staff investigate the matter, some mollifying word to accommodate him, but it was apparent that State Department policy was not to acknowledge the situation.

Marshall decided to let the matter drop for the time being. He had posed a frank question; Bunker had given him an emphatic answer. Diplomatic rules required that the subject be dropped to avoid unpleasantness.

When Marshall's limousine arrived before the JGS building without sirens, jeeps, or soldiers heralding him, Marshall could sense the welcoming group's disappointment: surely no important man would arrive in such a manner.

Yet General Tran, on the steps waiting for him, understood: a man who dispensed with pomp was confident of his power. The tall general, as formidable looking as a Manchurian warlord, moved to open Marshall's door, but before he could, a Marine jumped from the front seat and blocked him.

Mead looked warily on Tran and the armed Vietnamese guards, hesitating so long in opening the door that Marshall finally did it himself. He stepped around Mead and shook hands with Tran.

"Your entourage—effective as it is," Tran said without smiling, nodding toward Mead, "has disappointed my men. They were expecting you to be carried in on a sedan chair like a Roman emperor. Here, power is associated with circus trappings." The general's manner was almost threateningly fierce.

"In my country too," Marshall answered lightly.

Tran nodded. "I haven't been to Rome, but I suspect one might find such things there even now. Indeed, isn't the pope carried about in a golden litter?"

Marshall decided to let that pass without comment. "I think my entourage is ill at ease. I don't think he feels that he has enough bullets."

"Surely he wouldn't confuse us with the gooks?"

Marshall could not tell from Tran's impassive face if he was joking, but he saw immediately that he was dealing with an intimidating man.

Tran led Marshall inside the somewhat dilapidated building to a small conference room. "I did not prepare a formal briefing because I wasn't sure you wanted one. Perhaps you have specific questions to ask."

"Yes," Marshall said, easing into a chair at a small table, sitting directly across from Tran. "I'd like to talk informally. I'm in Vietnam to bring impressions and ideas back to President Johnson. He already has plenty of data."

Tran said blandly, "Secretary McNamara is a fountain of it."

"Indeed," Marshall said with matching aplomb. "However, sometimes numbers and figures don't tell any story."

Tran's eyebrows raised perceptibly. "My children used to paint by the numbers. They were very pretty pictures, but probably not great art."

Marshall nodded. "Secretary McNamara hasn't made a very great war, has he?"

Tran opened his hands. "He is neither artist nor general."

Marshall smiled appreciatively. Frankness was obviously

not going to be a problem, he thought, so he decided to go directly to the heart of what he wanted to know—could the war be won? He leaned forward, elbows on the table. "I was told today that there could be no political victory. Do you agree?"

Tran said evenly, "There might well be a political victory, but there is only one Vietnamese politician, and Ho Chi Minh is not on our side."

Tran sat perfectly straight in the style of a mandarin, his palms flat on the table. "I will speak as a Vietnamese, not as a soldier. French rule lasted here until the country was divided thirteen years ago. The South fell under the Diems, who were cruel, vain, corrupt, inspired only by hatred and contempt, and were backed by your country.

"The Diem brothers were assassinated four years ago. Since then there has been coup after coup, with no government having popular support. In the North there has been one man who has fought for national unity for forty years—he fought the French, the Japanese, puppet emperors, and now he is fighting the unpopular government here and the Americans."

Tran turned his palms up. "You tell me who would win the political fight."

Marshall sat back, slightly stunned. "Why are *you* fighting Ho Chi Minh?"

"I am a Catholic, and I do not like communism. In your country, communism means something terrible and all people unite to fight it. You have many words—'election,' 'democracy,' 'freedom'—that have a common meaning everyone understands. Here those words are meaningless. If you go into a village and shout those words, no one would have any idea what you are talking about. So, you end up talking to people who use your magic words—'freedom,' 'justice,' 'democracy'—and manipulate your tongue. You think you are having a dialogue with them when really you are only hearing your own monologue parroted back at you."

Tran smiled for the first time. "*I* know what those words mean, unlike most of my countrymen, and *I* have hopes that someday there will be democracy, justice, and free elections in this country; I also know that these never will be under communism."

Marshall nodded. "So that means you must win the war. I have been told that you will need H-bombs and nerve gas for that. Do you agree?"

Tran continued to smile. "Will President Johnson lend us H-bombs?"

"Probably not. But can you win without them?"

"Yes, in time, if there is enough time—if you are willing to stand by us for that long. But you are a very impatient people. We who lived under the Chinese for a thousand years, and the French for a hundred, are more stoic about time than you Americans. Everything happens so quickly in America—you believe in change, and things *do* change quickly. One hundred years ago you were cowboys; two hundred years ago you were revolutionaries; three hundred years ago you were pilgrims; before that you were savage Indians. Here things do not move so quickly. You think we are inscrutable when in fact we are just slow. Our perceptions and perspectives are different. You operate on schedules, we do not. Your political life is measured in four-year cycles, presidential elections—the life of a moth to us."

"You understand us very well," Marshall said.

"You are not complex: an election is on the horizon, your president grows nervous."

"Yes, one of those damnably free elections the results of which are not predictable."

"Very aggravating, I'm sure. Not unlike wars in that regard. Unfortunately, I cannot accommodate President Johnson by defeating the NVA by election time. In fact, I think the war is going to get much worse by then."

"General Westmoreland is optimistic."

Tran nodded. "So am I. But again, the measure of time differs. Time passes quickly when one follows the hands of a clock, much slower when one watches the calendar."

"I was afraid of that," Marshall said. "You are talking years."

"Many, unless we resort to H-bombs and nerve gas and invasion. The NVA too see the struggle in years; Ho and Giap have fought for forty years—what are a few more? But

Ho Chi Minh is an old man leading other old men in a communist cause that is wrong and unworkable. Time is not on their side—unless you cede time to them, unless you grow impatient and distracted."

Tran's face was an impenetrable mask. "You have come to me for answers to questions that only you yourself can answer, questions of commitment by you. Are you willing to support us for many more years?"

"I suppose that would depend on the course of the war and people's perceptions about victory."

"That is what worries me," Tran said. "I believe the communists will soon launch a great offensive, risking the loss of many men for the *perception* of victory."

Tran's face crinkled with wile. "The problem with an open society that airs its dissents is that it is open to all who care to look. Moscow and Hanoi read the same newspapers President Johnson does. They know there is opposition to the war in America, and that an election is coming up. The manipulation of perceptions is called psychological warfare, a potent weapon the communists have mastered. By striking unexpectedly, after America has been lulled into believing the war is being won, they intend to destroy America's will to fight on, or support us much longer."

"Have you expressed this to General Westmoreland?"

"Often. But he is convinced that such an attack would be too costly. Giap is a cautious, plodding strategist—truly an inscrutably slow tactician. So, would he attack with surprise and daring, hoping to inflict an unexpected and powerful blow that would crush the enemy's will to fight? The American generals and I disagree on this."

Tran shrugged. "It is a professional difference of opinion. On their side they have Giap's past and military record, and the buildup at Khe Sanh, which to them looks exactly like Dien Bien Phu."

Tran's eyes narrowed to slits. "But Khe Sanh is a ruse. Dien Bien Phu was thirteen years ago and against a weak foe incapable of quick deployments, reinforcements, or resupply. Giap would never try such a tactic against the Americans: he knows it wouldn't succeed. But what he's counting on is your vanity. He knows the Americans desperately want just such an attack so that they can prove their superiority—he's hoping that while they concentrate on Khe Sanh, they'll ignore other buildups. There will be a major attack soon, either at Christmas or a month later during Tet. So if we continue to assert that the enemy is too weak to attack, psychologically he will win simply by mounting the attack."

Marshall felt his heart plummet. Such an attack would destroy everything he hoped to accomplish. Lyndon Johnson would take such an attack personally; he would never withdraw while under siege for fear of being thought cowardly. Only in a position of strength, giving the appearance of magnanimity, would he withdraw.

Marshall pushed his chair back, signaling the end of the meeting. "Thank you. You've given me as much as I can digest now. I have to think about it all."

Tran stood. "You are a wonderful audience. I have never had an American listen so well before. You only asked questions."

"I came to learn. I had nothing to say."

"That seldom prevents people from talking."

When Marshall returned to the embassy, security had been downgraded to match that for Ambassador Bunker—the lobby was not cleared, but guards hustled him through to his private elevator. Seeing that Mead knew the guards, Marshall told him to wait with them until he came down.

In his office, Waggoner went over messages and the following day's appointments.

"General Westmoreland's office called. Colonel Romer will be reporting in the morning."

"Good. Do you know him—Robert Romer?"

"I've heard of him, but we've never met."

"He'll be traveling with me to visit outlying areas that were part of the COVIA study. His duties will not conflict with yours."

"Yes, sir. Also, Westmoreland's office said your plane and pilot are standing by. You have a jet and a chopper; a Lieutenant James Magnuson will be your pilot—a Marine sent down from Da Nang."

"Fine. Colonel Romer will handle all that. It will be like field and headquarters operations—you'll manage the headquarters here. And along those lines, would you get me two things—data on recent enemy infiltration, and a study on General Giap's strategy at Dien Bien Phu. I'd like them as soon as possible."

"I'll get to work on them tonight. Is there anything else?"

Marshall shook his head, and Waggoner left the office.

After turning off the light and drawing the window curtains, Marshall sat on the sofa. He liked quiet, dark repose. Now, staring across the dimness, everything muted except his thought, he saw that Tran was right—he was looking for answers in the wrong place. He and Lyndon Johnson and all Americans had to deal with the question: Did they care enough about Vietnam to risk a long commitment?

Forget the rhetoric—do we care enough to let our youth die for this cause?

Ryan. Suddenly thought was gone, and he imagined Ryan as a baby there on the rug, a silly baseball cap askew on his head, drool trailing from his mouth. Then he saw a hundred Ryans, as in a time-lapse camera: infancy flickering to childhood, then youth, a montage of faces—laughing, crying, curious, hurt—until there were too many impressions to handle and he stopped the rush on the image of an eighteen-year-old youth, angry and defiant.

Ryan. Who would be coming here soon.

And there in his mind were the coffins at Tan Son Nhut.

No, I do not care enough. I do not care at all.

Then thought returned, coldly shutting out emotion, erasing all the cluttered impressions.

If he were to succeed in this mission, if he was to convince Johnson to withdraw the troops, he had to prevent an enemy attack. An attack would add years to the struggle, rooting Johnson deeper into a commitment he did not want to make.

So somehow he had to make contact with the North Vietnamese. He had to convince them that an attack would create just the opposite of what they sought. But how? How could he secretly meet with the NVA? Who could arrange such a meeting?

An intermediary? Maybe. But could he find such a person?

He stood up. Yes, this would be his first priority.

Saying good-night to his staff, he left.

When the elevator doors opened downstairs, the Marines stopped talking and snapped to attention, then escorted him outside to his car.

The young men depressed him. They too were someone's sons, and so were those in the coffins: all the dead on both sides. That's what war was, he realized—other men's sons; it was not caring for them; it was caring for your own before them.

Lyndon Johnson was a good man, Marshall thought. But did he care enough to risk his own name and reputation— election—for freedom in Vietnam? He cared for the men fighting and dying, but did he care enough to risk his election to save them?

Suddenly there was a tap on the car window.

"Sir, you left this in your office," said a State Department civilian, handing him a shopping bag.

Lost in thought, Marshall accepted it distractedly, not noticing the shocked look on Mead's face.

The limousine started off. Absently, Marshall peered into the bag. He pulled out the Cinderella doll, then a box of Kotex.

He looked puzzled, then he put them back in the bag and handed it up to the front seat.

Mead did not turn, but head down, he reached back and mumbled, "Thank you, sir."

The limousine left the embassy compound and sped toward Marshall's villa.

In a world of philosophical doubts, there was one cosmic certainty, Bernard Lacouture thought—God was not a Frenchman. No French God would allow His language to be spoken the way Wilson Abbot Lord abused it.

Perhaps God was English. Or perhaps the devil was, and

this was some exquisite punishment. For here he was on the terrace of the Continental waiting for Bui Cao Kim, and instead Wilson Abbot Lord approached him speaking CIA French.

Lacouture could barely contain himself.

"Let's talk about money," Lord said.

Just like a street whore! Lacouture thought, shuddering.

"If we are going to talk about money," Lacouture said, "let's speak its proper language—English. How much money?"

"More than you can imagine," Lord persisted in French.

Lacouture wiggled his fingers. "I can easily imagine a million francs," he said, but instead he imagined the Côte d'Azur and bikinied savages.

"Far more than that."

"Ah," said Lacouture, putting Kim out of his thoughts, and resigning himself to Lord's French.

"I am talking about one million dollars, or the equivalent in whatever currency you desire, placed in escrow in a bank of your choice. But the task is complex and must be carried out exactly. If it is done according to our agreement, the money is yours. The details of payment, and whatever safeguards you require, will be followed to the letter. But I stress that the task must be perfectly executed."

"A task too perfectly executed often makes the executor irrelevant," Lacouture said smoothly.

"A man of your expertise and longevity in this field could surely establish for himself the safeguards that would guarantee his . . . continued relevancy. I don't expect you to trust me, but for one million dollars I expect you to be able to work out conditions that would provide you with sufficient protection. The man I want you to terminate is worth that amount dead to me."

"A termination? Oh, dear, they are usually very messy," Lacouture said disdainfully.

"Your hands will remain clean, of course."

"I insist upon it. Yours too, of course."

"Naturally."

"Then who is going to do this messy business?"

"Why, the enemy, of course."

"Ah. But the question arises—*who* is the enemy?"

"The NVA. The communists."

Lacouture tapped his head. "How foolish of me; naturally. But what enticement will be offered to the enemy?"

"They will be happy to kill this man; they will be inflicting a major blow against their enemy—the United States."

Lacouture opened his hands and stared into the spread palms. "Let me see if I grasp this: you want me to make contact with the NVA, persuading them to help lure an important man to a place where they will . . . 'terminate' him, something they would want to do, and which would coincide with your 'plans.'"

Lacouture folded his hands on the table and said serenely, "After contacting the NVA to set up this termination, I am to contact the important American to ensure he gets to the right place at the right time. All you require is the location and time of the meeting so that you can monitor events to make sure all goes smoothly."

"Bravo, Lacouture! Encore."

"The difficulties will be in getting your important man to the location, but that can be achieved by my convincing him that he is there to secretly meet and negotiate with the communists—who are there for an entirely different reason. The man will be portrayed as a dupe and fool for exposing himself to such danger, and the communists as perfidious double-crossers. You will have rid yourself of a trouble-maker while scoring a propaganda victory over the communists. I am to arrange this meeting between your man and the communists, a meeting you will have advised against—giving you . . . deniability."

"My dear Lacouture, you astound me. It is a pleasure to deal with a man of your grasp and understanding. I waste so much time with others trying to convey subtleties, which you seize instantly."

"Well, all we're talking about is ambush and murder," Lacouture sniffed. "Hardly anything subtle."

At that moment, Bui Cao Kim stole up the stairs of the Continental.

Seeing him, Lacouture gasped and rose out of his seat.

Kim mistook the reaction as a warning, and seeing the

CIA agent with Lacouture, he turned and darted down the steps.

Lacouture lifted out of the chair. "No, no!" he cried.

Lord jumped to the side, fearing an attack, but when he saw that the disappearing man was Kim, he nonchalantly sat back.

"I see that you have another appointment," he said smoothly. "I must be going." Then he stood. "I think we understand one another. I'll contact you soon, after you've had a chance to dwell on what we've discussed."

Lord saw that he had lost Lacouture's attention. The man was always nervous and flighty, but Lord had never seen him like this. What could be making him so frantic?

If he was going to use Lacouture, he had to know—only a fool played with an unmarked deck.

Lord extended his hand, but Lacouture was too distracted to take it.

"Good day, my dear Lacouture; I shall be in touch."

Lacouture did not even see him leave; he was still staring after the vanished Kim. The wretched, wretched little gook! He did that just for spite. Now he would have to track Kim down. He had to know about Le Sauvage. Especially now. Yes! He would buy him! Shower him with gifts. He would take his million dollars and live forever on the Côte d'Azur with his savage who would wear little black bikinis.

Oh, exquisite! He shuddered and sank down in his chair.

Maybe God was French after all.

CHAPTER
• 17 •

In the underground bunker, the candle flame flicked at the air, spitting wax. The noise startled Bishop, lying in his skivvies on his poncho, caught between sleep and consciousness. He watched the candle sputter, flail wildly, then drown.

Brock slept in another corner, and across the bunker, the radio operator, Landis, huddled against the wall, dozing.

Bishop stared at the planked ceiling, thinking nothing as his palm glided over his bare chest, massaging damp flesh. His hand dropped to his abdomen, rubbing its flatness, then glanced over his wakening groin, to his thighs, stroking muscle. He drew his eyelids tight and saw a woman over him, her hand caressing him, her mouth moving over his, and in response his mouth opened unconsciously, then he groaned and sat up quickly, casting it all away.

Landis looked up, and understanding what they all suffered, shook his head in commiseration and rested it back on his knees.

Bishop looked at his watch; it was five A.M. and he had not slept since the enemy probe hours earlier. He put on his fatigue trousers and boots, then he crossed the bunker and knelt beside Brock, touching him gently. Brock's eyes opened immediately, wary and hostile.

"It's five," Bishop said. "I want you to take the patrol out before dawn—just three men; I'll go get them."

Bishop went up the stairs. At the bunker entrance he stood a moment, like an animal coming from its hole, trying to sense danger, then satisfied it was safe, he emerged.

The morning was still as a pond. He urinated in the sand, splashed water on his face, then stretched his arms and legs.

For a moment he gazed to the south toward Khe Sanh, then he started across the hill.

Only a few men were awake, staring dully at the desert and the ridge. The darkness was lifting gradually, as if brush strokes of lighter gray were sweeping the horizon. Fog drifted toward the hill, seeming to ooze from pores in the earth, and soon the hill was enveloped in mist.

Frizzell was on guard at one of the bunkers. His head began to droop, but a muffled whimper from Sutherland startled him. It was a choked sob wrenched from within. He had often heard others cry in their sleep and wake with a frightened snap, so he supposed he did it himself, but he had been surprised when he had first heard Sutherland cry out: Sutherland always seemed so sure of himself.

Disturbed by a noise, he whirled with his rifle. He saw Bishop approach and smiled, pleased to have the loneliness broken. He whispered so as not to wake Coney and Sutherland, "What ya doing out, Lieutenant?"

"I love the war so much I wanted to get an early start today."

Frizzell grinned. He loved joking, even when it was directed at him, and he had been surprised when he found officers joked too.

"Sure is quiet, ain't it, Lieutenant?"

Bishop peered into the darkness, felt its calm, then crouched beside him. "Yeah, mornings are nice." His fingers drew in the sand; times like this were the hardest for him—choosing who was to go, then telling them. "You have any coffee left?"

Frizzell handed him lukewarm coffee in a canteen cup. "Do we have patrol, sir?"

"Yeah," Bishop said into the cup.

Frizzell sighed. "I was hoping we wouldn't have to go out today, but Coney knew we would. I was thinking that it'd be nice if for one day we—"

Bishop took a deep swallow. "I know. I wish we didn't have to go either, but if we didn't send out patrols, they could sneak up on us."

Frizzell studied him a moment, the man who controlled his fate, then he faced back to the wire. "You think we'll be getting out of here soon, sir?"

"I hope so," Bishop said.

They drank quietly, then Frizzell turned to him. "How long was it before you made lieutenant, sir?"

"It's different for officers. Right after college I went to OCS. That was ten weeks. Then they make you a second lieutenant. But you have to go to Basic School for four months to learn all the things you're supposed to know—artillery and tactics and weapons."

"Ten weeks?" Frizzell was incredulous. "How old are you, sir?"

"Twenty-two."

"Is that all? That's only four years older than me and only two years older than Coney. I thought you were about thirty. I didn't know you could be an officer so young. I been a PFC now for nine months. I don't think I'll ever get to be a lance corporal even."

"What's wrong with being a PFC?"

Frizzell shrugged. "Nothing, but it's kind of like this job I had in a restaurant once, clearing off tables and bringing people little baskets of crackers. People would come running in, and I'd bring them those fucking little baskets, then they'd leave and have someplace to go, and I'd still be there, cleaning up plates. I couldn't do that for long. I mean, a guy's gotta do something he can be proud of."

"You think being a lieutenant is something?"

"Sure." Frizzell grinned. "But maybe I'm just a PFC-type person."

"Well, second lieutenants are just the PFCs of officers, you know."

"I never knew officers joked. I always thought they—"

"Were just old and ugly and cranky, huh?"

255

Frizzell laughed. "Well, yeah, kinda. Who else is going on the patrol?"

"I was thinking of just sending you, since you think I'm so old."

"How about Coney and Sutherland too, sir? We're all buddies now. We have this pact kinda thing, and we know we're gonna make it if we all stick together. So would you send out all of us?"

Bishop considered; he had not planned to send the three, but men who felt the closest usually worked the best together. As in sports, a special bond could make all the difference.

"All right," Bishop said, and nudged Coney's sleeping form with his boot.

Coney groaned. "Kick me again, motherfucker, and I'll knock you on your ass."

Frizzell was horrified. "Dennie, it's the lieutenant."

Coney scrambled up. "I didn't know, I mean . . ."

Bishop feigned anger; he and Coney were similar in size, but Bishop had more muscle. He pushed bare-chested up against Coney. "What'd you call me? And what are you going to do to me?"

Coney stepped back. "Sir, I didn't know it was you. I never . . ."

Bishop grinned. "Jesus, first Frizzell tells me I'm an old shitbag, now you call me 'motherfucker' and want to kick my ass. I can hardly wait to see what Sutherland's going to say."

A voice came from under a poncho: "Sutherland can't say anything—he's gone and won't be back, and he left no forwarding address. But if he *was* here, he'd say, 'Take the patrol and shove it. Sir.'"

"I may have to court-martial this whole fucking post," said Bishop.

"Oh, no!" said Sutherland from under the poncho. "Then they might send us to Vietnam and make us eat C rations and go on patrols."

"Ten minutes," Bishop said. "You got ten minutes to have your asses ready and at my bunker." He walked off, shaking his head.

Sutherland threw off his poncho. "You asshole," he said to Frizzell. "What'd you tell him we wanted to go for? I don't want to go. You can take that buddy shit and eat it."

"What!" shouted Coney. "You told him we wanted to go? You *volunteered* us to go on a patrol? To the ridge? Are you out of your fucking mind?"

"Somebody's got to go," Frizzell said defensively. "It's better we go together."

"You dumb fuck!" yelled Coney. *"Nobody* should go out there."

Frizzell looked surprised. "That's not true. Patrols are important; we gotta have them. If we didn't go out there, the gooks would take over."

"You stupid jackass! What difference would it make?"

Frizzell's eyes set harder and his voice came with menacing control. "If they get this hill, then they'd take Hill Five Fifty-eight. Then maybe Khe Sanh. Then they'd get the whole country."

"Oh, for Christ's sake," Coney said with disgust.

Frizzell's anger flared. His eyes fixed intensely on Coney. "We gotta help these people. We gotta stop the enemy here."

"Jesus! You ignorant asshole, nobody believes that."

Frizzell's voice rose in genuine anger. "I believe in my country, and I'll die for it if I have to. I'm not ashamed to say that. If you don't feel that way, why'd you come over here?"

Coney said contemptuously, "Because I couldn't stand my wife anymore. To get the fuck away from her. And everybody else is here because they were drafted. And you're here because you're so fucking dumb you don't know better."

Frizzell lunged. He knocked Coney to the ground and fell on him. Coney was so surprised he could only curl up, shielding his face. Frizzell struck him repeatedly until Coney, larger and stronger, finally pushed him off.

Coney jumped up, then stepped back from the fury in Frizzell's face. "Les, stop it. Les!"

Frizzell's face was transformed into hatred, and he did not hear.

"Les! Les!"

Finally Frizzell relaxed. He looked dazed and confused, as though coming from a trance.

"Tut, tut, tut," said Sutherland, who had watched the two curiously. "Real buddies shouldn't fight like that."

Coney put his hand on Frizzell's shoulder. "Hey, forget what I said. I didn't mean it."

Frizzell dropped his head and said dully, "You shouldn't talk that way, Dennie. What we're doing is important. We're fighting for our country, and to help these people."

Coney looked to Sutherland, who rolled his eyes. "I know, I know," said Coney appeasingly.

Sutherland readied his gear, checked his rifle and bandoliers of cartridges, then lit a heat tablet to warm a can of C rations. Beans and franks were his favorites, and he saved them for days he had patrol. After the liquid began to bubble, he brought the can to his corner and started to eat with a plastic spoon while watching Coney and Frizzell gather their equipment.

Their belongings were stacked in their corners; Coney even had his letters arranged by date.

Sutherland looked to his own corner where gear, letters, centerfolds, and magazines were strewn everywhere. He pulled a few loose items toward him but gave up immediately, losing interest, and he turned back to Coney, a flash of envy rising in him. He wished he had a woman waiting for him, someone who really loved him. Toni was just the last of many girls he had had, someone to be with, drive around with and have a good time, someone just for sex—even he knew that—but not like . . . love. A wife. Coney railed about his wife and his child, but Sutherland knew that was just a pose, like the amulet around his own neck that he absently fingered—you didn't let on about the really important things.

Sutherland lit a cigarette and said casually, "You know, you never told me about your wife and kid."

"Holy shit!" said Frizzell. "Don't get him started on that."

Coney turned from his rifle, which he was oiling, and looked at Sutherland, trying to gauge his intent. "What do you want to know?"

Sutherland shrugged. "I just want to know." He pointed to the centerfolds. "That's just cunt. And I have this girl, Toni, but . . . well, I can't see marrying, and having a kid. That's so . . . heavy."

Coney nodded; he understood Sutherland's need, for he felt it himself at times like this. Before a patrol, before leaving the wire—crossing that line of safety and entering the arena where death waited, where evil was alive and tangible, and you were just nothing, a bug to be squashed— there was a desperate desire to make human contact, to just touch.

"Want to see a picture of my kid?"

"Sure."

Coney laid aside the rifle and reached for his pack. He searched through his pictures and handed one to Sutherland.

Sutherland stared at it.

"Well?"

He tried to think of something to say. "Yeah," he said.

"Yeah what?"

"Well . . . it's . . ."

Coney was truly angry. "Fuck you. Gimme my picture."

"Aw, Christ, Coney, it's a great kid."

Coney grabbed. "Give it here."

Sutherland pulled away. "It looks just like you. How's that?"

"It doesn't look a bit like me. It's bald and ugly."

Sutherland stared at the picture, then grinned. "It really is, isn't it?"

"All babies are ugly, asshole, but you don't tell a guy *his* kid is ugly—you're supposed to lie and say something nice, like it's cute."

"You said it first." Sutherland handed him the picture. "Hey, don't be pissed. It's a great kid, really. Talk about ugly—man, you should see pictures of me as a kid."

Sutherland smoked reflectively, lost in recollection. "They were in this old album, and sometimes I'd look at them. I used to like that, all by myself in the house, nobody yelling or screaming. It was the only time I liked being in the house. I'd stare for hours at those pictures. I don't even

259

know most of the people, just people in old clothes, a long time ago, most of them dead, I guess. But there were pictures of my folks when they were young, joking and happy. They don't look anything like that now. And there was this one picture of my mother when she was a little girl, wearing a white dress and staring at the camera with big, shy eyes. I used to stare and stare at that picture, because once it was real: she was a little girl and she was in that garden, and I wasn't anything. But in a way I was. I was in her, what was going to be me. It's all there, the future I mean, in the past or the present. You just can't see it."

He looked to Coney, suddenly embarrassed. "Anyway, I was ugly."

Coney took the cigarette from him and dropped down in the sand beside him. He drew deeply and let smoke drift into the darkness. "You know, we got pictures too. There's one of me in a football jersey, all smiling and puffed up." He shook his head. "I hated football. You run your ass off at practice then get the shit knocked out of you."

"Why'd you do it?"

Coney shrugged. "You had to do something. You can't see me playing a fucking clarinet, can you? And next to that football picture there's one of me in uniform, just after boot camp, with no more hair than an egg and looking like a complete asshole, but still smiling and proud." He hit his forehead. "God, what a jackass."

He stared at the picture of his own child, then put the photo back in his pack.

Frizzell, who had been listening carefully, said softly, "I used to play the piano. Not real good, but a little."

Then they were silent. For a moment they sat in their separate corners quietly, cradling their rifles, thinking their own thoughts, then Sutherland stood. "I guess we better go."

The three looked to the wire, then they began toward the underground bunker, weighted down with ammunition, their rifles at their sides, their boots digging into the sand.

When Bishop returned to the underground bunker, Brock was sorting through a stack of C ration cans.

"Frizzell, Coney, and Sutherland. They'll be here in a few minutes," Bishop said.

Brock grunted in disapproval, then in satisfaction when he found a can of pork slices.

From his pocket he pulled an opener and a plastic spoon crusted with food.

"Aren't you going to heat it?" Bishop asked.

Brock snorted. "Warm shit taste any better than cold shit?"

Bishop leaned against the sandbags and watched him. Juice spilled from Brock's mouth; he wiped the drippings from the back of his hand, grunted again—a remembering grunt, for Bishop could distinguish them that well—and reached into his back pocket. He tossed his wallet to Bishop.

They performed this ritual each time Brock left the wire.

Bishop looked at the wallet he knew contained a few pictures, four dollars, an identification card, and a folded envelope that bore the careful script, "For my wife in case I am killed," and he placed it carefully in his field jacket.

"What's your wife like?" Bishop asked respectfully, for at times like this he keenly felt his youth and inexperience. Brock knew men and war; he was the "old Corps" of whom Marines always spoke—the embodiment of tradition, custodian of the sacred duties of drinking, whoring, and bitching. His direct descendancy in the line of hardened professionals was not questioned by the younger troops or officers.

Though thirty-five, nearly twice the age of some of the men on the hill, at times like this, preparing to meet the enemy, there was no age about him at all—he was the timeless warrior.

Raised by his grandmother in St. Louis, at fourteen Brock tired of ciphers on a blackboard, of hours in detention, of the old woman's shrill exhortations, so he left. He worked his way west, stealing, selling his body, then at sixteen he killed a man in a knife fight in Colorado. The juvenile court saw the futility of an institution for delinquents and ordered him to join the Marines.

He found his home in the Marines. At seventeen he

married a woman four years older. At eighteen he was in Korea, and divorced. He loved combat and rose quickly in rank, but peacetime brought boredom and routine, which he escaped through drinking, fighting, and entanglements with violence-prone women. Brock went up and down the ranks, and through scores of discordant women.

"Which wife you talking about, Lieutenant?" he asked, wiping juice from his mouth, his eyes narrowing on Bishop.

"The wife you got now; the one you write three times a day—the one who nailed your dick to the floor."

"What do you want to know for?" he asked suspiciously.

"Because you give me this goddamn ratty wallet every time you go out; I'm trying to figure out what she's like that makes you this way."

Bishop was curious about Brock's wife because he never spoke of her—other women, his first two wives, but not her.

Brock tossed the empty can in the corner and considered Bishop. There had been many women in Brock's life, but he never believed he would find one to love: love was for movies and country-western songs, for women and for faggots.

Yet he had fallen in love. He met her three years ago at Pendleton where he was taking a course, a requirement for promotion to gunnery sergeant. She taught the course in grammar and saw that though he was crude and rough, he actually wanted to learn. She was shy, and not pretty, thirty-one, yet in her he saw a love and trust and decency he never knew existed. For her he was an escape from dullness and lonely nights at home listening to the gentle, maddening, damning proddings of her mother, wondering if there would ever be a man.

When they married, his aggressive, expedient lovemaking turned to tenderness, and she became everything in his life. They had been married nine months when he was sent back to Vietnam.

He did not talk about her because fate might overhear—he didn't fear the gods' jealousy as much as he did their perversity.

He shrugged. "She's a wife—after you've had a couple, Lieutenant, you'll know what I mean."

"How come you don't have any kids?"

"They might turn out like the assholes here."

"Did your wife cry when you left?"

Brock smiled. "Yeah. A lot. She kept saying, 'I'll never see you again, I'll never see you again.'"

"She probably won't."

Brock grinned maliciously. "Don't worry about me, Brown Bar. You got anybody but your mommy waiting for you?"

"Plenty, Gunny. Did I ever tell you about the woman I picked up in D.C.? I was on leave and—"

"I don't want to hear any goddamn fairy tale about you getting laid, Lieutenant," Brock said in dismissal, then hearing the three men at the bunker entrance, he shouted, "Stay up there—I don't want you tracking up my bunker."

He grabbed his rifle, crushed his years-old bush hat on his head, and went up the stairs. Bishop followed.

Brock checked Coney's, Frizzell's, and Sutherland's equipment, then he led them, silent as mules, down the slope.

Bishop watched them move through the mist, each figure gliding into the vapor until they were enveloped, and only he was left to stare after them.

Shivering, he shoved his hand into a pocket and looked to where the men had disappeared. He cocked his head, trying to sense what would happen, but there was no harbinger in the morning stillness. He cast a final glance toward the ridge, then went back down the stairs.

Huddled in a corner, fighting sleep, Landis sat next to the radios. He yawned, brushed hair from his eyes, and called each of the posts for security checks, then he rested back against the sandbags and thought again of the car he would buy when he got home. This occupied his time, and he gave long thought to the type, color, and interior features. At times he pondered what he would do *after* he got the car, but no prospect seemed interesting. There would be something, though, and for now the car was enough.

He yawned again and rested his head on his knees.

Bishop watched him from the stairs. Landis made a fist and rubbed his eyes, then he snuggled back. Besides Brock,

263

Bishop knew his radio operator best, but the gulf between them was so great.

Bishop went to the figure and stood over him. "Landis?"

The head lifted.

The bunker was oppressively quiet, and Bishop's words hung in the heavy air. "How old are you?"

"Eighteen, sir."

"You have a girl waiting for you?"

"Yes, sir."

Bishop nodded. He wanted to ask about her, yet he did not want to know anything. His hand reached out to stroke Landis's hair, and he felt the contact with another being. Landis stared up at him with dark, quiet eyes, then Bishop withdrew his hand.

"I'm going to sleep awhile," he said.

"I'll get you up if anything happens, sir."

"Don't fall asleep."

Landis was hurt. "I won't, you know that, Lieutenant."

"Yes, I know."

Landis pulled his poncho around himself. "I was just thinking about my car."

Bishop dropped down on his sleeping bag. "What kind is it?"

"Well, I ain't got it yet, that's what I was trying to think out—what kind to get. What kind of car do you got, Lieutenant?"

Bishop looked into the eager face, then he closed his eyes and lay back. "I sold my car before I came over here."

Landis nodded solemnly. "It's a big thing to get a car. I gotta think lots about it."

Bishop's voice echoed deadly in the bunker, and the words from his mouth seemed not his at all. "Yes, it's very important."

At the wire, the four men crouched for several minutes, listening, then Brock pointed to Sutherland. "You take point."

"You're really trying to get me killed, aren't you?"

Brock shrugged. "Better you than me."

Sutherland's body tensed as a spasm of excitement rippled through him. He gave himself to every sound and sensation in the dark, closing out all thought except of the terrain and the enemy, then he leapt, moving easily over the wire. Crouching, he moved to the triggered trip flare and found four sets of footprints.

He pointed them out to Brock, then following the prints, he led the others toward what was known as no-man's-land, the open area between the hill and the ridge, a mile of moonscape, defoliated and cratered by bombs.

Less than five hundred meters from the wire, Sutherland found more prints that seemed to come from the ridge but led due east, giving wide berth to the hill. He knelt in the middle of the trail and motioned Brock forward.

Coney and Frizzell spread out while the other two examined the prints.

"How many?" Brock asked.

"I can't tell for sure. Maybe thirty-five or forty."

"You only saw three last night."

"These aren't going toward the hill—they're going behind it."

Brock stood. He had not considered that because Khe Sanh was behind them—yet Khe Sanh was three miles away, much too far for a quick response to a surprise attack in the middle of the night.

"And look at these," Sutherland said, pointing to deeper prints. "They're carrying heavy gear—mortars, machine guns, ammo."

He moved off to scout the terrain farther north, leaving Brock by himself, but in a moment came back and led Brock to another trail.

"Here's another thirty or forty. The place is crawling with the fuckers. We gotta get out of here."

Brock knelt beside him. "How recent are these?"

"Hours. They must have moved in last night. And who knows how many came in before—prints don't last more than a day out here. Gunny, they got a hundred men behind us. They been going past us every night. Those probes are just to throw us off what they're doing."

Brock knew he was right. He stood, tightly controlling his anxiety. "Let's go."

Sutherland did not move. "Where?"

"The ridge."

"Are you crazy?"

"We have to search it; the only way to know what's there is to go."

Sutherland exploded. "You're out of your fucking mind! They got a goddamn staging area up there—I'm not about to walk in on a thousand gooks. We gotta get out of here. They'll have listening posts out all over the place. And what about the trails? There's a hundred gooks behind the hill."

Brock said coldly, "You don't seem to get the idea, Sutherland—we got a job to do, and it doesn't make any difference if you don't want to do it, or if you're scared. I said we're going. Now move out."

They crouched face-to-face, eyes locked. Sutherland turned slowly toward the ridge. He considered it a long moment, sounding for danger. He fingered the amulet around his neck, weighing it against death. His eyes narrowed, searching for death in the mist on the ridge.

He turned back to Brock. "All right," he said. "I'm going to be all right, but I hope your ass is wasted."

"It won't be. Now move."

Coney and Frizzell closed the gap behind them, and the four started across the waste that separated the hill from the ridge. On point, Sutherland used the mist to edge the patrol to a position on a small knoll several hundred meters from the slope of the ridge.

Brock lay on his stomach and contemplated the terrain behind him. The hill loomed like an island in a ghostly sea. Fog shrouded it, and he almost expected to see some ancient schooner slip out of the vapor.

What was now wasteland had once been jungle and rain forest; defoliation, air strikes, and shelling had left the area barren and arid. For miles in all directions, along the entire Demilitarized Zone, the land was blighted and scarred; it looked like the surface of a hostile dead planet.

Behind him, Brock saw the hill, isolated and prominent, a lonely fortress on the wasted plain.

Before him was the ridge, a rocky promontory covered with scrub brush and mangled, burned trees.

Suddenly, beside him, Frizzell brought his rifle to his shoulder and squirmed into a firing position.

Brock followed the barrel and saw distinctly on the ridge an enemy soldier gazing casually toward the hill.

The figure was in Frizzell's sights. He blurred the image so that he saw only the blade of the front sight in the center of the man's chest. Frizzell's arm was steady as he squeezed the trigger, pulling the flange as he had a thousand times in training on the rifle range. His mind was so intent on the discipline that he was not aware that it was a man in the sights—he saw only the blurred black tip of the centered blade. The mechanics of the act took control and he concentrated on the trigger squeeze.

Brock watched the textbook demonstration of marksmanship in fascination, then he looked across to the unsuspecting man who had only seconds to live, but suddenly the man dropped out of sight.

Frizzell lowered his rifle in disgust.

Brock motioned the other three and pointed to the ridge. Covering one another, leapfrogging the distance, they worked to the base of the ridge and crouched in the brush.

Brock edged up the slope alone, then signaled the others to follow.

The four gathered at the crest and peered into the clearing on top. Before them was a large, nearly completed bunker complex with two mortar sites.

Brock crept into the clearing and crouched beside the mortar sites; the aiming stakes were pointed toward the hill.

The enemy had never moved in this close. They'd need only two more nights to complete the bunker, then the position could withstand even a direct air strike. And with the enemy also behind them, the hill would be completely cut off.

Sutherland dropped beside him. "This place is swarming. Get us out of here," he hissed.

"No one's here," Brock said. "They're still working on the bunkers—they wouldn't risk showing themselves in the day."

"What about the gook we saw? You forget about him, you dumb *old* lifer," Sutherland taunted.

Brock grinned evilly. "I've fucked tougher pussy than you, Sutherland. We're staying." He motioned Coney and Frizzell to him. "Tear down the aiming stakes and booby-trap the bunker—we can't leave it like this."

"What about the gook?" Sutherland insisted.

"He's sleeping. Or ran away. They have shitbirds on their side too. I can tell one when I see one—he looked just like you, Sutherland. Now get busy."

"One of these days I'm gonna kill that motherfucker," Sutherland said to Coney.

For two hours they worked in the clearing, dismantling mortar sites and booby-trapping the bunkers with hand grenades.

When they finished, Brock pointed north, farther up the ridge.

"No way," Sutherland said, holding his rifle ominously tight.

Coney and Frizzell backed away instinctively, watching Brock and Sutherland square off.

Brock stepped in front of Sutherland, so close their faces nearly touched. "You still don't get it, Sutherland—it's our job. I said go."

There was no distance between them; they were as close as lovers. Neither moved, and their eyes were steady on each other. So casually that there could be no mistake that the move was without fear or intimidation, Sutherland turned, cocking his head, then lifted his face as though sniffing the air. Finally he turned back, his lips almost against Brock's.

"Okay, *this* time, motherfucker," and he moved. It was a liquid motion so smooth that he seemed to merge with the terrain, poured from an upright vessel into a pool that flowed over the ridge.

The others followed, spreading out behind him. They moved quickly, checking bunkers and concealed tunnels.

Then, with amazing speed and assurance, Sutherland raced across a clearing into a treeline and dropped into the brush. He was drenched with sweat, but he shivered as his own heat made contact with the air. Adrenaline pumped wildly through him; his excitement was beyond sexual—it was ferocious: jungle and animal fused.

He was on the edge of the main enemy position, he knew; the enemy, prey and predator, was beyond the trees. Instinctively he grabbed his amulet; he stroked the shrapnel furiously, then gripped it so tightly he lost feeling in his hand, yet from it came bursting power.

A single mistake, a misplaced step, would end with a bullet exploding his skull, he knew. He feared a head wound the most, an eye ripped away, his brain splattered into the dirt, some irreparable disfigurement so that his coffin would have to be closed.

He stared into the trees. And there it was, his coffin. He saw it clearly, and himself in it, the gray metal lid coming down, locking him forever within, at nineteen, sealed and trapped.

He closed his eyes, and when he opened them, the coffin was gone. It was going to be all right, he knew; he was not going to make a mistake. His breathing quickened and his skin prickled. His eyes narrowed and he drew himself tighter. His fear was gone, and in its stead, as though flowing from the weapon into his hands, came an ancient zeal. Everything was familiar to him now; it was as though he had been here forever.

Beside him, Brock watched the transformation; he had seen it many times, when a man passed beyond thought into pure feeling. It was all animal, the spasms before orgasm, the mad moment of murder, loins thrusting, hands slashing —the frenzy of fucking and killing.

Just as Sutherland leapt, Brock grabbed him; he threw himself on top and held him down. Sutherland strained up, eyes wild, but Brock pressed his arm against his throat until Sutherland collapsed.

When Sutherland regained his breath, Brock pointed to the treeline.

At first Sutherland did not see, so well hidden were the mines. They were camouflaged in the branches, aimed in a trajectory to sever a man in midtorso. He had not looked in the trees, only searched the ground for trip wires. There were no visible buried wires, these mines were triggered by weight.

He rolled onto his back. Suddenly he couldn't breathe,

and he clutched his sides, thinking he was going to be sick—that close had he come to death, and he hadn't known it.

Lying on his back, Sutherland looked up submissively to Brock. He could be dead now, he knew. He wanted to hug Brock.

Brock said impassively, "You *owe* me, asshole." Then he handed Sutherland his rifle. "Let's go."

Frizzell took point and led them down the ridge, then back across the open terrain to the hill.

When they reached the outer perimeter, Brock told Frizzell and Coney to go in. "I want to talk to you," he said to Sutherland.

Brock waited until they were alone, then he said almost fatherly, "I don't want you to get spooked by what happened out there. It was just one of those things—it could have happened to anybody."

"I could have been killed," Sutherland said, still upset. "I *would* be dead if you hadn't stopped me. How did you know?"

"As you said, I'm an old lifer. But sometimes that isn't all bad. I been around a long time—just lasting counts for something. You were so busy looking down that you forgot to look up—it's like looking out for the little things: when you do that, it's the big things that turn to shit. But when you look out for the big things, it's the little things that turn to shit. You gotta keep your eyes on everything, Sutherland."

Sutherland shifted awkwardly, unaccustomed to any demonstration of gratitude. "Well, you're right, I owe you. Thanks."

"Look, we're here for each other—no one could make it on his own in this shithole. You gotta learn that better; there's no shame in making a mistake, or letting someone help you. I was even younger than you when I went to Korea, and I'm still around. You're a lot like I was. You're good, I mean that, and that's why I don't want you spooked by what happened. Don't let it bother you, or make you too cautious—that's just as dangerous. Trust your instincts, just make sure you look up as well as down. Okay?"

Sutherland nodded gratefully.

Brock put out his hand to shake.

Sutherland smiled and reached for it, but as soon as he did, Brock punched him in the gut, so hard that Sutherland doubled over, then he flipped him onto his back so that he lay sprawled in the sand.

Brock jammed the rifle butt into his throat and placed his boot heavily on Sutherland's crotch. He stepped down at the same time he pressed the rifle into his throat.

"Don't you ever call me motherfucker," he snarled. "Don't ever call me Brock. You call me Gunnery Sergeant, got that? Next time I'll crush your balls into the dirt." He stepped harder, then let up and walked away, leaving Sutherland writhing in the sand, moaning and clutching his groin.

In the underground bunker, Brock told Bishop what they had found.

"You get on that radio, Lieutenant, and tell them what's on that ridge, and what's behind us, and you tell them we want out of here. We want out now. I'm not bullshitting you, Lieutenant—we haven't got a chance against what's out there, and I'm not about to die for this fucking hill, and I'll be goddamned if I'm gonna be buzzard bait."

"All right, all right, Gunny. I'll call."

"The ridge is crawling with the bastards; they got bunkers and mortar sites, and a fucking superhighway they're using to go past us. I'm no coward, but I'm thirty-five years old, and I got a wife, and in two years I can retire with twenty years in the Corps. I got a lot to live for, and I'm not going to throw it away on this goddamn hill, or because someone doesn't have the brains or balls to do the right thing."

"All right, Gunny, I said I'd call."

But Brock would not leave it. "You gotta make them understand, Lieutenant. They're killing us if they leave us here. They wouldn't leave us if they knew."

Bishop said quietly, "I don't know, Gunny. It may not be that simple."

"Well, it is that simple, Lieutenant. We're gonna die unless they get us out of here."

"But there's Khe Sanh—"

"Fuck Khe Sanh! It's a hill like this one, just a little bigger. It's ground. Dirt. We're men. Men shouldn't die for nothing; men should die for . . . important things—their children. Their women." Then he added softly, "Each other."

Bishop contacted the company commander on the field radio. He outlined the enemy buildup, told of the trails, and requested immediate withdrawal.

The company commander asked several questions, then said he would pass the request on to battalion.

Bishop put down the radio and stared at the sandbags.

"They won't leave us," Brock said confidently. "They can't."

Bishop went up the stairs. The midday sun was intense, the glare on the sand mesmerizing. In the distance he could barely see the ridge, just a faint shimmering on the horizon.

Behind him, out of sight, was Khe Sanh.

And in between, and all around, the enemy.

Then he saw Sutherland coming over the crest, limping toward his post. Coney and Frizzell came out to help him. They talked a moment, then Sutherland gestured toward the bunker. When they saw Bishop, they looked away quickly and moved on.

As Bishop watched, Brock came up the stairs. He looked confused, almost dazed, and he held a piece of paper loosely in his hand.

"They said no," he mumbled. "The CO just called; he said to tell you the request was denied. He said he wants you to"—Brock glanced at the paper—"'interdict.'" He looked up. "What does that mean? I wrote it down because I never heard it before."

"Interdict? It means stop them—intercept them."

Brock stared at him blankly. "He said battalion had no intelligence on enemy troop movement. I *gave* him the intelligence—what more do they want, names and addresses?"

Bishop said soothingly, as he would to a child, "All we see is our little part of this, the hill and the ridge—they have to think of the whole area of operations; it's a lot bigger than just us."

Brock was contemptuous. "Spare me that shit, Lieutenant—the trails are out there; there are tunnels and bunkers all over the ridge. We're going to be wasted if we don't get out of here."

He caught sight of Sutherland, who had turned back to look at them. "You can push men too far, Lieutenant. We can't go much further."

"You talking about them, or yourself, Gunny?"

"Everybody. When you get to that line between life and death—when a man knows he's there, when it's drawn right in the dirt before him, and you tell him to cross over it . . ."

Bishop waited; he saw Brock staring after Sutherland, then he asked, "What, Gunny?"

Brock stared hard at him, straight into his being. "When you tell a man to cross the line, you've reached that line yourself, Lieutenant—and the other guy may decide he doesn't want to cross over; he may send you over instead."

"You talking about fragging, Gunny?"

Brock shook his head. "I'm talking about those ethics we discussed once before, Lieutenant."

Brock said solemnly, "It's not right, Lieutenant, them telling us to stay here—it's wrong. They're not being brave, they're only asking us to be brave. It's like those cunt politicians in Washington always ready to send the Marines —that's *so* easy to do."

He spoke with pain, as though he had been betrayed by those he had trusted. "This is wrong. I'll do what they say—I'm just a gunnery sergeant, and I'll do my job, but they're asking us to die for nothing."

Bishop smiled and punched him playfully on the arm. "You're too much of a philosopher for me, Gunny. I'm just a Marine grunt who wants to fight and fuck—just like John Wayne in the movies, doing his duty, charging that hill, balls to the wall."

Brock spat. "I seen that movie—*The Alamo.*"

CHAPTER

• 18 •

Mead woke with Sung snuggled against him. The touch of her, the soft flesh, made him groan, and he pulled her closer, almost crushing her into him.

Sung did not resist or respond, simply lay with closed eyes, waiting.

His erection pressed against her; he hurt from desire and need, but when he rolled over on her and saw her face, her teeth biting into her lower lip, he pushed himself away.

She opened her eyes, then nestled against him, grabbing his erection and stroking him sensuously. He tried to pull away, but the sensation of her hand on him was too great, and he began to thrust his hips. She brought her other hand around and squeezed tightly.

"Oh, Jesus," he moaned and ground into her, thrusting powerfully until he came. He continued to pump his hips until he shuddered a second time and finally lay still.

He rolled onto his back and pulled her to him. "Thank you," he said. "But you don't have to do that, or anything. That's not why I brought you here."

She lay completely still beside him.

"Are you all right?" he asked. He turned to her, then raised up on an elbow and looked into her face. Her eyes were closed.

"Look at me," he said.

She tried to keep her eyes closed, then finally looked at him.

He quickly turned away, for all he saw in her eyes was terror.

He looked at his limp cock and saw her hands, no longer on him, but still clutched tightly, dripping semen, and he felt remorse and self-disgust. "I'm sorry," he said, and sat up.

He took her hands and rubbed them until they relaxed. "I won't ever hurt you," he said. Then he looked down on her face, into her eyes, and he stroked her cheek. "Don't do that again," he said softly. "Don't do anything you don't want to."

Then he jumped up and went to the shopping bag in the corner. He brought the boxed doll back and sat cross-legged on the sleeping bag next to her.

"I got you this," he said, handing the box to her.

She looked at him without understanding.

"It's for you," he said, thrusting it into her hands. She merely held the box until he sat her up and helped her open it. Even then she just stared at it.

"It's a doll," he said, taking it out and putting it in her hands. "Cinderella, I guess. You ever heard of her? She was a princess, and something happened to her. She fell asleep and some prince kissed her."

He shook his head. "No, that's not right. That was someone else. Snow White. Yeah, that was Snow White. I got it all fucked up. Cinderella was the one with the sisters and the glass slipper, and there were mice. I remember it now. Gus was my favorite, a little fat one. And there was a dance and the pumpkin."

He was excited and happy at the recollection. "And she lost her slipper at the dance because she had to leave early, but the prince found her, of course, and they lived happily ever after."

Then he felt silly, telling a fairy tale, sitting naked on the sleeping bag. "Anyway, that was Cinderella." He shrugged nonchalantly. "Your other doll was getting kinda ratty, so I thought . . . maybe you'd like another one."

She stared at him for a long moment, no longer with fear,

but still with apprehension. She looked at the doll, fingered the silk gown delicately, and touched the tiny glass slippers on the doll's feet, then looked back at him.

She opened her mouth to speak, but no words came until she wet her lips and swallowed. "Thank you," she whispered.

"She's got a crown too," he said, pointing to it awkwardly, "but I don't think they're real jewels."

She did not take her eyes from him to look, and he grew embarrassed under her gaze.

"Are you feeling okay?" he asked. "You're gonna hurt for a while longer, but do you feel better now?"

"Yes," she said, still in a whisper, the word painful in her throat.

"Can you make it? It's really hard, I know. I did dope too, but I never got hooked. I guess it made everything easier, being on dope, but you don't need to do it anymore. But if you do, I mean really need to, tell me, okay? If you really need it, I'll get some for you. If you gotta do it, tell me. It's okay—I know how things hurt sometimes. Just tell me so I can be with you."

She nodded but did not say anything.

He jumped up again and went to the corner. "I got you some candy too." He brought her a bag of Hershey's kisses and sat down, ripping open the package and unwrapping foil. He put one in her mouth. "I gave Han five bags. She probably ate 'em all already. No wonder she doesn't have any teeth."

The faintest smile flickered on Sung's face. "Han is a good woman," she said falteringly.

"I know," Mead said. "But she still doesn't have any teeth."

He unwrapped another candy, which she ate greedily. "I'll bet you're starving. I'll get you some food tonight, but I'll give Han some money so she can go out and get you something now."

He touched her torn blouse. "I'll get you some clothes too." Then he remembered his ordeal at the PX. "I'll just give you some money and you can get the things yourself."

He looked at his watch; it was six forty-five. "I better go," he said. "Can I get you anything before I leave?"

She shook her head.

He went to his clothes and dressed. When he finished, he lingered a moment, not wanting to leave, but not knowing what to say.

"Well, I gotta go," he said from the door. She did not look up but stared at the doll in her hands.

When he knocked on Han's door, Bill Catton shouted for him to come in.

Catton was blousing his boots and gestured in disgust to Han, sitting at a table littered with mounds of silver foil.

"What'd you give her all that fucking candy for? She almost OD'd on Hershey's kisses last night. I thought she was going into insulin shock. I got enough foil here to open an aluminum siding business."

Han did not look well. She smiled weakly and got up. "I go see Sung," she said.

"You should have seen her last night," Catton said. "She was eating those Hershey's kisses like a fucking robot—her hand would reach out, she'd unwrap one, pop it in her mouth, smack her gums on them, then whirrrrr, her hand would reach out again. Five goddamn bags, about ten thousand Hershey's kisses. I was getting sick just watching her. Next time you're gonna buy my woman something, pick something else—or get her some toothpaste and Pepto-Bismol too."

"I only did it because she was helping Sung, you know."

"I know, I know—no problem; just next time, don't buy her five bags. She was up half the night moaning and groaning—I didn't sleep worth a shit and I got duty the next three days."

"She's all right, isn't she?"

Catton finished dressing and grabbed his rifle. "Yeah. It was just a different diet for her—usually she just eats rice and cock." He grinned. "Maybe that gook doctor can help her."

"What gook doctor?"

"The little gook that came to see Sung yesterday. Han said

277

he was a doctor, but he looked more like a corpse." He checked his appearance in the mirror and turned. "Ready? You want to share a cab, or aren't you going to the embassy?"

Mead put his hand on Catton's shoulder, stopping him. "Wait a minute. Tell me about that gook."

"I just did. A gook—you know, your standard, everyday, regulation gook: little, old, ugly—he was with Sung yesterday morning. I went in to get Han. She was with Sung, and there was this old gook with her. Han said he was a doctor—well, more like a medicine man, I guess. He was giving Sung something—tea, I think."

"Did you see him giving her tea?"

"No, man, I didn't see anything—I could barely see the gook. My head was killing me." Catton shook his head in happy memory. "You should have been with us that night— funniest thing I ever saw. Taggart was so fucked up! We were going to some whorehouse in Cholon and Taggart decided to drive. He pulled the driver out of the cab and threw him in the backseat, then he took off. I don't think we were ever in the street—once we drove right through some fucking noodle shop, in the front door, and out the back. People were screaming and chasing us with knives, noodles everywhere, and the driver . . ."

He started to laugh but Mead pushed him, an angry shove that knocked Catton against the wall.

"I want to know about the gook."

Catton was furious; had it been anyone else, he would have struck back, but the burning rage in Mead's eyes stopped him.

"Ron, I just told you, I can't remember much. We got all screwed up the night before. I woke up blind. I went to get Han. There was an old gook in with them. He was sitting or kneeling over Sung—that's all I remember. Han told me he was helping her. What's the matter? He wasn't doing anything to her."

It had to be the Vietnamese who was outside the building yesterday morning, Mead knew. He was no doctor or medicine man; but what did he want with Sung? Yet she was better, that was certain—could Han have brought someone in to help her? Han would never tell him, and Sung probably couldn't, so he might never know for sure.

It could be legitimate, maybe just coincidental, but an inner sense told him that it was not.

The man had been there because of him. Mead had total recall of the encounter that morning—the surprise and anxiety in the guy's face, the request for a cigarette with teeth brighter than any Vietnamese he had ever seen, the pose of not understanding. He was there because of Mead. But why?

It had to be because of Marshall. They were trying to get at the ambassador through him. What else could it be?

This was a security matter he had to report. But to whom? This was too complex for the Marine guard; they were not set up for anything like this. Security breaches were supposed to go to Naval Intelligence, but those guys were worthless farts.

So then, yeah, he knew whom he had to see; he had to see The Phantom, Mr. Lord. He would know what to do.

The presidential palace in the heart of Saigon was to Marshall an incredibly bland building that perfectly mirrored its occupant and the government he represented. Despite its great size, the palace looked inconsequential, just a large white building taking up space at the end of the street.

The interior, expansive, airy, and cool, was likewise without majesty; it was dull and spiritless. Nothing captured the imagination, or gave an inkling of the richness of Vietnam's history, Marshall thought.

There was no past here, he decided, nothing to evoke centuries of art and creativity; there was no color—no gold or cinnabar, and there were no dragons or phoenixes, no unicorns or tortoises, no fabled creatures that figured so prominently in their mythology. And there were no Buddhas sitting on lotus leaves or Bodhisattvas; no religion. It was a building of the lackluster moment, without past, and without future, sterile and lifeless.

Where were the temple dogs and jade, he wondered; the scribes and eunuchs? The concubines were gone, emptied into the street where tight-skirted whores hustled drinks and gave blow jobs to soldiers for a dollar. The mandarins in their richly brocaded robes of brightly colored silks, with long sleeves and elaborately tied sashes, in steep-sided black bonnets, were replaced by dull men in dark suits and oxford shoes.

Marshall finished his courtesy call on President Thieu and Vice President Ky profoundly discouraged. Talking to Thieu was like trying to catch soup with a net—the platitudes slipped through and lay splattered on the floor. Ky recited the same speech he gave Johnson in Honolulu the year before, one written for him by personnel at the embassy.

A half million American men and billions of dollars were keeping Thieu and Ky in power; a mere hour with them convinced Marshall that the commitment was wrong. During the meeting, Marshall kept wondering how this had come about: why do we align ourselves with such people? Why the Diems and Batista and Somoza? What flaw makes us comfortable with runty dictators, hucksters, and zealots? Surely one can choose better friends, he thought—they don't always have to be fools and knaves. Yet Thieu and Ky were not wicked men, he knew, nor were their policies odious; they were simply dwarves.

He sat for a full minute in his car in the driveway. There would be no political victory, he now knew. And that is what he would tell Johnson.

Finally the driver asked, "Do you want to go back to the embassy, Mr. Ambassador?"

It was late morning; he had cut short his visit, and he did not want to return this depressed to the embassy. He needed something to raise his spirits.

He would go see Teresa Hawthorne, he decided; that would restore and fortify him. He fumbled in a vest pocket and passed a slip of paper to the driver. "Take me there."

The driver glanced at the address, then turned to Marshall. "This can't be right, sir. You don't want to go there, that's in Cholon."

"The address is correct," Marshall said. "Go there."

"But sir . . . that's a very bad area. I don't think you should go there." The driver turned to Mead in the front seat beside him. "He wants me to take him into the center of Cholon. You know what's there—only cathouses and dope dens. I can't take him there. Tell him."

Mead said apprehensively, "Sir, he's right, you really shouldn't go there, it's very dangerous."

"I'm not going to a whorehouse, I'm going to an orphanage."

"Sir, that's not the point. It's . . . well, it's a completely unsecure area. Anything could happen down there and I . . . I don't think I could protect you there."

"I'll take full responsibility, Corporal."

"That's fine, sir, but I'm not worried about that, I'm worried about protecting you." He didn't know another way to put it: "I'm not worried about my ass, sir—I'm worried about yours."

Marshall smiled. "Thank you for your concern, Corporal."

"Well, I'm worried about all our butts," said the driver.

"All you have to do is drop me off," Marshall said. "Now that's enough—take me to that address."

There was no demarcation between Saigon and the suburb of Cholon, but Marshall knew immediately when they passed into it. Suddenly the city changed, and one entered a maze.

For centuries Cholon had been the Chinese district, mysterious and labyrinthine, without base or bottom, the fugitive's lair—for here the rules and laws of the city did not apply. Cholon was a cabal of deceit and intrigue, betrayal and murder, sin, flesh, dope, and money. Shadows cast shadows; everything was murky and anything could be bought, and the buyer could himself become the commodity at the flick of an unseen hand. Everything had a price, but one could never be sure of the merchant or the merchandise.

The surface was all flesh and drugs, a carnal bacchanal, but beneath roiled an undercurrent of violence, an ancient underworld where arms and information were exchanged, where murders were arranged and deaths bought. Cholon was an intricately carved ball of evil set inside another, then another, then another.

The limousine plowed through the streets choked with bicycles, carts, pedicabs, and pedestrians. No one moved out of the way and people pressed against the windows, peering inside. The car was rocked and the door tried.

"This is bad shit," muttered the driver. "We gotta get out of here."

Mead's anxiety mounted as the car moved deeper into the district; the danger was overwhelming, and he knew he could not protect Marshall if he was attacked here. He kept thinking of the Vietnamese man outside his building—what if he had followed them here? They could kill or kidnap Marshall easily in Cholon.

The car turned onto a side street, narrower and more crowded, then onto another.

"This is the street," the driver said, glancing at the paper again. "What are we looking for?"

"An orphanage," Marshall said calmly. In Syria he had seen even angrier crowds.

On the next block they came to the address, but the building was boarded up.

"I can't stop here," the driver said. "They'd strip the car in five minutes."

"Just drop me off. I'll take a cab back."

The driver placed his head on the steering wheel and moaned. "I can't leave you here, Mr. Ambassador. They'll court-martial me if I go back and tell them I let you out here. This is totally unsecure."

"Hand me your dispatch log," Marshall said. In it he wrote: "Ordered back to the embassy after dropping me off in Cholon." Then he signed and dated the entry.

He opened the door to get out, but before he did, Mead was already in front of him, pushing people away from the stopped car.

As soon as Marshall emerged, beggars, women, and children pressed closed to him, shouting and thrusting out their hands. A few children ducked under the others and grabbed onto his trousers and tugged. The swarm grew, overwhelming him, and he tried to get back into the car, but then they were behind him too, blocking his retreat.

Suddenly a powerful hand grabbed his shoulder and pulled, yanking him from the grasp of the mob.

Mead elbowed and kicked a passage toward the building, thrusting Marshall forward, then he pulled him down an alley, slashing with the butt of his rifle to clear the way.

Marshall saw that his guard was transformed—murderous and methodical, and brutal. A beggar reached out a hand to Marshall, but Mead slashed it with the rifle barrel, then raised it quickly, parrying for another thrust. Mead was behind Marshall, between him and the alley entrance, yet he moved so quickly that at times he was in front of him, clearing the way, and continuously forcing Marshall on with his body, guiding him toward a door at the end of the alley.

Just as they reached the entrance, Mead pushed Marshall out of the way and entered first with raised rifle.

Women screamed, then Marshall was grabbed and jerked inside so that he stood beside Mead facing a roomful of terrified women and children.

The room was psychedelically bright, crammed with a hundred beds and cribs on which sick and wasted women with babies screamed and shrank from them.

Coming from another room, marching toward them with a stern, determined look, was Teresa Hawthorne.

Only when she was upon Marshall did she recognize him.

"My goodness," she said. "What a dramatic entrance."

Fear and adrenaline coursed wildly through Marshall's body, then suddenly crashed, and he almost collapsed in relief. He could not catch his breath and said a little hysterically, "Yes. Quite dramatic. Sorry to intrude. Good to see you again. Corporal Mead. You remember. My God, I can't breathe." He leaned back against the door and held his chest.

She rushed to his side to support him. "Are you all right?"

He took deep breaths, then nodded. "Yes. I'm fine now."

Mead had already crossed the room, rifle poised, eyes darting from right to left, ignoring the screaming women. He ran up the stairs, checked the ward, then ran back down and searched the other rooms. He had checked the entire building and was back at the door by the time Marshall caught his breath.

"Please put down the rifle," Teresa said to him. "You're terrifying the women. There's no one here. This is a clinic—there are only women and children here."

She turned beseechingly to Marshall. "Most of the women here have had very traumatic experiences. When they see a soldier with a rifle, it's profoundly disturbing. I assure you, there's no need for weapons here."

Marshall pulled himself straight. "I'm sure she's right, Corporal; I don't think there's any danger here." Then he patted Mead's shoulder. "You were quite remarkable—thank you. If I ever get in a firefight, would you make sure to be there beside me?"

"Maybe we should try to stay out of firefights, sir," Mead said disapprovingly, indicating clearly that he meant places such as this.

"Why don't you wait here, at the door," Marshall said, "while Miss Hawthorne and I talk."

"I'll get you a chair," Teresa said.

Mead shook his head. "That's okay. I'll just stand."

"But a chair would be so much more comfortable. Let me—"

"No, ma'am. I'd rather stand."

"Well," said Marshall, adjusting his jacket and trying to be casual, but then seeing the squalid conditions, the wasted women and pathetic children, all words died on his lips.

Teresa took him by the arm. "Let me show you about. I'm very pleased you came to see us—I never expected that."

She stopped. "Or would you rather not see? Perhaps you don't have the time."

He smiled. "I have the time. I'd like very much for you to show me about."

She looked about with concern. "Well, it is a little depressing, I'm afraid. I should warn you about that."

"That's all right, I've had a depressing morning anyway."

She took a breath and said brightly, "This is one of the wards. There's another upstairs—each ward has about seventy-five women and children."

284

"How long do they stay?"

"Oh, they come and go—it's hard to tell. Some women come a month or so before their babies are due, and some stay on a while, another month or so, but some leave the day after delivering. Some leave after a few days, then come back, often without their babies, who have probably died. Some women never stay at all, they just bring a newborn baby and leave it with us."

"Are all the babies interracial?"

"Most of them. That seems to be our clientele. They know we will take them, where they would be turned away elsewhere."

"And the women are all prostitutes?"

"I have trouble with that," Teresa said. "I suppose that technically they are prostitutes—they sleep with soldiers for money, or cigarettes or food. But how would they survive otherwise? They don't have any skills, and there is no economy—I mean, there aren't any jobs where they can find employment, no industry; what are they to do? There are two million soldiers here—a half million of them Americans, healthy young men, the only ones in the country with any money, and they are happy to spend it on . . . women who desperately need it. It is for most of the women the only way to earn money."

"What would happen to the women and babies if you didn't take them?"

"I suppose what happens to all those we don't and can't take—they give birth in the street, or in sewer pipes or ammunition boxes, and they die, or their babies die, or somehow they scratch out an existence."

Marshall gazed about the ward, which had settled back to normal. Babies screamed, women whimpered and moaned, curled into themselves on their cots, while others stared blankly at the walls.

"Dear God," he said.

"This is the part of war that people never think of," Teresa said. "Sometimes I read old magazines or newspapers, and there are always stories about the soldiers, terribly sad ones about how they are killed or wounded or maimed, and about their families and loved ones, and it's all true and sad, and there are pictures and stories about bombed cities and civilian casualties, and orphans roaming the streets, and all that is true and awful too, but then there's this—no one knows or hears about it, and I can't say it is any worse or sadder, but it's terrible nonetheless. Maybe I feel worse about them here because no one knows or cares."

She led him through the ward where he nodded and smiled to frightened or indifferent women, and he held diseased and emaciated babies. She showed him the differences wrought by their ailments—retardation, malnutrition, drug addiction, venereal disease—and at the end he was overwhelmed.

Yet Teresa's manner was brisk and undaunted; she smiled and soothed, comforted and laughed, giving Marshall the impression that he was making morning rounds with the head nurse in the well-baby clinic.

"And this is where we are," she said, bringing him to the converted supply room where there were six cubicles for the staff. "That's the kitchen, and over there the delivery room. In here are women ready to deliver—our maternity ward, so to speak; we try to separate them so they can get a little more rest. And in here," she said, bringing him into a small room filled only with cots, "is our . . . intensive care unit."

Teresa introduced him to a shy, smiling young Vietnamese woman. "We are lucky to have Trieu. She's a registered nurse."

Marshall tried to converse with her, asking if she spoke French, but the woman made no acknowledgment. When they left, Teresa told him that Trieu had spoken only a few times in the year she had been at the clinic, and never with a male, not even Father Dourmant.

"Trieu's mother and sisters were raped and murdered, and she was taken away by the Viet Cong and forced to live with them. She's wonderful with the infants, but she never speaks except to comfort the babies."

Teresa sighed, momentarily letting down her guard. "It's all so hard—such awful suffering, and not just the diseases, but the wounds to the heart and soul."

Marshall could not say anything, but Teresa caught herself immediately. "We're having lunch soon. Could you join us?

286

It's not very elegant, just soup and noodles, but it's not bad, really."

"That would be very nice, except I would like to talk to you privately. Perhaps I could take you to lunch, someplace where we might talk. I know you're busy, but maybe just for thirty minutes or so."

When she hesitated, he took her hands and said almost pleadingly, feeling like a boy before her, "Please. It would mean very much to me."

"But there are hardly any . . . restaurants like you would . . . be accustomed to." She laughed. "There aren't any menus or napkins—no amenities, let's say."

He did not let go of her hands. "Anything would be fine. I just want to . . . talk with you."

She was genuinely pleased. "Won't that be lovely. I never go out to lunch." She laughed. "Or to dinner, or anywhere. There are hundreds of little eating shops, mostly Chinese— we'll find a nice one."

Suddenly there was a loud commotion at the entrance and an indignant voice booming French. "Let me in! Fascist! Nazi! Get out of my way, infidel! Barbarian!"

"That must be Father Dourmant," said Teresa sweetly.

"And Corporal Mead," murmured Marshall, releasing her hands reluctantly.

At the door, Mead barred the priest's entrance. He blocked the passage with his body and held the priest at bay with his rifle.

"How dare you?" shouted Father Dourmant, trying to push his way in, but the frail old priest just bounced off Mead.

Not understanding anything the priest shouted, and intent on searching him before allowing him in, Mead pinned him against the wall with one hand and frisked him with the other.

"Sacrilege!" the priest howled in outrage.

"Corporal, it's all right," said Marshall, rushing to the doorway. "He's a priest; let him go."

Mead stepped away reluctantly. Teresa was at Father Dourmant's side, smoothing his cassock and comforting him with soothing words.

287

"How good of you to come by, Father. There's someone I—"

"What's going on here?" the priest shouted. "I heard there were soldiers. I rushed right over." He pointed furiously at Mead. "And then . . . this! Is everything all right? Have they hurt anyone?"

Marshall stepped forward and extended his hand, saying in excellent French, "Please accept my apologies. I'm Bradley Marshall. I came to visit Miss Hawthorne and see the clinic. Corporal Mead is my bodyguard. He's an extraordinarily competent young man who takes his job quite seriously. He was only doing his duty; he meant you no harm or insult."

"This is the man I was telling you about, Father—Ambassador Marshall, the man at the embassy who was so kind."

"Charmed," grumped the priest, shaking his hand, not charmed in the least. "I don't suppose you've come to offer any help, have you? I told Teresa not to expect any. Am I wrong?"

"Father . . . ," Teresa said reprovingly, "that's not polite or gracious."

"Certainly not very diplomatic," Marshall said lightly. "I see why you're here and not in the Curia in Rome."

Father Dourmant considered him sharply, then smiled faintly. "You must be Catholic. Or were, as seems to be the fashion these days"—that directed at Teresa.

"Won't you come in?" Teresa said. "We were just going to lunch. Will you join us?"

"Thank you, no," he said. "I just came to see if everything was all right. Several parishioners ran to the church to tell me that soldiers were here. I was worried. I feared they might be bayoneting babies—but apparently it's only priests." Then, eyeing Marshall narrowly, he said, "Your French is . . . adequate."

"It's the language of diplomacy. I am, I fear, merely an adequate diplomat."

The priest pursed his lips and gave a slight shrug. "Actually, it's not bad," he allowed.

"Thank you. Won't you reconsider? We'd be delighted if you'd join us for lunch."

Father Dourmant shook his head, but he said almost pleasantly, "Thank you, but no. I'm sure there's some foolishness at the church I should be attending. Wars, famines, and pestilences come and go, but the Ladies' Auxiliary is undaunted. Perhaps another time, though."

"I would like that very much," Marshall said. "I often wonder if I am listening to the right people. It's not often I get a chance to talk to people such as you and Teresa."

Father Dourmant said dryly, "That shouldn't pose any problem—just have your young storm trooper throw them up against a wall; then you can talk to them at your leisure."

The priest bowed, then said to Teresa as he left, "You were right, he does seem nice. But if I'm wrong, and he offers you any help, I'll pay for the lunch."

"He says awful things," Teresa whispered after the priest was gone, "but he's a wonderful man. We could not survive without him."

"I liked him very much," Marshall said. "How long has he been here?"

"In Vietnam? Oh, forever—since he was a young priest, and he's quite old now, surely in his seventies." Suddenly she wiped a tear from her face. "Well, I just love him. He's the only person who makes me wonder if there's a God after all—if I made a mistake leaving the order. I couldn't stand it if something happened to him."

"Is there something wrong with him? Is he unwell?"

"No, not that I know of anyway." She smiled. "I'm just being foolish—as if there aren't enough real sorrows and tragedies. Well, enough of that, let's have lunch."

She considered him a moment, then said hesitantly, "Maybe you should take off your jacket and tie. It's just that you might be . . ."

"Conspicuous?" He smiled, then shed his jacket and tie. "Do you think they'll notice Corporal Mead and his M-16?"

"Oh, dear," she said. "I forgot about him. Does he have . . . I mean, of course I'd love to have him join us . . . but . . . well, the rifle . . ."

Marshall turned to Mead. "I know you'd love to join us, but I'm going to send you back to the embassy."

"Sir, I can't leave you . . ."

Marshall raised his hand. "I know, I know, Corporal. You're absolutely correct. I shouldn't do this, it isn't safe, it's very foolish, anything could happen. But I'm going to—I am sending you back. I'm aware of your feelings and reservations. If you want, I'll write you a note like I did for the driver."

Mead's frustration burst out. "Sir, I've never disobeyed an order in my life, but I can't leave you here. I'm supposed to guard you and make sure you're all right, whether you like it or not, and not just when you want me to. Sir, it isn't right you should do this to me—just tell me to take off, as if I'm just some dumb dog that didn't have feelings or care about what was right. It isn't fair to me, sir. I mean, what if something happened to you? How am I supposed to feel then?"

Marshall had not heard so many words from Mead in all the time they'd been together.

"Well," he said. Then he grabbed Mead's shoulder. "You're right, and I apologize. This won't happen again, and when I get back to the embassy, I'm going to rethink this whole security business, but I'm still going to send you back now, and this is why. No one knows I'm down here, and if I walk down the street looking for a place to eat with you behind me, carrying an M-16—well, I'm just inviting trouble. I think that in this case, Miss Hawthorne and I would be safer on our own and would attract less attention than with you guarding us. I can catch a cab back."

"A cab?" Mead said incredulously.

"Corporal, if I can hail a cab in New York and Rome, I can manage one here." He turned to Teresa. "You know, I once got a cab in Beograd, and nobody does that."

Still Mead hesitated.

"Corporal, go. I'll be fine. Don't you think Miss Hawthorne can take care of me? I'm sure she could slap the shit out of any VC."

Teresa turned her head to hide a smile, and finally Mead

laughed. "All right, sir. When should I say you'll be back, so they'll know when to send out the search party?"

"I should be back by three."

"Yes, sir." Mead saluted and nodded to Teresa, then left, deciding to go directly to Wilson Abbot Lord. Something had to be done about this—if the VC didn't get Marshall on purpose, they were going to get him by accident. That Vietnamese outside his building, the one with Sung, had been there for a reason. He might only be a corporal, but he knew that the personal representative of the President shouldn't be going into noodle shops in a combat zone.

He would tell Lord everything. The Phantom would know what to do.

291

CHAPTER

• 19 •

"He seems like a very nice boy," Teresa said about Mead as they left the hospice.

"He is," Marshall agreed. "And he's right—I hadn't thought about his feelings."

"Are you really so important that you should have a bodyguard wherever you go?"

He shook his head. "It's all symbolic. What I do is far less important or significant than what you or Father Dourmant do. President Johnson asked me to come here and bring back some advice. I deal at a high level—General Westmoreland, and President Thieu this morning—but it doesn't mean anything. I don't *do* anything—I don't help or comfort anyone; I don't touch anyone. It's just politics, petty and grubby, self-serving, and dirty—you make me feel almost unclean."

She laughed. "That's silly. I'm sure you do very fine things."

At the alley entrance he stopped and put his hand on her, turning her to him. "No, I don't. And Father Dourmant is right—I can't help you. I tried; I raised the issue with Ambassador Bunker, but they will not help you. I'll try again in Washington—I promise I'll discuss it with President Johnson—but . . . I can't give you any reason to hope. I'm sorry. I truly am. I feel terrible about it."

"That's all right," she said softly. "I shouldn't have put you in that position. I know you want to help, and I don't want you to feel guilty or—"

"Teresa, stop it." He laughed. "I've never been around a saint before. No wonder they burned them—you make us feel awful."

She brought her hand up as ingenuously as a young girl, and he almost expected her to giggle. "I'm hardly a saint," she said. "I think one of the criteria is a belief in God."

"Oh, no, that's just for official certification—the paperwork part."

He let go of her arm. "Well, which way? Why don't you lead?"

The sidewalks were too crowded for them to walk side by side, and he had trouble keeping up with her; she was accustomed to snaking through the mass of people, while he was jostled and blocked and buffeted about. Finally he overcame his hesitation and pushed his way through. He had no trouble keeping her in sight as she was a head taller than the Vietnamese, but he was out of breath by the time he caught up with her, and wet from perspiration; his shirt clung to his back and sweat dripped from his brow.

She looked into a couple of small places and finally selected a third. "Will this do?" she asked him. "It has tables—the others didn't."

"Wonderful," he said at the crowded, garish Chinese restaurant.

There were no individual tables so they sat at a large one where other diners, engaged in animated conversations, totally ignored them.

Rushing between tables, waiters carried huge trays stacked with steaming baskets, shouting what it was in Vietnamese.

"I haven't had dim sum in years," Marshall said.

"Do you want me to translate?" she asked. "What's coming around now is pork and eel."

"I'll have what you have," he said. "Just flag him down."

Despite the noise and chaos, or perhaps because of it, and their need to sit close together in order to hear one another, the setting seemed entirely private, almost intimate.

She raised her hand, and two plates were placed before each of them. She said something else and two pairs of chopsticks were tossed on the table.

"People usually bring their own," she explained. She bent over the steamed dumplings and savored them, then she looked up to Marshall and smiled. "This is very exciting. I've never dined with an ambassador before."

He laughed. "What a treat this will be for you then. You'll see that we spill our food just like everyone else," and he proceeded to drop his dumpling onto the floor. "Damn," he said, reaching down for it and putting it back on his plate, trying again with the chopsticks.

Finally he got it into his mouth and chewed delicately. "Excellent. Once I was having dinner with the Queen of Denmark. We were having artichokes, and I had a particularly tough one. I was pulling a leaf off and flung the whole damn thing into the Queen's lap. She was gracious, but not amused. Queens rarely are, and are even less often amusing."

He speared another dumpling. "Do you really not believe in God?"

"No," she said softly. "I can't reconcile him with what I see every day. He is either very wicked or he doesn't exist. I choose to believe that he doesn't exist."

"You must drive Father Dourmant wild; he looks easily excited."

She laughed. "I do, and he is." Then she looked downcast. "How do you explain it all?"

"Oh, dear," he said. "Are we going to have a deep philosophical discussion over dim sum?"

"Oh, no. It's just that you're a very wise person who has seen so much. You dine with presidents and queens and generals—I thought perhaps you could explain everything to me, like why there's so much suffering. Why war? Why the orphans?"

He said quietly, "I think it's in the very nature of presidents and queens and generals, and the rest of us who serve them, and those who seek to usurp them."

"Human nature," she said.

"I am afraid so. Corporal Mead is, as you say, a nice boy.

294

But he has killed others—many others I think, at least it appears so from his medals and decorations. And he would kill again. Yet he is, I am sure, capable of love, and laughter and kindness. Lyndon Johnson is—and I believe this—a good man with good intentions. He does not want to see anyone hurt, including all those in your clinic. Yet look what he has wrought. Why is it then that the nice boy kills and the well-intentioned man allows the carnage and suffering? I don't think they can help themselves—neither is strong enough to overcome his nature. Johnson's terribly afraid of being thought afraid, he's never been to war, never borne arms, never proved himself in combat—he fears being called cowardly or unmanly. It is a curious phenomenon that the most ardent hawks, the fiercest proponents of wars, are invariably men who have never seen combat. They are vociferous in calling for strength and toughness—but only if others will do the fighting."

He motioned the waiter bearing another tray, and two more steaming baskets were placed before them. "But the depressing thing is that men *like* war—they like fighting and struggling; it's exciting and erotic. And women don't help matters much. There aren't any cheerleaders for the chess club or the 4-H club—the girls are out there for the football players, and they're chasing after the boys with the fastest cars and the most money. I think it's called natural selection."

"Why is it you never married?" he asked suddenly, popping a dumpling into his mouth.

She looked startled, then blushed. "It had to do with natural selection—I wasn't very pretty. And that was hardly a diplomatic question."

"Well, I didn't want to talk about men and war any longer; I wanted to hear about you. I'm curious about your decision to leave your order—how did you decide there was no God?"

"I hate to talk about myself," she said. "It seems so unimportant. Rather like the order and God. I suppose that's the answer—I don't remember ever making a decision about leaving the order or not believing in God. I was just overcome with their irrelevance."

She held up a dim sum. "I really like this one. Try it in the *nuoc mam,* the fish sauce."

As he did, she contemplated him, then asked, "What is it you want?"

The question surprised him. "Nothing. I have everything —money, position, health, even love."

"Then why aren't you happy?"

"Does it show? No one ever guessed that—or perhaps they were too diplomatic to bring it up."

He finished the dim sum and stacked the plate on top of the other, then he motioned toward the door. "I know the misery and despair out there—I didn't need to see the women and children in your clinic. I know how cruel and unfair the world is. But I can't *do* anything about it—I can't even help you. Nor can I do anything about the horrors lying in wait for me—age, disease, death. I know too much to be happy."

Another plate was placed before him. He picked up a dumpling precisely with his chopsticks and held it aloft. He focused his attention on it and with his other hand made a sweeping motion of the world around it. "Do you know, in all the depictions of God, anybody's God, I have never seen him happy. Don't you find that curious?"

"Not at all," she said. "What kind of God do you think Father Dourmant would paint? What kind of God created this situation which you have come to set right? God is probably Lyndon Johnson. Would you paint him with a benevolent smile?"

He laughed. "Did you leave the nunnery, or were you *driven* out?"

She held out her hand and showed him her wedding ring. "I didn't divorce God. I'm hoping the differences aren't irreconcilable. Perhaps it's just a trial separation."

He put down his chopsticks and pushed his plate away, suddenly very serious. "What are you going to do? The problem is going to worsen—more diseased women, more babies, more horror. What are you going to do about the woman who threatened to set fire to herself and her child?"

Teresa sighed. "I don't know. About the overall problem,

we'll do the best we can for as long as we can. But about Lin, I don't know."

"You're not considering for a moment—"

"I'm trying not to think about it at all," she said. "The child will absolutely die—it's deformed and brain damaged, syphilitic and drug addicted. God is not going to miraculously save this child."

She was silent a moment. "Yes," she said at last. "I've thought of letting her set fire to herself and the baby in front of the U.S. embassy. I've thought that it couldn't hurt, and might even help."

She reached for his arm. "Would it be wrong? What's one more dead 'gook' baby? And is it possible, just possible, that it might do some good, that it would cause such a sensation that the government would then have to help?"

Marshall did not say anything for a long time. He stacked his plates carefully and brushed at the table. "It seems to be one of those damnable questions of ends and means," he said finally.

She smiled. "Perhaps you can help me after all. Ends and means are matters for politicians and diplomats to decide— where do they usually side? You should have considerable expertise, Mr. Marshall."

He considered her; was she mocking him? "Actually politicians and diplomats don't make distinctions between the two: there are only ends."

"That settles it then; we'll burn the baby."

"I wish I could be sure you were joking," he said. "But more, I wish I could help you; I wish I could offer something besides solace and high-sounding phrases—but as a diplomat, that's all my expertise allows. Were the fate of that child left to diplomats, it would be neither saved nor burned—it would die of neglect."

"But you are different," she said. "You want to help; you would if you could."

"Yes, I do, and I will if I can. I want to help you, and I want to end this awful war. I don't want Corporal Mead to kill anyone else. I don't want there to be any more orphans or cripples; I don't want there to be any more suffering. And most of all—God forgive me—I don't want my son harmed."

He signaled the waiter to pay. "And now, forgive me, I must leave. Please ask him how much I owe, and should I leave a tip? How much? Oh, never mind, here's some money, you pay him, and keep the rest for the clinic—just promise not to buy gasoline to set fire to any children."

He stood. "I enjoyed this immensely. Will you join me again sometime?"

"I would like that very much," she said. She glanced at the money in her hand and offered it back. "This is a great sum of money. I don't—"

"Please. You should have it—it's money I embezzled from the government."

"Oh. Well, in that case, I'll take it," she said, and stuffed the bills into her pocketbook after paying the waiter.

Outside, he thanked her for accompanying him and said he would contact her shortly, but told her to call him if there was anything he could do.

They stood on the sidewalk, anchored it seemed, oblivious to the crowd jostling past them.

"Will you . . . see me again?" he asked, then laughed. "Or did I already ask that?"

She smiled. "You did, and I said yes."

"Well," he said, again feeling like a boy. "I guess I should be getting back. Or you should, since you're the one doing the good works."

She took his hand. "Thank you," she said. "Thank you for coming to see us. Thank you for lunch. And thank you for . . ." She lowered her head, then turned abruptly and disappeared into the crowd.

He stood long after she was gone, still feeling her presence, not wanting to lose it.

He had never met anyone like Teresa, nor had any woman ever made him feel this way, tentative and almost shy. There was an overpowering sense of goodness about her, something his own wife surely possessed, but this was without Catherine's stridency and righteousness. This was stronger because it was purer. Here was a woman of immense feeling and limitless love—a woman of intelligence and humor, without pretension, absolute genuineness—and far beyond him.

The crowd pressed past him, almost caught him in its swirl. He ran into the street and hailed a cab—with far less trouble than he had ever had in New York.

Only as he approached the embassy did he realize that he had left his suit coat and tie at the hospice.

Teresa threaded her way quickly through the crowd. What was wrong with her? she wondered. She had been so foolish—running away like that. Just like the goose her father had called her. And why was she running now? she demanded of herself, and forced herself to slow down. And why was her face on fire?

"Oh, dear," she said aloud, and stopped on the sidewalk because she knew what was the matter—she was feeling what she had never felt before.

And she was annoyed with herself; it was too silly for words, and she blushed at the thoughts that had no words.

He was a *nice* man; a good and kind man. He was strong and decent, with depth and understanding. Of course she liked him. What was wrong with that? she asked herself in front of a bicycle shop. Nothing, she said to her reflection in the window.

Then she sighed at her reflection. There she was—plain and horsey and simple.

He was handsome and powerful, confident and assured. He dined with queens.

He accomplished things.

He had affairs with beautiful women.

She sighed again at the image staring back at her. She fingered her threadbare dress and touched at her hair.

Then she took a deep breath and turned away.

Well, it had been a lovely lunch anyway. And she started back to the clinic.

CHAPTER

• 20 •

Earlier another cab dropped Mead at the embassy.

At the guard booth inside, he checked the directory for Mr. Lord and found there was no office listing, only a telephone extension.

Mead did not want to be overheard, so he walked down a corridor until he found an open office where the secretary had stepped out.

When he dialed, the phone was answered on the second ring.

"Extension three seven two four," said a bored voice that Mead recognized as Lord's.

His decision to talk to Lord had been all of a sudden, and he had not thought out what to say. Confronted by Lord's voice, and his aura of mystery and power, Mead stammered nervously. "Mr. . . . sir, this is Corporal Mead, Corporal Ronald Mead, with the Marine guard. I was wondering if . . . I mean, could I . . . well, talk with you, sir?"

There was neither interest nor hesitation in the response. "Room two sixteen in fifteen minutes." The phone was hung up.

Two sixteen was right above him, one of many unassigned all-purpose rooms used for small interviews. Lord's cool, matter-of-fact response gave Mead second thoughts; perhaps he had overreacted; it was all just coincidence. Lord would dismiss him contemptuously. Mead saw now that he had been foolish—seeing plots and conspiracies where there had just been an old gook; Mead had envisioned a clandestine meeting with The Phantom in the "Bubble," the most secure, electronically swept, inner heart of the embassy, but instead they were going to talk where visa applicants were interviewed.

He reached for the phone to call Lord back. Why had he done this? he berated himself. He wished he could disappear; what was he going to tell Lord? About Sung and the whorehouse? He hadn't thought of that.

But Mead couldn't summon up the courage to call and cancel the meeting. Shit, he thought, the whole thing was a mistake; so he'd just pretend nothing had happened. He'd go up to Marshall's office and tell Colonel Waggoner that the ambassador would return around three, then he'd go back to the barracks.

Mead was stepping out of the office when he encountered a Marine officer coming down the stairs, a tall, powerful-looking lieutenant wearing aviator wings and sunglasses. A Marine officer, except for the embassy detachment ones, was a rare sight, and he had never seen a Marine pilot at the embassy.

"Good afternoon, sir," he said as he passed.

The lieutenant glanced at him and said distractedly, "Hi," then continued down the corridor.

Mead stared after him; pilots were more casual about rules and regulations than other officers, he knew, but he would never have imagined one saying "Hi," and for a moment he wondered if the man really was an officer. Perhaps he was a CIA agent; he was coming down from the second floor, where Mead was supposed to meet Lord— maybe the man was just masquerading as a pilot. Then Mead caught himself—he was doing it again, dreaming up plots and conspiracies that did not exist.

Yet what was a junior officer, a pilot, doing on the second floor, using a back stairway? He had not imagined that. Now intrigued, and once again anxious about Marshall's safety— he hadn't imagined that old gook either—he changed his mind again and decided to see Lord. If Lord laughed at him, well, it wouldn't be the first time he had made a fool of himself. He checked his watch; there wasn't enough time now to inform Colonel Waggoner about Ambassador Marshall, or even to run down to the snack bar and grab something to eat, so he went upstairs.

He came upon Lord in the stairwell, absorbed in thought, and seemingly caught unaware. He did not look surprised or annoyed, but his usually totally indifferent manner was slightly discomposed and his gaze flicked to the stairs. Mead sensed that he had intruded, and that Lord was concerned that he had seen someone on the stairs. Lord would not have expected him to use this back stairway. Fully recovered in an instant, Lord gestured to the left. "This way," he said, and walked off.

Only while following him did it occur to Mead that Lord had agreed to see him immediately, without asking any questions, and that he had recognized him on sight.

Lord opened the door and went to a chair at a long table, leaving Mead to close the door and wait, standing for a full moment while Lord scrutinized him, literally X-rayed him with searingly cold eyes, then motioned Mead to a chair two down from his.

Mead sat, rigid and uncomfortable, waiting for a word, but there were only the intent eyes. Lord sat forward in his chair, elbows on the table, chin resting on his hands. After a moment he raised his head slightly and opened his hands, inviting Mead to speak.

"I wanted to see you about Ambassador Marshall," Mead began. "Not really about him, just something strange . . . well, maybe not even strange, just something that bothered me that I wanted to talk to someone about. And I thought that you . . . well, I guessed that you . . ."

Mead dropped his head, exhausted by the strain of finding words and embarrassed by what he now was convinced was his foolishness; he was also overwhelmed by Lord's presence and intensity.

Lord made no effort to ease Mead's discomfort. He merely waited.

"Okay," Mead said, braving it all with one fast outburst. "I have this girl that I met in a whorehouse and she's on

302

heroin, and I brought her to live with me and she's getting better, and yesterday this old gook was outside my building and then I found out that he went into my room, and he was with her and I just think there's something wrong about it and it has to do with Ambassador Marshall. There was something about this gook that was just wrong. I know it sounds stupid, but I just have this feeling. He was just an old gook and he asked me for a cigarette, but he had perfect teeth, like, I mean, they were perfect, not even with betel nut stain and all gooks have that, and he had all his teeth, and I never seen that. Then later he was inside with Sung, that's the girl, and my buddy Bill Catton, PFC Catton, found them and his girl told him that the gook was a doctor, but that couldn't be. And this morning, Sung, well, she just acted different, and I can't help but think that somehow this has to do with the ambassador, like maybe they're following me to get at him."

Mead dropped his head again. "I know this is just fucking crazy, and you probably think I'm on dope, but . . ." He looked up again, very earnestly. "You know how you get a feeling? It's just something that happens—you know it's wrong. You can be fine and everything's straight, and then . . . you just know."

Mead's eyes transformed, and he was suddenly lost in memory. "You can be moving through the bush with everything quiet and no sight of the enemy, then suddenly you just know—you can feel it in front of you, a trip wire, or something out of place. Or sometimes you know that it's all right—the enemy is there, right in front of you, but you know you're going to make it. You know, just know, the enemy is down the tunnel, and you're standing there over it, and you can't see down into the darkness, but yet you can—you see clearly, and you feel it's going to be all right, that nothing is going to happen to you."

Mead's voice was an intense whisper; he was standing over the tunnel, looking down. Then the spell broke and he shrugged. "Anyway, that's how I feel about all this."

Lord rested his chin back on his hands and watched Mead with unchanged expression. Then he spoke; raising his chin slightly, only his lips moved. His eyes were unvarying, his body perfectly still, and his voice low and flat. His manner was mesmerizing, as hypnotic as a snake's, and his words were so softly spoken and precise that Mead unconsciously leaned toward him.

"I am talking now about a Frenchman. You probably have seen him. Think about it carefully. Try to see this man in your mind: an older man, around sixty, short and round, very elegantly dressed, probably in a white suit. Do you see him? A short, fat little Frenchman in a white suit. His hands are always moving, like a girl's; he is very excitable—he moves around a great deal, he can't sit or stand still. And of course he is queer, you can sense that—you just know."

"Yeah," whispered Mead, lost to the picture, and suddenly seeing the Frenchman beside him in the taxicab. "Yeah, I saw him."

Then Lord's hands opened slightly. "Tell me," the hands said, and his chin lowered back onto them.

"I saw him a couple days ago. The day before the gook came. Yeah! Jesus, just like you said. He was in a cab that I jumped into, and he squealed just like a little pig. And that's what he looked like, a little fat pig in a suit. And you're right, it was white, and he kept squirming around on the seat like he had worms or something. And he asked me to go to dinner, or some fucking thing, and sure he was a faggot and I told him to shut the fuck up, and he didn't say anything else and I got out of the cab, and that was it."

Lord continued to stare, waiting patiently, letting Mead work it all out—spit everything out at random, feeding and building on his own recollections.

"I jumped into the cab just a block from the ambassador's house. The Frenchman was already in it and I told the driver to take me back to my place, and that's when the Frenchman started moving on me, and then . . . sure, we went to my building, and the Frenchman paid and I got out. Oh, shit! The cab waited there until I went in and he got my address. And the next day the gook was there."

Mead looked at Lord with awe. "How did you know? Jesus, that's fantastic. You put it all together in two minutes—the ambassador, the Frenchman, and the gook." He shook his head in wonder. "God damn."

Mead waited for some response or a question, but Lord sat as before, his face impassive.

"Well, I guess that's it," Mead said. "Except for Ambassador Marshall. This doesn't have anything to do with the other thing, just that I gotta talk to somebody about it and . . . well, Jesus, am I glad I talked to you. You'll see what I mean about this too. I mean it's nothing bad about the ambassador—in fact I hate to say anything because he's been so decent to me, I mean, really nice. I never expected that; I thought for sure he'd be a prick, but he's nice to everyone."

Mead had never talked so much in his life; suddenly everything burst from him and he wanted to tell Lord how he felt and what he thought. He wanted to pour out everything to this man who understood so much.

"Anyway," Mead said, catching himself, "I think he does some really dangerous things, and he's scaring the shit out of me. He never even wanted a bodyguard, you know—yeah, you were there, I remember, when he and General Abrams almost threw hands over that."

Mead shook his head at the memory and laughed. He felt wonderful, talking to The Phantom, who knew everything and who was listening to everything he said; he felt almost light-headed at the intimacy. "Shit, I almost died when General Abrams shoved my ass into the car. But he, the ambassador, I mean, still doesn't want a bodyguard, and he got rid of the rest of his security. That's what bothers me. You see, I'm supposed to protect him, but I don't think I can. Like today—he ordered his driver to go into Cholon. I mean, right into the middle of it, down back streets and alleys, down to an orphanage or hospital or something."

Mead shook his head. "I mean, it was bad—anybody could have nailed him, and I couldn't have done nothing. He sent his driver back, then told me to leave, ordered me to go, and then he and this woman . . ." He added quickly, making sure there was no misunderstanding, "The orphanage lady, or whatever—she's old and . . . well, kinda . . . not really pretty; I mean, it's not . . . well, you know, they're not . . . They're just friends; he's trying to help her. But there he is, all by himself down in Cholon, and I told him that was really dangerous, but I don't think he really understands how it is here. How . . . well, how you can get zapped so easily."

He shrugged again. "That's the other thing I wanted to talk to you about—he's gonna get waxed unless he's more careful, but there's nothing I can do, he's not gonna listen to some corporal."

He stopped, then sputtered on a little more as Lord continued to stare at him.

"Sometimes he just sends me off, tells me to go to the PX, and there's no one with him. It really worries me, especially now with the Frenchman and the gook."

He finished, indicating that he had nothing more to say by exhaling loudly, as though he had just completed a race, and he fell back in the chair.

Lord sat back also. His eyes eased and his features gave the faintest indication of warmth and friendliness, such a contrast to his previous behavior that Mead was as overwhelmed as a puppy.

"Thank you, Corporal," Lord said in an almost pleasant voice. "You have been intelligent, observant, loyal, and extraordinarily helpful. Is there anything I can do for you?"

Mead flushed with pleasure. "Oh, no, sir. I'm just glad I could do something."

Lord nodded. "If there ever is anything you feel I might be able to help you with . . ." A rare smile flicked across his lips. "Or even if there is something you *don't* think I could help you with—come to me."

Then he leaned forward, and with wizard's eyes drew Mead forward too, and he whispered, "I sense things too. I *feel* things—that's how I live; it's kept me alive a hundred times. It's in you too, I know. It's a priceless, rare ability. We need that."

The "we" sent shivers through Mead. The man he held in most awe, The Phantom, who in minutes had taken an obscure incident of an old Vietnamese and magically transformed it into an absolutely true tale of diabolical intrigue —this man had used the most compelling words Mead could hear: "we" and "need."

If he had just said "you," Mead's happiness would have

been complete. The CIA was beyond mystery and glamor; it was beyond the Marines and the FBI. For Mead it was a holy shrine of manhood; to be in that order was beyond his imagination, and yet Lord had intimated . . . surely he had . . . that there was a possibility.

Mead would do anything for that chance. He wanted to tell Lord that, but he was too embarrassed; maybe Lord had not meant that at all and would laugh at the mere suggestion that Mead could actually work for him.

Mead was held by Lord's gaze; drawn close, he whispered back, "Sir, if there is anything I can do, just tell me."

"I will," said Lord. "Count on that. One of these days. Soon."

Mead nodded.

Lord brought his hands up, a magician casting a spell, and he said, "But you must never mention that we talked."

Mead, trancelike, shook his head. "Never."

Then Lord broke the spell. He stood quickly, erasing the intimacy, and his face and manner were as impassive as before.

"Thank you," he said, nodding dismissal.

Mead jumped up. "Yes, sir. Good day, sir," he said, and left the room.

He almost ran down the back stairs, unable to contain his excitement and relief. He had talked with The Phantom. Maybe he was going to work with him. And everything was going to be all right—he had told Lord about the old Vietnamese and Marshall, and Lord in a second by himself had put it all together. It was unbelievable.

He was so distracted that he couldn't focus when he was pushed up against the wall.

"I'm talking to you, dirtbag. Don't ignore me. Who do you think you are, asshole?"

Mead was staring into a snarling black face. Gunnery Sergeant Robson Holman pushed him again; his head hit the wall. "Your shit don't stink now that you work for the big honcho? You see me, boy, and you say, 'Hello, Gunnery Sergeant,' 'Good day, Gunnery Sergeant,' 'How are you, Gunnery Sergeant?' "

Mead grabbed the man's wrists in so viselike a grip that

Holman could not move his hands. Holman tried to bring his knee into Mead's groin, but Mead placed his leg between Holman's so that he couldn't move.

"Fuck off, Gunnery Sergeant. Eat shit, Gunnery Sergeant. Suck my dick, Gunnery Sergeant."

The two men faced each other with murderous eyes, then Mead released his grip. Neither moved; their breath was hot and their necks bulged, but then Holman smiled evilly.

"That wasn't smart, Mead. That's gonna cost you, white boy."

"You want the nickel now, nigger?"

Holman whistled softly. "Dumb. Real dumb." Then he walked away.

Mead stared after him, then turned, sensing someone behind him, and there was Lord at the base of the stairway, watching him, his eyes as impassive as always, then Lord inclined his head slightly in what might have been a nod, and he walked off.

Mead glanced at his watch. It was almost two; Marshall might be getting back at any minute and he hadn't even reported in to Waggoner. He was famished but there wasn't time to eat. He ran down the corridor to the lobby, then to the elevators, Holman forgotten, and elated again at the thought of Lord and working for the CIA.

The guard at the glass booth waved him through. "Where's the man?" he asked.

"Beats me," said Mead. "I'm just his bodyguard."

He walked into the reception room to report to Waggoner.

Dolores Toland looked up in surprise, and the man leaning on her desk familiarly pulled away quickly.

It was the Marine aviator Mead had seen earlier. "Good afternoon, sir," Mead said to the lieutenant, then asked the secretary if Colonel Waggoner was in.

"Of course he's in," she said curtly, recovering her composure. "He works here. We *all* work here—when we don't have mornings and afternoons off and go to the PX, like you do." She turned to the lieutenant and said, "Corporal Mead is the ambassador's bodyguard, although one *rarely* sees them together."

"Lieutenant Magnuson," the officer said, extending his

308

hand to Mead, and looking at him curiously, trying to place where he had seen him before. "Good to meet you, Corporal. I'm going to fly for the ambassador."

Hearing voices, Waggoner came into the room with Lieutenant Colonel Romer.

"Where's the ambassador?" he demanded.

"I'm not really sure, sir," Mead said. "After we left the Presidential Palace, Ambassador Marshall decided to go to Cholon."

"Cholon?"

"Yes, sir. He wanted to visit a clinic, or orphanage, where that woman is—the one who was here the other day."

"Jesus Christ," muttered Waggoner.

"Then they went to lunch. He told me to come back here."

"Ambassador Marshall is in Cholon without any security?" shouted Waggoner.

"He ordered me to leave, sir. What was I to do?"

Waggoner turned to Romer. "Can you believe that? The goddamn personal representative of the President of the United States is running loose in Cholon—that's like having a rabbi run naked through Mecca."

Romer laughed. "If you'd seen him with General Westmoreland, you'd believe it."

Just then Marshall entered the office. The three officers and Mead jumped to attention.

Marshall considered them, then asked, "Is it a coup?"

He noticed his secretary behind them. "Or is Miss Toland teaching you all shorthand? They're not bothering you, are they, Dolores?"

Waggoner stepped forward. "We were about to send out a search party for you, sir."

"Well, thank you, but there won't be any need for heroics today. However, Corporal Mead is going to have to go rescue my coat and tie—I left them at the clinic. Unfortunately, Corporal, the address of the clinic is in the jacket pocket. I have no idea where it was. Perhaps the driver can recall it; better check with him. All I remember is that it was near Saint Francis Xavier Church, where the priest came from."

"That's the church where the Diems were assassinated,"

said Waggoner. "Cholon is extremely dangerous, Mr. Ambassador. The place is crawling with VC."

"I know," said Marshall. "That's why I'm sending Corporal Mead for my coat, rather than going myself."

Magnuson laughed, then caught himself immediately. "I beg your pardon, sir."

Marshall stared at him, and Waggoner said quickly, "This is Lieutenant Magnuson, sir. He has been assigned by MACV to be your pilot—he is qualified to fly fixed-wing aircraft, jet and prop, and also helicopters."

Marshall shook his hand. "That's impressive, Lieutenant. I know we'll get along very well."

He moved to Romer and shook his hand. "I'm delighted to see you again, Colonel. I never doubted General Westmoreland's word, but I know how loath he was to release you to me." He turned back to Magnuson. "So loath that I have to ask—are you really a pilot? I wouldn't be surprised if he sent me up in the air with the commissary officer."

Magnuson smiled. "Yes, sir, I really am a pilot. I was with the Marine Air Wing at Da Nang."

"Why did they send a Marine pilot from Da Nang?" Romer asked.

"I don't know, sir," said Magnuson. "Maybe just to rotate the stock—for the same reason they sent Corporal Mead down from the DMZ." He smiled. "They have army colonels for the brainwork—I guess they need a couple Marines for the dirty work: getting coats and taxiing the ambassador wherever he wishes to go."

Mead was the only one who did not laugh. How did Magnuson know that he had come down from the DMZ?

"Well," said Marshall, "I'm glad to have all of you. I think we have a very good team." He gestured to the other room. "Let's give Dolores her room back. Corporal, if you could retrieve my coat from the VC, I'll see if I can't get you some decoration." He reached for his wallet. "You'll have to take a cab because I'll need my driver shortly. Just bring it in with you in the morning—I won't need you the rest of the day. Damn! I don't have any money, I gave it all . . . Can someone lend me some money for Corporal Mead?"

They all reached for their wallets.

"That's okay, sir. I have plenty," said Mead.

"Get him a voucher," Waggoner said to Dolores. "He can pick up some money on the way down."

"No," said Marshall. "This is personal, not government. Are you sure you have enough, Corporal? All right then, I'll pay you back tomorrow. Dolores, would you remind me?"

Marshall wanted this brief, so he directed them to Waggoner's office and sat casually on the desk.

"Colonel Waggoner will shape my calendar and schedule —arrange all briefings, meetings, and appointments. Colonel Romer will coordinate all my field visits. You know where I want to go, Colonel—arrange it, and anywhere else you think I should see. Tell Lieutenant Magnuson, and he'll get us there. Working together, this should be a very smooth operation. You do all the work, tell me where and when to go, and I'll supply the body. Are there any questions? Good. I need to do some thinking."

He stood and started for his office, then turned. "Does anyone ever think about ends and means anymore? I mean, after sophomore year in college? Or do they even discuss it in college these days? You're closer than the rest of us, Lieutenant—tell me, do you think about ends and means?"

"Well, sir, I played football in college. The idea, the end, was to score. I remember the coach warning us not to draw a penalty—I think that about summed up the means."

"It's the same with women and war," Romer said. "It's not how you play the game, but whether you get laid or killed that counts."

"Probably, probably," murmured Marshall, turning away and going into his office.

Indeed, he thought, closing the door, what did it matter, ends and means? Sophomoric mind teasers; slogans for Boy Scouts; matters for the tribunals of victor nations—hardly a concern for those starving, suffering, and dying.

"Cholon," said Waggoner incredulously to the closed door. "Borrowing cab fare from a corporal. Jesus God." Then he shook his head and sighed. "That's the man you work for, Lieutenant."

Magnuson frowned and unconsciously voiced what troubled him very much. "Yes. But I like him."

Wilson Abbot Lord, easily the coldest bastard he had ever met, Magnuson thought, hadn't warned him of that possibility. Lord had spoken vaguely about "a special mission," but he, Magnuson, knew all too well what that meant and he had indicated to Lord his discomfort with this work. He had said he hoped he was finished with it, but Lord's manner was dismissive. He had been brought down from Da Nang to make a "drop," but the CIA hadn't brought him down for an ordinary one. Not to unload an NVA suspect into the ocean—this was going to be something else, something extraordinary. He had a feeling that he had been brought down to "drop" the man he was going to work for, Marshall, the special envoy of the President.

But Magnuson decided that he liked Marshall. He had never known any of the men he had dropped, not that it made a difference, he knew—he had had no choice, any more than he had a choice now. He could never tell Wilson Abbot Lord that he refused the mission—that would be suicide. He knew he would do exactly what he was ordered to do.

A complication, he realized, was going to be the corporal: he obviously wasn't very bright, but he had seen Magnuson coming down from the third floor where the CIA was. He would have to tell Lord that he might have been compromised; he'd let Lord handle that problem.

CHAPTER

• 21 •

Though no one would have guessed it from his languor, Wilson Abbot Lord did his best thinking while in motion.

Everything about the man was deceptive—ennui masked restlessness, and strong beliefs boiled beneath surface detachment.

Now, after meeting with Mead, he had to move. His thought was so active that it needed release; he had to work off the energy bursting within.

He left the room and walked down the stairs just in time to see the confrontation between Mead and Holman; he watched coolly, then moved on. The Marine could handle himself, he saw; he could be very useful, though Lord did not like to work with or depend on anyone so stupid or troubled, and a twenty-year-old youth with a previous drug problem, living with a Vietnamese whore, could be trouble. He would have to think this out carefully, he realized.

Lord knew he was called The Phantom, but the sobriquet was misleading. He did not come in at the loneliest hours and stalk corridors in the middle of the night out of stealth, but to think; he literally walked out problems and found solutions physically, as he would now. He would have liked to give thought speech, but that was not possible, so legs replaced tongue.

Silence, the inability to talk about his work, was the

hardest part of his life. It was worse than being a monk, for what did a monk have to talk about? What excitement was there to convey? What secrets burned the lips? There was no need for words in a monastery—but in his world, what tales could be told: lies, murders, intrigues to baffle a Borgia.

Yet there was no one he could tell them to. He had had such a person once, but his shark-mangled body, bound in barbed wire, washed up off Inchon seventeen years ago.

He had had no one since. One could never tell a wife secrets, not for fear of betrayal, though that was always possible, for no spy ever had a good marriage, but for her own protection: what she did not know could not hurt her or him—but what she did know could be lethal.

There was no one in the Agency to talk with, not about anything intimate or personal.

Quis custodiet ipsos custodes? Who guarded the guardians? They guarded themselves. Fear and treachery guaranteed watchfulness and restraint: like a self-cleaning oven, Agency mistakes and spills were quickly turned to ash.

Yet what secret agent did not wish to talk about his work and tell everything? Who wouldn't want the attention— look, look how clever I was, cleverer than all the others. What good is brilliance if no one knows it? That was the hardest part, he found, swallowing ego, accepting that no one could ever know what he did—silence. Like a perfect murder, that hardest part was *keeping* it perfect.

He wished he had someone to talk to now, someone with whom he could thrash out all the possibilities and complexities, for what he had just learned was more intricate and portentous than anything he had ever encountered.

The time had come to take Jeffrey Gibbon into his confidence; now was the time to test him. He had chosen Gibbon carefully. He liked his background—Dartmouth, his athletics, his military service, his politics—and he knew Gibbon's esteem for him, but he would have preferred more time to work with Gibbon before putting him to such a test. But there was no more time. Because of Marshall, the war might never be won, thousands of men would have died in vain.

What America stood for—democracy, justice, freedom

—was right; communism was wrong. It was black and white; yes the black could be lightened, and the white darkened—there could be overcast days and star-bright nights—but it was a sorry fool, he thought, who could not tell day from night, and white from black. Marshall was such a fool.

Lord walked briskly down the corridors and concentrated on the problem before him: Mead's "old gook" was Bui Cao Kim; it could be no one else. His teeth were his vanity, and consequently his undoing. That the man never realized what a giveaway they were, or learned the simple procedure of blackening them, mystified Lord.

And the "little fat pig in a suit, with worms" was Bernard Lacouture, of course; a perfect description, Lord thought—give the dumb Marine credit for that at least.

What a pair, Lacouture and Kim. But what were they up to? Lord wondered. Could Lacouture be infatuated with the Marine? Yes, that would explain his distraction at their meeting. Of course! Lacouture's agitation had not been fear but love. Christ, he had fallen in love with a Marine.

What an incredible stroke of luck, Lord thought: one couldn't hope for better leverage than love and lust. He, Lord, owned the Marine whom Lacouture wanted. Perhaps he would give Lacouture Mead—and that would save him the time-consuming legerdemain of bank accounts and the pretense of transferring money. Then later he would let the poor buggered Marine kill him in revenge. All very tidy. Moreover, with Mead in Lacouture's bed, he would be able to keep track of everything Lacouture was doing and ensure that Lacouture didn't double-cross him somehow in setting up the meeting between Marshall and the NVA.

That meeting—or rather Marshall's belief in the legitimacy of it—was essential, Lord decided: it would thoroughly discredit Marshall as a dupe of murderous, treacherous communists—thinking he was on a peace mission, like Hitler's poor mad Hess, while in reality Lord lured him into an ambush.

Also, that scenario solved the troubling problem of Lieutenant Magnuson, whom Lord had just discovered was regrettably bothered by his conscience. The man had been useful in the past and would be too in this mission, but now he would have to be taken out—bad consciences caused guilt, remorse, and worst of all, the need to confess; that was an unacceptable, and fatal, flaw.

Conscience was not something that troubled Jeffrey Gibbon, he felt certain, but now was the time to find out, to see if he, Lord, was right about Jeff.

Lord always had a backup plan. Rarely did an operation go as planned. There had to be a contingency for every step. Gibbon would provide the contingency in case the meeting between Marshall and the NVA fell through.

He climbed the stairs up to his corridor.

Gibbon, leaning back in his chair, feet on his desk, jumped up as Lord entered.

"Afternoon, Mr. Lord." He held up a manual he had been reading. "I was just going over the Huey."

"Learn anything?"

Gibbon shook his head. "It's like looking at centerfolds— I've seen the real thing, I don't need pictures for reminders."

"Come with me," Lord said curtly. "We're going for a walk." He left the room.

Gibbon tossed the manual on his desk and followed quickly. He knew this was serious; he had often observed Lord walking corridors and knew that was when Lord did his thinking. He had been waiting for this. Until now Lord had treated him with courtesy and consideration, but he had maintained a great distance; Gibbon knew he was on trial. He sensed that the trial period was over—now he was going to be tested.

Lord walked down to the first floor, then through the lobby and outside, Gibbon a respectful half-step behind him.

Gibbon put on his aviator sunglasses.

"Take those off, Jeffrey. I want to see into your eyes when I talk to you."

Gibbon put them back in his jacket pocket.

"I joined the CIA in 1947," Lord said flatly. "After I graduated from college."

He didn't say Harvard, Gibbon noted, though Gibbon

knew that was where he had gone. This was not a practiced recitation, he realized; he had a feeling that maybe he was the first person Lord was ever telling this.

"That was my first job, my first venture into the real world; I came from a fairly wealthy family. By then Bradley Marshall—we are the same age—had fought in the Second World War, made twenty-three beach landings in the Pacific, had a Silver and Bronze Star, and had been wounded twice. His family was even wealthier than mine. Why do you suppose he joined the Marines at seventeen?"

"To get away from home," Gibbon said. "His father was an alcoholic and his mother a bitch from Newport."

Lord nodded. "So in 1947, I went to work for the CIA, and Marshall went to Harvard. In the early fifties, we both ended up in Korea; I was on my first overseas mission—but why was he there, Jeffrey?"

They had walked behind the building and were alone on the vast expanse of lawn.

Gibbon took off his jacket and slung it over his shoulder. "I know you don't like my sexual references, sir, but the only thing I can compare war to is fucking. How do you describe that—it feels good? The earth moved?"

"I don't mind your sexual references, Jeff, I just keep hoping for more articulate and intellectual expression."

Gibbon said matter-of-factly, "There is a Goya painting, *Saturn Devouring His Son,* that depicts war. Saturn, in the act of eating his own children, has a frenzied, rapturous look on his face. War *is* rapturous—it is the selfish gene unleashed, screaming its existence. We love war—more than anything; it's more compelling than sex. War is man stripped bare, pulsating, crystallized. Marshall went back to war because he loved it."

Lord stopped walking and stared at Gibbon.

Gibbon grinned. "And you thought I was just a pretty boy."

Lord studied Gibbon's eyes. "Why is Marshall so dangerous?"

Gibbon didn't flinch under the scrutiny. "Because he's afraid of what he's learned. He doesn't want to like war. He took a bite of the apple and now he wants to regurgitate it; he wants to stuff the pestilence back in the box, rejar the genie."

Gibbon shook his head. "But it can't be done. Man can't forget or unlearn war—for that the child would have to forget his hand and unlearn his fist." Gibbon smiled, almost tauntingly. "And never find his dick."

Lord stared at him for a long minute, then he smiled with genuine warmth and pride, and he resumed walking.

"I was about your age when I went to Korea. I really believed in what we were doing. I was young and filled with passion."

He spoke with a fervor Gibbon had never heard in his voice. "It truly was cloak and dagger back in those days, and there really were trench-coated Russians and secret meetings. I was teamed with a man I'd known for years. We'd gone to college together, even double-dated together. His name was Brent Harwood."

He shook his head, lost in memory. "Jesus, it was scary. We were on a mission having to do with the Inchon landing. We were way behind enemy lines, and we were terrified. A hundred times we thought we were going to die. We bared ourselves to each other, and at night we'd sleep huddled like lovers for warmth. We talked of growing old together."

Lord stopped and faced Gibbon. "He was the only man I've ever been close to. The Chinese caught him. They wrapped him in razor-sharp barbed wire and tossed him alive into the ocean."

Lord took out his own sunglasses and put them on, his voice matter-of-fact. "What was left of his body washed up days later. He had struggled to get out, cut himself bloody, then the sharks had hit."

He resumed walking. "I never let myself get close to anyone after that. Nor have I ever told anyone about Brent."

He didn't speak for several minutes. They reached the back fence of the embassy grounds and walked the perimeter.

"Communism is a malignancy I've fought for twenty years," Lord said with barely controlled anger. "It's in the lymph nodes and has spread everywhere. Now it's in Vietnam, and if they win, they'll turn this country into a prison camp like Russia, China, and North Korea."

The anger broke through, and its intensity surprised Gibbon.

"Marshall is going to let it happen. He's thinking about his son, as if no one else had a son, and he's wrapped himself in principles and conscience and ethics, and he's going to let the communists take over this country."

Lord said furiously, "My job is to see that he doesn't succeed, and I don't give a shit how it's done. I'll leave conscience to the historians—after I've guaranteed it's our historians who write the history. I'll let them indulge themselves in the niceties of right and wrong, good and evil, ends and means. I'll let the academicians debate the minutiae, let the liberals argue the indistinctions, as those in the tumbrils on their way to the Concorde questioned the new calendar—was it Fructidor or August that their heads were going to roll? And as so many Jews argued rabbinical points in the boxcars on their way to Dachau."

He stopped and took off his glasses. He looked into Gibbon's eyes and his voice was calm. "I don't like violence. It brutalizes people and makes them stupid. Force and violence dull intellect and reason. Terror destroys sense. I am firmly opposed to the Phoenix Program and expressed my reservations all the way to Langley."

"I didn't know that, sir. I thought everyone was behind the program."

"Everybody is, except me. It's going to get out of hand— violence always does. By letting low-level field CIA agents and local Vietnamese authorities identify and terminate VC cadre, the program will soon become nothing more than random murder. Soon there will be competitions for identifying enemy cadre, then quotas set, and the goal— intelligence gathering—will be lost as the 'body count' becomes all-important."

Lord shook his head. "Violence is almost always counterproductive. And it's also irreversible. You can change your mind, alter an idea, revise a theory, but you can't undo a violence. It causes wounds and makes enemies. It's so easy that people begin to rely on it, then become inured to it."

He looked intently into Gibbon's eyes. "It is almost always wrong. I want to impress that on you; I want you to learn that."

"Yes, sir."

"But there are times when it is absolutely necessary—when there is no alternative."

"Yes, sir."

"I think now is such a time. I am going to ask you to do something, but I want you to understand that you do not have to do it. You are not a robot; you are not my puppet. I am not a robot, or anyone's puppet. I have refused assignments—not only is that our right, it is sometimes our duty. Do you understand that?"

"Yes, sir, I do."

"And I swear to you, on Brent Harwood's dead body, which I pulled from the ocean, that I will not hold it against you if you refuse. It will not change our relationship or the fine opinion I have of you."

"Yes, sir."

"I want you to sabotage Ambassador Marshall's helicopter. I want it to go down, and in such a way that the malfunction can never be traced."

Gibbon looked directly into Lord's eyes and he did not hesitate. "When do you want me to do this, sir?"

"I will not stand by you if something goes wrong. I did not order you to do this. In fact, we never had this discussion."

"I understand, sir."

Lord nodded. "I will tell you when."

Gibbon did not look away. "I have never kissed anybody's ass in my life, but I want you to understand this, Mr. Lord: I believe in you. Thank you for taking me into your confidence, sir. I would do whatever you said, sir."

"Thank you, Jeff. Thank you very much," Lord said genuinely.

Bernard Lacouture felt his pulse; it was racing. He held his chest; his heart thumped wildly.

Oh, the wretched gook; he's killing me, Lacouture thought wildly. A man's heart was good for only so many beats, and he was using up a year's worth waiting for Bui Cao Kim.

He was overheated too, and he fanned himself with the newspaper that he had been too agitated to read. There were crumbs all over his suit, and jam was smudged on his jacket. The damnable Kim—where was he? He was doing this on purpose of course—perversity, that's all there was to it, oriental cruelty. Torture! And cassis jam too! It would never come out, Lacouture thought.

He clutched his chest. The palpitations were irregular; he was going to have a heart attack. It was all that coffee, of course—morning chicory coffee, café au lait, then espresso. How many cups had he had waiting—seven, eight? And all that sugar—jams and pastries; no wonder his pulse was like a Rossini overture.

He had sat on the Continental terrace for five hours, since midmorning, through lunch with the Americans. I should be dead already, he thought. The vulgarity! The din!

Kim had done that on purpose too; the evil, sadistic dwarf. He would pay for that!

Oh, dear God, he thought, realizing that he couldn't feel his legs; he had sat so long they were asleep. He tried to push his chair away, but his numbed legs anchored him. He could not move. He would be here forever. He would have to sit through dinner with the Americans! He struggled and shoved, nearly falling over backward, but at last he was able to get his chair far enough from the table so that he could massage his legs. They moved. At least he would be able to get away.

If only his heart would calm.

It had been altogether a wasted day. He had not been able to read the paper or concentrate on anything, even his discussion with Lord.

He shuddered at the thought of Wilson Abbot Lord. What a reptile! An American Bui Cao Kim, only not as trustworthy. Completely treacherous because he believed in what he was doing.

Imagine!

He was a zealot. God spare me the moral man, he thought: give me the immoral one any day.

All Americans were zealots; they were frightening. It was because they were so young and immature, Lacouture thought.

Germans were frightening too, but in their case it was arrested development—true anal fixation. And the Chinese and Vietnamese were fearsome, but they were just bloodthirsty—primitives.

Americans were simply dangerous—all that nonsense about ideals and principles; all that religion. Like Santa Claus and tooth fairies—perfectly harmless in children, but disturbing in the postadolescent.

And all that energy—busy, busy, busy. Ideals, beliefs, morals—too exhausting!

The hypocrisy! The self-righteousness! The stupidity!

He felt his chest and checked his pulse. Much better.

Contemplating Lord and the Americans helped.

Lord. To think, Lord actually supposed he would trust him to open a bank account and transfer money.

Exquisite!

The Americans wanted to kill their envoy—whom else could Lord be talking about?—a reasonable desire no doubt, certainly nothing out of the ordinary, but to expect *him*, Lacouture, to help on the promise of a bank transfer—absolutely outrageous!

He was expected to trust a CIA agent to deliver on a promise? His word? The mind positively reeled.

He checked his pulse again. It was nearly back to normal.

Cash! Half in advance, that is what he required. The money would be handed over in person, laundered neatly through Hong Kong, and deposited in his secret Swiss account; then and only then would he dangle the bait before Marshall and set the plan into effect.

His part was easy; politicians and diplomats were hopelessly gullible. The hard part—the pilot, getting the plane on target, and the enemy's hitting it—depended on others. Chancy indeed; that is why he required his money up front—he wasn't about to forgo it because of map error, or a nearsighted soldier using a Russian rocket that would probably malfunction.

Yes, cash. Cash for him and his savage. If Lord was serious, he would pay it—simplicity itself. If Lord hesitated with the money, then there was no deal.

He would have enough money from the communists anyway—not as much as Lord was going to pay him, but enough for retirement in Cannes. The communist offer, he felt sure, was legitimate—when they offered money, they meant it. Money was almost a foreign tongue to them; they were not glib about it like the Americans, so when they spoke of cash, it was genuine.

He had made contact with the communists immediately following his talk with Lord, and their response had been remarkably quick, though not in the way Lord would have expected. Yes, they would help arrange a time and place to meet with this important American—but for a real meeting, not an assassination; they wanted to negotiate with him, not terminate him.

Now both parties, CIA and NVA, were going to pay him to arrange the meeting. He would do that. What actually happened at the meeting—negotiation or termination—was of no consequence to him. All he had to do was keep Wilson Abbot Lord in the dark about the true motives of the NVA—a risky proposition, but he was confident.

He felt his wrist; his pulse was perfectly normal. He took a deep breath and exhaled happily; he was going to live after all.

But then, coming up the stairs, literally stealing up them as in some ridiculous melodrama, was Bui Cao Kim, and Lacouture suddenly couldn't breathe and his chest pounded furiously.

Kim looked about stealthily.

Idiot! Lacouture wanted to scream. You do this every day—everybody from here to Mandalay knows who you are and what you're doing.

Kim crept closer.

Fool! Lacouture clutched his chest; he was going to die before the wretched gook got to the table.

Finally Kim reached his side; he looked about a final time, then pulled a folded piece of paper from his pocket and set it before Lacouture.

Lacouture grabbed, nearly ripping the page in half as he opened it. His hands shook so badly that he couldn't read a character, except to see the house was upside down. Imbecile!

He pushed himself away from the table and nearly fell trying to stand, his legs having fallen asleep again. He righted himself and stuffed the piece of paper in his jacket. "Come," he said, throwing some bills on the table for the waiter and making his way haphazardly across the terrace, kicking his leg every third or fourth step to bring it back to life, at the same time trying to keep his dignity and cover the jam stain on his jacket.

"Where have you been?" he fairly shrieked when he finally reached the sidewalk.

Kim answered in Japanese.

"What?" screamed Lacouture.

Kim repeated it patiently in Japanese.

"Well, Mr. Lord saw you too," Lacouture said in exasperated French. "He knows you, just as you know him. And speak French; I can't think in Japanese."

People turned at Lacouture's raised voice and watched the two of them walk down the sidewalk. Lacouture, with his strange little kicking step, walked into the street and was nearly hit by a pedicab.

"Well?" he demanded when he scrambled to safety.

"He lives there," Kim said cryptically.

"Yes? And?"

"I think you should be very careful. He is dangerous; he is a very hard man."

Lacouture shuddered with pleasure. "And?"

"He has a woman."

"Pah."

"She is a whore."

"Of course she's a whore!" he yelled. "What else could she be?"

"She is a dope addict."

324

Lacouture nearly stopped on the sidewalk to throttle him. "Of course she is. What whore isn't? I didn't send you there to find out things I could have figured out on the terrace."

"He took her from a brothel just a few days ago."

Lacouture grunted at that breach of economics. "It's cheaper in the whorehouse—no overhead."

"But not so convenient," Kim pointed out.

Lacouture nodded. Convenience and cost were weighty matters for individual determination, not really arguable points. He opened his hands and shrugged. "Is she pretty?" he asked, and his mind flooded voyeuristically.

Kim shrugged. "She is dirty."

That fueled the fantasy—the savage and a dirty slut. Exquisite! Lacouture swooned.

"Her teeth are stained," Kim added.

The fantasy fell in shards to the sidewalk. "Tell me the rest," he said in disgust.

"He works at the American embassy during the day."

"What is his weakness?" Lacouture asked.

Kim had anticipated that question. He had avoided Lacouture not out of perversity, but in order to think this matter through carefully, then he had labored the entire day putting it on paper in his beautiful calligraphy that was now crumpled in Lacouture's pocket. He did not mention the important American.

"The girl is his weakness, I think," said Kim. He tapped his chest. "Love."

"A whore?" Lacouture was incredulous.

"Many men love whores," Kim said. "Some even marry them."

Lacouture stared at him balefully.

They were on Tu Do Street where they both felt comfortable, the midway of the carnival before the show started: whores milled together on the street without makeup; brothel-keepers lounged with upturned faces, soaking up the last sun before disappearing into their dens. Drug peddlers cruised lazily; the beggars were picking out their places, putting down their mats and arranging their displays. The freak show was setting up; the lights were out, no neon flashed, no noise blared from the bars.

"You must help me," Lacouture said.

"It will not be easy," Kim answered. "This man is not like . . . others." He meant Lacouture's Legionnaire. "Money may not be enough."

"Nonsense," said Lacouture. "Money is always enough. Even reason has a price—it's called cost effectiveness."

But he could see that Kim was worried; he was going to have to coax him.

"My dear Kim," he said. "We are talking about an impoverished, ignorant soldier. I want to barter for his meager assets—though I hardly imagine them to be meager. I want to make a business proposition. I want his body. I want him to sell it to me. I will pay for it. What is the problem?"

What could be more reasonable? he thought.

Kim was doubtful. "He is an American."

Lacouture drew himself up indignantly.

"Are you suggesting," he said coldly, "that only the French and Vietnamese sell themselves."

His look was withering. "You think Americans don't? To be sure, they sell others first, but in a capitalistic pinch, they would certainly not hesitate to sell themselves."

Kim could not explain it, though it was clear in his mind, and any explanation he gave would only aggravate Lacouture more. How could he say that yes, the French and Vietnamese were whores, but the Americans were—what was it the gap-toothed whore had said? Not principled, but . . . heart. Yes, they had this weakness of the heart. This American had a heart; he was going to be difficult and dangerous.

"Perhaps there are other ways," said Kim.

"Besides money?" Lacouture was dumbfounded. "What?"

"Force maybe. It might be necessary to . . . take his woman."

"What would I want with his wretched woman?"

"Kidnap her."

"Ah," he cooed in understanding. "A hostage."

He considered it a moment. "It would certainly be cheaper, wouldn't it. All I'd have to do is feed her."

"Drugs," Kim said.

"My dear Kim, you are quite wonderful. Dope her senseless. What could he do? Report it? Who would care about a missing whore? Oh, excellent, my dear Kim. Let's do it. Kidnap her immediately!"

Kim was not prepared for that. While no one would care about a missing whore, if the bodyguard to this important American complained, there might be trouble. And Kim was not yet ready to tell Lacouture about the important American his savage guarded.

"First you should offer money," said Kim. "That is the easiest way."

"I suppose it would be," said Lacouture after considering a moment. To shelter a drug-addicted whore would not be simple or inexpensive or without risk.

"All right, all right," he said in exasperation. "What amount should I offer?"

Kim said with intended irony, "You would know the exchange rate better than I."

Lacouture curled his lip, both at Kim and the thought of money. Was nothing sacred? How could anyone discuss money over such a matter—love?

It would have to be a large sum, of course, an amount the soldier could not turn down—no point wasting time bargaining. He would have to handle this himself; certainly he could not allow Kim to know the amount of money he was prepared to pay.

A large sum in an arrangement he negotiated himself—how exciting! All he needed was a plan to make contact so he could offer his proposition. The money was no problem—with what Lord and the NVA were going to pay him, he could purchase a battalion of soldiers.

Then, surprising even Kim, and sending him into near panic, he grabbed his arm and dragged him across the street to confront Wilson Abbot Lord, whom he had observed following them since they left the Continental.

Lacouture took out his handkerchief and mopped his brow, then he flapped it in Lord's face.

"Cash, my dear American. Only cash—no checks, banks, promissory notes, or used tires. Half in advance, in my hand, *chéri. Au revoir, au revoir, chéri.*"

Waving the handkerchief, he flounced away.

CHAPTER

• 22 •

Landis watched the rat scurry across the underground bunker. Rats were his only company at night. He opened a C ration can and threw chunks to where it had darted between field packs. Then he placed a piece of meat in a trap and slid the trap toward the packs.

Rats weren't stupid, he knew, and it had seen him set the trap, so it was fair; what it did was its decision. He waited, making radio security checks without taking his eyes from the trap.

The rat crept out, tentatively inspected the bait, then moved back behind the packs.

Landis glanced at his watch, stood, and went to the corner where Sergeant Brock slept. He bent over, but as always, before his hand touched the sergeant, Brock woke warily.

Landis stepped back. "It's five."

Brock closed his eyes. "Okay. I'm awake."

Landis went to the other corner. "Lieutenant?"

Bishop stirred, rolled toward him, and focused.

"It's five, sir."

Bishop scrunched tighter. "All right. You can leave now."

Finally released, and outside, Landis took a deep breath, filling himself with the crisp morning, and started toward his own bunker, crossing the dark terrain with eyes closed, trying to maneuver without seeing, stumbling only once.

Although he had been up all night, he was not tired. He wanted to run or wrestle or scream at the top of his lungs—anything to give life to himself, expression to the exuberance he felt. But there was nothing in the darkness, and none to share with, only a few men wrapped in ponchos, staring dully toward the wire.

At his bunker he hesitated; he didn't want to go in, but there was nothing else to do. He thought he might write his parents, but letters took so long, and he remembered, he had written yesterday. He had a book from Coney, but he could not get past the third page because there were too many words he did not understand, and the story didn't make any sense anyway. Coney told him it was about a whale, but he really wasn't interested in whales. Everyone else was asleep, he wasn't hungry, and he had decided about his car—black exterior, and black interior—so there was nothing to do.

He dropped to the sand to do push-ups. He would count to ten, then start over, so he never knew how many he did—that way there was no goal. When he tired, he rolled over and did sit-ups, counting in the same manner, doing them at amazing speed, his body flexing like a spring. Throughout the day, whenever bored, or pent-up, he exercised. He possessed incredible strength and speed, and the others teased him about his muscular development, saying he looked like those models in body-building magazines who everybody knew were queer.

He grunted from the strain and his muscles ached, but he drove harder, because he had been told exercising never did any good until it hurt.

An angry voice called from inside the bunker. "What's going on out there?" Josh Martin crawled to the opening. "It sounds like pigs fucking out here."

Landis stopped. "I thought you were sleeping."

"I was, asshole." He pulled back and crawled under his poncho. Landis followed inside, crouched against the wall, and palmed sweat from his body. "Hey, I was listening to the radio and heard about a patrol that got ambushed. One of the guys is MIA. The gooks took him. You know the tortures they got? I heard they cut your fingers off joint by joint, then poke out your eyes. Or jab a needle down your dick. You think I wouldn't talk? Man, I'd tell them anything they wanted to know. They couldn't get me to stop talking."

Martin dug deeper into his poncho. "You don't know anything."

"I could draw them a map."

"Shit. They know where everything is, it's their fucking country."

Landis tried to think of something he knew that the enemy might not. At last he shook his head. "You're right. Snuffies don't know anything." He brightened. "Then they wouldn't have to torture me."

"You're right. They'd just shoot your dumb ass."

Landis looked at him smugly. "Well, they ain't gonna capture me." He dove on Martin. "I got you. I caught you, you dirty Marine. I'm gonna cut your balls off."

He jumped up and down on the struggling figure until they both collapsed laughing. Then they talked about what ration cans they would open for breakfast. Afterward, they washed and shaved, then tried to think of something to make the day pass faster.

In the main bunker, the two men lay unwilling to rise. At last Bishop rolled over. He clasped his hands behind his head and stared up at the planked ceiling. "What are you gonna do when you get back, Gunny?"

"Fuck. Eat. Eat and fuck. Fuck and eat."

Bishop traced the cracks above him. "I can't decide what to do."

"I thought you were going to play football."

"Not for a living. I wasn't that good. Maybe I'll go back to school—get a master's degree. Or maybe I'll stay in. There could be worse things."

"What?"

Suddenly there was a snap, a single high-pitched scream, the trap thrashing against the field packs, then silence.

"God damn that Landis," Bishop said in disgust. "I've told him a hundred times not to do that. One of these days I'm gonna set a trap for that son of a bitch. Now I gotta clean it up. What does he want to kill rats for anyway?"

"Rats are dirty," Brock said.

"Not to other rats. Maybe he had a family."

Brock looked over at him from under his poncho. "Maybe you better stay in, Lieutenant. I don't think you're going to make it in the real world."

The radio crackled; Bishop flung off his poncho and went to answer it. The call was for routine logistical information. Bishop snapped off the answers to the company commander, then repeated his request for withdrawal. The response was negative again.

Bishop tossed down the handset and bent over to make coffee, lighting a heat tablet under a can of water. "That's it then. I gotta go up there."

"Where?"

"The ridge. Remember 'interdict'? Well, this is it."

"You looking for another medal, Lieutenant?"

Bishop poured the boiling water into his canteen and stirred in a packet of coffee granules. "I have a plan."

Brock pulled his poncho about him. "You better get the guy who makes the plans for the gooks." He disappeared in the poncho. "I don't want to hear no lieutenant's plan."

Bishop ignored him. "I'm going to put a two-man killer team on the ridge tonight. When the gooks come down, they'll ambush them."

There was no answer.

"Two men with sniper scopes. I gotta do it; it's the only thing that will give us time."

Brock's voice came from the poncho, "Stop playing games, Lieutenant. You're gonna get two men killed. Two more."

"I fucked up once, Gunny, I know that. I can't just sit here and wait till they hit us again; I have to hit first. This is my chance to make up for the last time."

"Or to fuck up even worse."

Bishop shook his head. "Two men can do this, Gunny, I know it. Just two men. Someone who's been there. Sutherland or Frizzell? Which one, Gunny?"

Brock turned away. "I don't want any part of this, Lieutenant."

Bishop remembered the look in Frizzell's eyes. "Frizzell. And one more. Somebody you could trust completely." He thought a moment. "Landis. Frizzell and Landis. They could do it."

"You know you picked the two dumbest men on the hill?" Brock asked.

In early afternoon Bishop left the bunker. The sky was clear, with no sign of the approaching monsoon season. The night would be perfect for sniper scopes.

Landis was reading a comic book when Bishop crouched at the bunker opening. Bishop saw him intently following the cartoon blocks, his eyes slowly traversing the page. When he heard Bishop, Landis looked up with pleased expectancy.

"What you reading, Matt?"

"It's about Wonderdog. He's my favorite. You want it when I'm done, Lieutenant?"

Bishop smiled. "Yeah. When you're done."

Landis pointed to a pile neatly stacked in a corner. "Anytime you want, you can borrow one." He held up a heavy book. "Or you can have this fucking thing. It's Coney's. About some whale or something, but I can't get anything out of it."

Bishop stared into the eager face that carried not a trace of age or anxiety. "I got a special job for you, Matt. I want you at the bunker in an hour. Bring rations for one night."

Landis nodded, but before he could ask anything, Bishop was gone.

He found Frizzell sitting outside his bunker with Coney. He bantered with them a moment then said seriously to Frizzell, "I want you to show me the enemy positions on the ridge. I want you ready in an hour. I need someone who's been there before. I hate to have you go again so soon, but I need you."

"I don't mind, Lieutenant."

Bishop stared at him curiously. "Don't you?"

Frizzell smiled. "I ain't got anything else to do."

Bishop studied his face carefully. In it was only innocence, a completely smooth, clean face, unlined and unconcerned. Bishop turned to the ridge, then back again to Frizzell. "You like the killing, Les?"

Frizzell shook his head. "It ain't that, Lieutenant. I just like to go out there. It makes the time go faster."

When the two came into the bunker, Bishop was strapping on his ammunition belts. He handed Landis and Frizzell rifles. "These are sniper scopes. They're infra-red so you can see at night."

They brought the rifles to their shoulders and stared through the scopes to the dark corners of the bunker.

Landis whistled. He brought the rifle down and handled it admiringly. "What's infra-red?"

"Something like X-ray," Bishop said. "You can see in the dark, but no one can see you. We're going to find a good ambush site, and you're going to stay there until they come down tonight."

Frizzell stared at him dubiously.

"They won't see you in the dark, and you'll be able to get off at least ten shots before they can react. Then toss grenades and run like hell. We'll check the area carefully before to make sure no one is there. They won't come down until late. When you start firing, they'll scatter. You'll be gone before they have a chance, and I'll call artillery as soon as you get out."

Landis was impressed. "I think it's a great plan."

Frizzell thought a moment, then shrugged. "Okay."

"I picked you because you're the best shots we have, and because I trust you guys."

They looked pleased and fondled the rifles.

"This is real important. Everyone is depending on you." He patted them on their shoulders and pointed to the stairway.

Outside they waited on the crest of the hill, staring at the darkening sky. "Afraid?" Bishop asked Landis.

Landis smiled. "Nope," he said, and punched Frizzell playfully. Bishop thought of a child, a healthy, happy child with a rifle.

In Frizzell's face, Bishop saw the mask forming. The face was not cruel, but it seemed as if a hand was passing over it, smoothing the mold, tightening the muscles about the eyes and mouth. I was right, Bishop thought, looking at the two almost proudly—a killer wolf and a murderous child.

The three of them moved down the hill, through the wire, and by dusk reached the base of the ridge. They searched the area quickly, until Bishop was satisfied the enemy was not there.

Frizzell led them to the bunker complex. He knelt and found the booby traps intact. "No one's touched these since we were here. Why didn't they come back?"

Bishop pondered the enemy position. It made no sense for the enemy to have abandoned the bunkers to a few uncomplicated booby traps. He glanced skyward, watching the remaining light being squeezed out by the horizon. He motioned north.

They moved up the ridge and stopped on a small knoll overlooking a clearing. Frizzell pointed to several mounds on the opposite crest.

Bishop knew the danger; snipers could be watching, just waiting for them to cross, for this was the main enemy site.

The other bunkers had been a decoy.

He rubbed his eyes and held his breath. Either the enemy is there and I will die, or they are not there and I will live. I am betting my life on this. He concentrated, then slowly let out his breath.

He opened his eyes and tapped Landis. "We're going across."

Landis chewed gum and glanced casually to the mounds, then he nodded unperturbed.

Frizzell squinted at the hill. "I think they're there."

"No," said Bishop, then he looked at Landis. "Ready?"

Landis smiled. "Keep your ass down, Lieutenant."

They bolted, running a wide dodging pattern. Bishop ran ear cocked for a rifle crack, then dove for cover on the other crest. Landis surveyed the hill and hid in the trees. Bishop motioned Frizzell across, and the three explored the ridge extension.

The entire area was a huge, nearly complete bunker complex with mortar sites and stacked ammunition. The bunkers could easily hold a hundred men. In another day the enemy would be able to launch an attack the hill could not possibly withstand.

Bishop's blood pumped wildly. The night was closing in; the darkness was alive with movement and sound. A short distance from the complex, he found a small rise concealed by heavy brush. "This is it," he said. "You've got perfect line of fire and plenty of cover."

Landis and Frizzell positioned themselves and sighted through the scopes. Bishop walked to the bunkers and studied the ambush site, then went back. "They won't be able to see you."

They looked at him anxiously. Even Landis was afraid now.

"You know what to do," Bishop said. "They won't be down until late. I don't have to tell you what this means; you can see what they're doing here." He touched them both on the shoulder, then stood, glanced about a final time, and moved rapidly down the slope and disappeared.

The two sat motionless as a light breeze rustled the foliage. Landis stroked the cold metal of the rifle; he shivered as tensing pleasure rippled his body.

Frizzell repositioned his legs to ease growing numbness. His fear and anxiety were gone; he knew that if the enemy had observed them, they would have struck by now. He nudged Landis. "What time is it?"

"Nine-ten."

Frizzell rubbed his sides under the flak jacket. "I'm freezing."

They huddled closer. Landis brought the rifle to his shoulder, squirming into a better position. Through the scope he could see the clearing starkly illuminated. He lowered the rifle. "We're gonna get 'em, I know it." Excitement welled within him. He tried to check his agitation, but he had never remained still for so long. He took a deep breath and sighted it again. "Christ, I wish they'd come," he said.

"What time is it now?"

"Nine-twenty."

"Are you sure that thing's working?"

336

Landis brought the watch to his ear. He nodded, then chanted softly to himself, "C'mon, c'mon."

"It's too early," Frizzell said. "They won't come for another hour at least."

"Jesus, I don't think I can stand it." Landis laid aside his rifle and fumbled in his trousers for a can of rations.

"How can you eat?" Frizzell asked in amazement.

"I'm hungry."

"Christ, if I ate, I'd throw up. Aren't you worried?"

Landis scooped meat into his mouth. "It's a good plan." He ate contentedly, then belched.

Before them the brush rustled, and they brought up their rifles. Landis peered through the scope, then relaxed when he saw a lynx. He grinned at the image and squeezed his finger off to the side of the trigger, forming a silent bang with his lips. The animal passed through the clearing and disappeared.

Landis lowered his rifle. "I got it. He's dead."

They sat silently for several minutes, then Frizzell asked, "What time is it now?"

"Nine-fifty."

"Jesus, is that all?"

Landis's hand played nervously with the rifle, then he felt in his trousers. He remembered he had already eaten his rations and whispered to Frizzell, "You gonna eat your chow?"

"You pig."

"Man, I'm hungry. If you ain't gonna eat yours, can I have it?"

Frizzell handed him the can. Landis studied the label in the dark. "What is it?"

"What do you care, you'd eat shit balls. Anyway, it all tastes the same."

"I just like to know what I'm eating." Landis busied himself with the can. When he finished, he wiped his mouth with his arm and placed the can beside the other. Then he put it on top. Unsatisfied, he changed the order and finally again placed them side by side. He stared at his work, then placed twigs about the cans. Satisfied, he sat back to wait.

Frizzell shivered. "I'm freezing." He sighted through the

rifle, breathed deeply, then took it from his shoulder. He wished Coney were with him. He didn't like being out like this. He knew it was important, and he guessed it was a good plan, but he didn't like ambushes. He didn't really want to kill the enemy, and deep down he hoped they wouldn't come. If they did, well, he would kill them, but it would be better if nothing happened.

He sighed and cradled the rifle close to his body. He shivered against the cold and tried to think of something to pass the time, but unaccountably, a powerful sexual urge passed through him. He sat up straighter and asked irritably, "What time is it now?"

"Ten-fifteen."

"Jesus, this is the longest night in the world."

Landis sank back in disgust. "Maybe they won't come." He grew angry. "Fuckers. What if they don't come?"

"It's still too early."

Landis sighted again. He could see the clearing perfectly. He imagined the enemy before him and he squeezed on the trigger, silently forming the words—blam, blam, blam. He turned eagerly to Frizzell. "Oh, man, wouldn't it be fantastic if they show up?"

Against his will, excitement gripped Frizzell. They would be heroes. They would really have done something important; even Coney would have to admit it.

The brush stirred. They brought their rifles up. For five minutes they watched the clearing, bodies vised with tension, but they saw nothing and there was no further sound. Landis lowered his rifle and Frizzell leaned back, drawing a deep breath to relax.

Landis's hand stroked the rifle absently, the metal warming to the friction, sending pleasure through his fingers. "I'm going crazy." His restlessness grew. He felt desperately alive. His hand thumped the rifle stock nervously. When he was this charged, he always exercised, but now there was no outlet.

With his fear, Frizzell's coldness was gone too. He felt sweat on his hands and wiped them against his trousers. His legs ached and he stretched noiselessly, rubbing his calves and thighs. The touch made him acutely aware of his body.

He continued to massage his flesh until he felt sexual arousal. He stopped and pressed into his groin, squirming in frustration.

Landis leaned closer. "What's wrong?"

Frizzell said sheepishly, "I'm horny."

"Here? Now?"

"I can't help it. I keep thinking about women."

Landis said proudly, "I had clap four times."

"What do you screw, dogs?"

Landis grinned. "Anything." He sighted into the clearing with his rifle. "If you're horny, beat off—I don't care. Except it might slow you down—I never jack off before a patrol. I'd hate to get killed over something like that. Probably you oughta wait till you get back. You and Coney do it together?"

Frizzell was affronted. "Fuck no."

Landis brought his rifle into his shoulder. "Shhh."

Almost imperceptibly there was a change in the night, noises disharmonious with the softer sounds of the brush, movement heightening the air. There was gentle, tentative pressure on the vegetation, rustling that could not be the wind. They scanned the clearing, a surrealistic image of whites and blacks filtered through a rose optic.

Suddenly Landis jumped at the magnification of a man crouching in the opposite treeline. He nudged Frizzell. Neither breathed as they watched the enemy soldier. They could see his mouth tighten as he moved into the clearing, going swiftly to different bunkers, stopping a few feet from them. His image was so large in the sights that they could see the pupils of his eyes.

Frizzell aimed at the bridge of his nose and waited for the man to give a sign of discovering them. If he even raises his eyes, I'll blow his head off, he thought, but the soldier turned and whistled softly.

Immediately twenty men emerged from the trees and entered the bunker complex. Voices and orders filled the night.

Frizzell and Landis waited until they were sure the entire element had arrived, then Landis pointed to a group clus-

339

tered together and indicated himself. He motioned to another group and tapped Frizzell. Frizzell nodded and shifted his rifle to them.

Landis focused on seven men huddled around a bunker. He sighted on them a full minute, trying to decide the best way to get as many as possible, calculating different angles. If he shot the two men in the entrance, their bodies would block it and he could pick off the others easily. Two men stood side by side, and he wondered if he could kill them both with one bullet. He squirmed with excitement, then steadied himself and closed his eyes, drawing in his breath. He opened his eyes, refocused on the sights, and saw the bead resting on the back of a man's head. Slowly he let out his breath.

Frizzell saw the men so clearly he could distinguish buttons on their clothing. It was happening just as the lieutenant had said. He watched them set up aiming stakes for mortars. Bastards. Mortars had killed Snags and Miller. His mind closed out everything except the scene before him. He saw only the enemy in the rifle sights. The barrel was steady, his body relaxed. He blinked his eyes closed, and when they opened, they were locked in the sights, centered on a man's chest.

Landis exhaled. "Now." His rifle exploded, and he saw his target thrown backward. He shifted position, fired again, then again, and again at men seeking shelter. His fifth shot went through the throat of a man screaming orders. The scene was like a negative exposed to blinding light, freezing terror.

Frizzell methodically shot six men. His last bullet caught a man in the spine as he raced into the trees, dropping face forward, flopping like a decked fish. The entire sequence did not take more than ten seconds.

Screams and return fire rent the night.

Landis ripped a pin from a grenade, threw it, then two more. He yelled to Frizzell and they jumped up, their legs buckling from the cramped hours. They broke through the brush, racing to the treeline on the knoll. Behind them they heard shouts and bullets scattering wildly. Without stopping, they streaked down the hill and across the open field, charging up the opposite slope and throwing themselves in the brush. They gulped air, pressing the ground, hearing shouts and enemy fire.

Landis pounded Frizzell's back. "We did it! We got the motherfuckers. Oh, Jesus!" He was ecstatic, bouncing up and down. "Oh, man, we did it, we did it."

Frizzell's fury gave way to control. He listened to the cries and confusion, then motioned Landis, and quietly they slipped away, running the entire distance, stopping in the open field to signal with a green flare. When they reached the wire, they were pulled through, then dropped in exhaustion to the sand.

Bishop and Brock pushed the others away and knelt with them.

Landis gasped the story. "It was just like you said, Lieutenant; they came down the ridge, started on—"

"How many?"

"About a hundred, all coming down, just staring at the—"

Frizzell said evenly, "There were twenty-three, Lieutenant."

"Yeah, twenty-three, and we waited for a long time watching them, then opened up, and it was just like you said, they couldn't see us and we just shot the shit out of them."

"How many?"

"Six each, and the grenades got some."

Bishop searched their faces. "For sure?"

"I saw mine go down."

Frizzell nodded. "They're dead. We were so close we couldn't miss."

"Did they fire back?"

"Yeah, but they were shooting wild. Jesus, it was just like you said, Lieutenant. Everything happened exactly right. They never knew what happened."

Bishop went over the story again while Brock studied the two men. When he finished, Bishop told them to go back to their bunkers. "I'm going to write you both up for medals."

Landis shook his head. "I don't want no medal."

"You got twelve of them; you probably saved our asses.

341

That's worth a Bronze Star." He slapped them on their backs and they left, happy, eager to tell the story to everyone else, again and again.

Bishop watched them go. "What do you think, Gunny?"

"If they say they got twelve, they got twelve. You did okay, Lieutenant. Maybe they'll give you a Silver Star." He shook his head and motioned to the ridge. "But they'll be back tomorrow. They'll start all over again; they're not going to give up just because of this. They want this hill, Lieutenant, and sooner or later they're going to get it. And God help the poor bastards who are here then."

But Bishop was happy and felt vindicated. "You're getting old, Gunny."

Before dawn Bishop checked his rifle and ammunition, strapped on his first-aid pouch, and crossed to Brock, asleep in the corner.

Brock stirred at his approach, groaned, and curled tighter.

Bishop knelt beside him. "I'm taking a few men up to the ridge to see how many they got. You want to go?"

Brock rolled away. "I'm not walking three miles to see a bunch of dead gooks. I ain't risking my ass to count bodies."

Bishop woke Landis, Martin, Frizzell, and four others. In fifteen minutes the patrol gathered on the forward slope. It was still dark as the men made their way through the wire.

At the base of the ridge they waited until faint light penetrated the morning, evaporating the mist, lifting from the ridge like a veil. There was no sound. They moved up the slope, walking through brush still smoldering from the artillery Bishop had called in.

They picked their way carefully through foliage and craters until they reached the knoll overlooking the enemy position. Bishop sent his men over one at a time, then they circled the clearing and waited until Bishop was sure there was no danger.

When he signaled, they moved into the clearing where the bodies lay undisturbed.

Landis ran from corpse to corpse. "See. I told you we got them." He rushed to one lying on its face and turned it over with his boot. "I got him right in the head." He ran to another, checked inside the bunkers, then counted them all. "Sixteen. Jesus! Sixteen."

Frizzell examined the men he had killed. He knelt beside them and looked up to Bishop. "I didn't miss a single one. I wish my DI could see this."

The others pressed around the two men, studied each corpse, examined the wounds and listened again to the story of the ambush.

Bishop walked to the edge of the clearing. He looked to the position where the two men had hid, then to where the dead lay. It had been a perfect ambush. Pride flashed through him. He climbed the small rise and knelt, staring down at the clearing where the men were gathered. He placed his rifle on the ground, and his hand went to the empty ration cans neatly stacked and camouflaged. He fingered the tins and watched bugs swarm in the remaining juices. Then he looked at the clearing.

Frizzell and Landis were kneeling over the enemy soldiers. Bishop watched the others search through their clothing. Then his gaze returned to the ration cans. In his mind he saw the scene—the two waiting calmly, and the enemy moving unaware into the clearing. He looked on the faces twisted in death—a face blown off, a neck ripped open, exposing the fragile web of existence. One man had been shot in the chest and the bullet had thrown him backward so that he sat against a bunker as if dozing; another lay facedown with his hands reaching behind to clutch his severed spine. He tried to imagine what it had been like, unsuspecting, suddenly under fire, then systematically killed.

He sat in the brush, listening to the insects and the murmurs from the men below. The knoll was quiet except for the toneless voices. He looked to the sky, a brilliant blue pavilion, then to the dead on the ground. From where he was, they seemed hardly distinguishable from their killers kneeling over them. The sight filled Bishop with lonely wonder, and all the faces intermingled.

He looked again to Frizzell and Landis.

Landis's face was animated; he pointed to the dead,

laughed, and raised his rifle in demonstration, then he grinned happily and reached into his jacket for a pack of cigarettes.

Frizzell's face was as clear and unlined as polished marble. He was chewing gum and his teeth broke from his lips, spreading into a quick grin. There was no malice in his face; he looked happy, proud, and, Bishop thought, clean.

Bishop closed his eyes on the blood and brains and splattered membranes. In the darkness of his mind there was no horror; it was peaceful, and all he could hear was the soft murmur of men, like hushed acolytes in a sacristy.

When he opened his eyes, he was staring into Landis's face; his mouth was moving but Bishop could not hear him. He looked curiously at the face.

He saw no guilt, no evil, no cruelty. He was staring at a pleased and happy youth.

"Gee, Lieutenant, I asked if you want us to bury them?"

Bishop looked blankly at him, then to the bodies stretched before him. "No," he mumbled, then he yelled to a man jabbing a corpse. "Martin!"

The man jumped as if shot.

"Leave him alone. The rest of you get your gear, we're leaving."

"We just gonna leave them like this?" Landis asked.

"You want to take them with you?"

Landis looked solicitously on the dead. He had gone to so much trouble to kill them that he was reluctant to abandon them. Finally he shrugged and followed the others from the clearing.

The patrol made its way from the knoll, then carefully down the ridge. Bishop was absorbed in thought, too distracted by what he had seen to concentrate on the patrol's movement; he dropped behind and followed the others absently.

Frizzell slowed his pace so that he walked beside him. "Lieutenant?"

"Yeah?"

Frizzell looked away in embarrassment, then said almost inaudibly, "Do you think it makes any difference if you're circumcised?"

Bishop stared at him blankly.

"I mean, everyone knows it's better for women and it's cleaner."

Landis, who had dropped behind to listen, asked, "How is it better?"

Frizzell shook his head derisively. "Boy, you don't know anything."

Landis fell silent, then brightened at his unforeseen luck. "Well, I'm circumcised."

Bishop stared at them incredulously, then he turned away. Anger surged in him, but it burned out instantly, and he sighed. "I don't think it makes any difference," he said at last, and quickened his pace so that he broke free of them and walked alone.

On the crest of the next ridge he looked back to where the dead lay. Above, far on the horizon, he saw dark clouds, the first threat of the monsoon.

He watched his men start down the ridge, Landis and Frizzell last of all, pushing one another, jabbing and punching playfully.

"Christ," he said. "Christ. Christ. Christ."

When Bishop returned to his bunker, he tossed his rifle, flak jacket, and helmet into his corner.

"You're just in time," Gunny Brock said. "We're going to be saved." He was heating C rations near the radio and spooned peaches into his mouth.

Bishop whirled excitedly. "Is that right? When did they call?"

Juice spilled from Brock's mouth; he wiped it away with his sleeve. "Twenty minutes ago."

"When?"

"When what?"

"When are they pulling us out?"

"I didn't say anything about pulling us out."

"You said—"

"We're being saved. I didn't mean by battalion. I didn't mean headquarters was going to save us. I meant God."

"What are you talking about?" Bishop demanded.

"They're sending us a chaplain. A Protestant chaplain is

choppering in. He's going to give a service. We're all going to be saved—if he can beat the gooks here. Hallelujah, Lieutenant!"

"You asshole," Bishop said in disgust, taking off his T-shirt and mopping his chest with it.

"That is not being respectful to your elders, Lieutenant. Hardly a Christian response. You better get dressed too—I can't imagine the reverend wants to see naked officers."

"Kiss my ass. What the fuck are they sending us a chaplain for?"

"Probably to give us the last rites. Want some C rats?"

"Shit," said Bishop, unblousing his boots and stripping off his trousers.

Brock blew on his bubbling rations and smiled. "Doesn't sound like you had a real good morning, Lieutenant. Was it a disappointing body count?"

Bishop dropped onto his sleeping bag in exhaustion. "Sixteen," he said without enthusiasm, then sorrowfully, "Jesus, it was awful up there."

Brock finished with the C rations and tossed the empty can in a corner. "Better them than us," he said simply.

Sutherland and Frizzell sat outside their bunker watching the sky darken; massive black thunderheads rolled from the north.

"You know," said Sutherland, "Snags told me once that he saw it rain for fifty-two straight days. That's worse than the goddamn Flood."

"If I saw a sky like that at home, I'd run for the storm cellar," Frizzell said. "I never seen a monsoon."

"It's gonna be a real turd-floater, count on that."

Above them came the clattering of a helicopter. They watched it circle the hill, then drop ponderously to earth near the main bunker.

Lieutenant Bishop ran out, saluted a man emerging from the vibrating hull, then they shook hands. The chopper rose immediately; the two stood talking on the forward crest, Bishop gesturing toward the different posts, then across to the ridge.

346

Sutherland bent forward and squinted. "It's a chaplain," he said, making out the silver cross on the man's helmet.

Frizzell strained anxiously to see. "A priest?"

Sutherland stood. "Priest, chaplain, what's the difference?" He turned away and went into the bunker.

For a long time Frizzell stared across the hill, then watched Bishop and the other man disappear into the main bunker.

A priest, he thought. Into his consciousness came images of cassocked men, incense and solemn masses, the panoply of ritual in which he had been raised and had until now forgotten. He remembered Saturday confessions and fasting before communion, hushed voices, purple and red vestments, and bells. Death too, but different from here: quiet death, without terror, wounds, or agony, with garlands of flowers, a Madonna gazing beatifically, soft light refracted through stained glass—gentle death, the repose of the soul.

His head jerked up. His soul. What if he had died? There was sin on his soul, mortal sin.

The realization was more terrifying than death. He began to catalogue them—petty faults, thoughts, desires—then he stopped. He had killed; yesterday he had killed six men. No, he thought, that wasn't a sin, he had had to do that.

He looked to the main bunker, then he stood and walked down the slope to be alone to think.

Inside his bunker, Sutherland went to his rifle.

Coney looked up from a magazine. "Where's Les?"

Sutherland began stripping the rifle. "I think he went to see the chaplain. Or priest, or whatever." He took apart the rifle and inspected the chamber. "A fucking chaplain just choppered in. A lot of good he's gonna do. Hope he can shoot straight."

Coney lowered his magazine. He had been raised in a firm faith, taught to love and fear God, accepted unquestioningly all tenets of his parents' faith, yet he had not thought of God since he had been here. He cocked his head, puzzled. How was it possible in the midst of killing and his fear that he had not once thought of God?

Absently laying aside the magazine, he thought of the first

man he had killed, an enemy soldier cowering in a tunnel. He had watched, intrigued by the man's fear and his own power; then there had risen in himself, welled from deep inside, an overpowering desire, and he had shot the man. He had wanted to do it, and he felt no remorse later.

Where was God that moment? Coney thought. When I pulled the trigger, where was God for that man? Or for me?

His face set in deep concentration. Or didn't God care? Was God's absence the cause of this horror, or was it His doing?

He strained at the thought, then gave up, turning to Sutherland, intent on his rifle. "You believe in God?"

Sutherland looked up. "Sure." He waited expectantly, but when Coney said nothing else, he asked, "Don't you?"

"Yes."

The exchange puzzled Sutherland. Everybody believed in God. Then he shrugged and went back to his rifle. What sense was there in anything if there was no God? He stroked the amulet around his neck. That was from God; it sealed his private pact with God.

Across the hill, the chaplain sat on an ammunition box drinking coffee, unaware of the discomfort of the two men with him.

Bishop was not sure what to call him; the man was a naval officer, a commander who considerably outranked him, yet it didn't seem right to call a minister "Commander." "Reverend" was the proper title, but he was in uniform and wore rank insignia.

"How long do you plan to stay, sir?" he compromised.

The chaplain looked at his watch. "The helicopter will return at fourteen hundred."

Brock studied the man carefully. He was tall, his own age, thirty-five, with a high, receded hairline that left only a patch of closely cropped hair flecked gray. His face was full, and his wire-rimmed glasses were partially hidden by thick eyebrows.

"I'd like to visit the men, spend a little time with them before the service. Sometimes they like to talk alone; things are on their minds—family problems, wives, or simply fear. Just having someone listen is often a help—the religion doesn't matter, not on a battlefield. The battlefield is nondenominational."

"How about heaven?" Brock asked.

"Are you worried you won't get there?" the chaplain asked with a smile.

"Not a bit," said Brock. "God *needs* gunnery sergeants. It's officers I'm worried about. Especially lieutenants who drink hard liquor and chase whores in Da Nang."

Bishop crimsoned.

"They *should* be worried," agreed the chaplain, winking at Brock.

Bishop stood up. "I'll take you around to the men, sir."

He led the chaplain up the stairs, then he excused himself and ran back down and hissed at Brock, "You bastard, I'll get you for that."

Brock's hands were pressed piously and his eyes raised heavenward. "I'll be praying for you, Lieutenant."

The chaplain was waiting on a knoll surveying the hill. "How many men have died here?" he asked when Bishop returned.

Bishop thought back. "Seven, maybe eight."

"Aren't you sure?"

Bishop turned away. "I try not to remember."

"Are you afraid?"

The sky was completely overcast and the air cold. Across the wasted plain Bishop saw the ridge. In his mind he saw the enemy dead, their rubber flesh and upturned faces exposed to the elements. "Yes," he said, thinking of the dead, and his own men. It was not a physical fear, but one of more sorrow.

The chaplain, mistaking his fear, glanced about nervously, aware of the vulnerability of the remote outpost. "Will it be safe?"

Bishop looked at him quizzically. "Will what be safe?"

"To hold a service."

Bishop looked at him blankly. The chaplain pointed to the ridge.

"Oh. Yes, it'll be safe. They never attack in the daytime."

The chaplain continued to stare at the ridge. "I think you're all very brave."

Bishop said tonelessly, "We don't have a choice."

At a small bunker, two men lay unclothed, asleep next to one another. Bishop kicked their feet. "Get up, there's a chaplain here. He wants to talk to you."

Landis and Martin scrambled up and attempted to cover their nakedness, then struggled into their trousers.

"I'll be outside," Bishop said, leaving them.

The bunker was cramped, the air heavy with humidity and the odor of the two men.

The chaplain sat on the ground, his back resting against one of the sandbags. He motioned for Landis and Martin to sit also. "How are you boys doing?" he asked.

Martin nodded. "Fine, sir, real fine."

"Yeah, great," said Landis.

"Where are you from, son?" he asked Martin.

"Newark, New Jersey, sir."

"That's a fine place. You getting along okay?"

"Fine. Just fine."

"I'll bet you'd rather be in Newark, New Jersey."

Martin grinned. "Yeah, well, I guess I would."

"How about you, son? Where are you from?" he asked Landis.

"Fort Lauderdale, Florida. And I'd sure rather be there, sir."

"Well, so would I," said the chaplain. "Is there anything bothering you boys? I mean anything I could help you with? I mean things like mail, or personal problems—not much I can do about the war. How about books to read? Do you have Bibles?"

Landis reached for the book Coney gave him. "I got this book," Landis said. "It's about a whale."

"There's a wonderful story in the Bible about a whale. Have you heard about Jonah? He was swallowed by a whale."

"It sounds better than this one," Landis said. "More exciting anyway. How'd he get out, sir?"

"The Lord saved him. The Lord God Almighty can save us all—Jonah from a whale's belly, and us from sin. All it takes is for you to accept Jesus as your Savior. Pledge yourself to Christ and you will be saved. Will you do that?"

He reached out and took each by the hand. "Can you declare yourself for Jesus Christ? Is there room in your heart for Him? Do you want to be saved?"

They both nodded.

"Then say, 'I accept Jesus into my heart as my Savior. Save me Jesus.'"

They repeated the words, then the chaplain stood. From a satchel he carried he took out two small Bibles and handed one to each. "Believe me, this is a better book than what you've been reading. It is God's holy word. It is sacred. Every word is true."

At the entrance he said, "God bless you both. You are saved." Then he left and went to Bishop, who was sitting cross-legged in the sand.

"They seem like very nice boys, Lieutenant."

"They're very young," Bishop said, standing, and brushing off sand.

The chaplain smiled. "You all are."

At the next bunker, heavily sandbagged and with a sign over the entrance reading "No Solicitors and No Gooks," Bishop stuck his head in. Coney and Sutherland scrambled to stand. "Where's Frizzell?"

"Outside, sir. Down by the wire. He was looking for that priest, or whatever the fuck he is."

"He's a chaplain," Bishop said. "And he's here to see you." Bishop turned to the chaplain hidden behind him. "I think you really need to talk to this one."

When Sutherland saw the chaplain enter the bunker, and saw his rank, he covered his face in horror. "I didn't mean that, sir. Actually, he said it." He pointed to Coney.

The chaplain smiled and looked for a place to sit. Sutherland spread a poncho for him. He dropped down and motioned them to sit across from him.

They sat tense and respectful, eyes intent on him.

These two were very different from the others, he felt. He looked about the bunker. In the corners were piled their rifles, packs, and rations. Loose ammunition was strewn everywhere. He studied them, one dark with thick shoulders and a large, coarse chest, but with a boy's face, only sadder and worn; and the other, lean with glistening skin, features so clean they could have been a girl's except for the eyes, which burned hard, flicking restlessly as if he had been caged and starved.

He noticed Coney's ring. "You're married."

"Yes, sir."

"Any children?"

"We got a little boy."

The chaplain nodded. Children with children. "I'll bet you miss them very much."

"I never seen my kid. I left before . . ." His voice trailed off.

The chaplain turned to Sutherland, struck by the porcelain skin and hypnotic green eyes. "And you?"

Sutherland blushed and looked away. "Naah. I ain't married."

"Have a girl?"

Sutherland averted his eyes. "Yeah." Then compulsively he said, "Her name is Toni." And again. "Maybe we're gonna get married when . . ." The words were swallowed by the dark bunker.

They lapsed into uncomfortable silence. The chaplain could not think of anything to say, felt the awesome distance; and they—struck dumb in the presence of rank and surrogate divinity—sat mute before him.

"Is there anything I can do for you?" he asked. "I mean about mail, or personal problems. There's not much I can do about the war—I'm not consulted on strategy."

Neither spoke.

The chaplain was transfixed by Sutherland's eyes. "I'm sorry about the men who were killed. I'm going to hold a service for them. Were they friends of yours?"

Sutherland said evenly, "Yes." Then his voice turned cold. "Snags and Miller were my friends. Conrad too. And Blake and Wheeler and Perez. The gooks got them all. And they want to kill me too. But they're not going to." His eyes were green lasers. "Because I'm going to kill them first. I'm going to kill every fucking one I can."

The chaplain tried to hold the gaze, but he had to turn away. "You shouldn't hate others," he said softly.

"Then how can I kill them?"

The chaplain turned to Coney. "Do you want to kill them?"

Coney's jaw set. "No. But I have to. Don't I?"

The bunker was still. At last the chaplain stood; he fumbled in the satchel and took out two Bibles that he handed them wordlessly. "Good-bye," he said.

Outside he breathed deeply, then closed his eyes and rubbed his forehead. When he opened his eyes, Bishop was standing beside him.

"The bunkers are very cramped, Lieutenant."

"Yes."

He sighed. "I should find the man who was looking for me."

"Frizzell. He's down by the wire."

They moved across the hill under blackening clouds. Wind from the plain blew sheets of sand into them and swirls whirlwinded in the emptiness.

Bishop pointed to a man sitting in the sand with his back turned. "I'll have the other men gather for the service in fifteen minutes."

The chaplain nodded absently, then walked toward Frizzell. A few feet away, he stopped; the young man was crying.

The chaplain feigned noise in the sand.

Frizzell turned, and seeing the insignia, he jumped up.

"I didn't mean to startle you."

Frizzell brushed at his eyes and looked away.

They stood before each other; the chaplain's hands twisted anxiously until he clasped them tightly together, and he asked uncertainly, "Can I help you?"

For a moment Frizzell stood undecided. Then his doubts and fears, all he had shored within, broke, and he convulsed in sobs.

The chaplain was caught unaware. He started toward Frizzell, then held back. "Stop." He moved closer, spoke louder, more uncertainly, "Don't."

Frizzell began to choke with deep coughs. The chaplain grabbed him. "Look at me."

Frizzell slowly raised his eyes. The chaplain stared into the face; tears coursed through dirt.

"What is it?" he asked.

Frizzell shook his head, then said dully, "I don't know. I just began to think . . . about . . . about all of it—Snags and Miller getting killed, and about going home, and . . ."

The chaplain waited, but no more came. "Is that why you're crying?"

"I don't know," he said, dropping his head. "I get all mixed up."

The chaplain stared at the head bent in submission. "How old are you?"

"Eighteen, Father."

"Oh," he said; then, "I am not a priest. I am a Protestant chaplain. But that doesn't make a difference here. Father Todd is a good friend of mine. We take turns visiting the field. He talks to Baptists and Methodists and Lutherans. Right now he's probably with some young man just like yourself who just happens to be a Protestant. He's helping that young man, just as I would like to help you. Tell me about yourself."

Frizzell riveted his gaze to the sand. He shifted and mumbled, "There isn't much to tell, sir. Once I was an altar boy. I never missed a mass, not once." He kept his eyes down and said nothing more.

The chaplain watched him, then asked, "Are you afraid to die?"

Frizzell glanced to the ridge. "Afraid?" He lowered his eyes. "I don't want to die. I want . . ." There were no words.

"There is nothing to fear with God. You have accepted Christ as your Savior, haven't you?"

"Yes. I believe in God, and in the Church, and forgiveness of sin and the Resurrection."

"Are you prepared to die?" the chaplain asked gently. "I mean, your soul? I know that Catholics believe in confession and the forgiveness of sin. I can't hear your confession or grant you absolution, but I know that if you are truly sorry for your transgressions, you will be forgiven. I think you have to say a special prayer, but I can't think of the name of it."

"An Act of Contrition."

"Yes. A priest doesn't have to forgive you; God can."

354

"But what about terrible sins?" Frizzell asked.

The chaplain did not answer for a long minute. "I think that would be between you and God. He is a very great God; I suppose he can forgive very great sins if the sinner repents."

There was a pause, then Frizzell looked up beseechingly. "But I killed."

The chaplain was startled. "When?"

"Here. Yesterday I killed six men."

The chaplain drew a deep breath. "Oh." Then he sighed. "It is all right."

Tears dropped from Frizzell's face, and he shook in sorrow. "But isn't it wrong?"

The chaplain looked away. "God understands," he said to the plain. "It is wrong, but not your doing. You are without malice, you are"—he wanted to say "pawn," "instrument," but that was too harsh—"without guilt. The sin might be others', but not yours. He will not punish you for that. I think if you say a genuine Act of Contrition, you will be forgiven."

He patted Frizzell on the back. "Do not be afraid; God is with you." He looked to the menacing sky, then took a Bible from his satchel and handed it to Frizzell. "I must go now. I have to prepare for the service in a few minutes; it is for the men who died here."

Frizzell watched him leave, then he knelt in the sand to pray.

Bishop gathered the men outside the main bunker, and they stood when the chaplain approached.

The chaplain briefly explained the service and asked them to follow in the books he passed out.

The wind grew to a howl, and the men could barely hear him. Frizzell tried to concentrate on the service, spoke the answers in his book, but his mind wandered, wondering whether God had forgiven him. Martin turned the pages for Landis, who could not keep his place.

The chaplain looked at the sky, then to his watch. He said in a strong voice, "It is a privilege to come out to see you fine men, and I want to tell you how much we all appreciate what you're doing here. We are all grateful, and I know the people at home are proud of you. You are doing a fine job; an important job; a necessary job. You are helping ignorant people wage war against a godless enemy."

Bishop watched his men carefully, then his gaze rested on Frizzell and Sutherland, both intent on the words.

"There is a design and a purpose to what you are doing. It is not necessary that you understand it, for there is much we cannot know. We cannot know why God moves in the way He does. We cannot know His plan because we are only small figures in it. I cannot tell you why these fine men were killed. We must merely have faith that it is in God's plan for all men. You must trust.

"But I tell you that these men are this day with Jesus. They are dead in a way not to be feared, but envied—because they are with their Savior. They are sheep returned to their Shepherd; they are in glory. You *will* die—not in this war we hope, not for a very long time; we hope when you are old and surrounded by grandchildren and great grandchildren. But nevertheless, you *will* die. The trumpet *will* sound.

"Accept Jesus Christ as your Savior, and you will be with Him in glory, and truly, you will never die. You will live in eternity. Pledge yourself to Christ. Accept Him as your personal Redeemer, and you *will* be saved."

When the service ended, he collected the books, then stood alone with Bishop waiting for the helicopter.

They did not speak for a long time. Gusts of sand reeled across the plain. "It is a lonely place," the chaplain said finally.

Bishop's voice was low and sorrowful. "Yes."

The chaplain placed a hand on his arm.

Bishop sighed. "Is it all a game, sir?"

"No."

Bishop looked across to the ridge, stared until his eyes welled and tears rolled down his cheeks. "Christ, I hope not," he said.

Above, carried by the wind, came the clattering of rotor blades.

The chaplain looked over the hill, at the barbed wire, the

bunkers, the men already preparing for the darkness. He wanted to say something, wanted to help, but . . .

The engine roared closer. He turned to Bishop. Their eyes caught, then the chaplain turned away. "I must go," he said.

The helicopter hovered, then descended, churning sand. The chaplain bent into the storm and climbed into the chopper; it lifted immediately.

The chaplain strained to look out the window. He saw Bishop with his back turned, shielding himself from gusting sand, and he saw all the bunkers and some of the men looking up.

He raised his hand to wave a benediction, then brought it down quickly and clutched it in his lap.

The machine arched rapidly and in a moment disappeared.

CHAPTER

• 23 •

Like a fine, antique mechanism, Lacouture was usually reliable; unaccountable lapses too quixotic to be considered malfunctions merely contributed to his charm.

Every afternoon at precisely three-fifteen, Lacouture had coffee and cognac on the top-floor terrace of the Majestic Hotel on the quay overlooking the Saigon River—except when he inexplicably did not.

Knowing this, Lord waited for him there; though certain Lacouture would arrive, Lord would not be surprised if he did not—the movements of a jeweled Empire clock were precise, but sometimes the clock stopped nonetheless.

Yet as Lord knew he would—or would not—Lacouture stepped onto the terrace at exactly three-fifteen, fastidiously dressed in white suit and paisley cravat, silk handkerchief not arranged but sprouting from his pocket, and spats on highly polished black shoes. His attire was neither new nor a dapper affectation, but suitably worn and elegantly correct, as comfortably proper for a French colonial in the tropics as old tweeds for an Englishman in the highlands.

His entry onto the terrace was confident, his short steps and fluttering hands assured, his sharp eyes and raised nose aristocratically haughty.

The maître d' met him immediately and escorted him to the table that for nearly twenty years had been his, and where Lord had been waiting for twenty minutes, having told the maître d' that Lacouture was expecting him.

Too gracious to frown, but too well bred to hide his displeasure, Lacouture paused before sitting. His annoyance expressed without rudeness, he was now exonerated from a hypocritical greeting, or having to make any acknowledgment of the intrusion.

Lord was polite enough to wait until the waiter brought the coffee and cognac before saying anything.

Knowing Lacouture and his habits so well, the waiter was not surprised that the Frenchman, contrary to his usual behavior, gulped the cognac and placed it on the left, signaling that it was to be refilled. The Frenchman did not like his routine interrupted; a second cognac would restore him.

When the waiter left, Lord said, "Have you given thought to the arrangements?" trying to mask his anxiety for Lacouture's help.

"No arrangements are necessary, *chéri*. As I told you— cash; half in advance. Nothing could be simpler or less complicated. Only cash. Dollars—no rockets, bombs, or hardware for me to peddle on the black market. Just money."

He sipped coffee delicately.

Lord nodded. "That can be arranged. But for cash, I am going to need more from you than assurances. If I am going to invest such a sum, I will need something concrete. You can understand that I cannot—invest, shall we say, without a complete prospectus. I need a viable plan that offers a return on my investment. I can't advance you that much money without some guarantee that you have a plan that will succeed."

The waiter brought Lacouture another cognac. He sniffed it, then savored a swallow.

"You want to kill Bradley Marshall, the U.S. envoy. I have researched him. I will soon be able to provide you with the details for a plan that will succeed."

Lacouture did not mention that he had failed in six attempts to contact Marshall on the phone. Each time he had been thwarted by some military aide. Marshall took no calls personally. His secretary—Lacouture had a perfect picture of her in his mind, some tight-twated bitch with peroxided hair who fucked her superiors while wearing stiletto heels—answered the phone in a low, seductive voice, then hearing Lacouture speak, became insufferably rude and connected him dismissively to the military aide who demanded to know exactly what business Lacouture sought to conduct with Marshall, and then unsatisfied with the answer, hung up on him: six times.

"Is there anything personal you could tell me about him that might be helpful?" Lacouture asked.

Lord reflected. "He is very worried about his son, who has joined the army and will be coming here shortly. Marshall fought in World War Two—against the Japanese, as a matter of fact. He saw a great deal of combat, and it had a powerful effect on him. He is very opposed to war—what we call a dove. He would be receptive to an overture to conduct secret peace negotiations. More than anything, however, he is concerned about his son."

Lacouture finished the cognac. "Leave the rest to me."

"I will," Lord said blandly, inwardly relieved that Lacouture was going to help. He added coolly, yet also trying to convey urgency, "But your time is limited. He will return to the United States before Christmas, and in the coming month will be traveling throughout the country."

"I appreciate the necessity for a quick resolution," Lacouture said.

"Good. When you have arranged a meeting, or convinced him that there will be one, you will get your money. When the meeting is set, I'll pay you—cash. Probably he'll check with me about you. I will tell him that you are disreputable and not to be trusted. It will grieve me to say that"—he smiled faintly and put his hand over his heart—"but you can understand the necessity."

"Of course. I forgive you in advance for such outrageous lies."

Lord stood, bowed slightly, and left.

Lacouture was too confident, Lord thought, the little faggot was up to something. He had to find out what it was, and the only way he could do that was to get Mead into his bed. He sensed a double cross, and he couldn't risk that; this was too important. It might be better to end this quickly and surely by having Gibbon sabotage the helicopter. Yes, he decided, that would be the primary plan; Lacouture and the meeting would be the contingency one.

When Lord returned to the embassy, he called Marshall's office.

Dolores Toland answered the phone after many rings.

"Well, at last. This is Palmer in passports," Lord said in one of his favorite voices—the prissy bureaucrat. "There's a Ronald F. Mead up there. He must come down immediately to room two sixteen."

"Corporal Mead is Ambassador Marshall's bodyguard. He goes where the ambassador goes. I don't see room two sixteen on Ambassador Marshall's afternoon schedule."

"My dear, Corporal Mead is not going anywhere unless he straightens out his passport difficulty."

"What passport difficulty?"

"Oh, just the trifling matter that he doesn't have one. How is he going to accompany the ambassador in the very likely event that the ambassador travels someplace with his bodyguard where a passport will be required? Hmmmm? No one has thought of that, have they? What happens then, I ask you? Hmmmmm? What good is a bodyguard if the host nation won't allow him entry? Hmmmm? You just send his fanny down here right now so we can avoid *lots* of problems and embarrassments later on. Room two sixteen."

He hung up before she could, but she slammed the phone down anyway, just as Romer entered the office. He looked at her curiously.

"I am so sick of . . ." She shuddered.

"What?" he asked.

"Homosexuals."

"Homosexuals are calling you? Why in the world would homosexuals be calling you? How do you know they are? Are they identifying themselves?"

"You can just tell by their voices. Some awful Frenchman

has called a dozen times asking to talk to the ambassador, and now some dreadful man in passports wants Corporal Mead."

Romer smiled. "Corporal Mead is getting phone calls from homosexuals?"

"Apparently Corporal Mead doesn't have a passport."

"Soldiers don't need them," Romer said. "Their ID cards are good for travel here and to the States."

"The man said that he might need one if he accompanies the ambassador outside the country."

"Ah. That's a good point," Romer allowed. "He would need one if he went to the Philippines or Japan or almost anywhere. You better send him down, just in case. Never mind, I'll go tell him."

"Room two sixteen," she said.

Romer crossed the hall to the small room that had been cleared for Mead at Marshall's order. The room was not much larger than a closet and contained one chair and a wall locker.

Mead was polishing his boots when Romer entered. Seeing the colonel, Mead jumped up, dropping the boots.

"Dolores said some homosexual would like to see you down in room two sixteen."

"Sir?"

Romer laughed at the shocked expression on Mead's face. "Do you have a passport, Corporal?"

"No, sir."

"Well, somebody on the ball downstairs realized that you might need one in case you go traveling with the ambassador, so go on down to room two sixteen and get it straightened out."

"Yes, sir."

"But don't stay down there too long or Dolores will get suspicious. By the way, has anyone told you what's going on in the next couple days?"

"No, sir."

"The day after tomorrow, Ambassador Marshall will start making field trips. For the next month or so, he'll be traveling throughout the country. We'll start down in the Delta and work north. The first trips will be day ones, but when we go up to the highlands and into I Corps, we'll be staying over. There'll be four of us—the ambassador, myself, the pilot, and you. You won't need anything except your rifle—everything else will be provided. I want you ready to leave here for Tan Son Nhut at six A.M. Thursday. We'll pick up the ambassador at his residence. Any questions?"

"No, sir."

"Good. Now go get your passport."

Mead's first thought was that Lord had sent for him since it was the same room, but if Dolores had said it was a homosexual who had called, then it certainly wasn't The Phantom.

He went downstairs disappointed, but curious.

When no one answered the knock, Mead went in. On the table was a passport application. He was reading it when the door opened and Lord entered.

He was exactly as before, cold and impersonal. He didn't acknowledge Mead but sat down and gestured to the paper. "Fill that out and have a superior endorse it, then bring the application to the passport section."

"Yes, sir."

"Sit down." This was going to be a minor challenge, Lord thought.

Mead dropped into the same chair as before, two down from Lord's, and he tried to check his mounting anxiety.

"The Vietnamese man is Bui Cao Kim. He works for the Frenchman, Bernard Lacouture. Lacouture is going to try to kill Ambassador Marshall. He is trying to make contact with him. I think he will succeed."

Lord leaned forward, his eyes commanding, his voice harsh. "You're going to help me." The dummy will say, "Yes, sir," Lord thought.

"Yes, sir," Mead said quickly, almost rising out of the chair. "Anything, sir."

Lord sat back and considered him intently. Mead fought to hold still under the scrutiny. No challenge at all, Lord thought.

"You have no training," Lord said.

Mead tried to hide his disappointment.

"I've read your record; it's impressive," Lord said flatly, not at all impressed. "But this . . . what we require, is different."

His eyes bored into Mead's, and his voice was low and intense. "It is hard to ask you to help without skills or training. I would be afraid for you."

Mead leaned forward. "I can handle myself," he said fervently.

Lord stared at him. *This is too easy; he's too stupid,* he thought.

"Let me try," Mead said almost pleadingly.

Lord said nothing for a long moment, then he leaned forward, his eyes drawing Mead toward him, his voice a conspiratorial whisper.

"What we do is not easy, or without risk."

The way he said it—the intrigue and exclusion that he conveyed—made Mead shudder.

"Sometimes we have to do things we don't like. Our enemies do not play by any rules—the game is made up as we go along."

Mead nodded.

When Lord spoke again, his torso moved slightly, a perceptible swaying like that of a cobra, and Mead unconsciously mirrored it.

"Not only are our rules different, but sometimes there are no rules at all. What appears to be real may not be real."

The softly spoken words cast a mysterious spell. Mead, trancelike, watched Lord's hands shape and erase reality.

"No rules, and no rewards. No medals for your uniform —no Silver Stars."

His hand slowly unloosened his tie and unbuttoned his collar, then pulled down the shirt, exposing an ugly scar on his throat.

"No Purple Hearts," he whispered. "No glory."

Mead stared at the wound in fascination, then he whispered back, "Yes."

"It is lonely work."

Mead nodded.

"Lonely and unhappy work."

Mead nodded again.

"Lonely and unhappy and unpleasant work. Sometimes it is very unpleasant."

"Yes," Mead said.

"You understand? Lonely and dangerous, and unpleasant."

"I understand," Mead said.

"Could you do unpleasant things? Things you hate? Things that go against your principles if you knew they were important? Can you stand loneliness and unhappiness?"

Mead nodded solemnly, then he said firmly, "Yes."

Lord leaned closer; they were only inches apart.

"No rules," he whispered, and his wizard's hand erased rules. "No laws." His hand wiped away law. "No punishments."

He brought his hands together and held them up for Mead, offering him the treasure. "There is only our mission; that is all that matters."

Mead stared into his hands.

"No one cares how you complete the mission. No one wants to know. All we want is your help."

"Yes, sir," Mead whispered.

"The Frenchman is trying to kill Ambassador Marshall. We must stop him."

"Yes, sir."

"You must find out his plan."

"Me, sir?" Mead asked in hushed surprise. "How can I?"

"You are going to meet with him. He is going to contact you. He is going to offer you a great deal of money."

"For what?"

Lord stared at him so intently and for so long that Mead finally understood. He wanted to look away, but he couldn't.

"It's time to grow up, Corporal," Lord said. "The world is an evil place."

Mead could not move. "But, I mean, I . . ."

"The mission, Corporal—that's all that counts. We deal in lives—our country. We don't care about your delicate feelings."

Mead nodded, stammered, "I, uh . . . I mean . . . I'll be leaving with the ambassador Thursday. I, I won't be able to . . . for a while."

Lord sat back. "Do it when you return," he said sharply. Then he raised his hand, a magician waving a wand. "You must never . . ."

Mead nodded slowly. "Say anything."

Lord brought his hand down, breaking the spell, and his voice was brusque. "Good day, Corporal." Thursday, he thought: he had to see Gibbon immediately.

Mead jumped up. "Yes, sir." He started for the door, then went back to the table for the passport application. He lingered nervously before Lord.

"Sir, I . . ."

Lord raised his hand. "I need to know the Frenchman's plan—nothing else. I don't deal in cheap shit, Corporal; I'm not interested in personal problems." His eyes were cold and passionless, then the hand came down in dismissal. "You will do it."

Mead turned and left the room. He was halfway down the stairs before he took a breath, then he stopped and held on to the railing. He felt as if he had been kicked in the stomach, and his mind was in such turmoil that he could not focus on a thought. But he didn't want to—he did not want to think at all.

He returned to the top floor in such distraction that he forgot to check in with the secretary until he realized he still had the passport application in his hand.

He crossed the corridor and entered Dolores Toland's office just as the phone rang.

When she heard the voice, she put her hand over the receiver and looked directly at Mead. "God damn," she swore vehemently. Then she said sweetly into the phone, "One minute please," and put her hand back over the receiver.

"Go get Colonel Romer," she said urgently to Mead. "It's that French queer. Hurry!"

Mead froze.

"Hurry, stupid!" Then in exasperation she jumped up. "Never mind, I'll get him." She dashed from the room, returning in seconds with Romer.

She pointed to the phone in disgust.

366

Romer picked it up and said in French, "Hello. May I help you?"

On the other end, Lacouture took the phone from his ear and stared at it. The last thing he expected upon calling the U.S. embassy was to hear well-spoken French.

"Hello?" he answered. "Ambassador Marshall?"

"No," Romer replied. "I am his military aide. How can I help you?"

"You can help me, and Ambassador Marshall, by letting me talk to him."

"Could you please tell me the nature of what you wish to discuss with the ambassador. Perhaps I could help you instead."

His French is too good, Lacouture thought. No American speaks it this well. Then he made the connection—this had to be Robert R. Romer, Jr., the man he saw at the Continental the other day; he must be Ambassador Marshall's aide.

"Ah, Colonel Romer," he said. "What a pleasure it is to speak with you. At first I thought I had made a mistake and called the wrong embassy—your French is that good."

It was Romer's turn to be surprised. He had not given his name, and as far as he knew, no one outside Westmoreland's office and the few people here knew that he was working for Marshall.

"My name is Bernard Lacouture, Colonel. I am of your father's generation, and it would be uncivil and ungrateful of me not to pay homage to the memory of your father, despite the fact that you are probably weary of such tributes. Nevertheless, it would be improper for any Frenchman not to acknowledge what your father did."

"Thank you," Romer said graciously, for he could sense that the words were sincere.

"I have sought for two days to speak with Ambassador Marshall. I am somewhat ashamed that I cannot tell you the nature of this call, for I know you are an honorable man, and I would very much like to confide it to you, but I simply cannot. What I have to say is solely for the ambassador—I am charged to secrecy. Perhaps you better than anyone can understand, for you should appreciate that if I could tell anyone else, it would be you, the son of the man who helped liberate my country. I can only assure you that what I have to say is extremely important and that the ambassador would be very interested in my message. After all, he can always hang up the phone, can't he?"

"I suppose he could." Romer laughed. "Bernard Lacouture?"

"Yes."

"If you'll wait one moment, I'll see if the ambassador will take your call. Or perhaps you could leave a number, and he could return your call?"

"I'll wait. Thank you very much."

Romer put down the phone and walked toward Marshall's office, leaving Mead and Dolores staring after him.

Mead had caught the name, Bernard Lacouture, the same one Lord had mentioned only minutes ago. Lord had said he would be successful—and right as Lord always was, now Colonel Romer was going in to the ambassador to establish the contact.

Mead was stunned. How did Lord always know everything? And he had said that Lacouture was going to try to kill the ambassador. And Lord said that he needed help. He asked him for help—to save Marshall's life; to help his country.

He was ashamed of himself. Why hadn't he said something?

Romer returned. "Monsieur Lacouture? The ambassador will speak with you. Let me connect you." He pushed a button. "Mr. Ambassador? Monsieur Lacouture is on the line." He waited until he heard both speak, then he hung up.

"Now you won't be bothered again," he said to Dolores.

"Colonel Waggoner wouldn't let him talk to the ambassador," she said censoriously.

"The ambassador can always hang up, can't he? And he'll tell you not to take any more calls if he doesn't want to talk to him again."

Romer turned to Mead. "Did you get your passport?"

Mead held up the application. "I have to fill this out, then you or Colonel Waggoner has to sign it, sir." He lowered his head.

"Bring it in when you're ready," Romer said, and returned to the other room.

Mead closed his eyes, almost in pain, then he left.

"Ambassador Marshall, I have a very important message to convey. A most urgent one; however, I can't give it to you over the phone."

"Could you give me some idea what it is about?" Marshall asked.

Lacouture lapsed into rapid French. "I am a conduit, Excellency. Your CIA thinks I am disreputable, but they will also tell you that my sources are many and reliable. In this case, I am strictly an intermediary, paid to give you a message, paid even more to arrange a meeting between you and this other individual whom I cannot name for obvious reasons."

Marshall answered in French. "This sounds very intriguing, Mr. Lacouture; however, I would need more information before I could meet with you."

"The individual who wants to meet with you is a high-ranking North Vietnamese. He has lost two sons in the war. He is a disillusioned man, and bereft by his sons' deaths. He has other children, another son who will soon have to join the army, and daughters who are always vulnerable to the air attacks over Hanoi. He would like to meet with you to discuss . . . possibilities. I can give you more details in person, and proof of the legitimacy of the man's intentions."

"Very well," Marshall said. "Let's say tonight at eight at my residence. It's at—"

"I know where it is, Excellency. Thank you very much. I will see you then."

When Marshall hung up, he considered calling the CIA chief of station to inquire about Lacouture, then decided against it. First he would hear what the Frenchman had to say, then he would check on him. Though the coincidence was uncanny—an intermediary appearing exactly when he wanted one—he knew from experience that legitimate contacts could arise from anywhere.

Peace talks in Paris were imminent, Marshall knew, but he knew too that they could drag on forever because, once public, each side would have to posture and pose; theater would dominate.

As remote as the possibility was for anything to eventuate from a meeting with Lacouture, Marshall had to take the chance. After all, was it inconceivable that an enemy felt for his children as he did for his? What a stroke of luck, Marshall thought, suddenly almost buoyant. Here might be his opportunity—his chance to save Ryan; to end the war.

He had been reading the report on General Giap's strategy at Dien Bien Phu, but now he couldn't bring his attention back to it. Besides, it seemed evident that only the most superficial comparison could be drawn to Khe Sanh.

General Tran was right—Khe Sanh was a ruse to divert attention from other buildups and a major attack that would sabotage American support for the war.

But the NVA underestimated Lyndon Johnson, Marshall knew. An attack would only prolong the war; it would make the President intransigent.

He had to contact someone to convince them of that. And now, Lacouture offered such a possibility. He had to risk it. Marshall did not believe in fate, but this could be a godsend.

He turned off the lights and said good-night to his staff, then he crossed the hall to get Mead.

The corporal was hunched over forms, biting his lip as he labored filling them out. Since he didn't have a desk, Mead sat on the floor, using the chair as a desk.

Sensing someone in the doorway, he turned. Seeing Marshall, he jumped up, spilling the papers in all directions.

"I'm in no hurry," Marshall said. "Take your time—finish what you're doing. I decided to quit early. I don't suppose I deserve it, but to hell with it anyway. Finish what you're doing—I'll go down to the snack bar. Do they sell beer there? I could use one."

Mead stammered, "Sir, you can't do that. You can't wait for me. And ambassadors don't go to the snack bar. It . . . well, they just don't."

"I didn't ask you for permission, I asked you if they sold beer there."

"Well . . . yes. Yes, sir, they do."

"Good. I'll be having a beer. Come get me when you're ready." And he left.

"Damn," Mead said aloud. He couldn't believe Marshall had just wandered off again.

He flung the papers in his wall locker and slammed the door as Colonel Waggoner came in. Oh, no, Mead thought.

"What are you doing here? I thought Ambassador Marshall left."

"He did, sir. I mean . . . he went to the snack bar."

"Where?" Waggoner shouted.

"The snack bar, sir." Mead cringed at his own words. "He said he wanted a beer. He told me . . . to finish what I was doing."

"What the hell are you doing?"

Mead gestured weakly to his wall locker. "Some paperwork. My passport form, sir." Shit, he thought; why am I always fucking up?

"You jackass! Your job is to guard Ambassador Marshall. Can't you get that in your goddamn head? He's not supposed to be running loose through Cholon, or soaking up suds in the snack bar while you're up here doing 'paperwork.'"

Mead grabbed his rifle. "Yes, sir."

He rushed to the door but couldn't get past Waggoner. "I'll go get him, sir. If you'll just move, sir . . . ah, thank you. Good day, sir." He ran out of the room. Fuck! he wanted to scream; I can't do anything right; they always think I'm stupid.

The basement snack bar was a large room with a long counter and serving line, and many tables and chairs. Though the room was half full, there was a wide radius of empty places around Marshall's table, so noticeable upon entering the room that one would have guessed it a source of contagion.

Sidelong glances indicated that everyone knew who he was, but no one dared venture near.

Mead ran into the room, then stopped when he saw Marshall by himself, drinking a beer, attempting to be casual while the focus of all attention.

371

Mead walked over to him and stood awkwardly.

"That was quick," Marshall said. "Sit down."

Mead sat stiffly, keenly aware of everyone staring at them.

"Have a beer," Marshall said.

"Thank you, sir, but . . . I can't drink on duty, sir."

"Oh. I guess I shouldn't either then. Do you suppose there's some rule about that? I wonder if it's written down—ambassadors and corporals can't drink on duty? What do you think?"

"Well, I don't know about ambassadors, sir, but I'm sure there's one about corporals. There seem to be an awful lot of rules for corporals."

Marshall laughed. "Go get a beer. It's impolite for me to drink alone, and impolite for you not to join me."

Mead went to the counter and returned with a bottle of beer, fully expecting Colonel Waggoner to walk through the door with the Commandant of the Marine Corps and the shore patrol to arrest him.

"Prosit," said Marshall, raising his bottle when Mead sat down. "That's what the Germans say. I wonder if the Vietnamese say anything. Every society says something, so I suppose they must. Actually, this isn't bad beer. I wonder why they call it '33.' It's a strange name for a beer. Do you know why?"

"No, sir. I usually drink the Filipino beer."

"Is it better? Mind if I have a taste?" He took the bottle from Mead and drank a swallow, not even wiping it clean first. Mead had been told that it was insulting to a Vietnamese if you asked for a glass for your beer; it implied that the bottle was dirty. He saw how that could be so, for he was oddly flattered that the ambassador drank directly from his bottle.

"It is better," Marshall said. "But probably the French started this brewery, and they're not real beer drinkers—only in Alsace, and half the time that's Germany anyway."

"You know about almost everything, don't you, sir?" Mead asked somewhat timidly.

Marshall laughed. "You should talk to my sons. They don't think I know anything. According to them, I'm really quite stupid."

"That's what kids always say."

"Really? Maybe I should have you talk to them—you can tell them how smart I am and that they should do everything I say. Think it would work?"

Mead grinned. "Probably not, sir."

Marshall drained his bottle. "I could use another one; I'm feeling much better." He went to the counter and brought back a Vietnamese beer for himself, and a San Miguel for Mead, who felt very self-conscious about being served by the ambassador with everyone watching, though Marshall himself appeared oblivious to the attention.

"If they're going to court-martial us for one beer, we have nothing to lose by having two." He raised his bottle. *"Nasdrovia*—that's what the Russians say." He took a long swallow, then thought back. "What did we used to say in the Corps? There must have been something, but I can't remember. Is there something?"

"You usually just drink to the Corps."

"That's right."

"Were you really a corporal once?" Mead asked.

"Oh, yes, back when I was your age, but I don't think I was as good as you are. I was kind of a shitbird—couldn't march, call cadence, wasn't much of a marksman, and spent most of the time scared to death. But I had a good time. I liked being a corporal much better than being an officer."

"Really, sir?"

"It was much more fun. You could bitch and moan and sit around with the guys. Being an officer is lonelier. I remember once in Korea after some pretty hard fighting, all the men sat around drinking beer, talking and joking. I was the platoon commander, but I couldn't be a part of them. I really wanted to, but they would have felt funny about it. It would have ruined everything for them, so I just sat off by myself. There was no one for me to be with."

"I never thought about that," Mead said, and for some reason Lieutenant Bishop came into his mind.

"You looking forward to going out in the field?" Marshall asked him. "It should be interesting, and the time will go faster."

"Yes, sir. I never been anywhere in Vietnam except here

373

and on the DMZ. In fact I was just thinking about that when you were talking about being a lieutenant. I had a real good lieutenant up there. That's why I'm here—he sent me down; he was afraid I was gonna get killed. I really liked him. I been wondering what happened to all those guys."

"Where are they?"

"Up around Khe Sanh, sir."

"Oh? Would you like to go see them? We can drop in up there—I want to see that area anyway."

"Really, sir? You mean we might go up there?"

"I'll make it a point. I'll tell Colonel Romer to arrange it—all he needs is the name of the unit."

Mead beamed happily. "You really would do that? I mean, go up there for me?"

"Well, I have to go up there anyway. But yes, I'd go there for you."

Mead turned away in embarrassment. "I can't believe that. I'll see Snags again, and the gunny, and Lieutenant Bishop—all the guys. Jesus, they won't believe it—a goddamn ambassador . . . I mean . . . you, sir, and me choppering in with you." He downed the rest of his beer in a single swallow. "I gotta tell you this, sir. I just never expected you to be like this."

Marshall smiled. "We'd better go before you have a third beer and tell me what you really think."

Mead shook his head. "No," he said seriously. "I mean it; you really been decent to me—like no one ever has. I just want you to know I appreciate it. And . . . ah, well, I'd do anything for you, sir."

"Thank you very much," said Marshall, standing up. "But I hope that won't involve too much—I'll see if I can stay out of trouble, or at least not cause you any more problems like in Cholon."

Mead jumped up. He had been thinking of some way to raise this casually, but he hadn't been able to, and now this was his last opportunity. "That Frenchman on the phone sure bothered Miss Toland today." He wanted to tell him about Lacouture, but he couldn't disobey Lord.

Marshall eyed him curiously, knowing Mead's comment was not casual. "What are you getting at?"

Mead shifted uncomfortably. "Just that . . . well, it's my job to protect you, and if . . . someone's bothered about . . . I mean, she said he's been calling you a lot, and I thought maybe I should . . . well, know about it."

Marshall smiled. "You really are conscientious, aren't you?"

"I don't know what that means, sir," Mead said sheepishly.

Marshall patted his shoulder and steered him toward the door. "It means you do a very good job, Corporal. It means that I appreciate you too. But don't worry about the Frenchman."

By not saying more Mead felt as if he were betraying Marshall, but surely Lord knew best.

After accompanying Marshall back to his villa, Mead caught a cab and returned home.

He paid the driver and was starting up the stairs when Lacouture rushed toward him from the sidewalk.

"Mr. Mead. Wait! Stop! Dear Mr. Mead, wait."

Mead turned in amazement to see the little fat Frenchman running toward him, flapping his handkerchief. Mead brought his rifle up reflexively, not into his shoulder but to ward off an attack.

"Don't shoot!" Lacouture squealed, stopping dead and covering his head, while daintily holding out the handkerchief, as if it could shield him from a bullet. "Don't shoot! I'm not going to hurt you."

That being the most incongruous possibility Mead had ever heard, he laughed and lowered the rifle.

Lacouture peeked out from the handkerchief. Mead laughed even louder at the cowering little fat man in a white suit.

Offended, Lacouture straightened, stuffed his handkerchief into his pocket, and walked toward Mead with dignity.

"It is rude, crude, and unattractive to make fun of others. You should be ashamed of yourself. Besides, how do you know that I am not a ninja expert, capable of thrashing you soundly?"

Mead had never encountered anyone like this in his life.

Amazement gave way to fascination, but he could not stop laughing. "Thrash me?" he said. "Okay, go ahead." He rested his rifle against the stoop.

Lacouture stood in front of him, nearly a foot shorter. "You are a very brave man. I shall spare you. In fact, I shall reward you for such heroism." He reached for his wallet.

"Forget it," Mead said, picking up his rifle.

"Oh, please. You must come with me. You must!" He clutched his chest. "I shall perish."

The little man was curious and horrible, Mead thought, like some awful troll in a story, or the county fair where the freak on the stage talked to you.

"What the fuck do you want?" Mead asked.

"Well, I can't tell you *here*." Lacouture looked about with disdain. "It's so ugly." He reached out to grab Mead's arm, then remembering how Americans loathed touch, withdrew quickly. "Come have dinner with me."

Mead stared at him incredulously. This was the man who was going to try to kill Marshall? This funny little fag? This was the man on the phone to Marshall? How could he be dangerous?

"Please," said Lacouture. "You must. Just this once, then I won't bother you again."

Mead shook his head. "Maybe some other time. But I gotta go now; I gotta see someone."

"Yes, I know, your woman. Go see her, then have dinner with me. You simply must. Nine o'clock. Here." He thrust a large bill at Mead. "For cab fare. Nine P.M. That will give you plenty of time with your woman. Nothing is going to happen to you; no one is going to hurt you. Say you'll come. Please. Nine o'clock at the Coq d'Or."

"The what?"

"The . . . never mind. Here, I'll write it for you, and the address. You'll come?" He clutched his chest. "Oh, say you will."

"I'll think about it," Mead said.

"Nine P.M. Say yes. You must, you must."

"I said I'll think about it."

Lacouture put his hand over his heart. "I shall perish."

Then he waggled a finger at Mead. "Or I shall come back and thrash you soundly." He made strange chops at the air with his hands.

Then he turned and fairly danced down the street.

Mead watched in amazement.

It had happened just as Lord had said it would. How had he known? The phone call, contacting Marshall, and now this—just as Lord had predicted. And what else had he said? That there are no rules, and what appears to be real may not be real at all.

Lacouture disappeared, vanished around a corner; the savage was going to come—he knew it; he was going to have him! Then he stopped on the sidewalk, overcome with doubt and dread. The savage had said he would "think about it"—he wouldn't come; he had said that just to get rid of him. He had a woman; he was disgusted with a creature like himself, Lacouture knew. It would come to nothing, he thought in despair, and wanted to throw himself into the street under the wheels of a car.

No! He drew himself up. He would come; he just knew it; it was going to work. Everything was going to be all right. He was going to convince Marshall to meet with the NVA, he was going to get his money from them and Wilson Abbot Lord, and best of all, he was going to have the savage. He just knew it! And he rushed out into the street shouting, "Taxi!"

Lord sat on the metal folding chair in Gibbon's office.

"You are positively glowing, Jeffrey."

"I'm in love," Gibbon said with a grin.

"You're not in love, you're just perpetually horny."

"Love, horny—it's the same thing, isn't it?"

"I think Elizabeth Barrett Browning had a few more definitions."

"I'll bet she was a lousy fuck anyway."

"She was a cripple, Jeff." Lord reflected a moment. "Or maybe it was consumption, that's what everybody seemed to have back then."

"Even worse—then she couldn't suck."

377

Lord stared at him, then he smiled. "You do this just to aggravate me. So who's the woman you've fallen in love with, and what happened to Ca Li?"

"Ca Li is fine. The woman though is Marshall's secretary. Have you seen her?"

Lord frowned; something was always happening that was never foreseen, he thought. But of all things, he should have anticipated this—Jeff and a beautiful woman.

"You must have a divining rod between your legs," Lord said. "But this time you hit shale. Stay away from her."

"Oh, no," Gibbon moaned. "You mean she's one of ours? And she's Marshall's private stock?"

Lord shook his head. "Marshall wouldn't be interested in Dolores."

"Jesus, why not?"

"She's too obvious and crude."

"Exactly," said Gibbon. "Everything about her—her mouth, her eyes, her ears, her nose—says 'Fuck me.' She's gorgeous."

"She's not Marshall's type," Lord said. "Some amateur picked her and sent her here—someone with taste in women like yours. Marshall prefers the more subtle type, with a little more finesse—someone who doesn't wear a sign, 'Twat,' around her neck."

"You mean he's not fucking her?"

"No. He would sense right away that she was a setup. He's not a stupid man, Jeff; he's a professional."

"Then why can't I move on her?"

"It would cause complications. Stay away from her," he said simply. "I don't want there to be any contact between us and his office. Besides, you're going to be busy. Marshall is leaving Thursday on a field visit—he'll be taking his chopper, the Huey 1B we talked about. I want you to—do whatever is necessary before then."

Gibbon leaned back in his chair nonchalantly, trying not to betray any concern. "That means tonight. What about the pilot—the Marine aviator?"

Lord looked at him blankly. "What about him?"

"When I had an important mission, I stayed with my aircraft—I slept with it the night before."

Lord smiled ever so faintly. "He'll be sleeping with someone else tonight."

Gibbon considered Lord for a long minute, then he shook his head.

"Let me guess—Dolores?" Then he laughed. "You think of everything."

"Oh, no. I'm quite appalled by what I miss and overlook, but in this case, it's just a matter of checks and balances: Magnuson checks Marshall, Dolores checks Magnuson."

"Maybe you need someone to check Dolores," Gibbon said, pointing to his crotch.

"Thank you anyway, but that won't be necessary."

Gibbon leaned forward, all business now. "What's the security around the chopper?"

Lord said gravely, "Very tight; it's kept with Air America planes."

Gibbon grinned and relaxed; Air America was the CIA's own airline.

Lord stood and went to the door. Nothing more would be said—Gibbon knew that Lord did not want details, and Lord liked Gibbon's laconic manner about his work; he never shut up about women, but he never talked about a mission; he just did the job. Lord was utterly confident that the chopper would crash on Thursday.

"Good day, Mr. Lord."

"See you tomorrow, Jeffrey."

CHAPTER

• 24 •

"Ohhh," Teresa cried sharply as burning liquid spilled over her hands.

She was in the kitchen, ladling soup, when a woman who had just been served dropped her bowl and stumbled backward in a faint.

Though her own pain was excruciating, Teresa ran to the woman's side. She steadied her while trying to hold back her own tears.

"Are you all right?" She tried to hold her up, but the burning pain was too much and she had to let go.

The woman righted herself, but when she saw her soup splattered on the floor, she began to sob.

"It's all right," Teresa said soothingly. "There's more. Here." She grabbed another bowl from the stack and handed it to her. But now Teresa could not handle the ladle.

"Would you serve the soup for a few minutes?" she asked another woman. "I think I'll go wash off."

As soon as she got out of the kitchen, she brought her hands up. They were blistering red; she shook them, blew on them, then brought them under her armpits and tried to squeeze out the pain.

"Oh, God," she moaned, and rested back against a wall, her eyes brimming with tears.

Thinking she was alone, that everyone was eating in the

other room, she indulged her pain. She brought her hands up to her face and wept softly, then she wrung them in the air and cried aloud. "Ow, oww."

But then she saw Lin sitting on a cot across the room watching her. She brought her hands down quickly and wiped away her tears with the backs of her wrists. Her hands dangling at her sides, she crossed to Lin.

"I burned myself," she said. "I think burns are the worst pain of all. Oh, goodness, that hurt." She flapped her hands in the air again, then sat on the cot beside Lin.

Gaunt and pockmarked, Lin seemed not to notice Teresa, or even the emaciated child in her own lap. She merely held the infant and stared dully.

"You must eat," Teresa said. "Why don't you go get something while I hold the baby."

Lin did not respond.

Perhaps she was on drugs again, Teresa thought. It was impossible to keep track of all the women. They wandered in and out, disappeared for days, and often came back almost comatose from drugs.

Lin's history was like so many of the others'. She could not even remember how many abortions she had had. She was twenty-four, born during the Japanese occupation, and she grew up a street urchin in Saigon, entering her first brothel at eleven, though she had been first molested by an older Frenchman when she was six.

Teresa knew that there had been no love, no kindness in her entire life; it had been unremitting hell.

Only drugs brought temporary relief, or madness. Death was the only other salve. The soup in the kitchen, Teresa knew, only sustained the agony.

Teresa stroked the infant's brow with her still hurting hand. "You haven't named her," she said softly. "She should have a name."

Lin stared at the child blankly.

"Everyone should have a name," Teresa said. She lifted the baby from Lin's lap and cradled her in her arms. Her voice was friendly and interested, neither solicitous nor condescending. "Did you have a sister? Or maybe a friend when you were young, someone you played with? There are so many pretty names. Lin is a beautiful name. Let's think of a lovely one for the baby. Is there some name you can think of?"

Teresa was not sure that Lin heard her, her expression was so distant, but then she suddenly frowned. "No name," she said.

Teresa saw that Lin was not on drugs but had, on her own, managed to escape momentarily, finding a detached peace that she, Teresa, had ruined.

Lin's frown deepened. "I don't want her to live even if she could live."

Teresa stared into the infant's face, the malformed nose and mangled mouth, saw the moronic eyes, and all comforting words failed her.

"It is not her fault," Teresa finally said. "You should give her a name, Lin."

"Maybe it is her fault," Lin said, studying the child curiously. "What was she in another life? What did she do to come back like this?"

Lin raised her eyes to Teresa's, and her question was serious. "What could anyone do to deserve this? What horrible thing? What things worse than *they* do?" She gestured toward the window, meaning the world outside, the soldiers and whoremasters, the thieves and politicians.

Then she looked away and asked in detached wonder, "I wonder what I did."

Teresa gazed upon the child. What indeed, she wondered, could one have done in some past existence to deserve this? But karma was like souls and faith and heaven and hell, meaningless to her—a child pressing cookie molds on the ocean, painting pictures on the wind.

Teresa took Lin's hand and placed it on the baby. "Not wanting her to live and suffer is very different from killing her."

Lin rested her hand on the child for a long minute, then she took it away and looked at Teresa. "No," she said simply. "It is the same thing."

Teresa took a deep breath, then let it out slowly. "I don't know," she said at last. "Some people call it mercy killing—

there is a big word for it even, 'euthanasia,' and I suppose it has been practiced for as long as people have been sensitive to suffering, and could not bear to see others suffer."

She put the baby back in Lin's lap. "But this baby is not suffering, Lin. She is in no pain and has no anguish. Only you do, and *your* suffering does not give you the right to kill this child."

There, she had said it. She smiled suddenly, for it was that clear. Father Dourmant was right—she could see it—and there it was, as clear as right and wrong.

Lin held the child limply, then shook her head at the deformities and the Negroid features. "She will suffer. Shall I wait until she does?"

"Maybe she never will," Teresa said. "Maybe she will die on her own. Who knows what can happen in the future."

Suddenly Lin said with bitter determination, "I don't want men on me anymore."

Teresa stroked her arm gently. "Father Dourmant can help you. He can find you work."

"I don't want the men on me anymore—here," she said, and clutched her head, then shook it wildly, as though trying to cast them off. "They are always inside."

She brought the baby tightly to her breasts and jumped up. Her eyes widened in fear; she shook her head violently, and before Teresa could restrain her, she ran from the room.

After everyone had been fed and the wards were quiet, Teresa went to see Father Dourmant.

At eight P.M., the streets of Cholon were as crowded as during the day, only the movement was not as frenzied. As the night advanced, movement became more furtive and ominous, but at this hour the mood was relaxed, almost casual. Business was over, shops were closed, and night had not yet begun—doors were not sealed; people strolled and talked.

Father Dourmant lived in the dilapidated rectory in back of the church with two other priests and their housekeeper. Because of his advanced age, Father Dourmant had the downstairs bedroom, but the drawback was that when the housekeeper was out, he had to answer the front door.

Since it was his week to offer the early-morning mass, he had retired after supper. He had just finished his prayers and had climbed into bed when Teresa knocked.

"Damn," he said, knowing he was alone, and that whoever was at the door would knock until he got up. He put on his worn flannel robe and tattered cloth slippers and padded to the door, a stocking cap on his head, muttering disgruntedly.

"Oh, Father, I'm sorry," Teresa said when he opened the door. "I woke you, didn't I?"

"I was in bed," he grumped.

"I can come back tomorrow."

"I'm not in bed anymore," he grumped again. "Might as well stay." He shut the door and shuffled toward the kitchen, then stopped and turned anxiously. "Is anything wrong?"

"No, not at all. I just wanted to talk a few minutes."

"At this hour?"

She smiled. "It's only eight o'clock, Father."

She followed him into the kitchen where he turned on the stove and fumbled in cabinets for cups and teabags.

She was sorry she had come; he looked old and haggard, a man who would not live much longer. She wished she had not seen him like this and realized what a good front he put on during the day.

The kitchen was cluttered and small and harshly lit by a single bare bulb. Father Dourmant sat at the table, holding his palsied hands in his lap, waiting for the water to boil.

"I just came to tell you that you were right," Teresa said, sitting across from him. "About Lin and the baby, I mean. I can't let her immolate the child."

"Well, I hardly expected you to do otherwise. It's one thing to give up the church, quite another to encourage women to roast their babies on Tu Do Street. If you came here for me to congratulate you on that decision, I am afraid you came in vain."

She laughed. "You're getting crankier every day."

"I'm getting older every day—that in itself is enough to make anyone cranky. Listening to nonsense, and supposedly sane women debate the merits of torching infants, hardly adds to my tranquility."

Then he ran his hand through his thinning hair and said more gently, "But I'm glad you've come to the right decision."

"I guess I was just being silly," she said, "pretending there was a dilemma, when there really wasn't."

"That's common," Father Dourmant said. "Right and wrong are simple matters, usually very straightforward—there isn't any mystery about them. So we make it difficult to decide to do what we know we should. We make a drama out of it. That 'To be or not to be' nonsense is just that—nonsense. You know the fool isn't going to kill himself; nor should he. It's all just palaver. It's the foolishness of martyrdom—rewarding people for doing what they're supposed to do."

Teresa got up to get the kettle. "Goodness, your judgments are harsh. I'm glad you won't be deciding my canonization."

"I doubt anyone will be, since the church is rather fussy about making saints out of heretics."

"That's exactly what I told Ambassador Marshall."

"Spare me," said Father Dourmant, holding up his cup, but his hands shook too much, so he put it back on the table for Teresa to fill.

"Do you mean to tell me, Father, that the martyred saints shouldn't be saints?"

"Personally, I don't give a damn," he said. "But intellectually, I never saw the sense in glorifying someone for doing what he or she was supposed to do, and for what they knew they were going to be rewarded for anyway. Where's the sacrifice? Where are the heroics? People who expect to be rewarded aren't heroes; neither are brave people—they're only doing what comes naturally. It's the cowards who do something extraordinary, something completely out of character, who are the heroes. It is the person who makes the sacrifice without any expectation of reward who is the saint—the heretic."

"Then I have a chance after all?"

The priest smiled. "Only if those who decide such things think like I do. Or if God does—which isn't likely: the Lord and I seem to be at odds about everything."

Teresa poured the tea and sat down across from him again. "And what are you expecting in the way of reward, Father?"

The priest blew on the tea, tried a sip, but put the cup back down. "You mean after all the degradations ahead of me—senility, and incontinence, cancer, pain, diapers, and death? Why, I expect to be wafted to heaven on the wings of angels where I'll be restored to youth and vigor, and where I shall drink sauternes day and night, and eat nothing but foie gras."

"What if the cuisine is English?"

"I'm sure it is—in hell; but I'm talking about heaven."

Teresa finally managed to drink her tea. She nursed a few sips, then said casually, "Lin thinks that the baby's condition might be its own fault."

"Karma." The priest snorted. "Actually it's not much different from what Christians believe. Being rewarded or punished for a past existence—being rewarded or punished for what one does in this one: it's hard to ridicule one of those beliefs while espousing the other."

"It's heartless—blaming an infant for its deformities, saying that it's being punished for what it might have done in a prior life."

"It's heartless to punish people eternally for things they do in this life that they can't help."

Teresa laughed. "I thought *I* was the heretic."

"You are. *I'm* the kind, compassionate parish priest—like in those silly American movies. Except I can't sing."

"Then I have come to the right place," Teresa said. "I need your help."

"I knew it! I knew you didn't come here just to tell me that I was right. You dragged me out of bed for ulterior purposes."

"Bing Crosby would be happy to help."

"Who? Oh. Yes, but he was at St. Mary's with Ingrid Bergman, not in a tropical hellhole with a heretical ex-nun."

"All the more reason for you to help," Teresa said sweetly. "Think of the sacrifice and glory, not to mention the reward, Father."

"Oh, dear God," he said resignedly. "What do you want me to do?"

"I talked with Lin, but I don't think that I convinced her. I think it's possible that she still may kill the child. I don't see any alternative except to take the baby from her."

"But what would that do to her?" Father Dourmant asked.

"I don't know. It might drive her to . . . well, I just don't know; but I can't let her harm an innocent child. Lin needs help, but first the baby has to be considered—it has to be brought to safety; then we can help Lin."

"Yes, I think that's right," the priest said. "You want me to find a home for the baby?"

"Yes, a temporary one, until we can get through to Lin."

"I can do that. Bring me the child and I'll find someone to care for it. Send Lin to me and I'll find a place for her too. I told her I could get her work, but she wasn't interested. Perhaps if you tell her that she can have her baby back if she gets a job and finds a place to stay, it might encourage her."

"I'll get you the baby immediately—tomorrow morning. We'll have an examination of all the infants—weigh them, note their problems—and I'll slip out with her during the checkup."

"The woman could be hysterical, maybe violent," he said.

"Do you see another way, Father?"

He considered a moment, then shook his head. "Bring her to me in the morning."

Teresa stood up and brought her cup to the sink. "Thank you, Father."

"Oh, must you go? Surely not after dragging me out of bed, you're not going to just rush off."

"Well, I can see that you're tired."

"Not at all. I was thinking of singing."

She brought his cup to the sink, washed and dried them both. "Go to bed, Father. You need your strength to do the Lord's work."

"I wouldn't if He managed things better," he grumped.

"Good night, Father," she said, patting his arm. "I'll let myself out."

She returned to the clinic just as the mood of the streets turned ominous. Her passage back was accompanied by the sounds of shutters clattering and doors being barricaded. The business of night had begun.

After letting herself in, Teresa locked the clinic door. The lights were not yet out, but most women were in their cots. She walked through both wards, talking soothingly, pulling a cover over a woman, helping another with her infant, rocking a child. Only when she was passing back through the downstairs ward on her way to bed did she notice that Lin was not in her bed.

She checked the bathroom and the kitchen, then asked the women in nearby cots if they had seen her.

"Gone," one said.

"Gone where?" Teresa asked.

The woman cast open her hands in disappearance. "Just gone," she said.

Teresa looked under Lin's cot. Everything was gone—her little satchel, and everything for the baby.

Oh, dear God, she thought, she is going to kill the baby. Teresa ran to the door and fumbled with the key, then she stopped; she couldn't look for her, not at night. Nor would she even know where to begin.

She clutched the key so tightly in her hand that it throbbed. Opening her palm and staring into it, she saw how red and inflamed it still was, and just remembering the pain made her hand hurt all the more.

Then she had the most awful vision: she saw the baby consumed in fire, its screams mingled with the licking sound of flames searing flesh, and she saw the infant's tiny hands reaching up out of the inferno, then simply crumpling like paper, charring, turning to ash.

And suddenly she had the most terrible feeling; she was struck with the certainty—it was true; it was going to happen.

Mead knew that he was going to meet with the Frenchman. He thought of contacting Lord, but Lord had clearly told him that he only wanted to know Lacouture's plan—he didn't want to hear personal problems; he wasn't interested in details.

When he opened the door to his room, he thought for a second that he had made a mistake. The room was clean; there were no sleeping bags on the floor, and in the center was a card table and two chairs. The smell of vomit and sickness was gone.

Sung was in the corner on her knees with a sponge and a pail of water; seeing him, she rose, but too quickly, and she staggered against the wall.

Mead rushed to her side to steady her, but as soon as he put his hand on her, she flinched and closed her eyes. He let go and stepped away.

"Are you okay?" he asked.

She nodded, opening her eyes, but averting his gaze. "You came back early," she said in an unsure voice. "I wanted to finish."

"You shouldn't be doing this," he said. "You're not well enough; you should rest."

"I felt better. I wanted to do something."

He looked about the room; she had cleaned and straightened everything except for his clothing in a corner—she had not touched that. In another corner, carefully stacked, were the boxes of Kotex and the bag of candy. In front was propped the doll.

He stood awkwardly beside her, not knowing what to say or do. "Are you hungry?" he finally asked. "Do you want to go get something to eat?"

She shook her head. "Han gave me rice before. I can't eat much—it makes me a little sick."

"You have to eat; you're really thin."

"I will. Tomorrow I'll eat more."

"You have to get some clothes too," he said, and pulled out his wallet. "Tomorrow, go out and buy some things." Then he felt in his pocket for the bill the Frenchman had given him and he handed it to her. "Get something with this."

She stared at the money, then looked up at him. "Why are you doing this?"

"Well, you need to get some things. Everybody has to have clothes."

"No, I mean everything. Why are you . . . being nice to me? Han's man is not so nice to her. And she tells me the other men . . . they are not so good to their women."

He looked away in embarrassment, then shrugged. "I don't know. I just . . . I guess I just wanted to help."

He moved away from her, went to his corner to change, but somehow felt awkward about taking off his uniform, so instead he went to the table and sat down.

"Han said we could use it," Sung said. "She has four tables."

Mead laughed. "Her room's like a warehouse—she's got shit stacked to the ceiling. She gets every new guy to buy her another roomful."

Sung said mildly, "Women have to protect themselves."

"I know that," Mead said. "I know what she's doing—she's just trying to scratch out a life, humping a bunch of assholes so she won't starve. Christ, she must be forty-five years old, and all she's got is some card tables and a couple transistor radios. I don't blame her for what she does; she's just trying to make it."

He looked at her directly. "And I don't blame her for bringing that old man in here either."

Sung looked away, then lowered her head.

He went over to her. He stood silently for a long minute, looking down on her. "I won't hurt you," he said. "I never will, I promise."

"I don't know who he was," Sung whispered.

"What did he want?"

She shook her head. "I don't know. I don't remember everything. Just that he hurt me, and he said . . . he said that I should make you happy."

"Why?"

"I don't know."

"What did he want?"

She shook her head again. "I don't know. That's all he said to me."

"And is that why . . . why you . . . yesterday . . . ?"

She nodded.

He let out his breath, then lifted her chin with his hand and waited until she met his eyes. "I don't want you to do anything you don't want to do. I mean it. I don't want you to be afraid of me; I couldn't stand that. My old man used to knock the shit out of all of us. He'd get mad or drunk and . . . just tear into the nearest person—usually it'd be my mother."

"He would beat her?"

"Oh, yeah. And he was big. I don't guess he ever really hurt any of us—I mean, no broken bones or knocked-out teeth, but we learned to stay out of his way. Except my mom—she didn't have any place to run to; I could take off and stay gone a day or two, but she couldn't. She'd just have to take it, and you could see the fear in her. Sometimes she was terrified of him. I hated that the most, seeing her afraid of him—creeping around so as not to disturb him, hushing us, smiling and pretending everything was all right. Well, I don't want that. I don't want you to be afraid of me. That would make me feel . . . I don't know, sick or something—like I was diseased."

She nodded and said softly, "My father . . ." She fell silent and lowered her head.

"What? I don't know anything about you. Tell me. Where is your father? Your family?"

She closed her eyes and shook her head.

"Are they dead?"

"Yes," she said, her eyes shut tight. Then she took a deep breath and looked up. "They were killed. My mother and father and brothers."

"Who killed them?"

"Soldiers."

"Americans?"

"No; from the North. My father was a landowner."

Then she began to cry; she went slack and simply sobbed.

He put his hand on her tentatively. "Don't," he said, but she couldn't stop. He stood in front of her and put his hands gently on her shoulders, letting her lean forward, resting her forehead on his chest.

In a moment she stopped, wiped at her eyes, and drew away from him.

"I'm sorry," he said.

"I try not to think of it," she said.

"No. You should. You should think about it and cry until you can live with it without crying. It's like heroin, you gotta face it, and get over it on your own."

She looked at him curiously. "All the men before . . . the ones in the brothel, they were not kind. You are different."

"No," he said. "Sometimes I . . . wasn't kind either. I hurt people too. It's just that when I saw you . . . I don't know, I just saw that you were hurting, and I had been hurting too. And people have to help each other. I guess that's it—after all the talk and everything that's in books, it's just that we have to help each other."

She nodded, then reached out to the wall for support. He guided her to a chair.

"You should lie down," he said. "You shouldn't have been cleaning." He brought the folded sleeping bag from a corner and spread it out. "C'mon, lie down. You want anything? You really should eat something."

She remained seated.

"You never said anything else about the man," Sung said.

Mead shrugged. "What's there to say?"

"You didn't ask me to tell you if he comes again, or if he wants something."

Mead sat down at the table across from her. She was so pale and gaunt that beside her he looked even larger and more powerful, yet his manner was gentle and shy. He shifted nervously and said, "I can't ask you for anything. People have to take care of themselves—like Han. Sometimes people have to do things they don't want to do; you can't blame them if they're just trying to get by to live."

He shrugged and said softly, "I done things I didn't want to do. I guess I'll do them again."

She studied his face; again she was struck by how young he was, yet there was such sadness in the features sometimes —pain and weariness that seemed so out of place on a face so strong and healthy.

"I will tell you if he comes again," she said. "I will tell you what he wants."

"Just don't let him hurt you. And . . . do what you have to; it's okay—I understand."

She said solemnly, "I will tell you; I will never lie to you."

She bowed her head. "I'm sorry I didn't tell you. You have been very good to me. I am ashamed." Then she looked up and said sincerely, "I want to earn your trust back, Ron."

That was the first time she had said his name.

"Thank you," he said, looking away in embarrassment. Then he went to the window. "I'm going to be gone for a while. Sometimes I won't be coming back at night. I'll make sure you have enough money, and if you need anything, Han can help. You could ask Bill too. He's kind of an asshole, but if you need anything, go to him, he'd take care of you—I mean if anything came up, or someone bothered you, he'd help you."

He concentrated on his hand, pulling on his fingers, as though making sure they were still there. "But if you . . . uh, I mean if you decide to take off, well, I'll understand. I mean if you leave . . ."

"I have no place to go," she said. Then more gently, feeling guilty, and not wanting to hurt him, she added, "I will be here. Thank you."

He finished with his fingers and looked up shyly. "I . . . I hope so." Then he got up. "Well, you oughta lie down. And I gotta go out for a while."

"Yes," she said. "I will lie down."

She stretched out on the sleeping bag but did not close her eyes. She watched him at the window. He stared out it for a long time, leaning against the wall, and he looked even more sad and troubled than ever, she thought. She wanted to help him, but she could not keep her eyes open. She was so tired, and soon she fell asleep.

CHAPTER
• 25 •

When Lacouture's cab neared the villa, he had the driver circle the block; he needed to clear his mind. He was not nervous about the meeting but was preoccupied with the soldier—would he show up at nine? Would he take the money? What would he be like in bed?

Lacouture was only faintly interested in Marshall; he had dealt with many diplomats over the years. They were uniformly boring; vain and pompous, or bland and equivocal. Moreover, none of them knew anything; their lives were as sheltered as academicians'. They spent so much time guarding each step and word that they were as smooth and colorless as river-washed stones.

Vietnamese police guarded the entrance to the villa. They checked Lacouture's papers and opened the gate for him.

At the front door, a Vietnamese servant ushered him into the foyer.

"Monsieur Lacouture? His Excellency is waiting for you. This way please."

The gracious reception, and not being made to wait, surprised Lacouture. So often a game was played to put him at a disadvantage—his papers would be scrutinized; he would be looked at suspiciously, or lightly ridiculed (he was aware of his effeminacy); or he would be forced to wait uncomfortably while the dignitary tended to weightier matters. But here there was no pretense, and when he was brought into the salon, the ambassador rose quickly and crossed to him.

"How do you do, I'm Bradley Marshall."

"Bernard Lacouture," he said, bowing slightly and shaking hands.

"Would you care for something to drink? They've supplied me with rather shabby wines, but inadvertently I'm sure, with quite good champagne—vintage Moëts."

"Wonderful; that's getting hard to acquire these days. The black market isn't what it used to be: bullets, bombs, helicopters, condoms—nothing you really need, like good champagne."

"What do you suppose I could get for a case of Moët?" Marshall asked, pouring a flute for Lacouture and handing it to him.

"Santé," Lacouture said, raising the glass and sipping delicately. "Well, *I* would give you two tanks and a helicopter for a case of this."

"No French envelopes?"

"Pardon?" Lacouture asked blankly.

"French envelopes—condoms."

"Why," he enunciated carefully, obviously miffed, "are they called that?"

"That was the English name for them." Marshall smiled. "Who can account for them?"

"Indeed," sniffed Lacouture.

"Perhaps it was flattering French worldliness, just as Americans used to refer to . . . explicit photographs as 'French postcards.'"

"How charming," Lacouture said curtly. "Are you sure you're a diplomat?"

Marshall laughed. "I'm not a diplomat at all, I'm an envoy—we don't even have to be civil." He raised his own glass and drank. "By the way, I was asking earlier today if the Vietnamese have a toast, anything they said before drinking—do you know?"

"They say the same dreary things everybody does—toasting health, one another, ancestors. What makes it insufferable is that they drink very sweet wines, or a sickening rice one, or tea." He shuddered. "I would suggest you bring your own champagne wherever you're invited. Although not to meet with the North Vietnamese—they don't drink, or they make a pretense of not drinking, which would be even worse."

"You don't sympathize with them?"

"I am not paid to sympathize, only mediate. But how can one sympathize with humorless, obstinate people? And they're so moralistic—even worse than Americans. I wouldn't fit into such a society," he said demurely, blotting his lips with his handkerchief.

"Surely you don't sympathize with us?"

"Of course not, don't be silly, though I admit Americans have a little more humor, and they do drink, and I suppose I could fit into *some* periphery of society."

"Why, you would be a lion in certain circles."

Lacouture eyed him dubiously.

"Do we pay you too? I haven't checked with our people on you yet. I will of course, but I wanted to speak with you first."

"Form your own impression."

"Of course."

"Everyone pays me; I deal in information and services. Your CIA is particularly stingy, but when you check, you will indeed find that I am a contact, a paid informant."

"What will they say about you?"

"That I am unreliable. Which will only mean that they don't consider me sympathetic to the American cause."

"Which is true."

"Which is irrelevant. A whore performs a service—you are purchasing her time and . . . ministrations. She's not selling you love or fidelity. If you want that, you should have a—"

"Wife."

He waved his hand dismissively. "So American. A mistress. That's the problem with you Americans. One of the problems," he amended. "You are so insistent on being liked or loved. Love is a very fickle emotion, subject to whim and mood, and often as fleeting as an erection. There are so many more dependable and satisfactory, and certainly stable, bases for trust."

"Such as?"

"Money. Fear. Usefulness. Expediency."

"And on which of these am I to base my trust of you?"

"All of them. I am being paid a considerable sum to arrange a meeting. I fear—no, am terrified of what they, the Viet Cong and the NVA, and what your CIA would do to me if I double-crossed them. I am hardly inclined to incite professional assassins to anger. As for usefulness and expediency, my stock and fees are based on my successes. Good clients enhance an agent's reputation."

"And whose agent are you in this matter?" Marshall asked.

"So quick to the point; so businesslike. So American."

Marshall refilled both their glasses. "You have told me that you are not sympathetic to my country's cause and that you are being paid by the enemy, but that I am to trust you anyway."

"I am not sympathetic to *anyone's* cause—I preferred the French one. Alas, that died a colonial death many years ago. Now I am being paid by 'the enemy' only because I am useful to them. I would be delighted to accept money from you too, but you haven't yet approached me with any work. I see this as a business, only that; I don't know why Americans insist on some emotional attachment with them. You want to be the richest and strongest, have everything your way, and you want to be loved besides—it's very juvenile. It's also very dangerous—you open yourselves to machinations and manipulations; you will be played with like any lovelorn youth. I am not insulting you with a pretense of loving or admiring you. I could do that, play the flatterer or the coquette, but surely you don't want that."

Marshall smiled. "Surely not; I'd much rather be reviled honestly."

"No, no, no. It's not a matter of reviling at all. Don't make it an either/or proposition. Certainly I would prefer that the Americans prevail in this war since it can't be us; I certainly don't look forward to the communist victory. It's going to be awful; I'm going to have to leave. That's why I'm grubbing for money like any streetwalker—I've got to earn enough to retire to Cannes; I won't be able to live here."

"The communist victory is inevitable?"

Lacouture drained his glass and blotted his lips. "Of course." Then he fluttered his handkerchief coquettishly at Marshall. "Oh, do give me some more champagne—I'll flatter you shamelessly for it."

Marshall emptied the bottle in his flute, then walked to the door and called to a servant to bring another bottle. "What would you do for a bottle of Dom Pérignon?"

"Why, I'd go out in the trenches myself and fight for an American victory."

"But it would do no good—the cause is lost?"

"Hopeless," Lacouture said. "A river of Dom Pérignon won't alter that."

Marshall took the bottle brought in by the servant and showed it to Lacouture for approval, then he stripped the foil and wire and twisted the bottle expertly, allowing only a faint hiss to emerge as he pulled the cork away.

"I've been told that H-bombs, nerve gas, and an invasion of the North might have a decisive effect."

"No, not at all," Lacouture said, holding up his glass, giving a little squeal of pleasure as the liquid frothed in the glass. "H-bombs and nerve gas would only delay the inevitable—not change the outcome. The wretched little gooks are destined—determined—to be ruled by the communists. America should simply face that and strike the best possible bargain it can by offering to withdraw."

It was all true, Marshall saw; this strange little man was right—the war was hopeless. Johnson knew it, and he knew it—the war was a slough they could never cross; they *had* to get out. But how? Johnson had put his faith in him, and human lives, thousands of them, depended on his success—the toll mounted daily, yet he had not the beginning of a solution. Was it really possible that this strange colonial relic could be bringing him one?

Lacouture savored the champagne, drawing it back over his tongue, then letting it cascade down his throat. "Don't you think I'd rather see you win? Do you think any North Vietnamese official would offer me good champagne, or listen for a moment to anything I had to say? Communists never listen to anyone. I've spent my life here—I grew up here. Why, the stories I could tell." He brought his handkerchief up and fluttered it at Marshall.

"I was born here. Can you imagine? Tahn Thai was the Emperor—absolutely mad. My family was extraordinarily wealthy—I could have bathed in Dom Pérignon; there were servants for the servants, endless debauchery and license. We destroyed this country, not without their help of course; the court in Hue had been rotten for a century. There is absolutely no tradition for sensible or just government; that's why you get the freakish mishmash down the street. I mean, what kind of a government is it, Ky and Thieu, or vice versa? It's certainly nothing you want to support; it certainly won't last."

Marshall felt his despair mounting—it was worse than hopeless. How had his great country fallen into such a morass? How had our good men with good intentions brought on such a tragedy? Hubris and blind ignorance, he sighed inwardly.

But how to undo it? he wondered, refilling Lacouture's glass. He had to come up with a solution. Could this man possess an answer? Patience might tell, Marshall thought, settling back: patience, the great lesson diplomacy taught, a lesson he hoped he had mastered.

"Ho Chi Minh left Saigon harbor on the *Admiral Latouce-Treville* fifty-six years ago," Lacouture continued. "Not last week or ten years ago, but *fifty-six* years ago—that's how long he's been struggling, and he wasn't the first who fought against the French and the puppet monarchy."

Lacouture raised his glass to the light and watched the tiny bubbles stream ceaselessly to the top. "It's a mystery to me—science, I suppose—where these little bubbles come from. There's nothing at the bottom of the glass; where are the bubbles coming from?" He shook his finger at Marshall. "Don't tell me. I'm sure you know the precise explanation, but I don't want to know it."

399

Lacouture lowered his glass. "Ah," he said, peering into it, inspired. "Use the champagne as a metaphor for the enemy. You can bomb North Vietnam flat, erase the Ho Chi Minh trail—use nerve gas and H-bombs if you wish—but they'll still keep coming. They're here already, in the glass so to speak, part of the society, they'll keep churning up. It is a historical imperative, I'm afraid. We lasted a hundred years here, a flick of time. We built schools, roads, had businesses and trade—just like the British raj in India. And poof, it is gone. Your American conceit is even more incredible, thinking that you can come here without understanding a single thing about the history or culture, and refashion this country in your mold. It just won't happen, here or anywhere else you attempt it."

It *was* conceit, Marshall acknowledged—and we probably won't stop with Vietnam, he thought, not as long as the zealots among us keep seeing the world in blacks and whites.

He suppressed a sigh, for as fascinating as this discourse was, Lacouture was not telling him anything he did not know.

And at any moment Johnson would begin pressing him, he knew—cables, phone calls—and what would he have to offer? Unless maybe, Lacouture was bringing the possibility of an opening to the North Vietnamese.

He had a gut feeling it just might be. This effusive, almost comical little man might have it. He savored the bud of hope but sat back under a totally bland facade.

Lacouture put his glass down and spoke expansively, opening his hands. "I'll give you a small example of what I'm talking about because it is amusing. Your 'pacification' program—people thought it was terrible that villagers and farmers had no toilets. How primitive these Vietnamese are—poor savages who just squat down on the ground. We will build them toilets! So they did—nice wooden booths where they could sit in peace and privacy; no plumbing of course, just an outhouse, lots of them all over the province. When the Americans checked back, they found they had never been used. Stupid, hopeless primitives—can't even learn to sit on a toilet!"

He picked up his glass and sipped. "When they went back

again, the toilets were gone altogether. Ungrateful savages! All that money we spent, all that wood, all that labor."

"And the problem was?"

"Cultural. The Vietnamese in the provinces could not imagine anything more unclean or disgusting than sitting in the same spot where someone else had bared his buttocks, or to sit over a steaming pile of human manure to add one's own. They found the practice of the Westerner unsanitary and unwholesome. They didn't want to put their naked derriers down where someone else had had his; they found it much cleaner and more natural to go out into the fields and squat down. The point is, of course, that outhouses could sprout up around the country like mushrooms, but the people would never use them; they would tear them down and use the wood for something practical—like shelter. The peasants were grateful for the wood, but not the outhouses. Your good intentions went for naught—they merely thought you were wasteful and dirty. It is, I am afraid, an often repeated tale."

"Thank you for the discourse," Marshall said, getting up to pour more champagne.

"I don't mean to be rude or insulting," Lacouture said. "You have been very gracious; I feel guilty about responding with such impoliteness, but I am just trying to be frank."

"No offense taken whatsoever; I quite agree with you, that is why I am here—to learn, and to seek a solution to what seems to be an endless quagmire."

"Get out as quickly as possible; just go. Admit it was a mistake, blame the French, say you won—anything, just untangle yourselves. The North Vietnamese will eventually win; you can't prevent that. Then they will make a dreadful botch of everything; they will be corrupted from within— the Vietnamese are like the Chinese, much too enterprising to remain communist for long; only a truly dull people, like the Russians, could remain communist—and then everything will work out pretty much as you want it. Take the longer view of history; have confidence in our greedy, capitalistic natures—it will win out in the long run."

He folded his hands over his paunch. "You've let me babble on forever; how delightful of you. And you've doused me with wonderful champagne. You are a diplomat nonpareil; how could I have doubted it? Now I am at your service."

"You have brought me a message?" Marshall prompted.

"I have. I have been commissioned by a certain party to arrange a meeting with you. It is all very delicate, as these things always are, of course—so tedious."

"The sooner we get to specifics, the faster this can be accomplished; and consequently, the sooner you will be remunerated."

Lacouture finished the last of the champagne; he shook his head when Marshall offered to refill it, then he sat forward. "Do you know the name Xuan Tien Khanh?"

Marshall shook his head, encouraging Lacouture to continue.

"Khanh is commander of all NVA forces in the Saigon area. He is the most able NVA general. He was a schoolmate of General Giap at the Lycée Albert Sarrault. Sarrault, by the way, was governor general of what was then called Indochina; he was a friend of my father's. Then Giap and Khanh went to law school together at the University of Hanoi; they joined the communist party together and have fought unstintingly for independence for forty years. Giap masterminded the Vietnamese victory at Dien Bien Phu, and now he directs the overall war. Khanh is his chief lieutenant in the South."

Marshall, forcing himself to hold his excitement in check, said evenly, "General Khanh wants to meet with me?"

"Ah. That indeed is the question. You see, General Khanh supposedly died two months ago from dysentery. In any case, South Vietnamese intelligence—such as it is—and your CIA, believe him dead. I doubt they laid hands on the corpse, but his demise is an accepted fact. I myself have seen neither him nor his cadaver, so I cannot assert that he is alive or dead. I can only tell you that I have been approached by a supposed trusted confidant of Khanh who tells me he is alive and wants to meet with you. He says he has proof that Khanh is alive and that this proposed meeting is legitimate."

Marshall, his chin on his hands, scrutinized Lacouture's

eyes, hands, body movements. He listened intently to the tone of his words, alert for any false inflection, the slightest unctuousness. This was almost too good to be true. Eagerness surged within him despite his efforts to restrain himself, to not succumb to false hopes. Careful not to betray his excitement, he said calmly, "Go on."

"The North Vietnamese are planning a major offensive soon; needless to say, I was not given the exact date or times, only that an attack is imminent. The surprise will be enhanced because the South Vietnamese and Americans believe that Khanh is dead. Any hint that he is alive could alert the South Vietnamese and the Americans."

"And General Khanh is trusting you with this vital information?"

"Trusting me? Of course not. They have threatened to kill me in the most egregious manner if I divulge this information to anyone except you. And I have no doubt whatsoever that they would murder me. So in that sense, yes, I suppose they are trusting me."

"And they are trusting me not to divulge this information to anyone? Trusting that I won't go directly to General Westmoreland?"

"I don't think it is a matter of trust rather than it is a gamble on Khanh's part. He is risking a great deal in the hope of gaining a great deal. It's preferable to wager a penny to win a dollar, but sometimes you have to wager a dollar to win a dollar; sometimes you have to risk a lot more just to stay in the game."

It rang true, Marshall thought. But he was afraid to believe it. He leaned closer, eyeing the man with all his power to pierce a subterfuge.

"General Khanh is charged with the success of this attack. Very simply, he doesn't want to launch it."

"Why?"

"I was given three reasons. Number one is that he doesn't feel it will succeed. He has no illusions that the attack will defeat the Americans or overthrow the Thieu government. He thinks his army will suffer huge losses—he doesn't want to sacrifice his men."

Lacouture held up a second finger. "Two: Khanh believes

403

that an attack would backfire by stiffening American resolve. His reasons are psychological, and you better than I
could judge their merit. I wouldn't presume to know, but
Khanh feels that the more effective his strike, the more
entrenched the Americans will become. His goal is to force
American withdrawal—he thinks a major offensive would
be counterproductive."

Marshall nodded blandly, but he was stunned at the
perceptivity of the assessment. *That is exactly what would
happen.*

Lacouture shrugged, as though dismissing the third reason. "Three—this is personal. General Khanh has lost two
sons in the war. His wife and daughters are subject to the
daily bombings of the North. He was destroyed by the
deaths of his sons and cannot bear any more sorrow. I
myself find this hard to accept—a general so disturbed by
death, softened by losses—but that is what I was told. I'm
afraid you'll have to take that for what it's worth—whether
a man who lost his sons in war would be willing to negotiate
with the enemy rather than redouble his efforts to seek
revenge."

Ah, thought Lacouture, watching Marshall's reaction
carefully, *that struck home; Lord was right—Marshall's
own son was his vulnerable point.* Lacouture had been very
pleased with his own performance thus far, though it had
been aided, he knew, by both Marshall's intelligence—the
man was far more clever and facile than he had anticipated
—and Marshall's desire to meet with the NVA. He,
Lacouture, actually had had an easy job, he thought—trying
to persuade Marshall to do something he very much wanted
to do.

This meeting was going to succeed, Lacouture thought
excitedly—*the ploy about the sons guaranteed it. Very
clever of Lord,* he acknowledged.

Lacouture shrugged again. "A sensitive general? I find it
strange."

Of course Lacouture would find that strange, Marshall
thought—*he has no children. But what kind of man with
children would not be moved by their deaths? Would we*

deny an enemy such humanity? If this General Khanh thought the same way he did, surely he could *feel* the same way. The third reason could possibly be the strongest one, Marshall thought. The man had lost his sons; he could not bear any more loss or sorrow. That is exactly how he would feel.

Yes, he understood this man, a man who felt and cared as strongly as he himself did, a man who would help him achieve a just end to this war.

Lacouture had not made this up, Marshall was convinced. It was true—here was the possibility for peace; his solution. He dared not let it slip by, yet he had to take care and not betray his desperate eagerness.

"What proof is there that this man is alive?" Marshall asked indifferently.

"I suppose the question could be turned around," Lacouture answered. "What proof is there that he is dead? It would certainly be possible, even likely, that the NVA would plant rumors about Khanh's death merely to deceive the enemy."

"True, but you said there was concrete proof of the legitimacy of his proposal."

"Yes. But it is like Khanh's third reason, it doesn't make much sense to me. For verification, you are supposed to go to the most unlikely source—General Huy Chi Tran, who has recently been appointed area commander for the South Vietnamese army."

Marshall nodded noncommittally. "I should write these names down; I don't know if I'll be able to remember them."

"My sources tell me that Tran is a remarkably competent general, perhaps the only one. I can't imagine how he ended up as area commander; he certainly won't last if he is competent," Lacouture said. "Thieu isn't about to countenance that for long—someone really competent would overthrow him as the first order of business. Anyway, I'm told that Tran is loyal and utterly opposed to the communists. You may become the intermediary between them. Khanh wants to meet with Tran, apparently for the same reasons. Obviously any meeting between the two would be dangerous, not just personally but politically. Both would require absolute secrecy and assurances of safety. They will communicate through you—once you have allayed their suspicions and established their sincerity, they will meet."

"I believe I understand," Marshall said. "I do not know if Khanh is alive, or if this proposal even comes from him. To verify both, I am to approach Khanh's primary foe, his hated enemy, who believes Khanh is dead. With information you provide me, I will convince Tran that Khanh is alive and wants to meet with him. I will transmit a series of communiqués between them that will assure them both of the earnestness and reliability of each. Their acceptance of the good faith of the other is my proof. If they will trust one another on the basis of my good offices, then I should trust General Khanh too."

"Exactly," Lacouture said. "It took me a while to figure that out. I never would have done it with four glasses of champagne—my congratulations to you."

"It sounds unnecessarily convoluted."

"That's what I think. But would you agree to meet him without some proof or verification? Would you take my word for all this and let me set up a meeting in the jungle somewhere?"

Marshall smiled. "Probably not; at least not without another four glasses of champagne."

"Well, if you can think of a simpler method, I will be happy to transmit it. General Khanh indicated that he would be willing to provide any kind of proof or verification you would like, except coming forward personally, of course. You can appreciate his reluctance to meet you here in downtown Saigon."

Here it was, Marshall thought: exactly what he'd hoped for—a breakthrough, a chance. Success was possible. If he could sit down across from General Khanh, if they could look into each other's eyes, if they could see into each other's hearts, they could end the misery and suffering of this war—two fathers who cared for their sons could stop the slaughter.

He had to meet with this man; it meant everything.

Not that he had any delusions—there would be hard

bargaining, interminable negotiations. Yet here was the first step, and only yesterday that had seemed unattainable.

"I will give this serious thought," Marshall said blandly.

Lacouture did not move. " 'Squeaky,' that is what you are to say to General Tran. I have no idea what that means. Supposedly it will have significance to Tran, who will then respond accordingly. And so on and so forth until the tedious business is resolved." He reached into a vest pocket and took out a business card. He handed it to Marshall. "You can reach me at that number—assuming the phones work; or send a message to that address."

Lacouture stood. "Thank you for seeing me; thank you for the champagne, and your graciousness." It had worked, he thought in self-congratulation—Marshall was convinced—and his mind fantasized bank notes and bikinied savages.

They shook hands, and Marshall walked him to the front door.

"Have you had an opportunity to travel in the country?" Lacouture asked.

"Not yet."

"It's a gorgeous country. You must take the time to go to Da Lat and to Hue. Da Lat is simply paradise; it was formerly the hunting preserve of the emperors. Even now it's unspoiled. And Hue—the Citadel, the Imperial Palace, the River of Perfumes—you would have to go to Angkor Wat in Cambodia to see something more remarkable."

He shook his finger at Marshall. "And go to the tombs of the emperors outside Hue. It's quite stunning, not just architecturally, but intellectually. Each emperor built his own tomb. They would go there before their deaths for peace and contemplation. I found that intriguing, that men would go to their graves before death for quiet repose and meditation—leave the pleasures of their palace and concubines to sit upon their tombs and ponder . . . what? I don't think I could do that; could you?"

Marshall envisioned a robed emperor sitting alone in his sepulcher, his guards at a distance. Indeed the paths of glory and power lead but to the grave, yet what kind of man would stroll that path before his time to gaze upon his crypt?

Lyndon Johnson might oversee the construction of a

massive mausoleum for himself, and revel in its size and magnificence—but sit on his headstone and contemplate mortality? No.

Nor would he himself, he realized.

"You might gain a better understanding of this culture and what you are dealing with by going there," Lacouture said.

"Then I shall make it a point to go," Marshall promised. "I will make a special pilgrimage there."

They shook hands and held the grip an extra moment, locking their gaze.

Marshall smiled, not bothering to hide his pleasure, but the smile did not begin to express the happiness and hope he felt. He would save all the sons.

Lacouture bowed, then went down the steps daintily, trying to restrain himself from rushing to the street to hail a cab.

It was nearly nine! What if he missed the savage?

CHAPTER

• 26 •

"Hurry!" entreated Lacouture after giving the restaurant address to the cabdriver. "I must be there by nine; I will pay you double if you can do it."

"Fly!" he shouted, then fell back against the seat as the cab raced forward.

He had made all the arrangements earlier; he had been dining at the Coq d'Or for twenty years. Wars, governments, regimes, coups—none of these could alter his habits. Only a few things were sacred and inviolate—a fine restaurant was one. What did the politics matter if the food was good? Conversely, wretched food was not helped by good government. He believed a good chef more valuable than a good minister, and much worthier of loyalty.

He knew the best table had been set aside, his intimacy guaranteed; the food would be perfect.

He collapsed in the seat. What if the savage didn't come? Of course he wouldn't; there was no hope. He might as well go home now, or fling himself into the river. The savage would not show up; his dreams were dirt—it was all hopeless. He couldn't stand it. In despair in a heap in the backseat, he could not even summon the energy to tell the driver to take him home.

Yet the savage had accepted the paper with the name and address of the restaurant; he had said he would think about it. Maybe he would come. He would! He knew he would! He sat up. "Hurry!" he shouted to the driver.

The cab jostled and bounced through evening traffic; shops were closing, people were going home, and as they left the city, others were arriving—the night inhabitants—and the bars and brothels and discotheques were opening. Neon flashed and music blared cacophonously from every other doorway.

It was six before nine, and they were at least ten minutes away. Lacouture wanted to wrestle the wheel from the driver. The savage would leave! He clutched his heart. He couldn't stand it. He pulled out his handkerchief to fan himself, but instead he chewed on it.

The savage would not be there; he had a woman. He would be repelled by someone such as himself. Indeed, he had laughed at him, ridiculed him. He sank into the seat, then took the handkerchief from his mouth and dabbed his eyes. It was hopeless—another cruel joke. He sobbed at the injustice.

A feeling, like a leviathan hand squeezing his chest, brought a sensation so intense he closed his eyes. It was always the same fantasy, in which he gratified a handsome youth who never touched him in return, who merely reclined, lying still, eyes sheathed, watching. The act, his love, could not be reciprocated; the youth must remain motionless, mute, ungiving. He fantasized a perfection he could not possess, a perfection that would be destroyed the moment he touched it.

It was, he knew, because he had to love what could not love him in return, what had no need for him or his love. The youth was a god who had to be pleasured, ministered to, who returned only contempt. If the savage, his god, wanted him, he would no longer want the god.

Lacouture saw the fantasy as a representation of his life, a hell of unattainable love—loving what could not love back, and worse, his wanting it this way, requiring it so. He was doomed to love what by its nature must despise him.

That is how it had been with Jacques, he remembered, his centurion god in the Foreign Legion; he had worshiped him, no priest before any altar had supplicated more devoutly, and yet the only touch Jacques ever returned was vicious and abusive. Yet, and Lacouture knew this with pain in his heart, had Jacques returned his love, caressed him, then he, Lacouture, would have fled the temple and sought another god.

From this torment he had developed the cosmology that man's worship of God was homosexual, to love what must find him weak and contemptible, to need the love of what cannot be possessed; it was debasement and defilement—man on his knees before a beautiful god creature, begging for love from what must hold him in contempt and revulsion.

He wanted the savage so badly, yet he knew the disgust the youth would feel for him. Lacouture wanted him so badly to be there at the restaurant, yet he knew it would be better if he did not come.

Torn, Lacouture sat immobile in the cab when it pulled up in front of the Coq d'Or.

Then excitement and anxiety took over; he paid the driver and leaped out. The Coq d'Or was on Rue Catinat in the center of the French quarter. Though it had certainly seen better days, the restaurant was still fashionable and expensive, and because of its loyal clientele and formal service, it managed to affect a hauteur that spared it the invasion of soldiers and prostitutes.

The savage was not in sight.

Lacouture rushed inside. The maître d' met him and bowed. "A pleasure as always, Monsieur Lacouture. You are well? You look wonderful. The kitchen is at your command, and your table prepared. Please," and he started away.

"No," cried Lacouture. "I am waiting for someone. He has not arrived?"

The maître d' looked mournful in commiseration.

"I'll wait outside," Lacouture said, and rushed through the door.

He paced back and forth in front of the entrance, then lengthened the distance until he was covering the entire block, his anxiety mounting with each step until he was overcome with desperation. His savage wasn't coming; he wanted to weep, to throw himself in front of a car. Life was cruel and unfair. He couldn't bear it.

Then he appeared—just there suddenly, rounding the corner, and Lacouture could not believe his eyes. He clutched his chest and nearly fell into a shop window.

"Oh," he cried, and rushed forward. "Oh, oh, oh."

Mead was in fatigues, his only clothes, and he stopped when he saw Lacouture run toward him. He watched curiously as the small, dapper, fat man bore down on him, taking out his handkerchief and flapping it as if to give him more thrust; for a second Mead feared that the man was going to rush into his arms.

"Bien, bien. How wonderful! You came! I knew you would, oh, I just knew it."

Lacouture had to restrain himself from grabbing Mead to test his physical reality. He wanted to clasp him in gratitude. He was so wonderful; the most perfect man he had ever seen.

"Have you eaten?" Lacouture asked, trying to calm himself, knowing that he would make Mead nervous with his behavior.

Mead shook his head.

"Are you hungry? You must be. This is an excellent place. Do you like French food?"

Mead shrugged. "I don't know; I never had any."

Lacouture clutched his chest. "What? Never?"

"Well, french fries," he amended. "I like them."

Lacouture looked at him quizzically. "Pardon?"

"French fries."

Lacouture said the words. "I don't know them," he said at last.

"Everybody knows french fries," Mead said. "Potatoes, fried up."

"Potatoes," Lacouture mused. *"Pomme de . . .* Ah! *Pomme frites!* French fries? Why that . . ." Then he shook his head and muttered, "French envelopes, French postcards, now french fries. Is there anything else French you like?"

Mead shrugged again. "I never ate anything French before. What kinds of things do you eat?"

"What do you mean, what do we eat?"

"I mean, do you eat meat? Steaks, things like that?"

"Of course we eat meat. Beef, pork, chicken, duck, rabbit." He grabbed Mead's arm to lead him inside, but feeling the muscles stiffen, he let go immediately. "Come, we won't poison you."

Inside, Lacouture displayed him triumphantly to the maître d'. "He arrived."

The maître d', a tuxedoed middle-aged Vietnamese who had once lived in France, inclined his head to them both, smiled happily for Lacouture, and properly ignored Mead's attire.

Lacouture followed the maître d', and Mead trailed them both, beginning to feel very awkward and out of place; he had never eaten in a place like this, with real flowers on the tables, and tablecloths, silverware, and shining crystal. The lighting was dim, the atmosphere quiet, and all the other diners were dressed in civilian clothes with ties, and none of them looked American.

At a separate table at the far end of the dining room, the maître d' held the chair for Lacouture, then rushed to help Mead sit. No one had ever done that either, and Mead felt very unsure of himself.

"My young friend has never eaten French cuisine," Lacouture said.

The maître d' looked at him in mild astonishment, then nodded as a surgeon might over a critically ill patient. "Then he must have the *menu dégustation*."

"I quite agree," said Lacouture. "Myself also. And the entree is?"

"*Canard.*"

"Wonderful. An aperitif?" he asked Mead, then said quickly, "A drink? Oh, let me do it. Champagne for my guest. I just drank some marvelous Moët, so I simply can't have any more. I'll have a little sauternes with the foie gras. Then a Puligny-Montrachet; after that, we'll just see."

The maître d' bowed and left them.

413

Lacouture wanted to reach over and grab Mead's hand, both in happiness and to reassure him—the youth looked so nervous and stiff. "If you don't like the food, don't eat it. You won't hurt my feelings at all. Maybe a little champagne will make you feel more comfortable."

"I think it would take a lot of champagne," Mead said. "But I've never had any of that either."

"That I think you will like. And you may have as much as you wish." Then he shook his head. "Never had any champagne? Really?"

Mead grinned faintly. "It's not a big drink in Arkansas. Or the Marines either."

"The Marines? That is like the navy—on the ships? And Arkansas? I don't know that at all."

"It's probably not on French maps."

"Ah, a joke," Lacouture said happily. "How nice: a real man who makes jokes. But I probably won't understand your jokes because I don't know any Americans—just one or two. They try to speak French, and I don't understand that either." He waved his hand to erase the memory of Wilson Abbot Lord's French.

Mead smiled. "Well, you won't have to worry about that with me."

Lacouture brought his hands together. "Oh, you are too lovely." Then he lowered his head. "I shouldn't say that. It makes you nervous, doesn't it?"

"Well, it's . . ."

"You don't like it."

"It's just . . . well, I guess I'm not used to it. I mean, I don't know any . . ."

"Homosexuals?" Lacouture whispered. "You don't know *any?* None at all? Impossible. Maybe you did, but just didn't know."

"Well, I don't know anyone who bragged about it."

"Hah! You are so amusing. I am already in love with you." He covered his mouth again. "I won't say these things."

A waiter came with the drinks and set two small dishes of *amusegueules* before them.

Lacouture raised his glass. "To you."

Mead raised his, then drank.

414

"Do you like it?"

Mead thought a moment, took another sip, then nodded. "Yes. Is it alcohol? I think I could drink a lot of this."

"I won't lie; yes, it is alcoholic. And that, I believe, is oyster. Don't chew it, just lift it up and swallow, like this." He demonstrated.

Mead did the same. "It's okay," he said.

"*Bien.* Many wouldn't even try such a thing, though I can't imagine why, it's just from the ocean."

They stared at one another, then Mead looked away nervously.

"Well, now we must converse," Lacouture said. "That's required over dinner. We will talk about your work; what do you do?"

Mead stiffened and looked wary.

Lacouture said quickly, "I am just trying to be polite. I am not a spy, or rather, I am not professionally interested in the nature of your work. My interests are quite otherwise, I assure you. If you don't want to talk about what you do, for heaven's sake, we'll talk about something else."

"What do you do?" Mead asked, relaxing slightly.

"Well, actually, I am a spy, though that really isn't an accurate description. I exchange information—buy a little something here, sell it somewhere else. I don't work for anybody, no particular government, so I don't really qualify as a spy. I just try to make do as best I can; some people sell gold, some automobiles, some refrigerators, I sell information. But I am not interested in that kind of information from you. Unless you happen to know something particularly useful, then I shall purchase it from you. Do you have any secrets to sell me?"

Mead laughed. "I'm a corporal; I don't know anything worth selling or buying, or even worth knowing for that matter."

Lacouture shook his head in appreciation. "You must be wonderful with women—you have that perfect . . . how shall we say it? Easy confidence that comes out as humility."

Mead drained his glass.

Lacouture motioned the waiter, gesturing faintly toward Mead, and in a moment another glass appeared.

"You trying to get me drunk?"

"I would love to. Is it possible?"

Mead grinned, rather enjoying this in spite of himself. "I've been drunk before."

"Do you get violent?"

"Yeah; a while back I beat the shit out of a couple whores, so I've tried to cut down on drinking."

"You're making me giddy. Well, now we know what I do, and what you don't do, so what shall we talk about?"

"Who's the old gook, the one you sent to my room?"

"Oh, you figured that out. Kim will be hysterical; he prides himself on his stealth. What was it that gave him away?"

"His teeth."

"Of course. Stupid little man; I've told him a thousand times that he's the only Vietnamese on earth who has all his teeth, and they're as bright as flashlights. But I can't get him to do a thing about them. Vanity, vanity—there's some useful saying about that in the Bible, I think."

"My mother could tell you."

"Oh, dear."

"You have a mother like that too?"

"Quite the opposite. My mother was . . . hardly a religious woman. She was a woman who . . . how shall we say *that?* Who devoted herself to pleasure. Sometimes with my father, usually not."

"So why did you send the gook to my room?"

"To find out about you."

"Find out what?"

"To find out who you were, and where I could find you, and just anything that might help me."

"Help you what?"

"Well, really! Do have some more champagne. Ah, our first course. Do you like fish?"

"I've had some bluefish and catfish; I liked them."

"Bluefish? Catfish? But no Frenchfish?" He giggled. "That is a joke I just made—the Americans seem to have a French everything."

The plates were set before them and the wine poured for Lacouture to taste. He nodded and two glasses were filled.

Mead sampled his and Lacouture could tell that he did not like it, though Mead politely took another sip.

"No, no," said Lacouture. "Don't drink it if you don't like it. Tell me what's wrong."

Mead shrugged a little sheepishly. "I know it's probably great, and costs more than I make every month, but it's . . . just kinda strange to me—a little . . . sour."

"I understand. It's a white burgundy, not at all to everyone's taste. But you like the champagne?"

"Yeah, that was great. Or beer; I like that too."

Lacouture motioned the waiter and ordered a bottle of champagne.

"Much better," said Lacouture when the bottle arrived. "Now we don't have to share; each one of us has his own."

Though ravenous, Mead was careful to eat slowly, and he noted which utensils Lacouture used before picking up his own. "The fish is really good," he said. "I just had fried fish before."

"Is all your food fried?"

"Nah, not in the mess halls, but Mom used to fry most everything. I think farm people eat lots of fried foods. She had a big skillet on the stove; in the morning she'd fry bacon or ham, then eggs, and later she'd fry pork chops or chicken, sometimes steak. In fact, I guess she fried about everything, except vegetables, though sometimes she'd fry okra."

"It certainly didn't do you any harm," Lacouture said. "You grew up big, and you look strong and healthy enough."

"We ate good. We didn't have any money; I mean, there never was any cash. Mom hardly ever went to a store." He took a long drink. "I guess it was really hard for her—I mean, never getting to go anywhere, and when she did, really counting pennies. I remember sometimes going with her, and she'd secretly count up what she had, then try to add up what she was buying."

"I will cry," said Lacouture, pulling out his handkerchief.

"Don't make fun of me," Mead said, drawing up.

"No, no! You don't understand—I *will* cry. I can't stand sad stories. I see everything in pictures—it is my misfortune. I see your mother in a peasant dress standing—"

"My mother isn't a fucking peasant," Mead said proudly.

"Oh, dear, oh, dear," said Lacouture. "It is a cultural misunderstanding. A word in French means something different in English. I was not insulting your mother. I told you, I don't know many Americans; if I say something that offends you, it would be completely unintentional."

Mead eyed him narrowly. "Anyway, we ate good, but we weren't rich."

"My family was. They didn't deserve it, and didn't work hard, but that's how it usually is, or was, in Europe. I grew up having everything I wanted—except my parents; I never saw them. I was surrounded by servants, but I was very lonely. I always played by myself; I never had any friends." He took out his handkerchief and dabbed his eyes. "You see, everything makes me cry." He blew his nose loudly. "Did you have friends? Were you lonely?"

"I don't guess I was lonely," Mead said, trying to remember, for he was not given to reflection and seldom thought of his childhood. "I remember working a lot, on the farm, I mean. My old man was always hounding us. Maybe I was too busy to be lonely. And in school—yeah, I had friends. I was always playing ball—baseball or football or basketball —and there were always guys I was with."

"And girls?"

Mead smiled. "Yeah, later."

"Why did you leave the farm?"

"Jesus, have you ever been on a farm?"

Lacouture laughed. "No. That bad?"

"Pretty bad, unless you like pig shit."

"That is why you joined the . . . Marines?"

Mead nodded. "There wasn't much else for me to do. I mean, I couldn't go to college—not with my grades, and well, there really was no other way I could get out. I would have been drafted anyway, so I joined up. As it turns out, I should have stayed on the farm and shoveled pig shit."

"You do not like Vietnam?"

He drained his ever-filled glass. "Vietnam? I don't know anything about Vietnam. All I seen is some jungle and a little bit of Saigon. It wouldn't be fair for me to say anything about the country, or the people; I don't know any of them, except a couple women."

"That's a very mature thing to say; wiser than what men much older, and who have perhaps been to college, would say. What you are saying is that you don't like war."

Mead frowned. "Well, that's the funny part; sometimes I really did like the war."

Lacouture nodded. "That has been my experience with soldiers—they decry their lot, but deep down they seem to like it very much. I knew a boy, a young man—you remind me a great deal of him, that is what first struck me, that and your handsomeness—who was in the Foreign Legion—"

"There really is a Foreign Legion? I thought that was just in movies."

"Oh, no, it is for real. Men run off to join it, murderers and thieves, and who knows what else. They don't ask any questions—if you are strong enough and can stand the hardships, that's all that matters. Anyway, he was a very . . . tough young man, and he complained so much about the Legion and the military, but he just loved it. I suppose men love to be soldiers—carrying spears as on old, shattered Greek vases, or as grenadiers for imperial armies, or as Jacques was as a Legionnaire. Or as you are."

"But not you?"

Lacouture laughed. "Can you see me on a Greek vase with a spear? Or in the Foreign Legion? Or the Marines?"

Mead did not answer.

Lacouture lowered his head. "No. I never played with a ball." He heaved sadly. "I never should have been a boy." He looked at Mead. "I should have been a girl. It's true; I was born wrong. I couldn't help it. I should have been a girl. I always wanted someone like you to take care of me—to hold my hand and protect me. I would have liked to walk down the street with someone like you with his arm around me."

Lacouture dropped his head. "I am ashamed of what I am and how I act. I know I must disgust you. Do you hate me?"

Mead said softly, "Hate you? No. I don't hate you. Why should I? You just told me you can't help the way you are."

Lacouture sobbed slightly at the table. Mead looked about in embarrassment.

"Mr. . . . Mr. La—"

"Oh, call me Bernard," Lacouture said, shoulders shaking.

Mead swallowed. "Bernard, don't . . . I mean, stop crying. Jesus, people are—"

"I don't care. All I ever wanted was someone like you. And you are so kind and wonderful."

Mead was mortified. He poured another glassful and drained it. "You gotta stop this. You're getting your food wet."

Lacouture stopped, looked into his dish, then giggled. "You're right, I am." He wiped his eyes and sat straight. "But life is so unfair. Why should that silly whore have you? Why can't I?"

Mead stiffened. "She's not a whore," he said. "I don't want you saying anything about her."

"I'm just jealous. She's probably a nice girl; many of them are—they have no other way to make a living, then they are drugged by the brothel keepers. They have babies, or get diseases." He sighed. "Life is not fair to them either."

Their entrees were placed before them and their glasses refilled.

"It is duck," Lacouture said. "Have you ever had that?"

"Yes. My old man and I would go out duck hunting. We'd freeze our asses sitting in duck blinds in early morning. It was always cold and wet; really miserable weather, but you know, it was the only decent time I can remember with my father. I mean, he was sober and quiet."

"I never spent any time with my father," Lacouture said.

"If that's going to make you cry too, don't get started on that."

Lacouture laughed. "You are so amusing. You are going to break my heart."

"Let's not talk about that either," Mead said, taking a bite of duck. "Hey, this is good. My mom never cooked it like this."

"Did she fry that too?"

He thought back. "Well, yeah, sometimes she did. But she'd roast it in the oven too. What else can you do to a duck?"

"Well, the Chinese do lots of things. I think the best duck I ever had was packed in mud and baked in the oven. This one was . . . well, see that over there? That's a duck press. They put the carcass in that, after they've cut away the breast and legs, and squeeze. It crushes the bones and squeezes out all the juices."

"Oh," said Mead, turning back to his plate, and putting down his fork.

"I think we have done our duty conversing," said Lacouture. "Now we must talk."

Mead took a deep drink.

"Certainly I am not going to seduce you, nor am I interested in getting you drunk and taking advantage of you. So I suppose we should just make this as painlessly business-like as possible. I want to buy you."

Mead broke into a wide grin. "You can't buy me. I'm not a fucking duck—I'm not for sale."

Lacouture made a tsking, hushing sound. "I am talking business. Just listen. I mean your body—and not sell; let us say, rent. I want to pay you rent for your body."

Mead stifled his laughter. He stared at the ceiling, then looked at Lacouture. "Man, this is crazy. Look, I've had kind of a neat time. I thought this was going to be awful, but it's been fun. I liked talking to you, but . . . well, let's just leave it at this."

"You are embarrassed."

"Well, yeah. I don't want to talk about things like this. I mean, I'm not . . ."

"I know you're not a homosexual. I wouldn't be interested in you if you were. I am not expecting you to love me."

Mead shifted uncomfortably and looked about nervously, feeling that everyone was listening in on their conversation.

"This is business. I expect to pay you. I *want* to pay you. All you have to do is tell me how much money you want."

"Mr. La . . . Bernard, get this straight: I don't want any money from you. This has been nice, having dinner, let's leave it like this."

Lacouture said petulantly, "But I want to go to bed with you."

Mead laughed. "You want to what?"

"Sleep with you."

Mead laughed again. "Ah . . . that's just not possible."
He was neither angry nor affronted, and he tried not to treat
it as a joke for fear of hurting Lacouture's feelings. "Bernard, I don't go to bed with guys. I don't want to offend you,
but I just don't want to do that kind of thing. I mean, you
pay whores to go to bed with you: I'm not a whore."

"But I will pay you—"

"I just told you, I don't want money; I don't care if you
paid me a thousand dollars."

"But you must!"

"Well, I won't, damn it. Now cut it out, I don't want to
talk about it anymore."

"You are angry."

"No, but I will be if you keep this up. Look, I really don't
care what people do together—that's their business. If you
like guys and like getting fucked in the ass, that's okay by
me. I got my own problems in my own life—don't add to
them. Let's just be friends."

"Friends?"

"Yeah, friends. You know—get together and have a drink,
champagne; have dinner once in a while. Talk. That kind of
thing. But nothing else."

"You would be my friend?" Lacouture said in wonder.

"Sure."

"And see me again? And have dinner again?"

"Yeah. Sure."

"I don't disgust you?"

Mead let out his breath slowly. "No. I've done some
pretty awful things. I mean, killing people isn't at the top of
anybody's do-gooder list. I see things a lot differently since I
came over here. I seen guys die—I mean, just disappear.
Joking and laughing, then . . . gone. I don't understand any
of it—why we're here or where we're going or what it's all
about. And I know I never will."

Mead drained the last of his glass and set it aside. "I wish I
hadn't seen death." He sighed deeply. "I can't explain it, but
once you see death—I mean, really see it: awful and bloody,
muddy and wet, standing over somebody ripped and
twisted, and knowing it could be you—knowing it *will* be
you someday . . . well, it just makes everything different. All

the things that bother people, all the petty bullshit—none of it seems very important. We're all going to end up the same way, so I don't see any point in worrying about a lot of things. I guess I learned . . . well, it sounds kinda stupid, I know, but I learned that you oughta care for people. You oughta be nice."

He shrugged in embarrassment. "So, yeah, I could be your friend."

Lacouture sat back. "Well," he said.

"Hey, I really should be going. I know I shouldn't just leave like this, but probably it would be best this way. Should I pay you anything for all this food and champagne?"

Lacouture stared at him, absolutely struck dumb. He shook his head.

Mead stood up and held out his hand. "Thanks a lot, I really enjoyed it—really I did." Then he turned and walked out.

When he left, and after a respectable moment, the waiter came to the table. "Is everything all right, sir?" he asked.

Lacouture stared after where Mead had disappeared. "I don't know," he said at last. "I've never been in love before."

He looked across to where Mead had sat, could feel the presence so profoundly that it hurt his heart. "Is it all right to love?" he asked, looking up.

But the waiter was gone, and he sat alone.

CHAPTER

• 27 •

Rain had fallen continuously for three days, flooding the bunkers on the hill. Cold and wet, the men passed their time playing cards, reading, and sleeping.

"I never seen anything like this," Leslie Frizzell said for the hundredth time, sitting in the bunker entrance watching the steady fall.

"At least we won't have patrols," Dennis Coney said without looking up from a magazine he had read three times. "The gooks can't attack in weather like this, unless they have boats."

Scott Sutherland was curled asleep in a corner, a position he had seldom moved from in the past two days; it was as though he had switched off his system. Frizzell, bored to distraction, could not get him to do anything. Frizzell didn't expect Coney to play—he was older, twenty-one—and had a wife and child; he was an adult to Frizzell, part of the grown-up world he didn't think he would ever enter, but Sutherland, nineteen, nearer his own age, joked and played.

Glancing toward him hopefully when Sutherland turned over, Frizzell sighed when he saw that Sutherland was only shifting sleeping positions. Then he reached beside him and grabbed his helmet; he placed it outside the bunker upside down and watched it fill with rainwater. He leaned over and grabbed Coney's helmet and put it outside also. Both filled much slower than he expected in such rain, but at least watching them gave him something to do.

Finally they were sufficiently full. He brought them in carefully and with one in each hand he crawled toward Sutherland; Coney watched from over his magazine.

Sutherland groaned and yawned, then as if on cue turned toward him, eyes closed.

Frizzell threw the first helmetful directly into his face. Sutherland jerked up, gasping, then Frizzell threw the other helmetful, but the helmet slipped out of his hand and hit Sutherland in the head, knocking him backward.

"Oh, shit," Frizzell said in horror.

"You motherfucker," Sutherland screamed, jumping up, holding his head, but Frizzell was already gone, scrambling out of the bunker.

"I'll kill you," Sutherland cried, clawing his way after him.

"I didn't mean it," Frizzell yelled, racing across the hill.

"Bastard," screamed Sutherland, chasing furiously.

They ran up and down the slopes, around the bunkers, until Sutherland finally caught him close to their own, throwing himself in a desperate tackle, catching Frizzell's trouser cuff, tripping him. They rolled over and over until Frizzell began to laugh; then he clutched his sides, convulsing. Sutherland jumped on his back in fury, but Frizzell had rolled into a ball, choking with glee. Sutherland sat on him, felt his anger drain away, and thumped him in the side halfheartedly. "You prick."

Frizzell rolled over, tears streaming from his eyes. "You were so mad. You should have seen your face when the helmet hit you."

"Asshole," said Sutherland. Then he felt himself; his uniform was soaked and he was covered with wet sand. He stood and stripped off his uniform; Frizzell shucked his too. Then they saw Coney watching them from the bunker. They glanced at each other and nodded, then ran up the slope toward him. Coney tried to block their entrance but they overpowered him and dragged him outside, rolling him over and over, snapping him with their wet uniforms. Then they ran off.

Coney tore off his uniform and gave chase.

From the entrance of the main bunker, Bishop and Brock watched the three run through the rain, shouting and leaping, knocking each other down.

"What jackasses," Brock said.

Bishop smiled. "Didn't you ever play in the rain?"

"Not when I had somewhere dry to go."

Below them the radio crackled; both went down to get it. The message was in code from company headquarters at Khe Sanh.

"Whoa," said Brock. "Coded—that'll fox the gooks for sure. Bet it'll take them at least ten minutes to figure it out."

When the transmission ended, Bishop went for the code book, but he couldn't find it, only the outdated one.

"Shit," he said. "What are we gonna do?"

Brock had lost interest. He went to the corner for a can of rations.

"We'll have to ask the next gook that goes by what the message was."

"Maybe Landis knows where it is," Bishop said, reaching for the field radio, calling his post. Landis told him it was with the spare batteries, and after twenty minutes' work, Bishop held the decoded message before him.

Intelligence indicates large enemy staging area grid 1979 or 2579. Aerial surveillance unable to detect. Completion endangers TAOR. Send five-man patrol to confirm or deny. Do not engage enemy. Acknowledge receipt and dispatch of patrol.

Bishop read the message twice, then handed the sheet to Brock. He read it without expression, then handed it back.

"I don't need to send five men," Bishop said. "You ought to be able to handle it yourself, Gunny."

When Brock didn't say anything, Bishop ran his hand through his hair and asked softly, "What would you do, Gunny?"

"I'd acknowledge the message, tell them the patrol just left, and call them back in five days and say the patrol didn't

426

find anything. You can't send five men out there—that'd only leave thirteen men here, not even two men on each post. The gooks wouldn't even have to attack; they could just wait until everybody fell asleep, then they'd walk in and cut your throats."

"It's the same as the time they ordered me to send out a listening post, isn't it? And Snags and Miller got killed."

"You got it, Lieutenant. War's always the same old shit." Brock opened a can of rations. "The food's the same too—I think this is the same shit I ate in Korea."

Suddenly Bishop got angry, something Brock had not seen. He kicked over the ammunition crate he'd been sitting on and crumpled the message in his fist and shoved it toward Brock's face. "Okay, you're the professional soldier. Cut out all this crusty old gunnery sergeant bullshit and tell me what I'm supposed to do. I'm a goddamn second lieutenant; I'm twenty-two years old leading a bunch of dumbasses who know even less than I do. I get an order telling me to do something I don't like—you're telling me I'm supposed say, 'No, I don't agree with this order, I don't think I'll follow it; and besides, my tough but lovable gunnery sergeant doesn't like it either, so we're gonna pass on this one'? I'm a Marine officer, and you're a Marine gunnery sergeant."

Bishop shook his fist. "Here's the order. I don't know if it came from President Johnson or the Commandant or the regimental CO, or just Captain Willis, but it's a valid order from someone superior to me."

Bishop stuffed the paper into Brock's pocket. "And now I'm giving you the order. Take four men out there. If you want to go hide in a cave with them, or defect to the North, that's your fucking business, but I'm ordering you to take a patrol out there to see if there's a staging area or not. I'm tired of all this shit—sick of the rain and the war and trying to decide what's right and wrong. Fuck all of it. I just want to get all this over with and go home and not think about any of this shit for as long as I can. But *until* I get out of this shithole, I'm gonna follow orders, salute smartly, and do my job."

Brock stared at him expressionlessly. He glanced to the paper sticking out of his pocket, then he went back to his C rations.

"That was pretty good, Lieutenant. What OCS course did you learn that in—Platoon Drama?"

Bishop drew back furiously, then he laughed. "You asshole."

"You know I can't read a map worth shit," Brock said. "You're just gonna have to point me in the right direction and tell me how many hours to walk that way, then I'll turn everybody around and walk back."

"Take Sutherland—he's good with a map. In fact take the three of them, Sutherland, Coney, and Frizzell, and Landis too, he's the best with a radio."

"Sutherland will probably shoot me."

Bishop shrugged. "It's a Purple Heart. I'll make sure they send it to your wife."

Brock threw his rations against the wall and stood up. "I'm gonna be so pissed off if I get killed before you, Lieutenant." Then his eyes narrowed. "But it's not gonna happen, Brownbar—I swear it. I'll be *goddamned* if some shitass puppet lieutenant outlives me. Sir!"

Bishop looked at him quizzically. "Have I got your wife's address? Before you go, make sure you give it to me so I can send her the medal, along with that ratty wallet of yours. How about your fuck books and the *Playboy* cunt? You want me to send that to her or give it to Sutherland?"

Brock glared at him, then finally he smiled. "You know, I hope we both make it, 'cause when this is over, I want to meet you in the real world, Lieutenant. Then I'm gonna kick the shit out of you."

Bishop laughed. "Well, I don't think I'll let you do that, but I'd love to get drunk with you."

"And chase pussy?"

He put out his hand. "Deal."

Brock took it. "You're on, Lieutenant. But you're buying."

"You come back from this patrol okay, and I will."

Then Bishop got out his laminated map and the two went

over it carefully, plotting coordinates and establishing checkpoints.

"Two days, maybe three up, then two back."

Brock copied the coordinates and checkpoints on his own map, then went up the stairs to tell the others.

Crossing the hill, he stopped twice to gaze through the rain toward the hidden ridge. A heavy foreboding pressed him, and he could not shake it. Everything about this mission was wrong, he felt; everything about the war was wrong. He had liked Korea; he had understood that war. The South Koreans had fought hard and there was an identifiable enemy and everybody had fought like they were supposed to; there were great generals—MacArthur and Ridgeway and Chesty Puller—and great battles. But this war, he thought, was just bullshit: the South Vietnamese weren't fighting, the enemy—hell, he didn't even know who the enemy was—and there weren't any great generals and no battles, and they were just sitting on hills and behind perimeters.

Well, one for two isn't bad, he thought, and since this was the only war there was, there was no sense bitching about it—you take what you can get. After all, he had joined the Marines to fight, and they had obliged him with another war—not a great war, but a war nevertheless.

He was a professional. All his adult life he had been in the Marines, and though he did not like this mission, he would do what he was told; he was, after all, just a gunnery sergeant.

At the bunker on the rear slope of the hill, Brock took a deep breath and thrust his head into the entrance.

Landis and Martin were sitting cross-legged, playing cards.

"Get your gear," Brock said to Landis. "You're going on patrol."

"Now?"

"Now and for five days."

Landis was incredulous. "You're kidding me."

Brock said emotionlessly, "I want you at the bunker by seven. Bring ammo and rations for five days."

Martin watched him disappear, then he turned to Landis and taunted, "You're gonna die."

"Don't say that."

"Good thing you talked to that chaplain and got saved."

"Cut it out, Josh." He turned away and began to gather his equipment. He put aside rations and broke out his ammunition, then he dismantled his rifle and lubricated it against the rain. In the middle of his work, he stopped and stared absently out into the steady gray drizzle.

All he wanted was the car he had thought so much about, the black Firebird with black interior—he had finally decided about it. He strained to see it in his mind through the rain, low to the ground, powerful and mean, and he strained to see himself in it, but the rain was like a dark veil, and he could not conjure up the image.

Across the hill, Coney was finishing a letter to his wife when he heard Sutherland whimper in his sleep and draw himself tighter.

He put his pen down and stared at the two men curled asleep.

The war was right for them, he thought: Frizzell didn't know any better and didn't have anything else to do; he was the simplest individual he, Coney, had ever know, and Sutherland—despite all his bitching and moaning—deep down liked the war because it was exciting and he liked fighting, and if he wasn't fighting here, he'd probably be doing it in L.A.

But he, Coney, had made a mistake. He shouldn't be here: he knew better, and he had a wife and child. He had run from that responsibility. He shouldn't have; he should have stayed and made it work: he had dropped out of college to get married, then dropped out of marriage to join the Marines. He smiled to himself: he wished he could drop out of this too. Then he picked up his pen to write his wife that when he returned he was going to try to be a good husband and father; he was going to try to make the marriage work.

Suddenly Brock was in the entrance; he pointed. "Wake them up."

Brock wiped rain from his face and shook his poncho.

"I'm only going through this once. You're not going to like it. I don't like it either but there's nothing we can do. Five of us, you three, Landis, and me, are going on a five-day patrol to find an enemy staging area. We'll be in enemy territory most of the time. Bring ammo and rations for five days. I want you ready by seven tonight."

They stared at him unbelievingly.

Frizzell finally smiled. "It's a joke, ain't it?"

Sutherland threw off his poncho and jumped up. "It's not a joke. You bastard, you're trying to get us killed."

Brock was steady, his voice controlled and even. "I told you, I don't like it either. I think it's a stupid idea, but we don't have a choice. The CO just sent a message."

Coney put down his letter. "How come us?"

"Because for this you need men who can work together, who trust one another completely, and won't make mistakes. If anyone makes a mistake, we'll all be dead."

"We'll be dead anyway."

"Maybe. That's why we're not charging you bunker rent, and we're giving you all the pork slices you can eat. Now, you got any more questions?"

Brock waited another minute, then backed from the entrance. "I think I'm finally gonna get you this time, Sutherland."

He disappeared.

They sat mutely, then Sutherland slammed his fists into the ground. "Oh, Jesus, no."

Coney shook his head in disbelief.

Only Frizzell accepted the patrol calmly. "We'll be all right. Landis is good, and Brock won't make any mistakes. And when we come back, we'll have five more days out of the way."

"When we come back! You simple jackass, you aren't coming back!" Sutherland's fury erupted against Frizzell. "You know what you are—a baby Brock. You're a fucking lifer in his first year. If you lived long enough—if you weren't going to get killed on this patrol—you'd end up a gunnery sergeant someday, you dumb shit. Gunny Frizzell. You asshole!"

Sutherland fell back and pulled his hair. "Five days

431

behind enemy lines! We won't last one. They can't do this. They can't send us out like this." He sat up furiously. "That's murder, that's all it is, just murder."

He shook with anger, then he said with cold determination, "I'm gonna kill him. So help me God, this time I am."

Coney watched dispassionately. He had seen Sutherland's act many times; it was, he knew, the way Sutherland psyched himself up for a patrol. He tossed him his pen. "Hey, write it down that I can be your body escort so when you get blown away I can bring your body home." He pushed Frizzell. "We'll all be escorts. You'll be in so many pieces, Sutherland, the whole fucking platoon can bring back a piece."

Sutherland threw his helmet at him. "You won't even have a coffin, Coney. We'll just glue what's left of you to a postcard and mail you home."

Brock returned to the bunker and wrote his wife. He told her there would be a lapse in his letters because he was going on a long patrol. He told her not to worry, that he would be safe, and that he loved her very much. Then he set to work on his equipment. He broke down his rifle, saturated it with oil, and laid aside rations and ammunition.

By midafternoon the rain was so heavy that visibility was only a few feet. Brock tried to sleep but finally gave up. "There's no sense waiting till night; it's dark enough now."

Bishop sat across from him on the ground, his knees bracing his elbows. "Maybe it won't take five days."

Brock grunted. He called Landis on the radio and told him to get the others now.

Landis reached down to wake Martin. "Hey, I gotta go. They changed the time." Awkwardly he held out his hand. They both smiled nervously, then Landis was gone.

After cleaning his rifle and laying out his equipment, Frizzell went back to sleep.

Coney tore up the letter to his wife and began another. He closed his eyes and sat listening to the soothing fall of rain. He tried to envision the child he had never seen, knowing him only from the one picture his wife had sent. He took the picture from his wallet and held it in his hands. He pressed his eyes closed. Please, God, make everything all right. Give me that, just that, and I won't ask for anything else. Let me see my child.

Sutherland could not sleep. He sat with his arms clasped around his knees and watched the rain. Rivulets gorged into channels and streamed down the slope of the hill. Anger had given way to fear. He knew he would not survive five days behind enemy lines. His mind struggled for a way out but saw he was trapped; his only escape was to admit cowardice. When he realized this, he eased into resignation, but then the dead came back to him, filling his mind. Soon tears dropped from his face into the sand. He wanted to go home.

The bunker entrance filled.

Sutherland turned quickly and brushed at his eyes.

Landis lifted the hood of his poncho. "Brock said to come now."

Coney jumped. "What?"

"We're leaving right away. Get your gear."

"For Christ's sake, it's raining like a bastard." Coney pointed to the deep puddles of water. "There're probably sharks out there."

Landis shook his head. "Brock said it was dark enough to leave now." He backed from the bunker and pulled the poncho hood over his head. "Better bring some shark repellent."

Sutherland reached for a can to throw, but Landis was gone. Sutherland stared at the downpour, then laughed. "They've been waiting for this, you know that, Coney. They waited till the worst goddamn day in the whole fucking war to send us out."

Coney sighed, put away the letter, and reached over to wake Frizzell. Then the three gathered their equipment and left the bunker.

Brock waited quietly for them. Bishop sat across the bunker watching silently.

The stairs groaned under the weight of the four men. They came into the bunker and stood uncomfortably.

Bishop gave them the message to read. "It's an order, and we haven't got any choice. I can't add anything to it. Maybe

433

you'll find something, maybe you won't. Work at it as best you can. Don't engage the enemy unless you have to. You won't have a chance out there if they see you."

Their eyes were intent on him. "Take two extra radio batteries. Keeping the radio dry is the most important thing. If you lose radio contact with us, the patrol is off—you can't stay out there without contact. I've got it covered so it shouldn't get wet."

He stared at them, then opened his hands. "I guess that's it."

Brock motioned them up the stairs and followed. At the top he fumbled for his wallet and tossed it to Bishop. "Don't send the fuck books or pictures," he said, then was gone.

Bishop dropped wearily onto the ammunition box. He held the wallet for a long time before putting it in his trousers.

The five men were drenched before they reached the wire. Brock stopped them at the break, shouting over the wind, "You might as well get soaked before we leave, then you won't have to worry about staying dry. And leave your helmets—they're not gonna save you."

They looked to each other, then began joking, jumping up and down, squishing the water already in their boots. Sutherland opened his jacket and let rain wash his chest. In a moment they were thoroughly wet and cold, and their clothing clung heavily.

Without a look back, Brock motioned them through the wire. He signaled Coney to cover the rear, and they moved north.

Progress was slow. Twice Coney halted them when he thought he saw figures following, but when they formed ambushes, there was nothing.

After several hours, Landis began to stumble under the weight of the radio. Frizzell found a bunker and they fell into it for an hour's rest. Landis lay exhausted while the others ate wordlessly, huddling close.

They were east of the ridge, skirting it, in a charred jungle of dead trees. Brock radioed a security check, then continued the patrol north. They picked their way cautiously through the brush, moving almost in a crawl, waiting every few moments to listen, but they heard only the wind driving rain through the dead branches.

Shortly before midnight Sutherland fell, dropping the machine gun in mud. They waited an hour as he cleaned it in the dark, ramming mud through the barrel and uncaking the bolt. Then they shifted the weight and continued for three more hours until Brock knew they were becoming careless.

An hour before dawn he signaled Frizzell to search for shelter. Frizzell moved off by himself and returned to lead them to a camouflaged cave.

Brock radioed back their position, then collapsed against the wall to sleep. Coney and Frizzell drew together for warmth and were asleep in minutes. In a corner Sutherland made a bed from loose brush and fell into uneasy slumber.

Landis kept first watch. He sat hunched over the machine gun and peered tiredly into the darkness. In early morning he woke Sutherland, and they changed places.

Sutherland shivered in the entrance, staring blankly at the wet grayness. He tried to warm himself and could not shake his coldness. He gazed on the others. Brock was breathing lightly, his mouth open and his arms cushioning his head. Coney and Frizzell lay together.

Stupid bastards, he thought. No one can make it five days like this. He picked up a rock to throw out of the bunker when he saw approaching forms. He threw himself prone, hissing, "Contact! Contact!"

The others jolted forward.

Sutherland fumbled wildly with the machine gun and inserted a belt of ammunition. He pulled back the bolt and let a round slide into the chamber. The others switched off their rifle safeties and sought positions in the cramped bunker.

Brock crawled to the entrance and crouched beside him. "How many?"

Sutherland shook his head frantically, unable to count them all.

Brock pressed into the opening and saw a large force

moving directly toward them. He felt Sutherland's heavy breathing, saw his hands playing with the trigger. Sutherland turned to him, his eyes betraying fear Brock had never seen in him before. Sutherland began to shake and his voice broke. "They got us trapped. All they gotta do is toss a grenade. We can't do anything."

Brock studied their movement, then put his hand on Sutherland's shoulder. "Take it easy; they don't see us."

Suddenly the unit leader pointed in their direction.

Brock caught his breath. They couldn't suspect a patrol out this far.

The leader signaled and his men began moving steadily toward them. As they drew close, Brock saw how tired they were. They walked slowly, without purpose or caution, their rifles slung carelessly.

Brock whispered, "Don't move, don't fire."

The soldiers were so close the men could hear their voices, weary and irritable. The unit leader shouted at his men. One was so close they heard him curse under his breath. In a few minutes, the enemy had moved beyond them.

For another five minutes no one moved or spoke. At last Brock sat back. He grabbed the radio and contacted the hill, giving the enemy sighting and their direction. When he finished, he looked to the others and shrugged.

Coney put down his rifle. "You got any shitpaper? I just went all over myself."

Landis let out a deep breath. "Jesus, that's the closest I ever came. I counted forty of them. I just knew they had us."

Sutherland cleared the machine gun. He wiped sweat from his face and rested his head against the weapon. "You gotta get us out of here, Brock. That was just a scouting element. Soon as we stick our heads out, they're gonna blow us away. We can't go any further."

"What are you worried about? They didn't see you."

Sutherland's anger flared. "Jesus Christ, there were forty of them."

Frizzell fumbled nervously for a cigarette, found them completely soaked, and threw them aside. "You think they're going towards the hill?"

Brock shrugged, then pointed at him. "You take watch.

436

We'll stay here till dark." He lay back, propping his head against a stone.

Sutherland crawled to him. "Get us out of here. I'm no coward, but Jesus, we don't have a chance."

Brock closed his eyes and ignored him.

Sutherland grew furious. "You after a medal? Is that it, we're doing this just to get you a medal?"

"Yeah, that's it," Brock said without opening his eyes. "I'm gonna send it home to my wife, then I'm gonna retire and live off what it's worth."

"Then why the hell are we doing this? No one will know if we hole up here. This fucking war doesn't mean anything, you know that."

"I'll know if we hole up. And maybe the war does mean something."

Sutherland exploded. "You asshole! You stupid son of a bitch. You lifer motherfucker! You're gonna get us killed."

The others looked to him warningly. Coney turned away against the expected outburst, but Brock merely opened his eyes and stared at him impassively. "Sutherland, shut up. Let me run this patrol. I'll get your worthless ass back safely."

"Get your own dumb ass back—I'm not going on. I'm not following you, Brock. You're a has-been, an old lifer not even smart enough to hold a real job in the real world."

Brock's face drained white.

Frizzell nudged Sutherland, yet Brock only eased his head back and breathed easily. "All right, we'll vote on it. How's that? Just like in a fucking democracy."

Coney grinned. "I vote that everybody goes except me— that's democracy."

Brock glared at him, then turned to the others. "All those who want to quit, say so now. You know this is your job, that it's an order, but if you want to quit, I won't say anything." He looked to each man. "I don't know about things— Sutherland's right, I'm an old lifer—and I don't even know what this is all about, but a man . . ."

The words—something vague and mysterious like duty and honor and courage, fear and manhood—were lost in his mind. A fathomless chasm opened before him and he did not understand what it was that drew him in and allowed him no escape.

Coney stared into the rain, a silk screen masking the world from him. Frizzell and Sutherland looked to him, the older man, the one with wife and child, to make the decision.

I don't understand any of this, Coney thought. I don't know if it's important or if it means anything. He sighed. Am I going to die because I'm ignorant?

He looked out of the cave and could see nothing. He closed his eyes. He had dropped out of college and dropped out of his marriage; he had fled everything difficult, he knew. But he was going to change—he was going to make his marriage work and go back to college.

He lowered his head and felt the complete silence of the cave.

Finally he looked up and said softly, deciding that he would not drop out of anything again, "I'll go."

Frizzell nodded. "I think it's important; we gotta do it."

Landis remembered his fear, thought of the enemy so close he could still hear their breathing. But then he thought of Martin, of his mother, and suddenly of a single girl, and he could not even remember her name. Then there was the car—black and mean and bad—and he smiled. "Let's go for it," he said, for he was caught too by the ethic of male valor and deed, by the myths and stories and histories he did not even know, and by some germ in his being, and all options were foreclosed and he shrugged too. "Shit; dying ain't the worst thing."

Sutherland stared at them, then sat back in embarrassment. "All right. If that's what everybody votes, I'll go too. I just don't want to die."

Frizzell pushed him lightly. "I always knew you were a pussy."

Coney said quietly, "That's what we're all afraid of."

Landis looked at him quizzically. "What does that mean?"

Sutherland said maliciously, "It means you're gonna die pretending to be a hero."

438

"No." Frizzell shook his head. "We're buddies—as long as we are, it'll be all right."

Brock snorted and lay back, closing his eyes. "Will all you buddies shut the fuck up. You only got four hours to sleep."

Sutherland thrust his finger before Brock's closed eyes.

The others grinned and settled back, but no one was able to sleep.

CHAPTER

· 28 ·

Mead, worried about being late, arrived at the embassy two hours early, at four A.M. The snack bar was not yet open so he couldn't even get coffee. The corridors were completely deserted, offices all locked, and on his way he realized that he might not be able to get into the special wing; he didn't know if the guard booth was manned at night, and he had no other access.

When he got off the elevator, he saw no one was at the guard booth, and he almost went back downstairs when he noticed the bulletproof door slightly ajar.

Perhaps there was a cleaning crew inside, he thought; or maybe the sentry went to the bathroom. He entered, careful to leave the door as before, then went into his room. There wasn't even a light in the cubicle, so he took off his field jacket and put down his rifle in the dark.

Dolores had a coffeepot, he remembered, and he was about to go across the hall to make a cup when he heard someone leaving Marshall's private office.

Surely the ambassador wasn't here at this hour, Mead thought—though it would be just like him.

Mead stood silent in the dark as a man walked past.

It was Mr. Lord, The Phantom; Mead recognized him even from the fleeting glimpse.

Mead almost stepped out to tell him about the Frenchman, but he hesitated. Lord might not like being caught.

Caught at what? it occurred to him. What *was* he doing in Marshall's private office?

Was he spying on the ambassador?

Mead remained standing in the dark trying to sort out his thoughts. He knew that he was in no position to question a senior official such as Mr. Lord, but he had an unsettling feeling about what Lord had told him. The Frenchman Lacouture was strange, a homosexual besides, but Mead sensed that what Lord had told him about Lacouture might not be true. The Frenchman did not seem that bad; in fact, Mead kind of liked him. It was just a feeling, but he trusted his senses.

When he was certain Lord had left the wing, Mead went to Marshall's door. It was locked. Then, going through the secretary's and Colonel Waggoner's offices, he found that door to Marshall's office locked too.

So then Lord had a key. Why? Did Marshall know?

He made coffee, trying to reason out an answer, but it made no sense to him, so he cleaned his rifle again and reshined his boots, and at five-thirty, Colonel Romer banged on the guard booth. Mead let him in but did not mention how he himself had gotten in or that Lord had been there.

"There's coffee made," Mead said.

"Good." Romer handed him several dollars in military scrip. "Go get us some doughnuts."

"The snack bar doesn't open until six, sir."

Romer merely stared at him.

"Yes, sir," Mead said. "What kind do you want? Jelly ones?"

"Whatever you can steal," Romer answered.

Mead went downstairs. He liked Romer; the colonel had been fair and considerate, and he didn't seem afraid of anyone. Mead had observed that his manner to Marshall differed from everyone else's; he was proper and respectful, but he did not seem intimidated. He also had a sense of humor.

Mead had heard that Romer was the son of a famous

general, but the famous name was only vaguely familiar to him.

Besides, the colonel didn't seem much affected by it.

Except Mead had noticed that Romer had a tendency to push too hard sometimes, and that bothered him. The doughnuts were an example. Colonel Waggoner would have waited until the snack bar opened, a matter of fifteen minutes or so. Only Romer would make a point of stealing the doughnuts if necessary. It was minor, Mead thought, but something to watch in a man who controlled your fate.

Probably it was for this kind of sensing things that Lieutenant Bishop had sent him down here, Mead reasoned —Bishop was afraid Mead was going to get killed, pushing himself into danger. Mead didn't think he had reached that point, but Bobby Yates had done just that, and Mead saw something of him in Romer.

When Mead had arrived in Vietnam, Corporal Yates was the platoon hero.

Wounded twice, Yates had both a Silver and a Bronze Star, rare for enlisted men. He was an authentic hero, but dangerous because he seemed compelled to live up to his reputation. He could not just go on a patrol—each one became an effort to engage the enemy or surpass another in length and danger.

He died unnecessarily. The platoon was infantry support in a resupply convoy of amphibious tractors, huge behemoths used in ship-to-shore landings. Fueled by giant pods of gasoline under their hulls, they were twenty-ton tinderboxes.

When one of the tractors hit a mine, the three-man crew jumped off and ran for cover.

As they ran from the machine, Yates ran toward it.

Everyone screamed for him to stay clear, and the crew yelled that there was no one inside, but Yates jumped onto the tractor and started for the hatch.

The fuel cells exploded at that moment, igniting a thousand gallons of gasoline.

Yates was sucked in like a rag doll.

The fire burned for six hours.

The platoon watched the inferno for thirty minutes, then

moved on, hearing later that when the machine cooled and others went inside, they couldn't even find identifiable human ashes.

Perez joked that they should send pork slices back in the coffin as a consolation prize. Everyone laughed because they thought Yates was crazy and his death inevitable, and they were relieved the suspense was over, and that he didn't take anyone with him.

There was something of Yates in Romer, Mead thought; he was glad Romer's job was administrative—he would steal doughnuts for him, but he wouldn't want to follow him on a patrol.

Yet he didn't even have to steal the doughnuts. Marine guards had access everywhere in the embassy, so he merely went into the kitchen and told them what he needed.

"Good work, Corporal," Romer said, peering inside the bag Mead had brought, then he raised his rifle in one hand and said, "Let's ride."

The limousine was waiting in front. Mead rode beside the driver while Romer jumped in back, munching a doughnut.

When they pulled up before Marshall's villa at exactly six A.M., Romer brushed confectioners' sugar off the seat and got out.

"Is he for real?" the driver asked when Romer left. "He's too wired. Is that sugar or acid he's eating?"

They saw the villa door open, and Marshall step out, bowing slightly to what looked like a little army of Vietnamese servants.

Mead and the driver got out to salute and open the doors.

"Good morning," Marshall said, getting into the backseat. He wore gray trousers, a white short-sleeve shirt without tie, and loafers.

"You didn't tell me what to wear, Colonel. What's appropriate civilian attire for a war? I don't have any fatigues; a three-piece suit seems a little formal. Slacks and shirt?"

"I didn't think of that," Romer said. "I should have got you some fatigues. I beg your pardon, but we can get some at the first stop, sir."

"I don't want fatigues, Colonel," Marshall said. "I suited up for World War Two and Korea—that was quite enough."

"I think you look fine, sir," the driver said. "I'd rather wear what you have on than what I do. You want to swap, sir?"

Marshall smiled. "Thank you, no." He felt perfectly at ease, even enthusiastic about going to the field. His expectations were not high, knowing that he was going to see only what Westmoreland and Abrams wanted him to see, but at least it would be away from a desk, and now that he had the possibility of a meeting with the NVA, the hope for a breakthrough, he did not mind biding his time.

The car sped through early-morning traffic. Military jeeps met the limousine at Tan Son Nhut and sirened its passage onto the flight line, past an incredible arsenal of jets and reconnaissance planes.

Marshall shook his head in wonder. "How can we lose with equipment like that?"

"We can't," Romer answered. "The problem is that we can't *win.*"

Marshall's hand swept over the flight line. "All that equipment and we can't win?"

"That's just gear, sir. Gear doesn't win wars." Romer tapped his chest. "Heart does. You were on the DMZ, Corporal," he said to Mead. "Are airplanes and bombs going to beat the gooks?"

Mead couldn't say anything. Romer, not really expecting or wanting an answer, asked the driver. "How about you, Stokes? What do you think?"

Stokes turned from the wheel and grinned at Marshall. "I think you better wear a helmet and flak jacket, sir."

Marshall laughed. "What's the point of my fact-finding mission if you've already given me the answers?"

At the end of the flight line there was a single helicopter surrounded by six air force policemen. Black except for the U.S. flag on the fuselage and the Great Seal of the United States on the tail, the chopper was an impressive sight so isolated and simply marked.

When the limousine drove up, Lieutenant Magnuson and another officer jumped out of the cockpit, and everyone saluted Marshall.

"Good morning, Lieutenant," Marshall said, shaking hands with Magnuson.

"Morning, sir. This is Chief Warrant Officer Jack Ridley; he's the copilot and gunner." He gestured to the aircraft in back of him. "This is a UH-1B, a 'Huey,' sir. It carries six men, though I can't speak too much for its comfort."

Marshall nodded solemnly. "I don't care about comfort as long as it's invulnerable to ground and air fire. It is, isn't it?"

"Absolutely, sir."

"You guarantee that, Lieutenant?"

"Double your money back, sir. Now if you all will get in, we'll take off. It's a short flight to the Delta, so we won't be showing a movie or serving cocktails."

"Where *is* Dolores when we need her?" Marshall asked, climbing aboard.

"You'll have to ask Lieutenant Magnuson that question," Romer said.

"What?" said Marshall in mock alarm. "You mean there's fraternization going on among the staff? Is that allowed?" he asked Romer.

"Dolores checked with me," Romer said. "I said it was all right." Then he said to an embarrassed Magnuson, "I didn't tell her you were married, however."

"You went through my file, sir?" Magnuson asked belligerently.

"You bet I did, Lieutenant. If my ass is in somebody's hands, I want to know about those hands. Whether you want to wear your wedding ring is your business—but I want to know about the man who has control of my life."

"Pilots have all the fun," Marshall said, defusing the tension between the two and fastening his seat belt.

Mead sat across from him, his rifle propped on the deck, looking to Marshall as if he were a permanent fixture of the craft, part of the manufacturer's specifications.

Romer got on last, still scowling from his exchange with Magnuson, and sat beside Marshall to brief him on the itinerary.

Marshall was surprised at Romer's reaction to Magnuson.

At first he thought it was jealousy. Dolores Toland was a beautiful woman; surely it galled Romer that she found the young pilot more attractive. Then he remembered stories of the elder Romer, a man of profound Christian beliefs who often knelt to pray on the battlefield and allegedly carried on conversations with God in a jeep. He was puritanical too, Marshall remembered from the stories, possessing that incongruous mix of religious belief and moral prudery that often goes hand in hand with carnage and pillage.

Romer was not jealous, Marshall decided—he was offended by the married pilot taking out another woman.

And himself? Marshall reflected. How did he feel? No, no moral outrage; he was not offended. He was just jealous.

"We'll start with a general overview," Romer shouted over the engine, handing Marshall a laminated map. "We'll fly over the Mekong Delta into Fourth Corps to give you a feel for the terrain. Can Tho is Navy-Riverine Forces and Seals, and there's some Army Special Forces there too. This afternoon we'll stop at My Tho, which is infantry."

The chopper lifted, banked to the left, then headed south.

Marshall glanced at the map, then turned to the window. The huts and shanties of the massive scab around Saigon soon disappeared, replaced by intense blues and greens of marsh and water. Below was a brilliant canvas, blindingly mesmerizing, reminding Marshall of an energetic child's watercolor—a splash of green with big blue snakes romping through it.

He smiled at the beauty, at the same time feeling an inner sense of joy at the prospect that his mission might succeed. Lacouture had brought him a possibility. And he could persuade Johnson to seize it.

After an hour and a half, Magnuson spoke over the intercom. "We're heading down the coast. At Vinh Binh, the mouth of the Delta, we'll go upriver into Can Tho. This is definite VC area."

Mead reached for his helmet and sat on it. When neither Romer nor Marshall got theirs, he unstrapped himself and pulled them out for them.

Romer waved his away disdainfully. Marshall accepted his but didn't seem to know what to do with it.

"To protect your . . . crotch," Mead yelled at Marshall.

Marshall nodded, placed it under him, balanced precariously for a few seconds, then withdrew it and put it back under the seat, deciding that though he knew the perversity of fate, he would take the risk—survival in two wars had made him a little cavalier.

The chopper dipped lower.

The sun sparkled off the azure sea so brilliantly that Marshall had to shield his eyes, but toward the mouths of the rivers and inlets, the view was marred by flotillas of sampans and junks and military craft darting over the surface like water bugs. The marshland looked dirty and brackish, and smoke billowed from a hundred fires.

The blue sky was lost in a haze of smoke, and even inside the chopper, Marshall's eyes stung in irritation.

"Defoliants," Romer yelled, wiping at his own eyes, and pointing to the barren smoldering banks of the river.

Hundreds of sampans and junks plied the waterways, steering clear of giant armored boats randomly spewing flames and cannon fire.

"Monitors," yelled Romer, pointing at one of the armored boats. "Part of the Mobile Riverine Force—that's navy. They patrol the rivers to try to keep them open to commercial traffic, all the rice going to the markets."

The chopper swung lower, almost skimming over the water and marshes, so close that Marshall could see the muck and mud, terrain totally inaccessible to infantry or armor; he thought of leeches and mosquitoes, malaria, and immersion foot.

But when the chopper landed at Can Tho, he saw only clean, starched uniforms and was given an upbeat briefing by senior army and navy officers on recent military operations.

It was, Marshall realized, the same briefing that must have been given to those on the COVIA study: the war in the Delta was being won and no one had any problems, though more men and equipment would hasten the inevitable victory, of course. Morale was good, casualties light, and the civilian population grateful and supportive.

Marshall had come to see the real war, to get behind the glib clichés, but within his first hour in the field, his fears were confirmed—he was going to see a well-rehearsed and sanitized view of the war, only what MACV wanted him to see. Though he had half-expected this expurgated version, he was annoyed and insulted at their presumption of his naïveté.

To his questions about Agent Orange and defoliants, he was told that, yes, they were an irritant, causing red eyes and an occasional skin rash, but not unlike regular crop dusting back home, and certainly not as threatening as a VC bullet.

When Marshall asked about the twenty-five percent drop in rice reaching Saigon, he was told that considering the three enemy divisions and eleven battalions operating in the Delta, a major VC stronghold, a drop of only twenty-five percent was encouraging, and sure to improve.

Marshall could not penetrate the veneer. He saw battle-ready equipment and well-fed, motivated men who were clean and dry. He toured different units—Navy Seals, Army Special Forces, the Riverine Forces—ate lunch at an officers' club, saw a demonstration of firepower and was shown captured enemy weapons, plus a variety of enemy mines and booby traps, and all the while the message was repeated: the war was being won but could be won faster with more troops.

The Delta was too important to be ceded to the communists, it was one of the most productive rice-producing areas in the world, and a third of the nation's fifteen million people lived here.

After several hours of antiseptic spectacle, Marshall's exasperation broke through.

Before boarding his helicopter, he called Magnuson and Romer aside.

"Cancel what's next. Take me somewhere else. I am not about to be subjected to another dog and pony show. If they know in advance where I'm going, they'll have a production staged for me; the only way I'm going to really see anything is if I surprise them."

"But sir," Magnuson said, "all air movement has to be coordinated with the firepower people. I can't just pick a place and fly there—I have to get clearance. Otherwise I could fly you over an area where an air strike's been called, or where there's artillery fire."

"Lieutenant Magnuson is right, sir," Romer said. "We could fly into a real shitstorm that way. Besides, there might be some ground operations—patrols or ambushes—that could be compromised by an unscheduled chopper fly-over."

"I understand the difficulties," Marshall said. "Now let's surmount them. I am not going to make scheduled visits; I am going to see the real thing, no matter how many 'shitstorms' I have to fly through."

Magnuson grinned. "Well, sir, there's a saying—begging your pardon—that the baddest motherfucker makes the rules. Since you outrank everybody in this country, I guess if you want to fly to East Gookville, then that's where we go, and I get on the radio and tell them we're on our way and to hold the friendly fire."

Marshall nodded approvingly. "That's exactly what I wanted to hear."

Romer looked sharply at Magnuson. "Is that safe—taking off without a flight plan? It bothers me, Lieutenant, the personal representative of the President winging through hostile territory."

Magnuson shrugged. "Colonel, I can't control what the enemy does—whether they've got surface-to-air missiles, or some doped-up dink has an accidental rifle discharge, I can go down either way. That's just luck; your number is up. But I'm pretty sure that with the ambassador's call sign, I can get immediate clearance to wherever I want to go."

Romer turned to Marshall. "You're on an extraordinarily sensitive mission, sir. I really don't like the idea of your whereabouts being unknown. Someone should always have an exact fix on your position."

Marshall considered a moment, then decided. "I'll take the risk—no more prearranged, scheduled stops; we'll decide where we're going en route."

"Sir," Mead said hesitantly, "if we're going to be flying

over the badlands, I think you ought to wear a flak jacket and sit on a helmet—just for your own protection, sir."

Marshall nodded. "I'll wear the flak jacket, but sitting on a helmet is like trying to hatch a dinosaur egg—I'll risk getting shot in the ass, or elsewhere." He turned to Romer. "All right, Colonel, pick a place."

Romer turned to Magnuson. "There are all kinds of small-unit operations around here, especially towards the Cambodian border. Fly upriver until you see a small unit sweeping the area, then drop down on them."

Magnuson nodded. "That's okay by me, Colonel, as long as the ambassador understands the danger." He said respectfully to Marshall, "I'll still offer double your money back, sir, but this is a lot riskier, and if I head towards Cambodia . . . well, sir, that's an enemy sanctuary, and it could get scary." He grinned. "You might want to sit on that helmet like Corporal Mead suggests, sir."

They climbed into the helicopter and a moment later it lifted off. As soon as they were airborne, Magnuson radioed that their destination was changed, that instead of flying to My Tho as scheduled, they were heading upriver.

Within minutes there was a flurry of radio traffic, all of it demanding their original flight plan be followed, all coming from an escalating higher command. To each Magnuson said that "Viceroy," Marshall's call sign, would continue on. "Negative to your last," Magnuson said to each command.

Magnuson and Ridley smiled at each turndown, but Ridley flinched when he took the call from MACV, Westmoreland's headquarters.

"What the hell is going on, Viceroy?"

Magnuson politely explained that "Viceroy" himself canceled the stop at My Tho and directed the current flight pattern. He stated that he had advised Viceroy of the danger of the breach of procedure, but Viceroy was adamant. "Please advise," Magnuson said to the MACV controller.

"We'll get back to you" was the answer.

"They're not going to touch us," Magnuson said to Ridley. "They've had run-ins with Marshall before."

Minutes later, MACV radioed back. "Proceed as you wish, but keep us advised of location. Check in with us as soon as you return."

Magnuson started evasive movement, altering the altitude and speed, dodging and weaving the craft over the terrain.

In back, excitement suddenly surged in Marshall, an almost primal fervor, something he had not felt since Korea, and despite his effort to subdue it, it gripped him powerfully.

The Delta was now intermittently more densely jungled and more barren, with patches of heavy growth interspersed with cratered devastation from massive air strikes.

The chopper swept low over the rivers and inlets, so low at times that they could clearly see the expressions of the boatmen on the junks and sampans, but over the myriad villages that dotted the area, they flew at a higher altitude.

Finally they located an army unit sweeping through the marshlands in an area where Magnuson felt he could safely bring the chopper down.

The men on the ground looked up in surprise as the helicopter circled a few times then descended slowly.

Magnuson's main concern was that the ground was too soft and the chopper would sink so that he could not lift out. He hovered a minute before setting down. Finally he landed, and when the chopper embedded only slightly in the marsh, he let out his breath in relief.

Several troopers sloughed toward them quickly while others set up a guard perimeter—a chopper was an inviting target.

"You guys all right?" a soldier called over the dying engine.

"What kind of markings are those?" yelled the other, pointing to the Great Seal of the United States.

When Magnuson and the others jumped out, the soldiers were even more confused—Marine pilots, an enlisted man, army colonel, and a civilian.

"You guys lost?" the patrol leader asked.

Marshall stepped forward, his shoes sinking in the mud.

"I'm Ambassador Marshall," he said, shaking hands with both soldiers. "I'm visiting field units to get a feel for what's going on."

"How about saluting, troop," Romer said sternly. "And how come you're not wearing flak jackets and helmets? You look like you're on your way to the Winn Dixie, not on patrol."

"This is informal, Colonel," Marshall interceded, then turning to the soldiers who had stiffened in resentment against Romer, he said, "I'd like to talk to you; could you bring the others in?"

"Yes, sir," the patrol leader said. "But someone should provide security—a downed chopper causes a lot of interest."

"Give me your rifle," Magnuson said. "I'll go out there."

Romer took another one, examined it carefully, then said disdainfully, "You sure anything this dirty will fire?" but he walked out into the marshland with it.

The patrol leader, a young army sergeant, glanced at Mead and rolled his eyes, then he called the others in.

Marshall gathered them about him and told them to relax and smoke if they wanted.

"I want to ask you a few questions. There aren't any right or wrong answers—I'm just trying to gather information."

There were twelve soldiers, extremely young, Marshall thought, most no older than Ryan; they looked tired and raw from being pushed too hard.

"I was just at Can Tho," he said.

A tall black trooper, wearing a ripped green T-shirt, grinned. "We know—that's why *we're* not there."

"I don't understand," Marshall said.

The patrol leader explained. "We were supposed to go back yesterday, but they told us to stay out. I don't think they wanted us tracking up the area."

"I didn't see anybody with muddy boots at Can Tho." Marshall smiled. "One would never know a war's going on there."

"There it is," another said, affirming the obvious.

They talked for nearly an hour. Marshall learned they were from the 9th Infantry, patrolling and sweeping the area, trying to keep the VC out, a hopeless task they felt because of the terrain, over three thousand miles of waterways, because of the enemy's determination and skills, and because the civilian population was either with the enemy or afraid to resist them.

"Jesus," Romer said as they got back into the chopper. "What a sorry bunch. Don't get the idea that's representative of the army, Mr. Ambassador."

"I was impressed; I'd give them high marks," Marshall said. "They knew their jobs and seemed competent. They were just tired."

But inwardly he shared the pessimism of the troopers—no way for them to win, not without massive escalation. No other way, he had to meet with the NVA, he decided, boarding the chopper again.

The helicopter lifted without difficulty and Magnuson headed north, trying to keep a safe distance from the Cambodian border. Since all the ambassador wanted to do was talk to the troops, Magnuson tried to locate a camped unit where they could get coffee and a meal.

Skimming over the jungle and rivers, he saw a village with a large number of soldiers and some armored personnel carriers.

When the helicopter set down, no one approached, and stony-eyed troops stared at them balefully.

Mead jumped out quickly, yelling over the rotor blades to Marshall, "Stay on board, sir. Let me check this out first."

Magnuson got out to follow Mead, then Romer jumped out.

"You better stay here," Mead said to Magnuson.

"Why?"

Mead pointed at his lieutenant's bars. "Trust me, Lieutenant. And for Christ's sake, don't let the colonel come near."

Mead sauntered toward the men on an armored personnel carrier. His carriage changed—no longer coiled, he now walked loose and without swagger.

While Mead spoke with the men, Magnuson could barely restrain Romer, and finally Marshall got out and wandered over to them. "What's going on?" he asked.

"I'm not sure," Magnuson said. "But Mead told us to stay here."

"I don't normally take orders from corporals," Romer said.

Finally Mead walked back. "Sir, we better skip this visit."

"What's going on, Corporal?"

"Well, sir, this is what's called a boom-boom vil."

"Oh, shit," Magnuson said, stifling a laugh.

"It's a place . . . well, sir, where . . ."

Magnuson stepped in to save him embarrassment. "Mr. Ambassador, this is a place where the soldiers come for . . . recreation. They're all over the country, around all the major base camps. In cities like Saigon and Da Nang, there are special districts, but out in the boonies there are little villages that cater to—"

"I understand," Marshall said. "You're not offending my sensibilities. This is where the troops come to get laid. But why all the caution?"

Mead said in a lowered voice, "It's not just getting laid, sir. This is where they do dope—drugs, sir. Officers shouldn't stumble into an area like this. The men might think you're . . . going to cause them trouble. They could get pretty violent."

"What kind of dope?" Marshall asked.

"Anything, sir. Hash, heroin, opium, cocaine."

Marshall glanced to the men still watching them carefully. "Is there a lot of dope in Vietnam, Corporal?"

"Yes, sir, there is. And guys on dope are dangerous, sir. All you'll see here, sir, are guys wasted on drugs. You can't talk to them because they won't make any sense. And things can get out of control quickly when guys are hopped up. It's not like talking to people who know what's going on— somebody can misunderstand what you say, or suddenly just go wild. I'd pass on this place, sir."

"This wasn't in the COVIA study, Colonel. How come I didn't read about boom-boom vils?"

Marshall said it in jest, but Romer took it seriously, and he was profoundly disturbed by everything Mead had said.

"If this is what you say it is, Corporal, then these bastards ought to be arrested and court-martialed, and I'd like to do it myself."

"We couldn't fit them all on the chopper," Magnuson said dryly.

"We should fly directly to My Tho and tell the commanding officer what is going on here," Romer said.

"They'd just move to another village, sir," Mead said.

Marshall considered for a second, then shook his head. Everything he was seeing bore witness to the futility of the war. It was as Lacouture said, hopeless. He turned and headed back to the helicopter.

Romer was furious. "So far, Lieutenant, you've shown us some shitbirds and some dope addicts. What's next—a civilian massacre?"

"Colonel," Marshall said soothingly, "I've observed Navy Seals, Army Special Forces, and the Riverine Forces doing an exemplary job keeping the Delta from the VC. I've watched highly competent young men doing an extraordinarily difficult job—I've seen excellent things."

Then, getting into the chopper, he couldn't resist, and he called up to Magnuson, "Take me to a massacre, Lieutenant."

In late afternoon they dropped down near a village where a medical unit was working. As corpsmen checked teeth and rendered basic help—cleaning infections and festering sores, setting broken bones, and immunizing children— soldiers distributed food, threw candy and C rations to children, and played a game of stickball with them.

Another infantry unit was sweeping the mouth of the Rach Ba Rai River near "Snoopy's Nose," an area of heavy Viet Cong activity. They showed Marshall a cache of weapons and mines hidden in mud along the banks, and they demonstrated their search methods in the tunnels the enemy burrowed through the marshes.

"The gooks love the Delta," he was told. "They can scoot through this area like river rats. We chase them down one tunnel, and they come out a hundred other places. They just disappear into the reeds."

When Marshall asked if these men thought the South

Vietnamese could handle the Delta, the answers were uniformly negative.

"Would a lot more U.S. troops help?" he asked.

A soldier gestured to the vast marshland and pointed to a tunnel. "You could put so many of us out here that we'd trip over each other, but the gooks would still sink into the mud and pop out whenever they wanted."

Dusk began to settle over the Delta.

"You better return to base camp soon, sir," the unit leader said.

"Does the enemy own the night?" Marshall asked.

"They don't own it, but they're like vampires—they only come out at night. The dark equalizes everything. All the planes and tanks and boats don't do much in the dark—then it's just them against us. We could beat them at night, too, but the big brass likes all that firepower; they get kind of spooked when it's one on one. You see all kinds of generals and colonels during the day, but never one at night. And *never* out in the bush like this."

Magnuson added, "Especially ambassadors. He's right, sir, we should be going."

When Magnuson got everybody back on board, he looked at his watch and unconsciously revved the engine. Flying time to Saigon was an hour; count another hour checking the craft, filling out the logs, and he was never going to pick up Dolores on time.

Magnuson got an erection just thinking about her and last night, and he lifted the craft off the ground with such thrust that Ridley looked at him curiously.

"Got a date tonight," Magnuson said, grinning an apology for the takeoff.

They were airborne only twenty minutes when Magnuson felt an ebbing loss of power.

"What the fuck?" he shouted at the instrument panel flashing red in front of him. System after system was failing.

Ridley stared in disbelief as pressure collapsed and gauge needles swung to zero. "Holy shit," he said softly.

Magnuson furiously performed emergency procedures to bring the craft back to power, but nothing worked.

"You motherfucker!" he finally screamed at his plane.

"You bitch!" He slammed his fist into the panel. "You cocksucker!"

Then he turned to Ridley and said incredulously, "We're going down."

The chopper stalled in midair, at an altitude of a thousand feet. The engine sputtered, then died.

Magnuson shook his head. "This is really going to fuck up my evening," he said.

In back, Mead sat rigid and quiet, feeling the helicopter lose power, jerk and jar, then drop awkwardly. It was going down, he knew. He had seen charred wreckages of choppers that had crashed or been shot down, and he had heard that the bodies hit with such impact that limbs flew off and heads exploded.

He was as close to dying as he had ever been, he knew. The sensation was so strange that he examined it carefully in his mind, but he suddenly realized that he couldn't think at all. Sung was in his mind; that's all he could see.

Across from him, Marshall frowned in annoyance, then as the chopper bucked and rocked, and the failure became manifest, Mead saw Marshall's face ease. He appeared perfectly calm; there was not a trace of anxiety or fear in his features—even his hands were folded calmly.

Marshall turned to look out the window; the night was a black void, as he had seen bringing him toward death on the launch at Guadalcanal, in the shadowy snow at Chosin, but this time he was not afraid. He felt a contentment and peace about his life that he had not known when he was young and there was no desperation. A stab of sorrow passed through him, not for himself, but for what he would not now accomplish, for what he no longer could do to end the war.

He turned away, and his eyes met Mead's, then he smiled reassuringly at the youth.

It was such a warm smile that despite his stomach's bottoming out, Mead smiled back.

Then they plummeted.

CHAPTER

• 29 •

Brock crouched at the cave entrance listening a moment before motioning the others into the late-afternoon darkness; the rain had not abated. They were deep within the Demilitarized Zone, an area long ceded to the enemy.

On point, Frizzell led them across a wide savanna into a thick treeline where he waited cautiously, knowing that listening posts would surround a large enemy site, but that to locate one in the dark would be virtually impossible; it was far more likely they would walk into a sentry.

He was about to move on when the brush rustled. Footsteps drew near, then swerved away.

He waited a moment, then began to stalk the enemy patrol.

Suddenly a voice called out in the dark and the men they had been following shouted an answer. From the trees another enemy patrol emerged, then they moved off together.

Brock radioed the hill; he could barely make out Bishop's voice in the heavy static.

"We just spotted two patrols. They're moving towards you, about twenty men; that makes almost sixty we've seen heading towards the hill."

There was a long pause. "Roger. Anything else?"

"We'll get to the first position in about two hours. Out."

Sutherland took point and the patrol zigzagged north, reaching the first grid position after midnight, but a search of the half-mile area did not turn up anything.

Brock gathered them in a tight circle. "You sure this is it?"

Sutherland lay exhausted under a tree. "This is the place; I know what I'm doing."

Brock tossed down the map. "Shit! Take fifteen minutes, then we'll check in a wider circle. It's gotta be around here—I don't want to hike another fucking day to the other position."

But another search didn't reveal anything, so they started for the second objective.

By the time darkness began to lift, they were stumbling in exhaustion. Brock found the ruins of an old enemy camp, probably used against the French. He dropped into a crumbling bunker, testing the creaking beams, then motioned the others in.

Landis jumped in, his boot splashing water. "Shit! It's underwater."

Frizzell peered in dubiously. "There're probably snakes in there."

Landis rapidly clawed his way out, but Brock grabbed him by the collar. "There aren't any snakes."

Sutherland stuck his head in. "Terrific, Brock—if only we had scuba gear."

"Shut up, Sutherland." Brock dropped his pack into the water and sat on it. "Water won't hurt you. Get your asses in here."

They clambered in disgruntledly, easing gingerly into the water.

"Take first watch," Brock said to Landis.

Sutherland moved to the entrance. "Shit; I'll take it—I can't sleep in a fucking well, and I forgot to bring my surfboard."

Brock shrugged. "Suit yourself."

Sutherland sat at the entrance listening to the others fall asleep. His foot paddled in the water, and he dropped small rocks disgustedly into the pool. His head rested against the wall as he peered into the grayness. Only the cold and wet kept him awake; his entire body ached from fatigue and he cradled himself for warmth and blew into his hands.

Stupid bastards, he thought, staring at the others. Stupid, stupid bastards.

Suddenly the bunker rocked in an incredible explosion that slammed him against the wall. A string of detonations caved in the rear of the bunker and the overhead beams groaned, dropping dirt and rocks.

The others woke in terror, covering their heads and pressing into the water, then there was another series of blasts, and with a deafening roar, the bunker gave way.

A beam crashed down on Landis, pinning his leg.

He screamed out, and the others clawed at the debris and wrestled with the beam until they freed him. They dragged him to the entrance and cowered at the opening, watching the clearing erupt.

Trees and rocks hurtled through the air.

Above, planes streaked down in another run. The men dove to the ground as bombs ripped the clearing again, slamming huge metal fragments into the bunker.

"Those are ours," Frizzell yelled as jets strafed the trees, raining a fusillade into the deserted jungle, then streaked down again. The men hugged earth and water as the planes made two more passes.

The noise was tremendous and disorienting.

Long after the planes were gone, the men shook. Coney doubled over and Sutherland held his head between his knees; Frizzell shivered uncontrollably.

Brock crawled to Landis and felt his leg for a fracture. "Can you walk?"

Landis tried to stand but cried out and fell onto Brock.

"All right. Take it easy." Brock sank to the ground and looked warily to the other beams creaking above them.

Frizzell stared out in amazement to the smoldering clearing. "They could have blown us away. What if we'd been killed by our own men?"

Sutherland spat. "What difference does it make? Dead is dead. Who cares who kills you?"

"Those crazy sons of bitches."

"They're not so crazy. They're not up to their assholes in water, are they? They're dry and having hot meals. They're going back to the Officers' Club, and they've got—"

"Shut up, Sutherland," Brock ordered.

"Well, fuck 'em," Sutherland said. "I hate pilots—bastards flying up there about ten thousand feet, dropping bombs on people—even the gooks don't deserve that. Then one of them gets shot down and captured and we're all supposed to feel sorry for them. Screw 'em."

Coney shook his head in wonder. "Jesus, that's the worst thing I ever went through."

Brock squirmed to get comfortable and watched the others—numb, tired, and afraid—maneuver for positions in the cramped bunker. They had to sleep, he knew, or soon they would make careless, fatal mistakes.

But even before anyone fell asleep, Frizzell spotted an enemy patrol; all of them crouched at the entrance until the unit passed. Only when Brock went to call the hill did they realize the radio was missing. They dug in the debris for twenty minutes until they found it, but the handset was crushed.

"Well, that's it," Sutherland said in relief. "We can't go on without a radio. We gotta go back."

"We're only an hour from the second position," Brock said. "You heard the lieutenant. Besides, Landis can't go anywhere."

Brock knelt beside Landis. "Can you stand?"

Landis struggled up, grimacing, trying not to cry out. "I'll be okay," he said. "But I don't think I could keep up with you."

"Okay, everybody shut up," said Brock. "I gotta think this out."

Sutherland rolled his eyes. "We might as well shoot ourselves now and get it over with."

"Don't tempt me, Sutherland," said Brock. "Eat some chow and clean your weapons, and don't anybody say anything."

Brock studied them as they ate. No one had slept more than a couple hours in the past two days, and their exhaustion showed in their eyes and listlessness.

"This is what we're going to do," he said at last.

Sutherland brought his rifle up and pointed it at his own head.

"Landis, you got a choice: you can wait here till we get back, or you can start out on your own for the hill, and we'll catch up with you. The rest of us are going on to the second map site."

"That's even worse than I thought," Sutherland said. "They got some special school for strategy where they send old lifers like you? Terrific—split your men up, abandon the wounded, go on without radio contact. How about our weapons? You want us to leave them here? What about our uniforms? Maybe we could make clown suits."

Brock ignored him. "What do you want to do? Wait for us here or start back?"

Landis shook his head. "I don't know," he said softly. "If I started back, I could get a couple hours' head start and wouldn't slow you guys up much. But . . ."

"He'd be alone and couldn't protect himself and might get lost," Sutherland filled in.

"Well, yeah," Landis said. "I mean, there are a lot of gooks out there, and . . ."

"Okay," Brock said. "Stay here and we'll pick you up on the way back."

"What if we get lost?" Sutherland asked. "Or ambushed? What's he supposed to do then?"

"I didn't say I had all the answers," Brock said defensively.

"You haven't got any of the answers, you dumb old fart," Sutherland sneered.

"Look," Brock said. "We're going to check out the other area, that's all there is to it. We're this close, so we're gonna do it." He handed the map to Frizzell and pointed to the second objective. "Get me there. Landis, we should be back in about three or four hours. Just hang tight."

"Comforting words from your old gunny."

"Shut up, Sutherland."

They sat silently in the bunker until it was dark, then they moved into the rain and headed east, Frizzell on point, Sutherland staggering under the weight of the machine gun.

After an hour they crossed a large clearing into heavy trees, but another search yielded nothing.

Brock drew them together under a tree and wiped rain and sweat from his face. "We're gonna give it one last shot. Everybody go off in a different direction—shoot an azimuth and follow it for thirty minutes. If you don't find anything, come back; then we'll head in."

Sutherland sat up angrily. "Come off it, we're not going to find anything—maybe there isn't anything; and if we split up, we'll never get back together."

Brock turned to Coney. "What do you think?"

Coney shook his head wearily. "I don't know. I'm so fucking tired I can't think straight. Maybe Scott's right."

"Frizzell?"

Frizzell lay on the ground, breathing heavily, too tired to open his eyes. "I don't know. It don't seem right to quit, but . . . You promise this will be the last try?"

"Just thirty minutes more."

"And thirty minutes back," Sutherland said. "If we can find our way back, then another two hours back to Landis, then another eight hours back to the hill."

"So what's another thirty minutes?" Brock asked.

"All right, all right," Frizzell said. "But this is it—no more."

"Coney?"

"Okay," he sighed.

"I'm not even asking you, Sutherland. I'm telling you. Haul your ass up and take off." He pointed a direction.

Sutherland glared at him without moving. "If you haven't got any fucking sense, go ahead, but I'm staying here."

Their eyes locked, Brock's narrowing so closely that Sutherland thought he had closed them, but then he saw Brock tense, his whole body quiver, and instinctively Sutherland got up.

Brock's voice was so cold that Sutherland averted his glance. "Don't say another word. Just move out."

He left, then Brock pointed directions for Coney and Frizzell and watched them move away. Finally he shot his own azimuth with his compass and followed it into the trees.

Coney moved due north, stopping every few minutes to recheck his bearing. At first he was afraid, but gradually he grew accustomed to solitary movement. The night sounds became familiar, and he realized that he made less noise than with the others. Strangely, he felt more alert and less exposed.

Twice he thought he heard movement, but each time it came to nothing. After twenty minutes he stopped to rest. He braced against a tree and listened. The only noise was rain falling through the canopy. He placed his rifle on the ground and lifted his face. The rain was soothing; he spread it across his face and ran his hand through his hair, momentarily eased.

He sat for several minutes, not wanting to move.

Alone in the darkness in no-man's-land, he had a sudden vision of his life: I have a wife, a child, and my life, he thought—nothing else, nothing any man should want to kill me for. And there is nothing any man has that I want to kill him for. What I have is enough, he saw; and he almost laughed. What am I doing here?

The simplicity of his discovery was funny to him, and he stretched out, letting the rain wash him.

I won't go any farther, he said. He shivered, then sneezed, and wiped at his nose.

Immediately a rifle safety unclipped only meters in front of him.

Coney froze. Oh, my God, he screamed to himself.

A voice shouted a frightened command from a man in front of him.

Coney's heart thumped wildly as he pressed against the ground; he had almost walked into a listening post.

His mind raced, trying to think of a way out. If he ran, he would be shot in the back, but he couldn't wait, they would find him. The thought of capture made him sick to his stomach.

Before him, the brush yielded slightly, a boot crushing leaves.

Please, please, God, make him go away, he prayed.

But the steps came nearer. Coney grimaced against the nearness of the enemy soldier silhouetted twenty feet from him, moving steadily closer, thrusting his rifle into the brush.

Coney flattened himself into the ground, but the steps came unswervingly toward him. For an instant he glimpsed the soldier, a tense, frightened youth whose eyes darted over the brush. Coney tried to force fury into his mind, but even with death so close, he could not summon hate. He bit his lip. Please, God, please.

Coney heard the soldier breathing over him, saw the rifle quiver in his hand, then the barrel swing slowly toward him.

At that instant there was a howling in his head that drove out all thought, an incredible force bursting from within, and he sprang, knocking the rifle from the man, and he thrust his bayonet into his throat.

He withdrew the blade, jabbed it in again, then brought it down with all his weight, falling heavily on him. He pulled the bayonet out then stabbed it into his chest. It struck rib, jarring him, but when Coney moved, the blade slipped past bone into the heart.

The soldier gasped, then was silent.

Blood splashed Coney's face and flowed over his hands. He heard its rush and smelled it. He tried to wipe it away but only spread it more. He worked the blade free, then grabbed his rifle and ran.

To the east, after a mile of probing, Brock found nothing. He finally stopped in a clump of brush and cursed the rain and the enemy who eluded him. He was not going to be a hero—all he was going to return with was blistered feet from his soaked boots.

Sutherland was right: he was just a dumb old lifer past his time. He had given the Corps nearly twenty years and fought in two wars—he didn't feel old, but he knew he was. What had the lieutenant said mockingly—"the tough but lovable old gunny"? But it was just yesterday surely when he had been young like Sutherland.

He sighed unhappily, clutching his rifle, watching drops of water bead the metal. He wiped away the rain, then smiled at the sudden memory he had of long ago when he was seventeen, new to the Corps, forced at boot camp to hold his rifle aloft in one hand and clutch his crotch with the other as he ran around the drill field yelling, "This is my rifle, this is my gun—this is for fighting, this is for fun."

It was almost over, he knew; this was his last war. He wouldn't let on to anyone, but God was he going to miss it. What was he going to do? He was too old for anything else.

Sutherland was right about that too—he couldn't get a real job in the real world. And do what? Sell shoes?

God damn Sutherland. Damn him to hell. Damn him his youth and mockery. Damn all of them—Coney and Frizzell and Sutherland, Landis and the lieutenant. Damn them for being young. It wasn't fair. He should stay young; he wanted to fight some more. And drink and fuck, and never grow old.

God shouldn't make anybody a gunnery sergeant, he thought; he ought to keep us all lance corporals.

He wiped at his eyes and realized it wasn't rain, then he felt foolish.

Rising with a little difficulty, he spat in the direction where the enemy apparently wasn't, then he turned back.

Sutherland went only a few hundred meters before stopping. All he could hear was wind driving rain through the trees. He stared into the darkness listening intently, then he eased to the ground, drew his jacket about him, and sat huddled against a tree.

Fuck it, he said to himself.

The blackness was complete, and he sat for a long time listening to the night sounds. He was cold and tired and afraid.

Then, as always happened when he was alone, the dead came to him. He tried to remember each one, but he couldn't. He went over their names again but knew he had forgotten some.

He shuddered and clutched himself tighter. And me? What if I should die? How long would they remember me? How long before I was just another poor dumb bastard, dead and forgotten?

Oh, God, he shook, don't let me die.

Then he braced himself defiantly against the tree. I won't, he said to himself. I'm not going to die. I'll get out, no matter what. Let the others look for the enemy. Stupid bastards. Ignorant, ignorant bastards.

Then he felt guilt. The ethic drilled into him began to gnaw, and shame crept over him. God damn it, he said, struggling to his feet.

He stood a moment. It would be different if it were for my parents, or if I had a wife and it were for her, or for my country—I mean really for my country. But this . . . asking me to die for nothing . . .

He began to cry, in confusion and guilt, fear and sorrow, and then he wiped his face and continued on.

Landis was cold and wet, and his leg throbbed. He wished he had something for the pain; massaging didn't help.

He splashed his good foot in a puddle and stared out the mouth of the bunker.

He thought of his car—his mean, bad black car.

He thought of his mother. Even of his dad who used to beat him.

He thought of a girl, a special one, then others.

He thought about living, wanting desperately to live—not knowing what he would do with Life: just things—driving his car; having a Coke and some fries; a girl. Days; warm days and the beach. The ocean. Nights; cool, not wet and cold. His leg not hurting.

He was glad the chaplain had saved him, but that didn't seem very important.

He thought of Martin. And the other guys. He wished he was with them. He wished they were here now.

Then he heard sounds.

The brush outside the cave gave way. He heard many steps—more than Coney, Frizzell, Sutherland, and Brock.

He listened.

They were coming closer. He heard their voices.

It was the enemy. They had found him.

Oh, God, he wanted to live. They were coming closer. They were just outside the bunker.

And he knew he would never get his car—his wonderful, black, mean, bad car. And he would never see his mother again. Or anyone.

They were just outside.

He looked at his crushed leg. He felt his body. He loved his body. He touched his shoulder. His legs.

They were coming in.

He raised his rifle.

Frizzell was about to turn back when he came to a large break in the trees that stretched five hundred meters.

Beyond, in the opposing trees, a tiny light appeared, then disappeared. He was about to pass it off as a trick of his eyes when he saw it again, then others.

He had found it; he knew he had.

Coney raced through the trees. When he reached the clearing, Sutherland's rifle was pointed at him.

"Jesus Christ! I never heard so much noise. Tie your fucking elephant to a tree."

"Where's Brock?"

"You're the first one back. What are you running from?"

"We gotta get out of here. I just killed one of them. I stumbled into a listening post. He came at me, and I killed him." Coney fell against a tree to catch his breath. His face was tight from caked blood, and his hands were crusted. The smell of blood sickened him. "We gotta get out of here. They'll find him soon."

"Find who?"

They jumped at the voice and scrambled away, then breathed easier when they saw it was Brock.

"Find who?" Brock repeated.

Coney said evenly, "I killed one of them. About a mile out I ran into a listening post. He saw me, so I bayoneted him. The body's still there."

Brock took a long swallow from his canteen. "Were there others?"

"I didn't see any. I just walked into him. Another few feet and he would have shot me."

"Maybe that was the staging area. Did you see anything?"

He shook his head.

"Which way was it?"

Coney pointed north.

Sutherland knocked his hand away and snarled at Brock, "What's the matter with you? We gotta get out of here. They may have found him already. This place will be crawling with gooks. Fuck the staging area—get us out of here."

Brock stared into the trees, then he nodded. "All right. We'll wait for Frizzell, then go back."

Sutherland slumped down in relief. They spent another twenty minutes in tense silence before they spotted Frizzell moving into the trees.

Brock whistled softly and Frizzell ran to them excitedly. "I found it—there were lanterns, lots of them."

Brock checked his watch. "How long would it take to get there?"

"Maybe an hour."

Brock gathered his equipment. "All right, let's go."

Sutherland did not move. "Where?"

"To find what Frizzell saw. We got time—it's not even midnight."

Sutherland exploded. "What about the body? You know they found it now. What about Landis? He's back there all by himself. And if Coney walked into an LP this far out, how many more do you think they got closer in? And the radio, asshole—we don't have radio contact."

"I could get you to the clearing," Frizzell said to Brock. "But after that . . . Scott's right, they'd have listening posts all around."

"And the guy I killed," Coney whispered. "If they haven't found him yet, they will soon."

"And Landis. What about Landis?" Sutherland repeated. "We said we'd go back by now."

Brock looked at each of them carefully. "Our orders are to find the staging area. Maybe Frizzell just did, but we need to know how big it is, what size unit is there, and what kind of weapons they have. It's the enemy—you know they're trying to take the hill, and Khe Sanh after that. I guess it just boils down to that simple thing—they're the enemy and I'm a Marine. You guys can do what you want, but I'm going."

Sutherland almost collapsed in frustration. "You are the *dumbest* motherfucker I've ever met."

"The enemy doesn't know where we are," Brock said.

"They might not find the body till morning, and even if they already found him, they wouldn't know where to look for us. And Landis—he's not going anywhere; he'll wait for us."

Brock shrugged and said almost softly, "I can't explain it, but it's like the lieutenant said once, on his first mission. I remember it because I really understood it: he said he couldn't live with himself if he quit. Sutherland's right—I'm an old lifer, but that means I gotta go."

He started off in the direction Frizzell had taken.

"Oh, my God," moaned Sutherland. "What bullshit. Is this for real?"

Coney smiled. "I think I saw this in a movie once."

"I hope they shot the motherfucker," Sutherland said.

"Come on," Coney said, picking up his rifle. "We gotta go—you know that."

"Yeah," Frizzell said. He put his hand over his heart and said in mock seriousness, "I mean, I can't explain it, but well, we're Marines."

Coney and Frizzell headed after Brock.

"You assholes," Sutherland hissed. He waited the requisite moment, then he ran after them.

CHAPTER

• 30 •

"Mayday! Mayday!" Magnuson shouted into the radio. "Viceroy going down."

The helicopter dropped hundreds of feet in seconds before Magnuson was able to gain enough control to glide it with autorotation. Centrifugal force, and the rush of air upward against the blades, provided a measure of stability for the craft, just enough for Magnuson to steer and balance as they dropped.

He gave a location, as close as he could guess, where he thought they were going to crash.

"Saddle up and come get us—this is definite hostile territory." Then he turned to Ridley and said with cool anger, "It's the fuel line. No gas is getting to the engine."

"I didn't think to check it before we left," Ridley said. "What could have happened to it?"

"I don't know, but I'm going to check it carefully if I can get this bitch down without it catching fire."

Magnuson feared fire as much as a crash, for a fuel problem meant gasoline could be leaking, igniting on impact.

"Brace yourselves, gentlemen," he called over the intercom. "We'll be making an unscheduled stop here in the Delta for a little sight-seeing. You'll have a chance to stretch your legs. All trays up please, and extinguish cigarettes.

We've enjoyed serving you this evening, and hope you'll think of us when considering future travel plans. In the meantime, please grab your asses tightly—and kiss them good-bye—because, gentlemen, we . . . are . . . going . . . down."

After switching off the intercom, he said to Ridley, "Son of a bitch. I can't make out anything down there. Is that water or rice paddies?"

"It just looks like deep dark to me, Jimbo."

"Well, we only got one shot at this. I think it's paddies, and that means dikes, and that means I'm not going to get this fucker down level. Hang on, Jack—this is it."

The chopper glided in at high speed and hit with a terrific jolt, bounced several times, struck a dike, and finally came to a halt, tipped over, its blades embedded in the mud.

All the movement was a blur to Marshall, and he had no real sensation of halting because he was immediately in motion, literally lifted out of his seat and dragged, pushed, or pulled—he wasn't sure which—from the chopper.

A powerful hand propelled him through the hatch. He landed in water up to his calves; his legs buckled, but the hand on the back of his neck kept him going.

Then an arm went around his waist and he was pulled forward so powerfully that his feet weren't even on the ground at times. He tried to move his legs, but he couldn't keep up with the forward momentum. Then he was thrown to the ground, and he sank into water and mud, and before he could pull himself up, a crushing weight fell on him.

"Don't move!" Mead yelled.

Move? he thought. I can't even breathe.

Just when he thought he couldn't stand it any longer, Mead jumped up and jerked Marshall's head up by his shirt collar. "You know how to fire this?" he said, thrusting an M-16 into his hands.

Before he could answer, Mead grabbed it back, flipped off the safety, and shoved it back into Marshall's hands. "All you gotta do is pull the trigger. But don't move—I'll be back in a minute." Then he was gone.

Halfway back to the chopper, Mead found Romer. He was sitting in the rice paddy, stroking his leg, slightly dazed.

472

"You all right, sir?"

"Yeah. Where's the ambassador?"

Mead pointed. "You stay here, sir. I'll get the others."

Magnuson was on his knees, trying to get under the chopper, swearing furiously. "You whore cunt. You traitor bitch."

Mead grabbed his arm and tugged. "Lieutenant, you ought to come away from it."

"Something happened to the fuel line—I want to know what."

"Forget that, sir, we got a bigger problem—the gooks. They'll be swarming around here soon, and they'll hit that with an RPG. We got to set up a perimeter defense."

Ridley limped to them from the darkness. "Any way we can get her back up?"

Magnuson shook his head. "She's deep in the mud. We'll never get the blade out."

Mead jumped back into the chopper to get the rifles and flak jackets Romer and Marshall had left. "Is there a portable radio?"

"Not on this one," Magnuson said. "But we called in the location. They'll be out for us soon."

Mead jumped out. "Any other rifles, grenades, or signal flares?"

"In the cockpit. I'll get them," Magnuson said. When he got out, they started across the paddy, picked up Romer, and gathered with Marshall.

"Something happened to the fuel line," Magnuson explained. "I don't know if it broke, got clogged, if the fuel was contaminated, or what—just that suddenly no fuel was going into the engine. We were in radio contact all the way down, but it might take them hours to find us. That's all I can tell you."

Ridley spoke directly to Marshall. "I want to tell you, sir, that the lieutenant did a terrific job getting us down—not many pilots could land a chopper safely from two thousand feet in the dark without engine or instruments."

"Yes," said Marshall, feeling relief that bordered on euphoria. His survival was an omen. He'd been spared to complete his mission. He would end the war. "I'm delighted to be in one piece. I thought that was it for a while. I think even Corporal Mead believed we had . . . how would you put it, Corporal?"

"Bought the farm, sir."

"Grandstanding," joked Romer. "He couldn't find a massacre, so for the finale, he crashed the plane. You didn't fool me for a minute, Lieutenant." He smiled. "Well, maybe for a minute, when we dropped about a thousand feet. I think my lunch is still up there."

Marshall looked about the dark terrain nonchalantly. "So we just wait until they find us?"

The others glanced at one another.

"It's not quite that simple," Magnuson said finally. "You see, sir, MACV knows we're down, and the general area where we are, and they'll start an immediate search and rescue—"

"Maybe not," Marshall said. "They may let me stew out here for punishment."

"Well, sir, you can be sure the enemy has started a search. They monitor our radio nets; they know we're down. Plus they have eyes, and they might have seen us hit—they could be real close."

"Yes, sir," said Mead. "That's why we ought to spread out—a Chicom grenade could get us all. We need to set up a perimeter—not too far apart, so they can't pick us off one by one. And we need a password—lots of spooky things happen at night. You'll hear voices and swear somebody's creeping up on you, and there's a good chance we'll end up blowing each other away."

"I slept through all my infantry training," Magnuson said. "Just give me a rifle and tell me what to do—I'm an aviator, not a grunt."

Romer was the senior military officer, infantry besides, but he knew Mead's experience in this situation exceeded his own. "I suggest we do what the corporal says. Why don't you take charge and set us in as you think best."

Marshall himself would have suggested that, instinctively trusting Mead over Romer in the field, but he didn't say anything. He put on a flak jacket and held his rifle out from his body. Something seemed to flow from the weapon into his hands, an old, familiar feeling, and he brought the rifle close to him. It felt comfortable, and there passed through him a disturbing, pleasurable excitement.

Mead was surprised at Romer's deference to him. "Yes, sir," he said, then he addressed the others as he would a small patrol. "There's not much we can do except set in and wait. The gooks will see the chopper outline against the horizon, but they don't know if everyone was killed or if some are wounded or we all took off. They'll just have to guess what our situation is, but they'll come in real cautious. Except we don't know what direction they'll be coming from. So we'll set in a line, about five meters apart, the end men facing opposite directions, the three in the middle alternating directions."

"Not in a circle?" Ridley asked.

"Too dangerous," Mead said. "We'd end up shooting each other. Just a straight line is better, and we can cover all directions. Just remember who's next to you. Don't fire unless you absolutely have to. As soon as you do, the flash will give us away and they'll hit us with fire. I got a few grenades, so get the word to me and I'll toss a grenade where you think you hear something, that way they still won't know where we are. Anybody want a grenade? I have six."

Romer, Magnuson, and Ridley took one each. Mead checked all their rifles, gave them magazines of ammunition, and made sure they all knew how to fire their weapons, then he set them in.

"How about a password?" he asked.

"Motherfucker," Magnuson said.

"How about 'Dolores'?" Romer said snidely.

"'Dolores' it is," Mead said. "That'll give us something to think about."

"I don't want your thoughts to stray, Corporal. Or Lieutenant," Marshall said. "Let's keep our minds on saving my ass."

They laughed and then were quiet, and the quietness was suddenly overwhelmingly fearsome, and each man profoundly felt his vulnerability and exposure.

Marshall thought back fifteen years to the last time he had sat out like this, in Korea. He had been much colder then, and more afraid. It wasn't that the enemy threat was greater then, he realized, but that he was older now; death did not seem so frightening—there were much worse things. He hadn't known that before. He was all ego then, too young.

He sat cross-legged in the rice paddy, the rifle in his lap, and he tried to sound his feelings. No, it was not fear that he felt, but an awakening of a long-dormant sense of acute aliveness, as if he had been asleep all these years since he had lain in the snow at Chosin, cradling his rifle, waiting to kill the enemy. He ran his fingers down the barrel to the bore, then around the trigger housing. What he felt was animal, and wonderful, and he wished he did not feel that.

Down the line, Mead alone knew the true danger, and that Marshall's life, all their lives, depended on him. Lieutenant Magnuson had got the chopper down—how Mead couldn't imagine—and now it was up to him to save them.

He desperately wanted to save Marshall—not to prove himself, he knew, not even because it was his duty, but because Marshall had been kind and good to him. It was his chance to do something for Marshall.

Now his mind raced over possibilities, and he suddenly realized that he had made a mistake: sitting like this was the most dangerous thing they could do—the enemy would find them as soon as they discovered the chopper didn't have any casualties. Stupid! he thought.

The enemy would check the chopper first—that was the best time to intercept them. If the enemy had been monitoring the radio, they knew Viceroy was someone important, and they would race, hoping to get there before a rescue mission.

Damn! As soon as they saw that everyone had escaped from the crash, they would probe until they found them, and he knew that would not take long. They wouldn't have a chance against a VC sapper unit.

Mead crawled down the line toward Magnuson. "Dolores," he whispered.

"Fuck you," Magnuson said.

"We gotta go down there to the chopper," Mead said, "you and me." Magnuson was the only one he trusted. Anyone who could make a landing as he had wasn't going to panic in a firefight. "The gooks will go directly for the chopper; we have to ambush them, not wait for them to come to us."

"I changed my mind," Magnuson said. "I want Colonel Romer to be in charge."

Mead crawled to the others and told them that he and Magnuson were going to set up a two-man ambush at the chopper; then he reset Marshall, Romer, and Ridley.

He and Magnuson crept toward the chopper and found a spot about fifty feet away that gave them cover and good observation. The two sat shoulder to shoulder, their rifles in their laps. "You know how to throw the grenade?" Mead whispered.

"Just pull the pin and count to five and throw."

"Except don't bother to count this time—we got to get away as far as we can. Run back to the others as soon as I tell you, but don't forget to give the password—they're spooked back there and could blow you away. So yell 'Dolores' as you run back."

"Can you believe that asshole, picking that?" Magnuson said about Romer. "And checking my file?"

"You banging her, sir?" Mead asked.

"Nobody bangs Dolores," Magnuson said. "She's a pro—she could take a torpedo in her cunt and deep-throat a fire extinguisher. If she were out here with us, she could lift that chopper by just blowing up its exhaust."

Mead laughed softly. "Pilots have all the fun."

"Fun, shit. I could barely get to the flight line this morning; she wore my butt out. I escaped when she took a minute out to cool her cunt down."

Magnuson fell silent, listening, testing the air for any aberrant sign, but Mead, so accustomed to night ambushes, sensed immediately that there was no enemy near yet—the night sounds were reassuring: frogs croaking, insects calling, nothing hushed or expectant.

"How did you know I came down from the DMZ, sir?" Mead asked, that having troubled him since their first meeting, right after Mead saw Magnuson coming downstairs from what he was sure had been a meeting with Mr. Lord. "I know you hadn't read my file."

Magnuson did not say anything for a minute, then finally, "Luke Bishop is my best friend. I saw him in Da Nang just before I came down to Saigon. He told me to say hi to you." He paused a second. "Or maybe it was 'bye.'"

"You know Lieutenant Bishop? He's a good officer."

"Luke Bishop is a complete fuck-up. God, you should have seen him in Da Nang. I thought for sure we were going to be arrested."

"Lieutenant Bishop?"

"In college, Luke played football and chased pussy—I don't think he ever learned anything. And he sure looked like shit in Da Nang—what did you guys do to him up there?"

"That's just war, sir."

Magnuson shook his head, and looking about, he said ironically, "Yeah, I'm beginning to see—war sucks."

They were silent for a while, listening intently, but there was no change in the air or noises.

"How about Mr. Lord?" Mead said unexpectedly.

There was a long pause, then Magnuson turned so that he could see directly in Mead's eyes. Their faces were only inches apart. They studied each other for a minute, then Magnuson said, "You get me out of here alive, and I'll tell you. I'll sit down with you and we'll talk—I promise. I'll owe you that."

"I think we'd be even, sir. I owe you for getting us down safely."

"That's my job."

"This is mine."

Magnuson grinned. "Sounds like a Joe Friday routine. *Dragnet,*" he explained.

Suddenly Mead put his hand on Magnuson, a tight grip, turning him toward the chopper.

Magnuson couldn't hear or sense anything except the incredible change in Mead; he could feel the tension, the almost fissionable power building beside him, yet amazingly, Mead looked looser and more relaxed, seeming to ease into the reeds.

"What is it?" he whispered.

"They're coming. I can smell them."

478

Magnuson sniffed. "I thought you farted."

Mead laughed. "You're okay, Lieutenant. But it's their diet, all fish, so you can smell them. They can smell us too; they think we stink—it's the meat we eat. But they're upwind and won't pick us up. Concentrate. Smell."

Magnuson did, and Mead was right. He could smell them, a very definite odor of fish, and suddenly he could hear the change—the sudden silence, except for a rapid splashing of frogs disappearing.

"Get me out of this. Okay?"

"Just do what I say."

"Tell me fast, and make it real simple. I'm scared shitless."

"So are they," Mead said.

"I hope so." Magnuson shook so badly that he felt sure the enemy could hear him splashing in the rice paddy. I won't be able to move, he thought. Then Mead put his hand on the back of his neck, a strong, sure grip that calmed him, and turned his head slightly so that he was looking a little to the left of the chopper. Magnuson nodded, seeing two men creep through the marsh, and Mead let go.

His whispered voice was as sure and soothing as his grip: "They'll send up two men from each side. They'll check it out, then call the others in. As soon as they all gather close to decide what to do, toss your grenade at the chopper—try to hit it. Do it on my signal, then run as fast as you can, cause with any luck that motherfucker will blow."

Magnuson fumbled for the grenade, knowing he was going to drop it in the paddy, or worse, have the pin fall out from his shaking hand and detonate in his lap. No wonder Luke Bishop is a basket case, he thought wildly. Then Mead's hand was on him again, steadying him, turning his neck to the right, and exactly as he had said, there were two more soldiers moving in from that direction.

He watched in terrified awe at the ballet-precise movement of the two enemy teams. Even in his fear he saw the beauty of the fluid motion, silhouetted forms on a dark stage creeping toward a giant sleeping beast. He held his breath as they edged closer to the black dragon, and he suddenly was with them, and he could feel their fear.

One moved, then another, then together until they converged on the crippled chopper. They circled it quickly, searched inside, then jumped clear.

Then one called in a soft, low voice.

"Holy shit," whispered Magnuson as perhaps thirty soldiers rose out of the dark marsh and crept toward the chopper.

"Get ready," Mead whispered.

Gathered near the helicopter, the VC unit was being broken into search teams, Mead knew, each assigned a direction to look. Far in the distance he could hear the muffled roar of the rescue choppers.

"Now!" Mead said, pulling the pin on his grenade, tossing it, and ripping away a second pin by the time Magnuson threw his first. Mead tossed his second and bolted an instant after Magnuson, hearing the clunk of grenades against the chopper, and the third splashing in the marsh.

As Mead ran, he heard alarmed and confused shouts from the enemy, then there was automatic rifle fire and yells.

"Dolores!" he cried, and dove, tackling Magnuson by the ankles, throwing him to the ground as there were three sudden explosions, then a deafening detonation and blinding, searing light as the helicopter exploded.

The ground shook, shrapnel flew overhead, and flames shot sixty feet into the air.

Mead heard screams, and when he rolled over to look back, he saw men on fire, racing from the inferno, throwing themselves into the watery marsh. Screams and shouts filled the night.

The heat seared them and they had to shield their eyes from the brilliant glow, like a burning sun, before them.

Almost immediately the choppers on the horizon closed the distance and searchlights crisscrossed the paddy fields.

Mead watched the enemy soldiers grab their wounded and streak toward the village and treeline to the south.

Suddenly Marshall jumped up.

A hundred meters before him, silhouetted in the glow of the explosion, were three enemy soldiers. They had been approaching the chopper from behind and stood frozen in the harsh glare.

They were close enough that Marshall could see the shock and fear on their faces; then just as they charged, he brought his rifle into his shoulder and fired a burst.

As a man was thrown back, Marshall swung the barrel toward the second and fired, then emptied the magazine on the third.

Before he'd finished firing, Mead was up and charging forward. He found them sprawled in the paddy, two face-down, all dead, shot in the chest.

When he returned, Marshall was still standing, his face a mask. Marshall handed him the rifle silently; he looked at his hands, then he wiped them on his trousers.

"Jesus . . . ," Mead started to say.

Marshall looked past him to where the men lay. Finally he brought his gaze back to Mead.

"I don't want you to say anything about this."

"But, sir . . ."

"Not a word," Marshall said, then he turned to the others. "That's an order. Do you understand?"

"Sir, you got all three of them," Mead said in awe. "Right in the chest. They could have got us. You saved us. I mean, what you did was . . ."

Marshall shook his head. "I don't want you ever to say anything. I mean it. That's an order. I . . . I mean . . ." Then he fell silent, gazing into the dark, unable to articulate his feelings, unsure even what they were.

What *had* he felt? he wondered. Nothing; he could remember feeling nothing. It had been instinctive; rote. And what did he feel now? No joy, no elation. An immense sorrow. I thought that time was over, he said to himself. I did not want to know that I could still do this.

Nothing has changed, he thought sadly; the killing goes on and on. He looked at his hands: Guadalcanal, Chosin, and now here.

He faced the others, feeling that he owed them an explanation.

"I don't think the President would be pleased to know that his ambassador, the man he sent to find a settlement for the war, was having firefights with the enemy in rice paddies. It could . . . complicate matters. I can hardly conduct negotiations if the enemy knows I . . . that I've . . ." He could not finish, could not say "kill," because he did not want to think about it. Ever again.

"I never want to hear about this," he said. "You will never mention it; is that clear?"

They nodded, and almost immediately the night thundered with pounding rotor blades as the helicopters came in from the north.

Mead unclipped a flare from his jacket and popped it. There was a flash of green; it floated overhead, then dropped gently to the ground. Before he could pop another, several of the choppers peeled away from the enemy pursuit and arched toward them. The choppers circled, then others came, and three of them dropped down while others stayed aloft, their searchlights illuminating the entire area.

From the giant CH-47 Chinooks, squads of infantrymen jumped into the paddies and swept quickly toward Mead and the others.

"Everybody all right?" an officer shouted over the engine roars. "Where's Viceroy?"

Marshall stepped forward.

"Are you all right, sir?"

"Yes," Marshall said. "We're all fine."

The officer grabbed his arm. "Then if you'll come with me, sir, we'll get you out of here."

The officer told two squads to remain on the ground and search for wounded enemy soldiers, then he directed Marshall and the others onto a chopper, and it lifted before they fastened their seat belts.

The soldiers looked curiously at Marshall and the others, then one trooper shouted, "How'd you guys get out of that shit alive?"

Then a couple gave a thumbs-up, and others clapped.

Marshall tried to blank his mind, but the image of those soldiers at the instant before their death seared his brain. I will not think about it, he said resolutely, forcing the image away, fixing his thoughts instead on the meeting with the North Vietnamese. It had to occur, now more than ever. The carnage had to end.

But what would the enemy demand? What would Johnson

agree to? What could he ask of the North that they would agree to?

Talk, there'd be endless talk, points and counterpoints, proposals and ploys: old men babbling as young men died.

First, an immediate cease-fire, that's what mattered most —an end to the killing. Let that be the starting point: stop the bombing, stop the slaughter.

He was presenting imaginary proposals as the chopper approached Saigon and began its descent into Tan Son Nhut.

When he got off the chopper, Marshall saw an array of senior officers waiting for him on the tarmac.

"Jesus," he whispered to himself, but stepped toward them completely composed. Then he turned back to the helicopter where the crew and soldiers were standing.

"Thank you," he said. "You did a very impressive job. It was just a drill, you understand, but I'm sure that if we had been in any real trouble, we could have relied on you."

They laughed appreciatively.

"Thank you again," he said, then waved Magnuson, Mead, Romer, and Ridley toward him and brought them all to the waiting officers and State Department officials.

"I want all these men to have medals, not for saving me—which they did—but for incredible bravery. I don't know how Lieutenant Magnuson got that chopper down. And what he and Corporal Mead did was simply heroic— they stopped an entire unit of enemy soldiers by themselves. Then three enemy soldiers came at us from behind and Colonel Romer and Mr. Ridley shot them—you'll find the bodies only a couple hundred feet from where we were."

He turned to the men. "I'm really at a loss; how do you thank someone for your life?" He shook their hands, then put his arms around Mead and Magnuson and said to the two-star general before him, "I particularly want to commend Corporal Mead and Lieutenant Magnuson."

"Commend them?" joked Romer. "I think you ought to have them court-martialed, sir. He crashed the plane, then he fragged it."

"That's true—willful destruction of government property; I suppose we could deduct the cost of the chopper from their paychecks. And now, gentlemen . . . and Dolores," he said, seeing his secretary standing behind Colonel Waggoner.

"Jesus," whispered Magnuson to himself, seeing her look at him anxiously, unconsciously digging her nails into Colonel Waggoner.

"Dolores," Marshall said. "You saved us too—you were our secret password; I'm sure we'd be out there with our throats cut if it weren't for you. Now if you will all excuse me, I think I'll call it a night. And a day tomorrow, too—everybody else as well. Don't anybody come in."

He nodded to them all and walked toward his limousine parked on the flight line. "Get me out of here, Stokes."

The others watched the car drive off, then the general turned to Romer and the others. "Before you begin your holiday, we'd like a little debriefing, if you don't mind. Perhaps you could fill us in a little on . . . just what the fuck was going on out there."

It was nearly two hours before Mead was released; Romer and Magnuson were still there when he left.

He got a cab outside the gate and was dropped off in front of his apartment just before two A.M., nearly twenty-four hours after he had left for the embassy yesterday morning.

After paying the driver, he stood a moment on the sidewalk, too tired to move. Then he saw Bernard Lacouture racing up the block toward him. "Jesus," he whispered to himself.

Lacouture ran up, handkerchief fluttering, then he stopped in alarm. "*Chéri!* What happened to you? Your clothes are wet. And torn! Are you all right? Are you hurt? Oh dear, oh dear. Are you bleeding?"

"I'm fine," Mead said hoarsely. "Look, Mr. La—"

"Bernard."

"Yeah, Bernard. Look, Bernard, I'm really beat. I'm fine, really, not hurt at all—I just got wet. I don't want to be rude, but can we talk some other time?"

Lacouture pulled nervously on his handkerchief. "Of course. I shouldn't have bothered you. I just . . . wanted to see you. I wanted to know if it was true . . . that you could be friends with me."

He looked so sad and forlorn that Mead felt sorry for him. "Well, sure," he said. "It's just that right now I'm so tired I can barely stand up. Another time, okay?" Then he put his hand on Lacouture's shoulder. "I promise." He went up the stairs.

Lacouture watched him go. He felt the powerful grip on him still, yet it had been a fond touch, he knew. He swelled with happiness; maybe it was true.

As soon as Mead opened the door to his room, Sung jumped up from the sleeping bag on the floor in a corner. The lights were on and the room looked even less familiar than the day before—a cloth was on the table, and a vase of flowers on that. New curtains were at the window, and there was a throw rug on the floor.

When she saw him, she brought her hands to her mouth. "Are you hurt?" she asked.

Seeing her filled him with immense happiness; he wanted to grab her, but instead he backed up and said shyly, "No, I'm fine."

"But your face, and . . ." She looked at his torn, wet clothes.

He went to the mirror. His face and hair were caked with mud, and looking down on himself, it appeared that he had been hurt in a fight.

"I'm okay," he said. "Really."

He wanted to sit down, but he felt too dirty, and he saw that his boots had tracked mud into the room. "I'm sorry," he said, looking at the trail of water and mud. "I better take these off." But he felt shy about taking off his clothes, though he didn't understand why he felt that way before her.

He stripped off his fatigue top, then held it in his hands because he didn't know where to put it.

Finally she took it from him, then waited until he undid his boots. She put those in a corner, then took his trousers from him as he quickly crossed the room to put on dry skivvies.

"Do you want something to eat?" she asked. "Or to drink? I bought some tea with the money you gave me."

"No thanks," he said, and then he could not stop yawning. He dropped down on his sleeping bag.

485

"Are you all right?" he asked.

"Yes," she said, standing across the room, holding his clothing. "I am much better."

But he did not hear; he was already asleep.

It was nearly three A.M. before Magnuson got back to his BOQ room, having given a complete report on what had happened, and the entire day's events, including all stops, and everything he had heard Marshall say, and all his observations to three different groups, military, State Department, and an intelligence team.

He took a hot shower and was drying himself off when there was a soft knocking at his door.

Oh, no, he thought, thinking it was Dolores, but despite his exhaustion, he had an erection by the time he got to the door.

Wilson Abbot Lord pushed in, closed it behind him, and turned to Magnuson, noting the jutting erection Magnuson was trying to hide behind his towel.

"I trust you were expecting someone else," Lord said. "Miss Toland perhaps?"

"Jesus," said Magnuson. "Was it on the fucking news today? Everybody in Vietnam seems to know."

Lord went to an armchair and sat down. "Let's have a little chat, Lieutenant." He motioned Magnuson to the sofa across from him.

Magnuson wrapped the towel around himself and sat down.

"Tell me what happened to that chopper, Lieutenant."

You might know better than I, thought Magnuson, but he said, "It was the fuel line. It could have been anything—that kind of thing happens: contaminated fuel, a leak, an electrical problem; there's no way to tell unless you can examine the aircraft."

Lord nodded. "Spare me modesty: How lucky were you to land it safely?"

"To land it? That wasn't luck—that was skill. I'm good; besides, I didn't want to die."

"How many others could have done it?"

Magnuson shrugged. "Not too many. That's to land

it—but that it didn't blow up when we hit? That was luck. And getting out the way we did? That wasn't luck either—that was Corporal Mead. Without him, or with somebody else, the VC would have gotten us."

"It was a very near thing then?"

Magnuson laughed. "The President came within a cunt hair of losing his special envoy."

Do all pilots talk this way? Lord wondered, thinking of Jeff Gibbon.

Lord's face and voice were bland. He was upset at the development, but not unduly; glitches occurred so often in his line of work that they were the rule, rather than the exception. The plan didn't succeed, and there was no point in dwelling on it. Now he would have to effect the contingency plan—he would have to rely on Lacouture's setting up the meeting. He couldn't risk another "accident" with the helicopter. And this time he would see to the execution of the plan himself; he would oversee every detail personally.

The first step was to get hold of Bui Cao Kim. He had put a tail on Kim and discovered that he was running messages between Lacouture and the communists—too many messages. That and Lacouture's confidence increased his suspicion that Lacouture might be double-crossing him. Kim would, under duress, tell him what he needed, and for that he needed Magnuson.

"You came to me with the highest recommendation, Lieutenant; now we'll see if you warranted it. I have a special mission for you."

He said it so coldly that Magnuson understood exactly what he meant.

"I hate to coerce anyone," Lord said. "Are you amenable?"

As if I had a choice, Magnuson thought, but he said, "Yes, sir."

"Good," Lord said, standing and going to the door. "I'll get a message to you tomorrow. Be ready to fly the following night—don't make any evening plans."

He smiled without warmth. "Pleasant dreams, Lieutenant."

* * *

Marshall did not wake until after ten in the morning; he was stiff and sore and remained in bed another hour.

As he went downstairs, surrounded by luxury and servants, yesterday seemed like some bizarre, technicolor, pyrotechnic extravaganza more suited for a Saturday matinee for children; only his sore limbs gave credence to the reality.

The breakfast table was set with china and crystal and fresh flowers, the doors were open onto the garden, and the overhead fan wafted cool air and the fragrance of a thousand blossoms.

His mail had been sent over from the embassy; he sorted through it idly until he came to an envelope embossed with a picture of a Special Forces soldier, addressed in pencil, and posted from Fort Bragg. He ripped it open.

Dear Dad,

How's the war? Are we winning? Think there will be anybody left for me to kill or save by the time I get there?

Basic training was not as bad as I thought it would be—more psychological harassment than physical demand, and having been raised in an environment of constant psychological warfare, I was better conditioned than others. (Just joking, Dad.)

They gave the top ten percent of us our first choice—I picked Special Forces; no sense going halfway, right?

So far it's been real animal training—eating insects, that kind of thing, and I've learned lots of neat new words and sayings that I probably never would have at Brown, which just goes to show you that money can't buy everything.

I went home for a few days after Basic but all Mom did was sob, and every time I walked into the room she'd burst into tears about my shaved head, and I popped Chris when he said my head reminded him of his right testicle, but Sarah said no, it looked more like her boyfriend's (still Bosco) left testicle, so then I left—and may not go back till the war's over. Got any idea when that'll be?

Hope to see you soon—save a commie for me.

Yours in Christ, and the American Way,

Love,
Ryan

Oh, my God, Marshall said to himself, folding the letter and putting it under the stack. Then he read it twice more.

Special Forces! The stupid son of a bitch. God damn him!

He pushed himself from the table. I won't have it, that's all there is to it. I won't allow it!

He started for the door, then stopped.

What could he do? He looked about helplessly.

There was nothing he could do.

The horror was rushing headlong toward him. What if it had been Ryan out in the Delta last night? He would never have survived. He'll never make it, Marshall thought. He'll be out at night, terrified and alone, and the enemy will close on him . . .

Ryan. His son.

Oh, my God, he thought. A Green Beret. The stupid, stupid son of a bitch. He'll die.

God damn him!

Well, it wouldn't happen, that's all there was to it—he wouldn't allow it.

He crossed to the phone and called General Tran at ARVN headquarters.

An aide informed him that the general was not in, but if he left a number, the general would try to get back in touch.

Before he got to the table to retrieve his coffee cup, General Tran was on the line.

"After giving my aide hell and telling him to inform everyone that I'm not in, the fool seems to have taken me literally. He doesn't seem to know who *everyone* means. What can I do for you, Excellency?"

"A man wants to meet with me, and you also. I was given a word that is supposed to mean something. The word is 'squeaky.'"

There was a very long pause, so long that Marshall feared they might have been disconnected.

"I suspect that this line is not secure," Tran said at last.

"What line is? But I suspect that the word is."

"It is," Tran said. "It means something to only . . . one other man."

"And what would you say to him?"

"I'm not sure he could hear me. Or even if he could, that I would want to talk with him." There was another long pause. *"Goulue,"* he said finally with bittersweet sadness.

"Goulue?" Marshall repeated. *"Français?"*

"Yes."

"Thank you, General," he said gratefully. "I shall be back in touch with you."

It was coming together, Marshall thought, glowing inside. Lacouture was legitimate, the proposal to meet genuine. He would have something concrete to take to Johnson; there could be a cease-fire immediately. And Ryan? He would be spared. Marshall's heart soared.

When he hung up, Marshall took Lacouture's card from his wallet and dialed the number.

"Allô, allô," came the immediate answer, with such enthusiasm that Marshall smiled; at least one man in Saigon is happy, he thought.

"Monsieur Lacouture?"

"Ah, Excellency. How are you? How good of you to call."

"I have an answer. The word is *'goulue.'"*

"Pardon?"

"Goulue."

There was a pause, then, *"Bien."*

"I hope to hear from you soon," Marshall said, and hung up.

When Lord heard the playback of the taped conversation a short time later, he wrote the word down.

Goulue. Glutton, in French; he didn't even need to look it up.

He sat immobile at his desk, concentrating on the word, then he freed his mind, blanking it completely. *"Goulue,"* he

490

said softly, as though releasing it, and he let the word into his mind, gave it free roam, and watched distractedly from outside his thoughts as the word scented down all the corridors of his mind, searching memory for an association.

There was something, but so dim—a very old, cold scent. A woman. Yes, a woman. But none came from memory. He tried to focus on different types—fat women, nymphomaniacs, addicts, but he knew he was off the trail. The association was more ephemeral—softer.

He stood up. It would come; it always did when he was this close. He wouldn't push it.

There was a knock at the door. "Come in."

Jeff Gibbon entered, looking contrite and anxious.

Lord pointed to a chair and sat behind his desk.

"That's the first time I ever fucked up," Gibbon said.

"It wasn't your fault—it was just one of those things. You'd better get used to them, they happen frequently. The pilot landed the chopper without its blowing up; a Marine corporal drove off a VC sapper unit. You can hardly be blamed for not anticipating all that."

Gibbon nodded. "Thank you, but I'm sorry I let you down."

"It's just as well—actually that was my contingency plan. Now I'll go with the one I prefer anyway. I've got Lacouture setting up a meeting between Marshall and the North Vietnamese, except that it's going to be an ambush— Marshall only thinks he's going to a peace negotiation. Lacouture has already baited and hooked Marshall; the little frog fag has done a good job."

Lord leaned back in his chair and his face set harshly. "Maybe too good a job. He did it too easily, and the communists are too willing. The NVA never commits itself quickly, they're much too cautious, but in this case, there's been a rapid exchange of cryptic messages that indicates they want to meet with Marshall. I think Lacouture is playing both sides."

Lord smiled faintly. "You see, I almost 'fucked up' by not seeing that the NVA might actually want to meet with Marshall instead of ambushing him. I was getting so carried away with my plans and strategies that I almost overlooked theirs—that's like playing chess without considering the opponent's gambits. Do you play chess, Jeff?"

"A little," Gibbon responded blandly.

"Ah; you must be excellent. We'll have a game soon."

"What are you going to do about Lacouture's double cross?" Gibbon asked.

"I'm not sure it's a double cross yet; that's what I have to determine. I've got to get somebody in his bed so that he can whisper his innermost secrets to him." He stared intently at Gibbon. "You'd do it, wouldn't you?"

Gibbon swallowed but didn't look away. "If you told me to, yes, sir."

Lord smiled. "I already have someone, thank you anyway. And to ensure that Lacouture isn't double-crossing me, I'm going to pick up Bui Cao Kim, the one running the messages back and forth."

"What can I do?" Gibbon asked.

"Nothing for the time being, but I may call on you. You can help most by being my sounding board." He said sincerely, "It's nice to have someone to confide in, Jeffrey."

Mead woke with a jerk. He glanced at his watch, then jumped up, throwing off his sleeping bag and running toward his clothes corner.

It was one P.M. Jesus, he thought, he had slept the whole day. He'd be court-martialed. Waggoner would have his ass for this.

But where were his clothes? And what had happened to his boots? He picked them up in amazement. They were polished, but not spit-shined the way he did them, and they were wet. Then he slapped his forehead, remembering the day before, and that he didn't have to go in today.

He turned to see Sung staring at him cautiously from the table where she was sewing his ripped clothes. He put the boots down and went to the table, dropping in a chair across from her. "Thank you," he said.

She lowered her head.

He took the clothes from her. "You don't have to do that."

She didn't look up. "I . . . have nothing else to do." Then

she smiled faintly. "I never say the right thing. I should have said that I don't mind."

"No, you shouldn't say that. Only say what you mean. And do what you want. Even if you've got nothing to do, nothing is better than polishing a guy's boots and sewing his clothes."

"Didn't your mother do that for your father?"

"Yeah, but she shouldn't have, and I don't want you to be like my mother anyway."

He stood up and went to another corner, which was stacked with C rations and packets of coffee.

He returned with a couple of cans of rations and some coffee. "Hey, you want to go out today? I don't have to go to work. You want to go somewhere?"

He sat excitedly across from her again. "We could go downtown, or to the river. The zoo! Hey, how about the zoo? You ever been there?"

She shook her head shyly, still without raising it.

"We'll go there then. I mean . . . if you want to. Would . . . I mean, will you go with me? Or would you . . . rather not?"

She kept her head down, then said hesitantly, putting a finger on her ripped blouse, "My clothes are . . ."

"I told you to buy some new ones. I gave you the money."

She pointed to his trousers on the floor. "I put the money in your pocket. I couldn't take it for my clothes."

"Oh, bullshit," he said. "I mean, I want to buy you clothes—I don't need money. I never spend any; there's nothing I want."

He stood again, very happy suddenly. "Will you go if you have some clothes? We'd have a great time—they got animals there dumber than me." He laughed, something she had never heard, and she smiled at the sound.

"Great," he said. "In fact, why don't you borrow something from Han so we can go right away? I'll buy you something to wear later."

There was a knock at the door, and Sung stepped away quickly, edging toward a corner.

"Yeah?" shouted Mead.

The door opened, and Jim Magnuson stuck his head in.

493

Mead jumped up.

Magnuson looked about, smiled at Sung, and said apologetically to Mead, "Sorry to bust in, but I promised you a talk—I thought today would be a good time. I had a helluva time finding you. None of your buddies at the barracks wanted to give me your address. Why is everybody so suspicious of officers? You going to ask me in or not? Jesus, what a beautiful woman!"

He closed the door behind him.

Mead was too startled to say anything, but finally he turned to Sung. "This is Lieutenant Magnuson. He's a . . . we work together, sorta. Except he's an officer."

She nodded at Magnuson, then said to Mead, "I'll go see Han."

When she left, Magnuson whistled softly. "Want to trade? I'll swap you Dolores and my commission for her."

Mead grinned. "No thanks, sir."

"Damn," he said. "Corporals have all the fun."

"Sit down, sir. Can I get you something?"

Magnuson shook his head. "This won't take long. I don't want to keep you from what I know are more important things. Hey, really sorry about butting in, but I think we need to talk."

Mead gestured for him to sit. They stared at each other for a minute, then Magnuson said, "This is going to be difficult because neither of us can say anything, and in this kind of business, you shouldn't say anything, and you shouldn't trust a fucking soul."

Magnuson leaned across the table. "But after last night, I'm going to trust you."

They didn't speak for another moment, or break eye contact.

Finally Magnuson said, "I'm supposed to do something I'm not sure I want to do."

Mead stared expressionlessly, then said, "So am I."

"I'm not sure it's right," Magnuson said.

"Neither am I," Mead answered.

Magnuson nodded slowly. "Maybe that's as far as we ought to go right now—just touch base to let each other know that we're both in the game, maybe even on the same side."

Magnuson lifted his feet. "I think, Corporal, that we may be in some deep shit. It's too bad we had to blow up the chopper. I really wanted to check the fuel line."

"Why, sir?"

"Because there was another possibility besides contaminated fuel and electrical failure—somebody could have messed with it. But now I'll never know."

"But who would have done that, sir?"

Magnuson stared at Mead intently. "That's what we have to be real careful about. And that's what I'm trying to do—I'm trying to figure out the game and who's on whose side."

Magnuson stood and put out his hand. "I really hope we're on the same team; I think we are. If so, then we can get out of this. Like last night. But we better be careful, and before we do anything—like what we don't want to do—I think we should talk to each other."

They shook hands, then Magnuson slapped Mead's shoulder. "See you tomorrow." At the door he turned. "Sure you don't want to trade? I'll throw in my chopper too."

"Fuck, no! Sir."

"My new chopper—it's on the flight line." He grinned and left.

Mead sat back down. He was motionless for many minutes. Did he trust Magnuson? What did he mean about the fuel line? Who would have messed with it? Who would want Marshall killed?

He shook his head, trying to cast the confusion from his mind; he didn't know what to think.

He trusted Lord, yet something gnawed at him, and he thought he trusted Magnuson, yet Magnuson seemed to be hinting at something. He knew Lacouture was bad, yet his instinct told him that the strange little Frenchman could be trusted.

The only thing he knew for certain was that he wanted to protect Marshall. But now a disturbing question had been raised—protect him from whom? Suddenly everything had become murky, and he was no longer sure who the enemy was.

The door opened, and Sung stood shyly, wearing a light blue *ao dai* from Han.

He smiled when he saw her, for that was another thing that he knew for certain—he had fallen in love. He jumped up. "God, you look beautiful," he said.

She lowered her head.

"I'll be just a minute; let me put something on." Suddenly he was happy, everything else forgotten, insignificant to being with her, and going to the zoo.

CHAPTER

· 31 ·

Frizzell brought them to the edge of the clearing.

The four men spread out. Even in the light drizzle they could see flickering lights a quarter mile away in the trees.

This was it, Brock knew, but it looked bigger than he had expected, bigger probably than anyone at Khe Sanh suspected.

A large unit such as this would surround itself with sentries and listening posts, but he also knew that they would not expect a probe this far north. Their primary fear was of aerial surveillance and random bombing.

They would have been working since first dark so by now they would be tired and incautious, rushing to finish before light. Now would be the best time to move, Brock judged.

He gathered them close. "I want to cross. I think it'll be safe."

"Are you blind as well as senile?" Sutherland hissed. "That's it. Frizzell found it. Mission completed."

Coney nodded agreement. "That's a lot of gooks over there, Gunny. We're asking to get zapped if we go any closer."

"But we need to know how many there are."

"Four thousand six hundred and twelve, I just counted," said Sutherland.

"Listen to me," Brock said. "This is important. Suddenly

497

this is big time—I don't even think they have an idea back at Khe Sanh how big this is."

"Okay, it's big—I can see that. So we go back and tell them. We tell them there's a shitload of gooks up here. We tell them they're massing a huge fucking army up here. I'm a lance corporal, and I can see there's big trouble on the way. I'm sure some fucking general can figure that out too."

"Generals want to know how many, and what units they're from, and what weapons they have."

Sutherland pressed his face into Brock's. "If they're that fucking curious, they can come up here and see for themselves, and measure their dicks while they're at it—but I've seen enough. Now cut this shit out and get us out of here."

Brock pressed back. "We are going to move closer. We are going to see exactly what is happening over there, and then you and I are personally going to tell the CO at Khe Sanh what it is. And we will have done our jobs and saved a lot of guys' asses. Now, you want to take point or let Frizzell do it? But in any case, you are *always,* from this second on, going to stay in front of me so that I can watch you, just in case you have the idea to shoot me in the back. Not that you would—just in case, Sutherland, because I know you, and because I've been through two fucking wars, and because I want to see my wife again, and because—most of all—I want to live just as badly as you do."

Sutherland's mouth tightened. "Let Frizzell take point."

Halfway across the savannah, Frizzell stopped, suddenly disoriented. The rain had picked up and he could not see the lights any longer.

"What's the matter?" Brock asked, moving beside him.

Frizzell looked about in confusion. "I don't know, I just . . ." He closed his eyes and shook his head, trying to clear it, but when he opened his eyes, he knew he was lost. He looked about quickly, then began to panic. His hand went to his face; the skin was clammy. Warnings pumped through him; he was suddenly paralyzed with fear.

Brock signaled Sutherland. "Take over."

For a moment Sutherland stood in the middle of the marsh gripped with an intense image of death—cold, empty, terrifying—waiting for him in the trees beyond. He could not move his foot. He clutched his rifle so tightly that his hands shook. Then he saw his coffin.

In the far treeline, he saw it clearly before him, the coffin that he could not escape, that was relentlessly before him. He closed his eyes and his hand reached for the amulet around his neck. He stroked it furiously, then he opened his eyes.

The coffin was gone. He breathed in relief, and his panic passed. His eyes began to harden, as if coats of malice were applied; his mouth tightened, his entire body loosened as though it were melding with the night and terrain, then he moved—effortlessly, simply easing into the darkness.

He was moving so fast that the others could barely keep up, and even when he crossed the clearing he did not stop, moving unhesitatingly through the trees.

Then he stopped abruptly and threw open his hands, motioning them to cover. They dropped immediately, and for a moment Brock could not hear anything except his gasping breath, and he rested his head on the wet ground.

Then the sounds of digging came to him, then voices, and almost afraid to lift his head, he finally raised it to see lanterns all about them. They were so close that he wanted to bury his head; he was too frightened to speak or move— Sutherland had brought them into their midst.

They couldn't risk moving even to find better cover. Brock knew the enemy would go underground shortly, but now he was afraid a soldier would stumble over them on his way to hiding. They had no choice except to wait until daylight.

The enemy voices and digging were comforting; hearing them labor and curse reassured Brock that their presence was not suspected, but just before dawn came a burst of radio activity and Brock could tell from the operator's voice that something had happened.

Sharp, angry commands were issued over the radio, then relayed to the men working.

Everything grew quiet, then came hushed, anxious exchanges all about them.

The body, of course. They had found the sentry Coney had killed.

It was too late for them to search the area; the horizon was already beginning to lighten.

Brock tried to think of what the enemy might do, knowing a patrol was in the area. Would they leave teams above ground to search for them? Set up ambushes? Or withdraw into hiding?

He could not guess, he knew; he wasn't an officer and could not even for a moment put his mind into the frame of devising strategy or making tactical decisions. He never even knew for sure what the lieutenant was going to do—there was always something that he, Brock, had not considered.

He keenly knew his limitations; he was just a gunnery sergeant who had no business leading a patrol behind enemy lines on the Demilitarized Zone. He had made a bad mistake pushing the patrol on like this; he realized now that he should have turned back after Frizzell located the site.

And he shouldn't have left Landis; the poor bastard was probably terrified—a dumb eighteen-year-old left crippled in a cave surrounded by the enemy.

He hadn't thought through the dead sentry either, he saw now. American patrols never ventured this far north—and suddenly the enemy finds one of their soldiers with his throat gouged out right in the middle of a secret operation.

Jesus, he thought—what if the enemy knew they didn't have a radio and hadn't been able to notify anyone of the buildup or its location?

He began to panic. What if they had found Landis and the crushed radio and made the connection to the dead sentry? Of course they would—a soldier left behind because of a leg injury; the abandoned radio—no way to convey the information back to Khe Sanh.

All they would have to do is wait for the patrol to return to pick up their wounded man, then they would kill them all. They wouldn't have to track them, just wait at the cave for them to go back for Landis.

He dropped his head into his chest. Oh, shit, what am I going to do? I never should have come here, he thought. I should have gone back as soon as Coney killed the sentry, before they could have found his body or discovered Landis.

Landis. He moaned to himself thinking what they would do to him if they found him.

But they had just now discovered the body. If they had found Landis before this, they'd simply kill him. But if they found him now . . . Oh, my God, he thought. He had to get to him.

But that's just what they'd expect them to do; they'd be waiting. Shit, shit, shit, he cursed vehemently. What was he going to do? What would Lieutenant Bishop do?

The enemy voices grew louder; he could tell they were arguing.

Brock never awaited a sunrise more eagerly in his life; he could have run to the horizon and pulled it up himself if he could.

Jesus, he thought suddenly—maybe they won't go underground at all; maybe they'll decide they have to risk working in the daylight now because of the dead sentry. Maybe they'll risk that there won't be any aerial surveillance in this weather.

Sutherland was right again—the fucking pilots won't fly in this kind of rain; they'll sit back in their air-conditioned BOQ or go get drunk at the Officers' Club. The bastards.

He was making himself sick with worry, he realized. God damn it, if I was supposed to do this much thinking, I should have been an officer. Gunnery sergeants aren't supposed to worry and think like this.

The voices stopped arguing; more commands were issued, and there was a flurry of activity, then the sounds of equipment being put away and brush being moved.

They were camouflaging their work. They were going underground.

Some of those seeking shelter passed within twenty feet of the patrol, though the majority of enemy troops headed north. Brock decided that only a few men were being left for security, and the first hour would be the safest time to get away because the guards would be least attentive now, untensing from their night's work, eating rations, talking, and organizing.

Brock waited only ten minutes after the last soldier disappeared before signaling the others to move out.

They crept ten meters apart through the area; even in the faint light and despite the enemy attempt to camouflage their work, they could see the huge buildup. Shelters had been built for ammunition, and already they were half-stocked with mortar shells and RPGs. More ominous was a well-constructed canopy of trees and brush that hid a nearly completed launching site for middle-range missiles. Further concealed in the foliage were antiaircraft weapons, and beyond that they found a large cache of rice.

The enemy was obviously stockpiling weapons and supplies for a major assault; this was a main point of collection and distribution for what looked like a large attack on Khe Sanh. Certainly only a small percentage of what was already here could easily overcome their position on the hill.

Brock did not know what size unit was massing, but he guessed from the weapons and logistics that it was at least a regiment, which was the size Marine unit defending Khe Sanh.

As they moved through the area, each of them picked up whatever they thought might be useful for intelligence purposes. Brock found a personal letter and another piece of paper with markings on it; Sutherland found a web belt with a name and unit designation; Coney stripped the wrapping from an ammunition box, and Frizzell gathered loose items such as a discarded cigarette—something almost never encountered, indicating how well supplied the unit was—a ration wrapper, and a pencil.

It took thirty minutes to sweep quickly through the site, then Brock pointed to Sutherland and motioned south.

Sutherland peeled away, and the others followed single file, quickening their pace the farther they got from the site.

After a mile Brock stopped them, gathering them in a close circle under a tree.

"We gotta talk 'cause this concerns everybody. I'm sure they found the body—I think that's what they were talking about on the radio."

"Yeah, that's what I guessed," said Coney.

"Now we gotta consider about Landis. They might have found him; if they did, then they would have made the

502

connection between him and the guy Coney killed, and they'll know that we'll be heading back to pick him up."

Brock stared directly at Sutherland. "It means they might be waiting for us there."

The three stared uncertainly toward Brock as though not understanding what he was saying.

Finally Coney asked, "So?"

"I'm saying that they could have already killed Landis, or are holding him and they'll ambush us when we get there. I want you to be aware of that."

Frizzell looked at him curiously. "You're not suggesting that we leave him, are you?"

"No." Again Brock looked directly at Sutherland. "I just want to make sure everybody understands the danger."

"Oh, I get it," Sutherland said. "You're expecting me to say we should forget him and save our own asses. Look, Brock, I'm the one who said we should have gone back for him a long time ago."

Sutherland nodded slowly. "Yeah, I'm worried about my ass. I want to save it. But even if it were *you* in that cave, Brock, I'd go back. And it's not because I was being a hero, but . . . well, it's just that you don't leave a guy like that— even a dumbass lifer gunnery sergeant."

He stuck his finger out at Brock. "Fuck you," he said. "I'll take point, and I'll get us back there, and if they're waiting, they'll never see us because I'll get around them. Checking out a staging area like you had us do is one thing—dumb, and I wouldn't have done it—but leaving your buddy, that's different. So you try to keep up, old man, 'cause I'm gone."

And he grabbed his rifle and headed quickly into the trees. Coney and Frizzell scrambled after him, and Brock had to run to catch up with them.

Sutherland stopped only twice to check his compass for a bearing. Brock had no idea where they were, but when he realized that Sutherland was leading them in a wide zigzag, he knew that they were getting closer.

Still Sutherland did not slow his pace but moved with unerring certainty toward the hidden bunker.

Finally Sutherland stopped and signaled for them to

spread out. He waited a moment, then, motioning for them to give him cover, he crept forward, approaching the bunker from behind.

They watched him move with agonizing slowness, stopping every step to examine the surrounding brush. Then he moved back and circled behind, approaching from the other side.

Brock saw the worry in his eyes, not fear—that didn't register at all in Sutherland's face—but profound concern.

He moved forward in the same slow crawl and again stopped to examine every leaf.

Finally he came back and drew them farther away from the bunker.

"They've been here—a lot of them." He held out a handful of leaves. "See, they've been crushed—see the gook bootprint, different from ours. And not long ago, 'cause leaves go back into shape after a while, and these are still bent. But look, there's dew on them—it's not rain 'cause you can tell by the drops, so they came in the night, and either they're gone, missed him, and kept going, or they got him, and they're waiting in the cave."

Brock merely stared at the leaves, amazed and frightened.

"Call it, Gunny. What do you want us to do?"

Brock rubbed his face with his hand and shook his head. "What do you guys think?"

"What do we have to lose by calling to him?" Coney asked.

Brock shook his head. "If they don't know we're here, we don't want them to know because if they do have him . . . you couldn't stand to listen to what they'd do. They did that in Korea—they'd get a guy and bring him close to our lines, then torture him until he screamed to die and you went crazy hearing him. No, we can't call to him."

"I'll go get him," Frizzell said. "Cover me."

Sutherland grabbed him. "No. I'll do it."

Brock pushed them both down. "This is my fucking mess; I'll go. If something happens, you guys take off, understand? I mean it, don't stick around. Somebody's got to get back with the location and tell them what's going on—that's more important."

They all started forward, then Brock took the lead and moved steadily toward the bunker.

In all the time he had been in combat, he had never been as afraid as he was at this moment, afraid not so much for himself as afraid of what he was going to find.

He approached the bunker from behind on the left side. When he drew beside it, he leaned against it and listened. He listened until his ears thundered, but there was no sound except for the noise of insects and the soft rush of the wind through the brush.

He edged around the side and crept toward the entrance where he knelt and listened again.

Finally at the entrance, just to the side, he whispered softly, "Landis? Matt? It's Brock."

There was no answer. He called again.

Then louder. But there was no answer.

Only then did he notice the enemy bootprints in front of the bunker.

And blood.

He closed his eyes and turned away. Oh, God, he moaned to himself. Don't let it be.

A trail of blood led from the bunker, then ended abruptly —as if someone had wiped his bloody hands on his trousers.

Taking a deep breath, he jumped into the bunker entrance, his rifle at his hip.

He saw Landis immediately, and whirled away to shield himself from the sight.

Then he turned back. For many seconds Brock merely stared at him. Finally he walked to the body.

Landis was propped against a beam in a sitting position, his head tilted back, his genitals stuffed into his mouth. His fatigue shirt was torn open, revealing a massive wound that had blown out his heart. His trousers were ripped, exposing another bloody wound where his genitals had been severed.

Brock dropped to his knees before him. "Oh, God," he moaned.

Then the others were there behind him.

"Jesus," whispered Coney.

"The bastards," hissed Sutherland; he pushed forward and took the genitals out of Landis's mouth.

Frizzell knelt in front of the body and examined him carefully. "They didn't kill him," he said. He picked up the rifle beside him and felt on the ground for a moment, then held up the spent cartridge. "He shot himself before they got to him. They cut him afterwards."

"Fucking animals," Sutherland said furiously. "Faggots."

Brock stood up. He went to the entrance and leaned his head against it.

Sutherland went to his side. "We gotta get out of here, Gunny." He put his hand on Brock's shoulder.

The older man turned. They looked at each other for a long moment. Brock closed his eyes, and he began to cry, then Sutherland cried too. Then he shook his head and said between sobs, "It wasn't you. It's just the fucking war."

"Help me with him," Coney said to Frizzell. "I'll carry him first." Together they lifted the body and slung it over Coney's shoulders.

Frizzell picked up his rifle and made for the entrance. "You want me to take point?" he asked Sutherland.

Sutherland nodded, then tugged gently on Brock's arm, pulling him out of the bunker.

Frizzell led off; Brock followed, then Coney carrying Landis. Sutherland hesitated at the treeline. He turned to look back at the bunker barely discernible in the overgrowth. In his mind, he tried to see what had happened, the enemy closing on Landis, his fear and aloneness, the last second with his rifle pressed against his chest, pulling the trigger—then nothing.

He did not want to turn from the sight, release the bunker to the jungle—give Landis up—but at last he turned and hurried after the others.

Before long, they had to stop to shift the body.

The corpse began to stiffen, became more unwieldy, and they, more tired. Finally they rested. There was nothing to cover the body with so they merely placed it on the ground among them.

Sutherland tried to look away, but his eyes came back to the pitiful figure immobile at his feet with insects bloating themselves in the coagulated blood.

The beam could have fallen on him instead—on any of

them. Any of them could have been left behind; any of them could be dead. It just happened to be Landis—and that's all it was, Sutherland saw; just a matter of chance, where the beam landed; it was luck, or lack of it.

It wasn't Brock's fault, any more than it was the beam's fault for falling, or the pilot's fault for dropping the bombs —it just happened. Landis was just in the way; it wasn't his fault either.

It could happen to him any minute, and there wasn't anything he could do to protect himself. You couldn't even hide in a cave, Sutherland thought—a stray bomb could fall on it too.

You just had to hope your luck didn't run out and protect yourself as best you could. That's the only real thing you could do, Sutherland decided—you couldn't let anyone fuck with you.

No more, he promised himself—he wasn't going to let anyone risk his life anymore. He wasn't going to end like Landis. He closed his eyes and vowed, "I'll kill the next bastard who fucks with me."

Suddenly one of Landis's eyes flicked open.

The motion shocked Frizzell, then he realized it was a bug that had crawled under the lid, releasing the muscle.

He walked to the corpse, brushed the insects away, and closed the eye, suppressing a shudder at the hardening dead flesh, then he sat back down across from the body.

Suddenly he remembered what he'd been taught about death—if a man said an Act of Contrition, his sins would be forgiven; if truly penitent at the final moment, he would be saved. But what about the dead? Was it too late to be saved if the soul was gone? What if Landis had died with sin on his soul? Oh, God, that wouldn't be right. That wouldn't be fair to punish him after death, not after what had happened to him.

Frizzell started to pray, saying prayer after prayer for Landis all the way back.

When Frizzell carried the body, Coney walked behind, covering the rear. He saw Frizzell struggle under the weight, and the corpse jostled on his shoulders, as stiff now as a mannequin.

507

Coney knew about Landis's car, everyone did—the bad black bitch—that was what he called it, but he knew little else about him. That he was from Florida and worked out with weights, that he liked all the C rations and traded his cigarettes for peanut butter, but he knew hardly anything else.

But what did he know of any of them? What did they know about him? What if they were carrying him? he wondered. What would it matter to them? What was his life to any of them? Indeed, who would care if he had died? His wife, sure. Debby would be sorry, he knew, for there had been too much between them once for her not to feel that, but she would find someone else, and that would be the end of it; her life would go on. And for his little boy? Nothing at all; only a story.

Then he thought about the man he had killed—he had almost forgotten him already. Who cared about him? He seemed too young to have a wife. A mother would weep. And his buddies? They'd forget him as quickly as Landis would be forgotten.

God, he wished he hadn't killed him. Even with Landis dead and what they did to him, he wished he hadn't killed the enemy soldier. He was just as dead as Landis and had wanted just as much to live. He could feel his hand on the bayonet, then the blade slipping through flesh; he heard the soft cry of death. Oh, God, he thought, I don't want to live with that.

How can I? Will I forget that someday? Will I forget murder like I will Landis? Oh, I hope so, he thought.

Brock dropped behind to cover the rear as Frizzell took point. His grief and guilt were overwhelming; he felt crushed and old, and he had to force himself to keep up. He didn't care if he were left behind.

He had made so many mistakes. Landis didn't have to die; he could have saved him. If he had gone back as soon as he was hurt, as soon as the radio was crushed, Landis would have been all right. Or if he hadn't pushed them on, maybe he could have saved him. He tortured himself by replaying it over and over in his mind, doing it differently each time.

Every time he looked at the body he cringed; he would give anything to do it over.

He felt so old, and Landis looked so young. A boy, and that's all he was, Brock thought. That's what they all are.

He looked at Sutherland, Frizzell, and Coney. They are too young for this, he thought. They should not see this so soon. They are too young to see death like this.

What will it do to them? he wondered. What dreams and nightmares will they have?

How can they be young after this?

And then it was his turn to carry the body, and he carried it the rest of the way to the hill.

CHAPTER

• 32 •

"Goulue," Bui Cao Kim repeated to Lacouture.

Lacouture nodded, then pushed him away with his fingers. "And come to me with the answer no matter how late you return."

Then Lacouture motioned him back. "Be very careful," he warned, surprising Kim with a concern that betrayed a hint of solicitude. "I am afraid of Wilson Abbot Lord," Lacouture whispered. "Be careful you are not followed."

They parted on Tu Do Street in the middle of a crowd. It was early evening, and though Cholon, the site of the rendezvous, was only a few miles away, it would take Kim many hours of circuitous traveling before he was sure he had lost any tail on him and felt confident enough to approach the address he had been given.

He was being followed, he decided; there were three Vietnamese—Special Branch, which worked with the CIA —trailing him, but they were young, recruits probably, and no match for Kim, who had worked the streets and alleys of Saigon and Cholon for thirty years. He lost them in the first hour, but he feinted and dodged and evaded another two hours before knocking on the door of a dilapidated, vile-smelling, garbage-strewn hut on the outskirts of Cholon.

An old, unwell man answered the door and beckoned him inside to a squalid room lit by a single candle.

The man, in shabby, torn clothes, shuffled to a broken table and sat on a battered chair.

In the dim, flickering light, Kim studied the thin, haggard man who looked as if he had camped at death's door, and barely dragged himself away, and Kim tried not to tremble, because he knew who the man was—it was General Xuan Tien Khanh himself; it could be no one else. A great general would not send an old, sick man as his representative; he would not entrust a mission of such importance to a man as frail as this; indeed, Kim thought, he could not entrust a mission this important to anyone—he would go himself.

Kim lowered his eyes in respect before the aura of dignity and authority the man conveyed, despite his clothes and the surroundings. The ailing man sat with the subdued confidence and command of an immensely powerful mandarin.

Kim closed his eyes. He did not want the man to be General Khanh; he now knew things he did not want to know—even the suspicion of such knowledge was dangerous. To possess this knowledge, or even to be suspected of possessing it, marked him and put him in great danger.

"Goulue," he whispered at last, looking up timidly.

The man accepted the word as though he had expected it. He made a short, acknowledging sound in his throat, then he said, with the slightest, most wistful look on his face, confirming Kim's suspicion, "Nhay Dam."

Then the man stood, nodded a dismissal so slight that it was terrifying, and Kim fled the room.

It was nearly two in the morning before Kim stole up the steps of Lacouture's house and tapped lightly on the door.

Unfastening all the locks, Lacouture cracked the door.

"Nhay Dam," Kim whispered into Lacouture's sleepy face.

"Nhay Dam?" repeated Lacouture.

Kim nodded.

Lacouture grumbled something Kim did not understand, then handed him a folded wad of money and closed the door, and Kim stole away into the night.

Kim slept fitfully, fearful of the knowledge he had, but in the morning he felt better, with the sunshine, and the reality of the money in his hand, and certain that he had eluded his trackers.

The message was delivered, he had been paid, and no one knew of the meeting; he was safe, he decided.

He took a single bill from the wad of money and hid the rest, then he went to the market without undue anxiety. He was going to buy vegetables for soup, a celebration soup for his success, and he had to find just the right cabbage and carrots.

The black-market crowd, amorphous and anonymous, was comforting, and he moved easily through it, finding just what he was looking for, and he was so pleased with the price he got them for that he was not overly alarmed when two policemen grabbed him. At first, he thought it was a mistake—his main concern was that they would take his cabbage, or that he would drop it.

The police, who ostensibly kept order and managed everything from traffic control to routine criminal investigations, were basically ineffectual—they harassed and detained but were easily bribed and nowhere as formidable as the military or the Special Branch.

Kim was not frightened when the police grabbed him because he had had several run-ins with the police before. Because his papers were in order, he was quickly released each time. This was another harassment or mistaken identity and he did not resist them, or even bother to protest, because he knew that would do no good; he would explain when he was brought to the station. Now he was concerned with safeguarding his vegetables.

But before he was led from the market he realized his error—the policemen holding him, though they wore the white national police uniform, were either military or Special Branch; they were too young and hard for the national police, their manner too determined and professional. He was propelled in a painful grip that allowed no escape; when he tried to wriggle free, his neck was squeezed so powerfully that he feared they would break it, but that was nothing compared to the pain of his arm twisted backward up against his spine.

His seizure caused no interest; as he was led through the

crowd, people parted casually, then smoothed back like a wave on the sea.

On the street, he was pushed into the backseat of a waiting car, and before he settled and the car started, a needle was jammed into his arm by a third man.

His next recollection was being jostled awake, led hand-cuffed and gagged from some dank room to the dark outside where he was forced into the trunk of a car. A man peered down at him, leaned close, roughly pulled apart Kim's lips to examine his teeth, then nodded.

Though still dazed from the drug, Kim was positive as the trunk closed that the man was the American spy Lacouture had met with.

Wilson Abbot Lord had faith in the Special Branch; others in the Agency didn't, feeling the Vietnamese agents were either incompetent or, if competent, then compromised and most likely double agents of the North. Lord knew that the Special Branch had indeed been infiltrated by the communists, but there was a core with whom he worked that he felt were reliable, men like himself whose opposition to communism rested on a foundation far stronger and more enduring than principles and ideology—personal hatred, men who themselves or whose families had suffered at the hands of the NVA or Viet Cong. Lord only worked with men of whose suffering or losses he had documented evidence; thus far there had not been a single instance of difficulty or compromise in his dealings with his counterparts. The seizure of Kim had gone as smoothly as every other request he had made of them; in fact, he would have been surprised if it had not been Kim in the trunk, though of course he had to check the teeth to be absolutely sure.

At Tan Son Nhut, Lord was waved onto the air base without a search, and though challenged by guards on the flight line, and his special pass and identification scrutinized, he was allowed access and drove to the remote area where Air America craft were maintained.

He pulled up before a Huey helicopter.

Jim Magnuson jumped from the cockpit and walked over to the car. "Evening, Mr. Lord."

"Morning, Lieutenant," corrected Lord. "Help me with him."

He opened the trunk, and they pulled Kim out, pushing him into the six-man troop compartment, shackling him near the hatchway.

"You know the routine?" Lord asked.

"Yes," Magnuson said, watching Lord take a leather case from his pocket. He opened it, and the runway lights made the sharp surgical instruments gleam wickedly. "Jesus," whispered Magnuson.

"All necessary, Lieutenant," Lord said expressionlessly. He held out the case before Kim's eyes, then took out a pair of dental clamps and pliers.

"We may have to operate, Mr. Kim," he said in French.

Magnuson turned from the terror on Kim's face.

In the beginning, on his first missions, he had tried to hide his squeamishness; he had made a point of watching the torture and not registering his revulsion. After the third time, he stopped watching—now he couldn't bear it.

He had hoped it was over in Da Nang; surely Air America had pilots in Saigon for this type of mission, but he knew enough not to question or balk when Lord gave him the order to have a chopper ready at midnight with a flight plan that would take them over the South China Sea.

Indeed he knew the routine, but this time was different because he had never worked with anyone of Lord's rank, nor worked with only one other person; usually it was a three- or four-man team. But everything else was the same—the horror in the eyes of the Vietnamese, and the cold determination in the eyes of the American. What Magnuson saw in Lord's face did not differ from what he had seen in the faces of others in Da Nang—a cold resolution devoid of pity or cruelty, a look of conviction that reminded him of the fixed expressions set on the faces of worshipers during Sunday service at home.

"Then let's go, Lieutenant," Lord said, climbing into the compartment with Kim.

Magnuson did not see the cruelty in Lord's eyes, but Kim did: not sadistic cruelty—he had seen so much of it in his

514

life that he could distinguish the different kinds—but cruelty born of hatred, one seeking revenge.

Kim knew of this American, his position, power, and contacts, and knew there was only one way of saving his own life—convincing Lord that he was useful to him alive.

Even in his frenzied fear, he was able to think clearly, knowing that he had only minutes to live, and that those minutes could be agonizing.

He had been caught, that was all there was to it; it was a simple matter of fate, like the old whore knew when he had opened the door and walked in on her. Now it was his turn. The old whore had played the game well, bartered cleverly for her life; now he was matched against the American, who planned to kill him whether he got the information he desired or not.

Kim had no doubt that Lord intended to kill him, no matter what he promised.

He had heard about the helicopter rides at night and how no man ever returned from one. He tried not to tremble as he lay curled in fear on the floor.

He had faced death before, many times with the Japanese and French, but this was more terrifying. Before, his death would have been at the whim of his inquisitors, but now it was calculated and determined; this man meant to kill him, to throw him into the sea from this machine.

What was he going to do, what was he going to do? his mind screamed. He was going to be killed. Unless, Kim realized, unless he could convince the American that he could get the Americans even more valuable information; if he played a masterful game, and dangled the promise of helping them, then he might survive.

But he had no idea what the American wanted to know. How could he be useful if he did not know what he wanted?

His mind raced, and he could barely breathe from his terror. The American wanted to know about Khanh, Kim knew. He shuddered: he was going to have to be so careful.

"You really have beautiful teeth, Mr. Kim. I congratulate you on them. But I never understood why—in your line of work, shall we say—you advertised such an obvious trademark. Why is that?"

Lord removed the gag from Kim's mouth and waited for an answer.

Kim listened carefully to his words, especially his intonations, and though he had some trouble following Lord's French, he understood the question. He knew too that he had to answer, that with this man he could not play the ignorant "gook" or simple peasant.

He tried to speak, but at first only a strangled sound came from his dry, numb mouth.

"They are all I have," he managed at last.

Lord nodded. "It's remarkable you kept them in the Japanese camp, that they weren't knocked out, if they didn't rot out. With the French too. But perhaps that's how you survived, concentrating such care on them—they gave you purpose, something to live for."

Kim studied Lord's eyes and mouth; his face was now completely expressionless. The cruelty was gone, or perhaps it was masked by professionalism.

"Maybe they can save you again," Lord said. He held up the gleaming dental instruments before Kim's eyes. "I want you to concentrate on your teeth, Mr. Kim. I'm going to ask you questions. It's going to be like an examination—if you get one wrong, then I will rip out one of your teeth. If you get all the questions right—have a perfect paper, shall we say—then you shall keep your teeth, maintain your perfect mouth."

Then why the helicopter ride? Kim thought. If it were just a matter of torture, you could do that anywhere, even in the dark room where you drugged me.

The engine churned, the blades sputtered, then caught, and the chopper roared to life.

Lord slid the hatch closed, sealing out some of the noise, and the helicopter lifted from the ground.

"An easy question first," Lord said, brandishing the pliers. "Squeaky?"

"General Tran," Kim said without hesitation.

"I know that, Mr. Kim. I want to know what the word means. What is its significance?"

Kim felt sudden nausea. The American knew everything

that he did and was going to ask what Kim did not know. He had no use for Kim; fate was laughing at him.

"I only know what the Frenchman thinks."

Lord waited.

"It is a nickname for General Tran. When he was in law school in Hanoi he studied under General Giap. When Tran was asked questions, his voice would change, and his answers came out like a mouse's."

Lord stared and waited, but Kim knew better than to qualify his answer or explain further. He had said all that he knew, and it would either be accepted or not.

"*Goulue,*" Lord said after a long time.

The chopper arched high in the sky, away from the city and the glow from the lights below.

It was dark and cold and the machine trembled from the vibrations of the rotor blades.

"Again, I know only what the Frenchman thinks. He talks to me like he does to a caged bird; he does not want answers, but only to think aloud."

Lord's eyes were fathomless; there was not even a hint of impatience, but Kim sensed that he had exceeded his time for answering.

"Goulue was the name of a French dancer in Paris."

Lord snapped his fingers so quickly and with such force that Kim stopped speaking.

"Toulouse-Lautrec. *Moulin Rouge.* Jane Avril." Lord smiled, but it was not a warm smile at all. "I am getting old, Mr. Kim. Or sloppy. I should have remembered that. And now here I am talking to you just like the Frenchman does, but he's right, that is exactly who Goulue was. And what does he think the connection is with the other code word?"

"The Frenchman says there was a famous dancer in Hanoi many, many years ago who took that name too. He says that only those who were in Hanoi forty years ago would know that."

"General Tran was there then, studying under Giap."

"Yes."

"Who else was there also forty years ago studying under Giap who would know how Tran answered questions, and who also knew about Goulue?"

517

It was a rhetorical question; Lord knew who was there then—that was in their background files on Tran.

And Kim knew that it was a rhetorical question too; now the line was drawn, and his life lay on it. He had to redraw the line or pull himself away from it.

"There is another word."

Lord's eyes sharpened with interest, and suspicion too; the line wavered.

"Nhay Dam."

"The answering code word."

"Yes."

"What does the Frenchman think it means?"

Kim tried not to shiver, but it was so cold, and when he glanced out the window, he saw bobbing lights far below on the horizon; they were going toward them, out to sea.

Kim turned back to Lord and swiftly slashed a line. "He did not tell me because I only gave him the code very early this morning after I returned with it."

Lord did not say anything for a long time, for so long that Kim finally turned to the window. The lights from the junks and sampans were much closer.

"What does Nhay Dam mean?"

"I think it is a name of a place where people dance and drink; many years ago, when the French were here, there was a place in Saigon with that name too. It refers to the jumping way the French danced."

"The name of the place in Hanoi where Goulue danced?"

"Maybe the Frenchman Lacouture knows that; he probably does, but we did not talk this morning. I just gave him the words."

"And who gave them to you?"

How he said this would determine if he would live or die, Kim knew.

He felt as he did before—that morning with the old whore when he learned about the powerful American; he felt then that he stood in front of the lair of the dragon. But now it was worse; the beast had stirred—his burning red eyes fixed him, and Kim could feel his steaming breath, and smell rotting death.

Lord's face moved closer; his eyes glinted.

Should he hedge and say, *I don't know, an old sick man, but one who must be important?*

Or gamble: *He told me he was General Khanh.*

The lights were almost below them; they had reached the coast.

What could he do? He began to panic. He remembered that day when this horrible business began, the day outside the building when he encountered the soldier, Lacouture's savage. He had guessed wrong then by confronting the soldier for a cigarette; it had been his teeth then too that had caused the problem. He closed his eyes. What to do, what to do?

His mind raced ahead. Now they, the Viet Cong, would know that the Americans had taken him; they knew everything and had spies everywhere. What would they do to him? They would torture him to learn what he had told the Americans; then they would kill him.

His eyes flew open in terror. But the American would kill him first so that the Viet Cong would never know for sure what he had revealed.

He was going to die; he saw the dragon laughing. It had been decided long ago; there had never been a chance.

Suddenly a stiff rubber block was jammed into his mouth and he could not breathe, and he was slammed against the bench, a knee in his chest, and then his head was jerked down, and there was incredible pain, and his mouth was wet, blood running down his throat, and the block was taken out, but the pain grew worse, and his tongue found the gap where his tooth had been, and he shook his head back and forth, back and forth, and he moaned and moaned, but not from pain.

"Too slow, Mr. Kim. Who?"

But he only shook his head and continued to moan. What did it matter now? He had nothing left; the only thing that mattered to him was gone. He didn't care what happened now; the only thing he had was destroyed. He thought of the Japanese camps and all that he had endured there, how he had rubbed his gums with dull plant bristle and used pumice on his teeth. And in the French internment camp—the beating there too, and never eating the meat in the rice they were given, and rinsing and rinsing his mouth of their evil food, and polishing and polishing his teeth. And afterwards, all the pain and suffering, all the humiliations and degradations—yet there had always been his teeth; all that he had.

"Too slow, Mr. Kim, too slow." Lord rammed the rubber block into his mouth again, brought his knee into his chest, and ripped out another front tooth with the pliers. He pulled out the rubber and wiped the blood on his hand on Kim's shirt.

"One more time, Mr. Kim: who gave you the message for Lacouture?"

But that was a rhetorical question too because it could only be one man, and Lord knew that Khanh would never divulge his identity to Kim; Kim could only guess, and he, Lord, did not need guesswork.

Khanh was alive after all, the reports of his death a clever subterfuge that had worked. News of Khanh's death had heartened the South Vietnamese; only Giap's or Ho Chi Minh's death would have been more welcome.

After having gone to all the trouble to convince the enemy that he was dead, why would he now come forward? The code words were obviously meant to prove that he was still alive. But why?

Because he wanted to meet with Marshall; his offer was legitimate. He was taking an incredible risk to arrange a meeting.

Lacouture was double-crossing him; he was sure of it now. There really was going to be a meeting. The communists weren't going to kill Marshall, they were going to negotiate with him and were paying Lacouture to set it up. And Lacouture had cleverly used him, Lord, to exploit Marshall. It was he himself who had told Lacouture about Marshall's weakness, his son. Very clever indeed, Lord thought. The bastard.

And Marshall would fall for it too, yet he'd never see through it—he'd believe any story they'd try to sell him, some soft, sappy tale about saving lives. Yes, of course, he thought furiously, a pathetic tale about saving sons, and he—Lord—had even given them the bait. God damn! He himself had told Lacouture that that was Marshall's vulnerable point.

God damn, he swore again. He could just picture the scene: Khanh telling him about the loss of his own sons and how he could not bear to see any more sorrow on either side; and Marshall lapping up every word, shedding tears for all the dead sons, bleeding his liberal fucking heart all over the floor, then going back to Washington to the President to tell him about his secret meeting with the enemy battlefield commander; and if only he, Johnson, would make this small concession—pull back some troops, stop the bombing— then for sure there could be a negotiated settlement, a victory for peace, and not incidentally, Johnson's own ass saved, his reelection guaranteed.

The clever, clever bastards! All tied in perfectly with the peace murmurs from Paris, and the negotiation rumors whispered in the ears of every susceptible fool, like Palme in Sweden, and to every idiot journalist with an audience.

Indeed there was going to be a meeting, and he himself had helped set it up, had played right into their hands.

And it had almost worked.

He laughed at the irony: incredible, he was promising to pay Lacouture to set up a meeting with the communists, promising to pay him to arrange Marshall's murder by the communists when the last thing in the world they wanted was him dead. He was going to trust the communists to kill Marshall when they more than anything wanted him alive to take their poisoned apple back to Washington.

The communists had created a no-loss situation: if Khanh were believed dead, they would have lulled us and created an excellent opportunity to attack; if he were believed alive, they could convince Marshall and perhaps Washington to grant concessions the NVA would never gain on the battlefield.

This was art, Lord thought, as beautifully crafted as the carved ivory balls within carved ivory balls. What a mind to have conceived this, he marveled.

And such fools we are to underestimate our enemy, he

thought; they are more clever than we—diabolical and evil, preying on our weaknesses and good intentions, using any ploy to defeat us, counting on the gullibility of decent men.

Yet could he convince Marshall of that? Could he convince any of the war protesters or any liberal? Never. Would Vietnam have to fall, and Cambodia too, before they learned? Or would it take all Africa and Latin America, the entire Third World, Malaysia and the Philippines too? All were ripe and would one day be tested.

Why couldn't they see?

Well, he, Wilson Abbot Lord, knew the enemy. He would not let this happen; he would stop Marshall.

And he would settle with that bastard Lacouture.

He knew the enemy; for twenty years he had fought them, and rarely—oh, rarely—was he able to inflict a telling wound against them.

But now he could.

And he would.

Up front, Magnuson pounded on the bulkhead, the signal that the chopper was over the drop zone, and that he would circle until Lord pounded back.

Lord looked out the window; moonlight sparkled off the water below. The sky was clear and filled with stars. And he was cold.

It was a night just like this in Korea when they caught Brent Harwood and bound him in barbed wire and threw him into the sea.

Oh, yes, he knew the enemy.

He leaned close to Kim and said viciously, "It's payback time, Mr. Kim."

Kim did not hear him, nor even see him, and he felt only a dull blow on the side of his head with the metal bludgeon. He slumped forward, restrained only by the shackles, and when Lord undid them, his body fell to the floor.

Lord slid open the hatch and pushed the body out; all he saw was a small dark object falling through the sky, gracefully tumbling over and over.

The impact would kill him, break every bone in his body, Lord knew, which was too bad because he wished the sharks would hit while he was still alive.

Then he pounded on the bulkhead, and immediately the chopper arched toward the coast.

When the chopper landed, Lord jumped out without a word to Magnuson and went to his car.

He had a lot of work to do: a score to settle with Lacouture, and a fitting end to arrange for Bradley Marshall.

Magnuson stayed in the cockpit until Lord drove away, then he checked the passenger hold; there was only a little blood on the canvas seat and on the floor, and no urine or excrement like so many times in the past.

What could that little old man with the perfect teeth have done or known to deserve this? he wondered.

It had to do with Ambassador Marshall, he knew; Lord was personally implicating Magnuson, and testing him too. The next job, Magnuson was certain, was going to be the ambassador himself. And what was he, Magnuson, with all his collusions, going to do? What choice did he have? What would they do to him if he refused, or if he threatened to expose them?

He went into the hangar for a pail of water and soap, then he cleaned up the blood.

On the floor he found two bloody teeth; he wrapped them in a handkerchief and put them in his flight suit pocket. When all the evidence was gone, he washed his hands and left.

CHAPTER

• 33 •

Lacouture was in a panic, madly packing a box of prized ivory and jade pieces. He was on his knees on his Chinese silk carpet in the middle of his living room in a still-fashionable part of Saigon.

But what good would it do? What good would it do? he wailed aloud, and threw himself onto the rug in a heap.

He hadn't heard from Bui Cao Kim in three days; he was dead, of course—the wretched, wretched little gook had allowed himself to be captured and killed, he thought despairingly.

He had heard the news within an hour of Kim's seizure, but it took him the rest of the day to discover from inside sources that he had not been arrested by the National Police, despite the uniforms, and that no one knew where he was or who was holding him.

It was the Americans, of course; who else would be interested in the silly little man? Wilson Abbot Lord was behind this, he knew, and he would have gotten all the information he wanted from Kim, and then he would have killed him. The stupid, stupid gook.

But he loved Kim, and he shed tears onto his carpet. They were both survivors, had lived through the Japanese occupation and known each other for twenty years—they were almost brothers, and he sobbed, thinking of the dear, dear little man.

They would have tortured him, pulled out all of his teeth probably—that would be Lord's style—and then simply murdered him. The poor, poor man, he cried.

He pulled out his handkerchief and dried up the tearstains on the rug. Who was going to take the message back to General Khanh? He would have to be told, of course. What would he do, knowing that the plan was most likely compromised? And what about himself, Lacouture, now that Lord probably knew everything?

The damn gook! It was all Kim's fault for being captured. At the black market, in the middle of the morning! He deserved to lose all his teeth—one by one.

He heaved a deep sigh and began to unpack the box. He couldn't flee and couldn't hide; he would never get out if they—the Americans or the communists—were set on stopping him. And even if he, by some stroke of luck, managed to get away, he would never get his possessions out; his treasures—his life.

Wilson Abbot Lord would break every one, smash them to pieces before his very eyes. That would be just like him, the sadistic monster—he would force Lacouture to watch the destruction of his art, laughing as he shattered each object.

Lacouture shuddered at the image in his mind, and he clutched a carved nephrite crane of the early Ming dynasty to his chest. Then he grabbed a lapis lazuli horse figurine and held it protectively.

He laid them on the rug gently and looked about the room in despair. He would not be able to save any of it—the paintings and ancient scrolls, the porcelains and temple carvings, his treasured snuff bottles—some seven hundred years old—his mother's jewels, his father's coins and old clocks, the precious lacquer and enamel works, even the silk robes with gold threading that belonged to the emperor.

He couldn't stand it; everything he owned and treasured would be lost. The thought of that was worse than death itself.

He rose ponderously and went to his gramophone; *La Bohème* would soothe him. The record was old and terribly scratched, and the machine itself dilapidated and erratic, but he did not mind and would not consider replacing it. The black market was choked with wondrous machines that produced the finest sounds, but they were so *ugly*—all plastic and shiny metal, with knobs and buttons and lights. So mechanical and technical, so cold and robotic—so Japanese, and he wouldn't have anything Japanese in his house, even their art, pale and sticklike such as it was. He wouldn't even listen to *Madame Butterfly,* as much as he loved opera, especially Puccini.

The thin, reedy sound filled the room, but he only heard beauty and richness; music came from within, and what he heard in his heart could not be improved with the most expensive stereophonic amplification in the world.

He hummed, then sang, and all the wretched problems of Americans and communists disappeared. He was uplifted, transported—until he realized that Lord would destroy all of his records too. The brute!

He snatched the needle arm from the record. That was too much! All his prized records—his Carusos! Puccini, Verdi, Mozart, Donizetti! He reeled, seeing the discs flung against the wall, shattering into a thousand pieces. His Wagners! Tedious and interminable, but such moments! The shards of the broken records rained down on his head; he raised his arms to shield himself.

No! He wouldn't allow it. Lord had to be stopped.

He, Bernard Lacouture, would protect the art from such desecration. He would save the treasures; he would stop Lord.

But what could he do? How? How could he salvage the meeting with Khanh?

He assumed the worst—he always did, that was the safest way—Kim was dead and before dying he had told Lord enough for him to have reasoned out that Khanh was alive and that Lacouture had been arranging a genuine meeting between the general and Marshall, not an ambush to kill the ambassador. Lord would be in a murderous rage.

Marshall was Lord's primary target; that would remain,

indeed, become intensified as Lord sought to prevent such a meeting. Marshall was a marked man, as good as dead. And there was nothing that he, Lacouture, could do about it. He couldn't go to Marshall and tell him that his own CIA plotted his murder. Who would believe him? What proof did he have? And even if Marshall did believe him, what good would it do? The meeting had been compromised, nothing would be accomplished; Lord would still win.

Khanh would never risk a meeting now, not unless the tightest security could be guaranteed—not unless Lord was removed as a threat.

And himself? His heart fluttered at the fury he imagined Lord possessed.

Lord would be apoplectic; he would want revenge— torture and humiliation; suffering, dismemberment, death.

There was only one way to stop Lord: he had to be removed. That would save him and solve Marshall's and Khanh's dilemma too; they could have their meeting and he, Lacouture, would get his money, and off to Cannes he would go with his treasures.

But how? He could hardly face Lord in a cowboy shoot-out on the streets of Cholon, nor did he picture himself scaling walls and rooftops to ambush him in a back alley.

He couldn't put out a contract on him on the street; that would get right back to Lord, and besides, who would be foolhardy enough to assassinate a CIA agent, risk certain death and retaliation against one's family for Lacouture's money?

He could not fight Lord and the vast CIA apparatus. He had taken a chance and lost. But what choice had he had? Lord was never in earnest; he would never have paid Lacouture. He would never have allowed an accomplice in such a murder to live, so Lacouture had been forced to strike a deal with the communists. Besides, he rather liked Marshall, and perhaps, just perhaps, such a man could bring the war to some reasonable end.

No, no, he couldn't let Lord win; there had to be a way.

Kim would have helped him; Kim would have risked his life for him. Dear, dear Kim with his ridiculous teeth.

Tears rolled down his pudgy cheeks.

Kim was the closest he had to what could be called a friend. Kim was his only friend.

He began to sob. He didn't have any friends; no one had ever liked him. No one would even come to his funeral. What a disgrace; what a humiliation to be buried alone and friendless, no one to watch the coffin lowered into the ground or to grieve. He saw the cemetery, his coffin forlorn over the grave, no one in attendance except the gravedigger, a common paid laborer, and not even a handsome one, just an ugly old hunchback.

It was too awful, and he pulled out his handkerchief and blotted the tears.

If only he had someone he could go to, someone who would listen and help, someone who cared.

If only he had a friend.

Then he brought his hands together in his lap and sat perfectly still.

The savage had said he would be his friend, and he was not mocking him; Lacouture knew from his eyes and voice that he was sincere, that there was a gentleness and kindness about him that belied his manner and appearance.

Yes, he could go to the savage. He could talk to him, tell him, and he would listen.

But would he help?

Lacouture put his handkerchief into his pocket, eased back farther into his Louis XV chair, rested his hands on the armrests, and thought.

He was no longer sure Mead could be bought; perhaps—given enough time, and with much flattery and cajolery, and enough alcohol and drugs, yes, probably he could eventually get him into bed—once. But to bribe him to kill? To murder a fellow American? That could not be done, no matter how much money he offered.

No, Mead would not do it for money, but maybe for principle—for country, family, religion, for whatever it was he honored—and he would do it for his woman, or for his friends.

No, he could not make a catamite out of his savage, but maybe a murderer.

He is, he already was, one, Lacouture mused; a very accomplished one apparently.

He stroked the armrests and his gaze fixed on a jade temple dog on an Empire commode across the room.

Yes, the savage might be his hope; his only hope.

He jumped up quickly and ran into his dressing room, donned his vest and jacket, grabbed his wide-brimmed straw hat, fashionable thirty years ago, and after securing all the locks, left the house and hailed a cab.

Twenty minutes later he alighted before Mead's apartment and ran up the stairs.

When his knocking was not answered, he opened the door and looked in tentatively.

A young Vietnamese woman by the window stared at him in fright and backed toward a corner.

"Pardon me," he said in French. "I am looking for an American named Ron Mead. Does he live here?"

When she did not answer, he repeated the question in Vietnamese.

She only stared at him fearfully.

"He does, I know," said Lacouture in Vietnamese, closing the door and taking off his hat. He mopped his brow with his handkerchief, then sat at the table.

"Exactly as Kim described," he said aloud in French to himself, not thinking she would understand since she would have been an infant when the French left Indochina, and none of the young spoke the language any longer. "Beautiful. Like a princess. A beautiful slave princess for the savage."

Sung's fear eased slightly; the strange little fat man did not look as if he would hurt her.

"What is it you want?" she asked in French.

"Oh, dear," he said. "And good French too." He jumped up, the language itself bringing out his chivalry. "My dear, please sit down. I beg your pardon for the intrusion, but it is absolutely vital that I contact Mr. Mead. I cannot express how vital. It is a matter of life and death—regrettably mine."

She did not move any closer, but she was no longer afraid. "He is not here," she said.

"Do you mind if I wait for him; it is very important."

"I don't know when he will return; some nights he does not come home at all. I never know when he will return."

"But I must see him immediately." Lacouture grew very distressed and sat down, fanning himself with his hat.

"Perhaps you could leave a message for him. I will give it to him."

"You are very kind," he said almost tearfully. He dabbed his eyes with his handkerchief. "Pardon me, I really am quite upset."

He motioned to a chair at the table. "Please sit down; it's not proper that I should be sitting while you stand, but I'm too distraught to stand, so you'll have to sit."

She nodded slightly and sat down, hands folded, back very straight.

"You really are quite beautiful. And your French is excellent, as good as the ambassador's. Where did you learn?"

"I was tutored at home."

"Ah," he said, seeing the whole story. "Your family was very wealthy, yes? And the communists came. And you had to flee. Where are you from, my dear?"

"Ban Me Thuot."

"Exquisite place."

"You know it?" she asked, showing a spark of interest for the first time since the brothel.

"Oh, yes. I was there many times. My family was very wealthy too; I was born here. My father took me often to Ban Me Thuot when I was young. He had a large rubber plantation there and represented Michelin in buying from the Vietnamese. Probably my father knew your grandfather, or even your father. How curious!"

He was silent a moment, lost in reverie. "It was a beautiful place, so quiet and peaceful, and people seemed happier there than other places. I remember riding a bicycle through the villages and down the paths of the fields. But that was so long ago; I have not been there in many years."

Lacouture pulled a card from his vest. "We must get together and talk sometime. We could have coffee together on the terrace of the Continental. I would like to show you the beautiful parts of Saigon: you would appreciate them. Would you like to come? I'm sure Mr. Mead would not mind—he would hardly be jealous of me."

He pressed the card into her hand. "I never even introduced myself: Bernard Lacouture, and that is my address and phone number."

"I am Sung Le Vinh," she said.

"Imagine, Mr. Mead bringing us together—an American soldier, an old French gentleman, and a beautiful Vietnamese princess."

She blushed slightly and bowed her head.

"You will have coffee with me someday, won't you? We have so much to talk about. I would like to hear about Ban Me Thuot, though probably the memories are very painful for you, aren't they?"

She kept her head down.

"Was your family killed?" he asked.

"Yes," she said softly.

He sighed. "I am so sorry. What an awful, awful war. We, and I mean us, the French, brought such terrible misery to this country. Perhaps it will end soon."

"That's what Ron says too. He says the man he works for, the powerful man at the embassy, is trying to end the war. But do you really think it will happen?"

Lacouture folded his handkerchief carefully and placed it into his pocket. "Many people are trying to stop this war," he said smoothly, then with a benign look on his face ventured, "But it will take a very powerful man like Ambassador Marshall to end it."

"Ron says he is a very nice man; he likes him."

Lacouture tried to contain his amazement. "He *is* a very nice man, and very sincere."

"You know him?"

"Yes. I was at his villa just the other night—I drank too much champagne, I'm afraid."

"Ron says the house is very beautiful and he has many servants, but that he is kind to everyone."

"That is true. I don't understand though why I have never

531

seen Mr. Mead with the ambassador; perhaps it is because my associations with the ambassador have been social, and always outside of the embassy."

"I suppose. Ron is his bodyguard and goes with him only on business."

"I see," said Lacouture, pulling out his handkerchief and clutching it tightly in his lap.

My God, he thought wildly, this can't be true. He wanted to grab her hands and kiss them in gratitude.

Then he jerked upright. My God, Lord would kill him too! Marshall's bodyguard would be with him at the meeting with Khanh. His savage would be killed! And Lord had conspired with Lacouture to do it! The evil, evil bastard. His savage, this dear girl's protector—murdered.

He was too distraught to say anything, and when there was a loud banging on the door, and it flew open, Lacouture whirled in terror.

A huge burly youth, naked except for his skivvies, stood in the doorway holding a rifle.

Lacouture squealed and nearly fell off the chair.

"What the fuck!" shouted Bill Catton, kicking the door open and coming into the room, the rifle pointed at Lacouture.

"Who's this asshole? Get up!"

Lacouture scrambled up, holding on to the table for fear that he would faint.

"What's going on in here? Sung, you okay?" Catton crossed quickly to Lacouture and jabbed the rifle barrel into his belly.

Sung jumped up. "Bill, it's all right. He's not bothering me. He's a friend of Ron's."

Catton stared at the quivering man in front of him. "I doubt that very much. Who the fuck are you, fat ass?"

Lacouture could barely speak, but finally managed to get a few words out. "It's true. I know Mr. Mead from the embassy."

"I work at the embassy too, faggot—I'd have remembered someone like you coming in. You look like the Pillsbury Doughboy. He jammed the rifle deeper into

Lacouture's gut and turned to Sung. "First gooks, and now faggots—what's going on in here?"

"Bill, he came to see Ron; he knows Ambassador Marshall."

Catton quickly lowered the rifle. "Oh." Then he looked about suspiciously. "Where is Ron?"

"Still at work. I told Mr. . . . Lacouture that Ron might not be back for a long time, then we talked in French and he told me that he knew the place where I lived before."

"Yes, yes," Lacouture said quickly. "I was just leaving. I told Miss . . . Vinh to tell Mr. Mead that I stopped by to see him and give him the message. I told her that it was very important that I see him immediately—it has to do with Ambassador Marshall." He pointed at the table. "See, I gave her my card." He grabbed it and handed it to Catton, who glanced at it then stuck it in the waistband of his shorts. *"I'll keep it and give it to him."*

"By all means," said Lacouture, reaching for another card. "I'll give Miss Vinh another one—just as long as Mr. Mead gets the message is all that matters to me."

Then Lacouture drew himself up with as much dignity as he could. "Well, I shall be going now. It was charming to meet you, Miss Vinh, and I look forward to seeing you again. And good day to you, sir," he said to Catton, easing around him, and going quickly to the door.

Catton watched him leave, then he turned to Sung with a big grin on his face, holding up his rifle and pulling the trigger. It clicked harmlessly. "I just came in to borrow some oil to clean it. Where does Ron keep his cleaning gear?" Then he tossed Lacouture's card on the table. "Hope that little faggot wasn't important."

In the corridor going toward the steps, Lacouture had to hold on to the wall to support himself. He was so giddy that he thought he might fall down the stairs, but he wasn't sure if the giddiness was fear, Catton's near-naked body, or the information that he had just learned about Mead and Ambassador Marshall.

When he stumbled outside and got a cab, he collapsed

into the backseat and told the driver to drive anywhere. He needed to recover, and to think.

He had to contact Mead; the savage was his only hope. But would he help? Would his woman give him the message?

He pulled out his handkerchief to blot his face, but instead he chewed on it.

No one would help him, he despaired; they all despised him—see how the other youth reviled him?

But no, the savage was different; he was kind. He would help; he had to.

Teresa Hawthorne stood before the bulletproof glass sentry booth of the U.S. embassy. For days she had unsuccessfully attempted to contact Marshall; he was never in when she called, and because she didn't have a telephone, she couldn't leave a number to call.

Sensing the secretary's exasperation after so many calls, Teresa was afraid she would not put her through even if Marshall were in, so she decided to try in person.

She had looked everywhere for Lin, but no one had seen her.

Father Dourmant had not been able to help either. "I can't get anyone in the parish interested or concerned," he said. "No one cares about your clinic or those children. I can't get the bishop to allocate even a paltry sum—I have to steal it from the poor box."

Father Dourmant had sat her down in the rectory and shuffled about in the kitchen making them a cup of tea.

"It's not that they're heartless or unfeeling, but that they are more concerned with Catholic orphans, or legitimate Vietnamese orphans, those whose fathers died in the military and whose mothers died in bombings, or from disease. There are thousands upon thousands of these, with nowhere to go and with no support from the government. It is an overwhelming problem worsening by the day; there are hundreds of such orphans for every one of yours in the clinic. The tragedy is no more nor less, but your problems seem smaller and less significant simply because of the numbers."

He fumbled through mostly empty canisters of tea and brought one to the stove. "Probably she went back to the brothel," he said. "She may have just tossed the infant onto a trash heap."

"I'm sure she didn't," Teresa said. "I think she'd die before going back to the brothel."

"Well, she will die if she can't support herself. She needs money to eat, and there's only one way a woman like her can earn enough to live—and they don't have nurseries in the brothels; she'd have to get rid of the baby before she went back."

Teresa lowered her head and began to cry softly. The old priest ignored her, clattering cups down on the table with his palsied hands.

"I am seventy-three," he said. "I have seen enough misery and suffering and evil to make God blanch—or at least to feel ashamed about. And do you know, I don't understand any of it, no more today than I did fifty years ago when I was a young priest."

He tossed spoons onto the table. One bounced to the floor. "Damn," he said, groaning as he bent to pick it up, then he wiped it on his cassock and threw it on the table again.

"Yet I feel as deeply today as I did fifty years ago. I am not inured to the suffering that I have seen; my heart is not callused. But I have learned there is little that I can do, and that it does no good for me to wail or shake my fist in God's face. *I* don't like the world the way it is: *I* would not allow pain and suffering, but alas it is not in my power to change anything. Nor is it in yours, my dear, so stop crying and go get the kettle so that I don't spill boiling water over both of us."

Teresa sniffed, wiped her nose, then went to the stove and brought back the kettle.

He eased down on a chair. "You don't like God's world, therefore you reject Him. I don't like His world or understand what He's doing either, but I choose to believe in Him. It doesn't make any difference, certainly to God—it's just a matter of . . . comfortableness to us. For me, I decided long

535

ago that I would not fight Him—I couldn't win even if I did win, as you think you have by rejecting Him: what have you won? Understanding? Peace?"

He blew on his cup. "I took the harder route—to persist in belief no matter what. Doubtless I shall be rewarded."

She laughed and blew on her own steaming cup. "You think I took the easy way out?"

"Indeed. You gave up. It's easy to believe when all is going well. Job, after all, was tested for a reason."

"That is such sophistry, Father."

He smiled. "It's all sophistry, my dear; it's what I do for a living . . . and for salvation, of course. Karma, original sin, predestination—it's all the same; Eastern acceptance and resignation, Western faith and determinism—not a tea leaf's difference between them. And so it is with life and death; only a short time ago, but for eons before that, I was not alive—and in a very short time, but forever afterwards, I will be dead. My infinitesimal span is nothing to get worked up about. And so it is for Lin and her poor baby. My point, dear Teresa, is that you shouldn't take everything personally, because it is not directed at you, and there is nothing you can do. Let go, my dear. You can't help Lin, but there are others you can—go back to them."

But she could not give up on Lin and the baby, and now she stood before the sentry booth.

"Yes, ma'am, can I help you?" asked the Marine guard.

"Oh, I hope so," she said. "I need to see Ambassador Marshall."

"Do you have an appointment, ma'am?"

"No, I don't."

"I'm very sorry, ma'am, but you need a pass issued from the ambassador's office to get in—I can't let you in; I have specific orders about that. You could call his office and ask for one."

She shook her head. "That never works."

She started away, then remembered Mead and turned back. "Yes, you can help. There's a young man who works for the ambassador, his bodyguard. I can't remember his name, but he's a big man, bigger than you I think, and very fierce."

The guard smiled. "Yeah, I know him. That's Ron Mead."

"Yes, that's it, Corporal Mead. He knows me. I slapped him once—it wasn't his fault, of course, just a misunderstanding . . . oh, could you call him for me? He'd help me, I know he would."

"Well, ma'am, I'm not supposed to . . ." He looked into her pleading eyes, then reached for his phone. "Sure, I'll do it. What did you say your name was, ma'am?"

"Teresa Hawthorne. Thank you so much."

The guard spoke into the phone, waited a moment, then spoke again. She couldn't hear the conversation, only saw the guard grin and knew that he was talking to Corporal Mead, then he hung up and spoke through the grille to her.

"He told me to watch out for you, that you had a wicked right hand, but that he'd be down in a few minutes. You can wait over there if you wish."

"Oh, thank you," she said. "How nice of you all." She crossed the outer lobby to sit and wait.

Five minutes later she saw him come through the inner lobby and approach the sentry booth. The guard pointed to her, then released the sealed door, and Mead pushed through it and walked to her.

She jumped up from the chair, and he in mock fear threw up his hands to protect himself.

"How good of you to come down," she said, holding out her hand to shake his. "Thank you very much."

"Hello, Miss Hawthorne. How are you?"

"Fine, thank you. I'm sorry to bother you, but I didn't know anybody else who would help me."

"What can I do?" he asked.

"I have to see Ambassador Marshall, it's very important."

"Have you tried to call him?"

"Many times, but his secretary says he's never there."

"Yeah, that's Dolores—Miss Toland, I mean. She doesn't let anyone get through."

"I have to talk to him. Can you get a message to him?"

"Sure. You mean now?"

"Is he in?"

"Yes, ma'am. I'll go tell him you're here. Is that all?"

She smiled. "That's everything, and it would be just wonderful of you to do it for me."

"No problem. Do you want to come up? I can take you up."

"Oh, no, I'll just wait here, thank you very much."

"You sure? Okay; I'll be right back."

When he walked into the office, he told the secretary that he needed to see the ambassador for a minute.

"He's with Colonel Waggoner," she said without looking up.

"It'll just take a minute," he said, walking through her office.

"Wait," she said, but he was gone.

He knocked on Marshall's door. Waggoner opened it. "We're busy," he said on seeing Mead.

"Yes, Corporal?" Marshall said from behind his desk. "Come in. What is it?" he asked, knowing Mead would not intrude unless it was important.

"Sir, Miss Hawthorne has been trying to get through to you. She says it's very important."

"Of course," Marshall said, reaching for the phone.

"No, sir, I mean she's downstairs."

"Oh, well, have her come up. No, never mind," he said, looking at his watch. "We'll go to lunch—I owe her one. Colonel, we can finish this later. Tell me, where's a good place to go, a nice place?"

Waggoner shrugged. "I don't know, sir. I usually eat at the Brinks. I guess the Continental."

"No, that's too busy. I want a small place; surely there are some good restaurants in Saigon."

"I know one, sir," Mead said. "It's French."

"Perfect. What's its name?"

Mead stammered under Waggoner's dagger looks. "Well, sir, it's kind of a funny name. French, I mean. Something like . . ." He looked down, then away. "Something like . . . well, Cock Oil, sir."

Waggoner closed his eyes. "I hardly think that's where the ambassador wants to dine," he said.

"No, it's a really nice place. There's a chicken outside, on the door, I mean. A gold one."

538

Marshall frowned, then he smiled in recognition. "Coq d'Or."

"Yes, sir, that's it."

"Cock oil. Jesus!" said Waggoner.

"Wonderful," said Marshall. "Tell Miss Hawthorne I'll be right down, and have the driver get the car. Tell him where the restaurant is, will you?"

"Yes, sir."

The intercom buzzed, and Marshall punched the button. "Yes, Dolores?"

"Mr. Ambassador, Mr. Lord is here to see you."

"Oh, hell, I forgot," he said, then looked up to Mead. "This will only take a few minutes. Ask Miss Hawthorne to wait, please."

He pushed the intercom. "Have Mr. Lord come in, please."

Mead and Waggoner left together, and in the outer office they passed Wilson Abbot Lord. Lord nodded to Waggoner and looked right through Mead. He knocked on Marshall's office door and went in.

CHAPTER
• 34 •

Marshall rose to shake hands when Lord entered, then gestured toward armchairs across the room where both sat.

This was their first face-to-face meeting, and they studied each other with frank appraisal, both self-confident and relaxed.

When Marshall had received the call from Lacouture, relaying the message "Nhay Dam," Marshall called General Tran and repeated the words to him.

Tran hesitated, then said with what Marshall decided was a curious blend of anger and sadness, "It is he."

"You are sure?"

This time there was no pause. "Yes."

"Would you meet with him?"

"I will think about it," Tran answered.

Before returning a call to Lacouture, indicating his own willingness to meet with General Khanh, Marshall asked for a CIA briefing on the Frenchman. He was told Wilson Abbot Lord would give it.

Lord was the man he had been warned of in Washington; he remembered Andrew Maynard's intensity: "Be careful, Brad. He *believes.*"

Though Lord was listed as a consular officer, Marshall knew he was the CIA's senior operative, and he suspected that Lord acted independently of the station chief, answering only to Langley.

From Lord's utterly genuine assurance, without a trace of bravura, Marshall saw that Maynard was right—here could be a dangerously formidable foe.

"Why such high-powered handling on such a matter?" Marshall asked.

"The Agency gets nervous when ambassadors involve themselves with petty crooks and mercenaries."

"It's so reassuring to know that you people have an ear on everything," Marshall said dryly.

"What are telephones for if not to listen in on?" Lord answered lightly. "Lacouture's telephone had been tapped for years—in fact, it was hard to find a free space on the line, it has so many taps on it: French, VC, Special Branch. When the tapes played back cryptic messages between him and someone in the embassy, we got curious."

"Tell me about Lacouture," Marshall said.

Lord handed him a thick file. "Both of us have better things to do than go through all that, but I'll leave it with you to sample through."

"Just give me the highlights then, Mr. Lord."

Lord stretched comfortably in the chair. Having listened in on Marshall's conversation with Tran, he knew that what he told Marshall would determine whether Marshall would authorize Lacouture to arrange the meeting.

Lord said languorously, "Bernard Lacouture is sixty-two years old, intelligent, articulate, knowledgeable in art, and also a shrewd businessman and manipulator of people. Independently wealthy, he augments his income by dealing in information and intrigue; over the years he has provided information to Sûreté, the Japanese, the Viet Minh, NVA, Viet Cong, the South Vietnamese, and ourselves. His political leanings are . . . fluid, strictly opportunistic. His sexual preferences are for young men and tend towards the masochistic. We use him as a secondary source for substantiations of rumors and verification of primary sources. He has survived all the upheavals and regimes essentially because he is harmless. He is, more or less, a gadfly who would hardly warrant, as you say, 'high-powered' handling, except that he somehow seems to be trafficking in code with the personal representative of the President. Usually his contacts are drug dealers and minor intelligence agents fond of secret handshakes and mustache disguises."

"And code words?" Marshall said with a smile.

"Yes—things like 'squeaky,' and *'goulue,'* and 'Nhay Dam.'"

"Which mean?"

Lord shrugged. "I was hoping that you could tell me."

"I don't know what they mean," Marshall said. His gaze fixed Lord intently. "Are you sure you don't?"

Lord met the stare. "I imagine that it is part of an attempt to induce you to meet with a 'high-ranking' North Vietnamese official to discuss 'peace negotiations'—that's what it's usually all about."

"Usually?"

Lord looked bored. "The North Vietnamese are making a wide-scale effort to stop the bombing of the North and enter negotiations for a troop withdrawal. They're not going to let a possibility of using someone like you slip by."

Marshall leaned forward, his anger showing. "'Someone like me'? 'Using'?"

Lord, pleased that the insult had stung, and wanting to goad Marshall further, merely shrugged, as if the enemy's ploy and Marshall's gullibility were too obvious to bother with.

"And who, in your opinion, Mr. Lord, is the 'high-ranking' North Vietnamese?"

"General Xuan Tien Khanh."

"I thought he was dead."

Lord shrugged again. "So MACV believes."

"You don't?"

"Our intelligence estimates often disagree. It would be convenient if he were dead, but we tend to distrust opportune reports that cannot be authenticated."

"So your advice to me would be . . .?"

"I am not in a position to advise you, Excellency."

"But if you were?"

"I would caution you about your personal safety, and

suggest that you consider the possibility that you are being manipulated for military advantage and political gain."

Marshall sat back and considered him a moment. "You've been in Vietnam a long time, Mr. Lord—longer than any other official?"

"I'm sure there are others who have been here longer; but yes, a long time—many years."

"Can we win this war, Mr. Lord?"

"We *must* win this war, Mr. Marshall," Lord said evenly, consciously dispensing with any honorific.

"And how is this going to be achieved?" Marshall asked.

"Are you really interested in that as a goal?"

"I don't ask rhetorical questions, Mr. Lord. If you can enlighten me on how this war can be won, I will be happy to deliver your solution personally to the President."

"Send more men and equipment; allow the military to fight the war as they want; strike the enemy in his sanctuaries."

"Hardly novel solutions, Mr. Lord," Marshall said flatly.

"Is that what you're seeking, Mr. Ambassador? A novel solution—one that won't result in any dead? One without sacrifice? Something quick and painless? Expeditious and cheap?" Lord did not disguise his disdain. "No, *Excellency*, I don't have that kind of solution; mine requires dedication, commitment, perseverance—principles always do."

"Ah, yes," Marshall said, matching his tone. "And the principles are—let me guess—democracy and independence, supporting the freedom-loving government of South Vietnam, which is dedicated to truth, justice, and all that we hold dear."

There was a knock at the door, and Colonel Waggoner entered. "I beg your pardon, but we were just notified by Washington that the President would like to speak with you, sir. The line is being cleared now—he'll be on in five minutes. You'll have to go down to the 'Bubble,' sir; that's the secure communication center."

"Damn," Marshall said, glancing at his watch. "Send someone to tell Miss Hawthorne that I'll be delayed." He stood. "Thank you for your time, and expertise, Mr. Lord."

They did not shake hands, and Lord merely inclined his head as he left the office.

A fine, tightly controlled performance, Marshall thought, watching Lord leave—except for the slip about "squeaky." He had never spoken that word over the phone to Lacouture —it had been said in person at his villa, and once over his private phone to General Tran. Obviously Lord had bugged his, Marshall's, phones. But then, he thought, a man who "believes" so fervently would not hesitate to tap a telephone. Indeed, Marshall wondered, would he hesitate at anything?

Not this man, he decided; he was as dangerous as Maynard had warned. He would stop at nothing, Marshall thought, certainly not pain or sacrifice—or any number of dead. He was a zealot, dangerous and deadly, an implacable enemy to anyone who did not share his "principles," Marshall thought; a man who would be unmoved by youths —sons—dying for those principles.

He was the enemy, Marshall decided, affirming his dedication to meet with a representative of the North, to seek an end to the war, and resolutely he left the office to talk to the President.

Lord, too, was pleased with his performance. Surely someone of Marshall's intelligence and perception would fix on the mistake of "squeaky." That, his distrust of the CIA, and his overwhelming desire to negotiate "peace" would ensure that he authorize Lacouture to arrange the rendezvous.

The weak were so predictable, he thought; that made them even more disgustingly vulnerable. Men such as Marshall were the true enemies of democracy and freedom —bleeding hearts unwilling to stay the difficult course, weather the adversities, fight the long, brutal fight—men who mouthed principles, but who were unwilling to sacrifice for them; men who mocked others' dedication.

He, Lord, had been right all along; this meeting confirmed it, and reaffirmed his determination to stop Marshall.

On the next floor, he called Gibbon from a hall phone. Gibbon answered by repeating his extension number.

"Jeff, an important call is coming in from Washington—I want the transcript on my desk immediately. Get it." He hung up.

That left only the problem of Lacouture, and he would handle that one personally.

In the downstairs "Bubble," the most tightly guarded area in the embassy, the electronic hub, Marshall was led past rooms of communications equipment and brought to a soundproof booth.

"Where's the phone?" he asked, expecting to find the scrambler apparatus he was accustomed to using at other embassies.

"For White House communications, Ambassador Bunker uses this," an embassy official said. "You just sit inside, sir, and talk. When you're finished, just push that button and the door will open."

A red light went on. "The call's coming through now, sir."

Marshall closed the door and sat down before a desk in the closet-size booth, padded for soundproofing.

"Bradley! Is that you there, Bradley?" Johnson's voice screamed into the booth, literally raising Marshall from his chair.

"Jesus!" Marshall yelled. "Turn the goddamn volume down."

"What?" screamed Johnson. "What'd you say to me, Bradley?"

Oh, my God, Marshall thought—nobody can hear me, and he realized the volume was turned so loud in deference to Bunker's age. He put his hands over his ears. "Nothing, Mr. President. I was talking to someone else."

"Who else is there?" Johnson shouted. "Where the hell are you, a public phone booth?"

"No, sir, just a misunderstanding. What can I do for you, sir?"

The President's voice fell to a whisper that still resounded in the booth. "Help me, Bradley. I've been waiting to hear from you." He said it as if he'd been sitting before the unresponsive phone for years. Then he slammed his fist onto his desk and shouted, "I've got this goddamn CAVITY

545

study before me and I don't know what to do. They tell me they need more men, more tanks, more everything. They want to do everything except suit up Lady Bird and send her over with grenades. Bradley! What am I going to do? You're supposed to help me. I sent you over there to unfuck this mess." The President's voice caught in pain and betrayal.

"I've seen the COVIA study, Mr. President. I have serious reservations about it. In fact, one of the authors of the study and I have been making field visits to determine the accuracy of its findings. So far, nothing I've seen would substantiate those findings. I'll be going out to the field tomorrow, and I can give you a more detailed answer when I return. The situation is not so critical that you can't delay a decision for a while."

"You mean I can tell Lady Bird to unpack?"

"Yes, sir."

"Well, that's a relief, anyway. You know I have Westmoreland and Bunker here in Washington. Westmoreland addressed Congress and got them all charged up, and he's pressuring me with that damn COFFEE study, so I had to call you—since you're not talking to me, it seems—and find out what's going on over there. Are you *doing* anything, Bradley? I got that goddamn blackmail paper of yours hanging over my head, and my time's running out. You're supposed to be *helping* me, Bradley."

"I am doing my very best, Mr. President." Marshall wanted to mention the possibility of the meeting with General Khanh, but he didn't want to raise unrealistic expectations, yet now more than ever he was determined to meet with the NVA.

"I hope to have something concrete and positive for you shortly," Marshall said.

"Well, that's what I sent you for," Johnson said. "Hurry, Bradley! The wolves are closing in." He said it as if they were circling the White House lawn. "And I'm being crucified in the press."

Marshall could see the Christ-like hands thrown out, and Johnson closing his eyes from the nails being driven in.

"So this CAVIAR study is horseshit, is that what you're telling me, Bradley?"

"I'm suggesting that you defer a decision on it. I'll give you my recommendation on it very soon."

"All right, Bradley. I'll hold off. I'm counting on you, Bradley. Everything is in your hands." He said it as if the apocalypse hung in the balance. "And Dak To," he thundered. "I want to know about Dak To."

Dak To? wondered Marshall. He knew there was a battle going on there, but he had heard little about it.

"It's the end of the world up there," shouted Johnson, then his voice turned to a whisper. "Westmoreland is cutting short his visit here; I know it's because of Dak To. No one tells me that, of course, but then, I'm only the Commander in Chief, the last person to know anything."

"I'll find out for you, sir," Marshall said, then added gravely, "But if it's that bad, perhaps you'd better suit Lady Bird up again."

Johnson whooped, then yelled, "Tell me what's going on," and he hung up.

Marshall pushed the door release and staggered out of the booth, his ears resounding painfully.

"I'm sorry to have kept you waiting," Marshall told Teresa, greeting her warmly. "But I'm delighted you've come to take me up on lunch." He took her arm and guided her outside toward his car. "We'll hold Corporal Mead responsible for the food—the restaurant is his suggestion."

She stopped on the stairs. "Oh, no," she said in embarrassment. "I . . . I only wanted to . . . Ambassador Marshall, I . . ."

"Brad, please. Somebody's got to call me by my first name; I haven't heard it in weeks—I'm beginning to think I exist only as an honorific."

She was very flustered. "All I wanted was to talk with you for a minute. I tried to call, but . . . lunch . . ."

"You haven't eaten, have you?"

"No, but . . ."

"Neither have I, and we can talk, and I'll see to it that you get back to your saintly work without undue delay." He steered her to the car and ushered her in. "How have you been, and how is Father Dourmant, and your clinic?"

547

"Fine," she said, still in surprise at the speed with which everything was happening. "Everyone is fine. Well, most everyone." Then she laughed. "You know, every time I get discouraged, something happens to make me feel better. Father Dourmant would probably tell me it is God working His strange ways."

"If you are talking about me as an instrument of God, then it is a very circuitous way indeed."

The car left the embassy, and they chatted lightly on the short trip. When they pulled up before the restaurant, Marshall and Teresa got out. "What would you recommend on the menu, Corporal?" Marshall asked Mead.

"The duck's real good, sir. It's in this sort of orange jam."

"Sounds wonderful," he said. "Why don't you wait out here—or maybe they have a take-out service. Or maybe the driver could get you both something; we'll be here an hour or so."

Inside, the maître d' greeted them deferentially—he had seen the limousine—and brought them to a table in back.

After they ordered—Teresa declined wine—she told him about Lin's disappearance.

"Father Dourmant thinks she may have gone back to the brothel, but I don't. I'm afraid she's serious about burning the child before the American embassy."

"Is there anything I can do to help you locate her?"

Teresa shook her head. "A homeless woman with a baby in Saigon? There are thousands and thousands of them. She could be anywhere—in a back alley, by the river; she doesn't even need shelter, it's so warm. No, it would be impossible to find her."

Marshall sipped a glass of Chablis and tried to reassure her.

"Even if she did try to set fire to herself and the baby in front of the embassy, she wouldn't be able to—security is so tight that they would stop her before she could."

"You really think so?"

"Yes, I do. The embassy is very well guarded, and there are Vietnamese police on every corner for blocks around it. Besides, one doesn't just squirt a little lighter fluid to set oneself on fire—you need a large can of gasoline. I think the

Buddhist bonzes had help even, someone to carry the gasoline and pour it on them, then set the fire. It sounds terribly callous to discuss it like this, but I don't think a woman carrying a baby could manage the logistics of immolating herself and the child."

Teresa suppressed a smile. "That does sound terrible, but I suppose you're right. I never would have thought of all that."

"No cabdriver is going to drop her off in front of the embassy with a drum of gasoline, and I can't imagine she would be able to lug it across town, carrying the baby too."

"You've made me feel much better," she said.

"I'll have all the security people alerted; they'll be on the lookout for her in case she does try it. I'll have them apprehend her and get her and the child back to you. How's that?"

"You make everything sound simple; power is a wonderful thing."

"It could be," Marshall said. "But it seldom is, any more than things are usually simple. After all, returning Lin and the baby doesn't solve anything, does it?"

"Now you're depressing me again," she said.

"Then we'll stop discussing this war. Why don't you pick a topic?"

"Your family. Tell me about them. You must miss them very much."

"I do indeed. But that would be very boring for you."

She smiled. "I spend all my time with sick women and diseased children. I have no friends and talk to no one, except Father Dourmant. I've never eaten in a place like this, nor ever known anyone like you. How could I be bored?"

Marshall considered her a moment, then said softly, "Maybe you should go back to the nunnery, Teresa, whether or not you believe in God. I think the real world doesn't deserve you; it's too harsh. I would hate to see you hurt."

She bowed her head in embarrassment.

"Well, about my family! I have a wife and three children. My wife is also a saint—not as ethereal as you, more of a . . . bossy type saint: 'Do this, do that, it's good for you;

it'll help the poor, or whales or trees, whatever.' Actually she's more like a good queen rather than a saint. She's a wonderful mother, and a very kind person."

He paused a moment. "And I suppose a saint after all. I haven't been a very good husband."

"See," Teresa said. "This isn't boring a bit. You're going to tell me you've been terrible and unfaithful and had lots of mistresses, and that your wife has stood by you through it all."

He laughed and gestured for more wine. "You're supposed to be ethereal. I forgot you're a slum saint, dealing with prostitutes and soldiers and drugs and illegitimate babies."

"Do you still love your wife?"

"Oh, yes, and I admire and respect her. But rather than work through all the strains and stresses of marriage, it was easier to run off for some mindless affair. I haven't been very disciplined."

"But she's understood it?"

"Oh, heavens no, nor forgotten nor forgiven; she's much too strong and intelligent for that. She has her life and interests, her causes and projects, and we get along quite well—our relationship is very adult and no-nonsense—there just isn't any passion."

"That's too bad; I'm sorry."

"And my children? Dear God, I shouldn't talk about them at all; they drive me insane. I'll have to go back to the villa and drink myself senseless after this."

"I'm sure you have lovely children."

"'Lovely' is hardly the word that comes to mind. Ryan has dropped out of college and joined the Special Forces and will be over here probably sometime after lunch to get killed. Chris, who is fifteen, is a homosexual; either that or he's just maliciously trying to push me over the edge. And Sarah . . . she's sixteen and . . . well, she's just a father's nightmare."

"*I* was a father's nightmare," Teresa said. "Large and unattractive, never any boys. I never had a date; well, one, but that was just a dare on his part."

"That's a bad dream, not a nightmare. Sarah is a nightmare: she's beautiful and sexual, strong and willful and independent. All my children are that way."

"It sounds like you and your wife did a fine job with them."

"Far better to have them stupid and ugly and respectful; *that* would be lovely."

"You don't mean that."

"Right now I do. I can't stand the thought of Ryan's coming over here. If anything happened to him . . ."

"Is that why you are trying so hard to end the war?"

He considered a long moment. "I suppose it contributes to my urgency, but no, I want to end the war because it is wrong; it was a great mistake. And because we can't win—more children will die; there will be more Lins. You don't think we can win, do you?"

"I don't even know what you mean by 'win.' But I don't think it will be any better when the communists come; I can't imagine that they're going to take care of the orphans."

"What will you and Father Dourmant do?"

"Father Dourmant is an old man; he shouldn't be working as hard as he does. I imagine the church will put him in a home."

"And what about you, Teresa?"

"I don't know," she said. "I'll work here as long as I can. After that . . . I'll just have to see."

"The demand for saints is very great—there are so many places you could go: India, Africa, Central America. Why, there are probably even places in America where there's poverty, ignorance, and disease."

"You shouldn't make fun of me," she said, slightly hurt.

"I'm not; I was just teasing. I'm sorry, I shouldn't have. I guess it's just that I don't understand people such as you, those who do good works."

She laughed. "Are there people who do 'bad' works?"

"Indeed there are. Everyone I know is driven by greed and selfishness, or the promise of reward in one form or another. I really haven't had much dealing with self-abnegators—truly selfless people."

"You have a very discouraging view of people," she said sadly.

"I'm a diplomat; it doesn't pay to take the optimistic view—a fool and his principles are soon killed."

"Well, I don't think people are so bad."

"That's rather remarkable coming from someone who has seen what you have and who deals with what you do."

"The *babies* are not bad; neither are the women— probably the soldiers aren't either. As you said about Corporal Mead, he is a very nice boy even though he has killed many people. He *is* nice—you should have seen how kind he was to me, and genuine, but I suppose he could murder and rape and pillage."

"*I'd* certainly hate to be in his path," Marshall acknowledged, thinking of the other night in the Delta.

"But you, I mean figuratively, sent him here to do these things; I'm sure he wouldn't be murdering at home, but working in some job, married, raising his children, doing the best he could. I think most people are basically kind and good—they just get sidetracked, like you did in your marriage with your infidelities."

He looked away. Sidetracked. Did that describe him? No, and suddenly he felt jaded, almost unclean, soiled by the world and all that he had done. He had failed in so many ways; there were so many transgressions.

He felt that she could see into him with the purity of light, see the warps and worm holes, the rot. Yes, she would be kind to him, but she was of another dimension. His was one of pretension, cocktail people—queens and politicians. She had evolved beyond him; she was a kinder, gentler creature. She was what *should* be, while he was bogged down, limited, unevolved. She was beyond him—beyond queens and socialites, and Deborah at the Smithsonian.

Teresa frightened him. Catherine didn't. Catherine, for all her goodness, was part of his world, but Teresa soared— above trees and whales and wars. She was in a region of pure spirit that he only rarely and briefly attained.

And looking across at her at the table, he wanted her more than to like him—he wanted her to lift him into her world.

She folded the napkin in her lap. "Sometimes I think it would have been nice if I had had a husband and children, and a house, and I could have cooked meals and seen to their needs. But I don't really feel deprived. And I am happy."

She put the napkin on the table and smiled. "After all, good works *are* satisfying; they are their own reward."

Then she looked away from his intense gaze.

She *did* feel deprived; this minute she did. She wanted husband and children. And love. That's what she longed for most, someone to love her; forget all the nonsense about good works, sacrifice, and abnegation. Where was love?

Oh dear, she thought. Love. And her face reddened.

But that was what she wanted. And it was what she felt for this man. He was good and strong, kind and understanding, and he made her laugh. She had never met anyone like him; if there had been someone like him before—there might have been house and children. She would have cooked and cleaned. She would have loved and been loved.

But what would such a man see in her—homely and limited: plain and horsey and simple? She could not dress or make clever talk. She could not engage such a man.

It was all impossible. She sighed, then looked up. He was still staring at her.

They were the last two diners in the restaurant.

He sat silently, wanting to reach out to her, but instead he said, "Would you care for something else? Dessert or coffee?"

"I couldn't eat another thing; I've never had such rich food. It's been a perfectly wonderful lunch. Thank you so much."

When Marshall called for the check, Teresa buttered the remaining rolls in the basket and put them in her purse. "I wonder if those poor boys got anything to eat; we've been in here for hours."

Marshall stood. "We shall do this again soon, I hope. We talked all about me; next time I want to hear about you. Will you join me again?"

She met his gaze and said firmly, "I would like that very much."

He held the chair for her. They stood close together, then Marshall said, "Thank you."

"The next time is my treat; I choose the restaurant."

"No, mine," said Marshall. "This was Corporal Mead's choice; I haven't had one yet."

Outside, Teresa handed the rolls to Mead and Stokes.

"That was an excellent choice, Corporal," Marshall said. "Thank you for the recommendation." He held the door for Teresa, and when she got in, he leaned in the door and said to Stokes, "Take Miss Hawthorne wherever she wants to go. Corporal Mead and I will get back to the embassy on our own."

"Oh, I can't impose," said Teresa.

"I insist," Marshall said. "Besides, I need a little walk to clear my head after the wine. I enjoyed it immensely; thank you for joining me, and as soon as we hear anything about Lin, you'll be notified."

He waved and started down the sidewalk, followed by a very startled Mead.

At the corner waiting to cross, Marshall said, "I want you to do something for me. It is very important."

"Yes, sir."

He reached into his wallet, took out a card and some money, and handed them to Mead.

They started across the street. Mead had to listen hard to hear.

"I want you to go to the address on that card tonight. I want you to make sure you're not followed and that no one sees you. The address is that Frenchman you asked me about before, remember?"

"Yes, sir, the one who was calling Dolores."

"That's right. His name is Bernard Lacouture—it's on the card. I want you to tell him that I said all right—he'll know what I mean."

"Just tell him that: 'all right'?"

"Yes. He's going to arrange a meeting I want to attend. Tell him to be very careful about getting the message back to me—tell him not to use the phone."

"Is your phone being bugged, sir?" Mead asked, remembering Lord's coming out of his office early the other morning.

"I'm sure it is, and I don't want anyone to know about this."

"Is that all you want me to do, sir?"

"Yes. I'm sorry to involve you with this, but there's no one else I trust. Just make sure you get the message to him without anybody following you."

"Who would follow me, sir?"

"I suppose the same people who would bug my telephone; those who don't want me to have this meeting."

"Would the meeting be dangerous, sir?"

Marshall threaded his way among the pedestrians on the sidewalk. "There are some things more important than personal safety; I think you understand that. Besides, I'll have you with me wherever I go—what could possibly happen to me then?"

"Do you want me to report back to you tonight after I get the message to him, sir?"

"No, just let me know quietly tomorrow—but not in my office or in the car. I'm sure that's bugged too. And I also want you to be careful tonight—I really don't like involving you in this because it might be dangerous."

"I can take care of myself, sir."

"I have every confidence in you, Corporal, believe me. I'm entrusting you with a mission that's vitally important—not just to me or President Johnson, but one that could perhaps save many lives. But I'm afraid there are some people who don't want the mission to succeed."

"I'll get the message to him, sir, don't worry."

Yes, Marshall thought; Mead would get the message to Lacouture, but what happened after that was less certain. Lacouture was a clever man, but whether or not he was a match for Wilson Abbot Lord was quite another matter.

Beside him, Mead was filled with both pride and anxiety—great pride that Ambassador Marshall would trust him in such a way, but anxiety because it was all so confusing to him. Mr. Lord, The Phantom, had told him that Lacouture was an enemy agent who planned to kill Marshall. Mr. Lord knew everything; he was CIA; why would he lie? Was Lacouture deceiving Marshall? Should he, Mead, tell Lord what Marshall was doing in order to protect him against himself? The ambassador was often doing dangerous things—such as right now, walking down the main street of

Saigon where any VC on a motorcycle could race by and shoot him.

He had no reason to distrust Mr. Lord; so far he had been right about everything—every prediction he had made had come true. Mead wished he knew what to do. This was way above a corporal, he thought; he wasn't smart enough for this—Marshall, Lord, Lacouture, they were so much smarter than he was. All he could go on were his feelings, but he wasn't even sure he could trust them anymore. It was all as Mr. Lord said—he was right about that too—what seemed real maybe wasn't real at all.

He just wanted to do the right thing. But how could he be sure what that was? He wished there was someone he could go to whom he trusted; someone who would tell him what to do.

Suddenly he thought with great longing for Sung. He could trust her; he knew he could. He had never been in love before; is this what it was? he wondered—this rush of longing, not even sexual, to be with her? He wished he were with her now—just to be with her would make everything right. He could think everything out if he were with her.

That's what he would do, he decided; he'd go home first, before he went to Lacouture's, he'd go back and think things through and decide whether to tell Mr. Lord.

Just then Marshall stepped out into the street and flagged a cab, and they went back to the embassy.

CHAPTER

• 35 •

It was nearly seven, and almost dark by the time Mead returned to his apartment. He bounded up the stairs and threw open the door eagerly.

"Hey, Sung . . ." He stopped dead, for Wilson Abbot Lord was sitting at the table staring at him. Sung was across the room by the window.

"Get rid of her," Lord said, gesturing toward Sung. "We need to talk, Corporal."

"I'll go see Han," Sung said, edging around the room from Lord.

"Sit down," Lord said to Mead when she was gone. "I told you that I needed some information—I meant before the end of the war, and not at your convenience, Corporal."

"Yes, sir," Mead said nervously. "I been trying, but—"

"Excuses are like assholes, Corporal—everybody's got one; I'm not interested in yours any more than I'm interested in your personal problems."

"Yes, sir."

"I asked you for help, but it wasn't a request, Corporal. I expected you to get me some information—now I'm telling you: get it for me. Immediately. If that means you have to jump into bed with the son of a bitch, then do it. Understand? This is the big leagues—hard ball, and you're at bat. Got it? My job is national security; I take that very seriously—it's a lot more important than whether or not you want that bastard to fondle your dick. It's more important than any one life, no matter whose it is. Am I getting through to you?"

"Yes, sir," Mead said, very intimidated.

Lord leaned across the table, his eyes searing. "Let me make it perfectly clear so there's no mistake: that French faggot is working for the communists—they're paying him. Got that?"

"Yes, sir."

"He's a paid communist agent. He's trying to lure Ambassador Marshall into a secret meeting with the communists. He's trying to convince the ambassador that there's going to be a legitimate meeting to discuss peace and end the war. I'm afraid he's going to succeed—that the ambassador will fall for it despite our warnings to him."

Mead started to tell Lord that it had already worked, but Lord waved him silent. "The ambassador is a good man, and certainly not stupid—he means well, but sometimes when you want something badly, like he does to end this war, it colors your judgment. You know he shouldn't go running loose through Cholon and dismissing his security—well, it's the same kind of thing he's doing now with Lacouture; it's dangerous. Now you tell me, Corporal—you were on the DMZ, you know this enemy: are they interested in peace talks? Do you see them 'negotiating' to end the war? These are the bastards who send sappers with satchel charges into our wire. You've fought them, do you think they're interested in sitting down to compromise with Ambassador Marshall?"

"No, sir," Mead said truthfully.

"That's right, they're not. They're going to lure him into a meeting to kill him or capture him. And how's that going to look, the personal representative of the President of the United States captured by the enemy—with you there too, by the way?"

Mead nodded. It made sense. Lord was right again, as he always was—right even that there was going to be a meeting and that Marshall had agreed to it.

"Well, I'm not going to let it happen, Corporal. I don't

care if the ambassador wants to go to that meeting, I'm not going to let him; I've got a higher duty. I'm not going to let him get captured or killed, and you're going to help me."

"Yes, sir."

"I talked with the ambassador today, you saw me in the office, and I warned him about Lacouture, but I don't think I convinced him. I think he's determined to meet with the communists and he's going to try to hide it from us—he's going to run off to some secret meeting with them and do everything he can to prevent us from protecting him. You, one Marine with a rifle, are not going to be able to save him once he's surrounded by a thousand gooks. But you can save him beforehand; you might be the only one who can, because just by a stroke of luck, by unbelievable coincidence, that faggot Lacouture has fallen in love with your ass."

Mead looked away in great embarrassment.

"Hasn't he?"

"Well . . . yes, sir, I guess so."

"Look, Corporal, in this business you take what you can get—things aren't usually so easy or convenient. This is a godsend, and it's our only chance to find out exactly what is going on. You're going to get Lacouture to tell you, and I don't care how you do it . . . but *you will* do it. You *will* get me that information—if you have to fuck him in the ass, or if he wants to buttfuck you, I don't give a shit, just get me that information, understand?"

"Yes, sir."

"I want to know when the meeting is scheduled, where, and with whom. Got it? Who, where, when. Repeat that."

"Who, where, when, sir."

"You have any questions, Corporal?"

Mead shook his head, then asked tentatively, "How long do I have, sir, I mean to get the information?"

"Not long. Marshall is probably getting a message to Lacouture now, telling him that he's willing to meet with the communists. Lacouture will have to get the message to the communists, then they'll have to arrange the site and get everything ready, then get word back to Lacouture. I'd guess three or four days—no more than a week, so you'd better get busy. You seduce that son of a bitch so that he tells you everything."

"Yes, sir." Mead was too stunned to say anything else, or tell Lord that it was he who was taking the message to Lacouture.

"We understand each other?" Lord asked, eyes locked on Mead.

"Yes, sir."

Lord stood. "Good. Then there isn't any need for me to apply any pressure. I don't need to resort to anything crude like threats. I'm glad, because I hate that—I like reason and intelligence, not force and violence. You have to use violence when you can't reason, when intellect fails. I'm glad that's not the case here—otherwise it would get messy."

Lord glanced toward the door, then back to Mead, and his eyes were cold and vicious. "And she's such a beautiful woman."

He stared Mead down, forcing him to look away, then he walked out, closing the door softly behind him.

Mead would get him the information, Lord knew—if there was any information. With Kim dead, the communists would call off a meeting, fearing that it would be compromised, but that made no difference as long as Marshall still believed there was going to be a meeting, for he, Lord, would have his own people in place for the ambush. The Special Branch owed him many favors and were, after all, on the payroll. But it was essential to know what passed between Marshall and Lacouture so that if a time and place were arranged, it would be his people there, not the NVA.

Everything was falling into place, Lord thought; having the added leverage of Mead's woman was making this most simple.

Thirty minutes, he guessed—that's how long it would take Mead to leave for Lacouture's. He looked at his watch to time his accuracy after he had found a place down the street where he could wait without being seen.

He wished he could get inside Lacouture's house so he could hear that scene; the dumb Marine and that terrified little fag—that should be quite a show, he thought.

* * *

After Lord left, Mead sat perfectly still for several minutes trying to sort through everything.

Did he have any choice? No, he had to do exactly what Lord told him.

Though he somehow didn't trust Lord, he did see the sense in what he said: it would be just like Ambassador Marshall to fall for a trap like that. And Lord was right, the gooks weren't interested in any peaceful settlement—they were out to win. The one part of Lord's story that really bothered Mead was about Lacouture; he couldn't see the funny little Frenchman as a communist agent. Lacouture did admit that he bought and sold information, which probably meant that he got some money from the communists, but that would be like Han humping every different Marine—it was just to get by, not because she wanted to.

If Lacouture was setting up a meeting between the communists and Marshall, it probably was just for the money—he couldn't be in on trying to kill Marshall.

But what did he, Mead, really know? He hadn't been right about anything; he was always guessing wrong. Here he was just about to deliver a message for Marshall that would probably get him killed or captured.

Thank God for people like The Phantom, he thought, people who were really smart and knew what was going on, who could think ahead and outguess the enemy. Without them we would never win, he thought, because people such as himself weren't smart enough, and people such as Marshall—well, they could be fooled and tricked too easily, but no one was going to put one past The Phantom. He liked Marshall better, and maybe didn't even like Mr. Lord after all, but that didn't make any difference—some things were more important than liking.

Things like . . . with Lacouture. Homosexuality was as alien to him as geometry—he simply could not imagine it. Why would a man be interested in another man's body? That they kissed or were physical in the way men and women were together was beyond conception to him. It was so beyond his ability to envision that it was not even repulsive to him. Killing was terrible, but he knew about that and could understand it. Stealing, lying, all the bad things, he understood those—but not homosexuality; that was like child molesting—he knew it existed, but he could in no way identify with it.

Yet Lord had told him to go to bed with Lacouture. Could he? Could he touch him, or let Lacouture touch him?

But he had to get the information; he had to save Marshall. Every day he liked Marshall more; he would do anything to save him. It wasn't necessary for Lord to have threatened Sung, though he knew Lord meant it. There was no doubt in his mind that Lord would harm Sung if he didn't do what Lord wanted, and there was no way he could protect or save her from him.

He sighed and rested his head on his folded arms on the table. He wished he wasn't a part of this; it was too far beyond him—everyone was using him and he didn't understand it.

Suddenly the door opened and Sung came in quietly. She stood behind him, then tentatively reached out and touched his shoulder.

"Are you all right?" she asked.

"Yeah," he said without raising his head. "I'm just not smart enough for any of this. I wish everybody would just leave me the fuck alone."

"He is not a nice man," she said.

Mead shook his head. "No, I guess he isn't, but then I guess the nicest people don't come to wars, do they?"

"You came. I think you are nice," she said.

He looked up. She smiled slightly, and he was so overcome that he turned away, then he turned back and rested his head against her side.

"I'm so confused," he said. "I don't know what to do."

She stroked his head gently. "Do what you think is right, Ron."

"But I don't know what that is," he said agonizingly.

"I would trust you to do the right thing, whatever it is." Then after a moment she added, "But not that man."

Mead looked up. "Was he bad to you?"

She shook her head. "He just . . . looked through me. I liked the other man better."

"What man?"

"Oh," she said in embarrassment. "I forgot." She pulled Lacouture's card from her blouse and handed it to him. "This man came early today. He was a strange sort of man, but I liked him."

Then she brought her hand before her mouth to suppress a laugh. "He came to see you; he was almost crying he was so worried. He said he had to see you, that it was very important. We were talking, then Bill came in. He was nearly naked, carrying his rifle, and the little man nearly fell off his chair he was so frightened, and Bill was so terrible to him."

"I can imagine," Mead said, smiling.

"He is a Frenchman, and he begged me to tell you to go see him."

"And you liked him?" Mead asked curiously.

She considered a moment, then nodded. "Yes. He seemed nice."

Mead grinned. "Like me?"

"I do not think he is like you," she said with a smile, "but I think he is nice."

"What did you talk about?"

"About Vietnam. He has been here most of his life. He knew my home, Ban Me Thuot—maybe his father even knew my grandfather. He speaks good Vietnamese and just seemed . . . kind."

"Would you trust him?"

She thought a long moment. "Less than you, but more than the other man."

Mead took a deep breath and stood up. Now where was he? he wondered. He liked Lacouture more than Lord too, and maybe even trusted him more, yet Lord said he was a communist agent trying to kill Marshall. What was he to believe?

He pulled Sung close to him. She did not stiffen or flinch, but neither did she respond. He held her for a long time and leaned his head down so that it rested on hers.

"God, I don't want to leave," he said, pulling her tighter. "I don't want to do this."

She did not say anything, but sensing his sorrow and need, she brought her arms up around him.

He kissed her hair, then moved away. He grabbed his rifle, then went to the door. "I'll see you later," he said.

When the cab dropped Mead off on the street before Lacouture's house, he paced up and down the block twice, so distracted that he didn't notice Lord observing him from a car.

Finally he entered the immaculate courtyard and knocked on the door.

There was no answer, but Mead could tell someone was inside; he could hear faint stirrings and saw a window curtain move.

"Mr. Laco . . . Bernard, it's me, Corporal Mead."

There was an immediate scrambling at the door, and countless locks unfastened, then the door was thrown open and Lacouture rushed out.

He grabbed Mead, holding him tightly. "Oh, Mr. Mead, dear Mr. Mead! You came. I knew you would. You are so kind, so wonderful! You came to save me."

Mead stood stiff and awkward, but he did not push Lacouture away.

Lacouture held on. He was shaking, and when he looked up, Mead saw that he was stricken in fear and had been crying.

"Are you all right?" Mead asked.

Lacouture looked about quickly, then pulled him inside and fastened up all the locks.

When he finished, he clutched his chest, then turned to Mead. He clasped his hands in happiness.

"You came. You really came to see me." He hugged Mead in gratitude, and Mead forced himself to stand still.

"I knew you would come, I just knew it. I was so worried, but all the time I knew you would come." He grabbed Mead's hands. "And your woman—she is so nice."

Lacouture swatted him on the arm. "You must be good to her. I mean it; she is a lovely person." He swatted Mead again. "She isn't a whore."

"I know," Mead said, trying not to laugh. "I told you that."

Lacouture shook his finger in his face. "You be good to

564

her. Don't chase whores." Then he jabbed his finger into Mead's crotch. "You keep it in your pants, except for her."

"She liked you too," Mead said.

Lacouture held his hand over his heart. "Really?" Then he pulled out his handkerchief and dabbed at his eyes. "She is so lovely."

"Jesus," said Mead with a grin. "I only been here one minute, and already you're crying."

"I always cry."

"I know," Mead said.

"Some people *should* cry—if you were me, you would cry too."

"Does it do any good?"

"Oh, yes!" Lacouture said happily. "It's the only way I can bear things."

Then he grabbed Mead's hand and led him through the foyer. "I want to show you everything in my house—all my treasures. Have you eaten? I will feed you—I am a great chef; I can do . . . french fries. Hah! Your rifle, we must do something with it. Ah! The umbrella stand, put it in there."

He fluttered nervously about Mead, again and again reaching out to touch him, as though to test his reality.

"A drink!" Lacouture shouted, slapping his head. "What a host I am. What do you want? Ah! Champagne."

"A beer would be great."

"Pah! I have champagne—wonderful champagne, as good as the ambassador's. Have you drunk his too?" Lacouture shook his finger at him, then tweaked his cheek. "Hah! You thought I didn't know? That's why you didn't want to talk about your work."

"Didn't know what?" Mead asked.

"You didn't think I knew that you were Ambassador Marshall's bodyguard."

"Sure I did—I thought that's why you sent that gook to my place. You know, the one with the teeth. I thought you were trying to get to Ambassador Marshall through me."

"Oh, no," said Lacouture. "I was only interested in you—I told you, your body. I only just learned that you worked for Ambassador Marshall."

He turned anxiously to the door, then he sank down in a

chair and pulled out his handkerchief again. "And Kim, poor dear Kim is dead. Murdered!"

"The gook?"

"Yes, the silly little gook," sobbed Lacouture. "He was my friend. My only friend." He convulsed in the chair.

"Who killed him?" Mead asked, sitting down in a chair next to him.

Lacouture looked up, eyes flashing. "The most evil man in the world, the most hateful person—the same person who is trying to kill me."

"Who's that?"

Lacouture leaned forward and grabbed Mead's hands. "I mean it, he's trying to kill me. That's why I went for you. For help. You are the only person who can help me. You said you would be my friend."

Lacouture clutched Mead's hands desperately, and his eyes were pleading. "Were you mocking me? Were you making fun of me? You said you would be my friend. I don't have any friends. I have no one I can go to for help. Please help me. I am silly and foolish and a hateful homosexual, but please help me."

"Jesus," said Mead in embarrassment, trying to extricate his hands.

Lacouture clung to him. "Will you help me?"

"Yes. Jesus, okay, I'll help you."

Lacouture brought Mead's hands to his lips and kissed them over and over, until Mead wrenched them away.

Lacouture fell back into the chair, holding his hand over his heart. "You don't know what it's like to be so afraid. You're brave, a hero; I'm not. I shake constantly. Look at my hands—I can't even hold a glass. A car goes by—I duck. When you knocked on the door, I almost fainted."

Mead turned away to hide his laughing.

"Don't laugh at me, it's true. Brave men can face death—everything is different for them. When I was a little boy, I ran away from everybody, and everybody was always laughing at me. I couldn't help it. My father was ashamed of me, but I still couldn't help it. I was a terrible coward, afraid of everything and everybody—mostly afraid that people would laugh at me because of the way I was. I didn't want to be the way I was. I didn't want to be a joke."

He buried his face in his hands.

"But you got over that," Mead said kindly. "You were brave about that—being the way you were; that took courage."

Lacouture looked up. "You are a very wise young man," he said. Then he sighed. "I don't know if I was brave; I just learned to face it, to accept the way I was. I learned to bear the laughter and jokes."

He shook his head. "But I was always a coward otherwise—I could never fight. I could never hurt anyone; I would cry first. So you see, that is why this is so terrible for me—to live in such fear. I can't stand it. That's why I went to you—because you are so brave and strong, and because you said you would be my friend—"

"Who's trying to kill you? Who killed the gook?" interrupted Mead.

The clock struck, and Lacouture gasped, whirling about. "The most terrible man—I mean it, a truly evil man. I am terrified of him."

"Who?" demanded Mead.

Lacouture looked about nervously, as though afraid to say the name. "Wilson Abbot Lord," he whispered finally, shuddering.

"Who?" asked Mead.

"Wilson Abbot Lord. Oh, you don't know him, but he's the most awful person. He is with your American CIA, and he killed poor dear Kim, and now he's going to kill me."

Lacouture was too upset to notice Mead's surprised reaction. "Why is he trying to kill you?"

"Because . . . it's so complicated, but I will tell you. You *must* know because he is going to kill your Ambassador Marshall too. And *chéri*," he said, grabbing Mead's hands again, "he was going to kill you too."

"Me?" Mead laughed.

"Yes! You laugh, but you don't understand how wicked the world is. You don't know what people will do. Killing means nothing to some—a life is meaningless. Because we are different, we care and have feelings, we think everyone else does—but it is not so. People kill for greed and gain—for themselves, and these are dangerous people, but only if you have what they want or get in their way. But then there are people who kill because they *believe* in something and justify their murders for some righteous cause."

Lacouture shuddered. "These are the real killers, the truly wicked people. Do you see what I mean? If you kill somebody for anger or jealousy . . ." He shrugged. "We can all understand that; it's terrible and wrong, but we know the emotions. To kill somebody for money—for personal profit, jewels or to get rid of a competitor, that is horrible and they should be guillotined, but again, it is understandable—we are all greedy and ambitious."

He raised his finger before Mead. "But to murder others for a belief, for a cause or an idea . . . that is the worst— because then there is no wrong or sense of guilt; it is all smug and self-righteous. You can murder people for anything— your religion, your country, because you don't like Jews or homosexuals or Gypsies, because you don't agree with their politics or their art or the fabrics they use—it makes no difference. You kill people because they worship a Moslem god, or because they subscribe to a different newspaper, or because they wear sandals—it is exactly the same. You are saying that 'I am right and you are wrong and therefore I am justified in killing you.' Criminals who kill for profit don't cause wars—thousands and millions of women and children and young men aren't murdered by them but by holy men and prophets, by statesmen and politicians, by *believers*—by people such as Wilson Abbot Lord."

"I still don't understand why he wants to kill you—or Ambassador Marshall, or me."

Lacouture stood up. "Now we have to talk! I have to tell you some things—things you should not know because they are dangerous, but which you must know now. But first we must have a drink. I feel so much better that you are here. I may even be able to eat something—I haven't eaten for days, I've been so frightened."

He pulled Mead up. "And I will show you my treasures—

all my lovely things, though I know you don't care a bit and will be bored."

"No," Mead said, standing and looking about politely. "I'd like to see your things. I never seen so much . . ." He grinned. "Stuff."

"Art!" admonished Lacouture, opening his arms on the room. "Beauty. Treasures. But first the champagne."

He brought Mead into the kitchen and pointed to the refrigerator. "You'll have to open the bottle. I will tell you how."

He got glasses, then showed Mead how to twist the bottle from the cork. "Now the treasures," he said after both glasses were filled.

"Every one means something special to me," Lacouture said as he brought Mead through the house. "But I have no one to show them to."

"Everything is really beautiful," Mead said.

"Some of it is very old, hundreds and hundreds of years old," Lacouture said.

Mead picked up an object and handled it admiringly.

"You would choose that, wouldn't you," said Lacouture, smiling. "It is a dagger-axe, called a *ko*. It's bronze, with a jade blade, and inlaid with turquoise on the handle. It's about three thousand years old."

"Three thousand?"

"Yes. It is from the Yin dynasty in China, around the twelfth century B.C."

Mead put it carefully on the table, but Lacouture gave it back to him.

"Please," he said. "Take it. It belonged to some warrior long, long ago. You should have it."

"Mr. La . . . Bernard, I can't take that. Jesus, what would I do with something like that?"

"Stab Wilson Abbot Lord with it!" Lacouture laughed. "No, but it is fitting you should have it. Truly." He took it from Mead's hand and placed it under the waistband of Mead's fatigues. *"Voilà!* See, it is meant for you."

"Really, I can't . . ."

Lacouture opened his hands on the room. "None of this

belongs to anyone. Of course I collected it—technically, it is mine, but really!"

Lacouture picked up a large bronze object. "This is a wine vase in the shape of a buffalo, well over three thousand years old, and that is a jade incense burner. Good for what to me? To hold my ashes soon?"

He put the vase down and shook his head. "These things have given me pleasure, but they are not *mine*—I'm just holding them; I'm the custodian for a short time. It's like land, the earth—so preposterous to believe that we, who will be here for a few years, *own* it, that a little temporary suzerain gives us the right to bomb it or pollute it or destroy it."

He touched Mead's arm apologetically. "Forgive me, I am boring you."

Mead shook his head. "No. You and Ambassador Marshall are the smartest people I know—I like listening . . . even if I don't understand everything. It's just . . . nice to hear things, to have somebody talk to you like you did understand."

Lacouture just stared at him, then he dropped his head. "I would give everything I have for you."

He sighed and looked about the room, then to Mead. "Everything here is beautiful—it is art; bronzes, jades, jewels . . . but it is metal and stone, cold and timeless."

He reached his hand up to touch Mead's cheek, then a finger brushed his lip, and Mead did not move.

"But they are nothing compared to love and feelings. They are not touch. They are not warm. They are nothing, not even an unfaithful kiss."

He stepped back, then picked up a worn, frayed puppet. "This is the most important thing I have."

"It looks very old too," Mead said.

Lacouture smiled. "Oh, it is, very—it was my toy when I was a child. It is Pierrot." He hugged the doll to his chest, then kissed him gently. "He had a tear dropping from his eye—I rubbed it away long, long ago, when I was a little boy, because I could not stand to see him sad. I loved Pierrot more than anything; I still do, more than all my treasures. I talked to him and told him everything, all my secrets and dreams. And he talked to me, I know he did."

Mead said softly, "I had a bear like that."

Neither spoke, then Lacouture sighed deeply. "This is too sad! More champagne." He rushed back into the kitchen for the bottle.

He poured their glasses full, then raised his. "To your health. No! To *my* health."

"Is he really trying to kill you?" Mead persisted.

"Yes! And now I will tell you about it."

Lacouture ushered Mead to a chair and pulled another close to it and sat down. "I will tell you everything, but I warn you, it is dangerous to know it."

He squirmed back in his chair, looked around nervously, then started.

"I told you that I was a spy, but not a real spy, a person who buys and sells information. I have been here forever—I was born in Vietnam. I know everybody; I speak all the languages. I don't have any politics. You would find that hard to believe, but you see, I'm not on anybody's side. I just try to live as best I can—I am not an American or a communist or a Vietnamese; I think it is all stupid."

"Okay, I get that," Mead said.

"People come to me because I am in the middle—the communists come for information—I sell it to them; your CIA comes to me—I sell them information. When people try to get messages to other people, they come to me because I am in the middle, and everybody knows that I do not have a side. I am like a whore—everybody comes to me for a service. I take their money, but I do not love them."

"Got that too," Mead said.

Lacouture lowered his voice and raised a warning hand. "Now is the part that is dangerous—for you. A very important communist wants to meet with Ambassador Marshall. They came to me to make the contact. I went to Ambassador Marshall. Kim was the one who ran the messages—I hardly could sneak back and forth through alleys."

"Why does the communist want to meet with Ambassador Marshall?" Mead was looking for the flaw in Lacouture's story; the communists were the enemy—Lord was not.

Lacouture shrugged. "Maybe they have a peace offering; maybe they are hoping to trick the Americans into a concession; maybe this one communist disagrees with the ones in Hanoi—after all, there are people who disagree about the war in your country, maybe the communists do also."

"But maybe they want to kill the ambassador, or capture him."

Lacouture waved his hand in dismissal. "That wouldn't make sense. What good would that do?" He leaned forward in his chair. "You decide; you tell me: what good would it do the North Vietnamese to capture or kill Ambassador Marshall? Would the Americans give up the war? Pay ransom? Or would it just make the Americans furious—wouldn't they instead drop more bombs and send more men, and fight longer and harder?"

Mead frowned. That made sense; but everything that everybody told him made sense. When he listened to Marshall, he thought he was right; when he listened to Lord, he believed that. Now what Lacouture told him sounded reasonable and correct. What would be the point in capturing or killing Marshall? Nothing about the war would change. Marshall was important, but Mead could see that it really made no difference if something happened to him, any more than it would if something happened to General Westmoreland—they would just replace him with another general. At least corporals and generals were alike in one regard, he thought.

"The communists wouldn't harm Ambassador Marshall —they want this meeting," continued Lacouture. "They have everything to gain by meeting with him—and everything to lose if something happened to him. And Ambassador Marshall wants to meet with them—for the same reasons: he's hoping to end the war, negotiate a peace, and he too would like to win some concessions from them."

Lacouture tapped his chest. "And I want them to meet, mostly because I will get a lot of money for having arranged the meeting—but also because I want to see the war end. Remember, this is my country too; I was born here."

"So why does the CIA guy want to kill you and Mr. Marshall?"

Lacouture stared at Mead for a long minute. "You are so handsome," he said admiringly. "And so nice," he added wistfully. "What will happen to you after the war? I wonder. I dreamed of taking you to the Riviera once." He sighed deeply. "I never learned what happened to Jacques—he was the Legionnaire I told you about. I wonder what the fate of warriors is after the war is over. Did Jacques grow old? I can't imagine, and surely he couldn't. Did he grow fat and sloppy and have a tedious job and a miserable marriage and wretched children?"

Lacouture pulled out his handkerchief and dabbed at his eyes. "And you too, *chéri*, who are so young and beautiful— what will time do to you? I weep to think about it. In twenty years where will you be, my beautiful boy? Oh, happy, I hope. Maybe married to that beautiful, kind girl, and with lovely children and in a nice house. Oh, I hope so, my dear." But then he began to weep because he could not see that at all.

Mead shifted uncomfortably, not able to imagine any future, let alone twenty years.

"About you and Mr. Marshall getting killed," he prompted.

Lacouture blew his nose loudly and put away his handkerchief. "Now pay attention, *chéri*, and think hard. If the communists want to have the meeting, and Ambassador Marshall wants to have the meeting, and I want them to meet—then who would not want them to meet? Who would try to stop Ambassador Marshall from meeting with the communists? Who would try to stop him from negotiating a peace with them?"

"Someone who didn't want the war to end. Or someone afraid that Mr. Marshall would . . . be tricked. Or make a mistake." He let out his breath slowly. "Someone like . . ."

"Mr. Lord. The CIA. *Voilà.*"

"Is that really possible?" Mead asked softly, almost in awe.

Lacouture laughed. "Hah! Ask him what he did to my poor Bui Cao Kim."

"Did he really kill him? Why?"

"I would bet my life on it. Why?" He tapped his head. "I know how Lord thinks. I can guess what he is up to. He needs the information about the meeting and Kim had just returned from seeing the communists. He needs to know about the meeting so he can arrange to have Marshall killed there, then blame the murder on the communists, and make Marshall look like a fool to have trusted them."

Lacouture jumped forward on the seat. "And he wants to kill me because I know all this. And how do I know it? Because he—Mr. Wilson Abbot Lord—came to me a month ago to trick the ambassador into believing there was going to be a meeting so that he could kill him. Lord offered to pay me a million dollars to arrange that, and he actually thought I was going to help him. Probably the plan was to have Marshall's helicopter crash, or be shot down, and the incredible part was that you would have been on it—I who was madly in love with you would have been responsible for sending you to your death."

So *that* is what Lieutenant Magnuson meant about the fuel line, Mead thought in amazement—the chopper had been sabotaged; Marshall and everyone on board was to have been killed. But Lord? Was it possible?

Lacouture shuddered. "You see, I never knew until today, until your dear sweet girlfriend told me, that you worked for Ambassador Marshall."

"You really didn't know?"

"No! I only wanted your body. You jumped into the cab I was in—I didn't stop for you. I didn't arrange that: you stopped the cab and jumped in. That's how I got your address, and that's all there was to it—I sent Kim to find out about you, then I offered you money. And *you* said you would be my friend. No one ever said that. In my whole life no one ever offered to be my friend, so that is why I went to you—to see if you really would be my friend, and help me."

Mead didn't say anything for a long minute, then he shook his head. "Jesus. This is too deep for me."

Lacouture gasped and jerked backward. "What! Then you won't help me? Oh, God, what will I do?"

"No, no," Mead said, "I meant that this is so confusing. I mean . . . I'm just a corporal. I'm not smart—shit, I'm a dummy. . . . And all this . . ." He jumped up. "God damn! I don't know what to do. I don't know who to believe. Fuck!"

Lacouture shrank back in the chair. He cowered when Mead looked at him furiously.

"Jesus," Mead said, shaking his head and sitting back down. "I'm not gonna hurt you. And yes, I'll help you, but I don't know how."

Lacouture jumped forward and grabbed his hands. "You will? You really will?" He smothered Mead's hands with kisses.

Mead pulled them away. "Cut that out. Now I got something to tell you. I got a message for you from Ambassador Marshall. He says his telephone is bugged, so he sent me to tell you personally." He pulled out the card Marshall had given him and showed it to Lacouture. "He said to tell you 'all right'—those were his words. He meant about the meeting. He told me to tell you that he wanted to have the meeting."

"Then you knew everything I told you?"

Mead shook his head. "All I know is what Mr. Marshall told me this afternoon—that you were arranging a meeting and that he wanted to go to it. He also said there were some people who didn't want him to go, but he didn't tell me who they were, and I don't think he believes they're trying to kill him—he just said that the meeting was important and could save many lives and that there were some people who didn't want his mission to succeed."

"Well, he's right, and that person is Wilson Abbot Lord, and you'd better tell him that."

"He might already know that," Mead said quietly. "He knows about the phone being bugged, and maybe his car. He's a real smart man."

"Yes, he is. And smart men often take foolish chances and don't realize how dangerous things can be. Smart men, especially smart good men, often underestimate smart evil men."

"Well, what should I tell him about the meeting?"

"The meeting! There won't be a meeting now. Wilson Abbot Lord saw to that nicely. He murdered Bui Cao Kim, the messenger. How am I to get a message to the communists? And do you think they'll be willing to meet, to send their high official, now that Lord and the CIA know about it?"

Lacouture collapsed back into the chair. "Everything is ruined, and I'll never get my money. Lord poisoned everything—it was very clever. He didn't want Marshall to meet with the communists, and now he won't because they would fear a trap."

"So should I tell Mr. Marshall that the meeting is off?"

Lacouture thought. He pulled out his handkerchief and wiped his forehead, then fanned himself with it. He thought furiously, flapping the linen faster and faster.

"No," he said at last. "Tell him there is no return message. I'll do what I can to get back into contact with them and see if they're still willing to meet." He shrugged. "I'll just have to see; maybe they will, maybe they won't. I'll try tomorrow —maybe somehow I can salvage my money. Believe me, I'll try. All that money—my retirement to Cannes."

He smiled sadly. "I was going to have you come with me. I had such wonderful plans and dreams. They never come true, do they?"

"I guess sometimes dreams do," Mead said.

"Have yours?"

"Well . . . I don't guess I have any dreams. I can't think of any. Well, one . . . it's about Sung, as a matter of fact. I kinda hope . . . . that it might work out."

Lacouture nodded. "I hope so too, for you." He tucked away his handkerchief and said matter-of-factly, "My dreams have never come true. They can't. I dreamed of being loved, and taken care of. I dreamed of having friends."

"I'm your friend," Mead said gently.

"Yes. Yes, you are," Lacouture said. "A very great friend."

"And I'll try to help you."

"Thank you."

They stared at one another for a long time. Lacouture felt Mead's overwhelming power and masculinity. He closed his eyes, then looked up into Mead's. "Would you do me a special favor?" he asked.

Mead was silent, then he said softly, "Yes."

Lacouture lowered his head and said tentatively, "Would you stay the night with me?"

He looked up pleadingly. "Please. I am so afraid. I haven't slept in days." He edged forward on his chair. "Please stay. I won't bother you—you can sleep in my bed; I'll sleep on the floor, or a sofa. And I'll get you up in the morning in time for you to go to work—I'll make you breakfast. Just stay—so that I can sleep. Please."

Mead nodded. "Yeah. Okay."

Lacouture clasped his hands together. "You will? Oh, wonderful. You are so kind. So good."

"But I gotta get up early. I have to be at the embassy by seven."

"I shall set the alarms now! It will be like Notre Dame, all the bells ringing." He rushed about the room setting clocks.

"Would you like something to eat? Something else to drink? Tell me what I can do for you."

"Nothing," Mead said. "It's nearly midnight, and if I gotta get up before six, I should be getting to bed."

"Of course, of course. I will show you where everything is." He led Mead through the house. "That is the bathroom—there are towels and soap. A toothbrush! Oh, there are new ones in the drawer, and toothpaste—everything you would need. And this is the bedroom."

"Jesus," said Mead. "I never saw a bed like that—it looks like . . . a ship, with sails."

"It's a canopy bed. Do you like it?"

"Well, it's kinda . . . pink, and . . ." He poked the mattress. "It'll be okay."

"And I'll sleep there." Lacouture pointed to an ornate velvet loveseat.

"I don't think you can fit on that," Mead said.

"It will be fine. I will sleep wonderfully—just having you here will make everything all right." He looked about in concern. "Except I have nothing for you to wear—no pajamas that will fit."

"I don't wear any," Mead said, then amended, "I mean, I'll just sleep in my skivvies."

"Oh, this is so wonderful," Lacouture said, scurrying about the bedroom, gathering sheets and blankets for his loveseat. "I haven't slept a minute in three days. I have been so terrified. I hear every sound on the street."

After readying his makeshift bed, he got out his silk pajamas and looked at Mead nervously. "Do you want to use the bathroom first?"

"Oh. Yeah. I just need to take a piss and brush my teeth."

When Mead returned, Lacouture had already changed into his pajamas and was under the covers of the loveseat.

Mead went to the window and looked out. "Maybe you oughta have bars put on this," he said. "It's right on the street, and anybody could get in."

"Bars wouldn't stop Wilson Abbot Lord," Lacouture said.

Mead scanned up and down the street. Everything was quiet; a few cars were parked along the street, but he couldn't see into them. He stripped off his fatigue top, unbloused his boots, then shucked off his trousers.

Lacouture shuddered at the sight of him. "You are beautiful," he whispered.

Surprised, Mead turned, but he didn't know what to say, and now self-conscious, he went to the light switch and turned it off. Then he got into bed.

Outside, Lord watched the light go out in the bedroom. He waited a few minutes, then started the car and drove away. Tomorrow, he thought in satisfaction, Mead would give him the information—then he would get rid of Lacouture permanently.

For the longest time, Mead lay awake. He couldn't sleep for Lacouture's thrashing to get comfortable. Finally he said, "Mr. La . . . Bernard. You can't sleep over there. For Christ's sake, get into the bed."

"But I . . ."

"It's okay," Mead said.

"I will stay to my side," Lacouture said, bringing his

blankets and pillow across the room. Then he crept into the bed and curled up, far to the edge.

Finally Mead fell asleep, but he woke several times when he heard Lacouture whimper and cry out.

Mead lay awake on his back. He turned to see Lacouture shaking in his sleep.

People shouldn't live in fear, he thought; it was an awful thing to see a man shaking like that. There was so much sorrow in the world—Sung and Lacouture, all the dead.

Then they all came to him, and he saw them as they had died, and he heard their cries and screams, saw the men he had killed, and the man in the tunnel begging to die.

Oh, God, he thought; he didn't understand any of it, or what he was to believe or what he was going to do—what to tell Lord and Marshall, or what he could do to help Lacouture, or what was going to happen to Sung.

Oh, shit, he thought silently to himself in the bed. He wished he had never come to war. He wished he had never grown up.

And then to his surprise, he was thinking of his bear, a stuffed small teddy bear, rubbed and hugged so much that its fur was worn smooth—he hadn't thought of it in years. He hadn't thought of his childhood in a long, long time.

Lying in the dark, he thought there was so much he didn't know or understand.

Beside him, Lacouture cried out and whimpered in fear.

Mead gazed at the sad shaking form, then he reached over and pulled Lacouture to him.

He brought him close and let Lacouture's head rest against his chest; Lacouture sighed and snuggled into him.

Mead cradled him in his arms, and looking down on the sleeping head, he realized that though there was so much he didn't know or understand, there was nothing wrong in this.

Then he fell asleep too.

CHAPTER

• 36 •

Frizzell and Sutherland huddled together on the forward slope of the hill, staring out onto the dark plain. It was nearly midnight, but neither was sleepy.

"I almost wish we still had patrols," Frizzell said. "Then I'd be more tired."

"It's fine with me that we don't go out the wire anymore," Sutherland said. "Let the gooks come to us; I'm not interested in going out to them."

"But it's so fucking boring. And I've read those skin mags a hundred times. You can look at cunt just so many times."

"I could look at it forever."

Frizzell gazed up at the stars that he now knew were only hidden behind clouds on dark nights, and he remembered something. "One of Carver's magazines had a story on science in it. I'm kinda interested in science. I was thinking of taking one of those matchbook science courses. So I could get my high school diploma."

"What good would that do?"

"It'd be something; a guy's gotta do something. Anyway, there were things in the story that even Coney didn't know. God, that poor bastard—he's got bunker watch. When I had it the other night, I almost shot Brock. I ain't never heard anyone snore like that. I don't know how the lieutenant stands it."

Sutherland sneered. "I been through mortar attacks quieter than that. Stupid lifer. So what was in the story?"

"Lots of things. Questions you never even thought of."

"Like what?"

"Okay, see if you can answer any of them: which way does the Earth turn?"

"Whadda ya mean?"

"Which way does the Earth go round. East or west?"

Sutherland pictured a green globe from geography in his mind. "Ah . . . left I guess."

"You mean it turns west to east."

"Yeah. It turns east."

"You're right."

"Yeah?" Sutherland said with surprised pleasure.

"It turns on an axle west to east."

"How about that shit." He sat up straighter. "Ask me something else."

"Okay. How come a sundial isn't an accurate time measurer?"

"'Cause sometimes it rains."

"Well, yeah, but another reason."

"The sun don't shine at night."

"Yeah, but another reason."

"Well, shit, I just gave you two reasons."

"There's another."

"Okay, I give up."

"Because the Earth turns on an elliptical orbit."

"What does that mean?"

"I don't know, but that's the answer."

"That was a chicken-shit question. Ask me another."

"I can't think of any more."

Sutherland rested back and stared up at the stars. "I took a science course in school once. We cut up frogs."

"Why?"

"I don't know. I just cut the little motherfuckers up. You wouldn't believe the shit that's inside a frog. You were supposed to learn about all what's inside." He shook his head at the memory. "They really stunk. I hate dead things."

Frizzell was silent a moment, thinking of the dead and the priest. "Where do you think the dead go, Scott?"

"Home."

"No, I mean afterwards. To heaven, or something like that?"

Sutherland shook his head. "I can't see it—I mean playing a harp and singing. Who wants that shit? Heaven should be lots of cunt. And food." He groaned and sat up. "Oh, man, food. Can you believe we used to eat real food—hamburgers and fries. And breakfast. Oh, man—an egg. And bacon. I'd kill for some bacon."

Frizzell glanced at him slyly, then turned away and said casually, "Gee, I wish I'd known that, I could have got you some."

Sutherland looked up. "What? Bacon?"

"Sure. I'da had my grandfather send some seeds. They'd grow here."

Sutherland just stared at him. "What the fuck are you talking about now?"

"Bacon. We could have planted some."

"Planted!"

"Well, sure. How else you think you get bacon?"

"From a pig, you dumb fuck!"

Frizzell started to laugh. He grabbed his sides, then he fell over. "Oh, my God."

"What are you laughing at?"

"I'm laughing at you. A pig!" He rolled on his side, choking with laughter. "Bacon doesn't come from pigs."

Sutherland eyed him suspiciously. "Where does it come from then?"

"You really don't know?"

"I know all right: it comes from pigs."

"Jesus, Scott, don't ever say that to the other guys; they'd laugh their asses off at you."

"Then where does it come from?"

"A bush."

"What!"

"From a bush. A bacon bush."

Sutherland howled, "Are you shitting me?"

582

"No, bacon grows on a bush."

"You're putting me on."

"Listen, I know about farms. Where do you come from—Los Angeles? What do you know about farm things? Bacon comes from bushes, just like corn and wheat."

"I don't believe you."

"I swear to God. My grandfather has hundreds of them. Every spring we plant them. It grows on bushes, in strips, and when you harvest it, you pull the slices off the limbs. They have a hard covering, but they got machines that strip 'em, kinda like shelling them."

Sutherland was silent. He thought for a full moment trying to picture a bacon bush. Frizzell was too stupid to be putting him on, but . . . where had he heard about bacon? He stared into Frizzell's face, debating the possibilities, then he asked, "What comes from a pig then?"

"Pork chops, ham, that shit we eat in the cans—pork slices."

Sutherland considered him for several minutes. "Are you sure about bacon?"

"Of course I am. I planted and picked thousands of them. Who ever told you it came from a pig?"

Sutherland tried to remember about bacon. "I don't know," he said at last. "I just always thought it came from a pig though."

"Lots of guys who don't come from farms don't know about things like that. But I don't know anything about cities either. I mean, I'd be lost in L.A."

Sutherland studied his face again, then said dubiously, "I guess."

Frizzell heaved a deep sigh and lay back, his hands behind his head, staring up at the stars. "You know, tomorrow is Thanksgiving. I used to love that. The trees would have changed; everything was cold and crisp. Pumpkins. Fuck! Remember pumpkins? And we'd have this great dinner. And all my aunts and uncles would come. And we'd have the biggest turkey. My mom would start cooking it early in the morning, and all day you could smell it. And we'd sit around the table and my grandpa would give a blessing, mumble something nobody ever understood, except you really knew you were thankful, not like other times, just saying it to get it over with."

Frizzell shook his head in happy memory. "It was really special. Did you ever feel that way, Scott?"

Sutherland thought a moment. "Nope." Then he added in consolation, "But it sounds real nice. Around my house—well, there wasn't much at Thanksgiving. It was like most of the rest of the times. Usually just a lot of fucking noise and screaming."

"Didn't you even have a turkey?"

"My mom couldn't cook shit. I can't imagine what she'd of done with a turkey. Hell, she couldn't even fry bacon."

He was silent a long minute. Finally he said, "Les?"

"What?"

"Were you shitting me about a bacon bush?"

Frizzell closed his eyes on the stars and smiled. "Yes."

Sutherland nodded. "I knew it all along."

In the underground bunker, Bishop stared through the starlight scope to the seared moonscape. There was enough illumination from the stars to clearly see the ridge looming over the plain, forbidding and malignant. But there was no movement tonight, and he felt certain the enemy would not probe his position; the moon was nearly full, and the plain too exposed.

He lay aside the night-vision instrument and rubbed his eyes. Behind him, Coney made security checks on the radio, and in a corner, Brock was curled in his sleeping bag, snoring loudly.

Bishop knelt to light a heat tab under his canteen to make coffee. After the water boiled, he stirred in coffee granules, then held the canteen out to Coney.

Coney shook his head and nodded toward Brock. "That's enough to keep me awake, sir."

Bishop laughed. "I may have to call in an air strike to drown him out." Then he picked up the starlight scope to scan the plain again.

Coney watched him, then asked, "Do you think they'll overrun us, sir?"

"I don't know," Bishop said. Then he smiled faintly. "I'm just a lieutenant."

Coney could sense his exhaustion, and the responsibilities he bore, a man only slightly older than himself, in whose hands all their lives depended.

"Lieutenant," Coney said in the dark bunker. "I . . . I know you . . ." He stopped, not knowing how to express himself. "We . . . all know you been trying . . ."

He shook his head. "Shit," he said, unable to express what he felt.

But it was understood. Bishop put down the scope but did not turn. "Thank you," he said quietly.

Then Coney dropped his head onto his knees. "God, I've done so many dumb things in my life." His voice caught. "I want to get them right. I want . . ." He closed his eyes. "I want to see my kid, Lieutenant."

Bishop did not turn. He knew the tears he would see, and he tried to hide his own.

He let out his breath slowly, and he said, for all their dreams, for all their lives, "Oh, God, I hope so."

Just then the radio came alive. "Bravo One, Bravo Six."

Coney held the handset out to Bishop.

"Bravo Six, Bravo One."

"Bravo One, I want you to plan a Lima Papa for tomorrow night."

"Bravo Six, that isn't necessary. We can't go out more than five hundred meters, and the wire would pick up any movement."

"Bravo One, why am I always repeating myself to you? I want an LP out tomorrow. It's Thanksgiving. The gooks will think we're off our guard."

"Bravo Six, I don't think the gooks have any idea what Thanksgiving is."

"Bravo One, this is the *last* repetition—send out an LP tomorrow. Out."

Brock had rolled over to listen. "He's going to be a general someday. Imagine outguessing the gooks about Thanksgiving. I never would have figured that. But they're probably waiting for tomorrow. Be just like those sly little fuckers. I wonder how come they missed Halloween and Valentine's

Day? Lulling us probably. Crafty little bastards. Nobody's going to put anything past Captain Willis."

"Shut up, Gunny."

"I'm just admiring his way of thinking—officers are so much smarter than the rest of us. I guess it's college that does it. You really got to hand it to him. I guess that's why you'll be a lieutenant forever—you don't pick up on these things. You better start concentrating, Lieutenant."

The next night Bishop donned his field jacket and strapped the radio to his back. He checked his rifle and took two extra magazines of bullets.

Brock watched from his corner. "Now what, Lieutenant?"

Bishop blackened his face and arms. "I'm going on an LP."

"You?"

"I'm not going to send anybody out on Thanksgiving, not to sit outside the wire. Nothing's out there tonight. This is just bullshit."

"But an order."

"Right. So somebody's got to go. I'll sit out there. Hell, if anything happens, it's only five hundred meters—I can run that in a minute flat."

"Lieutenant, you shouldn't do this."

"I'm just moving the command post forward five hundred meters—it'll be an LP/CP."

"Jesus, Lieutenant. . . . I know, I know, it's an order." He struggled up, put on his flak jacket, and grabbed his rifle.

"Where do you think you're going?"

"On an LP, Lieutenant." Then he shook his head in disgust. "Officers are so fucking crazy."

They notified the posts of their movement, then threaded their way down the slope, through the maze of trip wires and flares.

They sat out for two hours, calling security checks, staring over the empty plain.

At midnight, Brock said, "Happy Thanksgiving, Lieutenant."

Bishop laughed.

Brock shook his head. "And merry fucking Christmas while we're at it."

In their bunker, before Coney and Sutherland went to sleep, Frizzell took a small package from under his gear and carefully unwrapped it. He fondled the small tin of turkey lovingly.

"Where'd you get that?" Coney demanded.

Frizzell opened the tin and smelled, closing his eyes to savor it. "My mom sent it to me. I been saving it."

"I'll buy it from you."

"No. Fuck no."

"C'mon. I gotta have some turkey and my wife didn't send me anything."

"So?"

"So I'll buy it from you. Ten bucks. Twenty bucks. C'mon, Frizzell. It really means something to me."

Frizzell held the tin to his nose. "Ah, man, this sure beats pork slices."

"You asshole."

"Why should I sell it to you?"

"Real buddies don't sell things to one another," Sutherland said from his corner.

"Okay," Coney said. "Then give it to me. If you were really a buddy, you'd do that, Frizzell."

"*Real* buddies wouldn't ask for something like that," Frizzell said. He cradled the tin of turkey in his hands. "I love Thanksgiving," he said simply.

Then he handed the tin to Coney.

Coney just stared at Frizzell. "You dipshit," he said finally.

Then he cut the turkey three ways and handed the meat to Sutherland and Frizzell.

CHAPTER

• 37 •

Mead didn't arrive at the embassy until after eight. Lacouture, an apron around his waist, had fussed endlessly over breakfast, setting the table, bringing out jams and breads, insisting that Mead eat properly before rushing off.

Then Mead got caught in traffic.

When Mead entered the office, Dolores Toland said sweetly, but very loudly, "Why, Corporal Mead, what brings you in? Is the PX closed for inventory?"

"Where the hell have you been?" shouted Colonel Waggoner, coming from his office at Dolores's voice. "The work day begins here at seven. Did you have another engagement? Are your duties interfering with your social life? I'm so sorry to be inconveniencing you."

"Sir, I'm sorry, I . . . I don't have any excuse, sir."

"I know you don't. Your job is to guard Ambassador Marshall—that means your presence is required. Do you happen to know where he is right now?"

Mead pointed toward Marshall's office. "In there, sir?"

Waggoner shook his head. "No. The personal representative of the President of the United States is waiting for you at Tan Son Nhut. The driver went early to pick you up this morning, first to the barracks, then your off-base hovel, but you couldn't be located. You see, the ambassador is flying this morning to Cam Ranh Bay; we thought it might be nice to have you accompany him."

"Cam Ranh Bay, sir?"

"Yes, Corporal—then to the Central Highlands. You see, the ambassador has a long itinerary, many places he must go this month. Foolishly, we didn't consult you on his travel plans, so the driver picked up Ambassador Marshall without you. He is there, Colonel Romer is there, the pilot is there, the helicopter is there—all waiting for you. Of course, I suggested they leave without you and let me court-martial your ass, but the ambassador said he would wait. Is it convenient for you now to go out to the air base?"

"I'm sorry, sir; I just didn't know."

"Did you know that you are supposed to be here every morning at seven to pick up the ambassador?"

"Yes, sir."

"Well?"

"No excuse, sir," Mead said, standing at attention.

Waggoner shook his head. "Jesus, and you look like shit—you haven't shaved, your boots and brass . . . where the hell were you?" Then he remembered Dolores was in the room. "Never mind, and forget about shaving; just get your ass downstairs. The car is waiting to take you out to the air base."

"Yes, sir," Mead said, starting for the door, then he stopped. "Is this going to be an overnight trip, sir?"

"Cam Ranh Bay? Corporal, this is for a week."

"A week, sir?"

"Is that inconvenient, Corporal?"

"Well, sir . . . no, sir," and he ran out the door.

Oh, no, Mead thought, racing down the corridor, then riding the elevator downstairs. A week. What about Sung— he hadn't told her a thing. What would she do? Who would take care of her? And she didn't have any money; nothing. And Lacouture. And Lord. He was supposed to see Lord. Lord had threatened Sung if he didn't get the information. Jesus, Jesus, he thought in agony.

He had to get word to Sung so that she wouldn't worry. Lacouture would just have to wait, and Lord would learn what had happened. Money, he thought anxiously; he had to get some money to Sung. He looked in his wallet and found only five dollars in scrip.

At the Marine guard booth he called the barracks. Bill Catton wasn't there, but he got another friend to promise to go by his place and tell Sung what had happened and to give her money.

"I'll pay you as soon as I get back, I promise."

"No problem, got you covered," his friend said.

"Make sure he does it," Mead told the Marine at the booth, "or I'll kill both of you when I get back."

"What has she got, a magic cunt?—I never seen you fall for a woman like that." Then he held up his hands to calm Mead. "Take it easy, just joking—we'll get her some money; she'll be okay."

Mead rushed through the door, then down the stairs to the waiting car, which pulled away as soon as he got in, at the same time that Wilson Abbot Lord's car entered the embassy compound.

Lord saw Mead drive off in the ambassador's car, but without Marshall in it. His first call upon entering his office ascertained the information about Marshall's departure and field visit.

Though Dak To was not listed on the ambassador's itinerary, Lord knew he would go there, and a visit to that military disaster alone would sink the COVIA study. Marshall had gotten Johnson to delay action on the study's recommendations on the mere basis of a suggestion; Lord now saw how influential he was with the President, and that an emphatically negative report to Johnson would kill sending the reinforcements.

Although he had not underestimated Marshall's influence, he was nevertheless surprised by its effect on the President, and to hear the bantering manner the two had. He, Lord, had been right about Marshall—he was the most dangerous man in Vietnam, and he had to be stopped at all costs.

"Shit," he said aloud, a rare expletive for him. He wanted the information about Lacouture from Mead, but it was too

late now to catch Mead. He did not have a week to wait until
his return; he had to know immediately what Lacouture was
up to, and to arrange the "meeting" between Marshall and
the NVA: Marshall had to be discredited, and he had to die.

It would help to know what Mead had learned, but it
was not essential—he could get the information from Lacouture. It would be messier this way, but if he handled it
himself, there would be no mistakes and there would be the
added satisfaction of personally getting even—and he
looked forward to that.

Mead scrambled onto the helicopter and saluted everyone
apologetically.

"I'm really sorry, sir. I beg your pardon for keeping you
waiting. I . . . I don't have any excuse, sir."

"You don't?" Marshall smiled. "Oh, surely there must be
some good story, Corporal."

Magnuson spoke over the intercom. "I want to hear it too,
so talk loudly, Corporal." Then he said snidely, "Colonel
Romer, since you're so interested in everyone's extracurri-
cular activities, you ought to check out Corporal Mead's
girlfriend—she makes Dolores look like leftovers. I'm surprised he showed up at all—I wouldn't have."

Then, as Mead crimsoned, Magnuson started the engine,
and the chopper roared alive.

Mead strapped himself in, then riveted his attention on
his boots.

Marshall watched him in amusement, confident that he
had made contact with Lacouture and would relay the
message to him as soon as they were alone. Surely by the
time he returned to Saigon next week, Lacouture would
have been able to arrange the meeting. It would mean
staying beyond Christmas, but that didn't matter if there
was a chance to negotiate peace. He sensed Johnson's
desperation and frustration over the phone, and he wanted
so badly to help. He realized what a presumptuous condition he had made to the President—that LBJ not seek
reelection and voluntarily step aside if he didn't withdraw
the troops on Marshall's recommendation. Even to himself

it reeked of sanctimony—and now he had the obligation to do everything he could to help Johnson end the war. This visit to the field should provide him with all the information that Johnson would need, he thought, and the observation at Dak To would give him a firsthand view of the fighting war.

Marshall's expectations for this trip were high because he had an understanding with Westmoreland—he would keep to his travel plans, and in return, Westmoreland promised that nothing would be staged for him.

"I've ordered everyone to make no special preparations for you; if you think you're being conned, let me know, and I'll court-martial the commanding officer," Westmoreland had said.

Looking out the chopper window as it skirted over the jungle that stretched to the coast, it was impossible for Marshall to think of Christmas only weeks away. But he didn't want to think about Christmas; Christmas was family, his children—Ryan, who would soon be flying over this same jungle, Ryan, who only yesterday surely squealed with joy at the tricycle Santa brought—oh, God, Marshall thought, the tricycle he had labored over for hours trying to assemble from directions written in secret code.

He laughed at that memory, on the rug before the Christmas tree, surrounded by tricycle parts, no two of which seemed to go together, and enough tools to build a Chrysler.

Oh, God, he thought again, the smile dying on his lips—Ryan, Ryan, you can't come to war.

Yet below, the war was as alien as Christmas.

The chopper had reached the South China Sea and was heading north up the coast. The white beach was like a ribbon separating the jungle from the brilliant azure water—a gorgeous scene of some Pacific paradise. Thatched huts and small fishing villages were the only signs of habitation, and they as removed from war as Polynesia.

The colors were mesmerizing, and Marshall leaned his head against the window—miles and miles of golden, untouched beach, an endless blue sea, and the jade earth.

There couldn't be a war down there, he thought; it was too

perfect, and there was beauty enough for all men that they did not need to fight over it.

He must have stared for over an hour, he realized, for suddenly he noticed the change—man's markings: spots of oil on the water, metal and plastic debris, then wreckage and shanties and the attendant litter of a major seaport.

As the chopper approached the massive military complex of Cam Ranh Bay, Marshall could hardly believe that in less than five years this natural harbor with its sheltered deep-water bay had grown from a sleepy fishing village to a twenty-thousand-man military base fifteen miles long and five miles wide—now the second-busiest port in Vietnam, with the third-largest air base.

There was no ceremony or honor guard upon arrival, and Marshall was met by the army and navy commanders, who assured him he could see whatever he wished whenever he chose—no preparations had been made for his visit.

"I was just on the phone with General Westmoreland," the admiral said. "I haven't been threatened with court-martial since I was an ensign."

They were shown to their billets in the Visiting Officers' Quarters, except for Mead, who was to be housed across base with the enlisted men.

"I hardly see the point of having a bodyguard two miles away; surely we can get him at least within sprinting distance. Besides, I need to keep my eye on him, and one of us here will have to give him a wake-up call—we can't afford to wait an hour on him again."

While his room was being readied, and the others got settled, Mead waited in Marshall's room.

"You should play poker, Corporal. Or be a diplomat—I can't tell anything from your face. Did you see Mr. Lacouture?"

"Yes, sir. I gave him the message. He said he would try to set up a meeting. He said he'd get a message to you."

"Thank you."

Mead did not tell him about Lacouture's fear, Kim's disappearance, and what Lacouture had said about Wilson Abbot Lord. He couldn't bring himself to implicate The

Phantom—besides, all he had to go on was Lacouture's accusations, and how could they be proved?

What he was going to tell Lord caused him great anxiety, and he was glad that he wouldn't see him for a week; he needed to think that out carefully.

The rest of the afternoon Marshall toured the harbor facilities where four thousand tons of cargo were unloaded daily—any and everything from bullets and bandages to stereo equipment and comic books. The troops might be away from home, he was told, but the supply line was bringing home to the troops—everything except their mothers and girlfriends. American troops in Vietnam were the best supplied in the history of warfare, they said, and he did not doubt it. He visited the Meadowgold dairy and ice cream factory, mess halls, clubs, recreation centers, and laundry.

Throughout the tour he kept wondering about the enemy —where were they? Hiding underground and supplied on foot by men sneaking down a jungle trail?

In the harbor he saw massive ships being unloaded, yet in his mind he pictured a barefoot man, artillery shells balanced on his shoulders, running down a path; he could even hear his footsteps and his labored breathing as he raced down the trail.

The next day that image was somewhat modified when he was briefed on the aerial war. He was told that earlier in the year, during a six-day bombing halt, the North moved approximately 25,000 tons of supplies down the Ho Chi Minh trail to the South—a daily tonnage that exceeded the unloading capacity of Cam Ranh Bay.

The CIA stated that the bombing was ineffectual—nearly a thousand planes had been shot down in the past year, and enemy MiG fighters were now so effective that more than half of the hundreds of Air Force planes that had been intercepted were forced to release their bombs early in order to get away. Even under the most optimistic damage estimates, the enemy was still moving more than five times what they needed to supply their forces in the South.

Though the statistics were staggering, the tonnage of bombs dropped beyond comprehension, one figure made an impression on Marshall—it cost ten dollars to inflict a dollar's damage to the North.

Marshall confided to Romer later that he had been naïve in his picture of the barefoot enemy soldier running down the trail.

"That's what they'd like everybody to believe," Romer said. "David against Goliath—except this David has surface-to-air missiles, rockets, MiGs, and a sophisticated supply system. Jane Fonda sees Sabu running naked down the trail, but Sabu is driving an eight-wheeler that was fork-loaded in Laos or Cambodia."

Early the next morning, the party took off for Nha Trang, the Special Forces headquarters.

"My son just wrote me that he's a Green Beret now," Marshall confided to Romer on the flight up.

"Jesus, what did you do to that kid?" Romer asked. "Even I with my nutty father stuck to the regular infantry. You probably shouldn't even see what goes on here—not that they're going to tell you what they're doing. And for sure you aren't going to be *shown* what they do."

Marshall looked at him questioningly.

"They're the CIA's private little army. Some of the units are legit, but some are no more than SS squads. That's probably been the main downfall of the Green Berets—they sold out to the CIA, or at least it's perceived that way; in any case, they work very closely together."

"The regular army doesn't like the Special Forces, do they?"

"It's the old story of elites and exclusiveness. When President Kennedy started them, everybody wanted to join—wear the green beret, jump out of airplanes; it was all macho and gung ho. Then it went to their heads, and a lot of resentment set in. It's still big in Hollywood and for PR, but it's a dead end for promotion: I wouldn't recommend it for your boy as a smart career move."

Marshall laughed. "I told him that in somewhat blunter terms. I think I used words like 'idiot' and 'jackass.' I may have thrown in 'dumb asshole' too—I can't remember clearly, since I was hysterical at the time."

"Well, at least you'll be able to meet his commanding

officers, and see the fine young Americans he'll be working with. You'll be able to chat about accommodations and food, recreational activities, hospital facilities—"

"If you say another word, I'll have you court-martialed. And seriously, don't mention that Ryan will be coming here—he'd never forgive me."

Just as at MACV headquarters, Marshall felt upon arrival that he had stepped onto a movie set, except here the sense of illusion was even more bizarre. In fact it was not so much movie as it was theater, he decided—Kabuki theater, with stranger costumes and makeup, exaggerated motions and gestures. Nobody walked—they strutted or swaggered or moved in some manner of stealth; nobody seemed to talk—they either shouted or used hand signals.

It was like some loony-bin Sparta—and all he could think of was his son arriving here in six weeks.

He was welcomed with gusto—everything was done with gusto—and not shown to his billet or asked if he'd like to rest or clean up, but taken immediately on a tour of the area.

Magnuson remained with his chopper, Romer and Mead were quickly separated from Marshall and put in a backup jeep, while three Special Forces officers rode off with him.

The first thing that struck Marshall was everyone's size— he had never seen so many large men—and the excellent physical condition they were obviously in. Then he was impressed with morale—the enthusiasm and esprit were not a show for him; it was real, he decided. These men believed in what they were doing; they liked it.

He saw training areas, watched hand-to-hand fighting, mock attacks on villages, practice ambushes, and obstacle-course movement with barbed wire and punji stakes. These were very tough young men.

In late afternoon they brought him and the others to their billets, and as they went up the stairs of the officers' quarters, two young men without rank insignia came out. They were laughing and pushing one another, but when they saw Magnuson, both stopped and called to him.

"Hey, Jimbo, where you been? We haven't seen you in a long time. You on some special op?"

Magnuson was behind Marshall and Romer so they couldn't see the quieting gestures he made to the two, but Mead did. Magnuson waved them off warningly; they picked up his meaning immediately and moved away.

"Good to see you again, Jimbo. Catch you at the club later—why don't you drop in tonight?"

"Who were the spooks?" Romer asked when they were gone.

"Just a couple guys I know," Magnuson said unconvincingly.

"So how do you know spooks, Lieutenant? You came down, so you say, from Da Nang. Okay, how come definite CIA types in Nha Trang know who you are?"

"What are you getting at, Colonel?" Magnuson said, taking the offense.

"It was a pretty straightforward question, Lieutenant—I want to know what your contact is with guys like that."

"Guys like what, sir?"

"Operatives: spooks, CIA agents, spies—those kind of guys, Lieutenant. I want to know your relationship with them."

"I don't think that's any of your business, Colonel—any more than who I'm fucking is your business. What you need to know is in my record."

Romer started down the stairs after Magnuson, and for a moment Mead thought they were going to fight, but Marshall said very commandingly, "Gentlemen, could you work out your problems on your own time?"

Romer turned and went back up the stairs. "We *will* discuss this further, Lieutenant."

Magnuson shrugged, and when Romer's head was turned, he rolled his eyes toward Mead.

"Rather than waste your time with a formal dinner, Mr. Ambassador," the senior Special Forces officer said, "we'd like to have you see as much of our operation as possible, and most of our work is done at night."

"I've already been on a night ambush, Colonel—down in the Delta last week; that was enough excitement to last me this war, thank you," Marshall said.

"That's not what we had in mind, sir. We'd like to chopper you out to some of our base camps. We do a lot of work with indigenous personnel—"

"Indigenous? You mean Vietnamese?"

"Yes, sir—Montagnards and others. It's perfectly safe, and I think it'd be informative. You could choose the location, and we'd drop in on them, see them as they really are, so to speak—see our young troopers working with the indig . . . Vietnamese. You could eat out there in the field— not as luxurious as it'd be here, but I think you'd find it palatable."

"Well, I'm here to see everything I can, so let's go."

"Excellent, sir. Since our pilots are more familiar with the area, we'll take you in one of our choppers—and you really won't be needing a bodyguard, sir. I hardly think you need a Marine when you've got us."

"Whatever you suggest is fine with me, Colonel. I'm sure Lieutenant Magnuson and Corporal Mead would rather stay here anyway. I'm sure they can find something to do."

"Good, then it'll be just you and Colonel Romer—how about in thirty minutes—will that give you enough time?"

"I'll be ready."

Mead was not happy when Marshall told him that he would remain back.

"Of all places, sir, I ought to be out with you in the field."

"Yes, but I think the Green Berets would be insulted if I took a Marine bodyguard with me—you see, they might get the idea that I didn't think they could protect me."

"Well, sir—"

"Corporal Mead, I want you to stay here. Go to the club, have a couple beers. You're not on duty tonight. Just don't get in a fight and hurt any Green Berets. If you feel some need to take care of somebody, keep your eye on Lieutenant Magnuson."

"Me, sir? I was planning to catch up on my reading. Maybe even go to chapel."

"Fine. Take Corporal Mead with you—I'll see you both in the morning."

Exactly thirty minutes later the colonel returned in a jeep and brought Marshall and Romer to the airfield. They were taken to a Quonset hut and introduced to another Special Forces officer and a CIA officer.

"We'll give you a short briefing so you'll know what to expect, then we'll take off, Mr. Ambassador," the colonel said, taking out laminated maps and spreading them on a tabletop.

"General Giap said that 'to seize and control the highlands is to solve the whole problem of South Vietnam.' That's been Giap's strategy for years, and that's how he beat the French. This whole area is called the Central Highlands. There are thirty-three primitive tribes here, which the French called Montagnards—mountain people. They've always been separate from Vietnamese culture and the old emperors left them alone. The French didn't have much to do with them either, and they've remained a distinct group."

The CIA agent took over. "Distinct, but not cohesive— they've fought continuously among themselves, and many tribes are bitter enemies. But in 1946, the communists made a concentrated effort to woo the Montagnards. They brought thousands of them to the North, training them as teachers and medical personnel, then sending them back as political agents. Though the communists have been successful, they haven't completely overcome tribal rivalries."

The third man began speaking in what was obviously a well-rehearsed performance. "Unfortunately, the South Vietnamese government hasn't been successful with the Montagnards. Their approach has been heavy-handed and corrupt, plus the government officials have the bad habit of referring to the Montagnards as 'moi,' which means 'savages.'"

The CIA agent interceded smoothly. "Our efforts began five years ago, and we've made good headway, especially with the Rhade tribe, which you'll see shortly, and the Hre tribe. Our approach is to live with them, adopt their methods and customs, and try not to force anything on them. This is one battle we are winning—even the Montagnards supporting the communists are realizing that a victory for the North will probably destroy their culture and that they have better hopes for autonomy with the South."

The colonel took over again. "The biggest problem, unfortunately, is with the South Vietnamese—we're having a helluva time getting the government and the military to respect their tribal and property rights."

Marshall nodded. "A situation somewhat analogous to our own dealings with our own 'moi.'"

The CIA officer smiled. "Exactly, and what we're trying to avoid is a Little Big Horn up here. Do you have any questions, sir?"

Marshall shook his head. "But I may after the visit."

The colonel gestured toward the door. "Gentlemen, let's go."

Indeed he did not need a Marine bodyguard, Marshall soon realized. There were two escort choppers, each with a platoon of Green Berets. The mood was so infectiously macho and upbeat that Marshall turned to the colonel and said, "Maybe we ought to scrub this visit and go up to Dak To. I hear that the 173rd Airborne is having a pretty rough time of it."

"Stupid Airborne bastards," the colonel said contemptuously.

But before he could add anything, the CIA officer interceded. "That's just professional competitiveness—the colonel feels his Green Berets could win it faster."

"Is it so bad at Dak To?"

The CIA agent shrugged. "I hear it's a good-sized battle."

Judging from that, Marshall thought, Johnson was probably more accurate in his assessment of the disaster than he realized; he would find out tomorrow.

When dropped into the Montagnard base, Marshall felt that he had entered a primitive world frozen in anthropological time.

While the Special Forces had equipped young Montagnards with camouflaged uniforms, given them rifles, backpacks, and boots, and taught them to use radios and call for artillery, the older men, the women, and children belonged to a near-naked society of bronze and bead trinkets and jewelry, body painting and tattoos, superstition and magic charms.

Marshall sat around a campfire in a tiny village of

thatched huts, with old men and women smoking pipes, and heard stories of gods and jungle demons, while behind him helicopters waited to whisk him away.

After a while, it made no sense to him and he could not concentrate on what he was hearing—the visual was too overpowering: air strikes, body counts, the Ho Chi Minh trail, communists, democracy, all drifted up with the smoke from the campfire around which naked children and bare-breasted women with teeth filed to the gums, earlobes stretched wide with ivory, stared at him curiously, alternating their glances from him to his helicopter in the clearing.

They returned very late; Marshall had no questions to ask when they landed, and when he fell asleep, he heard drums and reed music in his dreams.

Magnuson had banged on Mead's door earlier and barged in. "Let's go get something to drink—take your rank insignia off, and we'll go to the Officers' Club. No one will know, and no one will give a shit. Just make sure I get back safely, okay?"

"Yes, sir."

"And no 'sir' shit. We don't have rank tonight; all I want to do is get drunk. I don't have to fly tomorrow and you don't have to bodyguard, so let's get shitfaced. One thing though—don't let those guys we saw start talking to us."

"Aren't they friends of yours, si—"

"No more. I'm finished with that crap. I'm done with that CIA bullshit."

Mead leaned close to him and sniffed. "You been drinking already."

"That's right. You don't think officers get drunk? Jesus, you should have seen Luke Bishop. Talk about knee-crawling drunk . . ."

"Maybe we better not go to any club, Lieutenant. We could just get your bottle and sit around and—"

"Tell spy stories? You gonna tell me about Mr. Wilson Abbot Lord, Corporal?"

"I will if you will, Lieutenant."

"Sounds like we're gonna have us a real jerk-off session, Ron."

"I can handle that, Jimbo. If you're Lieutenant Bishop's best friend, I guess I can trust you."

"And if you saved his worthless ass, I guess I can trust you." Magnuson lurched toward the door. "I'll go get the bottle."

"We could go to your room."

Magnuson shook his head. "That's probably bugged; Romer's and Marshall's too. They didn't know you were staying here so they didn't have time to do yours. Besides, I don't want to puke in my room."

He returned in a few minutes, brandishing a bottle of bourbon. He handed it to Mead. "Go ahead—you're way behind me. Besides, I want to hear about that woman you're living with."

"You gonna tell me about Dolores?"

"What's to tell? She sucks and fucks, likes it up the ass, and talks dirty—no story there. Anyway, I'm a married man." He held up his ringless finger. "Aren't I?"

"That's what your record says."

Mead took a long pull on the bottle, then handed it back to Magnuson, who lifted it to his mouth and drank. They passed the bottle back and forth for several minutes without speaking, then Magnuson went to the sink and brought back plastic cups. "We better slow down, or we'll pass out before we get anything said. So tell me, you really a hero?"

"That's what my record says."

Magnuson laughed. "Records *lie*. There's nothing in mine about the CIA, Ronnie-bo."

"Mine either."

"Well, then, let's talk about what's not in our records."

"Who goes first?"

"I'm senior man. Hey, I'm a fucking officer even."

"A married fucking officer."

"That's right," he said, holding up his middle finger to Mead. "Oops, wrong finger. So I'll go first. I've never told anyone else this, except for Luke—this is between us."

"Got you."

Magnuson stared at him for a second, took a drink from his glass, and started. "In Da Nang, I flew some missions for the CIA."

Then he told Mead what he had done. "In October, I got orders to go to Saigon—in fact, just the time Luke came down from the DMZ."

"Why did they send you?"

"I don't know. It wasn't until I arrived that I learned that I would be flying for the ambassador."

"I saw you that day in the embassy, coming down from Lord's office."

"Yeah, I know. He told me that I'd been picked because I'd be needed for some 'special' work, but he didn't tell me what it was—but he made it real clear that I better be cooperative. You see, that's the trouble when you get started in this shit—pretty soon they have you by the balls, and you do whatever they say whenever they start squeezing. It was never said, but from the beginning I sort of knew that the ambassador was going to be the target—that I'd been flown down to . . . drop him. Then, after our little excursion to the Delta, Lord told me he had some special work for me. That's when I went to see you and told you we better talk before we do something we didn't want to do."

"What was it you didn't want to do?"

"I already did it." Magnuson grabbed the bottle back and drank from it directly. He shook his head and fell back on the bed. "Oh, Jesus, I had hoped all that was over."

He sat up quickly, his face a mix of fury and anguish. "I'm twenty-two fucking years old, from goddamn Boll Weevil, Oklahoma, and I played football—that's my life, and now I'm over here in some little handjob of a country dropping people out of airplanes in the name of . . . what is it? Democracy? Freedom? Fuck! And in a couple months, I'll go home to my wife"—he held up his ringless finger—"and settle into a cozy life of . . . what? Selling insurance? Or maybe I can get a job with the airlines. Terrific résumé: job specialty—unloading gooks into the South China Sea."

He shook his head. "That's what Lord wanted me to do—his special job for me the other night. Some poor old gook, scared shitless, that he was interrogating, a sad-looking old man, raggy clothes . . . and just pathetic, except for his teeth, that's what I remember—this poor old fuck with bright teeth . . ."

603

He reached into his flight suit pocket and pulled out a handkerchief. He unwrapped it and tossed a tooth to Mead, who caught it in his hand.

"That's what's left of him."

Mead held the bloody tooth in his palm. "Jesus," he said, then he tossed it back. "I knew him."

Magnuson stared at the tooth in his hand. "You can tell from one tooth who this is?"

"What happened to him?" Mead asked.

"Maritime casualty—fell into the ocean. Sorry, I shouldn't joke if he was a friend of yours."

"He wasn't a friend of mine—I just knew who he was."

"You want to tell me about it?"

Then Mead grabbed the bottle and took two long swallows. "Yeah," he said. "I need to talk about it."

Then Mead told his story: Kim and Lacouture, Lord's talks with him, and finally about the meeting Marshall wanted Lacouture to arrange.

When he finished, Magnuson didn't say anything for a long time, then he took the bottle and drank. "Jesus Christ," he said at last, wiping his mouth on his flight suit. "They got me dropping gooks into the sea, and you bunking down with faggots." He put his hand on his heart. "Some finer instinct tells me that this is wrong." He held up the bottle. "Or is it just the booze?"

"I didn't do anything with him," Mead said defensively.

Magnuson held up his hands. "Hey, whatever turns a guy on is okay by me."

"God damn it!"

Magnuson laughed. "Look, the point isn't what you did, but what they wanted you to do—and that you would have done it. And don't be so touchy about it—after all, I'm the one killing people for the bastards."

"So what should we do?" Mead asked. "I can't think straight anymore. Should we tell Ambassador Marshall?"

Magnuson held his head. "I'm having a little trouble focusing. What good would it do if we told him? I mean, besides me getting court-martialed for war crimes, you for crimes against nature, and both of us zapped permanently by the CIA—I think they bear grudges."

"Yeah, I see what you mean. But we gotta do something."

"Well, first we better figure out what Lord is up to—I think he's out to kill Marshall."

Mead dropped his head. "I still can't believe that. I mean . . ."

"It's our government, and we're the good guys, and all that kind of shit, right?"

"Well . . . yeah, I guess so. I mean, I believe in my country. I don't know much, but . . . Aw, shit," he said, wiping his eyes on his sleeve, and when he looked up to Magnuson, he was crying. "You know, I came over here when I was eighteen, and I been killing people for my country since then—one guy in a tunnel with my bare hands, some poor bastard bleeding to death, half his face blown away, and I . . . and I don't want to do it anymore. I want to go home. Even if it's just to my old man's dirt farm in Arkansas."

Magnuson let out his breath, then shook his head and looked away. "It's going to be a long rest of our lives, man." Then he stood up and went to Mead, patting him on the shoulder. "This doesn't have anything to do with our country, man. This is just . . . bullshit."

Then he crouched down so that his face was even with Mead's. "Hey," he said, making Mead look at him. "This is going to turn out all right. I'm glad we talked; we're in this together. We can beat that fucker—two Marines against that asshole; he doesn't have a chance. We'll figure out what to do tomorrow."

Then he took the bottle and stumbled back to his room.

In the morning, Marshall informed the Special Forces commander that he was cutting short his visit.

"I've seen all that I need; it's been most impressive and I congratulate you on your work, but there are many other places I want to see, and I have very little time. Thank you very much."

He sent Romer to wake Magnuson and inform him of the change in plans.

Romer found Magnuson sprawled naked on top of his bed, reeking of alcohol. He shook him awake.

"Lieutenant, get your ass up. We're leaving in thirty minutes."

Magnuson stared at him blearily. "Huh?"

"Think you can find Dak To, Lieutenant?"

Magnuson sat up. "Huh?"

"Dak To, Lieutenant. The ambassador wants to fly there immediately. Think you can find it?"

"Oh, Jesus," he murmured. "I don't think I could find my helicopter."

"I'll get you that far—you get us the rest of the way. There's a war going on up there, Lieutenant. Let's go!" He pulled Magnuson up and pushed him into the shower, turning on the cold water, and pushing on the sliding door so that he couldn't get out.

"Sober up, Lieutenant. Dak To, here we come."

606

CHAPTER

• 38 •

When Wilson Abbot Lord received word from the CIA station chief in Nha Trang that Marshall was on his way to Dak To, he knew he had to act immediately.

Dak To was a major military embarrassment. The enemy was supposedly incapable of launching a major attack, but they had at Dak To, and despite a huge counterattack with constant air strikes and artillery, U.S. forces had not been able to drive them out. Lord had followed the battle closely.

He knew Marshall would report negatively to President Johnson, who already was unnerved by the earlier attack on Con Thien, and the massive enemy buildup at Khe Sanh. Marshall's recommendation would have even greater influence with Johnson now.

But, Lord realized, after Dak To, Marshall would be even more eager to meet with the NVA, so it was imperative that he, Lord, set up that meeting before Marshall's return from Dak To.

Lord spent the remainder of the day completing arrangements, and in early evening he took a tape recorder and drove across Saigon to the fashionable district where Lacouture lived, parking several blocks away.

After determining that Lacouture was in, and seeing him pace nervously behind drawn curtains, Lord went to the door and knocked.

In a practiced voice that he knew was a good imitation of Mead's, he said, hesitant as he knew Mead would act, in a low, hushed voice, "Mr. Lacou . . . Bernard, it's me, Corporal Mead."

There was a flurry of unlocking bolts, and the door pulled open.

"Oh, Corporal Mead, dear Corporal Me—" Then he screamed when Lord pushed the door open wider and shoved a pistol into his face.

"Bon soir, monsieur. Pardon the deception, but we must talk."

"You! How dare you! I shall—"

Lord pushed him back, the pistol striking his forehead, and he closed the door.

"You didn't invite me in, Monsieur Lacouture, a terrible breach of etiquette. My, what a beautiful home. So much art. Such a collection. You must be very proud."

"What do you want?" cried Lacouture furiously. "Murderer. I know you killed Kim."

Lord continued to scan the room with arctic eyes. "Most regrettable. Terrible accident. He fell out of an airplane."

Lacouture gasped. Then he gathered himself, trying to calm his fears with as much dignity as he could muster. "What do you want? You are an evil man. I shall not cooperate with you."

Lord reached for a vase on a commode and juggled it in one hand. "Absolutely gorgeous. Museum quality. Oh dear," and he dropped it to the floor where it shattered on the marble.

Lacouture held himself in check. "I knew you would do that. Dear God, what is the point?" Then he shook his head. "But what is art to you? Or people? Or a country? Or life?"

"Oh, a great deal," Lord said, pushing a piece of Ming porcelain off the bureau. "It is because I care so much that I'm here."

"I'm sure that's what the Nazis said at Kristallnacht."

Lord smiled. "Don't flatter yourself; and spare me penny morality please—you, who are without morality or principles, you who would sell anything to anyone."

Lord seized a lapis lazuli figure and flung it against the opposite wall where it shattered.

"Stop! I can't stand it. Why don't you just shoot me and be done with it?"

"I need your cooperation. I thought we had an understanding." Then he sneered. "Squeaky, Goulue, Nhay Dam." He grabbed a jade incense burner and smashed it against the marble. "Tell me about 'dear' Corporal Mead. Was he a good fuck? Or did he fuck you?"

"You are disgusting," Lacouture said quietly.

"*I* am disgusting? You pervert." He grabbed a T'ang dynasty pottery bowl of brilliant polychrome glaze and sent it crashing against the wall. "You fuck boys and call me disgusting? I know Mead spent the night here in your bedroom. Tell me."

Lacouture knelt to pick up the pieces of clay. "This was over twelve hundred years old," he said in disbelief.

Lord hurled a celadon bowl against the marble. "Tell me."

Lacouture looked hopelessly at the destruction about him. Lord was going to kill him, he knew that with certainty, but strangely enough he was not afraid; he was more worried about his treasures. They were more important and valuable than himself—all that art and beauty destroyed, all that he admired and loved, shattered. What did his life matter to that? He didn't want to live in a world without his treasures. He didn't want to live in a world where art and beauty were trampled.

He didn't want to die, and oh, he was going to miss so much—life was such fun. He loved everything, and everything brought him joy and amusement. So many things—croissants and coffee and newspapers, intrigue and boys. Oh, wonderful, all of it.

Then he started to cry, not in fear, but for all that he was going to miss—not the art and beauty, they were enduring and transcended him, but the frivolous things.

He wept. He would not go to Cannes; he would never see his savage again. Dear Corporal Mead; what a sweet boy who had held him in his arms, that wonderful man who had comforted him. And here he, Lord, that wicked, wicked man who sought to make something dirty and ugly out of it. His dear savage! And what would Lord do to him? He would be next, Lacouture thought; Lord was going to kill him too.

No, he wouldn't allow that. He couldn't save himself, but he could do something for his savage; he would be brave for him, and suddenly into his mind came that wonderful scene from a movie, and he almost cried again. He remembered it so well, it was so touching, Ronald Colman as Sydney Carton saying, "It is a far, far better thing that I do, than I have ever done."

Lacouture wiped the tears from his eyes. "Yes, he stayed here; he spent the night in my bed. He was, as you say, a very good 'fuck.' He is very beautiful, the most beautiful of them all. But he is very stupid. He didn't learn anything—he doesn't have any information you want. The poor thing tried hard, but he was too transparent."

"I thought so," Lord said. "A smart man like you would see right through him. It really was an unfair match—him against you. Did he enjoy himself at least?"

"No. He likes women. He wasn't even able to come, despite all my efforts."

"And he learned nothing?"

"Nothing that would help you, I'm afraid. That's why I thought it was Corporal Mead at the door tonight—trying again."

"Well, too bad for you. On many accounts." He placed the barrel of the pistol against a seven-hundred-year-old scroll of the Yuan dynasty, a painting of bamboo and birds, and he ripped long gashes through it.

"Tell me about the meeting you've arranged."

"There is no meeting. There won't be any—you saw to that by killing Kim. Do you think General Khanh would meet now?"

Lord laughed. "No. But Mr. Marshall doesn't know that, does he?"

He pulled the tape recorder from his pocket and placed it on the table. "But you're going to tell him about a meeting."

"Without a bribe?" Lacouture asked sarcastically.

"No, Mr. Lacouture. No money, I'm afraid; it's too late for that."

"What then? What inducements for my cooperation?"

"A little longer to live—a few possessions to save." Then with unerring instinct, he went to the phonograph player.

"You know, I never appreciated opera—a lacking on my part, but nevertheless . . . ah, I've heard this one, *La Traviata*. So boring." He broke it over his knee and picked up another disc.

"Wagner. Oh, that's truly awful." He smashed it on the floor. "Let's make our own recording, shall we?"

He searched for another record. "Caruso. Oh, yes, very famous, and in very good condition." He raised it over his head.

"No! Not Caruso."

Lord hesitated, then laid it aside and picked up another and hurled it against the wall.

"We'll make our own record, but you'll be the only one speaking. I want you to say, 'A meeting is arranged for Friday, December twenty-third, at four P.M., near Hong Ngu on the Cambodian border, grid square' . . . here, I've written the script down for you. Read it."

Lacouture took the paper from him, his eyes nervously on the pistol, and the record too. He read from the paper.

"Again. Not so hysterically this time—you sound like someone is holding a gun to your head. Read in that elegant, haughty French you speak so beautifully. As opposed to mine, which I know you hate." He grabbed another record and hurled it against the wall.

"You're making me too nervous to read. Stop throwing things!" Lacouture cried.

"Just read it right, or I'll destroy everything in this goddamn room." Lord moved quickly to find something else. His eye fell on Pierrot, and he grabbed the doll. "What's this? Hardly a museum piece."

Lacouture gasped and ran to him, grabbing it from his hands, clutching it tightly to his chest.

"Ah, I see," said Lord sneeringly. "Your childhood toy. Well, perhaps it will comfort you. It had better, or I'll rip it to shreds. This is your last chance, Mr. Lacouture. Read."

Holding the puppet lovingly, Lacouture read from the paper.

"Better. Again."

Lacouture read.

"Very good. Now for the recording."

He punched buttons and held the machine to Lacouture, who spoke his words calmly, eyes closed, his hand stroking the doll.

Lord snapped off the machine, then rewound the tape and played it. "Excellent," he said. "This will be most helpful."

He gestured to the records, then to the other objects around the room. "To show you my gratitude, and prove that I am not an evil man, I am going to spare all of this."

Then he suddenly brought the pistol to Lacouture's forehead and pulled the trigger.

The bullet carried through his brain and hurled him backward where he crashed against a bureau, toppling everything on it to the floor.

Lacouture lay on his back, eyes open, a gaping hole in his forehead, his hands still clutching the doll.

Lord looked about, clinically dispassionate about the act, then he picked up the paper and put it in his pocket along with the tape recorder. He holstered the pistol, left the house, and walked casually up the street to his car, then drove away.

In midmorning, Lord called Marshall's office, imitating Lacouture's heavily accented, effeminate voice.

Dolores Toland answered the phone and readily recognized the man as the awful Frenchman who had called so often.

"Is Ambassador Marshall there? This is Bernard Lacouture. I have spoken with His Excellency before—he is *very* eager to hear from me."

"Yes, I know who you are," Dolores said with undisguised contempt. "But Ambassador Marshall is not here and I do not know when he will be returning."

"Well, I have a message for him. A *very* important message, one I cannot entrust over the phone, or to secretaries. I am sending the ambassador a tape. It is a sealed tape so that he will know if it has been tampered with. I am sending it the moment I hang up to the U.S. embassy by special courier. *You* will see to it that the ambassador gets it the moment he returns. I assure you that after he hears it, if he learns there was the slightest delay in his receiving it—*well,* I wouldn't want to be in his employ. Do you understand what I am saying?"

Dolores could barely contain herself, and she said seethingly, "Yes," and when he hung up, she slammed the phone down.

Forty-five minutes later, the tape was brought up by a Marine guard, who said it had been delivered by legitimate Vietnamese postal special delivery. The guard said it had been X-rayed and that it was a tape recording.

The seal was unbroken, and Dolores locked it in the safe.

CHAPTER

• 39 •

"Apparently you went to chapel service with Lieutenant Magnuson last night," Romer said maliciously to Mead, who sat in unconcealed pain as the chopper bounced and pitched toward Dak To.

Marshall suppressed a smile. His pilot and bodyguard were so obviously hung over that he felt sorry for them, especially since he had clearly indicated the night before that he wouldn't be needing them today.

"Are you sure he can fly?" he had asked Romer when he saw Magnuson, and after seeing Mead walk into a closed door.

"Never let on that I said this, sir, but he's a terrific pilot—probably better drunk than others sober."

Romer himself, Marshall observed, was in a fervor of excitement and eagerness, rushing everyone aboard, seeing to every detail, urging and prompting, keeping up a steady stream of rapid talk.

Marshall had never seen anyone so anxious to get to a battlefield; was it because he had never been on one, he wondered, or was it the same drive that had possessed his famous father? And it did seem a form of possession, Marshall thought—the man was in a hyper state, in control of himself and lucid, but somewhat manic. It was more than adrenaline propelling him—probably that indefinable ingredient so necessary for great military leadership, something beyond charisma and mere courage, that transcendental quality of warrior artistry found only in Alexanders, Wellingtons, and Napoleons.

"Viceroy requesting clearance to land in Dak To," Magnuson said in a voice so subdued it sounded bored.

Romer had told Magnuson to leave the intercom on so that he could hear all radio traffic.

The reply was instant and emphatic. "Negative, Viceroy. Repeat, Viceroy. Negative. Clearance denied."

Magnuson said in the same tired voice, "Viceroy approaching from sierra whiskey, ETA approximately ten minutes."

"Southwest, estimated time of arrival," Romer translated to Marshall with glee.

The ground controller's voice was a mix of fury and hysteria. "Negative. Repeat, negative. Clearance denied. You cannot land, Viceroy. LZ hot. Repeat, LZ hot."

"Landing zone," said Romer. "They're under fire down there." He strained to see out the window.

Mead, slumped in a corner, came alive suddenly. He whipped his helmet from under his seat and sat on it, then inserted a magazine into his rifle.

"ETA nine minutes," said Magnuson, suppressing a yawn.

Another voice, far more authoritative, came onto the net. "This is ground control—*the* ground controller: the LZ is hot, and your clearance is denied. You got a problem with comprehension up there? 'Hot' means real bullets, and 'denied' means get your ass out of here."

"Seven minutes," said Magnuson. "Hey, I see a lot of smoke down there—what's going on? You having a cookout?"

Romer laughed and slapped his rifle.

"You asshole!" the voice screamed. "I'm gonna shoot you down myself."

Then a very commanding voice came over the net. "Viceroy, this is Thor. You are in my area. I am unfamiliar with your call sign. Please identify yourself and state your mission."

"Roger, Thor," said Magnuson, knowing that he was

talking to the brigade or division commander, a one- or two-star general, or even higher. "Viceroy is the personal rep of U.S. One. That is *The* Six. Clearance for landing at Dak To not requested, clearance directed."

There was a long pause in transmission, then the voice again. "Roger that, Viceroy. I have you under visual. I am to your echo, about five hundred feet above. Can you see me?"

Magnuson looked to the east and spotted several choppers at a higher altitude. "Roger, Thor, I have a visual."

"Request you follow me to landing strip."

"The shit will now hit the fan," Magnuson announced to Marshall over the intercom. "This will be back to MACV by the time we land. By the way, I overheard a lot of medevac traffic on the net; they've taken heavy casualties down there."

When they touched down fifteen minutes later at the base camp, out of enemy mortar range, a two-star general and his senior staff ran over to greet Marshall. Frantic calls up and down the command net ascertained that, yes, the President's personal envoy's call sign was Viceroy, and while his expected destination was Pleiku, it was quite possible he was circling Dak To.

"What do I call the son of a bitch?" General Anthony Scarpoli blurted. "And how the hell can I run a war with civilians thick as gnats?"

"Call him Mr. Ambassador, or Excellency—MACV suggests civilians be given rifles and put in first assault wave."

"Mr. Ambassador, what a surprise," said the general, shaking hands. "I think they're expecting you in Pleiku."

In the background was a continuous roar of artillery and mortar fire, and even this far from the battle, the air was hazy from smoke.

"There's no battle in Pleiku," Marshall answered.

"I'm so glad we can accommodate you here," Scarpoli said without any attempt to disguise his sarcasm.

Marshall smiled. "General, I realize nothing could be more unwelcome on a battlefield than a visiting dignitary—"

"More enemy troops *might* be worse," Scarpoli deadpanned.

"But I'm here strictly to observe," Marshall continued. "I'm not here to evaluate or make judgments. The President asked me to come to Vietnam and bring back impressions to him. Since this is where the war is today, and the enemy rarely stages a pitched battle like this—I wanted to see it."

The general nodded. "I'll give you a flyover of the area and my G-3 will brief you on what's developed."

"Thank you, but I don't want to interrupt you if you're directing the battle."

"Mr. Ambassador, I wouldn't let the President interrupt me in a critical moment, and if suddenly my presence is needed, or I feel it necessary to bring you back, I will. MACV has made your position quite clear, but this is *my* battlefield, and what I say goes."

"We understand each other completely. My only request is that Colonel Romer accompany us—he's my military aide."

"Happy to have you, Colonel," the general said, shaking hands, then he directed one of his aides to make arrangements for an overnight stay.

"Mr. Ambassador . . .," Mead started.

"Do you think I'll need a bodyguard, General?" Marshall asked. "Corporal Mead worries about my safety."

"Apparently with good cause, but I don't think you'll need him on this leg; besides, if I take any more of your entourage, I'll need a jumbo jet."

As soon as Marshall and Romer took off with General Scarpoli, Magnuson and Mead climbed into the back of the chopper and fell asleep.

The G-3 briefing was succinct—two weeks ago, four NVA regiments, approximately twelve to fifteen thousand men, surrounded the town of Dak To. Fighting had been fierce and only now had the tide been turned against the NVA, who were entrenched on the high ground in well-built bunkers.

Casualties were high on both sides—seventy-five American KIA, and nearly four hundred wounded; NVA casualties were estimated to be three times more.

The heaviest fighting was on Hill 875, which the NVA held. Massive air strikes had failed to dislodge them, and an airborne battalion assault had not succeeded.

"We'll get the bastards," Scarpoli said. "If I have to flatten that fucking mountain, I will."

From the chopper, Marshall saw massive destruction—nearly three hundred B-52 missions and two thousand fighter bomber attacks had cratered the area. A hundred and fifty thousand artillery shells, napalm, and defoliants had turned the earth brown.

Marshall saw the battlefield clearly, a mountainous terrain with the enemy dug in on the hilltops, and the Americans on the assault.

"I don't understand what they're trying to do," Marshall said. "How do you explain it, General?"

"Explain what? The NVA attack on Dak To? The sons of bitches are trying to take the town—that would give them a foothold in the Central Highlands."

"But they've never attempted to hold any ground before—that would tie down their forces and put them on the defensive. I don't understand the purpose of this attack. They've always been on the offense; defense is contrary to everything they've done in the past."

Scarpoli grunted. "I think they expected to take Dak To without much difficulty, not anticipating our ability for rapid deployment. We can move battalions and regiments within hours—it takes them days and weeks. They misjudged. Then they weren't able to withdraw fast enough. It's easy for a patrol or platoon to slip away, but fifteen thousand men with all their equipment and logistics can't just vanish. They got stuck. Also, while the NVA are excellent fighters, and their strategy basically sound, they do make mistakes, and they are very slow to change or alter plans."

"You think Dak To is an enemy fuck-up?" Romer queried.

"No, Colonel, I don't. Those are excellent troops up there. *My* troops are excellent, and I can't kick the NVA off that goddamn hill. Their officers are good, and their generalship excellent. They're going to lose, but losing a battle is not a 'fuck-up.' Now if *I* lost, if I couldn't drive them out with everything I have at my disposal—*that* would be a fuck-up."

"You don't think they've calculated this scenario?" Marshall asked. "That this is part of a strategy to draw us from our main defensive areas to fight in basically insignificant places? My point is, after we win at Dak To—then what? Does everybody go back to where they came from, or do we set up a new major base here and try to hold it?"

Scarpoli laughed appreciatively. "You've been studying strategy, Mr. Ambassador." He shook his head. "I can't answer your questions—no one can. General Westmoreland has strong feelings about what General Giap is up to. Other senior commanders do not agree with General Westmoreland, but nobody knows for sure what Giap is doing. We're all just guessing; some will end up guessing wrong—that doesn't amount to a fuck-up, by the way—and somebody will have guessed right."

"And your guess is?"

"You're asking me to put my career on the line for a guess?" The general smiled. "I'll give you my considered opinion. There's been a huge intensification of enemy activity and infiltration here and in I Corps. Something definite is about to happen. Con Thien was hit a couple months ago; now it's Dak To. Next month will be Khe Sanh, and after that somewhere else. Do you realize where we are?"

He pointed to the west. "Twenty miles that way is Laos." He moved his finger. "Twenty-five miles that way is Cambodia. Just a few miles and the enemy has sanctuary where they can rest, lick their wounds, and come roaring back. What can we do? We bomb Laos and Cambodia, and all they'd do is move to China."

"You're not making a very strong case for our continued efforts here at Dak To, General," Marshall said.

"Mr. Ambassador, we'll get the NVA out of Dak To in a few days. Khe Sanh will not fall—they will not get us out of there. So the NVA won't be in Dak To, but we'll be at Khe Sanh." Then he looked at Marshall with an expression of Medici slyness and he shrugged his shoulders in dismissal.

Marshall laughed; he understood: Yes, we—the generals —can win the battles; we can defeat them at Dak To, and hold Khe Sanh. But to what avail? Then where will we be? The war is yours, Mr. Ambassador, Mr. President, and all civilians, to win or lose. We, the generals, can flatten this mountain or all the mountains; we can hold this hill or all the hills, but none of that will win the war. The war will be won or lost in Washington and in the rest of America. Victory or defeat will be a political decision politicians make on what they think voters want.

Just to make sure Marshall got the point, Scarpoli said, "We never would have defeated the Germans had we stopped at Normandy—we'd still be in Normandy, and Hitler would still be in Berlin. We never would have beaten the Japs if we hadn't hit Hiroshima—we'd still be on Iwo Jima, and the emperor would still be in Tokyo."

"He still is, General."

The Medici smile came with a faint shrug and an opening of Scarpoli's hands. "That was a political decision—see what I mean?"

"Indeed." Marshall looked at the destruction below, then sighed. "I assume this was once inhabited land. Where are the people now?"

"Resettled. The district and province governments set aside land for them and we move them there."

Marshall gazed on the smoldering ruin. The battle at Dak To would rage another week or so probably, he thought, then the enemy would flee and the Americans move on. People would begin to drift back, but the ruin—that would last all the lifetimes of those who only weeks ago lived in peaceful contentment; it might be two generations before the land was fertile again.

When he returned to base camp, Marshall found his accommodations not luxurious, but far from primitive. He had steak for dinner, watched *For a Few Dollars More,* and slept in private quarters on a comfortable bed, though sleep was limited because of continuous shelling of enemy positions.

At breakfast, Scarpoli told him that the battalion commander on Hill 875 was going to launch a major assault.

"It's not tied to your visit here," Scarpoli said. "I myself wouldn't risk it under 'presidential' scrutiny, but he's calling the shots—I don't interfere with combat commanders unless there's a compelling reason. He feels the enemy should be sufficiently softened up after last night's shelling."

Marshall nodded. "I can't imagine anyone slept up there last night."

Scarpoli smiled in mock sympathy. "I hope *you* slept untroubled."

Romer was ecstatic about the impending attack and quickly arranged for closer observation.

"I don't want to get closer," Marshall said. "It's neither my intent nor mission to engage in hand-to-hand combat with the enemy."

Romer brushed the objection aside. "Here's your opportunity to see our forces in action. All you've seen so far is the negative," he said, glaring at Magnuson. "This will be a classic infantry and airborne assault against a strong enemy. You'll be in an armored personnel carrier out of fire, but near enough to see the action."

He was so eager and insistent that Marshall relented. "However, I'll take my bodyguard."

Shortly, Marshall, Romer, and Mead were in an armored convoy bouncing over the rocky terrain toward Hill 875, accompanied by a platoon of infantry, all commanded by a young lieutenant very nervous about having a presidential advisor in his charge.

"Can't we get any closer?" Romer demanded when the lieutenant drew the unit into a defensive position on a hilltop some distance from the battle.

"It could get hairy if we got any closer, sir," Lieutenant Gould said.

"The ambassador could have stayed in America and seen this better on the *CBS News,* Lieutenant," Romer sneered.

"Well, I guess we could get a *little* closer, Colonel."

"Lieutenant, you better get us *a lot* closer. I want the ambassador to see this battle—I want him to *smell* gook blood."

As they redeployed, an artillery barrage started on the hill.

"That's the prep fire," Romer said to Marshall. "They'll start the assault as soon as it ends."

Urging the lieutenant on, Romer was able to browbeat him to the high ground adjacent to Hill 875, terrain that offered excellent observation but was exposed to enemy fire and vulnerable to attack.

As Romer predicted, the assault began when the artillery ceased. With binoculars, Marshall had a clear view of the battle and saw troops begin an on-line assault up the hill.

Enemy fire was withering, and soon the assault turned into squad and individual movement up the slope. He saw wounded being carried back and was deafened by automatic rifle fire and artillery shelling.

Turning from the hill, Marshall watched the men around him, so intent on the battle that they flinched at the enemy fire their comrades were suffering. It seemed to Marshall as though it were some grotesque tourney, a murderous forum, ancient and real, that he was observing, and that he himself was watching with the jaded detachment of a god at Troy.

He turned from it all and was surprised to see Mead sitting on his haunches watching him, seemingly not at all interested in the battle raging on the next hill, as indifferent as any god.

Their gazes met, statesman and warrior, seeking to penetrate the other—what was he thinking, what did he feel? For a long moment they stared at one another, a study of monarch and Ethiop, scepter and saber eyeing one another, the battlefield a bleeding tapestry behind them.

Then overhead, planes screamed down on the hill, and it erupted in an incredible string of detonations, and suddenly the men gathered on the ridge cried out in disbelief.

A five-hundred-pound bomb, released too soon, dropped on the American assault force, just above battalion headquarters; even from this distance, the screams of the wounded could be heard.

A contingent of enemy soldiers broke in terror from the crest and ran down the back slope, racing toward the hill from where the men were watching.

Romer jumped up wildly. "Here's our chance. Follow me!" He ran to the soldiers nearby and dragged them to their feet. "That's an order. Charge!"

The squads looked to the lieutenant in confusion, but Romer had run to Gould and started pushing him forward.

"Get those sons of bitches! Charge!" Pushing and pulling the lieutenant along with him, he rushed down the hill.

Seeing the two officers running to meet the enemy, the men jumped up and followed.

Marshall walked to the crest and stared down. Mead was beside him, and like two deities, they watched the folly below.

Seeing Romer and the others charging down, the enemy soldiers, already panicked, turned and ran back up the slope, chased furiously, rifles bursting automatic, by the Americans.

The enemy ran until they found cover, then they set in and returned fire, stopping Romer's assault. His men dove for cover, and the two sides fired furiously at one another.

Marshall watched a moment, then turned to survey the abandoned hill and vehicles.

"Christ," he said in disgust, then pointing at a vehicle, said, "I don't know how to drive one of those things, do you?"

Mead shook his head. "No, sir. But they'll be back in a few minutes—the way they're firing, they'll be out of bullets real soon."

And within minutes, the firing slackened, then tapered to random single shots, and they saw the men start back, running in a zigzag pattern to the hill.

"I don't see Colonel Romer," Marshall said.

"He probably went all the way to the top," Mead said, then added in disapproval, "That was pretty dangerous."

Then they saw the last man, Romer, running toward them.

When they all reached the top, Romer was jubilant. "We almost had those bastards. If we'd had more ammo, we could have taken the whole goddamn hill."

For another hour they watched the battle; the assault had been turned back and the enemy remained on the crest, while medevac choppers carried casualties away.

"I've seen enough, Lieutenant," Marshall said sadly. "I'd like to return to base now."

That evening he was briefed on the day's battle. Thirty

U.S. paratroopers had been killed by the prematurely released bomb—many of them were wounded earlier and had been withdrawn to the area near the battalion command post where the bomb had hit.

General Scarpoli did not try to conceal the dimensions of the disaster. "That's the worst thing I've seen in combat, Mr. Ambassador."

Marshall had visited battalion triage and seen the carnage; he knew the inadequacy of words. "I'm sorry too," he said, then shook hands. "I'm going to leave now. You don't need the added burden of my presence."

"A real fuck-up," Scarpoli said, shaking his head sadly.

"I'm afraid it didn't start here, General. Nor will it end here."

At the airstrip he told Magnuson to fly them out; he didn't care where.

"I can get us back to Saigon tonight, sir, if you'd like—it'd be late, but we can make it."

"Yes," Marshall said. "Let's go back."

Maybe Lacouture had been able to arrange a meeting. Dear God, I hope so, he thought. This has got to end.

CHAPTER

·40·

Magnuson brought the chopper down at Tan Son Nhut shortly before one A.M.

"I think we all deserve a day off," Marshall said, telling them not to report in for work in the morning.

Mead accompanied Marshall back to his villa and hailed a cab. He wanted to go home, but afraid that Sung would be gone and unable to face that, he decided to see if Lacouture was all right.

He never had a chance to tell him he was leaving, and now it had been six days; he knew Lacouture would have worried the entire time. He wouldn't spend the night no matter how much Lacouture pleaded; he would just see that the little Frenchman was safe, and if he had a message to take to Marshall.

The lights to the house were on when the cab dropped him off. He went to the door and knocked loudly. "It's me, Mr. Lac . . . Bernard. Corporal Mead."

He knocked again when there was no answer. "It's Corporal Mead, Bernard."

When there was still no response, he tried the door. To his surprise, knowing how many locks there were on it, the door opened.

He stuck his head in. "Bernard? Mr. Lacouture?"

Then he saw the shattered vase in the hallway.

"Oh, Jesus," he murmured. He unclipped his rifle safety and stepped inside carefully.

There was wreckage everywhere, and he knew what he was going to find.

Moving slowly, his rifle before him, he walked into the living room, littered with broken pottery, smashed porcelain, and shattered records.

In their midst, he saw Lacouture.

Mead knelt over the body. The corpse was cold and stiff, dead several days, he knew.

He bowed his head. "I'm sorry. I'm so sorry," he said.

Seeing the doll clutched in Lacouture's hands, he imagined the death, saw clearly the torment and ridicule, and pictured the cold murder. He turned away, tears welling in his eyes.

Then he stood. "That bastard. That motherfucker," he said to the corpse; "I'll get him. I promise." Then he turned and left, closing the door behind him.

It was nearly three A.M. before he got back to his apartment.

He stood on the sidewalk outside the building for a long time, afraid to go in.

Maybe she was gone, he thought. Or maybe Lord had hurt her.

He looked up to the dark window. Please. Please let Sung be there. Please don't let anything have happened to her.

The room was dark when he opened the door, but he heard movement. He raised his rifle and flipped on the light.

Thrusting the barrel at the movement, he shouted, "Don't move!"

Sung cried out in terror and covered her head with her hands.

Mead dropped the rifle and ran to her. "I didn't mean to scare you. I'm sorry, I'm sorry. Are you okay?"

She trembled, and he dropped to his knees before her. "I wasn't going to hurt you . . . I just . . . I was just afraid . . . Oh, God, I'm so glad you're here." He put his arms around her and held her tightly.

She stood still and tense, then feeling his arms, relaxed gradually. "You scared me," she said softly.

"I'm sorry." He stood and hugged her to him. "Oh, Jesus, I'm glad to see you." Then he kissed her. She did not respond, but he didn't care.

"I was so afraid you'd be gone, or something would have happened to you."

"I told you I'd be here."

"I know, but I wanted you to be here so badly that I was afraid it wouldn't be true. That's how things are: if you want it too much then it can't happen."

He moved back a step. "You look . . . oh, Jesus, beautiful."

She dropped her head. "Thank you." Then she raised her eyes. "You look . . . tired."

"Yeah," he said. "I guess I do. It's been a bitch of . . . I mean, a hard week. Is everything here okay?"

"Yes," she said. "Your friends brought me food and money—they were very nice to me. We have so much here—are you hungry? Can I get you something?"

He shook his head, overcome with her beauty, and so happy she was here. "I couldn't eat anything. Christ, I'm beat." And suddenly he was exhausted, utterly drained, his last reserves gone, and he dropped down on the sleeping bag, sighing contentedly.

He was asleep in a minute, having only the vaguest sensation of his clothes and his boots being slipped off, and he did not see her watching him sleep, a puzzled expression on her face because she did not understand the emotion she felt—she had never liked a man before.

It was afternoon when he awoke. Groaning and stretching on the sleeping bag, he looked across the room to her, and to his clothes and boots neatly stacked in a corner. He was surprised at his nudity and rolled over on his stomach, pressing his erection into the floor.

"I made coffee," she said, bringing him a cup.

"Thank you," he said, taking it from her and sipping, but he brought it away quickly.

"Too hot?" she asked in concern.

"No."

"Not good?"

He smiled. "You don't drink much coffee, do you?"

She shook her head. "I like tea."

He put the cup down on the floor. "I'll have to teach you how to make it. That's kinda strong."

Then he reached for her and brought her down to him on the sleeping bag.

She let him hold her, but she could not respond.

"I need you so badly," he said, pulling her close and resting his head against her breasts. "Oh, God, I need you. It's been so bad."

She felt both his need and his anguish and brought her hand up tentatively to stroke his head.

He looked up into her face. She smiled gently, and he smiled too, then he put his hand around her neck and drew her head down, touching his lips to hers.

He withdrew and looked into her eyes. "I won't hurt you," he said.

She nodded, then slowly unbuttoned her blouse and slipped it off.

He bent forward and kissed her breasts, taking a nipple gently into his mouth, and he shuddered at the warmth and softness.

She took off her slacks and lay still beneath him. He looked the length of her body, unable to touch her for a long minute, afraid that he would hurt her with the incredible power and urgency he felt.

Then slowly he reached out a hand and touched her face. Her eyes were closed, not drawn tight in fear, merely waiting. He stroked his fingertips down her cheek, then bent to kiss her neck.

He sought to go slowly, wanted to be gentle, trying to hold back, but the feel of her flesh, her scent, because it had been so long since he had been with a woman, and because he wanted her so badly, he could not restrain himself, and he pulled her to him roughly and ground against her, then moved on top.

She spread her legs for him, and he entered quickly. She was dry and the pain intense, but she said nothing as he thrust into her, and he continued to thrust long past his orgasm, his eyes closed tightly, lips drawn past his teeth in an expression of either pain or pleasure, she could not tell.

Finally he opened his eyes, and she was so shocked at the look in them that she flinched from the animal intensity, but then, almost instantly, the look was replaced by one of sheepishness and apology.

"I'm sorry," he said. "I didn't mean to . . . it's been a long time."

Then he withdrew and moved beside her. He lay still a moment, then his hands began to caress her body, and he nuzzled close to her. His mouth pressed her ear, only the tip of his tongue working in.

She lay perfectly still as he lightly traced her lips with his tongue, then moved down her jaw to her throat, tugging gently on the skin with his teeth.

Raising up on his knees above her, he kissed her breasts, then sucked on the nipples, drawing on them softly.

With eyes closed, she gave over to the sensation, freeing her mind from everything that had happened before, allowing herself to enjoy what she had instinctively known was possible.

She began to undulate slowly as his mouth worked lower, kissing her belly, and when he kissed between her legs, she parted them and raised up. He went slowly, bathing her with his tongue, and finally when his tongue entered her, she gasped in surprised pleasure. He buried his face between her legs and she grabbed his hair and pulled him into her, pushing up against him.

Finally she pushed his head away and grabbed his shoulders, bringing him to her, and this time she brought him into her, crying out when he entered. He withdrew to the tip but she arched up seeking him and finally grabbed his hips to pull him down on her, holding him tightly as she thrust against him. He held motionless as she bucked against him, then he began slow, deep thrusts, stroking faster as she jerked in spasms until he matched her wildness, and finally he exploded inside her again, and she shuddered powerfully, and they collapsed together.

For a long time they lay quietly, then he turned to her. "I think this is the happiest I've ever been," he said.

She looked at him, still puzzled by her feelings and response, then she gazed up at the ceiling.

"You're the only good thing that's ever happened to me," he said. "You're the only good thing in my life."

"No, Ron, that's not true," she said, turning to him.

"It *is* true. I don't have anything, here or anywhere—you're the only thing, that's why I was so afraid you'd be gone; I didn't want to lose you. I couldn't have stood that, not after everything else."

He leaned on an elbow and faced her. "I mean it, you're the only good thing in my life." He took a deep breath. "You know what I done since I been over here? Kill people. That's right, kill people."

She closed her eyes at his words and turned her face away, but he made her look at him. "I'm an animal, just like the bastards who killed your family—we're all the same. That's all I am, a dumb animal who kills people. That's been my life here, and I can't stand it anymore."

His voice turned intense and bitter; she had never seen him like this. He gestured to his sea bag in the corner. "Somewhere in that fucking thing is a medal I got from the President of the United States himself. They sent me down from the DMZ to Cam Ranh Bay when the President came, and he shook my hand with a glassy look in his eyes, then he made a speech. I listened to every word. It was all bullshit. He didn't believe it and I didn't, and nobody there did, and the gooks didn't, so why was he saying it? I was standing there like some goddamn dog trotted out to listen to bullshit nobody believed, then sent back to his cage. Good Ron, nice Ron, arf, arf. But I saw before. Nine months on the DMZ showed me everything; showed me what I am: a dumb animal."

She saw his incredible hurt and asked softly, "Why did you come over here?"

He laughed scornfully. "I didn't have a chance not to come. I'm from Arkansas, Sung. My father's a fucking farmer on somebody else's land. We lived in a shack with a tin roof and no toilet. We ate like pigs. Shit, we might as well been gooks. You probably lived like a queen compared to me. You talk better. I can barely read. I grew up dumb, Sung.

I am dumb. I knew only two books, the Bible and a book about King Arthur my grandma used to read to me about knights and honor and damsels and quests. That's all I dreamed about when I was a kid, knights and quests, but when I came here, I found out there weren't any knights, only dumb Marines and dumb gooks, and the damsels were all whores, and King Arthur is an asshole."

He was silent a moment, then he said softly, "I got all kinds of medals. That's why I'm at the embassy, because I'm a hero, and because I scared them in the field. They found out what I already knew—I didn't mind the killing at all. Sometimes I liked it."

She watched his face carefully. Suddenly he closed his eyes and lowered his head, and when he opened them, she saw tears.

"But I hate it too. Oh, God, I don't want to be like this. I was a kid when I came here. I believed in things. I'm not a kid anymore, and I don't believe in anything. It's like finding out there isn't a God, that there isn't anyone to believe in except yourself. And I know what I am. I thought I knew what being a man was—it was being a jock, a Marine, getting laid. I used to do that a lot, then I stopped because it was just animal too."

He grabbed her to him. "Until now—that wasn't animal. And that's why you're the only good thing in my life, the only thing that isn't animal. That's why I couldn't stand it if you were gone."

He was almost crying. "You see, I want to stop. I want to change; I don't want to kill people and hurt them anymore. I want . . . I want, I want to love. And you're the only person I can love. I wake up in the middle of the night dreaming of blood. I'm going to have nightmares the rest of my life—I'm never going to get over this. But I don't want it to be only that. I want something good and decent too."

He lowered his head and took a deep breath. "I don't want to die over here, Sung. I mean die inside. Don't let me, Sung."

Then he grabbed her arm and made her look into his eyes. "I want you to marry me. Will you?"

"Marry?" she whispered, staring at him. She was silent a

long minute, then she smiled and touched his face. "Ron, you can't marry me." Then she leaned close and kissed his lips. "I never thought there would ever be someone like you. You are a very good person. But you can't marry me. You must go home and find a lovely girl in America and have lovely babies. I . . . I can't marry you. I can't go to America. This is my home. Vietnam."

"Bullshit," he said. "There isn't any Vietnam anymore, and I don't want to marry anyone besides you, and I don't want any lovely kids, except with you. And why can't you come to America?"

She laughed at his anger, very real, but so harmless she saw, for it was true after all; he would never hurt her. "What would I do in America?" she asked.

"Be a wife."

"What does a wife do?"

"I don't know, I never had one. I guess they keep busy."

"Oh, Ron, that cannot be."

"Well, it can, god damn it. Listen, I'm not telling you the future, I'm just asking you to marry me."

She looked away, toward the light outside, and tears came to her eyes. She didn't think she would ever be happy again, but she was—this minute she was, no matter that nothing he said could ever be, just that for this minute there was . . . yes, it was as he said, love.

"Well, I know it's kind of a big thing, and sorta sudden," he said. "But I mean it, and I want you to think about it, okay?"

She faced back to him. "Yes. I will think about it."

"I mean really think about it."

"Yes, really." She smiled.

Then he rolled toward her, pressing his erection into her thigh. "Well, since we're engaged now—practically married almost, we ought to get used to each other more." He pinned her beneath him, his mouth searching hers, and she turned away, giggling, but only for a second, then she turned and sought his mouth.

CHAPTER

• 41 •

Mead did not see Marshall the next day, or for two days after that. The ambassador was in military and State Department briefings continuously, then returned to his villa.

During that time Mead stayed around the office or ran errands for Colonel Romer and Colonel Waggoner.

Once when he was alone with Colonel Waggoner, he nervously broached the subject of getting married and whose command approval he would need.

"Marry?" Waggoner asked. "Command approval? You don't need that; when you get home, marry anybody you want. Who gives a damn? What's her name?" he asked, more gently this time.

"Sung Le Vinh, sir. And that's the problem, sir—you see, she's not at home, she's here."

"You mean she's a gook? You want to marry a gook?"

"A Vietnamese woman, sir."

"No way, Corporal. Not possible. Forget it."

Then Mead went to the Marine barracks and started his way up the chain of command.

"Try that one on me again, Mead," said Gunnery Sergeant Robson Holman. "You're coming into my office to ask me for permission to marry a gook gash? You're doped up, right?"

"I want to put in the paperwork, Gunny," Mead said calmly.

"Haven't you got something better to do—kiss the ambassador's ass, or suck up to those colonels—than waste my time like this?"

"I'm requesting permission to put in some paperwork, Gunny."

Holman came from behind his desk and pressed his face into Mead's. "Well, we'll certainly let you do that, Corporal. I'll get you the paper and a crayon for you to fill it out with, but let me tell you this, fuckface, I will personally see to it that you get turned down. I knew you were dumb, but wanting to marry a gook—shit! Actually, I ought to let you do it—marry some sleazy whore and take her back to the States. Then she could set up shop at Camp Pendleton, walking around Oceanside with a mattress strapped to her back—but no, I got your best interests at heart, Mead, I got a duty to my men, even shitbirds like you—you ain't never gonna marry a gook."

Then Holman shook his head in disgust. "I hate your fucking guts, Mead—I think you're a puke, but I thought even you had better sense than this. What's the matter with you? You never dipped your stick before, and now that you did, you want to marry a whore?"

"She's not a whore, Gunny."

"I'm sure not; I'll bet she's a princess. Where'd you meet her? All that's got to be put down on the paperwork, fool. Where did this 'liaison' begin?"

"Okay, I met her in a cathouse, but—"

"Get out of here, Mead!"

"Permission to see the CO!"

"Sure, turd. He'll talk to you."

But Mead got nowhere with the detachment commander. The major was affable, amused, but adamant.

"You know how many requests I get like yours, Corporal?"

"No, sir."

"About three a month. A trooper goes off, finds some cunt that mesmerizes him, blows his boots off, and suddenly he's in love. Suzy Sinkhole back in Jerkyville, Tennessee, can't

634

suck and fuck this good, and since that's what life and marriage are all about—right?—then he's gonna marry this wonderful little girl over here whose only English is 'You buy me drink, big boy?' and 'Your cock number one, GI,' and Mama back in Jerkyville has a heart attack when the sweet little boy she sent off in the Marines comes home with some painted dragon lady with a parasol."

He pushed the papers back across the desk toward Mead. "So no, Corporal, I'm not going to grant permission—not to you, or any Marine under me. You're a grown man and by rights you should be able to do what you want, but you're overseas, the woman in question is a foreigner, so the rules and regulations of the State Department are in effect, plus Marine Corps policy, all of which are designed to save you from your dick. So forget about it, it will not happen. Besides, a Marine's cock isn't supposed to fall in love—it's a fucking machine; so go about your business, Corporal, but leave love and morals on the sheets. Dismissed."

Mead was stunned. They were all treating it as a joke, but the men over him had absolute power in such a matter—he could not marry without their permission; he could not take Sung back with him; she could not go to America. He had not considered the possibility that he would be denied—the impossibility seemed in finding someone to love, finding someone such as Sung, getting her even to smile at him, even to consider marrying him.

What was he going to do? He despaired. He loved her—it was real, not a joke or dirty like they made it seem. He wasn't some horny kid like they were talking about—he knew what life was about; he knew about people. He loved her.

But those who controlled his fate said no. They couldn't though, he thought—not on something this important; this was his life, the rest of his life.

There had to be a way, but he couldn't think of one. Rules and regulations overwhelmed him, and his world was one of strict obedience. It never even crossed his mind to go to Ambassador Marshall for help. Marshall had been kind to him, but his world was one of presidents and generals, war and peace—it was a world of power and authority, of thoughts and ideas—big things, Mead thought, not one of corporals and their women, not one of love.

Mead couldn't even bring himself to tell Marshall about Lacouture or Lord. He would if Marshall had ever mentioned the Frenchman again, but he hadn't. He, Mead, didn't understand anything that was happening; it was all so far above him.

That night, in agony over what he had been told about Sung, and unable to face her, he went into town to get drunk.

Marshall listened to the tape from Lacouture over and over again. It was legitimate, he decided, even though the Frenchman's voice was strained, and he sounded as if he was reading from a script. He wanted to verify the message's authenticity, but he could think of no way to do so without possibly compromising the meeting—he could not call Lacouture, and he did not want to use Mead as go-between again; he was too noticeable. He would simply have to trust the message on the tape.

An instinct for caution sounded alarms within him, and he challenged his judgment on the matter repeatedly—was he being duped? Was he being too eager for this meeting? Was he deceiving himself?

Finally he decided. It made no difference; he had to risk the meeting—it was the best, perhaps only, chance for peace. What did his safety count in the face of that? If he could stop the carnage—should he waver in caution, hesitate in fear?

He would keep his own counsel, he decided. He would make the rendezvous and tell no one.

In the interval before the meeting, he worked on his presentation to Johnson and attended MACV briefings.

Dak To was now secure, he was told. The enemy had been routed—322 of them had been killed, and a thousand wounded. Though Hill 875 was never taken, the enemy finally fled under the constant shelling.

"Where did they go?" Marshall asked.

Perhaps to Khe Sanh, MACV guessed, for that was where the enemy seemed to be preparing a major assault. Intelligence reported a doubling of enemy truck traffic on the Ho

Chi Minh trail and a concentration of troops along the DMZ. Moreover, a lone Marine patrol from an outpost beyond Khe Sanh had discovered a large staging area within the DMZ. The After-Action report indicated there was one Marine KIA on the patrol.

Another son, Marshall thought, scanning the brief report —not even a name, just a notation: 1 KIA. Holding the paper, he wondered fleetingly about the man—who he was and what dreams he might have had and whom he left behind. But then General Westmoreland was telling him about Khe Sanh, and Marshall laid the paper aside.

"Khe Sanh will be the crucible," Westmoreland predicted, and there he would destroy Giap. "I'll stake my career on this—Khe Sanh will never fall."

"I'll be safe there then?" Marshall said with a smile. "I plan to visit there shortly."

General Abrams leaned over to Westmoreland and said sotto voce, "Maybe we ought to reconsider our strategy and let them take the hill." Then to Marshall he asked innocently, "When are you planning a visit?"

After the briefing, Marshall asked Westmoreland about a battalion command for Colonel Romer.

"I'll see to it personally," Westmoreland said.

Back at the embassy, Marshall called his wife and learned that Ryan had completed his Special Forces training, would return home for Christmas, then would be sent directly to Vietnam.

"Can't you lock him in a closet?" he asked.

"I thought you were going to end the war," she said.

"I'm trying, for God's sake, but lock him in the closet just in case."

"I'm sure that with all his newly acquired combat skills, he'll be able to break the door down with his bare hands, Brad. Then, in a crazed frenzy, he might massacre us all."

"Catherine, I called to wish you a merry Christmas, not to listen to hysterical ravings."

"My son is being sent to war as a Green Beret—a Green Beret, Brad!—my son who was disconsolate when the fish in the aquarium died and who hid his head every time the wicked queen appeared in *Sleeping Beauty*—my son, Brad! —my baby, I don't care what idiot rag he wears on his head—my poor baby goes off to get killed, and you call me hysterical!"

"I hope you have a lovely Christmas, Catherine."

"I'll lock him in the cellar."

"Chain him, Catherine—with those chains you were going to use to chain yourself to the White House fence, remember?"

"Brad?"

"Yes, Catherine?"

"I couldn't stand it if something happened to him."

He sighed. "I couldn't either, Catherine."

"Well, thank you for calling. Neither Chris nor Sarah is in. They're out somewhere, but you don't want to hear about it."

"What do you mean? Where are they?"

She laughed. "You're so *easy* to stir up, Brad. I can't imagine how the enemy has any trouble with you."

"They're not as diabolical as you, Catherine—they're mere men."

"Then I should be there instead of you."

"I've said that all along. Well, I'll call again on Christmas —maybe somebody will be there."

"Let the phone ring for a while, we may all be out in the backyard learning hand-to-hand combat from Ryan."

"Good-bye, Catherine."

"Good-bye, Brad."

Dear God, he thought after hanging up; Ryan would be here in less than a month. It all seemed inexorable, some awful Greek tragedy unfolding in which he and Ryan were characters—the lines foreordained, the ending sealed, their fates long determined; they were merely playing out roles.

That was true tragedy: to have a foreboding, feel the premonition intensify, watch the doom clouds gather, and follow each irrevocable step of the disaster.

Yet there was still a chance to avert tragedy—the meeting Lacouture had arranged.

* * * *

Lord was impressed with the cool hand Marshall was playing; the ambassador had given no indication whatsoever of his plans or intentions. But Lord knew his man—Marshall had taken the bait; he would meet with the NVA.

A less confident or experienced man than himself might have pushed too hard, Lord knew: Gibbon could probably not have resisted an extra turn on the screw, or wiggling the bait a little more, but that would have only scared Marshall off.

Waiting was always the hardest part; patience was excruciating, but the best predators were never the fastest runners —they were the most patient stalkers.

"Those who stand and wait don't just serve, Jeffrey—they also live the longest, and feed the best," he told Gibbon.

"Exactly what Milton had in mind, I'm sure," Gibbon said.

"Why, Jeffrey, you amaze me—a literate pretty-boy spy."

Now Lord would just wait. The South Vietnamese Special Branch had men in place with a Soviet heat-seeking rocket to shoot down Marshall's chopper, and they would leave evidence on the ground that would incriminate the NVA. The Special Branch owed the CIA for its assistance with the assassinations of the Diems; they were just returning the favor.

On the morning of the twenty-third, Marshall worked a normal day, then shortly before noon he told Colonel Romer to notify Magnuson to have the chopper ready in an hour.

"Where are you going, sir?"

"Only I will be going, Colonel."

"May I ask where, sir? Someone should know."

"No, Colonel, no one needs to know. I'll give Lieutenant Magnuson the destination when we're airborne. I'm ordering you to strict silence and secrecy—I don't want anyone even to know that I'm gone."

"Sir, I don't think that's wise."

"Perhaps not, but those are my orders."

"Well, sir, at least take Corporal Mead—just in case something happens."

"I won't need him, Colonel."

"I'm sure not, sir, but as we both know, he's a good man to have around, just in case."

"All right. Tell him to be ready to leave in thirty minutes."

Romer crossed the hall to Mead's cubicle. "Get your ass ready, something's happening. The ambassador is taking off in a few minutes, and he's not telling anybody where he's going. I don't like it at all. I want you ready for anything, understand?"

"Yes, sir."

Mead barely had time to check his rifle and magazines before the ambassador left, and unlike any other time, Marshall merely nodded acknowledgment to him, riding silent and preoccupied to Tan Son Nhut.

Lord was already at the air base when Gibbon radioed him that Marshall had just left the embassy.

Lord knew that from here on he should let matters take their course, but he couldn't resist a final confrontation with Marshall. He wanted to put his opposition to the flight on record, personally distance himself from what was going to happen, and also he wanted to turn the screw one last notch and watch Marshall chomp the baited hook.

On the flight line, Magnuson saluted Marshall and said the helicopter was ready for takeoff. "Where are we going, sir?"

"I'll tell you when we're in the air."

As soon as they climbed into the chopper, Magnuson started the engine and the rotor blades began to whirl.

Just then Lord drove onto the runway and stopped before the helicopter. He signaled Magnuson to wait, then went to the passenger hold and slid open the door. Mead jumped when he saw him and tightened his grip on his rifle.

"Mr. Ambassador, I want to protest this flight."

Marshall, outraged at the man's gall, stared at him impassively. "I don't see that it's your business to protest anything I do, Mr. Lord."

"I've filed a formal protest about this mission," he said

arrogantly. "It's dangerous, and not in the best interests of the United States."

"Who are you to tell me what is in the best interests of the country?" Marshall snapped.

Lord smiled in knowing satisfaction. "The Frenchman and the NVA have set you up. This meeting you think you're going to is a trick—they've played you for a sucker. They're going to kill you. I've come to prevent that."

"You came to stop me from making peace," Marshall retorted. Then he caught himself, realizing how badly he had let his anger slip. "I've noted your protest," he said with clipped control. "Now go."

Beside Marshall, Mead said anxiously, "What meeting, sir? Is that where we're going—to the meeting Mr. Lacouture was supposed to arrange?"

"Yes, Corporal," Marshall said, annoyed that the whole arrangement was now in the open. "Now, good day, Mr. Lord."

"Sir, there is no meeting," Mead said quickly. "Mr. Lacouture's dead, sir. He never arranged a meeting."

"What?" Marshall said, turning on Mead, not believing he'd heard correctly.

Mead began to stammer, "I wanted to tell you, but you never, I mean . . . I thought you . . ."

Lord realized with a sinking feeling that he had overplayed his hand, violated his own rule against impetuosity, and he knew he had to intercede smoothly to end the discussion before his role was compromised. "Oh, there's a meeting all right, Corporal. Lacouture arranged one, but it's to have the ambassador killed."

"You lying bastard. You killed Lacouture while we were at Dak To."

Marshall felt confused, disoriented. What was all this?

"But I have a tape from Mr. Lacouture, Corporal, delivered the day we arrived. Dolores spoke with him."

"He was dead by then, sir. That's a phony tape. Mr. Lord killed him before then."

Lord shook his head in disdain. "What an impressive piece of business you've arranged, Mr. Ambassador—so professional: secret meetings, childish code words, ridiculous intermediaries, and an ignorant corporal arranging 'presidential' negotiations."

Marshall, stung and off balance, struggling to understand, to make sense of this, worried by how little time he had left to make his rendezvous, looked from Lord to Mead.

"Mr. Ambassador, I . . . I should have told you, but that night when I went to Mr. Lacouture's, after we came back from Dak To, he was dead, sir, and I didn't know what to do, and I . . ."

Lord shrugged. "Your bodyguard was very familiar with Lacouture, an enemy agent, Mr. Ambassador. He spent quite a bit of time with Lacouture. They were quite close, Excellency—Lacouture was paying Corporal Mead to sleep with him. He was sodomizing him."

"That's a fucking lie!" Mead yelled, leaping from his seat.

Magnuson came over the intercom. "Mr. Ambassador, Corporal Mead told me about spending the night with that Frenchman—he's telling you the truth, sir."

Marshall looked at Mead and Lord. Of course Mead wasn't lying, he knew, but he knew also that Lord did not want this meeting to take place—why then was he urging him not to attend, warning him of an ambush if there was no meeting? He glanced at his watch. There was no time left; he had to leave this instant or miss the rendezvous.

"Mr. Lord," he said, deciding that he could untangle the confusion on the way, "I am requisitioning your services on behalf of the President of the United States. You are to accompany me. Strap yourself in, please. Lieutenant, take off."

Lord seemed to hesitate for a second, but then coolly obeyed.

"Where to, sir?" Magnuson asked when they were airborne.

"Hong Ngu, near the Cambodian border. The grid square is seven eight four eight seven six five."

Mead unstrapped his belt and crouched in front of Marshall. "Sir, I delivered your message to Mr. Lacouture."

"And stayed the night with him," sneered Lord.

"Yeah, so what?" Mead said furiously, then he turned to Marshall, his voice pleading for understanding. "And the night we got back from Dak To, I went to his house. It was wrecked and he was dead. He told me before, the night I brought him your message, that there wasn't going to be a meeting because the CIA killed a gook messenger and that the NVA would be afraid to meet now. He said he would try to set up the meeting but he didn't think he'd be able to. Then he was killed. Mr. Lord killed him. He killed the gook messenger too."

Lord laughed and stretched out his legs comfortably. "This is just bizarre. Are all your diplomatic missions this fanciful, Excellency?"

Marshall had never hated anyone as much as he did Lord this minute, yet he could not decide what game he was playing.

"It's true about that gook," Magnuson said over the intercom. "I helped kill him. A few days before Dak To, Mr. Lord had me fly a gook over the South China Sea and drop him. I used to work for the CIA, sir, flying for them up in Da Nang. That's why I was sent down to be your pilot. I don't know what's going on now, sir, but I'd trust Corporal Mead, not Mr. Lord, if I were you."

"Don't go on, sir," Mead said. "Turn back."

Lord crossed his arms and smiled. "That is exactly what I have been saying—that's what I drove out to tell you."

Marshall glanced from Mead to Lord, then back to Mead. "Corporal, I believe everything you've told me, but I have to risk this meeting. Peace, the barest chance of it, is more important than anything else. Besides, Mr. Lord is so opposed to my making this trip, perhaps there is a meeting after all."

Mead shook his head. "That's just a trick too, sir. We're flying into an ambush."

"I have to take the chance," Marshall said. "If it's an ambush, Mr. Lord will go down too. But none of that matters, any of our lives, if there's a possibility for peace."

He patted Mead's shoulder and directed him back to his seat. "Lieutenant, fly to the destination," Marshall said, turning to look out the window, and trying with all his might to appear placid and statesmanlike.

Lord settled comfortably and closed his eyes. He had made a mistake, and now he was going to pay for it, he realized. He shouldn't have pushed his luck, but it was still going to work out—the chopper would be shot down, Marshall and his mission discredited.

His mind raced to think of a way to save himself, but there wasn't one without saving Marshall and his mission too.

He had made a foolish mistake, he knew; a fatal one—but if that was the price, he would pay it. He was almost relaxed; death was not something for which he was unprepared: he had been willing to die many times, had put his life on the line for twenty years—now the time had come. He had never had any illusions about the dangers of his profession, or that sooner or later the draw would have to go against him.

Across from him, Marshall analyzed everything he had just heard. Probably there was no meeting, he decided; perhaps he was flying into an ambush. Maybe he was a fool and had been duped—by Lacouture, the NVA, or the CIA, what did it matter? But maybe, just maybe, there was a chance for peace. Would he risk his life for that? If he could hand over his life to guarantee the safety of others—he would do it without hesitation. But he couldn't; he had to take a risk, and perhaps lose his life meaninglessly, yet he would do it for the mere possibility, no matter how remote, of saving lives.

He looked through the window to the blurred green earth below. Perhaps I am flying to my death, he thought. I certainly thought I was sailing to my death years ago on that launch off Guadalcanal; how afraid I was then, he remembered. And how unafraid I am now.

Watching them both, Mead marveled at their coolness; they were both willing to die, he saw—two men absolutely convinced that they were right, unwilling to compromise. And there was nothing he could do; he was trapped.

They flew for an hour in silence, neither Marshall nor Lord showing a trace of tension or anxiety.

"We'll be approaching Hong Ngu in about ten minutes," Magnuson said.

Lord yawned and stretched. Marshall turned from the window at the movement.

"I was thinking earlier today about Milton," Lord said. "Do you remember the lesson of *Paradise Lost?*"

"Pride, wasn't it?" Marshall answered.

"Yes."

"Is that the lesson to be learned here too?" Marshall asked.

Lord smiled, for he had been thinking that exactly, how his own pride and hubris had been his downfall—how he wouldn't be on this helicopter except for that. "All the good lessons are so stock, aren't they?"

"Tell me, Mr. Lord, whom do you see yourself as in the *Paradise* scenario?"

"Well, since you picture yourself as the righteous God, I suppose I'll have to be Lucifer."

Marshall shook his head and smiled faintly. "Too grandiose, Mr. Lord. Far too melodramatic, a common flaw in zealots. I'm afraid we're both just minor angels with bit parts."

"Five minutes," Magnuson announced over the intercom.

"Lieutenant, you gotta turn this thing back!" Mead yelled. "We're flying into an ambush."

"Corporal," Magnuson said calmly, "take it easy—let me fly this thing."

Marshall looked at Lord and said, "I have a son on his way here."

Lord met his stare. "I have a son already here."

"Ah," Marshall said in understanding. "How odd—fathers fighting instead of their sons." He smiled. "Maybe we're not minor angels after all—we might be archangels."

"Two minutes," Magnuson said.

"I am doing this for my son," Marshall said.

"And I am doing this for mine," Lord answered. "This war is right and can be won."

Marshall shook his head. "It is wrong and can't be won."

"One minute."

"We are implacable foes," Lord said.

Marshall nodded. "Opposing archangels, Hector and Achilles, and on and on—you are quite right, Mr. Lord: it's all very stock indeed."

"Jesus!" Mead said, pressing his face against the window.

"The strength of a belief is not of those willing to kill for it, but of those willing to die for it," Lord said, sitting back in his seat.

"Indeed," Marshall said, easing back in his. "That's the oldest lesson of all. Eons older than the lesson of Cain and Abel."

"It's the same story," Lord said, locking his eyes on Marshall. "Pride."

Marshall met his gaze. "Love," he said emphatically.

"You're both shitheads," Mead said furiously.

Marshall smiled faintly. "Ah. *That's* the oldest story—the God story."

"Zero, and hovering," Magnuson said.

Then Mead saw it. "Jesus Christ!" he shouted. "A rocket. They just fired a rocket at us."

Magnuson saw it too, the burst of fire and smoke from the ground, then the trail of the heat-seeking missile racing upward.

He cut his engine and at the same time pressed a button, firing a rocket.

The chopper plummeted in a free fall and the heat-seeking missile screamed past, chasing after the rocket, catching it in seconds, exploding both in a tremendous burst.

Magnuson immediately restarted the engine, and the blades, stabilizing in autorotation, caught and lifted the craft. Magnuson pulled the chopper to the left and sped it out of range.

"Now we're even," he said in the same calm voice to Mead. "You know, you're not the *only* fucking hero in this goddamn war."

"You see, Excellency," Lord said smoothly to Marshall. "I told you that you were flying into an ambush, that Lacouture and the NVA had set you up."

"You lying son of a bitch," Mead yelled. "*You* did that."

"*I* did, Corporal? *I* was the one who warned the ambassador about what would happen. I drove out to Tan Son Nhut to protest this flight for the very thing that happened. I told him over and over that the enemy was trying to kill him."

"That wasn't the enemy, that was you."

"Corporal," Lord said serenely, "that is all a fabrication of your *limited* mind and wild imagination. And certainly unprovable. My protest and warning are on file at the embassy."

"You motherfucker! You murdering bastard," Mead cried, throwing himself on Lord, slamming his knee into Lord's gut, his hands throttling his neck. "I'll kill you!"

Lord couldn't move, and he knew his neck was going to snap. He looked wildly to Marshall, but the ambassador just watched.

Mead pressed harder, squeezing out life.

At the last second, Marshall said, "No," then louder, "No, Corporal."

Still Mead did not release his grip.

"Stop!" Marshall heard himself yelling. "Let him go."

Mead pulled away. He turned to Marshall. "The bastard deserves to die," he said furiously. "More than anyone. Let me kill him."

Marshall shook his head. "Then we wouldn't be any better than he is."

Lord fell forward gasping for breath, clutching his stomach.

After a while he righted himself and said bitterly, "You *aren't* any better."

Marshall turned to the window, then he closed his eyes against the despair that he felt crushing in on him. He had lost; he would not end the war.

Rage burgeoned within him, and his eyes opened furiously on Lord. "I ought to kill you myself."

"You're too weak," Lord sneered.

Mead watched Marshall in fascination, then saw an incredible control take hold of the ambassador, a thing that so many times had gripped him too and allowed him to survive.

Marshall took a deep breath and eased back. "No, Mr. Lord. You are. Zealots are weak, desperate people. What you believe is wrong. What you do is wrong. The killing must stop. And it's going to stop right here."

He spoke with cold determination. "This was your point, Mr. Lord, but not the match. I am going to destroy you, and I want you to see it."

Then he turned to the window. His hopes were dashed; he would not succeed. He drew another deep breath. But he would try again.

That was the only hope men had, to not succumb; to keep trying. And he would, he resolved.

"Go back to Saigon," he said to Magnuson.

CHAPTER

• 42 •

Lord watched the shredder gobble the last of his papers. It was four A.M., and he was alone on the corridor, closing out his office. His flight back to the States left in a few hours.

He had kissed his son in his crib and did not linger, then he packed only a few belongings and told Ahne he was leaving.

"It is good-bye," she said.

"No," he said.

"You are not coming back this time, Wilson."

He smiled. "I go on trips five and six times a month; why am I not coming back this time?"

"Because you are packing things you have never packed before. Clothes can be bought anywhere," she said, holding up a manila envelope of photographs. "But you can't buy the past in any store."

"Oh, Ahne," he said, pulling her close against him.

"I know you would not do this unless you had to," she said. "And I knew it would happen someday."

She drew away and looked into his eyes. "We will be fine; do not worry about us. I will go back to my family."

He lowered his head and shook it. "I've forgotten how to cry," he said.

The machine spat out the final shreds, then returned to a low hum of inactivity, waiting to be fed more.

Behind Lord the door opened. He raised his head but did not turn; no one had ever entered his office without knocking. A chill passed through him. Finally he turned.

Gibbon stood in the doorway staring at him with cobra eyes.

Neither spoke for a full minute, then Lord said, *"Et tu, Brute?"*

Gibbon closed the door behind him and leaned against it, his expression gelid.

"No, Mr. Lord. You do me injustice; I am Antony."

Gibbon pulled a pistol from his jacket and held it casually. "Once you told me it was my right to refuse an order—my duty even."

He walked to Lord's desk and laid the weapon on it.

Lord let out his breath slowly. "So the order came down." He smiled faintly. "There's a lesson here, Jeffrey. Don't make mistakes."

"I knew *that* one, Mr. Lord."

Gibbon's expression did not change, and he did not take his eyes from Lord's. "I owe you loyalty. That means something to me."

"To me also, Jeff."

"I'm sorry it's ended this way, Mr. Lord."

"What?" said Lord with faint mockery. "A literate, *sensitive* prettyboy spy? That's not allowed. But I suppose you know that too." Then he shook his head. "You know, the strange thing is, I succeeded. I served well those who would . . ." He glanced at the pistol. "I accomplished what they wanted."

"There's a lesson there too, Mr. Lord."

"What is that?"

"Remember what flows down—it's seldom loyalty. Usually it's shit."

Lord smiled. "I knew that once; I must have forgotten it. So, Marshall called Johnson; Johnson called Langley, and . . ." He nodded toward the pistol. "The downhill flow started—and stopped at you."

Gibbon shook his head. "No, it passed me—it'll stop somewhere else, with someone who has a different sense of loyalty."

"I should have expected this. But in all honesty, I didn't." Suddenly Lord looked older, vulnerable for the first time, and his rigid carriage slumped. "You've given me a . . . stay of execution. A brief stay." He sighed. "I never expected to go that way. But I know too much; they'll worry that I might . . . compromise my knowledge."

Then he drew himself up. "Actually that was a smart career move you made, refusing that order, Jeffrey."

Gibbon smiled coldly. "I know. The job will get done; someone will do it."

"And you will be unscathed. Loyal. You will be trusted."

"Exactly."

Lord nodded. "You were a good student, Jeffrey." He switched off the shredder. "Well, the evidence is gone. All that's left is me—to be shredded neatly by . . . ? A bomb in my car? An assassin in a dark alley? Poison? I wonder how long it will take them. But soon, I would think."

Gibbon nodded. "I would expect so. Is there anything I can do for you?"

Lord looked into his eyes. "Would you?"

Gibbon did not break his gaze. "I would."

"Then would you see to Ahne and my son?"

"I will."

Lord inclined his head. "Thank you." He looked about the room a final time. "Then there's nothing else."

"Maybe Marshall won after all," Gibbon said.

Lord considered. "No," he said. "All he got rid of was me. And who will replace me—you? That would hardly be an improvement in his eyes."

Gibbon's eyes gleamed. "Maybe it *will* be an improvement."

Lord smiled. "You can tell me about it when we meet in hell."

Gibbon laughed. "Is that where we'll all be? Is that where spies go?"

"I hope so. I wouldn't want to share eternity with saints. Would you?" He eyed the pistol, cold and final on the desk. "You couldn't give me a hint as to when it might come, could you?"

"I would expect sooner rather than later. I would expect

651

very soon. I would guess that your last safe moments will be within the embassy."

Gibbon held out his hand and stared deeply into Lord's eyes. "Good-bye, Mr. Lord." Then he closed the door and left.

Lord stared at the pistol for a long minute, then he left the office and went down the empty corridor. After passing through the Marine sentry booth, he hesitated before going outside.

He stood a long while on the portico, looking out into the night. Finally he gave in to the pain he had held in check for so many years. He groaned slightly and started down the stairs, limping into the darkness.

Marshall took limited satisfaction in Lord's sudden and unexpected departure from the embassy, for he realized that Lord had won far more than a point—it might well have been the match.

What did he, Marshall, have to bring back to Johnson? An argument against the COVIA study, some personal observations, and a recommendation to end the war—hardly a breakthrough. Johnson had sent him to find a way out of the war; the President wasn't looking for data or arguments—he wanted a solution. And he, Marshall, didn't have one. Lord had destroyed the one possibility he had found.

The Christmas holiday provided an escape from his problems, and for diversion he attended receptions and parties, but afterward he sequestered himself in his office; he could not let Lord win; he had to bring back something meaningful to Johnson—what moral right did he have to demand the President step down because of the war when he himself could not come up with a way to end it?

He applied lawyers' logic and viewed the war over and over again from military and political viewpoints, but always he returned to the same point—the war could not be won without drastic escalation that would require an attack on the North. Johnson would have to become the invader or the peacemaker; he could not crawl through the tunnel any longer searching for its end, dragging the mounting weight of the coffins, followed by an army of amputees and disaffected, drug-abused youths.

This enemy could not be defeated; this ally they supported could not be propped. Sooner or later a president would have to make peace—better now, and better Johnson, Marshall thought.

His plan to find an intermediary had failed; there was no time to find another. He toyed briefly with the idea of seeking Teresa Hawthorne's or Father Dourmant's help in establishing contact with the communists, but that could endanger them. Though Lord was gone, there were certainly others in the CIA who shared his views, and they wouldn't stop at murder to protect their views, and what they felt was in the national interest.

Marshall knew that every step of his would be watched, and that powerful factions opposed to him would ensure that he never made contact with General Khanh, or anyone else who might negotiate an end to the war.

His only chance to bring about peace would be to convince Johnson to enter negotiations immediately. Marshall felt that he could, but only as long as the military stalemate continued. If the North attacked and sent Johnson on the defensive, the President would make no concessions.

He would have to make his case personally to the President, and before the military situation escalated.

As expected, the Christmas and New Year's truces held, and General Westmoreland was convinced that the North would honor the Tet truce also, so Marshall felt that he had a little time—a few weeks to wind down his mission, complete his report, visit the imperial tombs at Hue, which he had promised Lacouture that he would see before departing, and by then, Ryan would have arrived in the country, and he would be able to see him.

Marshall was in the final week of his mission when he received an urgent call from the White House.

When Marshall went down to the communications center, and before entering the soundproof booth, he directed that the volume be turned down.

"I'm sure everybody in Hanoi heard that last conversation," he said.

"Bradley! You there, Bradley?" Johnson boomed.

Dear God, thought Marshall; why are we bothering with all this equipment? Johnson could stand on the front portico and I could go outside and hear him.

"Yes, Mr. President, I'm here. How are you, sir?"

"Poorly, Bradley. Terrible, terrible poorly. Why don't you ever call me, Bradley?" he whined. "I keep waiting and waiting to hear from you, but you never call me. You know, the government *pays* for these calls."

"Well, sir, I haven't called because I'm returning right away; I planned to talk to you personally."

"Return?" Johnson shouted. "What do you mean? You can't come back here."

Now what? he wondered, but all he could manage was, "Sir?"

"Bradley, it's the Apocalypse."

"In Washington?" Marshall asked incredulously.

"At Khe Sanh," Johnson yelled.

"Khe Sanh?" Marshall repeated.

"Bradley, you're within walking distance of the end of the world, and you don't know about it? What are you doing over there?"

"Mr. President," Marshall said mildly, "I think someone must have exaggerated the situation at Khe Sanh. There's been an enemy buildup all along the DMZ, but no one here seriously thinks Khe Sanh is going to fall. General Westmoreland has shifted another fifteen thousand troops to I Corps—so enemy strengths and U.S. strengths are approximately equal, forty thousand men each."

"What about those enemy officers in Marine uniforms? They were shot right in the wire. What were they doing there?" he demanded, then thundered his own answer: "They were making a personal reconnaissance! They're getting ready to attack! It's Dien Bien Phu all over again, I know it is."

"Mr. President," Marshall said patiently, "General Westmoreland would like nothing more than a full-scale attack at

Khe Sanh—he's convinced he can hold the position. And I'm sure the Joint Chiefs concur. Haven't they reassured you?"

"No! Oh, they traipse in here three times a day and tell me how fine everything is, and they pat my head like some poor *doomed* hound dog ready to be put down—but I can see what's happening there. It's Dien Bien Phu! We're circling the wagons here, Bradley."

"I thought the NVA were in the wire at Khe Sanh, not in the Rose Garden."

"Bradley," Johnson said mournfully, "don't laugh at me. My presidency hangs in the balance."

"What can I do for you?" Marshall said resignedly.

"Go there! Tell me what's happening—I can't trust anybody else but you, Bradley. They're in the goddamn wire wearing our uniforms, and the Joint Chiefs keep telling me everything's under control. Son of a bitch! I'm afraid to close my eyes at night—if things get any more under control, I'm afraid I'll wake up in bed with Ho Chi Minh."

Johnson's voice became a whisper of craft and conspiracy. "Well, I've fixed those bastards."

"Which ones?" Marshall asked.

"The Joint Chiefs. I've had them put it in writing that Khe Sanh won't fall. I had each general sign a paper, *swearing* that. So if Khe Sanh falls, it's my presidency, but it's *their* asses."

"Well, what more can I do? Do you want me to sign a paper too?"

"Bradley, don't mock me. I'm trying to do my best. Bradley, do you *know* what rests on my shoulders? The Free World, Bradley—and I've got poverty and misery and disease and discrimination to fight; the old and sick and suffering, the poor and starving, they look to me, Bradley. And I need your help. Go to Khe Sanh for me. I can't sleep at night worrying about that goddamn place. I'm constipated because of that goddamn hill. You've got to go there for me."

"Mr. President, I think I could be more helpful if I returned. I've finished my mission here. I have concrete proposals and recommendations to make to you. I see a way out of this for you, but I need to talk to you personally. There's a way out of this war."

"I know there is," Johnson yelled. "If Khe Sanh falls, the war's all over. I'll be the first president to preside over a defeat. I'll be a laughingstock. I'll be reviled forever. I can't stand it!"

There was complete silence.

My God, Marshall thought, had he had a heart attack?

"Bradley." The President's voice was a choked whisper; it sounded as though he were dragging himself from the floor back into his chair. "I can't think with this hanging over my head. You've got to go there and tell me what's happening. Nothing else matters. This is the most important battle since Valley Forge. I've got Lady Bird saddled up and ready to ride."

Jesus Christ, Marshall thought, shaking his head. "All right, Mr. President, I'll go."

"Oh, Bradley, you don't know what that means to me. It's been awful here with everybody talking about Khe Sanh— it's in every newspaper and magazine. I can't sleep at night; I stalk the corridors here like Lincoln's ghost. I see all those dead boys . . ." His voice turned vehement. "I hate this fucking war!"

"Yes, sir, I know. But I don't think you should be too concerned about Khe Sanh; I think the military assessment is correct—it won't fall. But I'll go there for you, of course, and if I have the slightest concern about its falling, I'll contact you immediately."

"Thank you. Then you come right back and tell me how to end this war. I'll listen to you, Bradley. I promise I will."

The connection was broken.

Marshall sat for a full minute before moving. He understood Johnson's fixation with Khe Sanh, and that the President could not focus on anything else with this major battle looming before him. But now everything was out of his own hands, Marshall realized: he could not present his case to Johnson before Tet. Everything was now in the hands of the enemy.

He returned to his office and told Romer to prepare for Khe Sanh.

That morning, after they had made love, lying together quietly, Sung told Mead that she had missed her menstrual period.

"I didn't want to hide it from you," she said. "I had to tell you right away."

"Jesus," he said, rolling toward her, but careful not to touch her, as if he might do damage. His first response was joy, then immediately fear, then confusion. A baby, he thought—he would love to have a baby by her. But that was impossible; she couldn't have a child—he would be leaving soon. What would she do in Vietnam all alone with a child?

"Jesus," he said again. "What should we do? I mean, what do you want to do?"

"I thought . . . maybe you could help me. Are you angry with me?"

"Angry? No, of course not. I want to have a baby, but . . . well, maybe it would be better not to have one."

"Yes," she said. "I think it would not be good to bring a child to life here."

"I'll, I'll check around . . . okay? But don't worry, everything will be all right."

He went directly to Teresa Hawthorne, making sure to leave his rifle so he wouldn't frighten the women.

He paced outside the clinic for many minutes, then drew his courage and went inside.

She was in the kitchen, he was told.

When he went in, he found her sitting at the table having tea with Father Dourmant.

"Why, Corporal Mead," she said, smiling at him. "How nice to see you."

Father Dourmant raised his hands in surrender. "I'm unarmed. Tell him I'm unarmed, Teresa."

Mead started to back out. "Oh, I didn't mean to bother you . . . I mean, I didn't know you were busy. I'll come back some—"

"Sit down," Teresa said. "We're just having a tea break."

She smiled again. "You look so nice—without your rifle. Don't you think, Father?"

"Hardly recognized him," the priest grumped.

"No, I'll come—" Mead started to stammer, still backing away.

"Sit down," Father Dourmant barked.

Mead sat down.

"How have you been?" Teresa asked. "Would you care for some tea?"

"No. Thank you, I can't stay, I mean—"

"Have some tea," the priest ordered, and pushed a cup toward him.

Teresa poured him a cup. He resolutely kept his head down, and she and the priest exchanged smiles. "Well, what brings you here?"

He sipped, then sipped again, then sipped some more, his head bowed the whole time, then finally he said to the cup, "Well, I . . . I mean . . . I have a problem. I mean, I don't, but . . . this girl, she . . ."

"I see," Teresa said solemnly. "She's pregnant."

Mead flushed deeply. "Yeah, kinda."

"Kinda?" the priest asked.

Mead finally looked up. He drew a deep breath. "I mean, she just found out. I mean, she missed her period, you know, and . . ." Then he dropped his head to the table. "This is awful. I can't even talk."

Teresa laughed. "Corporal Mead, don't be embarrassed." She gestured to the clinic. "This is not an uncommon problem here. What can we do for you?"

He looked up miserably. "I don't know. You see . . . well, I love her. I really do. I want to marry her, but I can't. I mean, they won't let me, so . . . I don't know what to do."

Teresa nodded. "So you're thinking about—"

Father Dourmant stuck his fingers in his ears.

"—an abortion?"

"I guess," he said. "I mean, she shouldn't have a baby on her own, and they won't let me take her back to America. I want to take her, I . . . well, I really love her, but they all tell me it's impossible because she's Vietnamese."

"Yes," Teresa said. "I know, they simply won't allow such marriages."

"Why?" asked Father Dourmant. "What does love have to do with nationality? I thought only hate and killing were a part of nationality. Love doesn't have anything to do with borders. Or religion, for that matter."

Teresa stuck her fingers in her ears.

"Well, it doesn't," the priest said. "I haven't lived this long for nothing, you know. And you, you damn fool," he said to Mead, reaching into his cassock and pulling out some packets that he tossed to him, "use these in the future. Of course I expect you to abstain altogether, but in case you should fall from the path of righteousness, for God's sake, use rubbers."

Mead gathered them in embarrassment and remained head bowed, like a chastised child.

"Why don't you send her to me?" Teresa said. "I'll talk to her. Father Dourmant and I will both talk to her. I'm sure that everything will work out for the best, and that she gets . . . medical attention if that's her desire."

Mead stood. "Thank you. Really, thank you. I'll make sure she comes. And for money . . . I'll take care of everything."

Teresa smiled. "We won't worry about that now."

Mead backed away, thanking them all the way out the door, and that night he told Sung about the clinic and wrote down the address and the name of Teresa Hawthorne.

"I'll go with you if you want, but maybe you'd rather go on your own. They're really nice people."

"I'll go," she said. "Thank you."

Then he told her that he had just been notified that he would be leaving in the next few days on a long trip with the ambassador. "I really hate to leave you like this, but I . . . I have to go when they tell me. I'll leave you plenty of money and . . . will you be all right?" he asked. "I mean, pregnant and . . . maybe I can get out of it. I shouldn't leave you . . ."

She smiled. "Everything will be fine. And I'll be here when you return."

* * *

Marshall sat alone in his living room, a glass of wine cradled in his hands. It was nearly nine; he was sad and depressed, and for the first time in a long while, he was lonely.

He wished he had someone to confide in, someone to whom he could unburden his unhappiness—someone who would just listen and nod in understanding and commiseration. Poor thing, poor thing, she would say, stroking his brow—how hard you tried, how much you cared, how noble your effort.

He smiled at his self-indulgence and brought the glass to his lips. But he *did* care—more than anything he wanted to end the misery and suffering; he wanted to save all the sons. He had had such great hopes, but now they were like the legs of the wine in the glass, trailing to the bottom.

His valet entered the room and stood silently until Marshall looked up.

"Excellency, a lady is here to see you. A Miss Teresa Hawthorne."

Marshall was startled. He put the wineglass on the table and stood. "Show her in, please."

He straightened his clothes and adjusted his tie.

The valet led Teresa into the room, then he closed the French doors behind him.

Teresa stood just inside the room, slightly stunned at the opulent setting.

Marshall crossed to her quickly, very happy and expectant. "How nice to see you." He stood before her and awkwardly held out his hand.

She shook it and, inadvertently, both their gazes dropped to the contact. Marshall pulled his hand away first. "I'm so glad you came."

"Thank you for seeing me," she said. "Am I interrupting anything?"

"Only my despair. I was feeling sorry for myself. You are an angel of mercy."

She blushed slightly, then smoothed at her dress, but she couldn't find anything to do with her hands. Then she brought them to her mouth to cover the laugh on the verge of breaking from her lips.

She had been *so* foolish about this, she thought, worrying over her appearance, changing into all five of her dresses, arranging and rearranging her hair, even rouging her cheeks —then resolutely washing it off. And just before she left the clinic, Father Dourmant came to visit, and as soon as he saw her, he said, "Why, it must be love."

She had flushed more crimson than any rouge applied to her face, and she had said, "That's silly."

He had smiled. "Love is never silly, Teresa. It's a beautiful thing. People like you *should* love; and be loved."

"Father!"

"Why won't you admit it?"

"It's not love. It's just . . . a nice feeling."

"That'll do."

"I'm old," she said. "And not pretty."

He laughed. "That doesn't have anything to do with love." Then he smiled. "You are a lovely woman, Teresa; more lovely than any woman I have ever seen."

She was very embarrassed.

"See," he said. "That's love."

"Stop it!"

Now Teresa brought her hands down. "I just came to . . . well, I had a reason."

Marshall smiled. "I'd like it better if you had come to see me for no reason." He gestured to a chair and led her to it. "May I offer you something? A drink? Coffee? Please."

She hesitated. "A drink would be very nice," she said at last.

"Wine?"

"Yes. Oh, that would be lovely."

He poured a glass for her, then sat down in a chair across from her. "I'm so glad you came. I was wallowing in self-pity, being perfectly stupid. And there you are in the clinic—I'm humiliated."

She laughed. "Don't start the saint routine, it's hardly apt, and very embarrassing. We each find our niche in the world and do what we can—I've found mine here in Vietnam, and I'm happy. And very busy."

She smiled broadly. "That's why I'm here tonight. I debated it a long time. I'm breaking a confidence, though he didn't ask me to keep it a secret, but I thought you should know."

"What is that?"

"Corporal Mead came to see me."

Marshall laughed. "You too? My God, that boy is everywhere. What did he come to you for?"

"He's in love."

"Corporal Mead? One hardly associates him with the—more delicate emotions."

"He is a very sweet boy, as I knew all along. Even Father Dourmant thinks so. And he is in love with a Vietnamese girl, and she is . . . how did he put it? 'Kinda pregnant.'"

"Dear God," Marshall said, shaking his head. "Where does he get all the energy?"

"He's young. Young people have lots of energy."

Marshall sighed. "I'll take your word for it—youth is a dim memory to me."

"That's not what you told me before; what with all your infidelities, I would think you had considerable energy left."

"You're beginning to sound like my wife. Besides, we were talking about Corporal Mead."

"I just wanted you to know. He came to me for help. I told him to send the girl to me. Father Dourmant and I will talk to her, and take care of her in whatever way is best."

Then Teresa said forthrightly, "He wants to marry the girl."

"He does?"

"He says he is in love. He believes he is. I know it's all very complicated—but maybe, well, perhaps you can help him; he could use some sound fatherly advice, and you'd be a marvelous father figure for him."

"Thank you," he said dryly. "Just what I want to be—a father figure for a twenty-year-old boy with a pregnant girlfriend." Then he smiled. "I'll talk to him, of course."

She was very happy. "I knew you'd help. You are so nice." Then she was embarrassed and lowered her head to the glass. Finally she looked up and saw him staring at her intently. "Well," she said. "That was why I came." She finished her drink and started to stand. "I guess I should be going."

"No," he said, jumping up. "I mean, please don't go yet."

They stood facing one another, then Marshall said, "Oh, Teresa."

He went to her. For a full moment they didn't speak, then he touched her hair and whispered, "You are beautiful."

She lowered her head and smiled. "Is this a seduction?"

He shook his head. "I wouldn't know where to begin with you. Don't mock me, Teresa."

"I'm not. I've just never been seduced before."

He laughed. "You make it sound immoral."

She considered a moment. "I don't even know what morals are anymore. Perhaps I'm amoral."

"No," he said. "You are above all that; you are supramoral."

He took her in his arms and said softly, "I am in love with you."

She lowered her head and smiled. "I think you fall in love a lot."

"No," he said, stroking her hair, then letting his fingers brush down her cheeks. "I've never been in love like this."

"Your wife," she whispered.

"Yes. That was love. It still is." He sighed. "But . . . oh, so much has happened. There is so much baggage. So many hurts and wounds. It's scarred so badly. But this . . ."

He raised her face, then he touched his lips to hers. It was the softest, longest kiss, and when they broke away, they stared into each other's eyes as though sounding for a depth, but there was no measure in such fathoms.

He took her hands and gently pulled, leading her from the room, and they went up the staircase.

The bedroom was dark except for the soft lights of the garden, streaming through the open French windows.

She stepped out onto the balcony. Blossoms of bougainvillea, oleander, and orchids floated like clouds over a tranquil sea that was the pond, shimmering in the moonlight.

She drew a breath at the beauty. "That is how the world should be," she said.

"No," he whispered, standing behind her, taking her into his arms. "You are how the world should be."

"That would be a heavy burden if it were so," she said, closing her eyes, leaning back against him.

In his arms, she felt protected and safe as she never had before. This moment there were no cares or worries, no one to comfort or nurse; this moment was hers alone, and it was perfect.

All was quiet and warm, and all the love she had always known was within her welled up, and she had the briefest vision of another life, one of shared love, of children and home, a touchstone to a world she had not known, or ever would. But that was all right. She had this moment. It was an interlude from the world, a respite from sorrow and struggle, and it did not matter that it would not last.

He would not leave his wife, nor she her clinic—the parted waves would close over her life soon, but for this moment there was peace and contentment. It was a glimpse into another world, like this view of the garden. It was not the real world; there was still war and suffering and misery, but this moment the garden was real too—a tranquil atoll surrounded by a fearsome sea.

The garden *was* beautiful. Yes, beyond it were all the horrors of this world, all man-made, tended like the garden, but fiercely and without love, with hatred and strife and possessiveness. But still the garden gave her pleasure because she saw its essence that was not temporal, that would survive weeds and overgrowth and seasons.

What was in her heart was enduring too, an essence of love and beauty that was lasting and triumphant.

What did it matter that the garden would die, or that the moment would pass? It was here now, and this man was kind and good, and the moment should not be denied just because it was impermanent.

Her heart soared. She felt full of life and love. She wanted to give and receive, knowing that she would be expanded and enriched, and she turned to him.

They stood, looking over the garden, lips almost touching, and he said, "I've never made love to a saint. How does one do it?"

She touched a finger to his lips. "Quietly."

He rested his forehead against hers, then he smiled and said in a whisper, "Reverently."

They kissed again, without urgency, without even great need, beyond both urgency and need, with a sense of spirit as close as hearts and flesh can reach.

Then he led her to the bed that was bathed in the soft light from the garden.

In the morning, there was no reticence or embarrassment, and at breakfast they talked and laughed together as though they had known each other for years. Only when they finished was there a sad silence, for beyond the door was the waiting clinic, and the war.

He walked her outside to his car, but she told him that she would prefer to take a cab. "I understand," he said, then leaned forward and kissed her cheek. "Do I need to tell you what you have meant to me?" He shook his own head in answer.

"Good-bye," he said, and walked her up the driveway.

That afternoon, Marshall had second thoughts about Khe Sanh; it was far more important that he return to Washington. If the NVA struck at Tet, Johnson would not negotiate; there would be no withdrawal, and no peace.

The more he thought about Khe Sanh, the more convinced he was that it was a straw man designed to divert attention from other areas; if this was so, Johnson was falling into the trap, and he, Marshall, was being forced to go along.

He called General Tran and asked him if he still felt an NVA attack was imminent.

"More than ever. Captured documents showing troop movements and enemy buildups indicate there will be military attacks coordinated with uprisings in the towns and cities. Westmoreland has those documents—he thinks they were planted to deceive him; I believe they are legitimate because of the food, supplies, and ammunition being moved in."

Marshall arranged a late-afternoon meeting with Westmoreland and expressed his concerns about a Tet offensive, but Westmoreland discounted it, stating flatly that the enemy was not capable of massive, widespread attacks throughout the country, and because they would suffer huge and unacceptable losses. The threat was at Khe Sanh, but Khe Sanh would never fall.

"The President is . . . anxious," Marshall said.

Westmoreland laughed. "We have been in *constant* communication on that matter."

"I can imagine," Marshall said. "I tried to reassure him, but he wants me to make a personal observation. I told him that I didn't feel it was necessary, but he was insistent. I'm much more concerned with a Tet offensive."

"You are overly . . . anxious," Westmoreland said.

The morning of Marshall's departure, a patrol from Khe Sanh approached the ridge line of Hill 881 and was hit by enemy automatic fire. In less than a minute, twenty men fell. Just as the Marines in full force were ready to attack the ridge, the assault was called off by the commander at Khe Sanh.

At two P.M., an NVA officer appeared at the perimeter wire holding a white flag. The lieutenant said he was defecting and gave his captors a complete set of battle plans that indicated a huge enemy force was preparing to overrun Khe Sanh, sweep across the northern provinces, and take Hue, the ancient capital. The attack was to begin shortly after midnight.

The intelligence was flashed to Westmoreland, who immediately notified Marshall and persuaded him to delay his trip.

That night, just as the defecting officer had predicted, the shelling of the Khe Sanh outposts began. Thirty minutes after the barrage, three hundred NVA soldiers attacked Hill 861, two miles from the combat base. Using satchel charges, bangalore torpedoes, and automatic fire, they broke through the defensive wire.

The Marines counterattacked and the two forces fought hand to hand in the trenches until the NVA withdrew at five A.M.

Twenty minutes later, Khe Sanh itself came under intensive shelling. An enemy rocket hit the main ammunition dump, blowing up 1,500 tons of ordnance, slamming helicopters across the runway and collapsing buildings.

Another rocket hit the tear gas supply and the base was soon covered with the vapor.

Fires burned for hours, and large portions of the runway were destroyed. Within the first hours of siege, more than ninety percent of the base's ammunition supply was destroyed.

The following day, a bare fifteen percent of the required 160 tons of resupply made it in.

After only one day of siege, the condition at Khe Sanh was precarious.

Knowing that Johnson would be apoplectic, Marshall, despite the danger and Westmoreland's warnings, decided to fly into the combat base.

Because of the distance, Magnuson flew a fixed-wing craft to Dong Ha, 3rd Marine Division headquarters; from there, after a briefing on the military situation in northern I Corps, Marshall switched to a helicopter for an aerial overview of the positions along the Demilitarized Zone.

The DMZ was scorched earth; the terrain, flat and sandy along the coast, became more rocky and mountainous as it stretched westward toward Laos. Running along the DMZ was a network of bases from which the Marines operated patrols and sought to intercept NVA infiltration. The bases, set on the highest ground, looked from the air to Marshall like crude, dirt forts of besieged survivors on an alien landscape.

Khe Sanh was the last base in the network, only miles from the Laotian border. The massive hill sat on a defoliated plateau surrounded by higher mountains.

The day was overcast and cold when Marshall's chopper touched down. The Khe Sanh commander, Colonel Lownds, a medium-height man a few years older than Marshall, wearing helmet and flak jacket, greeted him and hustled him over to a trench alongside the runway.

Seconds later, artillery shells screamed overhead, exploding beyond the perimeter.

Marshall heard a chorus of obscenities, and looking out from the trench, he saw a pair of red panties being raised on a makeshift flagpole.

"Maggie's Drawers," Colonel Lownds explained.

"Yes," Marshall said, remembering the banner flown in the traditional, and humiliating, sign of a miss on the rifle range. He had seen many at boot camps years ago.

"This is the best show yet," Romer said, then to Lownds, "But one can always count on the Marines for Oscar performances."

Lownds smiled. "Yes, but there's a terrific supporting cast of NVA out there—twenty to forty thousand as best we can determine. Not really very fair since there are six thousand of us here—they're hopelessly outnumbered."

"How often are they shelling the base?" Marshall asked.

"This is the eighth day. They lobbed in fifty shells one day, five hundred another; usually it's a couple hundred every day. You'll see the effect on the men when we walk around. You'll be talking to them, but you won't be sure they're hearing anything. We call it 'the thousand-yard stare.' We've been expecting a full-scale attack every day for eight days; the idea that thousands of enemy soldiers are outside the wire waiting to kill you gets nerve-wracking. Everyone is up all night because the enemy only hits at night, but during the day when you're trying to catch a little sleep, they shell you with rockets and artillery."

"The siege is taking its toll then," Marshall said.

"Sieges generally do, and Marines aren't trained for this—we're strictly offense minded. Digging trenches and sandbagging bunkers is not the Corps' way of fighting a war. I hate sitting on this goddamn hill waiting for those bastards to hit me whenever they want—I want to go out and get them."

"Are you going to be overrun?" Marshall asked directly.

"Mr. Ambassador, any position can be overrun if the enemy is willing to sacrifice enough men, but I'm not worried. They would have to throw three divisions against us; and they would be decimated—no commander would do that, certainly not for something as intrinsically worthless as this miserable place."

Marshall looked about the desolate, dusty hill. "It is a pretty miserable place, isn't it?"

"A real shithole, sir. But it's mine, and I'll hold it."

"I can tell the President that?"

Lownds looked at him squarely. "Yes, sir, you can tell him that."

"Actually, I already have, but he's a little . . ." Marshall sought the right word—*hysterical,* though apt, did not seem an appropriate word to describe the commander in chief to a battlefield officer under siege.

"Anxious," Marshall settled on.

"There's not a man here who thinks Khe Sanh is going to be overrun. I know everyone makes the comparison to Dien Bien Phu, but there's no similarity. The French were completely isolated and had no air support or artillery; we control the air and have massive artillery support. Basically we're invulnerable, unless they decide to throw everything into the assault—human-wave type attack, but that's barely feasible."

"Then, Colonel, show me your impregnable hill."

For the rest of the day, Marshall viewed the base and walked the two-mile perimeter manned by two Marine battalions, U.S. Special Forces, and South Vietnamese Rangers.

Within the compound were miles of trenches over seven feet deep. Khe Sanh looked like a primitive underground city, or a throwback to World War I—indeed, with the land bombed and defoliated of color, the men themselves bleached, the sky a constant gray haze from the shelling, and sandbags wherever he looked, Marshall felt Khe Sanh was like a photograph of a scene on the Western front fifty years ago.

While talking to the men, Marshall saw the thousand-yard stare, a blank, almost hollow, look that would suddenly come alive to focus sharply on the distant ridges where the enemy hid.

Yet after walking the position for hours, viewing the defenses and fields of fire, Marshall shared Westmoreland's and Lownds's view—Khe Sanh was not going to be over-run: the enemy would have to attack uphill in exposed terrain against an entrenched foe who possessed vastly superior air and artillery support.

Of course Westmoreland wanted the NVA to attack, Marshall thought; but it would be the height of folly for them to do so, and they had never placed a foolish step.

Then why this massive concentration of forces at Khe Sanh? Marshall wondered. What else could it be except a decoy, a tactic to divert attention from other targets?

Lownds dodged Marshall's question on the matter. "I'm not competent to tell you overall NVA strategy—I see only my area of operations, and to me, it looks like the enemy is pretty serious about taking my hill."

That evening, from the underground command center at Khe Sanh, Marshall spoke with Westmoreland via radio relay.

"I think the situation is well under control here," Marshall said.

"May I pass that on to the President?" Westmoreland asked.

"Please do. My concern is not with what's happening here, but with the possibility of enemy attacks elsewhere during Tet."

"We're monitoring that carefully, Mr. Ambassador. We're confident that there won't be an attack—Tet is the Vietnamese's biggest holiday; the North asked for a cease-fire during this period—they'll honor it."

That would give him just the time he needed, Marshall felt. He would be able to bring Johnson reassurances about Khe Sanh and press him to negotiate from a position of strength.

It might all work out yet, Marshall thought—he would spend two days in Hue, seeing the palace and tombs as Lacouture recommended, then he would return to Saigon and see Ryan. By next week, he would be back in Washington, pressing peace on the President.

From the bunker headquarters, Marshall saw the hills that formed Khe Sanh's forward defense network.

"Hill eight sixty-one is the one three hundred NVA almost

overran last week," Lownds said. "This week, except for the shelling, it's been pretty quiet."

"Do you expect the NVA to honor the Tet cease-fire?"

"They've honored all the cease-fires in the past; but for us here, Tet will be business as usual." Lownds smiled. "I could give the men the night off, but I don't know what they'd do or where they'd go."

"Where is Hill seven forty-two?" Marshall asked. His question was not idle; he had asked Mead about his former unit, the one Marshall said they would visit, and Mead had said the platoon was on Hill 742.

"You can't see it from here—it's beyond eight sixty-one. Hill seven forty-two is the most northern outpost; there's a platoon up there."

"Why wasn't it hit the night they almost overran eight sixty-one? Especially if it's more isolated and has fewer defenders."

Lownds shrugged. "Perhaps for those reasons—they wanted to overrun a bigger outpost. Of course, Lieutenant Bishop would have you believe that it's because the enemy wouldn't dare attack him. Bishop is the commander there—good officer; they've seen their share of action, and maybe it's true the NVA are leaving them alone. Have you heard of Luke the Gook?"

Marshall shook his head.

"He's the Khe Sanh pet—this is a true story. There's an NVA sniper outside the perimeter. The little bastard has a .50-caliber machine gun and a rifle and he shoots at everything that moves. Fortunately he's a terrible shot or we'd all be dead. Anyway, we've hit him with everything we've got. Our own snipers have shot at him, we've fired mortars, recoilless rifles, and the other day we called in a napalm strike. No one should have lived through that—it was like lava out there and the whole area burned for ten minutes. And you know what? As soon as the smoke cleared, he fired a round at us. Everybody cheered—I mean it, every Marine applauded, me included. Now we worry about him—we don't want anything to happen to him."

"I guess not—they might replace him with somebody who can shoot straight."

"So that's our Luke the Gook. Maybe they feel the same way about Lieutenant Bishop and his men—his name is Luke too, by the way."

The following afternoon, after an intermittent sleep in which he had been toppled out of his cot twice from incoming rounds, Marshall told Magnuson to ready the chopper for takeoff, satisfied that Khe Sanh was secure and that there was nothing to be gained from staying on.

"We're going to stop in on Hill seven forty-two," Marshall told Magnuson, who knew that was where Bishop's unit was.

"I loaded six cases of beer on the chopper for them, sir. Lieutenant Bishop and I went to college together."

"Then this will be quite a reunion for you and Corporal Mead."

Without anyone knowing its destination, the chopper departed Khe Sanh in midafternoon.

After flying over the forward posts for a final view of the battle positions, Marshall's chopper approached Hill 742.

"Bravo One, Bravo One," Magnuson said on the net over the intercom so that they all could hear. "This is Viceroy. Do you read me?"

"Viceroy, this is Bravo One Alpha. Go."

"That's Gunny Brock," Mead said excitedly.

Magnuson's voice was its usual bored, supercilious self. "Roger, Bravo One Alpha. Viceroy will be landing in about two minutes."

There was a pause.

In the underground bunker on Hill 742, Luke Bishop opened a sleepy eye on Brock, who was flipping through sheaves of paper, looking for the classified one that listed the identifications of the call signs. He couldn't find it.

"Who the fuck is Viceroy?" he asked Bishop.

Bishop yawned and rolled over. "Beats me; it's not company, battalion, regiment, or division, so fuck him."

Brock keyed the handset. "Viceroy, you got business here? This is our siesta time. Go away unless this is important."

672

"Roger, Bravo One. Just dropping in on a beer run. We have six cases of cold beer—should we come back later?"

"Negative, Viceroy. You are cleared for immediate landing."

Brock threw down the handset and crashed into Bishop, who had jumped up from his sleeping bag, and the two men, dressed only in their skivvy shorts, fought each other up the stairway.

Everyone else on the hill heard the traffic on the platoon net, and the bunkers emptied as men scrambled outside to greet the helicopter already descending in their midst.

CHAPTER

· 43 ·

The men on the hill turned their backs from the spewing sand as the chopper landed; when the engine was shut off, they saw an army lieutenant colonel in starched fatigues jump out.

"Shit," Gunny Brock muttered under his breath, then said loudly, "Are you lost, sir? This is a Marine post."

"I could tell," Romer answered. "Army troopers usually wear clothes. Who's the ranking naked man here?"

Bishop stepped forward. "I am sir—Lieutenant Luke Bishop. Are you Viceroy, sir?"

"No. Viceroy is Ambassador Bradley Marshall, the personal envoy of the President of the United States." He gestured to Marshall, climbing out of the chopper. "This is Viceroy."

There was complete silence on the hill.

Then Magnuson stepped out of the cockpit and took off his helmet. "Hey, Luke, how's it going? Ambassador Marshall wanted to know why we're losing the war. I told him a quick trip here would explain it all. Glad you didn't disappoint me." Then to Marshall he said, "See, sir—ever seen such a bunch of shitbirds in your life?"

Bishop's mouth dropped open, and before he could react, Marshall spoke.

"Actually, the reason I'm here is because of Corporal Mead—he said he wanted to see some of his buddies."

Mead jumped out, grinning broadly.

"Holy shit," shouted Sutherland. "It is Mead!"

"We also brought some beer," Marshall said. "I would have brought uniforms too if I had known you needed them."

Bishop looked around at his men, almost all in their skivvies, and he stammered, "Sir, we have uniforms. Just in the daytime . . . well, it's very hot, and we . . ."

Marshall stepped forward and shook hands, then said to the men gathered around, "Gentlemen, I'm Bradley Marshall. I'm here at the request of President Johnson, but this particular visit is unofficial and informal. Please stand at ease."

No one moved, nor had any idea what to do.

Magnuson reached into the chopper and pulled out a case of beer. He tossed a can to Bishop. "Luke, relax. It's okay. Jesus Christ, you look even worse than the last time I saw you." He turned to Mead. "That's the time he was knee-crawling through Da Nang—single-handedly tore a cathouse apart. Luke, you really look awful—you better get out of this place."

Bishop was too surprised to move. He held the beer in his hand and just stared at Marshall.

Marshall took a can from Magnuson and opened it. He took a long drink to ease the tension, then he glanced about the hill. "I think I'll take a little walk. The enemy's that way, right?" He pointed toward the DMZ, then started off in the opposite direction.

"I'll come with you, sir," Romer said, grabbing a beer and following.

As soon as they left, everyone scrambled for the beer and gathered around Mead.

"The lieutenant's right," Mead said. "You are some sorry-looking motherfuckers."

"Yeah?" belched Sutherland after downing a beer and reaching for another. "Well, we ain't been eating real food and pussy like you have—we been fighting a war, you office poagy."

"Hey," Mead called. "Who's here? I see Coney and Frizzell, Martin, Whitley, Dorlander—where's Landis? And Snags—did he rotate?"

Then they told him what had happened to Snags and Landis and the others.

While the men talked, Bishop drew Magnuson aside. "Who the hell is he, and what's he doing here?"

"Marshall? Just what he said."

"How long's he going to be here?"

"You never know what he's going to do. I could tell you some stories you wouldn't believe. He rattles their cages so bad . . ." He laughed. "Ask him to stay the night; he probably would. Then we could talk, and I could tell you some real war stories. I'm a fucking hero, Luke. I may even get a medal." He put his hand over his chest and shook his head. "Oh, man, you don't know what I've been through." Then he cupped his crotch and grinned. "It's been hell, Luke."

"I don't want to hear about it, Magnuson. Hey, grab me a few beers before they're all gone while I go check on the ambassador—he shouldn't be wandering around unaccompanied. Who's the colonel with him?"

"His aide. I haven't figured him out yet—sometimes he's okay, sometimes he's just off the wall. Ever heard of Raging Romer?"

"The World War Two general?"

"Yeah. This is his son. He's got a good sense of humor, but he can be real hard-nosed; you never know what to expect. I've had a couple run-ins with him. He takes this military shit real seriously, but Marshall keeps him in line."

"What am I supposed to call him, 'Ambassador'?"

"Call him that, or 'Excellency'—that's the official way to do it, but I just say 'sir' or 'Mr. Marshall.'"

"Okay, I'll be back shortly. Gunny Brock will take care of you—he's been taking care of lieutenants for about a hundred years. Hey, Gunny—tell Lieutenant Magnuson your halls of Montezuma and shores of Tripoli stories—he was there, Jim, real living history."

When Bishop caught up with Marshall, he and Romer

were standing on the berm staring across the plain to the ridge.

"That's the badlands, sir," Bishop said.

"Do you ever go up there?" Romer asked.

"We used to, sir, but it's too dangerous now—we could get cut off too easily. Since the enemy buildup, we have orders from battalion and regiment not to go more than five hundred meters from our wire."

Marshall gazed at Bishop as he answered Romer's question; he was only slightly older than Ryan, with a freshness and eagerness about him that the war had not yet bleached. He was so tautly muscular that he looked as if he might rip open, and though Marshall could see the man's exhaustion and strain, there was no dullness about him, no thousand-yard stare in his eyes.

"I asked Colonel Lownds why the NVA didn't try to overrun this hill the night they hit Hill eight sixty-one. He said it was because you felt the enemy wouldn't dare attack you. Is that right?"

Bishop grinned. "Well, sir, we're just a bunch of grunts doing our best not to let the enemy overrun us."

"How about tonight? Think they'll overrun us tonight?"

Romer looked at Marshall sharply. "What do you mean, 'us,' sir? You can't stay here, Mr. Ambassador."

"Why? Isn't there room? You don't mind if we stop over, do you, Lieutenant?"

"Well, sir . . . no, not at all, but . . . it's kinda primitive here, sir."

Marshall looked about, then he smiled. "I like the . . . simplicity. Besides, it'll give you and Lieutenant Magnuson a chance to talk, and Corporal Mead can visit with his friends. I owe him that, at least. In fact, I owe you too, Lieutenant."

"Me, sir? How's that?"

"I understand you sent Corporal Mead down to Saigon."

"Yes, sir."

"Well, he ended up as my bodyguard. He's saved my life at least twice that I know of."

"Yes, sir, he saved my life too." Then Bishop saw Frizzell

sneaking across the hill, his hands loaded with beers, and he shouted, "Hey, Frizzell! Only two beers. You're not even old enough to drink—you'll get so dicked up you'll fall off the hill; the gooks won't even have to come up here."

Frizzell dropped the cans, then he scrambled to pick them up. "Yes, sir. I was only going to drink two, Lieutenant. I was gonna save the others for later."

"They don't send beer out regularly? I thought there was supposed to be a two-beer ration for every man," Romer said.

"That might be so," Bishop said, "but if it is, they owe us a lot of beer. I never heard of field units getting beer—I think that's just for rear areas."

Marshall nodded. "I've noticed there's a very different war going on in places like Da Nang and Cam Ranh Bay and Saigon, Lieutenant. But I suppose that's how it always is. I spent a little time in combat in World War Two and Korea, and we used to have great contempt for those in the rear. That was probably true at Troy and Jericho too."

"I'll ask the gunny," Bishop said. "He was probably there."

Marshall laughed. "Gunnery sergeants never change, do they? They're a special force in nature." And he thought, looking at Bishop and seeing himself in another war nearly twenty years ago, neither do lieutenants.

Then he saw Frizzell disappearing into his bunker. Neither do privates, he thought.

And looking out onto the plain, he was filled with sudden sadness. Nothing changes; nothing at all. And the young men keep dying.

"Well, I suppose I'd better call somebody and tell them where I am," Marshall said, turning back to Bishop.

In the underground bunker, Bishop radioed the company commander that Viceroy was with him and staying over; he requested the information be relayed back to battalion.

Several minutes later, the radio crackled, and a cultivated voice said calmly, "Bravo One, this is Dragon Six."

"Jesus, that's the regimental CO—he's never called," said Brock.

"Dragon Six, Bravo One, go."

"Understand you have a visitor there, a Victor et cetera."

"Roger that, Dragon Six."

"You understand about Victor et cetera?"

"Affirmative, Dragon Six."

"Good. May I talk with him?"

Bishop handed Marshall the handset. He keyed it. "Hello?"

The others hid their faces to stifle laughter.

"Hello back," Colonel Lownds said lightly. "What I said about safety and overrun positions applied to my position —not where you are. I recommend you reconsider your evening accommodations."

"Thank you," Marshall said. "I seem to be a little overdressed, but otherwise quite safe."

"I'll have to report this to Mike Alpha Charlie Victor."

Marshall looked inquiringly to Bishop.

"MACV, sir."

Marshall keyed the handset. "Give them my regards. Good-bye."

Bishop laughed. "Holy God, General Westmoreland will—"

"Shit bricks," said Gunny Brock. "Begging your pardon, sir."

"General Westmoreland and I have a good understanding," Marshall said. "He understands that I outrank him." He looked about pleasantly. "Well, now what do we do? Fill some more sandbags?"

"Well, sir," said Bishop, "we really don't have anything to do—we just sorta wait around till the gooks decide to attack us. Then we fight back, and they withdraw, then we wait some more . . ." He shrugged. "That's about it up here. The rest of the time we just sit around and listen to the gunny's bullshit stories."

"And tonight?" Marshall asked.

"All the men will want to talk to Mead. I want to hear what Jim . . . Lieutenant Magnuson's been doing."

"Have him tell you about Dolores," Romer said.

"And maybe the gunny can tell the ambassador what it was like at Jericho."

Suddenly an incredible barrage of artillery screamed

overhead. Everyone ducked instinctively, but the shells were outgoing and exploded on the ridge beyond.

Bishop laughed. "This is probably the safest place in Vietnam, tonight. They're scared something will happen to the ambassador, so they'll keep up a steady strike against the enemy. We could take the night off probably."

He seemed right, Marshall thought, as artillery and air strikes continued at close intervals.

Not wanting to inhibit them, and finding the air in the underground bunker stifling, Marshall went out frequently to walk the hill and sit on the berm, staring across to where the enemy waited.

The hill was utterly Spartan, almost purifying, Marshall thought. He lay back in the sand and stared up at the sky; the first evening stars were already visible, and closing his eyes, he heard laughter and the faint sounds of transistor radios. It seemed very innocent, but then the artillery started up and he could see explosions on the ridge.

Sitting alone in the dark under the stars, he thought back of many years ago, young and afraid, staring up at the Pacific sky, before a beach landing, wondering if he would die, if his body would be floating facedown in the water like so many others, and later, shivering from cold, huddling under his poncho at Chosin, staring into the searing void of night, knowing that he was only heartbeats away from merging with that void.

Once Bishop came to sit by him, having listened to Magnuson's stories and drunk more than his allotted two beers.

They sat side by side in silence, and Marshall was overcome with the sensation that he was sitting with a younger self, the strangest feeling that it was he himself who was not real, but only a faded ghost perched near the younger man, that it was Bishop who was alive and vibrant, if only for a short time, and then it would be he who was the ghost, and another young man would be sitting here, and on and on it would go, all of them sitting on the hill overlooking the dark plain, an army of ghost warriors.

And for the briefest moment he envied Bishop. He

wanted it to be his hill and his men. He wanted to be young again. And yes—damn it all, he wanted to be the warrior again. It was there suddenly in his blood and in the air he breathed, an incredible desire, primitive and atavistic, and overpowering.

He shuddered at the feeling quaking through him.

Then he laughed out loud, and he said, "Hopeless."

Bishop turned respectfully. "What is, sir?"

Marshall opened his hands, encompassing the plain below.

He didn't speak for a long time, then finally he said, "I was thinking about war, Lieutenant."

"Yes, sir?"

"It's an awful thing. Oh, God, the suffering and misery . . ." In his mind he saw the frozen dead at Chosin, and the bloated dead on the beach at Guadalcanal.

And Bishop saw in his mind the dead lying at his feet, and Miller's severed head, and he said, "Yes, sir, it is."

Marshall turned to him. "But the truly awful thing is that . . . you love it and would go back in a minute."

Bishop had not expected that, but he smiled. "That's what the gunny says—though not quite in those words; it was something about war being like his first wife, and how both could stiffen your dick."

Marshall laughed. "Well, there it is, God's very own truth spoken through the mouth of a Marine gunnery sergeant." Then he shook his head sadly. "Dear God, what a curse on us." He sighed. "And our children."

He stood. "I think I'll go visit the posts—I'd like to talk to some of the men."

"They'll probably be too afraid of you to say anything, sir."

"Oh, you'd be surprised how I can get people to babble at me."

The first bunker he came to belonged to Coney and Frizzell and Sutherland. When he stuck his head in, they jumped up frantically.

"You guys got anything to eat?" he asked. "Nobody's offered me anything since I got here; I'm starving."

"Sir, all we got is C rations."

"Anything wrong with them? Except of course that they taste like shit—I mean other than that?"

They laughed. "No, sir, nothing wrong with them, except for what you already know. We got pork slices, and beef slices—anyway, that's what's on the label—beans and franks, and ham and limas."

"Beef slices," Marshall said, moving into the bunker and sitting against the sandbags. He took the can and opener and surprised them with his ability to work it. "Same thing we used in Korea," he said. "We used to call ham and lima beans 'ham and motherfuckers'—what do you call them?"

"Same thing, sir," they said, sitting down.

"That's what I was telling Lieutenant Bishop—nothing ever changes." He scooped meat into his mouth and drank the juice.

Frizzell asked hesitantly, "Sir, what does an ambassador do?"

"I haven't figured that out completely," Marshall said. "I'm still working on it. We do a lot of listening. You see, President Johnson asked me to come over here and see what's going on, then go back to Washington and tell him."

"You really know President Johnson, sir?" Coney asked.

"Yes. He swears much worse than you guys. I am really thirsty. You got anything to drink?"

Frizzell pulled out one of his prize beers. "You can have this, sir."

"Thank you," Marshall said, opening it. "I'll get you some more—promise."

Soon the three were talking to Marshall without difficulty, and before long the bunker crowded with other men who had heard that the ambassador was there, talking and drinking beer.

"Somebody go tell Lieutenant Bishop that we need some more beer here. I brought six cases—that's a hundred forty-four beers, about five cans per man. Nobody's going to get drunk on that, and I want my share."

Marshall looked about the cramped bunker and asked, "What do you guys normally do to pass the time? Anybody play cards?"

A howl went up, and decks appeared out of nowhere.

"What are the stakes?" he asked.

"We can't take your money, sir."

"Oh, professionals, are you? I'll take my chances."

They sat in a big circle, taking turns playing, and while they played, Marshall talked to them about their feelings and concerns, listened to their problems and gripes, and gradually won all their money.

Yes, there was a lot of dope in Vietnam, but not on the front line—anybody who got messed up on drugs would probably get killed by everyone else for risking their lives.

Race too was a problem, but again not on the line.

"I can call Williams a nigger out here on the hill," Sutherland said, "and he can call me a redneck mother-fucker, and it's okay, 'cause we got bigger problems to worry about—like the gooks blowing our fucking heads off. But in the rear we'd be real respectful to one another, or else we'd square off in a second."

During the game, Marshall felt the eyes of several of the men on him intently. Their looks weren't hostile, but probing, as if he had the answers to the questions and doubts plaguing them, and he feared that soon someone would ask him one of the impossible questions—why?

And finally Martin did. He had lost his money an hour ago and did not take his eyes from Marshall or break expression even when Marshall glanced up at him and smiled.

They played till nearly eleven P.M. before Sutherland, the last man in, threw his hand down.

Marshall scooped the money to himself. "You guys let me win, didn't you? You were just being polite."

"Were you cheating, sir?" Coney asked.

"That's probably how he got to be an ambassador," Sutherland said bitterly. "He won it in a card game."

Marshall laughed. "Gentlemen, I've been playing cards since before you were born. This is probably hard for you to believe, but I'm even older than your gunnery sergeant."

There were jesting oohs and aahs.

"Anybody here born before 1942? See? I was a PFC in the Marines then, playing poker just like you guys are now. So you see, I have a little head start on you." He pointed to the centerfolds on the bunker walls. "We used to have pictures too—they didn't show quite as much flesh as those, but . . . they covered up the same things you guys dream about every night, and we dreamed about them too. And we had mothers and fathers, and wives and girlfriends, and we were lonely and homesick and afraid too."

There was complete silence in the bunker.

And then Martin spoke. "Sir, my best buddy got killed. His name was Matt Landis. I want to know why he died. I want to know if he died for anything."

And there it was, the awful question.

He looked from Martin to the others, all quiet and waiting in the silent bunker.

Words turned to ash in his mouth. All he could think of were the fearful lines from Kipling:

> Now all my lies are proved untrue
> And I must face the men I slew.
> What tale shall save me here among
> Mine angry and defrauded young?

They waited respectfully.

Marshall closed his eyes, and when he opened them, they were still waiting.

"I'm going to give you the most terrible answer," he said. "I don't know. My son, my oldest son—he is exactly your age, and I love him very much—is coming to Vietnam, this week I think. I did everything I could to stop him—I yelled at him and I pleaded with him, and I could not bear it if anything happened to him. If it did, I would ask the same question you are asking me, and I would still not have an answer."

Marshall drew a deep breath and leaned back against the sandbags. "I guess it is a question every man must answer for himself. It's like religion, and even women, I suppose. What you believe about God is probably different from what I believe, and what I believe is different from what everyone else here believes. I can't say that what I believe is right, any more than I could say that the woman I choose is right for everyone, or that the girl you choose is better than anyone else's."

He looked carefully to each man in the bunker. "I don't like this war. I don't want my son to be here. I don't want you to be here. Did your friend die for anything? I hope so, if only because there is something in him that lives in you. Every man who dies can live on in us. We can carry him in us and learn from him, and we can answer the question you ask in many different ways and still make his death matter. If you think the answer is no, that this war is wrong, then you can live with his memory and see that this never happens again—that no one dies in another war that is wrong."

He shook his head sadly. "I've been afraid for a long time that someone would ask that question. I wish I could give you a better answer. I wish I could tell you wonderful things about sacrifice and glory, but I can't. Forgive me."

He stood and started to leave.

"Your money, sir," someone said.

He turned and looked at it, stacked at his place.

"Would you do me a big favor, please? When you get off this shitty hill, would you all buy as much beer as that will get you, and get completely blitzed?"

Then he left.

He walked back across the hill exhausted and drained.

Romer was standing on the berm staring out on the moonlit plain.

"It's a beautiful night, isn't it, sir?"

Marshall shared the silence with him a moment; the dunes looked like a peaceful sea.

"Yes, Colonel," he said, nodding. "Good night."

Romer only vaguely noticed he was gone.

This is what had drawn his father, Romer realized. He understood now. It was beautiful and wonderful. He was his father, and his father was a warrior from times past. The old man had believed that, he knew, had often said he was warrior incarnate—that they all lived on in him, that he had been on the plains of war since time immemorial, that the blood of all soldiers past coursed through him. He had laughed at his father, but it was true after all. And now it coursed through him. He felt his father here. He was right beside him, the old man staring out on the plain defiantly, waiting to meet the battle.

It was a mystical place, this hill and the plain beyond, Romer felt.

Behind him he could hear men talking and laughing, and he could feel the ghosts of all the warriors on the berm with him.

He understood his father, and his father's love. And he felt the same love. This is where he belonged.

In the morning, after a surprisingly long and good sleep, Marshall ate C rations voraciously, brushed his teeth with his finger, and was almost reluctant to leave.

Romer drew him aside shortly before they did. "I would like to ask a great favor of you, sir, even though you've already done me one by getting me a battalion command."

They were standing outside, near the spot where they had been the night before. The day was overcast and cool.

"I'd like to stay here the two days you're going to be in Hue. You don't need me there—that's strictly sight-seeing, and I'd much rather be here."

"What would you do here?" Marshall asked.

Romer pointed to the plain, and the opposing ridge. "It's hard to explain; I just like it here—I'm not interested in seeing the sights of Hue, the ancient palace and temples, and besides, this would be better experience for me since I'm taking over the battalion in a few days. This would give me a better feel for the men and small units."

"I have no objection," Marshall said. "My work is done. All I want to do is visit a few historical sights, so it's all right with me, but you better clear it with Lieutenant Bishop and his superiors."

"I don't think that will pose a problem."

"Then it will be fine—just as long as you . . . how shall I put this delicately?"

"Mind my own fucking business and don't interfere."

"Precisely. This is Lieutenant Bishop's hill."

"I understand perfectly. I'm just an observer."

"Good. I'll have Lieutenant Magnuson fly up the day after tomorrow and pick you up before we head back to Saigon."

After a final walk around the perimeter, Marshall thanked Bishop and Brock and got into the chopper.

The men came to see Mead off, and after handshakes all around, and friendly jostling between Magnuson and Bishop, the chopper lifted off.

"What about Colonel Romer?" Mead asked.

"He'll be staying for a couple days while we go sight-seeing in Hue."

Mead looked out the window at the hill rapidly disappearing from view; he frowned so deeply that Marshall tapped him lightly.

"It's all right. It's Tet—the cease-fire. Nothing can go wrong."

CHAPTER

• 44 •

"What the hell are we supposed to do with him?" Gunny Brock asked Bishop when Romer left the underground bunker to check the perimeter.

Bishop shrugged. "He's just here to observe."

"Yeah? That's what my mother-in-law used to say."

"Which mother-in-law is that, Gunny?" Bishop taunted. "You have about eight of them, don't you?"

"My *first* mother-in-law." He paused in recollection, a smile spreading across his face, and he shook his head. "God damn, now that was a mother-in-law. Did I ever tell you about her, Lieutenant?"

"Oh, I'm sure you have, Gunny. But what with my other concerns—life and death, gooks and the war—it's somehow slipped my mind."

"I should have known about Laurie—that was my first wife—from her mother." He pointed admonishingly at Bishop. "Never marry a woman before checking out her mother first."

"Do you recommend fucking her, Gunny—I mean the mother?"

"I'm trying to give you sound advice, Lieutenant," Brock lectured. "Don't be a college puke. Anyway, I would not recommend fucking the mother. That's what happened to me. Remember, I was only seventeen, and Mama was about thirty-two when she came to visit."

"I probably don't want to hear about this, Gunny."

"It's a lesson in life, Lieutenant."

"If I wanted one of those, I'd turn on the radio and listen to a country-western song. In fact, it just occurred to me, Gunny—your whole life is like a country-western song."

"Those songs are true, Lieutenant; they're not made up."

"I know. And I've always been afraid that I was going to meet somebody from one of those songs. And goddamn if it didn't turn out that I've had to spend six months with one in an underground bunker."

"Well, better than marrying one. Now, as I was telling you about Laurie's mother—she'd stay in her room till Laurie'd go to work or shopping, or hell, just to check the mailbox, then she'd run out and grab me, throw me down, and fuck my ears off. Know how some women come in wild little bucks, sort of like a machine-gun burst, just humping crazy against you? Well, not Laurie's mama—that was like getting fucked by a motorboat; her cunt would just hammer your dick raw."

Bishop stared at him. "What does this have to do with Colonel Romer?"

"Like I said—he makes me think of my mother-in-law—he's here to fuck us."

"Naah," Bishop said. "He didn't want to go to Hue and look at temples. He's been with the ambassador for months—I think this is just a break for him; R and R. He's only going to be here two nights. Tell him some of your stories—he'll get out a lot sooner. Shit, tell him that mother-in-law story, and he'd start walking to Hue now."

Bishop cocked his head, then pounded a beat on the ammunition crates. "Hey, I like that—'Walking to Hue'—that could be a real chart buster."

Brock shook his head. "You been here too long, Lieutenant."

"And I'm getting short, Gunny—only another month or so, and I'm outa here."

"Bullshit. You'll be here longer than the gooks—if you live."

"I mean out of this platoon. Then they'll make me an 'XO'—you only have to put in six months as platoon commander. I'm getting short, Gunny."

"You know your problem, Lieutenant? You never say anything interesting—that's why I have to take up the slack by telling all these stories."

"Walk, walk, walking to Hue. Rock, rock, rocking to . . ." Bishop ducked a can of pork slices.

"I don't like him here," Brock said. "He's gonna want to go out there. You watch, he's gonna start bugging us about sending out a patrol."

"I already got that figured, Gunny. And I'm gonna let him—I'm gonna send him out with three men, and they're gonna sit out there five hundred meters from the wire, and we'll have some peace and quiet here."

Brock harrumphed, which Bishop knew meant that he was pissed because he hadn't thought of that himself.

"He wants to see some action—okay, I can dig it, so I'll send him out there with a couple guys to sit all night. He can't go anywhere—orders say five hundred meters, no further, so everybody's happy."

"Would you cut that 'dig it' shit. It's bad enough being out here with some brown-bar college know-it-all without him doing his hippie Beach Boys routine."

Bishop beat on the crates. "Gonna walk, gonna rock, gonna walk and rock to Hue. Hey! Hue!"

Brock pelted him with cans.

Bishop covered his head.

"Who you gonna send out there with him?" Brock asked.

"Coney, Frizzell, and Sutherland. They'll keep him in line."

Brock didn't say anything for a minute, then he shook his head. "That may not be such a good idea, Lieutenant. I'm a gunnery sergeant and *I* can barely handle them—he's only an army colonel, he'll never do it."

"I don't want him to handle them—I want them to handle him so he doesn't get carried away. You think Sutherland's going to let him take the patrol up the ridge or into the DMZ? I don't want him out past five hundred meters—those guys won't let him stray."

Brock harrumphed again, then he turned on the radio and turned up the volume very loud on a country-western song, one of his favorites, "I'm So Hungry for Your Love, I'm Waiting in Your Welfare Line."

"Phu Bai," Magnuson said over the intercom. "We'll be landing in a few minutes."

"Can you give me a flyover of Hue first?" Marshall asked.

"Roger that, sir," Magnuson said, and the chopper arched to the left.

"Phu Bai's the big base," Magnuson said, as though he were a tour director. "About six miles from Hue on Route One, the road you see below."

Marshall looked out one side, Mead the other. Magnuson flew low enough that they had a perfect view of the countryside, cultivated land and pine forests virtually unspoiled by the war.

Hue itself sparkled in the sun; the gilded roofs of the pagodas, temples, and the Imperial Palace blazed like crystal.

Magnuson lifted another five hundred feet and hovered to capture the full beauty of the surrounding land—the maze of lagoons protecting the city from the coast of the South China Sea, only three miles to the east, and the emerald mountains, called the Screen of Kings, to the west. Snaking through the city was the River of Perfumes, wending from the sea down past the tombs of the emperors, six miles from the city.

"That's where I want to go," Marshall said.

"You'll have to take the road, or a boat to the tombs, sir. I can't land there—a chopper is just too tempting a target."

"All right," Marshall said. "Go back to Phu Bai."

The reception there was like all the others, a respectful meeting by the senior officers, and an offer to show him whatever facilities he desired, but he told them his visit was personal, not official—all he needed was ground transportation to see the city and tombs.

"How about a guide, sir? Someone to take you through the Imperial Palace and some of the temples?"

"Yes, that would be helpful, thank you."

"And an armed escort."

Marshall shook his head. "I have Corporal Mead. Do you think it's that dangerous that I'd need security?"

"Hue is probably the most secure city in the country," the commander said. "Especially during Tet."

"You're not anticipating any trouble?" Marshall asked.

"No, sir. It's their New Year's, their biggest holiday. Today and tomorrow are the last shopping and preparation days; the markets will be jammed—people buying squid and rice wine and sweets—so it'll be a good time to see the Citadel and Palace. It's a cease-fire; they won't attack—that would be like us launching an attack on Christmas; it just won't happen."

In midafternoon, Marshall started his visit to Hue, outfitted in a shiny black sedan with a Vietnamese driver and scholarly guide who turned out to be a tourist's nightmare—a guide of immense goodwill and energy, boundless knowledge and chatter, proud and covetous of the culture and history, he alternated between obsequiousness and tyranny, giving Marshall no pause to reflect or enjoy.

He would not take Marshall to the Citadel, that was only to be seen in the morning, nor would he take him to the tombs, because they should be seen only after visiting the Citadel. Instead, he brought Marshall to myriad temples and pagodas, recounting the city's history.

Though referred to as the "Ancient City," Hue's cultural and political importance dated only to 1802.

Gia Long chose Hue as the capital because it was equidistant between Saigon and Hanoi, capitals of Cochin China and Tonkin, a compromise capital for the very different peoples of the north and south.

But independent Vietnamese rule was short-lived—the French arrived in 1847, and by 1883 they had effectively colonized the country. The last Nguyen emperor, Bao Dai, now living in Paris, abdicated in 1955.

Finally, at the end of the day, the guide presented Marshall with several books and directed him to study them prior to tomorrow's visit to the Citadel and the tombs.

When he returned to his quarters at Phu Bai, Marshall had a severe headache; he had dinner sent to his rooms, and he canceled his guided tour for the morning, directing that only a car and driver pick him up at nine. Tomorrow was the last day before the Tet holiday and he decided to visit the sights alone and undisturbed.

"I'm curious, Lieutenant," Romer said, sitting in the underground bunker, sipping coffee. "Why don't you send patrols or ambushes out at night?"

Bishop glanced quickly at Brock, then explained, "Well, sir, we're limited as to how far we can go beyond the wire—five hundred meters, that's orders from regiment and division. I'm not worried about a sapper attack—the NVA can't get into my perimeter without me knowing it; we've strung enough wire and booby traps so that Houdini couldn't sneak in. My concern is a full-scale assault. When that comes, a patrol outside the wire will only cause problems because then I'll have to worry about getting them back safely before I can open up on the enemy."

It sounded so sensible to Brock, listening across the bunker, that he was afraid Bishop had overdone it, and now Romer would not press to go out, instead staying in the bunker and badgering them all night.

"Can it hurt?" Romer asked. "Having a patrol out there?"

"I can't send a patrol out there, sir—a patrol means movement, and as I said, we aren't allowed more than five hundred meters beyond the wire. An ambush, or listening post, might be all right though."

Romer jumped at that. "I'd like to sit out there, Lieutenant. It'd beat sitting in here."

"How is that, sir?" Brock asked.

Romer smiled. "You don't really need me to explain that, do you?"

The two men were the same age, but when Brock ran away from home at seventeen to fight in Korea, Romer was finishing prep school, getting ready to enter college. Brock was married and divorced, with mother-in-law stories to tell, and had seen a war by the time Romer finished his sophomore year.

Brock had seen hundreds of officers—Bishop was perhaps the fiftieth second lieutenant he had served under, and there had been as many company and battalion commanders. He had seen them all from second lieutenant to colonel and had known several who had become generals. He understood Romer's desire—need—to go out: it wasn't anything he shared or admired because he himself didn't need to prove anything to anybody, but officers such as Romer seemed to—he had seen many even worse in their compulsion to disguise whatever inadequacy it was that ate at them.

"I can send three men out with you, sir," Bishop said, "but you have to understand the rules of engagement—we are not allowed more than five hundred meters from the wire. That's an order I have, a written one even." He pointed to the pile where the code books, call signs, and everything else important could never be found.

"I understand, Lieutenant. I just want to get a feel of it before I leave. I've been sitting in Saigon so long I was getting ashamed of myself. Being out here on the DMZ, well, it just does something to you."

"That's okay, Colonel," Brock said. "The lieutenant 'digs it.'"

"You should go out in an hour or so," Bishop said. "I'll go tell the men who will be with you. Gunny, go over the map with the colonel—show him where he could set in, and set up some standby artillery."

Bishop left the bunker and took his time crossing the hill. The night was cool and black; the new moon was two days away, and no stars lightened the sky.

"Gentlemen," he said, startling the three men in their bunker. "Your mission tonight, should you choose to accept it—"

"We don't," said Sutherland.

Bishop put his hand over his heart in deep wounding. "And let your country down? Let *me* down? Your mothers, wives, and girlfriends?" He pointed to the centerfolds on the wall. "All that cunt?"

"He's getting flakier every day," Coney said to Frizzell.

"You three have been chosen for a special assignment. In one hour you are going to take that army colonel outside the wire and sit there for a couple hours, then you're going to come back in."

The three just stared at him. "Why?" Sutherland finally asked.

"Because he wants to go out there—he's never sat in an ambush before. He thinks this will be good experience. He is going to get his battalion to command next week, and he wants to learn."

"The first thing that dumb motherfucker better learn is not to leave a safe place to sit outside the wire," Sutherland said.

"It's not a good idea to go out there, sir," Coney said doubtfully.

"You're right, but it's not dangerous either. I wouldn't do this if he didn't want to go out there, but he really does. And it might do some good—he might learn that it isn't necessary, so when he's calling the shots somewhere, he won't send men out like this."

Bishop dropped down in the bunker beside them. "I wouldn't send you out if it was dangerous; I wouldn't risk your lives for something like that, but there's no enemy movement, no sightings, no radio traffic. It's quiet out there. And all we're talking about is five hundred meters. Do you have any idea how far five hundred meters is?"

"The exact distance from here to hell?"

"Close, but not quite. Hell is a mile—the distance to the ridge; five hundred meters is a third of a mile. And that's as far as I want you to go. In fact, you're forbidden to go further. Once you leave the wire, walk five hundred paces—and I mean regular paces, Sutherland, not little elf steps—and then set in for the night. That's all you have to do. Just sit there for a couple hours. Give him a show if you like—jack him up a little—tell him you smell gooks, or hear them. Shit, you could have some fun. But stay within five hundred meters of the wire. He might want to go out further. That's the main reason I've picked you guys. He's a colonel—if I sent others out with him, he might run over them and scare them into doing something they shouldn't. You won't let him do that, will you?"

"Not hardly," said Coney. "No way I'm going more than . . . how far did you say, Lieutenant, fifty feet?"

"Five hundred meters. And for doing this, as your reward . . ."

They stared at him.

"You will have a choice of prizes. You may choose me singing my new song, 'Walking to Hue,' or the gunny will tell you the story about his mother-in-law."

"Jesus," said Coney. "I'll stay out there with the colonel."

"One hour," Bishop said, standing carefully so that he faced directly into one of the centerfolds, his nose up against her crotch. "I know this girl." He sniffed. "Yep, that's her."

Romer made such a production about cleaning and oiling his rifle, strapping on his grenades, and blackening his face that Brock had to leave, and when the three men came into the underground bunker for the briefing and saw him, they had to restrain themselves—Romer looked ready for an assault on Hanoi. He shook hands gravely.

"Who's going to take the radio?" Bishop asked.

"I will," Coney said.

"Who wants point?"

Frizzell and Sutherland looked at each other; both shrugged. Bishop flipped a coin. Sutherland lost. Frizzell chose point.

Bishop showed them the ambush position and again warned them not to go out farther.

"They've been quiet out there all day. But you guys know what that means—nothing. It's almost Tet. We haven't had sightings or warnings, but for all I, or General Cushman, knows, there could be ten thousand gooks hopped up and ready to ride tonight. Okay, any questions?"

"I want to go over that five-hundred-meter part again," Sutherland said.

"I think we all understand that," Bishop said. "Call sign is . . . anybody got a preference?"

"Peggy," said Romer. "That's my wife."

There was stunned silence, then Frizzell said, "Sir, we can't have a girl's name. It's . . ."

"It's just a superstition, Colonel," Bishop said. "No one even knows how it got started, but in this unit it's always been a taboo to have a female call sign, like apricots. I'm sure it's fine in other units—they probably have their own superstitions and taboos."

"Then somebody else pick one," Romer said good-naturedly, not at all upset.

But the three men were. The superstition had been challenged, if only briefly, and the taboo broken. The three looked to one another nervously.

"Dodgers," said Bishop quickly to ease the tension, and appease Sutherland, who was from Los Angeles.

"Tigers," said Coney, who was from Detroit.

"You're carrying the radio, so Tigers it is," said Bishop. "Check in every thirty minutes, and I want you to come in at zero four hundred. Time now is twenty-one forty-seven. Take off."

They left the bunker and, outside, tested the radio and checked each other's rifle and equipment, then they headed down the back slope toward the break in the wire—Frizzell first, then Coney with the radio, Romer, and finally Sutherland.

The three had treated this as a joke until Romer's slip; breaking the taboo changed everything. Suddenly this had become serious and grew worse as they individually thought about it, for things always seemed to go wrong when least expected—there was always a fuck-up in something simple. It would be just like the time Perez or Bowman or Miller or Snags or Tolson got zapped—out of nowhere.

Sutherland felt this keenly. He liked Lieutenant Bishop, even trusted him, but this patrol was just a joke to him, and it was a game to that colonel, but it *wasn't* a game—it was his life.

After Landis's death, Sutherland had sworn no one was going to play with his life again.

And this wasn't a game to the gooks either. They were out there waiting to kill him.

Death was beyond the wire, and he saw it clearly in his mind—a screaming skull leering, beckoning. Death was real—it was awful and ugly and forever.

He felt the amulet around his neck, rubbed it until it was hot in his hand, and when he let go, it burned against his chest. He closed his eyes for many seconds, then opened them.

And there it was—the coffin, gleaming silver, its lid open. He shut his eyes immediately and clutched the amulet.

They were at the wire. The other three went through, but Sutherland hesitated, so long that Frizzell and Coney went back to him. They waited with him tensely, sensing the night.

"We gotta go," Frizzell said finally.

"They're out there," Sutherland said.

They waited longer, knowing the importance of what a man felt, trusting his instincts for survival, especially some-one like Sutherland, who did not spook easily.

They looked to Romer, patiently waiting for them.

"He's bad luck," Sutherland said.

"He didn't know," Coney said. "He didn't mean any-thing."

"Yeah," Frizzell said. "Maybe it doesn't count if he's not one of us."

Still Sutherland hesitated. He had listened carefully to what Marshall had said to Martin. If this man thought the war was wrong—well then, what did it mean? Why was he here? Why was he risking his life? Those were just words about carrying the dead around with you. What good did that do Landis, or Miller or Snags, or any of the others? Dead was dead. And dead was nothing.

He was not going to end like that, dead for a joke, killed in someone's game.

He looked beyond the wire. The coffin was still there.

"No," he said.

Coney tugged on his arm. "You have to."

"C'mon, Scott," Frizzell hissed. "It'll be okay." He pulled on him until finally Sutherland relented and slipped through the wire into the enveloping darkness, but he could hear the skull laughing at him, and the coffin would not go away. He was closer to death than he had ever been, he knew.

They set out, Frizzell on point again, moving down the hill and to the west, coming into the ambush position from behind.

Usually they went quickly and surely, so familiar were

they with the terrain, but this night Frizzell crept slowly because he felt something was wrong; it was not just what Romer had said—something was different about the night; it was darker; there was something in the air, and the ground itself seemed hostile.

"God damn," Coney whispered once, feeling the eeriness too, and when he looked back toward the hill, he couldn't see it.

And no matter how many times Sutherland closed his eyes, he could not dislodge the image of the coffin.

The night was so black that it was disorienting; no landmarks could be discerned, neither the ridge nor the hill; they were as removed and isolated as if in cold space.

When they neared the ambush position, Frizzell went alone to check it; he left them a mere hundred feet away, but he had trouble finding them when he came back.

After setting in, they remained acutely tense because they were unable to establish any control—they couldn't see anything; nothing became familiar—it was like trying to mark water. They felt as if they were suspended, a spider hanging from the thinnest thread over an immense void.

Romer had no way of knowing that the three felt differently from other times; this was his first patrol, and it was exhilarating—more gut-wrenchingly fearsome and exciting than anything he had ever experienced. Nothing in his past compared to this—the sense of exposure, gamble, vulnerability—life—was overpowering. Every nerve in his being throbbed; mind and body quivered from concentration. He was the essence of being, distilled and purified self—no burdens, no past, no father—alone in the dark universe, not a part of it, not in harmony with it, but awesomely separate: the only thing in the universe; everything.

The intoxication grew, built to a sense of omnipotence, until he was barely able to sit still.

For the others, the usual calming that followed setting in did not come; the longer they sat, the more uneasy they felt. The air was malevolent.

There was no smell and no sound.

It was not the enemy.

Sutherland felt that intensely—it was not the gooks, but something even worse—not the enemy, but Enemy, something awful and horrible, some force with a fury and strength that dwarfed them, a godlike power of crushing brutality.

Sutherland shivered before it. He was alone, a distilled being too, but no feeling of omnipotence rose in him; he cowered before the immensity that loomed over him.

After two hours, Romer could not contain himself—the enemy was not going to come; he would have to go out for them.

"Let's go," he said suddenly, startling the others. "Nothing's going to happen here."

They thought he meant back to the hill, and Coney whispered, picking up the radio handset, "I have to tell them we're coming in so they don't blow us away."

"Not in," Romer said. "Further out."

"What?" said Sutherland, then quickly, "No."

"Just a little further, over towards the ridge—that's where they are."

"No shit," said Sutherland. "That's where they are, all right, and we're not going there."

"Colonel," Coney whispered, "we can't go further—we're out the maximum distance right now."

"Sir," Frizzell said, leaning close, "I brought us out five hundred meters, maybe even a little more. The lieutenant told us not to go past this. And it's early, we only been here two hours—they might still come."

"Besides," Sutherland said not very respectfully, "you don't move an ambush after you've set in. Once you're in, that's it till you're pulled back."

"I want to move closer to the ridge," Romer said, a senior officer unaccustomed to lectures from junior enlisted men half his age.

Coney started reasonably. "Sir, we can't. It's not allowed, and Scott's right—you never move an ambush after it's set in, it's too dangerous; the enemy, if they're out there, will spot the movement. You just have to wait for them to come to you."

Frizzell was placating. "Most nights you sit out and

700

nothing happens—you almost never make contact, sir, maybe one time in fifty. This is how it usually is."

"Well, they're out there," Romer said emphatically. "We know where they are, and we're not going to wait for them to come to us, we're going to them. You don't wait for someone to kick you in the balls before you protect yourself—it's too late then. We're going out there to get them."

The three men didn't say anything for a minute. Moving the ambush position was not a consideration, but they were trying to think of a way to avoid what each saw as a dangerous situation developing. They were low-ranking enlisted men, he was a lieutenant colonel, light-years above them. Sutherland could back-talk Gunny Brock, even go a little distance with the lieutenant, but a lieutenant colonel was different. If a lieutenant colonel gave an order, it was not up to Sutherland to weigh its merits or raise questions.

They were on the edge of receiving an order, they knew, an order that was wrong, dangerous, and probably unlawful, but an order nonetheless, and if they refused it, they risked court-martial. They were privates and corporals, he was a senior officer: whom was the military going to back? What chance did they have when their judges would be other senior officers?

"I want you to take point," Romer said to Frizzell. "Head towards the ridge."

"God damn it, no!" Sutherland said. "We're not moving."

"I'm giving an order, soldier," Romer said threateningly.

"Listen, you stupid motherfucker—"

"Scott!" hissed Frizzell warningly. "Colonel, we can't, we—"

"I said move out," Romer said. "I'll take full responsibility."

"You crazy son of a bitch," Sutherland said furiously. "I don't give a shit about responsibility—we'll get waxed if we move, can't you get that through your fucking head?"

Romer reached over and grabbed Sutherland by the neck, raising him up and pushing him out of the position, toward the ridge.

Sutherland tried to scramble back, but Romer pushed

him again, knocking him off balance, and he fell to the ground.

Romer, standing over Coney and Frizzell, said harshly, "Now move."

Before they could do or say anything, they heard a rifle safety click off, then an incredible explosion, and Romer's body slammed beyond them, carried by the impact of the bullet.

Then Sutherland was standing above them. He dropped down and immediately emptied his rifle in automatic fire into the darkness.

"Fire," he shouted to Frizzell and Coney.

They didn't even think, but fired into the night blindly.

The radio crackled alive, "Tigers, Tigers, Bravo One, Bravo One!"

Coney shouted into the handset, "Contact! Contact!" Then he continued to fire until he had to switch magazines.

"Where are they?" demanded Frizzell. "How many? I can't see shit out there."

Sutherland said between rounds, "There's nothing out there. I shot the son of a bitch. Keep firing." Then he grabbed Romer's dropped rifle and pulled the trigger; it didn't fire.

"Jammed! The stupid motherfucker!"

"Jesus Christ, Scott," said Frizzell. "You killed him."

"Fucking A I did."

"Tigers, Bravo One! Give me a sit rep," Bishop's voice demanded.

Coney looked at Sutherland. They stared at each other for an interminable second, then Coney punched the handset. "They got us pinned down, coming from both sides. We got a WIA at least. We gotta get out of here. Request withdrawal and medevac."

Frizzell and Sutherland snapped off a few more rounds.

"He stood up, all right? We told him to stay down, but he thought he heard something and got up. As soon as he did, they fired, and we opened up. Are you with me or not?" Sutherland asked.

"Well, sure," said Frizzell. "Jesus, he was asking for it—wanting to go out further, then pushing Scott. We gotta stand by him, Dennie. I mean, we're buddies, and the pact—remember?"

"Yeah, I know," Coney said. "But we got to get the story exactly right. We heard things, right? Noises, just movement, and suddenly he started to freak out, wanted to go get them. We told him to stay, but he wanted to go, then he stood up, and that's when he got waxed and we opened up. Everybody's got to say the same thing, and don't add anything. Okay?"

"Yeah, yeah, I got it," Sutherland said.

"Les? Tell me what happened."

Frizzell repeated the story.

Suddenly there was a crump of mortars from the ridge.

"Holy shit," Sutherland shouted. "Run! They saw the flashes."

"Grab him," Coney shouted, jumping up, struggling under the weight of the radio, and shouting into the handset, "Incoming! We're moving."

Frizzell grabbed Romer and lifted him onto his shoulders and began to run.

The first mortar rounds landed just short of the ambush, but the blast knocked Frizzell down and he couldn't get up with Romer's body on top of him.

"Help me," he yelled, and Sutherland was there instantly, lifting the body, then Frizzell jumped up and together they ran, dragging the corpse as more mortars crumped from the ridge, and suddenly there was automatic fire behind them.

"Shit!" screamed Coney. "They're in back of us. Get down!"

"No!" yelled Sutherland. "The mortars! Run!"

The mortars landed directly on the ambush site, and shrapnel flew past the three, struggling with the body and the radio.

"Tell them we're coming in the front," Frizzell yelled. "We'll never make it around back. Tell them to hold their fire, it's us."

"Bravo One, Bravo One, Tigers coming in, hold your fire, it's us in front, about a hundred meters out. Don't shoot."

They could see the wire now, the distance of a football field away, but the enemy was walking the mortars in from the ambush site, adding another hundred meters to every salvo.

"Negative! Negative!" Bishop screamed. "The mortars are right on top of you. You won't make it. Go around. Run to the left. Now!"

They changed course instantly and ran to the west, but it was like running in water, their boots sinking into the sand under the weight they carried, and when the rounds exploded, the impact knocked them all down, but they were up immediately, running to the west, circling around the hill.

The next rounds landed directly in the wire where they would have been, but they were safe, shielded by the western slope of the hill, and now artillery from Khe Sanh slammed into the ridge, huge 105mm and 155mm shells bursting orange and red, ripping the enemy position, sending the enemy mortar crews back underground.

The three staggered to the back wire where Brock and several others jumped through to help them, Brock yelling, "Who got hit? Who's hit?"

But none of them could talk; they dropped to the ground, rolling onto their backs, gasping for breath.

"It's the army colonel," Martin yelled in relief, and Brock and the others dropped beside them asking repeatedly, "You okay?" "You all right?" "Anybody else hit?" "Jesus, we thought you bought it that time." Then they pounded the three on their backs and slapped them happily.

Then Sutherland said between gasps, "They were out there, moving in, and we told him to stay down, but he jumped up, he just freaked out wanting to go after them, and as soon as he got up, they shot him, then we opened up, and—"

"Forget it," Brock said. "Get back to your posts—they may be getting ready to hit us. Get back up the hill right away. Two of you grab him and bring him to the bunker.

Later, after the shelling ceased and the threat of an enemy assault passed, Bishop called the three to the bunker.

He asked each to tell him the story and he listened without saying anything, and he didn't ask any questions, and then he let them go.

In their bunker, the three smoked nervously.

"He didn't believe us," Sutherland said. "He knew we were lying."

"He just stared at me," Frizzell said, shivering. "He knew it was bullshit. What do you think he'll do? Dennie, they could hang us for this. What do you think he'll do?"

Coney took a deep drag on a cigarette, then crushed it out. "Nothing. He won't do anything. We stood by Scott. He'll stand by us—that's what it's all about." He sighed and leaned against the bunker in exhaustion. "The colonel didn't have anybody to stand by him; the poor fucker was all alone." Then he shook his head. "Jesus, Scott . . ."

Sutherland dropped his head. "I'm sorry," he said at last, then to them, "Thanks."

He slipped Coney's ring from his finger, the emblem of their pact.

Coney took it. It was crusted with blood. He held it a moment, then he tossed it back. "Semper fi," he said.

"Yeah," Frizzell added. "We're still buddies. And we're gonna make it out of here. I know it."

"What do you think, Gunny?" Bishop asked when the three were gone.

Brock shook his head. "I'm just a dumb old lifer, Lieutenant—I don't think. You gonna think, Lieutenant?"

Bishop rubbed his face and ran his hands through his hair. "No," he said at last. "I'm not going to think." Then he sighed. "It wouldn't do any fucking good, would it?"

"Thinking never done me any good, Lieutenant. Every time I try, I get it wrong."

"God damn him," Bishop said angrily. "He shouldn't have done this to us. We didn't need this. The bastard . . . he shouldn't have come out here to us. Damn it!" he said furiously, shaking his head, because the fury was at himself for letting this happen, for letting something else get out of control, for the war, for everything that had happened. For all the dead, and now one more he had to carry for the rest of his life.

"Forget it, Lieutenant," Brock said, then he stood and went to a pile of discarded ration cans, and he picked up one and held it out to Bishop.

"Apricots," he said. "That's what he ate. I told him not to. I told him everybody who ate them got zapped. I told him it wasn't a superstition. I told him it was real. He laughed, Lieutenant."

Brock dropped the can. "He was doomed, Lieutenant. Maybe it was his old man or maybe it was the apricots—but he was doomed."

Bishop stood up; he needed air. At the bunker entrance he turned. "Is that all it is, Gunny? Just a matter of apricots?"

Brock shrugged. "Lieutenant, it makes as much sense as anything else, doesn't it?"

Bishop stared at him, then he turned and went up the stairs. The body bag lay against the bunker. He glanced at it, then walked to the berm of the hill. The night was black, the ridge obscured, and the enemy hidden.

"Apricots," he said softly to the darkness. Then he sighed. Yes, that's probably all the sense there was in it.

CHAPTER

• 45 •

The gardens of the Imperial Palace were unkempt, the ponds choked with weeds and stagnant water, the spired battlements in disrepair, the brilliant reds and golds faded and tarnished, yet Marshall did not find the Citadel sad or depressing.

The Palace was not in ruins, but disheveled and neglected, as if its occupants were gone on a long journey and the staff too tired and old to keep it up.

Marshall had arrived at the Citadel in midmorning to find it nearly deserted. It was the eve of Tet, but probably few people ever wandered in, he thought—it was not a monument to past glory, a shrine of loving memory, or a touchstone of hope; it was irrelevant, as faded in people's minds and hearts as it was in appearance.

But Marshall liked the Palace. Modeled after the Imperial Palace in Beijing, it was almost comfortable in its smaller scale, and all its ornamentation, whorls and ridges, ceramic dragons prowling the roofs and cornices, were not ostentatious, but complementary, giving the impression of perfection rather than splendor, as a Fabergé jewel was perfection in miniature but would be vulgar were it larger.

He spent several hours in the Citadel, after crossing the moat into the first of the three concentric cities within the walls of the fortification.

After the "Capital City," he entered the "Royal City," within the second concentric ring of walls, and he wandered the pebbled paths of the neglected gardens and passed before the Palace of the Spirits of the Six Emperors, the Temple of Generations, and the Halls of the Splendors of the Moon and the Glory of the Sun. He lingered on a bridge over a pond and watched carp splash, the sun reflecting off their shimmering scales, and he saw the reflection of temples floating on the surface of the water.

Though unplanned, it was almost exactly noon when he passed into the heart of the Citadel, the Tu Cam Thanh, the Purple Forbidden City within the third concentric wall where once the emperors lived in total seclusion with their families and concubines. Here was the Thai Ho, the Palace of Perfect Peace, a blaze of red and gold in the noonday sun, its steep, gilded roof seemingly on fire, the dragons snarling flames.

Across the courtyard was the imposing Longevity Palace, residence of the queen mothers.

Mead kept a respectful distance from Marshall, content to bask in the sun's rays, his rifle slung casually from his shoulder. He could not even imagine the life that had once throbbed here—to him it was all a postcard.

But Marshall could sense the life; he could almost hear the whispers of intrigue carried on the wind through the limbs of the trees, and closing his eyes to concentrate, he conjured the vibrancy and color that had been here such a short time ago—the flick of a feathered fan held by a eunuch, cooling an emperor.

Standing on the steps of the Palace, warmed by the sun, he was wafted back in time to an era of serenity and peace where mandarins in brocade robes ruled a bureaucracy that administered the country for a ruler who carried the mandate of heaven and before whom mortal men prostrated themselves.

Emperors had walked these very gardens, Marshall realized, their robes trailing on the path that had been cleared lest their thoughts or vision be marred by human imperfection, followed at a discreet distance by guards carrying spikes, barefooted, and wearing yellow, the color reserved for the emperor's entourage.

And now he was here alone, a foreign envoy to a deserted court, whose own guard tossed rocks into the pond out of boredom.

He gazed about in wonder—the emperors and mandarins were gone, the eunuchs and concubines had disappeared; the dragons looked down on him in mock ferocity.

"Did you like it?" Marshall asked Mead as they walked out of the Purple Forbidden City.

"People really lived here, sir?" Mead asked.

"Oh, yes. In fact, I think the dowager empress is still alive—the mother of the last emperor. She lives in Hue somewhere—absolute bitch from what I understand, but not long ago she lived in that very palace there," he said, pointing to the Longevity Palace.

"And the last emperor, Bao Dai, is very much alive—he's in his mid-fifties and lives in Paris, but once he lived here too. All the emperors did. There were thirteen of them, not such a lucky number for the empire, but it lasted in one form or another up until only twenty years ago."

Marshall shook his head. "How are we going to change a country that was ruled by emperors who had eunuchs and concubines only a few years ago?"

"Do you think we're going to, sir?"

At the gate they both stopped and looked back. Even in its faded majesty it was magnificent—exotic, and utterly alien.

"Do you, Corporal?" Marshall asked.

"No, sir."

When they got into the car, they broke open the food that the mess hall had sent along.

"It is getting late, Excellency," the driver said. "Perhaps you should visit the tombs tomorrow. I could not get us there until nearly four—the roads are very bad, so even if you stayed just a short while, it would be almost dark before we returned."

"No, I must go today," Marshall said. "I won't be there long; I know Tet begins tomorrow, and you want to get home to your family, but if I don't see the tombs this afternoon, I never will."

"You cannot see them all, Excellency, there are too many, and they are not in the same place."

"Yes, I know. I just want to see two—Minh Mang's and Tu Duc's, they are supposed to be the most remarkable."

Because of the holiday, there was little traffic on the road, and with the driver's urgency, they soon approached the tomb of Minh Mang, second emperor of the Nguyen dynasty. He was resolutely opposed to foreign intervention and initiated the policy of noninvolvement with the West. His formal Confucian training and scholarship made him intolerant of Christianity, and he began the persecution of the missionaries, which set the stage for the confrontation between the French and the Vietnamese.

"You must walk from here," the driver said. "It is still a long way, but I cannot go closer with the car." He looked nervously at his watch. "You must hurry."

Mead and Marshall got out and followed a narrow path to the top of a small hill.

"My God," Marshall said when he reached it and saw the scene before him.

Below, on the banks of the River of Perfumes, lay one of the most beautiful scenes he had ever beheld. He saw that he should have come by water, borne the way the emperor himself would have been from Hue.

Leading from the mooring on the bank was a grove of banyan trees spreading to the wide, crescent-shaped Lake of Scintillating Brightness, over which red-pillared pavilions were built that brought one to the burial grounds—an expanse of temples and shrines, and a garden laid out in the pattern of the Chinese character for eternity.

"That's a grave?" Mead asked incredulously.

"Yes," Marshall said. "But it's more than that. The emperors built their graves themselves, and they came out to them before they died—sometimes they lived out here, as if they were country palaces. That's what I read last night."

They walked down to the burial grounds, but Marshall saw that it would take hours to go through the site. Though the grounds were well kept and obviously required numerous workers, no one was in sight.

"He's buried beneath that hill." Marshall pointed. "The one with all those tangled trees."

The late-afternoon sun was dropping behind it and Marshall stared at the remarkable sight of the wild trees dominating the hilltop. It looked untamed, almost violent, as if nature were bursting from the earth, trying to grapple with the sky, and he knew that soon the sun would drop lower and appear as if it were entangled in the grasping trunks and limbs of the trees, and at night the moon too would be caught. And beneath, entangled in the roots, was the dead emperor.

The vision took his breath away—man, earth, sky, sun, and moon all entangled; all one, all in harmony.

Marshall stared for so long, stunned by the richness and complexity conveyed by the trees, a capturing of the eternal in a grove on a hill, that he was unmindful of the time, and only when Mead began to shuffle his boots in the gravel did he realize he had to go, yet all the way back he kept turning to look, and finally at the top of the hill, as he was about to leave, he saw the trees reaching, at last grasping the burning orb that would be brought down into the earth and not escape until tomorrow.

"Too long," the driver admonished as Marshall got into the car. "There's no time now to go to any other tomb."

"You must," Marshall said. "I have to see another one."

The driver slapped his watch. "Too late; soon it will be dark, Excellency. You cannot be out after dark; too dangerous. Tonight . . ." He was very nervous, more anxious than he should be, Mead thought, but Marshall did not notice.

"I don't care," Marshall said, taking out his wallet and handing him several large bills. "Take me to the other tomb."

By the time they reached the tomb of Tu Duc, fourth Nguyen emperor and last ruler of independent Vietnam, it was nearly dusk.

"Thirty minutes," the driver said. "No more." Gone was the respectful tone, and Mead bristled at the man's manner, but again Marshall did not notice—he had already started up the path.

At the top of the hill he saw a majestic scene below him in the glades spreading from the river.

He had come at the perfect time; the emperor himself would have chosen such a moment, he thought, when the shadows were longest, lingering over the land, and the last dying glimmers of the sun shimmered over the water.

The beauty was breathtaking, and for a moment he did not breathe as he marveled at the gilded pavilions and temples in the midst of a pine forest set within a series of lagoons, man and nature, caught in the moment that divided day from night. Again he saw it—man, earth, time—the universe in a single scene of perfect harmony.

He followed the path down to the tomb, unmindful of time, drawn by the beauty and mystery.

Again the grounds were deserted; they were completely alone.

Marshall crossed the lagoon over a covered bridge and passed through a bronze gate behind which were the trees and temples. He walked through a pebbled courtyard raked smooth, and just as he started to mount the stairs of the imperial tomb, Mead stopped him.

Mead whirled. "Jesus Christ!" He started to run.

"What is it?" Marshall called.

"The car! The bastard's leaving us. Wait here." He ran out the gate and raced over the bridge and up the path and out of sight.

Marshall stood a moment on the stairway staring after him, then looked about.

Beautiful, he thought, but not really where I want to be abandoned for the night, at a deserted tomb miles from anywhere.

He walked back toward the gate and in the dimness saw Mead returning.

Marshall sat on a stone and waited, though he could tell from Mead's furious gait that the driver was gone.

"The son of a bitch," Mead yelled from across the bridge. "I can't believe he left us here."

Standing before Marshall, he said incredulously, "He's gone, sir. He drove off."

"Did he leave the food? I'm famished."

Mead stared at Marshall in amazement, not knowing what reaction to expect, but not expecting calmness. Finally he smiled. "No, sir, the bastard didn't even leave us a sandwich."

Marshall gazed about placidly, then said to Mead, "All right, Corporal—how are you going to get me out of this mess?"

Mead looked about the burial grounds, to the closeting trees and dark sky, and he shook his head. "Well, sir, I guess all we can do is sit tight."

"You don't think we should start walking back?"

Mead was emphatic. "No, sir. The last place we want to be at night is walking along a road. We don't have much of a choice, sir. We better just wait here until someone comes. The only way into here is over that bridge, unless they want to swim across the lagoon."

"You're worried about Viet Cong?"

"Yes, sir. The driver was acting nervous all afternoon—he didn't want to come out here at all. I think he knows something is up. And for him to leave you here . . . I mean, what's he going to say when he returns with the car to Phu Bai, and you're not with him? He's not going back to Phu Bai with the car, now or ever."

Marshall thought a moment. "So no one knows where we are."

"Only the driver. And whoever he tells. But whoever he tells has to come over that bridge, and I'm going to be right here waiting. The problem is, I only have ten magazines—about two hundred rounds; we can't make much of a stand on that."

Marshall stood and smiled. "Corporal Mead, I think if Custer had had you with your two hundred rounds, that last battle of his would have ended very differently, and he probably would have died in obscure old age."

Marshall was unperturbed and unafraid; this development, after all, was nothing like the chopper crash in the Delta.

He started back through the gate. "I think I'll go look at

713

Tu Duc's tomb while I can still see. And with any luck, someone left a food offering—it's going to be a long, hungry night otherwise."

But there was no offering, only incense placed before the red and black lacquer altar, and from the top of the temple, walking the long portico, he could not see anything in the darkness, and presently he returned to the bronze gate where Mead had built a small fortification from rocks and wood planks pulled from the fence.

"Maybe I ought to do something about that bridge," Mead mused aloud; then he turned to Marshall. "Do you think I should wreck it so no one can get across? We'd probably be a lot safer."

Marshall could not sense any danger in the night; the situation seemed almost absurd to him. "Do you really think there's any danger? No one seemed around for miles, and if the driver were an enemy agent, he could have arranged something to happen anytime during the day. After all, it is Tet—maybe he just wanted to get home. Everyone keeps saying that there's no chance of an enemy attack during Tet."

"That's it then," Mead said. "I'm going to knock the bridge down."

Marshall restrained him. "Can't you barricade it, or booby-trap it? I'd hate to damage this place; it's a sacred tomb."

Mead considered, then nodded. "I could booby-trap it with a grenade so that if someone did come across, it'd blow the bridge—except I'd need to find some wire." Then he remembered the fence. "I know where there's wire."

It took him thirty minutes to rig the grenade on the bridge so that the pin would be pulled by anyone's crossing, then he returned and set up his rifle with a perfect line of fire on the bridge.

"It's going to be a long night," he said when he was finally satisfied and sat back to wait. "It's only nine-thirty; if you want to sleep, go ahead, sir."

"Strangely enough, I'm not really tired," Marshall said. Then he laughed. "And Colonel Romer didn't want to come because he thought it would be boring."

"I'll bet he's driving them nuts up there," Mead said.

"I'm sure he is, but your lieutenant looked like he could handle the colonel; the gunnery sergeant too. I liked them all very much—there are some fine men up there. I'm sorry about your friends who died there."

Mead didn't say anything for a long moment, then he sighed. "I knew Snags the best—we'd been there about the same time. I never thought anything would happen to him. And Landis was a good guy too—he used to always talk about this car he was going to buy, a black one; we used to joke it'd be a hearse." He sighed. "There it is."

He put his elbows on the fortification and stared toward the bridge and said softly, "It don't seem right, sir."

There was no answer from Marshall; he looked at the young man beside him, then to the silhouette of the emperor's tomb behind him. There was nothing he could say.

They sat silently for a long time, then Marshall said, "I can't imagine my son out here like this." He laughed softly. "I'm being unfair to him, I'm sure—fathers always are—but if he were out here instead of you, I think I'd shoot myself."

"Is he really coming, sir?"

"He may be here already. A Green Beret—I just can't picture it. That's the unfair part; parents always see their children as helpless and vulnerable. I'm always amazed when he gets home in one piece even when he's just going to the store. We remember all the dumb things and can't conceive the child can thread his way alone through the world."

"I'm sure he'll be all right, sir."

"I don't know," Marshall said. "He's not like you at all."

Mead grinned. "I sort of figured that, sir," he said in self-deprecation.

"No, no," Marshall said quickly. "I mean . . . he's never done anything; I can't see him knowing what to do. He's not stupid, of course, just that—he's never *had* to do anything, and it's not even that we spoiled him. We didn't spoil him, or any of our children, and it's certainly not a criticism of them that their lives haven't been difficult. They got good grades, haven't caused us any problems—until recently anyway—and if they had had to work, or struggle to survive, I'm sure they would have. God knows they've turned out better than a lot of our friends' children."

Mead smiled. "I'm sure my old man couldn't imagine me making it over here either. Not that he'd care any; he may have even forgot I'm here."

"But you see, that kind of background probably prepared you for life over here. Poor Ryan, he thinks it's just a game—he doesn't have any idea what it's like." Then he said in exasperation, "My God, he couldn't even throw a baseball; how the hell can he be a Green Beret?"

"You're probably being too hard on him, sir."

"I'm not! He never could throw a ball. Neither can Chris—but that's another depressing story altogether." He shook his head. "Chris. Dear God," he sighed. "I wonder what I did wrong?" he mused to himself.

"How old is he, sir?" Mead asked.

"Chris? He's fifteen."

Mead didn't say anything, and in the awkward silence Marshall felt the need to explain. "I think he's a homosexual," he said softly.

"Oh," said Mead, then after a long minute, "I guess there are lots of worse things, sir."

"Oh, I *know* there are, Corporal. It doesn't really bother me—I just don't want him to be unhappy. I don't want any of my children to be unhappy. That's what makes it so hard to be a parent—seeing them hurt or disappointed, rejected or not chosen, or God forbid, laughed at and humiliated." Then he bowed his head. "Or killed."

He dropped his head into his hands. "Oh, God, I couldn't stand that. I'm so afraid."

Mead had never seen Marshall exposed, the calm, confident exterior penetrated, and he was very moved and wished there was something he could do or say to ease him.

"I wanted so much to end this war. I wanted to help so badly. But I haven't done a thing."

"It's not your fault, sir."

"But it is. I let it happen; I didn't say anything long ago when it could have been stopped, before it really began. I should have known better—I *did* know better; I just didn't do anything. I was silent, and I let all the nonsense and stupid slogans become policy, and even when the sons were dying, I didn't say anything—only when it became my son. Ryan saw before I did how wrong this war was; he was wiser and braver. And now he may die for it."

Marshall looked up with tears in his eyes, and he laughed sorrowfully. "How can he survive if he can't throw a grenade? And I know he couldn't have booby-trapped that bridge without blowing himself to the moon. The stupid son of a bitch," he said angrily. "God *damn* him for coming over here." Then he smiled. "Maybe Catherine locked him in the cellar—that's my wife, she's certainly capable of it."

He shook his head. "Do you know that all I ever wanted my sons to do was play football? Isn't that asinine? Just be normal boys and toss a football around. They never did."

He looked at Mead. "You played football, of course."

"Yes, sir."

Marshall sighed.

"But my dad never cared; he never came to any of my games. I don't ever remember him saying anything decent to me, or any of us, specially my mom. He'd ignore us, or come roaring through and smack whoever was in the way."

"At least it taught you to be quick on your feet—maybe your father and I should have swapped kids for a while. Wives too—he would have only popped Catherine once."

Mead laughed. "Your wife sounds kinda neat, sir; I mean strong and interesting."

"Yes, she's all that for sure. She's a very fine woman, a very good woman. Much too good for me—as she'd be the first to tell you."

Mead was silent, then he let his breath out slowly. "My old man never said anything good about my mother; maybe when they were young it was okay, but in all the years I can remember, he'd just . . . treat her like shit." He shook his head and tried to stop the tears in his eyes. "She didn't deserve it; she was always kind, and never complained—I mean, we never had anything, and she never . . . Ah, shit," he said, wiping his eyes. Then he laughed. "I guess we better be careful, sir; with us both crying, the gooks could cross the bridge and we'd never see them."

Marshall smiled. "You booby-trapped it, remember?"

Then Marshall said gently, "Would you do me a very great favor, Corporal Mead?"

"Yes, sir," he said without hesitation.

"Let me help you."

"How, sir?"

"I haven't been able to do anything here—stop the war, even help Miss Hawthorne in the clinic, so let me do something for you."

Marshall took a deep breath. "You could have made it easy by asking for my help, but that wouldn't be you at all, so now I have to ask you. Miss Hawthorne told me about your visit to her."

Mead started. "She shouldn't have . . ."

"She wanted to help you, so when I saw her she told me about your girlfriend."

Mead looked away in embarrassment.

"She said you were in love with her; she said you wanted to marry her."

Mead couldn't bring himself to face Marshall. "Well, yes, sir, I do."

"You've thought about it carefully?"

Mead turned to him and said earnestly, "Yes, sir, I have. I talked to everybody about it, and they act like I'm some horny kid who doesn't know anything and that she's some whore who . . . but she's not, she's, she's . . . Well, I love her. She's smart, and speaks lots better than me, and she's good and kind, and she's not a whore. Her family was killed, and . . ."

Marshall put his hand on his arm. "You want to marry her?"

"Yes, sir," he said emphatically. "I love her."

"Well, wonderful. At last, something I can do."

"You can help me, sir?"

Marshall laughed. "I think so. An ambassador isn't good for much, but he should be able to arrange a marriage at least," he said solemnly. "I think I can pull enough strings to get you authorization to get married."

Mead was too overcome to say anything. He tried several times, but each effort sputtered inarticulately.

"There's just one small hitch, Corporal."

"What's that, sir?"

"You've got to get us out of here—the bride is in Saigon; the groom and the best man are . . . wherever the hell we are."

"Best man? You would . . ." He sputtered into inarticulation again.

"Well, I certainly hope you ask me." Then he touched Mead's arm again. "I want more than anything to help you. I want you to be happy." He looked to the sky with its first hint of moon, the new moon, the first moon of the Year of the Monkey. "I wish I could help everybody; I wish everybody could be happy. I want the war to end, and my son to live, and I want peace and happiness for everyone—but I'll settle for helping a man and a woman in love. That's certainly not a small thing." He smiled. "Maybe it's everything."

Then he looked about the night and to the tomb in back of him.

"I haven't done much better than poor Tu Duc," he said. "He lost an empire by not fighting. He gave in to the French, and his descendants have been fighting for their freedom ever since. He was a good man from what I understand, clever and intelligent, and he was only seeking to buy time for his people—he certainly didn't mean to send them into a hundred years of slavery and warfare."

Marshall turned to Mead and smiled. "Promise me you won't listen to politicians and you won't beat your wife."

Mead laughed. "I promise, sir."

"Then I can't ask for more. And you'll probably have a happy life." He looked at his watch. "It's after midnight. Happy Tet, Corporal. Actually this is a good sign, at least for me."

"How is that, sir?"

"The Vietnamese believe that the fortunes of the coming year are determined by the first person you meet after Tet begins. I consider you a very good omen."

"Well, you too, sir."

"Maybe this will be a good year then," Marshall said. "I can't think of a better way to begin it." He looked about, then smiled. "Well, maybe I could; but maybe not." He yawned. "I think I've worn myself out with talk."

"Why don't you go to sleep, sir? I'll get you up if something happens."

"Yes, don't leave me here alone, please. And if you get tired, wake me up—I couldn't do much, but I'd probably notice if the bridge blew up."

Marshall settled onto the ground, tried to make himself comfortable, and didn't even have time to be surprised at how quickly he fell asleep.

For a long time, Mead basked in happiness, warmed by thoughts of Sung. He tried to foresee a future, envision a life with her, looked for children and a house, but he could not conjure it. Yet that was all right, for he never saw into the future; he never planned ahead because he seemed to have such little control over his life—what happened just happened. He never expected anything he desired to come true. Landis could talk for hours about his car, describe every detail and tell you exactly what he was going to do—see it real in his mind—but he, Mead, could not do that. He had such diminished expectations from his childhood that hopes and dreams hardly existed for him.

Yet all he ever could have hoped for was going to come true. He never really thought he would fall in love, thought that the nerves for love had been cauterized, yet he did find someone to love, in this most awful place in the middle of a war, and she . . . well, maybe she didn't love him, but that was all right—it might happen someday—and now he was going to marry her, and . . . But that was as far as he could go. Yet it was enough, more than he had expected—as much as he could hope and dream.

Then suddenly everything was wrong.

He bolted upright and clutched his rifle tightly.

Something was happening—he could hear it and sense it and feel it, and it was massive and overwhelming. The air was electric; he had never felt such tension, but he could not identify it—it was amorphous and pervasive. And imminent.

He looked at his watch; it was 3:25 A.M.

Then specific noises came—troop movement on the water and along the banks; he could hear faint voices and commands.

He almost shook Marshall awake, but the movement was not coming this way—it was going upriver toward Hue.

At exactly 3:40, the sky was lit by flashes of light, and seconds later the ground shook in explosion after explosion.

Marshall jerked awake. He sat up and focused on the horizon, which seemed to be bursting apart. "What in the . . . are they celebrating?"

Mead shook his head. "Those aren't firecrackers, sir. That's artillery. Gook 122mms—big artillery."

Then the horizon was a bonfire; shells burst continuously and flames shot a hundred feet in the air.

"My God," Marshall said incredulously. "They're attacking the city—they're destroying it."

The shelling, even from this distance, was deafening, then it gave way to mortars and small-arms fire, signaling the troop assault on the city.

The firing went on and on, raging and subsiding, and all the while the horizon glowed.

"That's the most fighting I've ever heard," Mead said. "They're gonna take the city—that's a gook division out there, and all we got is some Marines at Phu Bai; they'll never get there in time, if they get there at all."

"What do you mean?" Marshall asked.

"I heard a lot of movement before, on the river and banks. We're south of the city—so's Phu Bai; they're gonna ambush any unit trying to get into Hue."

"So he did know," Marshall said. "The driver, I mean."

"Yeah—he's probably one of their mortarmen."

The fighting did not abate until nearly dawn, but even then, small-arms fire continued without cease. Then around eight in the morning, fighting intensified with barrage after barrage of automatic weapons fire.

"General Tran was right," Marshall said. "They completely fooled MACV with the Tet cease-fire. Now it's all over."

"The war?" Mead asked incredulously.

"No," Marshall said in resignation. "The peace, and any hope for it. The war will go on and on. The President won't listen to me or anyone. The deaths will go on and on."

Marshall listened to the battle rage, then turned and walked across the courtyard to the tomb. He sat for a long time on the portico, hands in his lap, head down.

Mead knew they were trapped; they couldn't move from here and had to stay until they were rescued.

The battle continued without letup all morning.

"If the NVA are in the Citadel, it'll take a week of hand-to-hand combat to get them out," Mead said.

"Surely someone will find us before then," Marshall said.

"Nobody knows we're here, sir, just that gook driver."

Then suddenly from downriver came the sound of a chopper at low altitude, and in a few minutes they saw the distinctive black helicopter above the trees, flying at an extremely exposed altitude. They shouted in relief and happiness.

Mead ran up the steps of the tomb and signaled; Marshall stayed in the courtyard, waving frantically.

Magnuson brought the chopper down into the courtyard. Running to get in, Marshall and Mead saw that the fuselage had been riddled with bullets.

Magnuson lifted off as Mead was still pulling himself in. "Were you finished sight-seeing?" he asked over the intercom. "Don't mean to rush you."

As Mead strapped himself in, he saw the green body bag under the seat.

"What happened?" Marshall said, out of breath, face pressed to the window, but before Magnuson could answer, he asked, "How did you find us? How did you know where we were? As stupid as this sounds, Lieutenant—thank you."

"I owe you two now," Mead shouted over the engine.

"Call it even," Magnuson said. "In fact, let's call the fucking game over."

"Absolutely," said Marshall. "And think of a good-bye present I can get you—whatever you want is yours, Lieutenant."

"Corporal Mead's girlfriend."

"Too late." Marshall laughed. "They're going to get married—that's my present to him. Pick another one—and not another woman, you have a wife. Colonel Romer was right—I read your record too. Where is he? He would have loved this."

There was a pause, then the chopper tilted to the left so they had a clear view of Hue. "I can't get closer, but see the Citadel—that's the NVA flag flying over it. They took the city last night, and hit every other one in the country, even Saigon. They even got into the embassy and killed a few guards. They hit everywhere except Khe Sanh—it's just a fucking disaster."

"How did you know where we were?" Mead asked.

"You told me you were going to the tombs—we flew over one, remember, and I said it'd be safer to drive out, or take a boat. When they told me at Phu Bai that you hadn't come back—they're frantic, by the way; they think you're at the Citadel—I flew down to the tombs. Do you know how many there are? That one was the sixth I buzzed."

"Is that where the bullet holes came from?"

"What bullet holes?" Magnuson deadpanned.

Then Mead unstrapped himself and moved toward the cockpit. "Are you all right, Lieutenant? Are you hit?"

"Really minor," he said. "Good thing there's no copilot though—they took out that seat."

Mead slid the compartment door open into the cockpit. Blood was splattered everywhere. "Jesus Christ."

Magnuson turned, his face white. "I'm okay, just a surface wound."

"Bullshit, Lieutenant," Mead said, dropping into the copilot seat; there were bullet holes through the door and Plexiglas.

"Get out of my cockpit, you dumb grunt—that's the worst possible luck, and close that goddamn door."

Mead slid the door shut so that Marshall couldn't see. "Are you gonna make it, Lieutenant?"

Magnuson held up his arm and pointed to his calf. "I'm okay—they're not bad wounds; I'm just a heavy bleeder—low factor eight. Now get the fuck out of here."

"What happened to Colonel Romer?"

Magnuson shook his head. "At the hill—he took out a patrol; they got hit."

"Who else?" Mead asked anxiously.

"He was the only one. When I went up for him yesterday, the body was already at Dong Ha waiting to be sent back. I told them I'd take it to Saigon, that the ambassador would want that, then I went to the hill to find out what happened. I had a long talk with Luke—Lieutenant Bishop. Just between you and me, I think it was Romer's fault—I think he asked for it."

"One of the men shot him?"

"Luke wouldn't say that. Officially, it was enemy fire on an ambush."

"And everybody else is all right? They weren't hit last night?"

Magnuson shook his head. "Not a single bullet was fired—it was all a decoy. You played football, right? It was just a feint, and they made an end run around Khe Sanh. Bishop and your buddies were safe—last night anyway."

Then he grimaced and stroked his thigh.

"Jesus," Mead said, adding worriedly, "Are you really okay, Lieutenant?"

"Now I am. I was getting nervous about the fourth tomb." He pointed out the window. "That's just a massacre down there—they hit the Marine company coming up from Phu Bai, then pinned down the company sent to rescue them; there are dead Marines all over the place. The gooks own Hue, and nobody's getting them out anytime soon—that'll take house-to-house fighting down every street."

Then he snarled at Mead, "Now get out of here, god damn it—grunts in the cockpit is worse than bad luck—it's a curse. Besides, Corporal—even if I wasn't all right, could you fly this?"

Mead looked at the myriad controls and instruments; he smiled. "No, sir."

"Go back and tell the ambassador about Colonel Romer."

Mead peered through the door; Marshall was asleep, propped against the window.

"I don't need to for a while, he's sleeping."

"Why don't you try to sleep too," Magnuson said. "It's going to be a slow trip back—this baby's shaky, but we'll make it."

"Take your time, sir," Mead said, leaving the cockpit.

Magnuson stopped him. "Congratulations. When's the wedding?"

"Soon as we get back, sir."

Magnuson smiled. "I'll see if we can't make a little better time then," and he pushed on the throttle.

CHAPTER

• 46 •

By the time Marshall's helicopter touched down at Tan Son Nhut in Saigon, the embassy had been declared secure.

At one-thirty A.M., a sapper team had struck the Presidential Palace but was turned back by guards; they retreated to an apartment building across the street where they killed two American MPs and took their machine guns.

At two-thirty A.M., another sapper team hit the U.S. embassy. Because of the Tet cease-fire, only two army MPs were at the main gate at the eight-foot wall that surrounded the compound, and three Marine guards were inside.

The VC killed the two MPs and raced toward the chancery. Two Marines barely managed to get the massive teak doors closed before antitank rockets ripped through the lobby. The third Marine was trapped on the roof with a pistol and six bullets, but he was able to radio security headquarters about the attack, and soon reinforcements arrived, killing or capturing all the sappers.

Though the Viet Cong and NVA attacked numerous targets throughout the city, including a three-battalion attack on Tan Son Nhut, by morning Saigon was secure. Only in Cholon had the enemy established a foothold, and there they began systematic destruction.

* * *

Shortly before dawn, a lone woman, strangely oblivious to the fighting throughout the city, approached the U.S. embassy. She had an infant strapped to her back, and she was carrying a two-gallon container of gasoline.

"Na Mo A Di Da Phat," the woman repeated over and over, intoning the Buddhist supplication for mercy, and then "Nam mo amita Buddha"—"Return to the eternal Buddha."

Lin had to stop frequently because of her burden, and because she was so weak.

It had taken her a month of begging on the streets to amass enough money to buy the gasoline and container; twice her money had been stolen by beggar children, and usually what she was able to beg during a day barely bought food to keep her and her baby alive. But at last she saved enough, and Tet was the perfect time for her sacrifice; it was a great religious holiday, and the merciful Buddha would look favorably on her act.

As she neared the U.S. embassy, small-arms fire intensified, but what surprised her was that there were no television cameras—she had expected a great crowd, as there had been for the Buddhist monks when they immolated themselves. She didn't understand why they had been there for the monks, but not for her.

Lin did not fear death; she had decided that it was better for her and her baby to die. There was no meaning in their lives, but there would be in their deaths. The world would notice; her act would make a great difference, she knew. But she didn't understand why there were no cameras.

A block from the embassy she saw armored vehicles and a cordon of police and soldiers.

They were going to try to stop her, she realized, and she started to run, carrying the gasoline in her arms.

Suddenly there were shouts; they were yelling at her, then they started toward her.

She stopped and started to open the container.

The soldiers halted and backed away as she knelt over the canister, then they screamed for her to stop but she didn't, and then suddenly there were shots and she felt incredible pain, then again and again, and the gasoline leaked everywhere, and bullets hit on the street, sending sparks, and then a burst of flames and she was engulfed in fire, and all she had time and strength for was to reach behind and grab the baby, cradling it into her arms.

"A massive defeat for the enemy," Westmoreland told Marshall at the afternoon briefing. "They tried to overrun the country and failed everywhere."

"Hue?" Marshall asked.

"That'll be over soon—all that's left is mopping up."

"Khe Sanh?"

Westmoreland sighed. "It seems to have been a diversion. General Tran was correct; they never meant to attack it. But if I hadn't reinforced the hill, they would have overrun it."

"A no-win situation then," Marshall said. Like the war, he thought.

"I'll be leaving in two days," Marshall said. "The first thing the President is going to ask me about is Tet."

Westmoreland smiled ruefully. "We've been in constant communication. He's under the impression that the bottom fell out here. And I'm afraid that's the message the media is going to convey—that this was a major defeat for the United States. My main fear is that this is going to be interpreted as an enemy victory. It isn't, Mr. Ambassador. They surprised us—I'll admit that, but what did they accomplish? They were able to raise the flag over the Citadel in Hue. No other city fell—there was no popular uprising behind them; the people remained loyal to the South Vietnamese government. The enemy lost thousands of their best troops without gaining anything."

"They gained the perception of strength and victory," Marshall said.

"What is perceived is what is *reported*—whatever the media decides to make of this will be the historical verdict. If all the anchormen and newspapers report that the enemy won, then the President and the people will accept that, despite all evidence to the contrary. You've got to tell the President what happened here—that the enemy staged attacks throughout the country, but only Hue fell. They were repelled everywhere else. Even worse than their military failure was that the army and people remained loyal to the government of South Vietnam."

"I understand, General, but I have misgivings about how the President and people will interpret this. Unfortunately, the President and people have been told often about the light at the end of the tunnel, and how victory is just around the bend—they won't believe that anymore; they'll see a long struggle ahead.

"When the sons begin to die, when the coffins start coming home, then the words and slogans are examined more carefully. The words are weighed against the metal caskets. The scale is very precise, General—and more empty words won't alter the balance in the slightest. A single coffin is heavier than all the slogans, and all the words won't fill a single grave."

Westmoreland looked haggard and troubled; the enemy offensive had obviously shocked him, and Marshall could imagine the pressure he was under from Washington.

"I'll convey your views to the President," Marshall said, "and I'll support your view that the Tet offensive was not an enemy victory. But before I leave, I have two favors to ask of you: there is an American woman in Cholon, Teresa Hawthorne, who runs a clinic for illegitimate children of U.S. soldiers—I want her and those children rescued."

"Done," said Westmoreland. "And the second favor?"

"My son Ryan just arrived here. He's a Green Beret. I'd like to see him before I leave."

Westmoreland's manner changed to genuine solicitude. "Of course, Excellency. Ryan Marshall? Special Forces? I'll see to it immediately."

"Thank you. And I won't trouble you further, General. Thank you for your help and consideration. I wish you success and happiness."

"Will you marry me?" Mead asked Sung. They lay exhausted on the sleeping bag. "Actually I'm not asking you, I'm telling you that we're going to get married and that you're going back with me to America in a couple days, and if you don't like me or America and you change your mind, then you can get a divorce and come back."

Sung laughed and pulled his chest hair, then the trail of hair down his stomach to his groin. "You are like a bear," she said.

"Did you hear me?" he asked.

"Of course. That was the longest sentence you ever spoke."

"Well?"

She pulled the hair around his navel. "That is such a strange place to have hair."

"God damn it!"

She sat up. "You are serious and this is true?"

"Yes," he said, sitting up beside her and taking her hand. "Please marry me. I . . . I mean . . . Aw, shit, I'll never say it right. That was my big sentence before. I want it to be forever, but I know how you feel . . . I mean, I know I'm not good enough for you, and hell, maybe you'll hate America. But if it doesn't work out, I promise, I'll send you back."

She smiled. "You are a very sweet person. Probably I never would have found a man like you in Ban Me Thuot. Anyway, no one as hairy."

"Does that mean you'll marry me?"

She nodded solemnly. "Yes."

He yelled joyously, then kissed her and eased her back.

"How about tomorrow?" Marshall asked Mead. "I'm leaving the next day. I've already made the arrangements with Immigration and Visa; there won't be any complications—most of the crap has been waived: medicals, interviews, family documentation—all she has to do is sign the forms. And get married, of course. So how about tomorrow?"

"Yes, sir. Anything you say."

"Good. Arrange that downstairs and tell me when and where—I'll bring the champagne. Maybe Miss Hawthorne will be there too—they're going out to get her."

"Who, sir?"

"The army."

"They'll fuck it up. Sorry, sir—but they will. I'll go."

"Bridegrooms don't go on combat missions, Corporal; let's leave it to the army."

"Sir, Miss Hawthorne is responsible for all this. I have to go; please, sir."

"I really don't want you to—I never should have let Colonel Romer stay at the hill. If something happened to you, I . . ."

"I'll be fine, sir. I'm getting married, I'm not going to let anything happen now. And I just have to go get Miss Hawthorne."

The army unit was happy to have him because he knew exactly where the clinic was and its interior layout, but as soon as they neared Cholon, they realized the fighting was far more intense than they'd been briefed.

Cholon was a battlefield; streets were barricaded, enemy commandos fired rockets and grenades at all movement, and snipers pinned down South Vietnamese and American troops.

Twice the unit commander radioed for reinforcements, and they waited until armored personnel carriers were brought in with self-propelled 40mm guns and more machine gunners.

Finally, they fought their way to the street where the clinic was and set up defensive positions on both blocks while Mead and others ran inside.

There was pandemonium within the clinic as the soldiers stormed in. Teresa Hawthorne, terrified that it was enemy troops coming to murder the women and children, blocked the entrance with two other nurses.

"It's okay, Miss Hawthorne," Mead yelled. "We came to get everybody. You got to help us. Tell all the women to grab the children and go out to the trucks."

Teresa started to question and protest, but Mead grabbed her and put his hand over her mouth. "God damn it, don't say anything, just tell everybody to get in the trucks. If you don't, we'll drag them out. Men are going to get killed out there if we wait. Now tell everybody to shut the fuck up and get outside. Now!"

Teresa looked at him in surprise, and then admonishment —no one had ever spoken to her like that, or put his hand over her mouth.

Then his fierceness eased, and he looked almost pleadingly at her. "C'mon, Miss Hawthorne, let us save you like we're supposed to. Tell everybody to grab a bag or whatever they want and go out to the trucks. Trust me. Trust Ambassador Marshall."

She turned and began speaking rapidly in Vietnamese, then she moved among the women, soothing and urging, and within minutes they all started out toward the trucks, clutching their babies and few possessions.

"I have to go get Father Dourmant," Teresa said, heading for the door.

Mead grabbed her arm. "Miss Hawthorne, you can't, there's no time. We have to get out of here. Those trucks are sitting targets."

"I'm not leaving until I get him," she said emphatically.

"God damn!" Mead swore, then he shouted to the soldiers that he'd be back in a few minutes. They tried to stop him, but Teresa had already run out, and Mead chased after her.

She was shocked at the devastation in the streets. Fires burned throughout the district and smoke billowed hundreds of feet in the air. Rubble and broken glass lay everywhere.

She started to run but was halted by the sudden explosion of nearby mortars and small-arms fire.

Mead urged her on, guiding her by the elbow, and they ran down alleys and back streets until they came to the church. She pushed open the rectory gate and ran up the stairs to the little house.

"Father Dourmant," she called, knocking on the door. There was no answer. She knocked again.

Then Mead slammed against the door, bursting it open. He ran in, rifle raised, and pushed through the kitchen door.

"Sacré Dieu!" said Father Dourmant, spilling his cup of tea over the table where he was sitting.

Teresa was behind Mead. "Father, you have to hurry. They've sent trucks for us. The whole city is on fire. You have to come with us."

The priest looked at them as though they were both mad, then he started to blot up the spilled tea.

"Father—" she started again.

"Teresa, my dear, I am flattered that you and Gunga Din have come for me, but I am perfectly content and safe here, and I am not . . ."

Mead ran to him and snatched him up.

Father Dourmant started to holler a protest, but Mead tossed him over his shoulder and started away, thrusting his rifle into Teresa's hand. "Carry this for me, and tell him to shut up. Please."

Then Mead ran out the door carrying the struggling priest, Teresa running after, holding out the rifle at arm's length.

"Do you cry at weddings?" Marshall asked Teresa. They were in a reception room of the embassy, hastily set up for the ceremony.

"I've only been to two others," she said. "I didn't at those. Do you cry at weddings?"

"I try not to, but I don't know about today," he said. "I feel like I have the most tenuous grasp on myself. If I start to weep or babble, please stop me. How are the children?"

"Very well. It's all quite strange for the women—we're in a dormitory type of building, and the toilets work and there's plenty of food and water. It's impossible to thank you enough. We keep hearing about the fighting in Cholon—I can't imagine what would have happened if we had stayed there."

"Probably they'll send you back when this is over," Marshall said, "but that won't be for some time—by then you'll be in the bureaucratic supply and requisition system."

"Yes, they've already sent doctors and nurses. Father Dourmant is very disgruntled to find that there are good Americans."

"I'm surprised he offered to conduct the wedding," Marshall said. "I didn't think it would be allowed—I mean, they're hardly the ideal young Catholic couple."

"She's very sweet, isn't she?"

"Absolutely lovely," Marshall said. "And Corporal Mead is right, she does speak better English than he does. I'm very happy about it. I suppose it's the only meaningful thing I accomplished over here."

He wanted to touch her, hold her close, remain beside her, but he couldn't. "Thank you," he whispered to her. "For everything good that has happened."

She was surprised, but she did not look up at him.

"I will see you again," he said.

Then she looked up at him and smiled because she knew that he would, because he accomplished things.

Father Dourmant came from a side room, then Mead in his jungle fatigues and Sung in a white silk *ao dai*.

A table at the front served as an altar, and behind were rows of chairs for the guests—everyone in Marshall's office, Mead's friends, and Han with several other Vietnamese women.

"I won't offer a mass," said Father Dourmant to the assembly. "This will be a . . . shortened version of the sacrament."

He looked at Mead. "Are you Catholic?"

Mead shook his head. "No, sir."

Father Dourmant frowned, then turned to Sung. "Are you Catholic?"

"No," she said.

The priest nodded. "Good. I couldn't marry a Catholic to a non-Catholic, but I don't know of any prohibition against marrying two non-Catholics, so will you please stand while we join this man and woman in holy matrimony under the loving, watchful, and probably dumbfounded gaze of our Lord Jesus Christ."

When it was over and Father Dourmant blessed them, Magnuson shouted, "Kiss the bride," and after Mead did, everyone stepped forward to congratulate them while bottles of champagne were opened and food was served by Marshall's household staff.

"I have a present," Marshall said to Mead and Sung, handing him an envelope. "A honeymoon gift, so to speak."

Mead opened the envelope and brought out two boarding passes.

"Hardly luxurious," Marshall said. "Not even first-class tickets, I'm afraid—just two seats on a MAC flight back to America tomorrow. Your tour here is officially over."

Everyone clapped and wished them luck, and drank all the champagne and ate all the food, and Marshall saw that Teresa Hawthorne did have a few tears in her eyes, and for a brief moment, he was very happy himself.

At the end, Lieutenant Magnuson, bandaged and limping, went up to Mead. "I don't have a present—the PX was closed, something about a war going on, but here's my address in the States. I'm not much for sentiment, but I want to keep in touch. Most of this fucking war I want to forget, but a few things I want to remember, and you and Luke Bishop I don't ever want to lose track of. Someday we'll get together and talk about all this. We'll get roaring drunk and laugh and tell lots of stories—and we won't even have to lie, will we?"

"No, sir," Mead said. "But probably we won't even believe it ourselves someday."

They shook hands. "May I kiss the bride?" Magnuson asked.

"No, sir."

Magnuson laughed, then he bent forward and kissed Sung lightly on the cheek.

Just before the reception ended, Mead left Sung and went up to Teresa.

He was flushed with happiness. "I just wanted to thank you, Miss Hawthorne. This is all because of you."

"No," she said with a smile.

"Yes, it is." He grabbed her, more strongly than he realized, and said as fervently as he believed, "You made my life. You and Mr. Marshall. I wish I could do something for you."

735

She felt tears in her eyes, and she brimmed with love and joy. "Oh, you have, Corporal Mead." Then she wiped away the tears. "I always cry at weddings," she said.

He looked at her with a sad, wistful smile. "I heard that crying helps."

She touched his hands. "Oh, it does, Corporal Mead. It does."

Marshall paced nervously in the VIP room at Tan Son Nhut. Through the window he could see his plane being loaded. A single silver coffin was being lifted into the cargo hold; he was taking Romer's remains directly back to Washington for burial at Arlington National Cemetery, beside those of his father.

Dead because of his father? Marshall wondered. Driven by some sense of inadequacy, or vainly seeking the father's glory and reputation? Perhaps, he thought. But how was that different from the other dead sons being sent home in their coffins? They were killed just as surely by their fathers—through silence or acquiescence, slogans or stupidity, but dead nonetheless.

And Ryan? It was his, Marshall's, fault that he was here. He, the father, had allowed this to happen. Fathers created wars for their sons to fight.

He had arrived in Saigon on a beautiful day of brilliant sunshine, and he was leaving with portions of the city in flames, and smoke curling to the sky. The Viet Cong still controlled Cholon.

In Hue, the enemy flag still flew over the Citadel; the "mopping up" was in its fifth day.

Early assessment of the destruction created in the Tet Offensive throughout the country estimated that 14,000 civilians were killed, with twice as many wounded, and a half million made refugees. Damage was in the hundreds of millions of dollars—certain cities such as Hue, Ben Tre, Ban Me Thuot, and Da Lat were destroyed beyond reconstruction.

Behind him there was a knock on the door; he turned to see a young man in a Green Beret uniform, a tall, lean, and muscular youth, clean shaven and short haired, a young man unfamiliar to him except for the warm and self-deprecating smile on his face.

"Dad?"

Marshall held a chair for support. "So your mother didn't lock you in the cellar after all."

"No, but she put on a great show—she cried and fainted and sobbed, 'I'll never see you again, I'll never see you again.' Jesus, what a way to send a son off to war—terrific vote of confidence. How about you, Dad—you going to stage a show too?"

Marshall just stared at him, then he shook his head. "I don't have the energy—the old man's done in, Ryan."

Then they walked toward one another, and Marshall put his arms around him.

"I'm going to try to be brave—though if it would do any good, I'd scream and faint like your mother."

They stepped away and appraised one another.

"You don't look so good, Dad; you look tired."

"Listen, I'm delighted to be ambulatory—another few days here and I'd be going back in the cargo hold." Then he sighed miserably. "And you—you look wonderful." He shook his head. "Absolutely wonderful in that uniform. You jackass!"

Ryan laughed. "That's better."

"Where are you stationed?"

"Nha Trang."

"I don't want to hear about it."

"Apparently you were quite a sensation there, Dad."

"You stay away from the CIA, Ryan; they're lunatics."

Ryan smiled indulgently. "Any more advice?"

"Lots. But would you listen? Would it do any good?"

"About the same as fainting."

Marshall grabbed him close again. "Oh, Ryan, Ryan." Then he placed his head on his son's shoulder. "I'm not going to be able to be brave after all. Oh, God, be careful. Please, please . . ."

Marshall stepped away and he was crying unashamedly. "I love you. More than my life, more than anything—if anything happened to you, I would want to die."

Then he said laughingly through his tears, "I wish I could

737

grab that ridiculous little beret off your head and snatch your rifle and take your place in Nha Trang."

"Hey, this is as good a show as Mom's."

"Stop that! Don't you dare mock my tragedy. This is the worst moment in my life—how dare you laugh at it?"

Ryan laughed. "Dad, I'm *going* to come home. I don't want to spoil all the melodrama, but I do plan to make it; I'll be home in a year."

Marshall stood slumped and agonized before his son.

Ryan patted him on the shoulder. "I'll be okay, Dad."

Finally Marshall looked up. "You know, I finally understand the God story—the one about how He loved the world so much that He let His son be crucified, watched him tortured and killed. Except in His case, since He was omnipotent, He must have known it was all going to work out fine in the end—a lovely resurrection and ascension; He could console Himself with that. But the idea is there—the awful suffering and agony, the sacrifice of the father."

"Oh, my God," said Ryan. *"I'm* going to get killed, and *you're* going to be the sorrowful victim? *I* die and *you* get to be the tragic figure? Spare me this, will you? If I get killed, I don't want you and Mom throwing yourselves on my coffin, robbing me of *my* tragedy. Don't steal my final scene. Let's keep the story line straight—it's *my* fucking death."

"God damn it, stop talking this way!"

"You started it!"

They glared at each other, then laughed.

"You'd *better* come home," Marshall said. "I'll never forgive you otherwise."

Ryan held out his hand. "Good-bye, Dad."

Marshall took a deep breath and braced himself, then he shook his son's hand. He started to say something, then changed his mind, turned, and walked out the door.

He nodded at the saluting honor guard, then climbed the stairs of the plane and took his seat, resolutely not looking out the window, and resolutely not thinking about the coffin in the cargo hold as the plane taxied, then lifted, and headed out to sea.

* * *

In another plane on the runway, delayed for the presidential aircraft, Mead and Sung sat together.

They spoke little as they waited, and out of nervousness, she clutched the doll he had given her.

Finally the plane was cleared for takeoff.

They did not hold hands as the plane taxied, but sat stiffly upright as though posed in an old photograph, a grandniece of the last emperor of Vietnam and a sharecropper's boy from Arkansas, staring out the window at the land rushing by.